A Life In Music

Wulf Müller

TABLE OF CONTENTS

FOREWORD

THANKS

ABOUT MY PARENTS

IN THE BEGINNING:
1955 - 1962
1962 – 1964

BERLIN
1964 - 1967
1967 - 1969

EBERGASSING
1969 -1970

VIENNA, PART 1
1970 – 1975

VIENNA, PART 2
1975 – 1978
1978 – 1980
1980 – 1983

VIENNA, PART 3
1983 -1984
1985
1986
1987
1988
1989
1990
1991

LONDON, PART 1
1992
1993
1994
1995
1996
1997
1998
1999
2000
2001
2002

LONDON, PART 2
2003
2004
2005
2006
2007
2008
2009
2010

MADRID
2011
2012
2013
2014
2015
2016
2017
2018
2019
2020
2021

A KIND OF DISCOGRAPHY
amadeo
Emarcy
OKeh Records

Copyright 2022: Wulfhardt Müller

All photos are from the Müller family collection, except when otherwise indicated. Some photos have been in my possession for many years and therefore I am not 100 % sure anymore who took them – me or family members or friends from all periods of my life.

KDP ISBN printed version with photos: 9798353190752

FOREWORD

During the second phase of the Covid 19 pandemic in 2020 and 2021 I wrote this chronicle of my life and the music that played an important part in it. From the early encounters at home, through my youth and student years, until I started to work in the music business and worked directly with artists and their records.

It is therefore not a biography as such, it's not a kiss and tell story either, as I keep what's private exactly that: private. But my personal life and my professional one cannot be separated, as they influence each other. Beside major events of a personal nature, the ones of global or regional impact play a part in the book as well. Events I remember directly or which had an impact on my life from further away. That's why I think 'chronicle' is the best word for what I wrote – a chronicle of my life seen through music and events and so painting a picture of the times I lived in.

I really enjoyed the process of writing all this down, researching some of the events and album releases in more detail and making connections between historic events and my life. I tried to be as accurate as I could, but in some cases I might have mixed up an event or a date, but in general I hope to have gotten it right.

Memories are a tricky thing, so wherever possible I tried to find facts to verify what I remembered. Websites like Discogs or Wikipedia have been extremely helpful, as has been my collection of release magazines and catalogues from the jazz department at PolyGram / Universal. From 2010 onwards I used a lot of the writing on my blog and integrated it into this chronicle. I started the blog more or less for myself, to remember concerts I had attended, records I had listened to and trips I had made in that phase of my life and I really enjoyed writing these blog posts and still do today. Meanwhile I have a few thousand readers per year and am happy if I can point them to a certain record I enjoyed.

The writing of the chronicle stops just short of my 66th birthday, but will continue in some form via my blog, as I will always have an ear for new music, especially new jazz records. I have been extremely lucky making my passion my job, to have a wife and daughter who love and support me no matter what and a family that has each other's back. With that background I truly lived 'A Life In Music'!

Special Thanks

-       To my wonderful wife Yolanda for her unwavering support, encouragement and invaluable help in correcting and editing my text, as well as selecting the right photos for the book. Te quiero para siempre!

-       To my beloved daughter Hannah for making me a proud dad and for giving her permission to use parts of the letters my father wrote to her, in the text. Big hug!!

-       To my amazing mother for everything and for telling me her story and to my incredible siblings for being the best brothers and sisters one can wish for – caring, fun and understanding.
          In Loving memory of our father and youngest brother, Thomas.

-       To all the artists I had the pleasure to work with, as without your creativity there would be no music business.

-       To the photographers, for approving the use of their art in my book, especially to my dear friend Rainer Rygalyk, may he rest in peace.

-       To friends, artist managers, booking agents, festival promoters, colleagues in record companies, road managers, club owners, etc. who are part of the business I describe and who helped me to make my work better.

-       To Sonny Rollins for spiritual guidance and encouragement.

-       To Fraser Kennedy for trying to find a publisher for me and for his friendship of many years.

ABOUT MY PARENTS

My father Wolfgang was born on December 24th, 1924. He wrote to my daughter Hannah about his life in a series of letters, which tell his story much better than I ever could do:

"When I was born in 1924 the inflation period was over and my parents and grandparents did well. We were a good bourgeois family, the grandparents officials at the city council or the post office. My uncles were officials, business people, including my father. And of course, war veterans, some of rank. And that is important. Being of rank in the army was socially important. On your business card, there was the name and then the army rank, orders or merits and only last the profession.

If the elders came together for any festivity (and it was often partied), or were just visiting for dinner or coffee, there was, for the men, after a maximum of 15 minutes, only one issue of discussion: War. They repeated all experiences and memories in endless variations, adding a few victims here and there. Showing off!

The emperor had abdicated and busied himself, as a refugee in Holland, chopping wood. But the 27th January, the emperor's birthday, was still celebrated by the elders. My grandfather, Magistratsbotenmeister in the City of Höchst, came to the celebrations in his Grand Ducal Hessian Peace Uhlan uniform with boots and spurs and sword, etc. They all met in Hessia, wearing their various uniforms: East African Protection Force, Prussian infantrymen, Hussars, pilots, etc., etc., singing 'Hail the victor's laurel', praising the monarchy - Wilhelm II in Prussia and cheering for frenzies, I can't even remember now.

The French were our arch-enemies, not only because they had occupied the Frankfurt area including Höchst until 1930. It all began with the destruction of the castle Heidenberger around 1689 and in 1693 with the devastation of the Palatinate (Pfalz) by Louis XIV and the occupation of the Rhineland by Napoleon. But French culture and language were appreciated in quite a different manner: One was Francophile.

My first toys were a helmet and a sword. Then tin soldiers, a castle, and then more soldiers, cannons and everything pertaining war games. Of course, I wore sailor suits, and, in my dreams, I was a cabin boy, sailor, Lieutenant, Captain or Admiral on all ships from U9 to the big battleships.

When I was 6 years old - 1930 - we were in the midst of the Depression in Germany and had about 8 or 10 million unemployed. I can remember the long lines at the employment office, both men and women who came every week to collect their dole money. My father was also unemployed. But going for the dole money was not on. He was too proud: To be unemployed was a disgrace. It was a terrible and political time. Conflicts were fought on the street, battles between Communists, Socialists, Nazis, Centrists and German Nationalists. Even in the schools the battles between the various youth groups continued. Sundays we went to church with our parents or with our youth groups and afterwards we fought.

There were cars and buses, which were particularly interesting for us children, on full rubber tyres, with Horn and gear stick set outside, they rattled over cobblestones. So slowly that we could attach ourselves with roller skates and then drove through the village or we were sitting on the spare wheel holder and let us be driven around. Also, we were able to attach our bikes to a truck, with ropes to which 6 or more bikes were connected. Impossible today.

Swimming and cycling I could before I went to school. I learned to swim in Mainz. There was a Flusschwimmbad (a public bath in the river Main) and we could lie in the sun in the grass on the banks of the river. The water was clean and there were fish in the Main. In Höchst there were still river fishermen. The fish tasted good and was even sold at the market in Höchst. On the Main wood was still floated. Trees from the Spessart to Holland. Long rafts with tents or even cabins for the rafters floated slowly downstream. Long poles were still used to steer the rafts. Often, we were allowed to climb onto the rafts and travel a bit with them. Then we had to either run back or try to get a ride back upriver on a tow boat. It was beautiful, but also a bit dangerous. Years later this was all over. The Main contaminated by chemicals, poisoned the fish and swimming in the river was prohibited.

In 1930 I started, 6 years old, elementary school in Höchst, staying with my grandparents. At the time Höchst was still occupied by the French. Moroccan Spays were there as occupiers. It was a real colourful picture when they rode through the city, in white robes and with spears on beautiful horses. But they were not popular, the 'Hutschebebbes' as they were called popularly.

My class teacher at my primary school was Herr Ferdinand Helfenbein, who had already taught my father. He, of course, was a reserve officer and had led his regiment's war diary. It was terribly easy to interrupt our German, History or Geography lessons with a question about the war and all German, Geography or History was soon forgotten and 'long live the war' was all he talked about.

For class trips we went into the woods but we did not learn anything about plants or listen to nature, we just played war games. We were divided into Germans and Frenchs and, with his umbrella and 'boom-boom' shouts, he killed every student in the class at least three times.

Why I do not know, but we went by bicycle from Höchst to Schencklengsfeld in Upper Hessia, where a brother of my grandfather lived, who was a stationmaster. Via Frankfurt, Hanau, Gelnhausen, Fulda, Hünfeld we cycled, 160 km in one go. I could not go any further than Fulda and sat the rest on the pole of my father's bike, who had my bicycle around his shoulder. But we arrived, with carbide lamps lit at night and tired. There I went for a few weeks to a mediocre school. I can't remember the school, but I do remember the sausage sandwiches, made of homemade sausages and bread and the honey from their own hives. When and how we were driven home, I cannot remember either. I then went back in to school Höchst and Sindlingen.

In 1933 Hitler came to power. He was democratically elected and appointed Reichskanzler by the old Generalfeldmarschal Paul von Hindenburg. In Germany, millions were unemployed as a result of the stock market crash in the U.S. When the democratic parties in the Weimar Republic failed, we had 12 Chancellors in 14 years, it was easy for Hitler's propaganda slogans, such as "work for all", "a powerful kingdom", "a new army", "restoring the honour of the old army", etc. (all lies), to get the people behind him. Many believed he would bring back the emperor from his exile in Holland and the good old days would be restored. Old Fritz, Bismarck and Hitler were the guarantors of a new Germany, with old traditions: far from it!

In 1933 I joined the Hitler Jugend, a youth organization for 10 to 14-year-olds. My father was in the Labour Front, a Nazi trade union organization, the same for all workers whether they were working with their hands or heads. Later he was in the SA. Life was organized; all took place more or less, in uniform.

From the beginning, we marched every Sunday in lock-step with flags and pennants to church. God bless the Führer, the people and the fatherland. All church youth organizations were banned, along with the Boy Scouts, as well as all other youth organisations that didn't belong to the NS Party. The ones, who were not for Hitler, were persecuted. Political parties of the opposition, social democrats, communists, etc., were prohibited and their leaders put into concentration camps, like Dachau.

Of course, we had as well idols and role models. The sportsman Max Schmeling was the only Heavyweight World Champion Germany ever had. That meant beatings and fist fights to prove that one was the best. And as an aviator Ernst Udet, who on demonstration flights with his biplane, picked up a handkerchief from the ground with the wing.

Even as a boy flying was a dream for me. You can't imagine the aircraft from that time looking like today's machines. Sports planes were constructed out of wood and upholstered wings. Commercial aircraft were made of corrugated iron and a so-called wide-bodied aircraft had space for 17 passengers. The biggest, the Do X was a 12-engine flying boat for 75 passengers and dining room plus stewards on board. I've seen it once as it landed in Frankfurt on the Main and then started again. And of course, there were the airships, which floated like fat cigars quietly and slowly through the air.

There was no television yet, but radio, mostly hand built with tubes and coils. Initially only for headphones, then with speakers. Mostly it hissed before you could hear a squeaky voice, or music.

But music usually would be heard on a Sunday afternoon and evening from the gramophone, pressed on shellac records and played with wood or steel needles. Salon Music, Goblins Parade and the like and classical music was played. Caruso sang and grandmother, your great-grandma, dropped the knitting needle. In the cinema there were the first films with sound. That was a great time – back in 1930, when I was 6 years old.

We boys were now playing war in uniforms, our heroes were soldiers whom we tried to emulate: Zieten, Seidlitz, Blucher, von Moltke, the airmen Immelmann, Richthofen, Udet, etc. There were many to whom we looked up to. We went for camping trips. We were fully involved and more in uniform than in normal civilian clothes. The parents only had a small saying in what we should do or not.

Then the Jews were persecuted. In Höchst there were quite a lot of them. I went to school with a Jewish girl, Ursula Schiff. The family Schiff lived near my grandparents. They were two brothers that owned a department store in Höchst. Both highly decorated military officers from World War I. Suddenly they were gone and the department store was called Conradi. That "Jews" (shameful use of a word as synonym of hatred and discrimination) existed, I only realized, when posters were put up hanging in all their shops: 'Germans do not buy from Jews'. And then there were less and less of them. The fact that the Jews were arrested or taken to concentration camps was sometimes talked about, but if at all, only in whispers and quietness and not just with everyone. Slowly fear took over. We boys did not notice much of this.

In 1936, the last shackles of the Versailles Treaty were broken and the German military sovereignty was restored. The first troops marched into Rhineland and also into Frankfurt. I witnessed in the city-centre of Frankfurt how the Traditions-Regiment, with drums beating and flags flying, and the Cavalry, also with drums, trumpets and banners, passed by. My father and grandfather had tears in their eyes and I was excited in my uniform. I am sure that this was an important moment in the awakening of my desire to become a soldier. It was the 9th of November of 1938.

Every day, I used to go to school from Höchst to Sachsenhausen. At the Hauptbahnhof (main station) Frankfurt I had to change trains. There I saw how Jewish shops were wrecked and looted. Still today, I keep in my nose the scent of a perfumery store shattered into thousands of shards of glass. In school, not a word was spoken about the matter. Not at home either. In Höchst and Frankfurt the synagogues were on fire.

At 14 years, in 1938, I moved from the young people organisation into the Hitler Youth proper for the 14 - 18 years old, the section for the air force. I should add as well that in 1936 my father, and of course many others, volunteered for military service to reach the level of an Officer of the Reserve. So, each year he would attend training in the army for 6 to 8 weeks. Employers were obliged to pay full wages and the "old gentlemen" would once again have a great time together, dressing in their brand-new uniforms and being somebody again.

In the Flieger HJ we learned Morse, sailing and of course how to use a wind glider. But not like today. This was the Prussian military and everything went according to a plan, an order that was set and given. Two hundred hours to build a model, neatly listed in a construction book. Two hundred hours to build the aircraft, a Grunau 9 or SG 38. We learned all the necessary crafts. And then, finally, the first flight off a slope.

By then, we were traveling daily between school and the hangars and on weekends, with the help of an old car used as a winch we were able to glide. We had the A-B-C exam and having 3 wings on your chest that really meant something. Flying, whether we took off from a slope or simply being towed by an old aircraft, was the absolute freedom. Of course, we had to learn how to shoot as well, first only with small calibre guns, then with carbines and soon the HJ shooting and sport medals were on the uniform as well.

Then the war started. My father was immediately drafted on 21st August '39 at 2 am. My mother was just at the spa in Bad Wörishofen. On September 1st 1939 the invasion of Poland commenced. We only heard the reports of victory and were proud of our soldiers. At home life changed. Air raids, cellars, ration cards.

The first bombs fell. Incendiary bombs fell on our house. The fire was put out. More friends and family members became soldiers. Support services were established, women required to work in production and repair lines. To school we attended less and less. There were always excuses: A fire here and there. The teachers couldn't do anything. In the tramway, when we went to school every morning, big and athletic in our uniform or in short leather pants, we always had the feeling that people silently asked: 'Why are you not a soldier?'

Beside the air defence we still had to go to the HJ and gliding drills, additionally we also were part of the "Kriegshilfdienst" (war support service) in a factory, manufacturing parts for submarines.

In early March, what had been predictable for a while finally happened: for unruly behaviour towards a teacher, I was expelled from school. But because of voluntary joining the Air Force, I generously received the so-called "Notabitur", a substitute for my A-levels. Without having to report to labour service, I was called up on 24th March 1942 for flying training at Regiment 32, based in Eger.

I have to make clear that we boys were by then totally smitten with the war. Reports of victory, bells ringing nearly every day after battles won. We heard nothing about concentration camps or killings in Poland, France, etc. Sometimes you heard, silently, carefully: "If the Führer would know about that!", of course, he knew everything but no one believed it.

From Eger in the Sudetenland, I was sent to France - Rochefort sur Mer - to an air base for my basic training. Work, work. No close contacts with the local population, going out to eat, visiting brothels and drinking, that was more or less all. Afterwards some more training as a pilot in Southern France - Mar de Marson - mornings at 8 with the breakfast milk onto the tarmac, training on a SG 38 Glider or a Grunau Baby, risen by winch or towed by an aircraft. It was a nice time, quiet, besides a little work and guarding the ME 109E we had nothing else to do. Then it was all over, I was expelled once again this time due to my lack of control of the aircraft, soon after I volunteered for the Para troops.

Which meant: Goodbye France and off to Russia. It was now October '42. We were forced to march and sleep on the bare soil at sub-zero temperatures and ride on wooden saddles. We did not get out of our uniforms for weeks; the stockings were rotting in our boots and we had lice. By then, we had seen hospitals attacked by Russian partisans who injured, raped, tortured and murdered nurses and doctors; we were afraid of these partisans.

Winter '42: now in the North Section, finally deloused and cleaned up, the lice-bitten legs looked after and bandaged, with what today we would only consider as toilet paper. But we were alive! We didn't find the war so wonderful anymore, now we had learned what it was all about: survival! From November to February, we were in Novgorod on the Volkhov in the so-called Fortress Alkazar, 3 km behind the main front, in a former convent, which was occupied by the 'Blue Division', a Spanish Regiment, which we replaced. War, opened graves, everything that could be moved was stolen: gold teeth, jewellery, clothing, shoes, etc. We were in dogfights with spades, guns. The Russians had unusual ideas to build mines: cigar boxes with rusty nails. There was nothing that was off-limits for them. Despite all, we had a lot of respect for the Russians. Through Russian propaganda we had heard about the fighting at Stalingrad. By that time, I was a seasoned soldier at the front - but cigarettes and alcohol I was not allowed, because I was not yet 18 years old – instead loads of chocolate. – My weight at the time: 50 kg.

It continued until the end of February 1943. I was seriously wounded over Pleaskau - Riga - Gdansk to Glöven. A shot through the face, I could not even speak. From Glöven I was sent to the hospital in Berlin - then to Gütersloh to a support regiment. People at home still had a life, but no more enthusiasm for the war, we dare not say that we might lose the war, but many silently believed we would.

Holidays in Höchst with my father, who had been stationed for duty in Yugoslavia, my mother was also there at the same airfield and uncle Luck came to meet me at the station, he had come from the front in Russia, already a Battalion-Commander.

From Gütersloh I was sent to combat training in southern France - La Courtine. In September '43 I was a paratrooper in the Monte Rotondo battle, we were supposed to storm the Italian headquarters and take Marshal Baltoglio prisoner. But we didn't succeed. In January '44 we went to Anzio /

Nettuno, before that to Monte Casino. We fought against the British, Australians, New Zealanders, Americans, Poles, Indians and so on. We had prisoners and smoked cigarettes with them and looked together at photos of our families. As humans, we were not enemies, as soldiers, we obeyed our commands. War was fighting and some even felt it was a sport. Who is the better?
I still remember an American Captain called Brown, who always used to shout: "Paras – shall we do a round together?"
Italy - March 1944 - Muletta gorge close to Anzio. We have also seen how civilians were arrested and later heard of shootings in the Pontine Marshes outside Rome. Still, we wanted to win. We were too young to understand that the war was already lost. At Pentecost 1944 I was taken prisoner and sent via Naples, Tarento, to Egypt, into a Prisoner of War camp at Ismailia. We were treated very correctly by the British, received our military pay and via the Red Cross even mail from home. When the Allies landed in France on 6 June, we dismissed these reports as propaganda and lies. In January 1945 our camp was moved to the desert of El Daba. While our journey went through populated areas, we were transported in Pullman cars, once out of human sight we were then loaded into cattle cars.
When the war was lost in May 1945, for us boys, our world had been destroyed. What had we fought, suffered or even, some of our comrades, died for? For Hitler, for Germany? No answer.
The English showed us the concentration camp film: "The liberation of Buchenwald". We did not believe it. We could not believe that our role models were murderers.
In May 1946 I was one of a contingent of 50 selected prisoners which were sent to England - Wilton Park, a University for POW's. It was there that, for the first time, we boys (we were 5 in my age group) learnt what democracy meant. We heard about the rules of democracy and learnt the truth about the Nazi party, about Karl Liebknecht and Rosa Luxembourg, Klara Zeltkin and all the others. In England, we were able to move freely. In 1946 I went to a Proms concert at the Royal Albert Hall in London, then to the Westminster Abbey and the House of Parliament. We learned a lot. And through that school it was easier for us to adapt later to life after the war. The gateway to the future was open."

My father came back from England in 1947 and went directly to Höchst, where his parents lived. He started to work at a dental surgery, as this was what he wanted to do, but the dentist closed his shop shortly after and my father decided to become a colourist in the textile industry and went to Reutlingen to study in 1948. One of the other students there was Hans-Joachim Bamler, who invited his younger sister Annemarie to a masked ball in Reutlingen in 1950.

My mother Annemarie Bamler was born in Berlin on July 5th, 1928. Her father Rudolf was an officer in the German military, who hardly spoke about his work at home. His job made the family move from one place to another, as it is common in the army. When my mother was 4 years old, they moved to Königsberg, a historic city, today part of Russia and known as Kaliningrad. They lived very close to the barracks where her father worked and she and her brother spent most of their time there as well, though mainly in the stables. Her brother had a horse and did ride some youth races, but my mother was still too young for that. But she knew her way to the stables and, as she wasn't at school yet, went there every day to be with the horses.

Then two years later, in 1934, they moved back to Berlin. Education and organisation of all the moves, finding new homes for them, schools for the two kids and so on, was the responsibility of their mother, Mary. Their aunt Gustl, short for Auguste, one of their mother's three sisters, lived in the same district of Berlin, Steglitz, and was married to an early member of the Nazi Party and of the SS. My grandfather couldn't stand the SS, therefore, even so being more or less neighbours, they didn't see her aunt that often then.

In 1939, my mother's family moved to Vienna, as her father was promoted to colonel and commander of the 74th Tank-Artillery regiment, stationed in Austria. They lived close to the Prater Park and city centre and, from what my mother remembers, she liked living there a lot. But their

German dialect caused a few problems at the beginning, living in occupied Austria. As my mother told me, she *"very quickly picked up the Viennese dialect"* to avoid being bullied in school.

But the good life in Vienna didn't last long, as in 1940 the family moved again, this time to Zoppot by Danzig. Zoppot, which today is a part of Poland and called Sopot, was a spa town with a Kurhotel and a seaside beach for the tourists and was the last family home for my mother. She didn't like the house they were living in, as they heard rumours that something terrible had happened to the previous owners, a Jewish family who had disappeared suddenly. School in Zoppot was good, with mainly young teachers, as the older ones were all called up for military service. In 1941 my grandfather was promoted again, this time to Chief of Staff in the 2nd Tank Army and was therefore involved in many battles of the war in that year. While he was sent to Norway in 1942, the family stayed in Zoppot. Having joined the Jungmädelbund (Hitler Youth for girls) aged 10, as all girls that age ought to, my mother didn't like the more military aspects of it and when, with 14, she was moved to the Bund Deutscher Mädel (League of German Girls), she decided to go to the BDM part that was supporting the Red Cross and work as a help or nurse in hospitals when needed. And as Zoppot was the first stop for most injured soldiers from the Eastern Front, my mother was called a lot from school to help out. Her mother had volunteered as well and helped the injured there too.

Her brother, Hans-Joachim, became a soldier in 1943, after voluntarily joining the German Wehrmacht, not to be called up by the SS, as he states in his memories. Only a year later my grandfather was captured by the Russians at the Eastern Front and became a prisoner of war. According to the biography of my uncle Hans-Joachim, his father was by then disillusioned with Hitler, his Generals and their unrealistic ways. The Nazis accused him of collaboration with the Russians and treason. His wife Mary was immediately arrested, based on what the Germans called 'Sippenhaft', which basically meant the whole family could be punished in such cases. While my grandmother Mary was first imprisoned in Danzig and then sent to the concentration camp in Dachau in 1944, my mother was saved from a similar fate by her aunt Gustl, who had come to live with her in Zoppot and swore to educate her in the best German way from then on. Having been married to an early member of the Nazi Party was helpful to succeed with this as well. My uncle Hans-Joachim was not arrested either, as he already served in the war as a soldier, as did aunt Gustl's husband at that time. According to my uncle, their mother could have gone free, had she agreed to divorce her husband, but that was no option for her and therefore she was first moved to Dachau and then to Reutte in Tirol, where she died in 1945 under circumstances that have never really been clarified, after the Americans liberated the camp, she was held in.

In the same year, aunt Gustl and my mother had to flee Zoppot from the advancing Russian troops and ended up in Beuren, close to Stuttgart. Some of aunt Gustl's friends from Stuttgart had fled to Beuren before them and they all lived in a closed down inn for a while. After these friends went back to Stuttgart, the two rented a room at an older widow's place, bath and kitchen to be shared with her. But the widow's daughter needed to come home shortly after and they had to move again. This time they found two rooms above the butcher shop, for whom my mother started to work. My mother took a sewing course in Beuren, which was meant to be more industrial orientated, but she as well learned how to sew clothes very well. Aunt Gustl's husband was one of thousands of missing soldiers, assumed dead, but without knowing for sure. Both, aunt and niece, had to work in Beuren, to manage their costs of living. At one point my mother wanted to train as a nurse, as she had enjoyed what she did in Zoppot at the hospital. Unfortunately, she had to recognise after a short while that she didn't have the strength required to do this job. Years of war and malnourishment had taken its toll. So, she gave up on that dream and started to work for the butcher again. After a short period as a prisoner of war of the Americans, my uncle made his way as well to Beuren, where the two siblings were reunited again under the roof of their aunt, who had as well managed to get in touch with their father, exchanging postcards while he was held in Russia. Immediately my uncle Hans-Joachim started to look for work and after a handful of jobs landed one working in textile printing in Stuttgart. It seemed to really have interested him and so aunt Gustl decided to pay for his studies in Reutlingen, the leading school for the textile industry at the time. And for the masked ball there in 1950, he invited his sister to come along.

On February 3rd 1950, Annemarie met Wolfgang thanks to her brother and she knew immediately, as she told me: *"that was it"*. My mother had found her man and they got married on August 11th 1950, being pregnant with their first child Marie-Louise, called Marlis, who was born on December 16th of the same year. They lived in Frankfurt/Höchst with my fathers' parents. Actually, in the beginning only with his father, as his mother was in Brazil for a year, working as a house keeper for an American family. She had worked for this family while they were stationed in Germany and when they had to move, they asked my grandmother if she would consider to come with them for a year. As jobs in Germany were rare and this one was well paid, she said yes. My father was working at the Farbenfabrik in Höchst then, but in 1952 they moved to Hünfeld, where he had found a new and better paid job. Their second daughter, Christine, was born there on May 28th 1952.

My grandfather was released by the Russians in 1950 and went to stay with Maggie, the older sister of his deceased wife in Wilhelmshorst, close to Potsdam, located in the Russian controlled sector of Germany. After my parents moved together, they went to Wilhelmshorst, along with aunt Gustl, to visit her father. Which even then was difficult, as for crossing the occupied sectors of Germany you needed approved papers. They did so illegally. Aunt Gustl decided to stay behind and my parents made it back to Frankfurt/Höchst. In December 1950 aunt Gustl married my grandfather – so being aunt and stepmother to my mother at the same time.

In 1954 my brother Jürgen was born on November 19th, the first son of the proud parents.

My mother and father could still visit her father and his new wife in Eastern Germany occasionally, but it was very complicated and difficult, especially as he was working for the newly built army there. The more the border with West Germany was closed off, the more complicated it became to visit or even stay in touch. And after the wall was built, and the Cold War was raging, any contact with her family was cut off completely for security reasons.

My parents, Wolfgang and Annemarie Müller, 2007

IN THE BEGINNING
1955 - 1962

1955 – Ten years after the end of WW II and Europe was still recovering and rebuilding. Winston Churchill retired, West Germany and Austria became sovereign countries again, Miles Davis performed at the Newport Jazz Festival, which led to A&R (Artists & Repertoire) man George Avakian signing him to Columbia Records. Louis Armstrong released his 'Satch Plays Fats' album. Erroll Garner his 'Concert By The Sea' and Clifford Brown & Max Roach recorded and released 'Study In Brown', all classic recordings of jazz now. In October of this year, the Four Aces dominated the US single charts with 'Love is a many-splendid thing'; in the UK Jimmy Young was top with his 'The Man From Laramie' and in Germany Silvio Francesco was #1 with 'He Mr. Banjo'.

And I was born on October 24th 1955 in Hünfeld/Hessen in Germany as the fourth child of Wolfgang and Annemarie Müller - a bit too early, as my mother (as the legend says) fell down the stairs to the cellar, when she was eight months pregnant with me.

But all went well in the end and here I am 65 years later, writing down some thoughts and memories.

My sisters and brothers are, in order of birth Marlis, Christine, Jürgen, then it was my turn, followed by Barbara and Thomas. Once asked why she wanted six kids, my mother answered that she had usually been joking about it, but as she always had loved being with kids, she wanted a few and after having three it was like having a kindergarten already and a few more wouldn't make a difference.

My father was, at the time of my birth, working as a textile printer and stayed in the industry for all his life, while my mother tried to educate us and keep us out of trouble. Not easy with six children running around, who needed to be fed, clothed and set off for school every day. These carefree days as a child in Hünfeld, the small town where five of us were born, brought lots of fun and outside activities and music only played a part of our lives through our parents. The music industry hadn't discovered kids as potential buyers yet. And there were no music lessons in school either, these would come later.

with my mother around 1957

There are so many memories from that time, even so, now and then, I am not sure whether what I do remember is really a memory or an image formed much later from stories told or photos seen. The little boy who at his brother's birthday misbehaved as he wanted as well some attention could be one – but I have heard this story being told by my mother so often, that again I can't be sure. Or the little boy sitting on his maternal grandfather's lap – sure not a memory as I only recall that one image – exactly as the photo that exists somewhere in my parent's collection. What is for sure is, that my childhood was protected and, in company of so many brothers and sisters, definitely not missed fun or action.

We lived in the two ground floor apartments of a house owned by the company my father worked for, divided by the common staircase and entry hall, which we had to cross going from the bedrooms to the living room and kitchen. It had a huge garden area all around and kind neighbours, all working in the same company my father worked for as well.

I do remember that we had to go to the company owner's home at Easter and Christmas and sing for them or recite poems – then we got small presents. Strange events for us kids, but kind of usual in these times.

Easter we would usually be allowed in the special garden next to the common one and look for Easter eggs and little presents – for us children very exciting – for my parents, especially mum, a lot of work and preparation. Christmas must have been the same – the six of us, in most cases not more than 2 years apart (my brother and myself only 11 months); and the tree and all the presents and all the food ... and grandmother (from my father's side) for whom my mother could never make it right (this is not a clear memory, this I was told by my mother in later years).

Six kids in front of the Christmas tree, eyes wide open, not allowed to move until all had said their poems – then a bell would ring (my parents still haven't told us how they did this with everyone in the living room and the bell ringing in the dining room, where the tree was placed ...) and off we went to the presents carrying our names. Sledges and snow pop up mentally, but that might be images from later as a kid, already in school.

A neighbour had a pig and on some sunny days she would let it out in her garden and we smaller ones would be allowed to ride on it ... that I remember, as well as the pigs in the farm not far from our house, which was situated kind of at the end of the village. Pigs we threw small stones at until the farmer would chase us away.

Trips to see our grandparents on both sides and even the grandparents of my father – I remember the old house they lived in with the garden, a little brook running through it. No faces there for me to remember, just the thought of good food – probably the first impression of that outside my mother's kitchen.

Images of how our flats were arranged and the furniture and of course remembering the many games we children played together – from jumping with the umbrella from the wardrobe in the boy's room, which we reached thanks to having bunk beds, imagining to be on parachutes or of playing cowboy and Indians and me getting caught, tied up and then my brother pulled my feet from the ground – what a scream initially and a headache afterwards! Football in the garden, hide and seek – running around the house or being on the wooden scooters we had – once falling and hitting a stone, breaking a tooth – when running inside to mum she had guests and to calm me down I got a sip of Coca Cola, my first ever! What a treat and the broken tooth was immediately forgotten.

around 1958 at my grandfather's place in the Russian Sector of Germany

With so many kids in the house we didn't need a kindergarten – we played together and looked after each other, forming the bonds we still have.

I do not remember my mother having someone to help her, but I have been told she had for some time, as it was simply too much to look after all the small kids. Especially after I was born, just 11 months after my brother, and Christine and Marlis were still small as well. The young girl got 25 Marks a month, but according to my mother didn't help a lot, as she *"had to explain everything to her"*. When one or two of us got sick, and with six kids around that was almost all the time, she had to keep the rest away from the ill ones, not to spread whatever child disease was around then.
I remember us kids being scared when the big storms hit, one so strong the plum tree in the garden was bend into the house and knocking on and breaking windows, me sitting in a cardboard box somewhere, hiding, keeping the dangerous outside world away from me.

Many other snapshots, frozen moments pop up while remembering – not unlike photographs – and from that period all of them are happy ones. A sign that my parents gave us the warmth and protection to develop as children and get ready for the world. As well a sign that as kids we really looked after each other – and obviously had our fights while building our own identities within the social cell called family. And emotional snapshots as well – some not connected to a picture, just an overall feeling of 'good' or 'exciting' as the times were for us kids. No fears endangering that happy little world - no clouds on the sky of childhood, these appeared later. First in 1961 with the building of the Wall in Germany, separating the West and the East of the country. My mother's father and brother were in the East and we in the West. At the time the Wall was build my father was visiting them and just made it back in time, thanks to the help of a friend and my grandfather. Many families were separated then and my mother couldn't get in touch with her father or brother, as the father was a highly ranked general and contact would or could have been dangerous for all of them. Only when the Wall finally came down in 1989, she could get back in touch with her family.

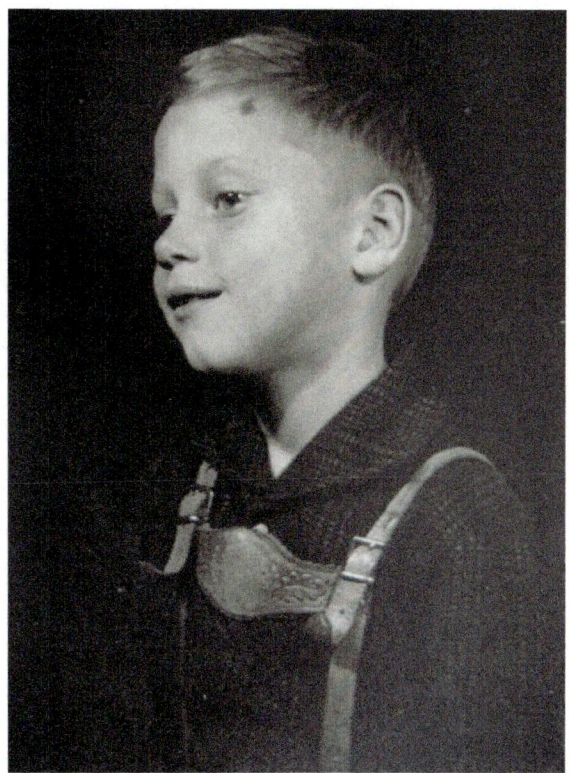
around 1960 / 61

1962 - 1964

1962 was the year when Aleksandr Solzhenitsyn's novella 'One Day in the Life of Ivan Denisovich' was published, The Beatles had an audition with Decca Records and got rejected, Bob Dylan released his debut album, Sonny Rollins his sensational 'The Bridge' and Miles Davis put two albums out, the wonderful 'Someday My Prince Will Come' and 'Live At Carnegie Hall', featuring Gil Evans' stunning arrangements. That year Marilyn Monroe died of 'probable suicide' and clarinettist Mr. Acker Bilk had with 'Stranger On The Shore' the first US Billboard chart # 1 for a British recording.
And I started school! The custom in Germany is, that on the first day of school kids get a 'Schultüte' filled with sweets and little presents and stuff for school to celebrate this new chapter in their lives.
I remember standing outside the old school building with mine and my satchel, in which I had my little blackboard and chalk, then walking into the building, in formation two by two and sitting down on the old wooden desks. I was excited, as my older brother and sisters already went to school, I couldn't wait to do so as well and this was the big moment.
Learning always came easy to me; I picked up things fast and enjoyed school, without having too much trouble understanding or any needs to study extra at home. This didn't change much during all my school time – even so later it became a bit more dependent on who the teacher was and how good he/she could explain and make me understand.
When I started school, I was seven years old – being born in October, I had to wait a year, which wasn't too bad after all. The school was in the old centre of town, close to the church and a mill, if I remember right, as a little brook was running there, leading right into the mill. Therefore, of course, it was strictly forbidden to play around the brook, which obviously made it even more interesting to do so … and we did. And naturally, I fell into the strong current of the brook, but my brother and a friend took hold of me and pulled me out quickly. How to explain that I was soaking wet to my mother, who had made it clear that the water was off limits as a playground? And how to explain that I was wet all over, except for my head, as falling of the little bridge I did turn around and fell

into the water feet first? So, we invented a big guy with a watering-can …. And we really thought my mother would believe us!

When not in school the garden around and behind our house was our main playing ground and often friends would join – from the house or from school. Even so I do not remember faces or names, there were two boys I still recall – one living close by and the other being the son of the owner of the local driving school. Once we did a trip together – I can still see in front of my eyes me sitting in the back of their car and getting travel sick. Strange to remember that – but then, can we pick our memories? Or do we filter and want to forget, push some of them into a far corner of our sub consciousness?

My parents both love music and were often listening to records, sitting on the living room floor with a glass of wine or whiskey and enjoying a collection of jazz singles my father had gotten from Joachim Ernst Behrendt, when he was working with him on some jazzy designs for printed table cloths. That was as well in 1962.

By then Behrendt was the most important jazz radio presenter, writer and jazz record producer in Germany. These singles are a snapshot of the history of Jazz - starting with The Reverend Kelsey and Mahalia Jackson. My father said about these two singles that he *"had never heard a better version of the evangelion than the Reverend's and never before or after felt more faith then when listening to Mahalia Jackson"*. There were as well singles by Pete Johnson, Satchmo, Bix, Shorty Rogers, Count Basie, Ella, Benny Goodman, Glenn Miller, the MJQ and others … this collection is now with me and I love to listen to these singles, as much as my parents did many years back.

But my parents had a few long plays as well – the first Columbia album by Miles Davis, with his timeless version of 'Bye Bye Blackbird', Stan Kenton, Acker Bilk, Dexter Gordon and Benny Goodman on the jazz side, as well as German marches, Nana Mouskouri and Freddy Quinn. A wide range of different styles, played all at certain times: Jazz late at night when the kids were in bed, Marches on Sunday morning (to get us out of bed …) and so on.

As kids we didn't like all of it, nor did we understand the music, but we were exposed to this variety without prejudice. Even when we grew up and started to listen to 'our' music, my father always was interested in what we were listening to and some of our records even became favourites of his collection, like The Moody Blues album 'Days Of Future Passed', or, much later, Sami singer Mari Boine's 'Gula Gula'. But I am going ahead of myself … Let's say we six grew up in a household that didn't know 'bad' music, as all music genres seemed to be equally existing next to each other – the tradition of the New Year's Concert being watched on January 1st opened each year with classical music, which was occasionally listened to in the evenings as well, otherwise it was Jazz or German Schlager or what we would call today 'World Music'.

1962 jazz design printed for J. E. Behrendt

We frequently did trips with my father as well – to see his parents in Kaiserslautern or later his mother in Bad Orb, or weekend trips to areas around where we were living – always fun and exciting – once we went to see some gliders and got the chance to get on one and glide over the area – I didn't! I simply couldn't stand the thought that I would fly simply on the wind and without engine … my brother Jürgen did, he loved it. Heights have never been my thing, neither has water been my element – I need ground beneath my feet to feel comfortable – being a Scorpio after all!

My parents watched the TV news about the visit of John F. Kennedy to Germany and heard his speech in Berlin. His words 'Ich bin ein Berliner', still resonate with me, even so I am not sure if it was from exactly that time or from later, when I did understand the context a bit better. This speech is considered Kennedy's best and the most famous Cold War and anti-communist speech as well. And it underlined the US support for West Germany after the construction of the Wall that separated East and West Germany.

We moved to a new school for my second year. A different way to get there, walking every morning with my sisters and brother. On our way to school, we had to cross a main road using a zebra crossing – I went first that one day in the fall of 1963 and a car came around the corner much too fast and, even so having done only the first step onto the road, it hit me. I can kind of remember being thrown into the air and landing on the street, lying there – seeing a car stopping on the opposite side of the road and people getting out. The driver of the car that hit me helped me up and asked me if I wanted to go to a doctor or to a hospital – "Hospital" was all I could say and got into the car. The next thing I remember is lying on a table to be operated on, a nun standing next to me praying (this was a Christian hospital after all) and then I saw the doctor pulling the handle of the car door out of my ribcage ……….

Meanwhile Christine was running home to tell my mother what happened, while Jürgen went to school as if nothing had occurred and when the teachers asked where I was, he just said: "He was run over by a car" (or so tells me my mother, whose shock must have been immense, as I have always been the one, they worried about – very thin, even so eating well). Five weeks later (just two days before Christmas) a slimmer version of me came home from the hospital. I was immensely glad to be back from this experience and able to celebrate Christmas that year with my parents and siblings.

my first school report - Hünfeld, 1963

Winter was always fun – the smell of freshly baked cookies and the Christmas tree, snowfall and building snowmen in the garden, going out sledging to a hill not far from the house and snowball fights with the whole family. The evenings with hot chocolate, baked apples with cinnamon and board games with all brothers and sisters and sometimes the parents as well.
And Advent – every day in December we would open a window in our calendars and every day there would be a little something in our shoes in the morning – a Clementine or a little chocolate or a small toy. Then, on December 6th, Saint Nikolaus would come and bring a toy for the kids that had behaved all year. I was scared every year when my father or a neighbour would come dressed up and tell us whether we have deserved a gift or not ……. as the ones who hadn't behaved throughout the year would get a few on their backside by his sidekick Knecht Ruprecht. Stories and myths like these are part of every childhood and seem to work, at least for a while, but in one way or another they keep as well the imagination going for the kid – for sure it was like that for me.

around 1959, with Sankt Nikolaus

Somehow, I do remember the images of the assassination of John F. Kennedy, showing on the little black and white TV in our living room and the discussions following this event. I didn't understand the meaning of it all, but it stayed with me as something important and when, a bit older, I read a lot about it, as well as another 1963 event of importance, the 'I Have A Dream' speech of Dr. Martin Luther King in Washington DC.
In the same year Duke Ellington, Charles Mingus and Max Roach released the album 'Money Jungle' – still one of the best small group jazz recordings ever. Ellington as well released the beautiful 'The Symphonic Ellington', while Thelonious Monk put out 'Monk's Dream', Miles Davis his 'Seven Steps To Heaven' and pianist Bill Evans the classic 'Conversations With Myself', all recordings which would later be part of the soundtrack of my life.

BERLIN
1964 - 1967

In 1964 my father got an offer from a company in Berlin and my mother, for the first time, packed us all up and moved, quite a complicated thing to do, but she had seen her mother doing it often enough to be ready for it. My father moved first to find a house for us and to start work. We kids were placed with family and friends or for some time in an inn somewhere before all was set for us to go to Berlin as well.
Thomas and I went with Barbara and Jürgen (if my memory serves me well) to an inn in a village not far from Hünfeld – a place that was as well the local butcher and had been used in the past to run the local cinema in the attic. When we arrived, it was already a derelict place, but still full of magic for us.
After that Thomas and I spend some time with Luck and Leni, whom we called uncle and aunt, even so they actually were my father's uncle and aunt. They lived in Frankfurt, he had been injured in the

Second World War and couldn't work and was in a wheelchair – so we had a lot of time with them together playing Domino a lot and, as it was summer, went out and had ice creams and fun in the sun. I still remember the orange colour of the ice cream – basically water with some orange taste … and I remember that Thomas and I really had a great time and we both stayed in touch with Luck and Leni until their passing many years later.

Then, finally, we were off to Berlin – our first flight (an Air France Caravelle from Frankfurt to Berlin) was a stormy one, which made me throw up, but I wasn't the only one. Unlike Thomas, who just slept through the whole trip, didn't pay any attention to the turbulences at all.
Looking back at this time, I think it was a real blessing to live more or less on the countryside in that age: the freedom to roam outside the house, going to the farms in the area and the woods not far off, was very important for me, in the same way as having the advantages of a village and its tight social network, as some of the neighbours were as close as family. Very different to life in the city of Berlin, as we experienced after the move.
How big that city was for us – being used to the small town of Hünfeld!
My start there wasn't that great: after the horrible first flight from Frankfurt, my father came to pick us up. Mum, Thomas and me and we went to his flat, as the house he had rented wasn't yet fully renovated. The flat was in one of the upper floors of the house and we took the elevator and put the luggage in, which obviously was too heavy and we got stuck in the elevator. The concierge had to call the fire brigade and they had to wind us down to the floor below. Which all in all took a few hours – I was tired and hungry and Thomas – sleeping!

While in 1964 Dr. Martin Luther King received the Nobel Peace Prize, Cassius Clay / Muhammad Ali beat Sonny Listen to become heavyweight champion of the world, the Rolling Stones and the Kinks released their debut albums and Miles Davis his 'Live In Europe' recording, we moved into the house in Lichterfelde, Steinmetzstrasse 7, and really settled into the city life. We learned to get around in Berlin and especially our area and finally got a dog for us kids to play with and look after. Poor thing didn't last long – ran away and was hit by a train ….
There is not much I do remember concerning this house, but there are a few memories: the library bus that came into the neighbourhood once a week, where we got all the books we wanted to read for almost nothing, a special place in a sense, introducing me to Karl May, Astrid Lindgren and her master detective Bill Bergson and many others. One time my parents went on holiday (think it was in the late 60's) and my father's parents looked after us: tough times for us kids, we had to stay at the dinner table until even the last tiny bit on the plate was eaten, whether we liked the food or not; they had a very old-fashioned way of discipline for everything and we were simply not used to this. But we loved the walks along the close canal and playing our games in the trees there, watching the ducks.

Then we moved to a bigger house in Devrientweg 22 – plus two new dogs to play with, a small garden in the front and one a bit bigger in the back of the house, a cellar for the kids to play and the boy scouts to meet and lots of space. It seemed like Paradise, with a football club around the corner and I started playing for them, aged 12, while doing gymnastics in school with some success as well, but football was my preferred sport and I spend a lot of time with my friends and my brother Jürgen at the pitch there.

Berlin, Devrientweg 22

School was fine as well, as when we moved house, we didn't have to change schools, so we were with the same friends. With one of them I started guitar lessons, but after just a few weeks I had to go to hospital, as while doing my maths homework I had accidentally inhaled a little plastic piece that was part of the cap of my fountain pen and it got stuck in front of my lungs. Unfortunately, plastic doesn't show in X-Rays, so the guys in the hospital didn't see anything. My mother took me to a specialist who as well didn't find anything, but mum insisted for me to stay in the hospital and after a few days I got really high fever and they looked for the thing again and couldn't find it and again and I got worse by the day. Then they decided to transfer me in an ambulance to the University Hospital on the other end of Berlin, where they found the plastic piece sitting in front of my lung and having infected my chest. At last, they could remove it and over the weeks following the operation I slowly got better and was released a day before Christmas to spend the holidays with my family. A very close call, I was told later!

The walks in the morning to the school were always fun as well, as we had half an hour to chat and always bought yesterday's Danish for almost nothing for our school lunch, as milk or a cold chocolate drink was provided by the school authorities for every kid.

I think we all became more conscious in Berlin, knowing about the wall that surrounded the city and in the first house sometimes being able to hear gunfire at night, when someone tried to cross that border and with getting older obviously new and other things became of interest, like football (soccer) or the American Apollo programme. Hertha Berlin was the team I followed and often went to the games at the Olympic Stadium to see them play in the Bundesliga, Germany's highest league. I especially remember their goal keepers, Wolfgang Fahrian and then Austrian Gernot Fraydl, both outstanding at times.

My father had for his job developed a machine that printed carpets and was working on it seven days a week. Sometimes he took me or any other of my siblings with him to help to clean the machine, as certain parts inside the big thing could only be reached by a child or by taking half of the machine apart – so we sometimes climbed into the monster and helped and got a few Marks paid to buy some candy or whatever we wanted.

Life in the house in Devrientweg was fun as there were always friends from someone around, the dogs to take care of and play with and lots of fun with my dad and mum. On weekends we always ate together and we played games or worked a bit in the garden or the house. We did little competitions, like who could do the most push-ups or just generally fooled around and when we needed money, asked if we could wash the car for a few Marks. Once being with some neighbour's kids, Hoffmann was their name I think, a smaller kid had his candy stuck in his throat and started to run out of breath. I don't know how I knew, but I took the kid turned him around and hit him on the back … and the candy shot out of his mouth. We all laughed about it and nobody did mention it again.

We continued as well the trips to my grandmother and sometimes my father took one of us with him on business trips. I went to Basel once with him and was treated like royalty there – had someone to take me to the zoo and a stamp collectors' shop, who showed me a very rare stamp from the UK. I was really impressed with what my father had arranged or had asked to be arranged for me.
Guess that's when I discovered a taste for good food, as the places we went to eat or were invited to, always seemed to be very top and I remember vividly how, once in one restaurant, my father explained to me how to properly cut a fish and how to take the bones out without breaking the fish apart or leaving bones inside.

Being six kids, we all developed a sense of being a team and always supported each other, but on the other hand we needed a sense of independence as well, as you had to stand on your own against the older ones or the younger ones, depending on the situation.
Arguments were fought either by discussion or by force. Jürgen and I had many fights, boxing, crying and usually he won. But once the argument was over, we moved on and continued to play and support each other as before. Having a lot of brothers and sisters was definitely a good school for life.
1966 was as well the year we found out through a newspaper article, that our uncle Hans-Joachim had been arrested in Paris together with his wife Marianne, for spying for the GDR. My parents had had no idea that he was in the West at all, nor about his line of work.

1967 - 1969

One of the news items of 1967 somehow got stuck in my head: the first human-to-human heart transplant by Dr. Christiaan Barnard, a South African cardiac surgeon. I thought of this as something outstanding and kind out of a science fiction movie. But it was real and a start of what somehow is a 'normal' procedure today. After hearing this news, I, the 12-year-old kid, wanted to be a successful surgeon one day as well.

When we entered the boy scouts, we did many trips with them – in Berlin over weekends and to the rest of Germany as well – camping, swimming and just enjoying being outside and playing games.
The cellar of the house we had was furnished to be the room where the group of boy scouts could meet and talk. Some of the older boys were already listening to rock music and that's how I came in touch with the music of the 60's. We started to listen to the radio as well and found our first favourites … simple pop like The Tremeloes ('Even the bad times are good'), local favourites The Lords ('Gloryland') and Dave Dee, Dozy, Beaky, Mick and Tich ('Bend It'), besides a few other groups and some other songs as well. I remember Anita Lindblom ('You can have her') and Wencke Myhre ('Beiss nicht gleich in jeden Apfel'). And then there was the question of the time: Beatles or Rolling Stones? Stones in the case of my brother Jürgen and myself. One of these older guys in our boy scout group, who was my eldest sister Marlis' boyfriend for a while, played us once 'My Generation'

by The Who – that must have been in 1967 – and we were hooked! This music was so cool and powerful. And there was so much to discover! Rock was then my brother's and my favourite genre.

In August of '68 we did a trip with our boy scout group to Scotland. First by train to Oostende and then by ferry to the UK, where the train ride continued. We had a camp in southern Scotland and then got the permission to hitchhike through the country and meet up again a week later in Inverness, so my brother and I went on this trip together and made it up there in time, seeing some Lochs, which reminded me of the Benny Goodman version of the song 'Loch Lomond' on the 'Live at Carnegie 1938' album.
On the way back we stopped in London before heading home. The return trip was just days after the Soviet Army had occupied Czechoslovakia and suppressed the freedom movement. Some of the older guys had put some posters up in the train against the occupation and we therefore got stuck at the Eastern German border for a few hours, had to change wagons, but could continue the trip home, where our parents were waiting anxiously.

In school we did generally fine, except that in the first year of college my brother had to repeat the course, as he was not paying too much attention. From then on, we went to the same class at school and had more fun together and could help each other out as well. We were playing and running around with the other kids and trying to fool the teachers whenever we could – same old story! Eventually, we got a bit interested in girls as well. I remember one especially, Margot Pohl. The one for whom I put a little chocolate bar on her desk in the breaks and didn't really make sure she knew from whom it was, as I was too shy. But she came to watch a football game I played in once. Then I found out she had a 'boyfriend' … we became friends and actually stayed in touch for some years after I had moved away from Berlin. Innocent feelings and games, not even a kiss, but then, we were only 12 or 13 years old at the time.

Stupid we were as well – boys challenging each other, sometimes going too far, like trying to steal something from a big department store and, of course, I was the one who got caught. I had to tell my mother and she went to the store, but they had already forgotten about it and didn't want to follow it up. I was deservedly grounded for a week and it never happened again, as I didn't want to disappoint my mother a second time.

For the big holidays we always were together as a family, plus some friends of my parents, the Riegers, which they had met on a trip to Spain and who didn't have kids of their own and spoiled us when they visited for New Year's Eve. They stayed close to the family ever since the late 60's when they first met.

We boys started to listen to Jimi Hendrix and other rock groups of the time like the Byrds, The Animals (with Eric Burdon), Cream and The Doors, which became one of our all-time favourite bands and begun to watch Beat Club, the rock music show on German TV at the time (1965 to 1972), were Iron Butterfly left a deep impression, beside others.

with my brother Jürgen, Berlin, 1968

We listened to Radio Luxembourg, a pirate radio station broadcasting from a ship in the North Sea and discovered rock bands like Mountain, Spirit and Wishbone Ash that way. Miles Davis had released two albums that would be part of my life for many, many years, but not just yet, 'Filles De Kilimanjaro' and 'In A Silent Way'. The end of the sixties arrived and with-it student protests and demonstrations in Berlin and other German cities. My sister Marlis was involved in some of these and my father was not pleased at all – he hadn't yet fully developed his liberal attitudes of later. I guess, that dealing with these circumstances helped, but Marlis, being the eldest, had the biggest struggle.

While in the U.S. opposition against the Vietnam war grew, violence again erupted in Northern Ireland, the first man landed on the moon in 1969. I vividly remember the pictures on TV, the excitement and awe about this achievement. This was as well the year when Led Zeppelin released their first album. Pink Floyd put out 'Ummagumma' and Willy Brandt became chancellor of West Germany, as well as Olof Palme of Sweden – both social democrats that would change politics in Europe for a long time. Woodstock was the event we all talked about: music and hippie culture and then the movie and the album came out and we all went to see the film and buy the record. Hendrix was amazing! And no-one even talked about another important music event that took place more or less at the same time: The Harlem Cultural Festival. The festival took place over six weekends and attracted a total of approximately 300.000 listeners and featured B. B, King, Sly Stone, Stevie Wonder, Nina Simone, Abbey Lincoln and many other top acts, but it was forgotten immediately. That was only to change many years later.
And this was the year two records that would become part of the soundtrack of my life were released: King Crimson's 'In The Court Of The Grimson King' and Renaissance's self-titled album, both debuts for each band, far ahead of its time, still powerful when listening to them today.

And for us things changed as well: my father lost his job and for some while didn't find another one. At one point he was so disillusioned that he started drinking and fights with my mother over money happened more and more often, up to the point when he hit her once. Police came to the house and we were all shocked. My father punished us kids occasionally with a slap or two, but he had never laid hand on our mother that way. He was shocked as well and realised that he needed to stop drinking the way he did at the time and get whatever job until something better would come up. He started to work as a night watchman, cooled his drinking down and finally the offer came. We were all called to a family meeting in the kitchen and discussed moving to Austria, close to Vienna, a place called Ebergassing. My mother, who as ever supported my father in these decisions and had forgiven him the one time he had lost himself, packed us kids, the dogs and everything else and got ready to move, as a generation earlier her mother did so often. Only Marlis stayed behind.

Late Sixties or early Seventies, dancing with my brother Jürgen and my sister Barbara

EBERGASSING
1969 - 1970

We moved back again to a smaller village, smaller even than Hünfeld was, much smaller.
We arrived and half of the town looked on when the truck with our stuff was unloaded – then we had a walk through the village and met two brothers, Siggi and Vickerl, who took Jürgen and me on their bikes to the football pitch and 'tested' us. A few days later we were members of the local club and started playing in the youth team, for which my father kind of became the driver on weekends when he was available. And as the local head of the police was the president of the football club as well, all police turned a blind eye when my father in his, with boys overloaded, car came back from a game.
Ebergassing kind of centred on the factory my father worked for, Eybl. Most of the people worked there or supplied it one way or the other with services. Therefore, and because of the football, we were integrated pretty fast and had a great time there.
Our School was in town as well for a year and my parents discovered the Burgenland, one of Austria's wine regions and only 20 km away. Trips to the local vineyards were common and usually a lot of fun.
And of course, my brother and I got more interested in girls. Still not yet seriously, but trying to steal a kiss here and there and maybe holding hands. But most of our time was spent at school or on the football pitch, a bit of training and on weekends the match we played and then watched the 'A Team' as well.

In Ebergassing everyone knew everyone and there were no secrets in that village. The café in the centre, which means next to the church, was as well the centre of information and gossip and the movie theatre was the place to meet a girl and disappear for a few hours.

The boy scouts had a place to hang out and play music or arrange a boxing competition, have a party and dance, preferably slow. More music to be discovered … through a friend we got into Uriah Heep and UFO, as well as some other rock bands including Led Zeppelin and Humble Pie. Summers were spent at the public pool and having fun and getting drunk at the yearly fun fair, which usually had a kind of cover band playing as well for the younger population of the village.

As in any small village, the mayor, police chief, priest, doctor and head of school and the teachers were the authorities. One teacher thought he could overstep boundaries, as one day he hit me with a cane on the hand for being a bit of nuisance. Caning is banned by law in Austria, but in the small villages it was still common and I told my mother when getting home. The next day she was heard in school screaming at the headmaster to control his teachers as otherwise she would sue the hell out of them and she meant it! The teacher was warned and didn't dare to repeat his actions at least not in our class and my mother got the respect of all the kids and some of their parents as well. When our parents went away for a day or two, they always arranged for us to have lunch in the inn across the road from our house. We just went there for lunch and dinner and all was sorted either before or after. And the food there was great.

For my parents Ebergassing was one of the best times they had in their lives. The feel of being part of a community, the trips to the Burgenland, the relaxed Austrian lifestyle, seeing their kids happy and healthy and no financial or other worries, surely made this time special for them and us.

VIENNA, PART 1
1970 - 1975

After a year of school there, in 1970 (the year Freddie Hubbard released 'Red Clay' and Miles Davis 'Bitches Brew', two albums that I am still listening to a lot) we started high school in Vienna. Both of us went for an entry test in a school for the airline industry with loads of physics, which we both didn't like that much and both of us obviously failed the test. Then our father spoke to a few people and, as connections are everything in Austria, got us into the high school for textile industries with the direction of economics, even so manufacturing and other less interesting topics were as well part of the syllabus.

Through the same connections somehow my father got tickets to the 1970 European Cup Winners' Cup Final, a match between Manchester City and Górnik Zabrze played on 29th April at the Prater Stadium in Vienna and my brother and I were allowed to go with him. City won 2:1, but unfortunately, we had such heavy rain, that it was no fun at all to be there. Still, a memory I cherish.

For me another memorable event of that year was Thor Heyerdahl's crossing of the Atlantic Ocean in his papyrus boat RA II, an incredible feat and inspiring for many. Austrian Formula 1 driver Jochen Rindt was killed in an accident when qualifying for that year's Italian race and became the first driver to be crowned champion posthumously.

The Who recorded 'Live At Leeds', Black Sabbath released their debut album and Pink Floyd their first chart topping album 'Atom Heart Mother'. Both Jimi Hendrix and Janis Joplin died that year. In 1971 Weather Report released their first album and Miles Davis released his soundtrack to 'A Tribute To Jack Johnson', for me the ultimate jazz/rock record, with both Miles and guitar player John McLaughlin rocking like crazy!!!!

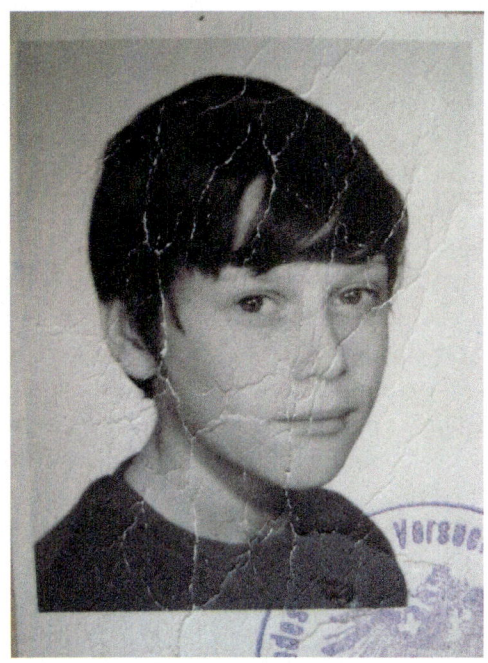
school pass photo 1970

program for European Cup Final 1970

In the beginning we took the bus every morning from Ebergassing to Vienna, but as so often at one point my father changed jobs again and the family went back to Germany and my brother Jürgen and I, as well as our sister Christine, stayed in Austria – the school had a boarding school attached, so no problem there. We were lectured every day from 8 am to 6 pm with a one-hour break for lunch, we could stay the weekend in the boarding school or stay at friends' houses – our parents gave us the necessary approvals when needed. But of course, the boarding school closed at a certain hour on weekends – much too early for us normally – so we had to find ways to either crawl through the basement of the school and find and open window to squeeze through or climb the 4-meter-high wooden gate, which on the way out was fine, but back in, after a few beers, risky!
And of course, we got caught coming home late and had to clean all the stairs in the 5-floor building down to the cellar. And got grounded – then, at least, we could play table tennis or billiard, as the boarding school provided both.
School was OK – we did fine, but not great. Had our problems with teachers – and they with us. Weak ones were tormented and strong ones left in peace – silly ones got silly answers and fair ones been treated friendly. Guess the same way as it used to be or as it is today – nothing much changes in the way people deal with each other.
On one of my brother's birthdays, he had an oral English exam. Our English teacher never figured out who was who between the two of us, so I volunteered to do the exam for him, as I had the better grades – we changed places within the lesson, he was called up and I went out, got him a reasonably good exam and sat down in his chair to start misbehaving until I was thrown out of class – or better he was, as the entry in the class register only mentioned him, not me.

The boarding school had guys of all ages and therefore some older ones had already more advanced tastes in music and we listened to the Dutch band Ekseption and to Procul Harum, or I got interested in Blood Sweat & Tears and Chicago, who by that time were still calling themselves Chicago Transit Authority and Al Kooper and the first kind of jazz fusion bands like The Flock, Mahavishnu Orchestra and Chick Corea's Return to Forever. Radio Luxemburg, as in the past, continued to be a good source for new music. There were as well some exciting German bands like Kraan, Amon Düül II and sax player Klaus Doldinger, whose groups Passport and Jubilee I really got to like.

Professor Johann Neumayer not only ran the boarding school, but was our teacher in History and German as well – an open minded and fair guy who took a liking to our class of 10 pupils, always having each other's back. We were a tight bunch and somehow, he respected that, but he surely underestimated the lasting effect Jimi Hendrix had on the music world, as once, when seeing the huge Hendrix poster in our boarding school bedroom, he exclaimed that in 10 years Jimi would be forgotten and nobody would talk about him anymore … not quite!!

And we started to sneak out sometimes to go to our first concerts – I will always remember the first gig I attended: Procul Harum with the Orchestra of the Munich Kammeroper, conducted by Eberhard Schoener and a boy choir was there as well … and the guitar player at the time was none less than Robin Trower … what a first gig!! Jethro Tull were next and extremely good too! We always loved that band and especially their 'Aqualung' album. Then Deep Purple (support act was the German rock band Kin Ping Meh) on the heights of their powers …. And before 1973 was over, the unforgettable show by Pink Floyd – first songs like 'Set The Controls For The Heart Of The Sun', 'A Saucerful Of Secrets', 'Astronomy Domine' and 'Careful With That Axe Eugene' and then the full 'Dark Side Of The Moon' album – music and light show par excellence. Santana rounded these first gigs off with a tremendous concert featuring jazz vocalist Leon Thomas – sensational!
Some of the weekends I stayed with a friend who lived just around the corner from school – others I drove with some class mates to their homes in all parts of Austria to either spend a weekend or a short holiday, as going to Germany was not always financially a possibility.

Then we started going to a disco called Wendeltreppe, which played rock on certain nights (Iron Butterfly, Steve Harley, Golden Earring, Alex Harvey, Manfred Mann's Earthband, Hawkwind, Supertramp, Wishbone Ash and many more) and met girls, went to parties …. enjoying life as a teenager. Girls and going out with them became a part of our lives, no serious relationships and for me at least no proper sex before I was 18 – not intentionally, it just happened that way.

1973 Pink Floyd in Vienna

The school offered a lot of sports too – I did for many years orienteering and cross-country skiing and run many competitions, with some success, but nothing major. Of course, I played football for the school team and other teams when having the chance and was in the volleyball team as well.
The sports teacher, Lackner by name, always encouraged us to be active, which was fine by me. Another professor who left a big mark in my memory for various reasons, was 'Joe' Weiser, whom we had in Maths and Physics. He couldn't really explain anything and we often had to ask other teachers to help us and he would sometimes even sing the math problems to us to solve … one day we had a trip in the surroundings of Vienna, walking through woods and he came in shoes several sizes too big and he had inserted little folded paper trays, which one would normally use to serve sausages on, into his shoes so they would fit…. A truly strange character, who once helped my brother and myself in his unpredictable ways – as our family was by then based in Denmark, we liked to walk in Traeskos, the wooden soled shoes they wear in Denmark a lot, but as the director of the school deemed them to noisy, he forbade wearing them in school … only for Joe Weiser to come in the next day wearing a pair of these … and the ban was lifted.

1973 was the year our uncle Hans-Joachim was released from a French prison and exchanged for French nationals imprisoned in East Germany and sent back to East-Berlin, where his wife was waiting for him, having been released the year before.

1974 was the year Willy Brandt resigned as German Chancellor and Helmut Schmidt followed in his footsteps … an almost impossible task. In China the Terracotta Army of Qin Shi Huang was discovered and always held a certain fascination to me, which didn't change once I had a chance to see some of these statues at an exhibition at the Guggenheim Museum in Bilbao many years later. It's hard to imagine the man power and time that has gone into this monument of human skills. America's leading composer Duke Ellington passed away that year, leaving behind countless hours of timeless music.
Germany won the FIFA World Cup at home and Muhammad Ali beat George Foreman in the Rumble In The Jungle. Weather Report released their 'Mysterious Traveller' album, Norwegian guitarist Terje Rypdal his outstanding 'Whenever I Seem To Be Far Away' and Ralph Towner the wonderful 'Solstice', featuring saxophonist Jan Garbarek, bass player Eberhard Weber and drummer Jon Christensen, three players who would go on to write jazz history in Europe.
Then hearing about a school newspaper in Salzburg at one point, some friends and I decided to publish one at our own school and after discussions with the director we finally got going.
The content was a mixture of school topics, politics – mainly educational issues – general stories and music, films and arts in general. The Spenger Spots, as the paper was named in respect for the name of the street the school was located on, became a success at our school and after a year or so we included two other schools and then in the end it was available at six schools in total in Vienna, if I remember right.
Together with Ewald Volk, a colleague at school and friend of mine, I started writing a bit about music – so learning more about it, listening more and with diversity, developing from my father's jazz to CTI Records and its great albums by Bob James, Freddie Hubbard, Grover Washington, guitarists Eric Gale, Jim Hall and Gabor Szabo plus many more. And of course, now really getting into Miles Davis, discovering Weather Report and Chick Corea's various groups, trumpeter Ian Carr's Nucleus and Colosseum, listening constantly, starting to buy books about the history of the music (including Joachim Ernst Behrendt) and through a friend got introduced to ECM records in 1974 via the Keith Jarrett, Jan Garbarek album 'Belonging'.
But once we came to our final year and started to focus on our final exams, we had to stop doing the paper and there were no younger pupils interested in taking it over and continue what we started, so it simply disappeared.

Vienna had a few great jazz clubs at the time (Willy's Rumpelkammer, JazzSpelunke, Uzzi Förster's Einhorn, JazzGitti and Jazzland) and I started to visit them, as well as checking the few international acts that came by, like Art Farmer, local groups and blues artists, but jazz drew me more and more in. 1974 we went as well to see the bigger rock acts coming to Vienna, including a powerful performance by Emerson, Lake & Palmer. Keith Emerson was for a long time a favourite of mine – the first ever LP I bought being' The Five Bridges Suite' by The Nice, the group he had before ELP.

1974, Keith Emerson of ELP and ticket to their Vienna gig

In the summer of 1975, we finished school with a wild and fun party – I was 19 years old then and because of the great experience with the school paper had decided to become a journalist and to study journalism and politics – and therefore enrolled at the University in Vienna. I haven't documented all concerts I did see that year, but I am sure there were a few ones including local jazz acts like The Spontan Music Trio, and shows by German rock legend Udo Lindenberg, Ike and Tina Turner, who performed at the Konzerthaus to raving reviews and electronic pioneers Tangerine Dream, arriving with six Moogs and seven keyboards for three musicians … an unforgettable show, the music coming from mostly their album 'Ricochet' and the follow up live album 'Encore'. Some friends and I had started to work as kind of security at concerts for promoter Jeff Maxian, making sure the artists had peace in the backstage area, and so I got a first glimpse of life behind the scenes.

I was always interested in poetry (especially Rilke and the German classics) and even as a kid I always was writing poems myself – for the special holidays or my parents or just for fun … nothing worth reading, but the habit stayed and I did much more writing in the 70's – some of the poems, when I look at them today, are actually not that bad at all. Christian Morgenstern was someone I admired for his truthful humour, singer and songwriter Konstantin Wecker for his straight social lyrics and I tried to write something in their style … just to get this out of my system. Which is a bit like when playing the sax – you need to go via Coltrane at one point ….
After finishing school, I never considered going back to Germany, as that would have meant having to go and do the then mandatory military service for 18 months and I saw absolutely no sense in that, besides: I loved life in Vienna.

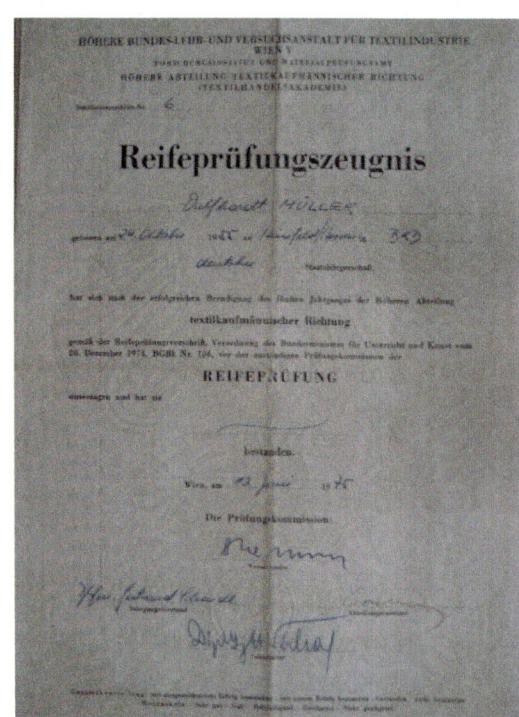

1975 Vienna, around the final exams and the report of these

In the summer holidays we usually went home to wherever my parents were living then … first in Germany again and then in Denmark, where we would work for the summer months in the company my father was running at the time, to make money for the next year of studies. Usually we would take the train, but sometimes we just hitchhiked home. My father was always interested in what I was listening to, less the rock side of it, but the jazzy ones and the more folk music-oriented albums. He was as well interested in some of the books we read, about society and labour conditions etc and liked to discuss these issues … how could you revolt against someone, who to a degree liked the books you read and the music you listened to? Our parents were always open and ready to learn, would leave us to ourselves when they felt we needed it, but were there in case we asked for them to be.

Reading always let me escape into other worlds - as a younger reader it was through the books by Enid Blyton and Karl May, then Johannes Mario Simmel and further on the German Classics like Goethe and Fontane, but as well modern writers like Hermann Hesse, Heinrich Böll, Günther Grass and, thanks to my older sister Marlis, J.R.R. Tolkien and Ann Fairbairn's 'Five Smooth Stones', which left a deep impression on me.

VIENNA, PART 2
1975 - 1978

I started University in the fall of 1975 – going for journalism and politics. The summer I had spent with my parents and meanwhile Christiane Reger, a colleague from school as well as a friend, had furnished a little flat for me, which I had rented from Herbert 'Herbie' Laa, another friend from school, for cheap – it didn't have a shower, but he lived next door and I could use his, so no major problem there. I was set and now just needed to find some jobs to get by studying. The obvious choice was of course working as a waiter in one of our favourite bars, but any other job would do as well – counting cars on crossroads or anything that brought a few Schillings for beer, food and rent. Going to the lectures was interesting and meeting new people exciting. I hardly ever had any money, but plenty of time to listen to and discover new music. And occasionally go to the movies – I still remember my favourite film from that year 'One Flew Over The Cuckoo's Nest' by Milos Forman, with an outstanding performance by Jack Nicholson as McMurphy, which won him an Oscar for best male actor and really kick-started his career.

The same year dictator Franco died in Madrid and Spain started to move towards democracy. Carlos 'The Jackal' and five more terrorists attacked the OPEC in Vienna and took many hostages, which were in the end flown out to Algiers and set free. The movie' The Rocky Horror Picture Show' was premiered in the US, while Jeff Beck released his album 'Blow By Blow, the Boss put out 'Born To Run' and Queen their single 'Bohemian Rhapsody', which became one of their most successful songs. Keith Jarrett released 'The Köln Concert', a beautiful solo piano recording, which became one of the best-selling jazz records of all time. Kenny Wheeler issued 'Gnu High', Julius Hemphill his powerful album 'Coon Bid'ness', featuring the composition 'The Hard Blues', which a bit later became part of the soundtrack of my life.

The first pub I was working in was the Stehbeisl – I had met Hannes, the owner, while hanging out at one of his previous pubs, called Augustin if I remember correctly and when he and his wife started the Stehbeisl in 1976, some friends and myself were there to help and work. We also started a football team with the pub and played some fun games and grew as a group of friends that became the centre of my social life. I remember well that once they did a little exhibition of paintings in the pub and asked me if I could be the DJ for this closed event – so I picked some cool jazz recordings and played mostly ballads and mid-tempo standards throughout the night, of course including Miles's 'Bye Bye Blackbird'. Never after did I make as much money in tips as on that night … what great music can do!!

The same year Chinese revolutionary Mao Zedong passed away aged 82; the Concord aircraft had its first commercial flight and Jimmy Carter was elected President of the USA, while saxophonist Jan Garbarek released his career making album 'Dis', trombone sensation Albert Mangelsdorff his 'Tromboneloneliness', composer and saxophonist extraordinaire Ornette Coleman 'Dancing In Your Head', bass wonder Jaco Pastorius his self-titled debut and Stanley Clarke his funky 'School Days' album. Besides a few other shows I went to see the Keith Jarrett Quartet perform, this one being the American group featuring Dewey Redman, Charlie Haden and Paul Motian. Simply amazing!

And while in Denmark with my parents I went to Aarhus to see and hear Herbie Hancock, whose group featured Wah Wah Watson and for that night only they had special guest Svend Asmussen on violin, improvising with them. An unforgettable concert for its sheer musicality and improvisational skills. A good year for music and especially jazz.

Studying was fun, I enjoyed not having much of a real schedule, except for when some work had to be done to earn some money or when an important lecture was scheduled. Otherwise, there was a lot of free time to read, enjoy life in general and play football with friends. Red Octopus Records became the shop of choice for new jazz records, where owner Karl Klebl always had a recommendation ready for me and occasionally the rare Japan import of a Miles Davis box or something else exciting. The best record store to learn and chat about jazz.
The 1970's were an interesting decade in German movie making with directors like Werner Herzog, Volker Schlöndorff, Rainer Werner Fassbinder, Wim Wenders, Eberhard Itzenplitz and others delivering some of their best work then and I went to see most of them.

When my brother Juergen came back to Vienna to study as well, we rented a small place from Helmut Schrammel, who was at the same school as we were and who had rented already the flat next to ours to one of our class-mates … again it had no water, not uncommon in the old Viennese houses, but the flat Hannes Steyrer, our friend, had rented did, so we shared the bathroom and toilet and spent a lot of time together listening to music or discussing topics of the time. My brother Juergen didn't really enjoy jazz, he was still a rock and blues guy, so we agreed to play music in the way that each of us would pick alternatively the record to be put on ... good for me, as I enjoyed his LPs as well, whereas he couldn't really go through a whole solo trombone album or the more experimental jazz I was listening to.

Being of German nationality and Austria not being part of the EU yet, we had to get a permission to stay in Austria every year. For that we had to prove that we got money from our parents regularly to be able to maintain our life as students without working, for which we would have needed a work permit. As our parents couldn't afford to support us every month, we had them send money once a year, a few weeks before we were due to renew our permission to stay in the country and went with that one transfer slip to the authorities. And we never had a problem – we were for sure better treated by the bureaucratic guys checking our application than most of the workers coming in from Eastern Europe.

For some time during our student years (mine lasted from 1975 to 1983) we worked in the company Christiane's mother had in the centre of town – helping with the delivery of furniture or whatever else they needed a pair of hands for ... interesting work with some interesting guys and good income for us. We did these unofficially, without a work permit, got paid in cash and had more or less an open schedule. As a student of journalism, I had to do some practical work as well and therefore started doing some freelance work for the Austrian radio company ORF.
At the Stehbeisl there were always a few guys from the radio station and they helped me a bit getting into it and gave me some valuable tips. I made stories for the program Radio Holiday, interviews and facts on whatever topic fitted the summer period ... like jogging in the morning heat or working with kids in the summer .... I simply did some interviews, edited them, added commentary and music and the story was done. The first few took me a while, but once I had the understanding of the 'how', it was easy earned money and fun.

the music corner in our apartment, about 1977

In early 1977 the first home computer, a Commodore PET, was demonstrated at the Consumer Electronics Show in Chicago and went on sale later that year, as well as the first Apple home computer. Spain was holding the first democratic elections for 41 years, won by Adolfo Suarez and his Union of the Democratic Centre and in Cologne the Red Army Faction abducted and killed Martin Schleyer, President of the German Employer Association. Shortly after this, three members of the RAF, Andreas Baader, Gudrun Ensslin and Jan-Carl Raspe, committed suicide in their prison cells.

'Annie Hall' by Woody Allen was released and won him international awards. The United Jazz + Rock Ensemble released their first album 'Live Im Schützenhaus' to critical acclaim and started touring Europe. This incredible band of band leaders featured over the years Wolfgang Dauner (piano), Charlie Mariano, Barbara Thompson, Christof Lauer (saxophone), Jon Hiseman (drums), Eberhard Weber, Dave King (bass), Volker Kriegel, Peter O'Mara (guitar), Ian Carr, Rüdiger Baldauf , Kenny Wheeler, Johannes Faber, Ack van Rooyen (trumpet, fluegelhorn) and Albert Mangelsdorff (trombone) and released all their records on their own label, Mood Records. I saw them a few times and always enjoyed their energy and original compositions. Al DiMeola released 'Elegant Gypsy', singer Radka Toneff the wonderful 'Fairytales' album with pianist Steve Dobrogosz and Keith Jarrett records the 'My Song' album with his European band, featuring Jan Garbarek on saxophone, Palle Danielsson on bass and Jon Christensen on drums and he brought that band to Vienna in October that year for an unforgettable performance at the Konzerthaus. The same year I had the pleasure to hear and see as well Austrian jazz legend Fatty George and Klaus Doldinger's group Passport, whose 1975 album 'Cross-Collateral' for me is a European classic. Stanley Clarke brought his funk to Vienna's Sofiensäle, but suffered from bad sound – a mixture of the wrong venue with a sound engineer who couldn't get it right. A sensational Jazz and Swing Concert! That was what the advert said for a truly special concert night at Vienna's Stadthalle featuring Ella Fitzgerald, Roy Eldridge, Joe Pass, the Oscar Peterson Trio and the Count Basie Orchestra. And special it was – true jazz heaven!!! To experience these Legends perform was a true pleasure and something I will always remember.

1977 David Gilmour, Pink Floyd. Photo by Tom Sebesta

In 1977 I saw Pink Floyd for the second time. They had just released their 'Animals' album and toured Europe with a mixture of their previous successes and the new music – the show was phenomenal!! The music great as expected, the lightshow beyond anything that toured at that time and 14.000 enthusiastic fans and a little smoke before the show, made that night really special.
Saxophonist Rahsaan Roland Kirk passed that year – I hadn't discovered his music yet, that would come a few years later when concert promoter Heinz Krassnitzer told me about a Kirk gig, he had the pleasure to attend and I started listening to his music. There are so many great recordings still available by this outstanding musician – my personal favourite is 'Blacknuss' because of its raw power, incredible performances and eclectic song choices.

The 1970's were in one way the continuation of the 60's with their fights for racial and gender equality, against the Vietnam war and for the environment, but in another way a new conservatism took hold of politics, culminating in the election of Margaret Thatcher as UK Prime Minister and putting question marks behind some of the achievements of the student movement of the decade before. Terrorism became a global threat, local and international and left a trail of blood on the world.
Meanwhile my studies continued, we started to go to a new pub called Das Lange where we made new friends, including Michael and Ernestine Dietl, with whom we would work a few years later. I had as well become friends with Heinz Krassnitzer, who was one of the guys at Live Performance Service, the most important jazz agent and promoter in Austria and he invited me often to see shows or we talked about new albums and artists. Together with some friends I had also started to work for Heinz as security for his concerts and festivals. I remember being in Velden with him, but can't recall much of the music, as we were stationed outside of the performance tent. The Brecker Brothers and B.B. King spring to mind, but not much more. Beside the festival in Velden (1979 to 1981) LPS as well produced since 1976 the Jazzfestival Wiesen, run by Franz Bogner, owner of the Jazzpub in Wiesen, in which he had concerts and jazz DJ's since 1972.

1978 - 1980

1978 was only the second year when three different Popes reigned the Catholic Church after 1605. Pope John Paul II succeeded Pope John Paul I, who only was in office for 33 days after succeeding Pope Paul VI. John Paul II was the first Polish pope in history, as well as the first non-Italian pope since Pope Adrian VI, 455 years before him. Reinhold Messner and Peter Habeler climbed Mount Everest for the first time without supplemented oxygen and Argentina won the FIFA World Cup at home, with Mario Kempes being their star player. Sony Corporation showed the Walkman portable cassette player for the first time in public. Chick Corea released 3 essential albums that year – 'The Mad Hatter', 'Secret Agent' and 'Friends'; Carla Bley her complex 'Musique Mecanique' and James Blood Ulmer his 'Tales Of Captain Black'. The drummer of rock band The Who, Keith Moon, died of an accidental overdose and Kate Bush was heading the charts in the UK with her composition 'Wuthering Heights', while I went and see as many shows as I could, including the Gary Burton Quartet, the outstanding guitar trio of Charly Byrd, Barney Kessel and Herb Ellis as well as Alexis Korner, whom I had the pleasure to hear three times in different settings – with his band, then in a duo with bass player Colin Hodginson and with Route 66, all three events unforgettable for me.
As the 70's came to an end, we witnessed some events in 1979 that would change the world forever, which of course at the time we didn't foresee: after the western backed Shah fled the country, Ayatollah Khomeini returned to Iran after 15 years in exile and took control. The rest, as they say, is history! Israel and Egypt signed a Peace Treaty and Philips Electronics demonstrated publicly for the first time the Compact Disc and found an immediate ambassador in legendary conductor Herbert von Karajan. Haruki Murakami published his first novel, 'Hear The Wind Sing', the first part of the so called 'Trilogy Of The Rat', which continued with 'Pinball' and 'A Wild Sheep Chase'. Douglas Adams

put out the first book in the five-part trilogy of 'The Hitchhikers Guide To The Galaxy', hilarious and funny books, that I discovered a few years later.

1979 program Jazz Festival Wiesen

I saw The Who perform at the Zeppelin Field in Germany in front of 90.000 rock fans, which was one of the first gigs with new drummer Kenney Jones ... and Pete Townsend surely smashed his guitar at the end of the amazing show ... on the same trip I saw as well a Woodstock Revival Festival, featuring Richie Havens and Joe Cocker, who was unable to walk onto the stage without help, managed somehow to do 5 fantastic songs and then had to be carried off again ... then that summer of '79 I went to my first jazz festival in Wiesen and truly enjoyed the atmosphere and music – many firsts that weekend, like Jan Garbarek with John Taylor, Bill Connors, Eberhard Weber and Jon Christensen or the Sun Ra Arkestra, Abdullah Ibrahim, Dexter Gordon and Old And New Dreams, who played an unforgettable set. This group consisting of Don Cherry, Dewey Redman, Charlie Haden and Ed Blackwell was paying a wonderful tribute to the music of Ornette Coleman. That was the beginning of many trips to festivals in Austria and then all around the world.

Meanwhile in Cuba 'The Havana Jam' took place, with Weather Report, Irakere, The CBS All Stars featuring Dexter Gordon, Bob James, George Duke, Stan Getz, Eric Gale, Arthur Blythe and many more, plus a group called Trio Of Doom, which featured guitar wizard John Mc Laughlin, bass wonder Jaco Pastorius and drum genius Tony Williams. The 2 tracks, featured on the 2 albums from this event, were the only recording available of this power trio until 2007.

Pink Floyd was premiering 'The Wall' live in L.A. and releasing the album later that year. The Crusaders were having a hit with the Joe Sample song 'Street Life', sung by Randy Crawford, Dollar Brand (Abdullah Ibrahim) released his 'African Marketplace' album, Pat Metheny 'American Garage', Jack DeJohnette his Special Edition and the group Old And New Dreams their self-titled first album. The world/jazz music group Codona, featuring Collin Walcott, Don Cherry and Nana Vasconcelos released their second album 'Codona 2', with a powerful version of the Don Cherry composition 'Malinye'.

Even so this decade opened the door into jazz for me, I was (and I am) still listening to rock and some of the best live rock albums come from that period of the late 60's and 70's. The main difference to later rock bands was, that then rock, at least live, had a lot of improvisation in it – just check out Cream 'Live', Humble Pie's 'Rockin' The Fillmore' as well as live recordings by The Doors, Ten Years After, Wishbone Ash, The Who, Blue Oyster Cult, Deep Purple, Allman Brothers Band, Frank Zappa, Colosseum, Grand Funk Railroad, Uriah Heep and many others to hear what I mean. These recordings are still part of my life's soundtrack, plus a few more added over the years.

Poster for Woodstock Revival Festival

1980 – 1983

With the death of Tito in early 1980 the break-up of the former Yugoslavia started and kept the region in turmoil for years to come. Lech Walesa became a Polish icon through the strikes at the Gdansk shipyard and finally the founding of the Solidarity trade union. Ronald Reagan was elected President of the USA. Pianist Bill Evans passed away, shortly after recording a run of concerts at New York's Village Vanguard and John Lennon was murdered in December that year. Germany became European champions at the Euros in Italy with players like Horst Hrubesch, Bernd Schuster, Klaus Allofs, Karlheinz Rummenigge and others shining in the tournament. The Police released their first album 'Zenyatta Mondatta', Pat Metheny put out the incredible '80/81' with Charlie Haden, Michael Brecker, Dewey Redman and Jack DeJohnette, whose 'Tin Can Alley' was as well released that year and James Blood Ulmer asked us 'Are You Glad To Be in America?'. Barbara Thompson released the sensational live album by her group Paraphernalia 'Live In Concert' and I discovered the Vienna Art Orchestra, who had just released their first album and playing around the clubs in Vienna, especially in the Jazzspelunke.
A few friends and myself went to see The Who and Led Zeppelin that year in Vienna – powerful (and loud!!) concerts with the bands in top form, expanding the songs to captivating rock improvisation In the middle of Jimmy Page's solo one idiot threw a little firework cracker on the stage, whi exploded close to the guitarist – the show was stopped until that guy was guided out of the ver and then Jimmy and the band thankfully continued their amazing playing. Unforgettable!!

My studies moved forward without too many problems and at the end of the year we started to help our friends Michael and Ernestine to build a new pub in Vienna's 8th district to be called 'u.s.w.'. Franz Maurer was also part-owner, if my memory serves me well, and Christian Hofbauer, Reinhard Mayr, Georges Kirtz and myself, plus a few more were to work there after the opening in early 1981. The long bar and relaxed atmosphere in the pub made it an immediate success in the area and beyond. When Christian and I were working we usually played some core jazz around the time the pub was to close for the day … and after a few weeks doing so, saw that there were a few guys coming in late to catch a bit of the music, which gave Michael the idea to check the neighbourhood for a smaller place to build a new pub with jazz music as theme. More or less around the corner he found the perfect place, which we then started to refurbish to what was to become the jazz café 'miles smiles'. Tom Sebesta, a friend and designer, created a painting based on the album cover of Miles' 'A tribute To Jack Johnson', which, almost life size, covers a wall in the bar.

While we were working to get the jazz pub open in the fall, the year took its course with assassination attempts on Ronald Reagan, Pope John Paul II and Anwar Sadat and AIDS for the first time was clinically mentioned in the US. We followed the band IVIRON, which friends of us had founded, Ingo Schleicher and Fritz Rainer, plus others including saxophonist Karl Takats, a great player and very nice guy, who continued to perform with some of Austria's leading pop acts over the coming years. Miles Davis made a comeback with the album 'The Man With The Horn' and started as well touring again. Another of my favourite trumpet players, Lester Bowie released his incredible 'The Great Pretender' album and Charlie Haden, Jan Garbarek & Egberto Gismonti their outstanding 'Folk Songs' and the Austrian Jazzzwio of Harry Pepl on guitar and Werner Pirchner on vibraphone released their 'Live Montreux '81' – an instant Austrian and European jazz classic. Another classic released that year came from guitarists Al Di Meola, Paco De Lucia and John McLaughlin and was their live album 'Friday Night In San Francisco', that set the standard very high for any guitar player.

That summer, while with George at a public swimming pool, I met x-ray assistant Eva Maria and we started to go out and soon she became my girlfriend. Late September we finally opened the 'miles smiles' and Heinz Krassnitzer helped us to get a live act for the opening night – Eberhard Weber and Bill Frisell.

'miles smiles' jazz café   photo by Rainer Rygalyk

Bass player Weber had booked a few dates in a duo with the then not much known guitarist Frisell, as Bill had before played his first European tour as a member of the Paul Motian band. The small place was packed and people were even listening to the music through the open windows while standing outside on the street. The idea was to have the occasional gig in the pub, but in general we would play music from LPs, which initially came from the collections of Christian and myself. And we always displayed the cover of the album that just played, so people could check that out. Heinz got us as well the second live act for the jazz café, as we called it, another duo, this time of violinist L. Shankar and tabla master Zakir Hussain. The two had played the previous day in Berlin in front of 1000 people and then came to Vienna to play for 100, packed in a small room, but enthusiastic and attentive. The music was powerful and touching, Zakir's fingers moving so fast that sometimes one couldn't see movement at all, just hearing the sound … and L. Shankar adding little melodies and violin wizardry. Absolutely amazing and a wonderful follow-up to the first concert. I had to pick up Zakir the day after the show to go to the Indian Embassy and there in his hotel room in his underwear, he gave me a hilarious impression of Miles Davis, with croaky voice and all … Zakir and my ways would cross again a few times in the future, but then I was just amazed how down to earth and kind that great artist was.

The 'miles smiles' became our new home away from home, our circle of friends either worked there as well or came by and we moved our football team to that pub and started to play more often. Christian and myself were running the place for Michael and Ernestine, and Christian looked together with them after the stock of food and drinks and I looked after the music – getting gigs or going to record companies to ask for the latest releases to be played in the jazz café and making sure the program of shows appeared in the various magazines in Vienna. At the beginning the two of us worked almost every evening/night, to connect with the new customers, but soon after we had a great team working with us. More concerts followed, but then by local artists mainly, like Karl Takats, marimba player Woody Schabata or pianist Gus Seeman, whom we knew from his work with the Spontan Music Trio. Our regular guests included beside Heinz Krassnitzer, the journalist Gunther Baumann, photographer and friend of mine from studying journalism, Rainer Rygalyk, musicians like Eric Trauner, leader of the Mojo Blues Band, comedians and people who simply liked jazz.

In April of 1982 I saw that Miles Davis was giving a concert in Frankfurt/Main in Germany. Heinz knew about that as well and wanted to go – so we spoke to my sister Marlis, who was living there at the time, and arranged to stay with her for one night, Heinz got us through an agent friend in Germany tickets and off we went – by train, overnight, as it was cheaper than flying. The first time for both of us to see Miles live – playing mostly the music from 'The Man With The Horn' with a band consisting of Mike Stern on guitar, Bill Evans on saxes, Marcus Miller on bass, Mino Cinelu on percussion and Al Foster on drums. Wow … that one I'll never forget (and now I can even re-visit it as often as I like on Youtube)! Heinz and I then spent the night at my sisters. We slept on her living room floor and the following day we went back to Vienna with another overnight train, where we arrived tired, but happy. And on the next tour Heinz and Fritz Thom, his boss and partner at the LPS booking agency, would bring Miles to Vienna!

1982 Miles Davis (with Mino Cinelu) Live in Frankfurt

That summer they asked me to be their festival secretary at the Wiesen Jazz Festival and I gladly accepted – so I was there all three days, working behind the stage, receiving the artists and making sure everything was running smoothly with Heinz, who was picking the artists up at the airport. I remember three things from that festival – 1. Andreas Vollenweider was to play there and as I had long curly hair at that time and was wearing a white shirt, a journalist mistook me for him and asked me for an interview ... 2. I saw Bill Frisell again, who really seemed pleased about that and from that on, I always tried to go and see him when he was playing in or around Vienna, and 3. Terje Rypdal, whom I really like and saw him there for the first time and truly did enjoy the concert. I drove with him and the band to his hotel and they were a bit complaining about the changing rooms (they all were in an old, but clean and well looked after, rail wagon ... a bit different and obviously not everyone's taste ...) and as I spoke a bit Danish, I did understand most of it, but didn't comment until I said Goodbye in Danish and they kind of knew that I had heard everything ...

After living for a while with Christian in the 6th district of Vienna, I had moved to a small flat in the 3rd district, which had a shower inside and one bigger room and a kitchen, but the toilet outside, shared with one neighbour. It was a bit off the centre, but I enjoyed living there, having known the flat from before, as my friend Harry Schwartz lived there, but when he moved in with his girlfriend, I took the opportunity and rented his.

The same year the world was looking perplexed at the Falkland war between Argentina and Britain, we went to the movies to see Ben Kingsley's impressive performance in 'Gandhi' or the wonderful movie by Jamie Uys, 'The Gods Must Be Crazy'. The first compact discs were manufactured in Germany and the first CD players sold in Japan, while Italy won the FIFA World Cup in Spain with Victory over Germany. Michael Jackson released his album 'Thriller', which still is the best-selling album of all times. Miles Davis released the live album 'We Want Miles', including a very cool version of his 'Jean Pierre', a composition he played as well when Heinz and I saw him in Frankfurt earlier that year. Chick Corea released his 'Touchstone' album, his first collaboration with guitar legend Paco de Lucia, who performs on two songs. Don Cherry and Ed Blackwell released their timeless 'El Corazon' album and Hungarian bass player Aladar Pege his outstanding 'Solo Bass' recording.

Rainer Rygalyk, drummer Rudi Staeger and myself started talking about creating a jazz magazine for Austria ... a late-night idea from the jazz café 'miles smiles', but at one point we really got into planning it and in 1983 we finally had the first issue in our hands, ready to be sold directly to jazz fans at the Jazz Festival in Wiesen and then per subscription. But it was hard work to get to this first issue – at that time we didn't have computers available as widely as we have now, so all we had was an electric type writer and lots of enthusiasm – and we learned by doing.

We decided that the first issue should have Austrian jazz legend Hans Koller on the cover and the magazine should have stories, interviews, LP reviews, a calendar with jazz gigs around Austria and a jazz gallery with photos from Rainer's collection and it should be in the A 5 format, to fit in the back pocket of a pair of jeans. We printed 15.000 copies, as we wanted them to be as well in jazz clubs, kiosks etc. but had to go down with the coming issues as subscriptions didn't meet our un-realistic target. Rainer and myself wrote most of the first issues, but had journalists like Klaus Schulz, a specialist in the history of Austrian Jazz, Werner Rosenberger and others to contribute. Then there was the issue with advertising – we needed these to survive, so everyone got to talk to their contacts – clubs, festivals, record companies, record stores … and we got enough to make it happen! We delivered everything to Bobby, our man at our printer Schreier & Braune and when done, Rudi took care of the distribution, except for the stock we went to sell at the festival in Wiesen, where Michael and Ernestine, meanwhile, had bought a house with tons of space, which every year for the festival gave us a place to stay. We sold well at the festival and the first step for this little Austrian jazz magazine, called "Jazz Live", was done. By then, the Austrians only had either the German magazine 'JazzPodium', or the US one, 'Downbeat', to get their Info's from. Subscriptions started to flow in and we got ready for the next issue – we had planned for 10 a year, with August/September and December/January covered by one magazine respectively.

VIENNA, Part 3
1983 – 1984

Wiesen '83 was a really good festival and from the many concerts I remember especially Oscar Peterson and Lionel Hampton, Charles Lloyd with Michel Petrucciani, Art Blakey and Herbie Hancock. I also went to the Jazz Festival on the Formula 1 track in Knittelfeld, which unfortunately didn't have many visitors, but great music by an expressive and captivating Sun Ra Arkestra, as well as two duo shows by Chick Corea – one with Gary Burton on vibraphone and the other with classical pianist Friedrich Gulda – both sensational, deep and touching. Meanwhile, my studies suffered from the work at 'miles smiles' and the magazine and that my professor, who was overlooking my final essay, passed away, didn't help either. Being in a fix relationship and working a lot at nights wasn't ideal and therefore I started to look around for a proper job and did send out a bunch of CVs to different companies for work I thought was interesting.

In 1983 socialist Chancellor of Austria Bruno Kreisky's reign came to an end, Swatch presented their first low price watches, the German magazine Stern published the Hitler Diaries, which turned out to be fake … fake news even then! Vanessa Williams was elected the first African American Miss America, while Metallica released their first album. Bass player Jamaaladeen Tacuma put out his amazing and groovy 'Show Stopper' record, Miles Davis his blues influenced 'Star People', Herbie Hancock his modern and cool and funky 'Future Shock' and Carla Bley and Charlie Haden their timeless 'The Ballad Of The Fallen'. ECM Records released their first Compact Disc – Keith Jarrett's 'Köln Concert' with an incredible sound, as the music was newly mastered especially for the CD, therefore not using the LP master, as had been done for many releases before and giving ground to the notion that the LP would sound better, but if the music is mastered for the new medium, it will be as good as … something some leading mastering experts had said for a while.

As we were working on the 'Jazz Live' October issue, I got a call from PolyGram, the Austrian branch of the international record company, to whom I had send my CV and they asked if I could come in for an interview … sure I could! There were lots of candidates being interviewed and I was the only non-Austrian, who would need a work permit in case he got the job … but to my surprise a few days later I was asked to come in for a second interview and then a few days after that I got the call that I could start on October 15th in the Import Music Service department.

And so started my career in the music business. PolyGram was then jointly owned by Philips Electronics and Siemens, who both brought their labels into the group – Polydor and Deutsche Grammophon from Siemens and Phonogram, Philips and Mercury from Philips. Polydor had their head offices in Hamburg, Germany and Phonogram theirs in Baarn in The Netherlands, where in the end the combined head office was, before being moved to London in the mid 1980's. In the Austrian branch, run by Wolfgang Arming, a seasoned music business executive and great boss and mentor, they used mainly the local label 'amadeo' for artists directly signed to the company, even so when expecting possible international sales, they used Polydor as a label. The department I was working in, IMS, basically did the following: distribution in Austria of all 12" singles from within PolyGram companies, which meant one had to follow the charts and be prepared to have enough stock if one of the singles, which were handled by the Pop division, became a hit. We could also import PolyGram repertoire from other countries, like Greece or France or Italy, if something had a bit of potential in our market, but wasn't big enough for the main repertoire division to take it on and last, but not least, we could sign indie labels for distribution deals in Austria. After learning the repertoire quickly and where to check the charts, I found out that we had the right to import all Fantasy, Milestone, Prestige repertoire via a deal in Germany and so we did that, which helped to raise turnover. After really getting into it, I signed a few indie jazz labels from the US for distribution in Austria, as in these cases I knew they didn't have a partner in the market – best of these was Gramavision, whose excellent recordings by John Scofield, Oliver Lake, Jamaaladeen Tacuma and Bob Moses, beside others, I really liked. Jonathan Rose, the founder, was surprised when I got in touch, but helpful and positive. We too had the rights for a little soundtrack from Ode Records in Canada, 'The Rocky Horror Picture Show', and sold very well every year … and especially great when they did a German version in one of Vienna's musical theatres. IMS did well, I was even sent to an international Import Meeting within PolyGram, where we discussed what was selling, who had which rights and if there was anything, we could do together … Eddie Wilkinson was running the UK operation for IMS then, Martin Davies was in France, and the guys from Germany and the US were there as well. Again, learning the ropes by doing. In 1983 PolyGram was talking to WEA (Warner, Electra, Atlantic) about a possible merger, but the talks failed. Philips bought most of the Siemens shares that year to have overall control of the company.

I was at IMS for about a year, before being asked to join the international pop division as product manager for UK/US repertoire. That was 1984 and in the January issue of that year I wrote in 'Jazz Live' a short portrait of Hungarian bass player Aladar Pege, a wonderful musician and really sweet person, who later that year would record his 'Solo Bass II' album at the jazz café 'miles smiles' and even dedicate a composition on this record to the place and its crew. I had stopped working there, but still was kind of involved and either with my girlfriend Eva or just with the gang, spent a lot of time there. I stopped reviewing records for 'Jazz Live', as I thought it would be a conflict of interest with working at PolyGram … but I continued to write articles and do the occasional interview. As the product manager for UK repertoire, I usually got an advance cassette with either the single or album to evaluate the potential in Austria and of course always checking how a certain single was doing in either the UK or Germany, both very influential markets for us. One of the first singles I got was 'Shout' by Tears For Fears and after listening to it with the team, we were not sure about it … and in the product meeting with all the other divisions (German and local repertoire, Classical) I said something like *"this will never be a hit"*, which sure enough two weeks later I regretted … the single was storming the charts in the UK and Germany and we almost missed the boat … I never repeated that sentence and took a valuable lesson: you can't predict how the listener will react!

The same year the Cirque Du Soleil was founded, France beat Spain to win the Euro '84 at home, the assassination of Indira Gandhi led to riots all over India and the first part of Edgar Reitz's film series 'Heimat' about a German family from the 1840's to 2000 was released. The Boss issued his 'Born In The U.S.A.' album, which was the first CD manufactured in the US and Prince released the album of the decade with 'Purple Rain'. On the jazz side, Chick Corea put out his wonderful 'Children Songs' recording, Bobby McFerrin made waves with 'The Voice', Bill Frisell delivered 'Rambler' and Miles Davis 'Decoy', featuring among others John Scofield, Branford Marsalis and Gil Evans, who arranged 'That's Right'.

And I went to my first international product and marketing manager meetings – first in Hamburg for Polydor and then in Baarn for Phonogram. Just before I left my boss gave me a single which was doing extremely well on the label Musica in Austria – Opus 'Live Is Life', as he had obtained the international rights and I should present it to all the colleagues from around the world. I never had a problem speaking in front of people, so I played the song, gave all the info and later spoke to the Polydor International guy, Michael Golla, about how to make the record available everywhere, as the response from my colleagues was really great and, in the end, this was a big hit for the band and us – single and album did extremely well internationally. But the biggest hit of the year came from Phonogram UK in form of Band Aid's 'Do They Know It's Christmas'. This single, written by Bob Geldof and Midge Ure and performed by the top stars of the time (Bono, Phil Collins, Boy George, Simon Le Bon, Bananarama, Status Quo, Sting, Paul Weller and Paul Young among others), was released as a charity single for famine relief in Ethiopia and sold close to 12 million units globally. And it topped the charts in Austria for a few weeks.

1984 was the year Milos Forman released his movie 'Amadeus', which was a huge hit in Austria, the land of Mozart. Short after the release and after I had seen the movie, I was playing football with some guys from the Burgtheater, the most important German language theatre and one of the guys said "Want to go out tonight, hang in bars without paying?" Surprised, I asked how he would do that … and he started laughing – exactly like Mozart in the movie, immediately recognisable. It turned out that he had synchronized Wolfgang Amadeus voice for the German version of the movie and therefore had the 'original' Mozart laughter ... and so we went from bar to bar and he did his laughter and everyone wanted to invite us ... it turned out to be a long night in the company of Mozart and a tough morning.

In June I wrote for 'Jazz Live' a portrait of Austrian saxophonist Wolfgang Puschnig – and that was the first time we actually met and talked. He was at the time part of the Vienna Art Orchestra and had some other band projects on the side, but hadn't recorded yet under his own name and didn't have then much urge to do so. When interviewing him I also met his wife at the time, singer extraordinaire Linda Sharrock and we as well got along great right from the start.

The Wiesen jazz festival had a bunch of great shows that year, especially Charles Lloyd with Michel Petrucciani (I will never forget the image Charles carrying Michel in his arms to the piano ...), Lester Bowie's Brass Fantasy with their jazzy pop tunes and of course Miles Davis, who at one point of the show was joined on stage by Chick Corea for a little jam. Excellent and unforgettable.

1984, Miles and Chick Corea, photo by Rainer Rygalyk

Another memorable event from 1984 was the 'Jazz Around The Clock', a 24 hours concert at the Technical University in Vienna, as a showcase of the strength of the local jazz scene in a situation where the Austrian radio and TV mostly, as well as the big record companies, neglected that genre. Originating in an idea by 'miles smiles' regular Herbert Pirchner, Fritz Thom and Heinz Krassnitzer took it on themselves to organise the 24-hour jazz marathon with all genres within jazz being represented. The radio station in the end participated and the local jazz musicians showed extremely high quality and musicianship. We from the 'miles smiles' volunteered to work there and so got to hear at least some of the music – especially the Karlheinz Miklin Trio left a strong impression on me. In November the percussionist and member of the groups Oregon and Codona, both some of my favourites, Colin Walcott, died in a car accident while on tour in Europe. I was lucky enough to have seen him with Codona in Wiesen and Saalfelden and with Oregon once. An outstanding and unique musician.

1985

The following year I worked on the album by UK band The Cure 'The Head On The Door' which included the singles 'In Between Days' and 'Close To Me'. We had the singer Robert Smith in Vienna for promotion, went to the scene restaurant 'Wiener' with him, as we would with most artists in town and then I went to London to see them perform – what a great band with a very unique sound.

PolyGram had signed a license and distribution deal with A&M and we had a meeting to introduce all the international marketing managers to them in London. Wolfgang Arming went with me, as he had other business to attend there, and when it came to us, I introduced myself with name and position and some nice words on their repertoire and artists, then Arming introduced himself and added "the two of us stand for A&M in Austria (Arming & Müller) and will make the label proud" ... and right he was! Sting put out his 'Dream Of The Blue Turtle' album on the label that gave us as well Bryan Adams successful 'Reckless' album, from which at one point we had 3 singles in the top 10 in Austria. A&M also released in 1985 Suzanne Vega's first and self-titled album, with the outstanding song 'Marlene On The Wall' included. I had seen her before at an international meeting, where she went out in front of the worst crowd possible, record business executives, and just blew everyone away.

Peter Pernica, my PR guy and myself worked on the album 'History Mix, 1' by Godley & Crème, which included the single 'Cry', for which the two did an amazing video clip. They came to Vienna for promotion and TV and we spend some time with them. They are really cool and nice guys and did roll the most perfect joints I've ever seen.
Other records we worked that year came from INXS, Elton John, Swiss group Yello, Bon Jovi, the Fine Young Cannibals, and rockers Magnum and Dio, among many others.

It was as well that year that I asked my boss Wolfgang Arming to get us a distribution deal for ECM. As he knew label boss and sole producer Manfred Eicher from his time in Germany, he set up a meeting for himself and me at the ECM offices in Munich. As this was and still is one of my favourite labels of all time, it was easy to convince Manfred that we could look after their catalogue and new releases and soon we started working with their music. Shortly after we took over distribution of the ECM catalogue and new releases, Pat Metheny played a concert at the Vienna Konzerthaus.

I went to say "Hi" and talked a to a guitar playing (as a warm up) Pat backstage ... then he played an incredible show for over 2 hours, only to be playing the guitar as a warm down afterwards again. They had planned a gig in Budapest the day after, which was cancelled for reasons I can't recall, so they asked me to get them to some of Vienna's jazz clubs, as they wanted to try to get a gig there instead. The Jazzspelunke had a local act booked for the day after and decided to postpone that one, so Pat could play there on that night ... and so he did!!! A really rare showing of a big jazz star in a small club – intense and deep.

Another ECM act, that came to Austria very often, was Lester Bowie and in 1985 he had released his incredible Brass Fantasy album 'I Only Have Eyes For You' and came to play the Jazzgalerie in Nickelsdorf, so I did some promotion before the concert in Vienna. Lester, all gentleman that he was, did all the interviews over coffee, cognac and a cigar and was fun to work with. We chatted a lot and got along pretty well, and from then on, I never missed a gig when he was in town or somewhere close.

1985 Pat Metheny in Vienna. Photo by Rainer Rygalyk

I had always wanted to sign a few local jazz acts to 'amadeo', as I thought they had enough potential to make it work financially – but Arming denied the request every single time. Then he did send me to a negotiating course with some guys from the unions and they taught me how to find the right angle in any deal you want to strike. A bit of preparation, the right moment and I left the boss's office with the OK to sign local jazz acts in the coming three years, but would not be able to continue after that, if I were to lose money on the project. Immediately I started to prepare the first releases for 1986.

And while I was doing that, Mikhail Gorbachev became General Secretary of the Soviet Communist Party; Vodafone launched the first mobile network in the UK; the Unabomber was active in the US and European football was in mourning after the Heysel Stadium disaster, which left 39 people dead and about 600 injured when Liverpool and Juventus met for the European Cup Final. The Schengen agreement was signed by Belgium, France, Luxembourg, The Netherlands and West Germany and created a zone without internal border controls. Another step in the direction of a united Europe. Commodore launched the first personal computer, Amiga, in New York and Microsoft released the first version of their Windows software. My favourite jazz albums of that year were Miles Davis' 'You're Under Arrest' with his versions of Steve Porcaro's song for Michael Jackson 'Human Nature' and Cindy Lauper's 'Time After Time'. Which apart from 'Jean Pierre' became one of his signature tunes in the later years of his life. Japanese bass player Nobuyoshi Ino released his duo album with trumpet star Lester Bowie, simply titled 'Duet', which features a touching and timeless version of Sting's 'Moon Over Bourbon Street', and Don Cherry released his reggae-influenced album 'Home Boy (Sister Out)' with him as well singing. Outstanding tracks for me on this recording are 'Butterfly Friend' and 'Bamako Love'. Marc Johnson's 'Bass Desires' and the rocky 'Chasers' by Terje Rypdal complete this list.

Around the same time my girlfriend Eva and I had decided to move together and found a cool little flat in Vienna's 4th district and all friends helped to take down a wall, re-paint the place and furbish it. Harry Schwarz and Michael Pribitzer designed and built a book and record shelf that would have lasted through many earthquakes, if necessary. Franz Maurer and his brothers helped too, as did in some ways the rest of the gang. The house warming party was a lot of fun and even included some of our new neighbours. We had a good time there together, spending time in each other's company, but as well leaving each other their individual space. Eva liked music, but wasn't really passionate about it, so only occasionally and when it was a musician we socialized with, like Wolfgang and Linda, she came to gigs with me. We both liked Greece and spent our holidays either there or with our parents.

At the 'miles smiles' we had a concert with guitarist Harry Pepl, vibraphonist Werner Pirchner and drummer Georg Polanski, which was really amazing and luckily, we had Christian Sodl, a friend from Austrian Radio ORF, recording the show, which was then released in 2003 as a CD. Other memorable concerts at the 'miles smiles' included one by Karlheinz Miklin, as when he did a solo, Christian's girlfriend Monika entered the jazz cafe with her dog, who started to bark at the sax ... and Charlie simply played along ... sublime!! Another concert was that of group AM 4, which stands for 'A Monastic Quartet' and actually was a trio of Wolfgang Puschnig on saxes and flute, singer Linda Sharrock and pianist Uli Scherer. This was an outstanding concert and the musical variety and deepfelt emotions these musicians displayed was very special. We recorded that show, but unfortunately there was a problem with the tape and it could not be used. But ECM later did a studio recording with this trio, which I think is a really great album, but I was, nevertheless, disappointed in some way when I heard the album for the first time, as for me it only showed a certain aspect of the group and not their complete potential.

The 'miles smiles' football team had as well started, on an initiative by Heimo Holzbach, to arrange twice a year a friendly tournament with a team from Darmstadt, which later was expanded to 4 teams. Once a year we would go to Germany to play and once the Germans would come to us. These events were always a lot of fun and we started every year to prepare something special for the final night, when the cup was to be handed out to the winner. As we had with Fritz Rainer, Tom Sebesta, Heinz Ruff, Reinhard Mayr and Karl Maierhofer a few musicians in our group, we started to do some musical numbers ... once a Spike Jones playback, which was hilarious ... then full live shows, like an Austrian music event, or the Blues Brothers and even the Rocky Horror Picture Show, but of course all with changed lyrics, all referring to our event. At one point we booked a studio and recorded a single about the tournament, which we then had manufactured in a limited edition, performed and handed out to our guests. Manfred 'Mani' Hofer, our coach and best player, was as well an active member of the group setting these events up, so were Josef 'Seppi' Dorrek, Robert Swoboda, Jutta Hofer and Tina Maierhofer, Werner Geisberger and many others. To plan these events and then do the performance once a year at the tournament in Vienna, really kept the group close and together.

celebrating a win with Franz Maurer, Darmstadt, mid 1980's

The jazz festival in Hollabrunn brought Miles Davis back to Austria with a strong gig and there were as well memorable performances by bass player Jamaaladeen Tacuma, Pharoah Sanders, Joe Zawinul and Duo Due, consisting of the brothers Christian and Wolfgang Muthspiel. They had in advance to this concert sent me their debut album, released on a small label in Graz. The duo show was absolutely brilliant and so I went backstage afterwards and told them that I would release their next album, after I had seen them perform. It was as well in 1985 that I met Paco De Lucia for the first time – he came to play at the Konzerthaus in Vienna in December that year – 2 sold out shows and as we had all his recordings via Philips, I went to say "*Hi*" and hear one of the shows. It was magical to see this guy perform wonders on his guitar and he was such a humble and kind human being. But the musical highlight of the year were the LIVE AID concerts in London and Philadelphia, with satellite shows in 7 more countries, raising an estimate £ 150 million globally in the process for famine relief in Ethiopia. Especially, the performance by the group Queen stood out, but The Who, U2 and David Bowie, Eric Clapton and many more played as well. I was glued to the TV set at home, watching this with a few friends … a very special and emotional event. In the cinemas, Sydney Pollack's 'Out Of Africa' and Steven Spielberg's 'The Colour Purple' were successful in a year when I celebrated my 30th birthday with a party together with my friend Herbie Laa, who had his birthday 3 days before mine and had a big hall where he manufactured I don't know what, but had moved everything aside so we could celebrate in style. All our friends were there, good food and enough beer and wine and music … dancing all night long.

The team at PolyGram in Vienna was a collection of wonderful and diverse characters, but extremely efficient and lots of fun to work with. Seasoned executive Wolfgang Arming led the company since 1979, after spending time in Japan and Germany, and was a well-liked and fair boss, openly called 'Charming Arming'. He would often come down to my office for a chat on football or give me advice on something about the business and so became my first true mentor in the music industry. My little international product and marketing department consisted of my assistant Christa Krenn, who kept order in my dealings and could run with a project on her own without a problem. Gabi Mihats as product manager with a smile and some great ideas, product and promotion assistants Heike Rupprechter and Karin Laber, brilliant both and smart and hardworking, like everyone else in the crew.

The PolyGram Austria International Pop Team – left to right: Robert Grass (Distribution Dept.), Karin Laber, myself, Bosi, Karin Helfert, Gabi Mihats (with cake) and Christa Krenn

The promotion team consisted of Horst Bichler, who as well was a drummer in a traditional jazz band, and he looked after some of our jazz releases, but soon would leave and work in publishing. Peter Pernica was the rock guy in the team and we worked a lot together and, at some stage, he came up with introducing us to acts we worked with as 'Peter and the Wulf'. He worked on Bryan Adams, Sting and many more with me and his open and straight way of dealing with people made it easy for everyone to like him. Karin Helfert did some local stuff and more pop oriented promotion for me and Doris Lang and Gwyneth Leatherborrow, called 'Bosi' by us, the more modern pop and groove stuff of the time. German language repertoire was handled by Peter Schilling, with the invaluable help of Eveline Höfer and local A&R was done then by Bernd Rengelshausen.

Peter organised as well the PolyGram football team, for which we sometimes hired guys from the 'miles smiles' team, when we didn't have enough players available. Ewald Markl, who had wonderful skills to use his language as long as it wasn't in front of a lot of people, was running the classical department and Charlie Bednarik the video division. Sales and distribution were handled by Gottfried Urschler and Hans Prückler, who was extremely good at listening to and discussing marketing ideas and often came up with great one's himself and who had everyone's respect; that's why we called him lovingly 'Uncle Hans'.

We were the most successful record company in the market because we had people working there with a passion for music and respect for the artists ... and always got great records from the UK and the US, pre-promoted with chart success there or in Germany. Over the years working with this incredible team, made me learn a lot – first of all that I had to let them do their work in the best way for them. I just wanted the results and things done, but how they would do them didn't matter that much. I believe that people are different in the way they deal with situations or tasks and I shouldn't ask them to work in a certain way, just because I might do something that way. I also believe that if given that freedom, they would do a better job and enjoy their work more. And given the pressure we were sometimes under; they would deal better with that too. But first of all, I believe that we should have fun working with music. Despite the stress, we all should be able to enjoy our daily work. And I think, as a group and as individuals, most of the time we did.

The most incredible campaign we worked on as a team was the release of the Dire Straits album 'Brothers In Arms', for whose release campaign and tour they partnered with Philips Electronics to promote the Compact Disc to a younger audience. In advance of the release, we had meetings in London, went a few times to Eindhoven to talk with Philips and got meters of telex from the band's manager Ed Bicknell.

Philips might be great engineers, having invented the music cassette as well as the CD, but they weren't the best in marketing, as the fact, that most people believed the cassette as well as the new CD format was an invention by the Japanese Sony Corporation, clearly showed. Therefore, PolyGram took the lead in the marketing of the album and the push of the CD to a younger audience and thanks to the incredible success of the record, it worked. Joint radio and TV spots, a bus with CD listening equipment on the road, shirts and tons of other merchandise as well as the first advance promotional only CD's with 4 tracks from the album – today a collector's item – were the tools we used.

The band's gig in Vienna was incredible and the audience went completely crazy ... and I handed the band their Gold Awards for sales in Austria and had a late dinner with the guys at the Vienna Hilton Hotel after the show. Nice and relaxed, with typical Austrian food and wine.

1985, Dire Straits / Philips campaign poster

1986

In 1986 my brother Juergen started to work at PolyGram in Vienna as well, initially as exploitation manager, meaning he would look after the export of local productions – mainly to Germany and Switzerland, but occasionally also globally.

The first local jazz productions I was responsible for, came out in '86, two by sax player Karlheinz Miklin, first 'Echoes of Illyria', which had some nice success at home and then 'Carlitos', recorded with a group of Argentinian musicians, which was a groovier and more Latin influenced affair. The third album was by marimba player Woody Schabata, an incredibly talented guy, whom I had seen playing with the Vienna Art Orchestra and who then played at the 'miles smiles' jazz café. The record is still one I listen to often and it hasn't aged at all. All three albums did fine, but nothing out of this world – good reviews and decent sales in Austria and a bit in Germany, but not much else … some of the international IMS departments took a few copies, but that was it. Jazz from Austria wasn't really on many people's radar! In general, jazz from Europe still had to struggle to get into the big festivals, which were focused on US artists mainly. But the first steps were done and the activity, that a major record company would produce and release local jazz musicians, was well received by all Austrian media.

Otherwise, the year wasn't the best: the Chernobyl disaster left many people dead or with long-term health problems, had families leaving the soil they worked on for centuries and left Europe wondering how much of a radioactive cloud the wind had brought to the countries in the east and north. The Swedish prime minister Olof Palme was murdered while walking home after visiting the cinema … a crime that had left the country and Europe shocked and was never solved.

Space Shuttle Challenger exploded shortly after the take-off, killing all 7 crew mem¹
Phil Lynott of Thin Lizzy passed that year, as well as Benny Goodman, whose 'Farr
Hall Concert' was one of my father's all-time favourite records and has been p
equipment ever since I bought my own copy sometime in the mid 80's. Arger
world champion at home by beating West Germany 3:2 in the final. Their c
Diego Maradona.

At the movies, Woody Allen's 'Hannah And Her Sisters' was a huge success and ...
and I worked on two bands and their records which we both liked a lot: Deep Purple and
Both had just signed with PolyGram and released albums that year.

Playing football with Deep Purple, first row, third from the left

Deep Purple came first to Austria on tour to support the release of 'House Of The Blue Light' and before the gigs in Linz and Vienna we arranged to have a football match of Deep Purple/PolyGram against a team of journalists from the Linz area – tickets were sold for a few Schillings, as the money was for charity and the match was broadcasted live on local radio. We had a lot of fun and played a lot to Ritchie Blackmore, by far the best player the group had, and in the end, we won 2:1, with goals by Ritchie and myself.

The Kinks came later in the year to Vienna for a concert to promote 'Think Visual' and, as it was December, one of the journalists who had an interview with Rays Davies, asked him what was the one gift he wanted for Christmas and never got and the surprising answer was: "A teddy bear". Next thing we decided was to buy him one and give it to him during next day's show – so Peter went out got a really cool teddy bear and gave it to Ray on stage while he was about to announce a song ... laughter and applause all around and Ray was smiling throughout the rest of the concert.
Another act who came to visit Austria that year for a gig and a few interviews, to promote his David Bowie produced new album 'Blah Blah Blah', was Iggy Pop. We had heard rumours that he could be complicated to deal with, but thought nothing of it, as we always treated our visiting artists like normal people and not like stars, which usually worked out well. And, as we knew that his wife Suchi Asano was coming with him, we picked the two up at the airport with a beautiful traditional Viennese flower bouquet. And from then on it was all smooth sailing and we enjoyed a relaxed time with Iggy doing interviews and an energetic and powerful rock concert by him and his band.

...g released his fabulous live album 'Bring On The Night' and toured Europe extensively, but didn't ...me to Vienna, so I headed with some colleagues from Germany to the gig at the Lorelei Festival to see him perform there an amazing concert. This was the first time I met Branford Marsalis, who was part of the band. That record is still one of my favourite Sting albums for its jazzy touch and incredible musicianship.

Bon Jovi's 'Slippery When Wet' was another one we worked on successfully that year, as well as Status Quo's 'In The Army Now', which had 2 hit singles, the title track and the first single 'Rollin' Home'.

1986 with my promo man Peter Pernica (on the left) and Status Quo

We had a UK meeting a few months before Status Quo released the single and it was held at Butlins, a famous UK holiday resort – very typical English family camp for the summer and Quo performed there, having as kids always had their holidays in these camps. Then Quo came to tour Austria and to do some promo, including a TV show and we had lots of fun with the guys, ending up with an amazing dinner at the Marriott Hotel. That dinner included Francis Rossi and Rick Parfitt ordering wine of the highest quality and to round up the meal a 70-year-old brandy ... I was shocked when seeing the bill, but was prepared to pay, except that the band had paid already for all drinks and just wanted to check if we would swallow the bitter pill of excess ... they appreciated that we would and, as they had been a successful act for us in the past, it wouldn't have been too much of a problem with my financial controller anyway. At the end of the meal, they virtually had to carry drummer Jeff Rich out of the restaurant, as he was too intoxicated to walk ... bass player John 'Rhino' Edwards, Rick and Francis, their manager, I think it was Iain Jones, and Peter and myself were all fine, but a bit loaded as well

We also worked new releases by Janet Jackson, Mylene Farmer, Joan Armatrading, Bronski Beat, Bananarama, Zodiac Mindwarp, Bob Geldof, Salt 'N' Peppa, Robert Cray and Magnum, to name just a few.

Friedrich Gulda, the famous classical pianist, was recording occasionally for 'amadeo' and especially his Mozart and Beethoven albums for the label are wonderful, but my favourite is his 'Variations on Light My Fire', a solo piano recording from 1971 for MPS (on the album 'The Long Way To Freedom'). I first met him when he came to our offices once to see Ewald Markl, who told me, that on one occasion Gulda had finished a recording for 'amadeo' and called him to get on a train and bring him the agreed advance in cash and then he would give him the master tape. Ewald travelled to Salzburg, then took a cab to get the Gulda's place a bit outside and delivered the money. And, of course, he asked for the master to which Gulda answered: "I don't trust you – I've sent it by post". He was a real character and in 1999 even circulated the news of his death, just to see what people would write about him. In 1986 he performed a duo concert with Joe Zawinul at the Konzerthaus in Vienna. Arming invited me to join him for the event, which I gladly did, as I hadn't heard Joe play acoustic piano before – it was absolutely incredible what the two guys did, either individually or as a piano duo. Two hours of divine music, performed by two masters of our times.

My favourite jazz records from that year include The Pat Brothers 'No. 1', another project featuring Wolfgang Puschnig; David Liebman's solo sax master piece 'The Loneliness Of A Long Distance Runner'; Abdullah Ibrahim's 'South Africa'; the Pat Metheny and Ornette Coleman release 'Song X' as well as Courtney Pine's 'Journey To The Urge Within', Miles Davis' 'Tutu' and Herbie Hancock's soundtrack for the movie 'Round Midnight', featuring the best of the best in jazz. And Fela Kuti's 'Teacher, Don't Teach me Nonsense' a powerful and rhythmically amazing album with a strong statement. Fela came as well to Austria and I saw him perform twice – every single show amazing in musical terms, colours and movements of the dancers and musicians. One of Africa's first strong musical ambassadors.

handing a gold disc to Mark Knopfler of Dire Straits

1987

Over the previous few years, I had worked with Konstantin Wecker, a singer/songwriter and pianist, signed to Polydor in Germany, but touring Austria every year. I liked his social critical lyrics and him as a guy, so we got along very well and when he turned 40 in 1987, he invited me to the birthday party at his Café Giesing in Munich, where musicians and German celebrities partied with the singer. His deal with Polydor in Hamburg had come to an end, but he wanted to record and release a live album from his tour in Austria, therefore I stepped in and signed the project on. I loved this band especially, as it had a bunch of wonderful jazz players involved. The touring band on these dates in May '87 included saxophonist Charlie Mariano, bass player Colin Hodginson, guitarist Frank Diez, pianist and keyboarder Wolfgang Dauner, who as well was the musical director of the group, drummer Pete York, tenor sax player Christof Lauer, cellist Hildi Hadlich and trumpeter Johannes Faber. The album was produced by the legendary promoter and label man Horst Lippmann, with whom I had a bunch of meetings to set everything up and who was the sweetest guy to work with, and full of stories. We released that album in late '87 and in Germany the following year.

We had a busy year in terms of international releases, working lots of records, including albums from Janet Jackson, The Mission UK, Bryan Adams, Level 42, Swing Out Sister, The Cure, Wet Wet Wet, Van Morrison, INXS and Def Leppard, which were all very successful in our market. But the biggest sales we had with Suzanne Vega's 'Solitude Standing', which included the hit 'Luka', and Austria was one of the first countries to hit # 1 with single and album. Suzanne came to do a lot of PR and TV, which obviously helped immensely. The second big album that year was Sting's 'Nothing Like The Sun', featuring the hit singles 'Fragile', 'Englishman In New York' and 'Be Still My Beating Heart'. Sting came to perform in Vienna and we ran a major advertising and marketing campaign around the release and tour – a campaign that landed me the following year the 'Label Manager Of The Year 1987/1988 A&M Records' award, something I was very happy about and celebrated with a few drinks with my team and the sales division.

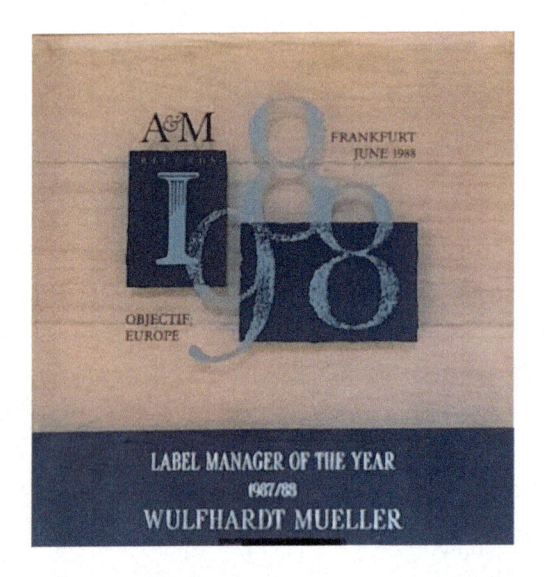

Another hit for us in '87 was the single 'Wonderful Life' from the album of the same name by Black, who actually was Colin Vearncombe, a British singer and songwriter. We immediately liked the song and thought it could do well for us and therefore brought Black to Austria to do interviews and TV. We were right and we had Colin over another time for promo on the second single, the excellent 'Everything Is Coming Up Roses'. On this second visit we went to see a band – I can't remember which one – and lots of people in the audience came and asked for his autograph ... he was surprised, but happy. 'Wonderful Life' became a big hit across Europe, but Austria was again the first country it went to # 1 in the charts. Another great record from that year is 'Deep In The Heart Of Nowhere' by Bob Geldof and Bob came to Vienna to promote the album. He was fun to work with and a very relaxed guy, with whom Peter and I did the typical late-night thing in Vienna, eating a sausage and having a beer at one of the stands that you can find all around the city. He loved it. When doing the interviews one of the journalists came with a bunch of albums and wanted to have them signed. I stopped it and told him that he was here to do an interview and not to have his album collections signed by the artist. I didn't like that at all and never myself asked an artist to sign an album for me, it was simply not part of the job description, in addition to that, I didn't want to take advantage of my position. To make things worse, the journalist had a bootleg recording of 'Live Aid' in there, which Bob immediately spotted and told the guy to *"fuck off"*, as he was supporting people who wouldn't pay the artists in the show or on the album. How unprofessional by the journalist, had he done his homework, he would have known how outspoken Bob was; especially when it came to 'Live Aid' and the many actions other people had done to make money for themselves out of the event.

Australian/New Zealand band Hunter (or Dragon as they were known 'Down Under') had an album out that year on Polydor titled 'Dreams Of Ordinary Men', and they came to Vienna in May for three concerts as support of Tina Turner, who toured her successful 'Break Every Rule' album. The brothers Todd and Marc Hunter had brought their families and we had a lot of fun spending time showing them, plus keyboarder Alan Mansfield, around Vienna. The real star in the band was the guitarist, which was Tommy Emmanuel, now considered one of the best on his instrument of our times. Great guys all of them. Unfortunately, the record didn't do much business, so they never came back to Europe, but still have a career in Australia, though without Emmanuel, who left after the European tour.

Around that time Shari Belafonte had some success as an actress in the TV series 'Hotel' and decided to make an album as a singer. Our label in Germany, Metronome, did the deal and Ulla Hope, their exploitation manager, called me to tell me that Shari would be willing to come to Vienna to do some interviews and TV. We checked and, as there was interest, said OK and then received a message from management asking for: a suite in the hotel with a 24 hours car service, no taxis. And that she would do only 2 interviews per afternoon and only one song on TV. I told Ulla, that we needed 4 interviews, with 30 minutes breaks between them and 2 songs on TV. This was in the end an unproven music act and we needed this to make steps forward. Shari and management refused. I had a chat with my boss and told him that if the act wouldn't do what we needed, I would not bring her to Austria, but spend the money on an act who actually wanted to work. He agreed and I told Metronome that if she didn't accept, we wouldn't bring her in. Next thing I know I have the guy running Metronome in Germany on the phone, saying *"You can't do this ….!!!"*, so explained to him that costs and work by the artists wouldn't stand in any relation and that *"Yes, I could do this"*. He called my boss, who backed me up. Then he called me again to offer that they would cover all costs if I bring her in, which was nice but didn't help with the fact that TV didn't want her if she didn't do 2 songs, which she refused. In the end, she stayed at home and we never looked back and worked a different act.

To commemorate the 25th anniversary of the A&M label, they arranged for a big meeting in L.A. to which all the product managers were invited and we had the celebrations at the A&M building, which was the old Charlie Chaplin studio, a historical place in L.A. Many artists performed over these few days, but I especially remember Joe Jackson's gig and John Hiatt, whose concert was at the 'Whisky A Go Go', the famous L.A. club, where as well the Doors, Led Zeppelin and many others had performed. The one evening we had off, my German colleague, I think it was Thomas Starkjohann, and I went to see Bon Jovi, which meant a 3-hour car drive on a 6-lane motorway to get to the venue – but the show was worth the effort!!

Then we had a BBQ at Malibu beach, at the house of Supertramp's Rick Davies. We played beach volley ball, ate well and listened to their forthcoming album 'Brother Where You Bound', the first one without singer Roger Hodgson, yielding the hit single 'Cannonball'.

The 'amadeo' jazz releases for that year were an album by the group Airmail, featuring guitarist extraordinaire Harry Pepl, saxophonist and flutist Wolfgang Puschnig, Mike Richmond on bass and drummer Wolfgang Reisinger, performing mostly Pepl's compositions and this was the first record that got a bit more international response. The album by Duo Due, by the brothers Christian and Wolfgang Muthspiel, 'Focus It', was next and started the European jazz scene to talk about these two extremely talented musicians. 'Weites Land' by pianist and keyboarder Hans Joachim Roedelius and saxophonist Alexander Czjzek was the third release and especially interesting, as it was more an ambient release than a jazz album, but of incredible beauty and musicality. Roedelius was then already a legend of electronic music as co-founder of the German group Cluster and according to

British music magazine 'The Wire', their album 'Cluster 71' is one of the "One Hundred Records That Set The World On Fire".

In the USA, AZT was approved for the use in the treatment of AIDS and was a step in the direction of finding a working cocktail of medicines to treat the disease. The world population was estimated to have reached 5 billion people and in October the financial world experienced the 'Black Monday', a sharp fall of the stock markets around the world, while Microsoft released their Windows 2.0 software and Starbucks opened their first coffee shops outside of Seattle, in Chicago and Vancouver. And 18-year-old German pilot Mathias Rust flew a small private plane from Helsinki to Moscow, evading the Soviet air defence systems and landing close to the Red Square – only to be immediately arrested. In his trial he stated, that he wanted to build an imaginary bridge between East and West with his action, but the court wasn't really interested in that and condemned him to 4 years in prison, only to be pardoned 14 months later (after some re-structuring of the Soviet Air Force).

Miles Davis had come back to Vienna in November 1986 to perform music from his latest album 'Tutu' and he gave a press conference the day before the show, unusual, but it truly happened. He had just changed record companies, leaving Columbia after 30 years and signing with Warner Music. Rainer and myself went to the press conference. I was for sure a bit starstruck, but thankfully there were other journalists around, who like us, were in advance instructed not to talk about the past (Parker, Coltrane, …) but about the present.

Miles press conference. Photo by Rainer Rygalyk

Miles told us that he left Columbia because they hadn't released his version of 'Time After Time' as a single and never re-issued the impressive jazz/rock album 'A Tribute To Jack Johnson', one of his favourites. Personally, I think that another reason for him to leave was the focus of Columbia on Wynton Marsalis, which surely wouldn't have gone down well with the legend Miles. I wrote an article about Miles and his press conference in 'Jazz Live' in early 1987. The magazine meanwhile had changed its format to the bigger A4, as in the newsstands and kiosks the smaller version got lost easily. New editor was Hannes Schweiger and Rainer and myself only occasionally wrote for the mag, having other work commitments by then. That article on Miles, probably one of the best I wrote for the magazine, was as well selected to be re-printed in the 15th anniversary edition of 'Jazz Live' in 1997.

'Good Morning Vietnam' ruled the cinemas and made Robin Williams a global star and Woody Allen released his 'Radio Days', a wonderful and charming homage to the Golden Age of Radio. In the pop and rock world Michael Jackson and U2 dominate the charts with 'Bad' and 'The Joshua Tree' respectively. The jazz world saw releases by Michael Brecker, simply titled 'Michael Brecker', being his first album as a leader and featuring Pat Metheny, Kenny Kirkland, Charlie Haden, Robby Kilgore and Jack DeJohnette; Ornette Coleman and Prime Time ('In All Languages'); the Don Pullen George Adams Quartet ('Song Everlasting'); and Miles Davis with Marcus Miller. Their soundtrack to the movie 'Siesta', featuring Ellen Barkin, Gabriel Byrne and Jodie Foster among others, is the perfect vehicle for the images.

1987 came to an end with a delicious dinner and New Year's Eve party at the Berliner Schauspielhaus, where Wolfgang Dauner and Konstantin Wecker had worked on music for a show I can't really remember and had invited me and Eva to join them that evening – something different and a lot of fun with these actors and musicians.

1988

Jazz within PolyGram had become stronger in 1988 with the resurrection of the Verve label under Richard Seidel, adding new releases to an already impressive re-issue strategy to make the vast catalogues the company owned available on CD.
In Japan we had Kazuhiko Yanagida at Nippon Phonogram releasing acts like Ray Bryant, Ron Carter and John Lewis (most of these produced by Kiyoshi 'Boxman' Koyama, who made himself a name for his re-issues and liner notes) and at Polydor Japan we had Hiroshi Itsuno working with some local acts and as executive producer for the German label JMT, run by A&R man and producer Stefan Winter, with whom Hiroshi had made a global deal.
In France we had Jean-Phillipe Allard and Daniel Richard, who step by step signed and produced local acts as well as international ones, like Helen Merrill, Stan Getz, Randy Weston and Dee Dee Bridgewater, to name a few.
 And then there was 'amadeo' with the records I put out. Centrally jazz was then part of the catalogue division, run out of Baarn by Cees Schrama, himself a great jazz pianist, who had recorded among others with Toots Thielemans and who hosted one of the Netherlands best known jazz radio shows. In 1988 Cees started to send out to everyone his Catalogue and Jazz new release bulletins, which could be ordered and given to retail.
The first issues featured in the 'new jazz releases' section, beside some Japanese productions, the new Verve US recordings by Shirley Horn, Nina Simone, Betty Carter and Charlie Haden's Quartet West.

Cees Schrama, photo taken from the PolyGram release magazine 1988

More or less, we had one big international marketing meeting, IMM, every year, where all marketing guys from around the world came together to be presented with new releases by all labels – there was then the UK with Polydor, Phonogram/Mercury and London Records and the US labels and, if you wanted, there was space given to local presentations, in case you had an act with international potential. I remember especially the meetings we had in Rimini in Italy and in Athens, Greece. In Italy we had tons of meetings, but every evening great dinners with special guests joining us, like Status Quo or Yngwie Malmsteen. Quo I remember as I had got to know them a bit and it was always great to meet up and chat and have a good glass of wine. Yngwie, I remember as he came with Joe Lynn Turner, the singer in his band at the time and at one point at around 3 am in the hotel bar, Bas Hartong, one of the guys at the head office, started to play a few jazz standards on the piano and Joe Lynn jumped in immediately and to everyone's surprise did sing these songs absolutely wonderful. An unexpected jazz experience at a global pop meeting!

The meeting in Athens was similar unforgettable for great food, amazing music and hanging out endlessly. At the time we went there, PolyGram could only own 50% of a local company and couldn't get money out of the country – therefore they spend it on a lavish IMM and inviting guest stars from all around the world. One image I will never forget was Robert Smith, frontman of The Cure, standing next to local superstar Nana Mouskouri – the perfect image to prove the diversity of PolyGram at the time.

Robert Smith (The Cure) and Nana Mouskouri, IMM Athens

Nana was actually really cool and nice and when she came to Vienna for a concert a few months later, we were hanging out after her show in a Greek restaurant until 4 am, telling stories, eating well, drinking Retsina and simply enjoying life.

One Sunday we were playing football and in the team opposite mine was Willy Resetarits, a well-known singer in Austria, who was the frontman of a band called Ostbahnkurti & Die Chefpartie. The history of this group is very peculiar: having been invented by a journalist, who mentioned a legendary concert in his radio show, before there actually was any group … he then created stories for the musicians in the band and so the non-existing band became a kind of cult group. In the end Günther Brödl, the journalist, decided to find someone to personify Kurt Ostbahn and Willy was the perfect choice. Soon Brödl had written some Austrian lyrics to famous rock songs, plus a few originals and the band had released their first studio album and then a live recording. As I really liked what these guys were doing, I asked Willy what was happening with the band's second studio album and whether he had seen someone at PolyGram already. "Refused" was his answer. I said, that I couldn't believe that and would look into it. Meanwhile, the head of A&R at PolyGram had left the company and my brother Jürgen was looking after the local department now – so we invited Günther, Willy and the manager Günter Grosslercher to a meeting and made the deal. The album 'A Schene Leich' was released in 1988 and started the incredible success of Ostbahnkurti – not yet in sales, but the story got rolling. While they were still playing small clubs with about 300 people, their next album 'Liagn & Lochn' would change all that. Songs like the title track, originally a Townes Van Zandt song titled 'At My Window' and Brödl's adaption of Springsteen's 'Factory', which became 'Arbeit', and the Austrian version of Steve Miller's 'The Joker', became hits and live favourites for the audience, which grew by the day. Gold and Platinum awards for high sales in Austria were the result. Jürgen was working closely with the band, but I always stayed in touch and still played occasionally a game of football with Willy. Apropos football – when their deal was up to be renewed a few years later we had a discussion about their royalty percentages and were haggling about 1 % point up or not. Then Willy proposed to have a football match to decide the matter – the band against PolyGram, indoors. And so we did! It was a close call, a great match with lots of fun and a draw until the end, so we had to play extra time. In the end PolyGram scored the final and decisive goal and we all went to have a beer or two together. Willy used most of the money he had earned as Kurt Ostbahn to found in 1995 the House Of Integration, an internationally recognised place to house and integrate immigrants or simply support and advise people in need.

The jazz releases for 1988 were by trumpet player Karl 'Bumi' Fian and Wolfgang Puschnig. The 'Fian' titled album, produced by drummer Wolfgang Reisinger, unfortunately remained the only album of this outstanding and powerful musician under his own name. I had seen him many times at the Vienna Art Orchestra and his energetic way of playing and his sound reminded me a bit of Bill Chase, whose group Chase released some incredible rock/jazz albums in the early 1970's. Beside the leader and Reisinger 'Fian' featured Robert Riegler on electric bass, Harry Stojka on guitar, Dejan Pecenko on piano and keyboards, plus singer Elisabeth Kraschl on one song. A really strong album that got great reviews and decent sales.

But it was alto sax player Wolfgang Puschnig's debut album 'Pieces Of The Dream', that really caught the attention of the media in Austria and abroad – for very different reasons. The album is a collection of duo recordings, showcasing the talents of Wolfgang and his ability to integrate various influences into his music. It was recorded in various studios and once the music was done, we started to look for a cover. For me a cover needs in some way to reflect what is inside … the music and the artist. In this case I had to hold the album's release back, as it took us six months to come up with a cover everyone was happy with. But it was worth waiting for and, in the end, Wolfgang's wife at the time, singer Linda Sharrock, come up with the final version of the sleeve artwork.

The album featured beside Wolfgang, his wife Linda, bass players Steve Swallow and Jamaaladeen Tacuma, guitarists Hiram Bullock and Harry Pepl, Hans Koller on tenor sax and, among others, Carla Bley on piano. With Carla Bley, Puschnig had decided to record his version of one of Austria's most famous songs – the Erzherzog Johann Jodler, in his arrangement called 'In Another Time'. To some people in Austria this song means more than the national anthem, and therefore a storm blew up over Wolfgang and Carla improvising on this theme. The biggest national tabloid, Die Kronen Zeitung, wrote a wild review of not having respect for the heritage and so on … which only made people more curious to hear this and off they went to buy the album! Thanks a lot – shows that even bad PR can be helpful, besides, this is still a landmark recording in Austria, being one of the first to mix the Austrian culture with jazz.

A few months after the release, my friend Heinz Krassnitzer produced a concert at the Kurhalle Oberlaa in Vienna, inviting the musicians on the record to come to play the program with Puschnig live. It was a truly special event, recorded by Austrian TV. This album was as well the first 'amadeo' record that got a slot in Cees Schrama's international release bulletin, so making the PolyGram world aware of this recording. As Puschnig already had a bit of a name in Europe via the Vienna Art Orchestra and the Pat Brothers, this album not only did well at home, but abroad too.

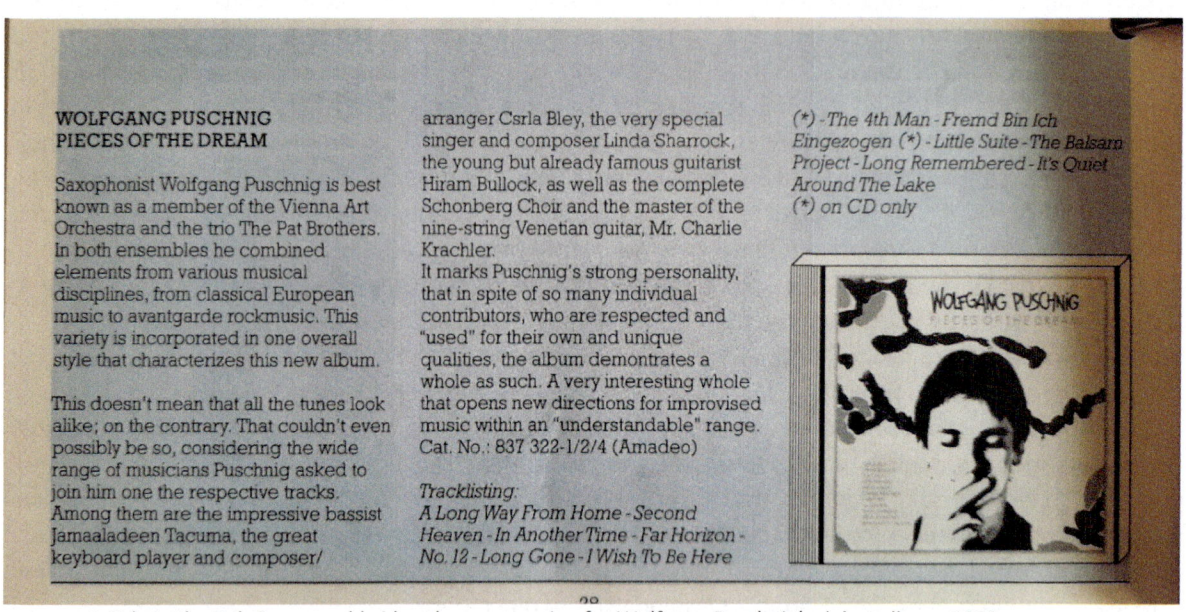

WOLFGANG PUSCHNIG
PIECES OF THE DREAM

Saxophonist Wolfgang Puschnig is best known as a member of the Vienna Art Orchestra and the trio The Pat Brothers. In both ensembles he combined elements from various musical disciplines, from classical European music to avantgarde rockmusic. This variety is incorporated in one overall style that characterizes this new album.

This doesn't mean that all the tunes look alike; on the contrary. That couldn't even possibly be so, considering the wide range of musicians Puschnig asked to join him one the respective tracks. Among them are the impressive bassist Jamaaladeen Tacuma, the great keyboard player and composer/arranger Csrla Bley, the very special singer and composer Linda Sharrock, the young but already famous guitarist Hiram Bullock, as well as the complete Schonberg Choir and the master of the nine-string Venetian guitar, Mr. Charlie Krachler.

It marks Puschnig's strong personality, that in spite of so many individual contributors, who are respected and "used" for their own and unique qualities, the album demontrates a whole as such. A very interesting whole that opens new directions for improvised music within an "understandable" range.
Cat. No.: 837 322-1/2/4 (Amadeo)

Tracklisting:
A Long Way From Home - Second Heaven - In Another Time - Far Horizon - No. 12 - Long Gone - I Wish To Be Here

(*) - The 4th Man - Fremd Bin Ich Eingezogen (*) - Little Suite - The Balsam Project - Long Remembered - It's Quiet Around The Lake
(*) on CD only

Article in the PolyGram worldwide release magazine for Wolfgang Puschnig's debut album, 1988

1988 was the year the Iron Curtain began to open up – Hungary was the first nation to allow free travel to Europe and so started the disintegration of this border between East and West. This was only possible because in Russia Mikhail Gorbachev had started his Perestroika (re-structuring) and Glasnost (openness) reforms of the political and economic system.

At Ramstein Air Base in Germany a crowd of about 300.000 spectators had gathered to see the shows of various flight teams from across Europe. When the Italian team, Frecce Tricolori, tried to create the formation of a heart, three of their aircrafts collided, crashed and left 70 people dead and about 500 injured.

Osama Bin Laden founded Al Qaeda that year, in which the Netherlands became European football champion in West Germany, with Ruud Gullit and Marco Van Basten their outstanding players.

Elton John sold some of his stage costumes from the past at an auction at Sotheby's, but before having invited the European marketing managers to a pre-listening session of his new album 'Reg Strikes Back' and a wonderful dinner exactly there – at Sotheby's auction house. Some of his clothes were on display then and overall, this was a memorable event in a very special place. Of course, we worked this album, as well as singer Sam Brown's debut album 'Stop' with the hit single of the same name. Sam, a truly great person, did lots of promotion for us and the single went to #1, even before it hit that position in the UK. I went to see the Hothouse Flowers perform their debut album in Dublin, and The Mission played Vienna with success, so did Robert Cray and Michelle Shocked to promote their releases of that year. Status Quo, Magnum and Level 42 all came to Vienna as well and had singles and records to work with.

Singer and songwriter Labi Siffre had some hits in the early 1970's and then kind of disappeared until 1988 when he released the album 'So Strong' and it simply blew me away and we decided to go for it and brought him to Austria twice for promo and in the end succeeded with the title track of the album and the song 'Listen to the Voices'. Labi is a very spiritual and kind person and was really grateful for all the work we did. His songs were covered by many great artists, among them Madness, Kenny Rogers, Joss Stone, Rod Stewart and Olivia Newton-John.

John Hiatt's album 'Slow Turning' was one of my favourites of that year from all the releases I worked on and in jazz it was Trilok Gurtu's 'Usfret', a world music influenced jazz recording featuring among others guitarist Ralph Towner and Don Cherry on trumpet. Bill Frisell released two great recordings that year with 'Before We Were Born' and 'Lookout For Hope', while fellow guitar star John Scofield made a noise with 'Loud Jazz'. Keith Jarrett released the live Trio album 'Still Live' with Gary Peacock and Jack DeJohnette and Jan Garbarek his wonderful 'Legend Of The Seven Dreams' featuring Eberhard Weber on bass, Rainer Brueninghaus on keyboards and Nana Vasconcelos on percussion. Verve released 'Look What I got' by the very unique Betty Carter. Sadly, both Chet Baker and Gil Evans, which I had seen over the years a few times live, passed away in 1988. Leaving a timeless legacy of outstanding music.

The two highlights of the year were two live events I was lucky enough to attend, of which the first was on June 11th at London's Wembley Stadium and was the Nelson Mandela 70th Birthday Tribute concert, which was broadcasted around the world. But the event, also referred to as 'Free Nelson Mandela Concert', had as well a strong political message, being outspoken against Apartheid in South Africa, which led the broadcast in the US being heavily censored. Some of the songs were known protest songs and made clear what the message was – these included Peter Gabriel's 'Biko', Sting's 'They Dance Alone', 'Free Nelson Mandela' by Jerry Dammers and a touching rendition of 'Amazing Grace' by Jessye Norman. But the one act that shone over all the big stars there (which included Dire Straits with Eric Clapton, Simple Minds, Salif Keita, etc.) was the almost unknown singer and songwriter Tracy Chapman, whose two performances were spectacular in terms of emotional content and audience reaction. Her songs were catchy and full of meaning and when she sang 'Talkin' Bout A Revolution' she had the sold-out Wembley audience in her hands.

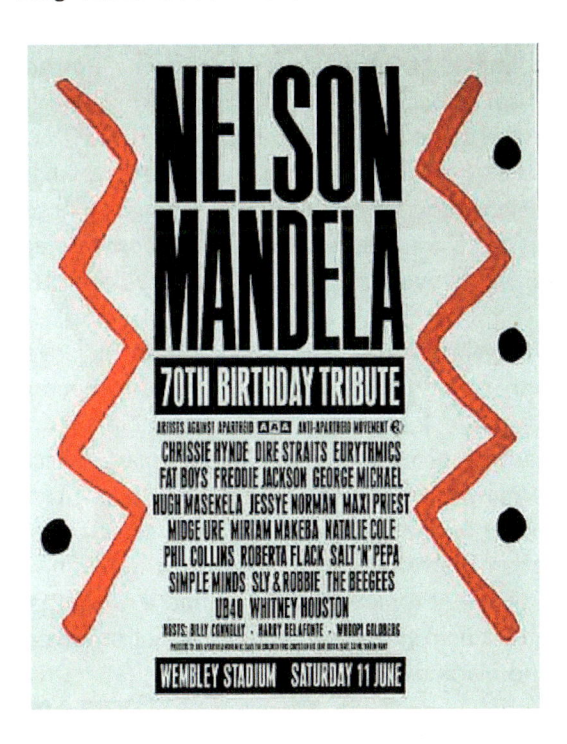

The second event was the Amnesty International Concert For Human Rights Now! in Budapest on September 6th. As Budapest is a beautiful place and not too far from Vienna, Eva and I decided to go there for a few days and enjoy the city as well as the event. The concert lasted about 8 hours and had some incredible performances by all acts, which were Sting, Tracey Chapman, Peter Gabriel, Youssou N'Dour and Bruce Springsteen, who alone played for more than 2 hours and got the 80.000 strong crowd going. Two local acts were invited as well to perform, Hobo Blues Band and singer/songwriter Janos Brody. All in all, the tour included 20 shows around the globe and put human rights and the work of Amnesty International in the spotlight. And gave a lot of people some unforgettable memories.

I can't remember exactly what year it was, but in the late 80's I am sure, when our parents visited us in Vienna for New Year's Eve, so we could celebrate together – Jürgen, myself and our girlfriends. As we always had seen our parents watch the New Year's Concert on TV, we tried to get them tickets for the real thing and as at that time the recordings were issued by PolyGram's Deutsche Gramophone label, we were lucky enough, thanks to Ewald Markl and his connections, to get a set of tickets. My parents were over the moon and really enjoyed the experience and spoke of it for many years after. And we were happy, as we made one of their dreams come true. When living in Ebergassing my parents discovered a restaurant in Vienna's 4th district, which they really liked and went there whenever they got to Vienna and so got to know the owners a bit. The place was Adi Berber's Montenegro Grill and was offering Balkan specialities plus wine from the region, of which we always had one from the Plavac grape. And after the meal a Šumadijski čaj – hot Slivovitz with sugar or honey. Whenever my parents came to visit us, we went to have a dinner there and even after many years, the owners, Adi Berber jr and his wife, would be extremely happy to see 'die Müllers'. The original owner, Adi Berber sr., was in the 1930's and 40's a famous freestyle wrestler and won 2 world championships and three European champion medals, but he was as famous as an actor, who appeared for example in the famous 'Ben Hur' movie, as well as some German Edgar Wallace TV programs and many more. He opened the restaurant in 1943 and run it until his death in 1966, when his son took over.

1989

1989 goes down in history as a year of change. The revolutions of Czechoslovakia, Romania, Poland, Hungary and finally Eastern Germany changed the political landscape in Europe and not only led to the overthrowing of the communist dictatorships in most of these countries, but as well to the fall of the German Wall and in the end the re-unification of the two German states. In November, when images of people breaking down the wall in Berlin were shown on TV globally, I was sitting in a hotel bar with the German group Camouflage, who had just given a concert in Munich in support of their new release 'Methods Of Silence'. This was one of the events everyone will remember where they had been … and so do I.

The same year saw Ayatollah Khomeini issued his fatwa against author Salma Rushdie for his novel 'The Satanic Verses' and later offered a $ 3 million bounty on his head. The writer had to live under police protection from then on. In China protests by over 1 million people demanding more democracy unsettled the Communist Party. Students led the protests in Tiananmen Square, which were violently suppressed with hundreds of dead and many more injured. The iconic picture from the protests is that of an unknown student standing in front of a tank. During a fatal human crush at the FA Cup semi-final between Liverpool and Nottingham Forest at the Hillsborough Stadium in Sheffield, 96 people lost their lives and over 700 were injured. It took until 2016 to find a ruling that the football supporters were unlawfully killed through gross negligence by the present police forces, who originally did everything to cover their faults up and blamed hooligans and drunken fans. On a more positive note, Frederik Willem De Klerk became president of South Africa and started to abolish the Apartheid system, which led to Nelson Mandela finally being freed.

The first English translation of Haruki Murakami's novel 'Norwegian Wood' was released. The original was available in Japan already in 1987 and was a huge success, selling over 1 million copies. The first English version, translated by Alfred Birnbaum, was made available as well in Japan only by the publishing house Kodansha as part of their pocket-sized English Library series, targeted for Japanese students of English. Only in 2010 an authorized second translation, by Jay Rubin, was published outside of Japan of this outstanding and touching story.

PolyGram bought two top independent labels that year – A&M Records, which we worked with already and Island Records, home of U2, Bob Marley, Cat Stevens and many other great acts. I was promoted to Head of International and National Marketing and therefore had to get a new work permit, as a change of position required that. For some unknown reason the guy working on this request denied it, stating that an Austrian could probably do that job as well. This obviously came as a shock to me and when I discussed this with Wolfgang Arming, he just told me to relax and that he would make a few calls. And so he did – actually he called his friend, the then mayor of Vienna, Helmut Zilk and told him of my problem. Zilk, of the Social Democratic Party, was married to singer Dagmar Koller, who had recorded some of her musicals with PolyGram, so the connection was two-fold. Zilk then spoke to a few people and about a week later I got a letter confirming my work permit for the new position for a year. Zilk, who was a well-liked politician, later got seriously injured when opening a letter bomb at his home. He remained mayor of Vienna until 1994, when he retired.

At PolyGram we had a very busy year with new releases like Elton John's 'Sleeping With The Beast', including his hit single 'Sacrifice'; Barry White's 'The Man Is Back', which brought him to Vienna for a great gig of soul and R&B; Janet Jackson's 'Rhythm Nation; Tears For Fears new album 'The Seeds Of Love', which featured fantastic singer Oleta Adams; Van Morrison's 'Avalon Sunset' and albums by the Neville Brothers, German rock singer Doro, Soundgarden, the Fine Young Cannibals and many more.

Singer Robin Beck had a huge success with her single 'First Time' from the album 'Trouble Or Nothin'. The success of the single was mainly due to it being used massively in a Coca Cola advert around the world. Robin came to Vienna to do some promo for the album, sang the single on TV and collected a gold disc award for it. The photo shows Gabi Mihats, myself, pr lady 'Bosi', Robins UK Label representative, whose name I forgot, plus, seated, our boss Wolfgang Arming and singer Robin Beck.

1989, Gold for Robin Beck

d six jazz releases coming out on 'amadeo': a soundtrack by sax player Karlheinz Miklin for ...nentary 'Fegefeuer / Purgatory' about Jack Unterweger, serial killer and writer. The ...luthspiel featured on their third Duo Due album 'TRE' and Christian on the album '...one Performance', recorded together with Swiss trombonist Roland Dahinden. Wolfgang Muthspiel released his first album under his own name, 'Timezones', featuring bassist Peter Herbert and drummer Alex Deutsch. I had meanwhile signed the Vienna Art Orchestra to a recording deal and leader Mathias Ruegg delivered their first album for us, 'Blues For Brahms' that year. A press conference was held for the release at the Café Brahms – where else?

Wolfgang Puschnig had met Korean percussion ensemble SamulNori on a tour and they became friends and wanted to play and record together. Heinz Krassnitzer was interested to set up a concert and we discussed a recording with Wolfgang and in the end decided to share the costs of flying SamulNori into Vienna, have them rehearse, then play the concert, which in the end was two shows, as the first one sold out very fast and Heinz added a second one and then go into the studio for two days to record the album.

We recorded at the studio of one of Austria's most popular singers, Wolfgang Ambros, with the excellent Hartmut Pfannmüller as the sound engineer. Beside the group of percussionists and singers from Korea, led by Kim Duk Soo, the band included Puschnig, his wife and singer Linda Sharrock, his friend and electric bass player Jamaaladeen Tacuma and his long-time musical companion and pianist Uli Scherer.

They called themselves Red Sun and the first album of this collaboration was titled 'Red Sun • SamulNori'. Hartmut had the set up for all instruments done in an hour and a half and off we went. Right in the middle of the first song Hartmut stopped the recording, pointing out that one key on the piano seemed to be stuck – over all the other instruments, especially the percussion, I hadn't heard anything, but that's why you go for a real good engineer.

We fixed that key and then recording proceeded fast, almost all tracks being done in one take. Ambros came by to check who was using his studio and as we knew each other from him recording for 'amadeo' as well, I explained the project to him. He asked when we had started recording and I said *"about 3 hours ago"*, to which he followed up with the question when we would be ready. My answer of *"tomorrow afternoon"* slightly shocked him, not being used to record an album in 2 days. But that's jazz!!!

Linda Sharrock designed the cover and once the album was released the guys got back together for some dates, this time I went to see them in Hamburg's Fabrik playing for an enthusiastic audience. With the exception of the more local releases by Karlheinz Miklin and Dahinden/Muthspiel, all of the records were featured in Cees Schrama's release bulletin and got international releases and sales. The Red Sun album was as well released in Asia, as the group SamulNori was very famous there and we had some good sales in Japan and Korea, and of course in Austria and Germany.

1989, in the studio with Wolfgang Puschnig

I had finally met Cees at an international meeting, where I had played some of the Wolfgang Muthspiel record to the pop guys, which surprised them a bit. Cees, as the catalogue guy, was in attendance and came later to me and said that it was great to hear some jazz in the meeting and we spoke a lot and stayed in touch, so the 'amadeo' stuff could be featured in his bulletin. With these releases we had reached the end of the first three years of producing and releasing jazz and, thankfully, had made a bit of profit with these – therefore my boss gave me the green light to continue making jazz records.

The Wolfgang Muthspiel Trio was invited to perform at the Montreux jazz festival that year – on the club stage, but still, it was an important first step and some recognition. As I checked the program for the festival, I saw that the day after Miles was playing there, so I decided to fly out and see the trio performing and stay for another day to see Miles Davis again, who played with Rick Margitza on sax, Foley McCreary on 4 string guitar, Adam Holzman and Kei Agaki on keyboards, Benny Rietveld on bass, Ricky Wellman on drums and Monyungo Jackson on percussion. A great show, Miles and the band were on great form and on the song 'Human Nature' they were joined by singer Chaka Khan. What else can one ask for???

Verve released that year Terri Lyne Carrington's 'Real Life Story, guitarist Ricardo Silveira's 'Sky Light', while from Japan we got releases from John Lewis, Helen Merrill and JMT delivered among others recordings by Geri Allen with Charlie Haden and Paul Motion; Gary Thomas, Greg Osby and Tim Berne. My personal favourites of that year include Pat Metheny's 'Letter From Home' and Keith Jarrett's 'Personal Mountains', a live recording from a 1979 concert in Tokyo featuring Jan Garbarek, Palle Danielsson and Jon Christensen. Jan released a wonderful folk oriented album with Norwegian singer Agnes Buen Garnas, 'Rosensfole' and Lester Bowie's Brass Fantasy their 'Serious Fun' album. Miles bettered everyone and put out two recordings that year: 'Aura', a suite composed by Danish trumpet player Palle Mikkelborg, which was already recorded in 1985, but only released four years later and is a modern classical recording with a jazz feel, as it features, beside Miles, his ex-sideman John McLaughlin. The second release was 'Amandla', a new recording produced by Tommy LiPuma and Marcus Miller and featuring Kenny Garrett, Don Alias, Mino Cinelu, George Duke, Foley, Omar Hakim, Jason Miles and others. Another modern Miles album of top quality.

1990

was invited by PolyGrams's Human Resources department to take part in a ... se in Nordwijk, the Netherlands. People from all over the world were ... er Kazu Koike from Japan being there and later working in London, plus an ... n. We were lectured all day and then got some homework to do or work on ... d in the end each group had to do a presentation on the future of the music ... xhausting two weeks with lots to learn and absorb. Our group did a pretty ... ought, focusing on the CD as the sole carrier, home and on the road with a ... ayer. No one was talking about the internet yet, but the bosses weren't too ... us on a one-carrier future (which turned out to be wrong, but for different reaso... nt company Philips Electronics was going to bet on a digital cassette format as the mobile carrier, called Digital Compact Cassette, DCC, with much higher sound quality than a standard music cassette. Honestly, we weren't sure that such a system or carrier was needed, when the CD was already portable enough.

After the course, Arming promoted me to marketing director of PolyGram Austria, with all repertoire divisions reporting to me, including the classical music department, now run by Gabi Kader, a very capable and knowledgeable manager and really nice person. And this time I didn't have a problem obtaining a new work permit.

German unification happened in 1990, or better the integration of the former East Germany into West Germany and my parents started to look for friends and family they knew lived in the former East. My grandfather had passed away in 1972, so much my mother knew, but her aunt Gustl, who had become her stepmother and her brother and his family were still somewhere in the now new states of Germany. After checking with the Red Cross and driving into the region they found both, my father's best friend and my mothers' family. I guess it must have been weird to meet them again after so many years, but afterwards they came together more often and her aunt even came to Denmark a few times, and so did her brother with his wife.

My mother and aunt Gustl, 1990

My uncle once asked her what we kids thought about him, having been a spy for Eastern Germany, but we couldn't care less. In his time, he made his choices and no-one knows what we would have done under the same circumstances. No problem there and when we met him, no-one talked about that, we just wanted to meet and get to know our mother's brother.

The break-up of Yugoslavia began and ended in a war between Serbia and other former Yugoslav states, that would last years and destroy the region. And with Iraq's invasion of Kuwait the ground for the Gulf War was laid. Mikhail Gorbachev was awarded the Nobel Peace Prize and finally Nelson Mandela was released from prison, while Lew Walesa became the first freely elected president of Poland.

Tim Berner-Lee created the first web server and Archie, the first web search engine was built, setting the creation of the world wide web in motion and in the USA the first digital camera was sold. Kodak used a Nikon camera to fit in their 1.3-megapixel sensor. It would take another 3 years before Kodak, Casio and Apple introduced cameras with direct computer connections and a price that allowed it to become a mass market product.

West Germany, in its last appearance under that name, won the UEFA football world championship in Italy by beating Argentina 1:0 and with it their coach Franz Beckenbauer became the first man who won the trophy as a captain of his team as well as a coach. On the eve of this World Cup final, three classical superstars performed together in a concert that was watched by an estimated TV audience of 800 million people around the world. Jose Carreras, Placido Domingo and Luciano Pavarotti recorded that event and the released disc became the best-selling classical album of all time.

We had at that time a specialised jazz marketing and product manager in all key markets, with Christian Kellersmann joining Polydor Germany being one of the last to complete the jigsaw. Because of the increase in new releases, Cees Schrama decided that from 1990 onwards the catalogue and jazz release bulletins would be split.

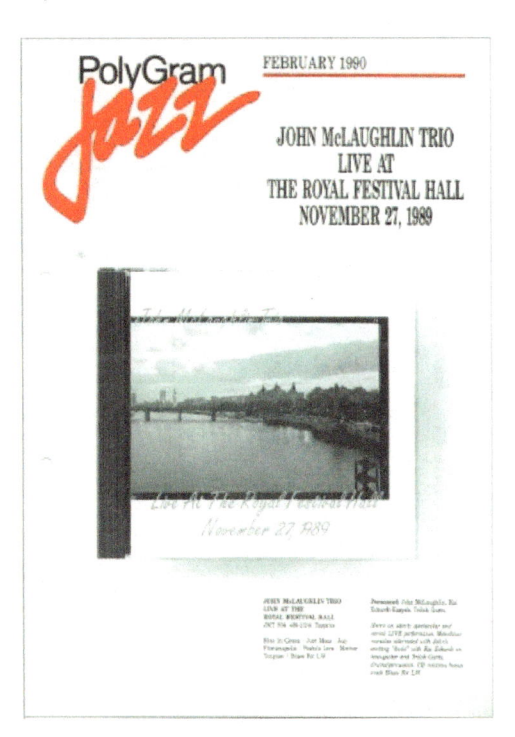

Therefore, from January onwards, we had a jazz release magazine called PolyGram Jazz, that featured all new releases from all sources plus all jazz catalogue re-issues and series, like the successful Compact Jazz mid-price CD series. Cees had also made a deal with the US company

MusicMasters and we put out their releases internationally on our Limelight label. Their releases were mainly archival, with a few new recordings on top. Artists included Benny Goodman, Duke Ellington, Mel Lewis and others.

JMT that year brought us the wonderful live recording by John McLaughlin, 'Live at the Royal Festival Hall' featuring bass player Kai Eckhardt-Kaipeh and percussionist Trilok Gurtu. Releases by Gary Thomas, Cassandra Wilson, Greg Osby, Hank Roberts and Paul Motian rounded up their program. Jean Philippe Allard and Daniel Richard from Paris released Randy Weston's outstanding 'Portrait' series, featuring the pianist playing three portraits in music – Duke Ellington, Thelonious Monk and a self-portrait. Abbey Lincoln's 'The World Is Falling Down' was another successful record for the French that year. Verve had a few releases as well, including Betty Carter's amazing 'Droppin' Things' and Toninho Horta's guitar masterpiece 'Moonstone' featuring Austrian violinist Rudi Berger on 2 tracks. The other one was from fellow Brazilian Joyce. Her 'Music Inside' ranks among her best recordings. Out of the Nippon Phonogram releases the Toots Thielemans album 'Footprints' stood out and A&M records started that year a new jazz series under the direction of producer John Snyder including releases by Cecil Taylor, Max Roach and Dizzy Gillespie, Sun Ra, Don Cherry, Gerry Mulligan and Art Blakey's last recording 'One For All'.

And I added a few on 'amadeo' as well, even so, I almost didn't ... We were just ten days from recording the new Wolfgang Muthspiel album in New York, with Gary Burton as a producer (Wolfgang was a member of Gary's band at that time) and jazz stars Bob Berg, Richie Beirach, John Patitucci and Peter Erskine hired for the session, when my boss got a message from headquarters that all local product should be put on hold, as overall European numbers were not as good as expected. He passed that message on to me and I told him that I could easily postpone the two other productions planned for the next few months, but not this one, as we would be hit with penalties and I would lose face and artists wouldn't want to sign with me anymore if I were to cancel this important release on such a short notice. He maintained that there was nothing he could do – order from above, for the next few months, then we could go back to it. I was afraid that I would lose my reputation as someone who kept his word and said to Arming that if I really had to do this, I would resign from my job. He asked me to sleep over it. Next day he called me and my brother and our financial director into his office and we spoke about it again. My brother thought I was overreacting and maybe I was, but I truly thought that this album was too important and maintained that if I had to make this call, it would be the last thing I do for the company.

Arming respected that point of view and asked the financial guy, Herr Rauscher, if we had somewhere a fund that we could tap into to make this recording happen. "Sure", was his answer. I was relieved, not sure if Arming had tested me or just played around, as he obviously knew that there were hidden funds somewhere; nevertheless, the second Wolfgang Muthspiel album 'The Promise' was released to critical acclaim at home and in Europe, even got an US release on the Antilles label and established Muthspiel as one of the young guitar players to watch out for. I didn't tell the story to Wolfgang at the time and I am not sure I ever did, I thought it was an internal matter of PolyGram Music in Austria and when solved, we all just silently moved on. At the time I got a lot of offers from local artists to release their music or make recordings with them, but I kept the artist roster small and exciting. One guy came to my office, I can't remember his name, and played me a tape of his guitar recordings. But somehow this sounded very familiar, until the penny dropped: Pat Metheny. I told the guy that he must have given me the wrong tape, as what I was hearing was from a Pat Metheny album, but he proudly stated that he could play any Metheny recording note by note. I asked him "who would want to hear that if they can listen to Pat's original recording?" He didn't really have an answer to that. I told him to come back once he had something that was his, as the guy obviously knew how to handle a guitar, but I never heard from him again. I had as well signed Vienna-resident singer Linda Sharrock and her first project for us was a funky and modern take on songs connected to Billie Holiday, titled 'On Holiday'. Produced by Jamaaladeen Tacuma, this album featured a rapper and was received very well. The Vienna Art Orchestra delivered their 'Innocence Of Cliches' for which my friend August Kraus designed the cover.

Guitarist Harry Pepl came to me one day with the idea to record a piano album. Which I found a bit surprising, but ... OK. Actually, it wasn't really a piano album, because he wanted to play the left hand and the right hand separately on his guitar into a midi computer, then transfer these files into a computer piano, so that the sound in the end was an original piano sound, even so played on the guitar. I like crazy ideas and this was definitely one - we booked the studio in the Konzerthaus in Vienna, had a Bösendorfer Computer-Piano 290 SE brought in, hired the band for the recording (David Liebman on soprano sax, Johannes Enders on tenor sax on two tracks, and Wolfgang Reisinger on drums) and made the record. It was truly a strange experiment seeing the musicians playing to the piano ... without a pianist! And then we set up a release concert in the smaller room of the Konzerthaus, this time with Wolfgang Puschnig on alto sax and flutes, Harry doing the pedals on the piano and drummer Wolfgang Reisinger. The album was called 'Schönberg Improvations', a mix of the two words improvisation and variation, as the album was influenced by Glenn Gold's 'Goldberg Variations'. Musically, I still find this album exciting, challenging and powerful. Unfortunately, when the first reviews came out, most writers focused on the technical side of the production and less on the musical part ... same for the concert. Only in 2004 the re-issue gave the album the credit it, in my opinion, deserved. It was just a bit ahead of its time when released.

Harry's partner in the Jazzzwio, composer and vibraphonist Werner Pirchner, had started his own label and offered us to release the album 'A-Naa-Nas Ba-Naa-Nas', with some of his compositions performed by the Vienna Brass. This being a more classical release, it still resonating with me today, due to its humour and amazing music.

The main ECM releases of the year came from Keith Jarrett, 'Paris Concert' and Jan Garbarek, whose extremely successful recording 'I Took Up The Runes' featured Eberhard Weber, Rainer Brüninghaus, Manu Katche, Bugge Wesseltoft and Nana Vasconcelos and included the touching 5-part 'Molde Canticle' and Jan's version of the famous song by Mari Boine, 'Gula Gula'. Around that time, ECM boss Manfred Eicher asked me if I would consider coming to Munich to work with him. I was truly honoured, but had to say "*No*" for two reasons: 1) Had I moved to Germany, the authorities would have called me up immediately to do my military service, a compulsory 18 months of wasted time in my opinion and 2) I actually enjoyed what I did in Austria too much to change and by living there I was out of the reach of the German army. Keith Jarrett came to Vienna again, this time to the Musikverein to perform with his Standards Trio, featuring Gary Peacock and Jack DeJohnette. Musical communication on the highest level!

Other jazz records of that year I remember or am still listening to are Bill Frisell's 'Is That You?', John Zorn's 'Naked City' and the first John Scofield album on Blue Note 'Time On My Hands'. The Red Hot organization released their first album to benefit AIDS research and relief – 'RED HOT & Blue', a tribute to Cole Porter, featuring a host of big-name stars performing Porter's songs, including Neneh Cherry, Salif Keita, The Fine Young Cannibals, David Byrne, Tom Waits, U2 and Annie Lennox. The first album set the tone for the series and was a big success around the globe, raising awareness and money for AIDS research.

In the pop division we worked among a lot of others the following records that year: Jon Bon Jovi's 'Blaze Of Glory', INXS 'X', the Scorpions and their hit single 'Wind Of Change', new records by Van Morrison, The Neville Brothers, Mother Love Bone's first and only album 'Apple' and Roger Waters 'The Wall – Live In Berlin'. My brother Jürgen went to see that show, getting there on bicycle on his way from Vienna to Copenhagen. A two weeks trip with a stop for great music. The concert featured Bryan Adams, Cyndi Lauper, Ute Lemper, The Scorpions, Van Morrison, Joni Mitchell and many others and was a huge success.

Dan Reed Network performed in Vienna as opener for the Rolling Stones. The concert was held in the Prater Stadium and attracted about 50.000 people. Dan Reed had released the previous year his second album 'Slam', with the wonderful single 'Rainbow Child' and played a great gig, appreciated by the fans waiting for the main act. We didn't hang around to see the Stones, but went out to hang with Dan and the guys. And singer Oleta Adams, known through her collaboration with Tears For Fears, released her own album 'Circle Of One', including the single 'Get here', written by Brenda Russell, which became a big hit for Oleta.

1991

The year 1991, was the year the first Gulf War began, after an UN deadline to withdraw from Kuwait was neglected by Iraq and therefore Operation Desert Storm was launched. In Europe the so-called Yugoslav Wars started and became a series of related ethnic conflicts and fights for independence that lasted until 2001, took the lives of over 130.000 people and was the deadliest conflict in the region since WW II. Having lived in peace for all my life, it was scary to see how fast people can turn on each other and start a war, this time right in front of our doorstep. The IRA attacked Downing Street and bombed the Paddington and Victoria train stations in London.

And Ötzi, the Iceman, was found in the Italian Alps, close to the Austrian border and after some closer examination it turned out that he had been living in that area around 3400 to 3100 BC. He is Europe's oldest known mummy, having been preserved well by the ice of the glacier. His body and the artefacts found with him are now displayed in the South Tyrol Museum of Archaeology in Bolzano, Italy.

Haruki Murakami's almost perfect novel 'Hard-Boiled Wonderland and the End of the World' was released in its English translation and Günter Grass published his wonderful 'Unkenrufe'. In the music world, Grunge had its popular breakthrough with releases by acts like Nirvana, Pearl Jam and Soundgarden, whose 'Badmotorfinger' I was working on in Austria. Singer and showman extraordinaire Freddie Mercury passed away from Aids related illness in November that year, just shortly after Miles Davis.

I was at home watching the Late-Night News when they reported his passing – I couldn't believe it! Miles' music had by then already been a constant in my life and would remain so, therefore the news were hard to swallow. I thought to go down to the radio station with some of my rare albums and bootlegs, but couldn't bring myself to do so. They broadcasted his music all night long and, as I was alone at home, I stayed up long and listened. I was lucky to have been able to see and hear him perform live so many times since 1982 and I will cherish these moments forever.

The Vienna Art Orchestra released their album 'Chapter II', as the band went through some changes and this was the first VAO album without saxophonist Wolfgang Puschnig. A powerful record with an unusual cover, based on a piece of art by trumpet player Herbert Joos, who as well had a name as illustrator

Wolfgang Puschnig also released a new album that year – we had been talking a lot about different ideas, but when Wolfgang mentioned in one of the dinners, we occasionally had together with our partners Linda and Eva, that he would like to record with a traditional Austrian brass band plus a few jazz musicians, I thought that this was really special and what we should do next. We set the recording dates, booked the studio and were ready to go.

The search for a brass band that could play 'jazzy' started immediately and Wolfgang called a few friends who he thought might be able to help him, including Robert Pussecker. He, unknown to Wolfgang, had his own ensemble, the Amstettner Musikanten and played fun fairs, weddings and dances with them. Amstetten is not far from the place Eva comes from, so she knew about them and when we went to the first rehearsal, she actually met a few friends playing in the band. Pussecker was not only the clarinettist and conductor but an imaginative arranger and writer and he and Wolfgang got into the music immediately. As usually, we recorded at the Powersound Factory with Hartmut Pfannmüller and beside the 14-piece brass band we had Jamaaladeen Tacuma on bass, Linda Sharrock on vocals, Bumi Fian on trumpet, Jon Sass on tuba and Thomas Alkier on drums. Most of the music was written by Wolfgang, some of the tunes together with Pussecker and then they recorded their version of 'Looney Tune', which is still crazy to listen to. When they performed 'March Of The Lost Illusion' we had a take that sounded good, but for me something was amiss ... so I asked Wolfgang to do it again, but slower and that was it – the feel of a funeral march was exactly what that tune needed. I am not a producer, I just listen and, in this case, we all agreed that the slower version would make it on the album, which was cool with me – I simply 'felt' that one more.

Linda again did the artwork, which was perfect for the record. If I remember correctly, their first gig was in Moers at the festival and the audience just loved it! Then Wolfgang got sick and couldn't play for a few months. His grandfather, who was very important for him, passed away and he couldn't deal with these emotions the usual way: by playing. But, in the end, he was given the OK to perform at the Saalfelden Jazz Festival and he brought 'Alpine Aspects', the name of the album with the brass band, with him. It was interesting to see how the audience reacted to this project at home: when the brass band came on stage, in Lederhosen and wearing sun glasses, playing a typical Marsch-Musik piece, people started laughing ... but the moment the six jazz players joined them and the music started to groove, every one of the 3000 people in the tent was on their seats screaming. I had heard Wolfgang play many times before, but never like this – all the tension of the last few months, the mourning, as well as the pleasure of performing again, came out of his horn. I was standing in the crowd, in tears, feeling the emotions in the music. The audience didn't know the details, but they heard and felt too that this was a special moment and none of them will most likely ever forget that experience.

Heinz had the crazy idea of having 'Alpine Aspects' play a real Volksmusik festival, or open for one of the more famous traditional bands. And it really happened ... but unfortunately the audience wasn't really open enough for such an experiment and soon enough eggs and tomatoes were thrown on stage and in the end the group had to abandon the gig ... with drummer Alkier bowing out by going to the microphone telling the audience: "thank you a lot – I never thought I would experience being booed off the stage, but you made it happen. Thanks!!".

When later performing in London, the audience there loved the show and it was a real great experience and success and it was the first time I had contact with the booker of the festival, John Cumming. The Amstettner Musikanten never wanted to get paid for the gigs or the recording, but Wolfgang and I did what we could to make them some money, as this would go to the fund for the band and the music school in Amstetten, buying instruments for example. They enjoyed especially the international concerts, travelling and seeing bits of Europe that way.

In 1991 PolyGram was approached by the Austrian Tabaco company to create a CD sampler named after one of their cigarette brands. The Memphis Music Edition was their way to work around a ban on tabaco advertising and bring awareness to their Memphis cigarette brand. The first and only issue in the series 'Jazz Around Midnight' was compiled by me and had all big names and a bunch of famous songs in it and a cover that was based on a photo by my friend Rainer Rygalyk. It actually didn't do badly, but the Tabaco company decided to focus more on sport events and let music rest after this first compilation.

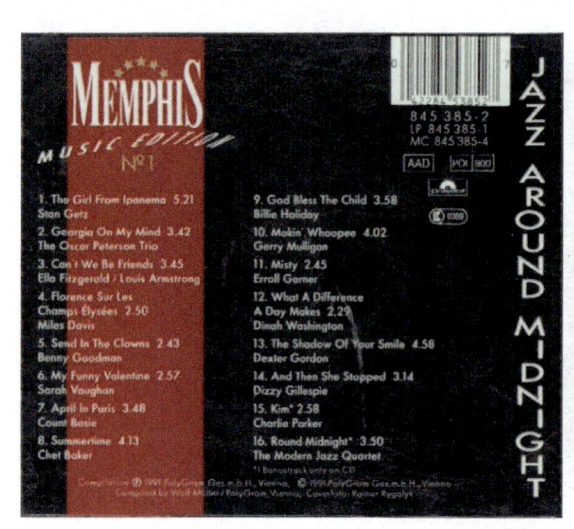

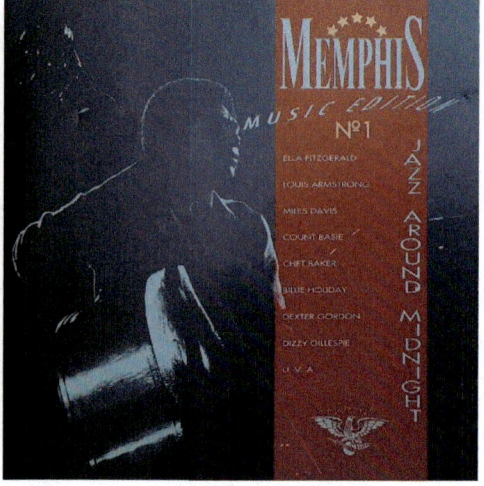

PolyGram Jazz kept me busy with lots of exciting releases that year from the various sources of repertoire. Verve delivered Shirley Horn's master piece 'You Won't Forget Me', with Wynton Marsalis, Toots Thielemans, Branford Marsalis and Miles Davis as special guests. Other Verve releases came from Joao Gilberto and fellow Brazilian Joyce. The Red Hot Organization partnered with Impulse Records, part of Verve, for a compilation of legendary Impulse! recordings to benefit their AIDS awareness and support activities. The 11-track album included some of the best recordings by John Coltrane, Pharoah Sanders, Alice Coltrane, Oliver Nelson, Charles Mingus and Archie Shepp and created a lot of money for the good cause and lots of awareness for the Impulse! catalogue.

Tim Berne, Gary Thomas, Paul Motian with Bill Frisell and Joe Lovano and the Cassandra Wilson 'Live' album, were the top releases for JMT that year and the French jazz division put out a collection of timeless recordings, including the final Stan Getz studio album, as Stan had passed away in 1991. He was as well featured on the outstanding Abbey Lincoln album 'You Gotta Pay The Band'.

Vocalist Dee Dee Bridgewater, a new signing to the French company, released her 'In Montreux' live recording, showcasing her immense talent in a powerful concert setting, accompanied by a trio featuring pianist Bert Van Den Brink, bass player Hein Van de Geyn and drummer Andre Ceccarelli. Japan brought discs by John Lewis, Sir Roland Hanna, Steve Khan and pianist Yosuke Yamashita and finally Limelight gave us more Duke Ellington and Lionel Hampton to look after.

ECM recording artist Keith Jarrett came to Vienna on July 1991 to perform at the sold-out Vienna Opera House, a concert produced by Fritz Thom and Heinz Krassnitzer. The solo show was, as all performances by Keith Jarrett, recorded by Manfred Eicher and was a rare show of the beauty of improvisation and therefore Manfred decided to release the album the following year.

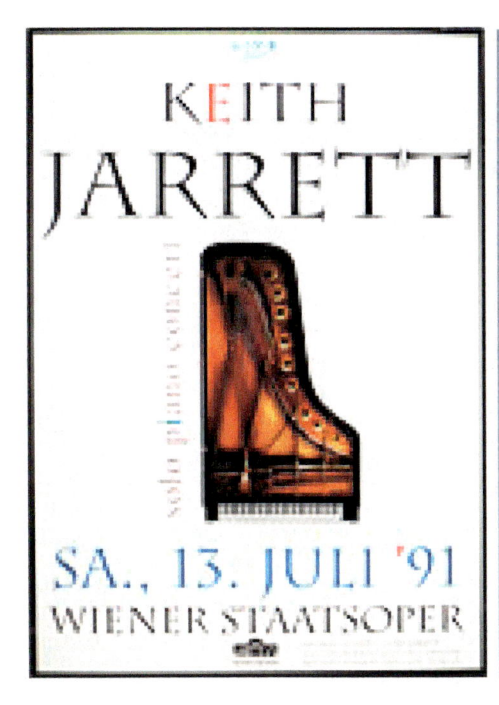

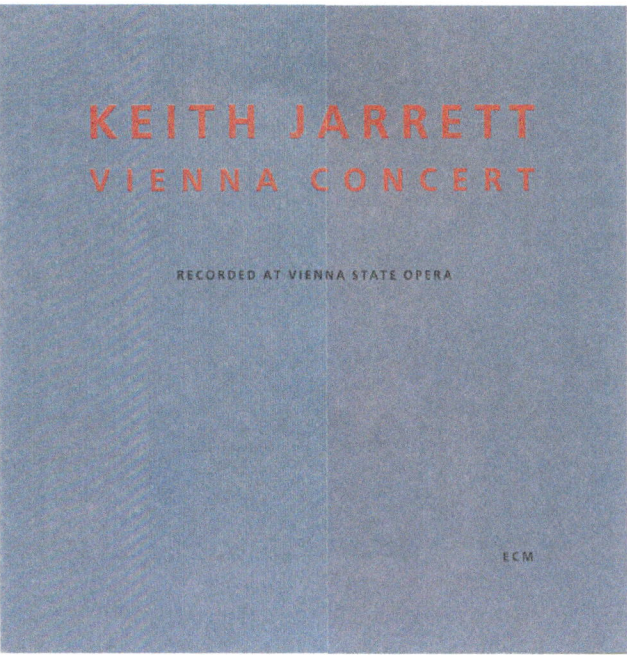

Jazz releases from that year I remember included, of course, the Miles Davis / Michel Legrand soundtrack to the movie 'Dingo' in which Miles acts as well. Not a huge success as a movie, but the music was and still is beautiful. Miles went into the studio with producer and rapper Easy Mo Bee and started recording what would be his final album, released posthumously in 1992, 'Doo-Bop'. Easy Mo Bee finished the album, which got mixed reviews on its release. Miles had seen the power and success of hip hop and rap and wanted to integrate these styles into his music. For me it's a cool record, making a step into the new, but not throughout satisfying.
Julius Hemphill's 'Fat Man And The Hard Blues' featuring among others saxophonist James Carter, was re-visiting one of my favourite compositions of his 'The Hard Blues', originally recorded in 1975 on 'Coon Bid'ness'. Percussionist Trilok Gurtu delivered with 'Living Magic,' another milestone in his career, and a beautiful album featuring among others Jan Garbarek.

he year when in the UK and Europe the first of the compilation albums under the banner Of The Cool' was released. The series featured music that combined jazz and hip hop and success. In the US, the first compilation was released with a slightly different track list in verall, seven records were made until 1998.

ar I listened a lot to the self-titled, black-covered Metallica album, which had the great Sandman', 'The Unforgiven' and 'Nothing Else Matters' included. That record made me a fan of the band and their music.

In my 'main job' as marketing director I worked on a bunch of great records that year with my team, above all Sting's 'The Soul Cages', which is another of his records with a jazzy touch and did very well for us in Austria. So did Swiss group Yello and the new Dire Straits album 'On Every Street'. They had again partnered with Philips Electronics for the album and tour, to promote the new Digital Compact Cassette, which Philips just had launched, as an alternative to Sony's Mini Disc. Both systems failed and were silently stopped a few years later. The same fate that happened to the Digital Audio Tape, DAT, but that at least was used for a while as a professional recording and storing system. INXS' live album and recordings by Crystal Waters, Ugly Kid Joe, Vanessa Williams and Aaron Neville were as well on the release schedule.

Locally my brother released the extremely successful Kurt Ostbahn album '1/2 So Wüd' featuring the wonderful single '57er Chevy'.

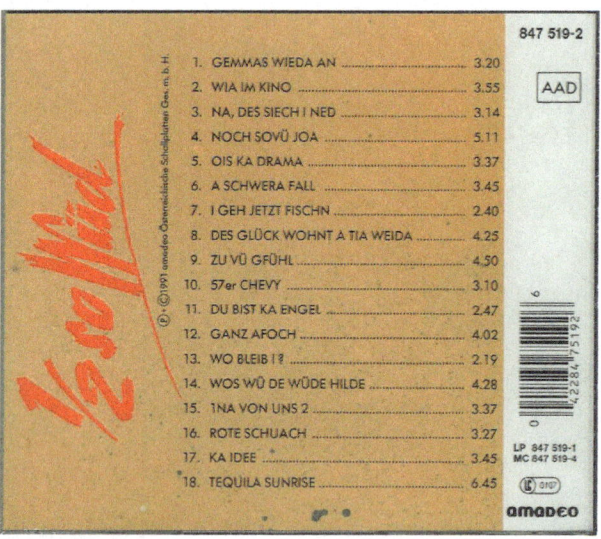

It was in 1991 that we were told that Wolfgang Arming would become Chairman, but stop running the day-to-day business of PolyGram Austria, which came as a shock to us, never having thought about it, as he always seemed to energetic and young in a sense. Lots of speculation about who would get the job. In the end, it was announced that Chris Wemcken, a German who had worked for PolyGram Australia and whom I had met on various international meetings, would be Wolfgang's successor. When Chris came, he did work for a few months side by side with Arming, before taking fully over. I had a lot of meetings with Chris, being the only one whom he knew in the company and we discussed a few possible changes which would streamline PolyGram Austria a bit. Arming had run a very well organised machine, but a few changes could surely improve how things were done.
Internationally Alain Levy, the Executive VP of PolyGram N.V. (under president Jan Timmer), brought in David Munns as Head of International, who started to set up his global marketing department. I had met Munns a few times on meetings, as he had been before the President of Polydor UK and was known not only for his A&R and marketing skills, but as someone who was good with people as well. It must have been late '91 or early '92 when he called and asked me to come to London, as he wanted to talk to me. Knowing a bit about his plans for the international office, I hoped he would

offer me something that had to do with jazz, as it was rumoured that he wanted to give structure to the various activities around the world in that area. But he was actually offering me the catalogue marketing job. I was honoured and thought I could do this, but had my eye on the jazz job, which he confirmed he would fill, but had the other jobs as a priority. I didn't need to think about it, I wanted to work with active artists, be part of the creation of records as I was with 'amadeo' jazz and not only compile Greatest Hits or Box sets, which is the main work in the catalogue division. I said "*No*" and Munns was a bit pissed off, as he had to look for someone else. But I was sure I had done the right thing for me.

A few months later I met David again at a listening session for the new Elton John album 'The One' and he still seemed a bit angry with me for turning him down. We were having a drink at a bar with some of the guys and I knew he hadn't appointed someone for the jazz position yet, so I brought it up. When he asked me *"What do you think this job would be all about?",* I told him that I had a hand written concept in the drawer of my desk in Vienna and he asked me to fax that through to him the next day upon my arrival in Vienna. I warned him that my handwriting might be hard to read, but he insisted that I sent it as it was – which I did and an hour later he called: *"Nobody can read this, have someone type it and send it again!".* Two days later he called again and asked me to get on a plane and come over, so we could discuss the concept and my deal! I flew into London, met him in his office and we discussed the deal, which was good in any case and agreed on the initial steps of my work. Then he gave me a pile of papers to go through and come back to him the next day to discuss what was in there that needed to be looked at. Two things stood out – JMT and MusicMasters. He asked me to change my flights and go to Munich to chat with Stefan Winter, the owner of JMT and later have a chat with Cees to inform him about my imminent appointment and talk about MusicMasters. Cees was great, he was happy for me and very helpful and Stefan Winter explained to me the way the deal with Japan was structured and after speaking to Hiroshi Itsuno there, we decided to continue.

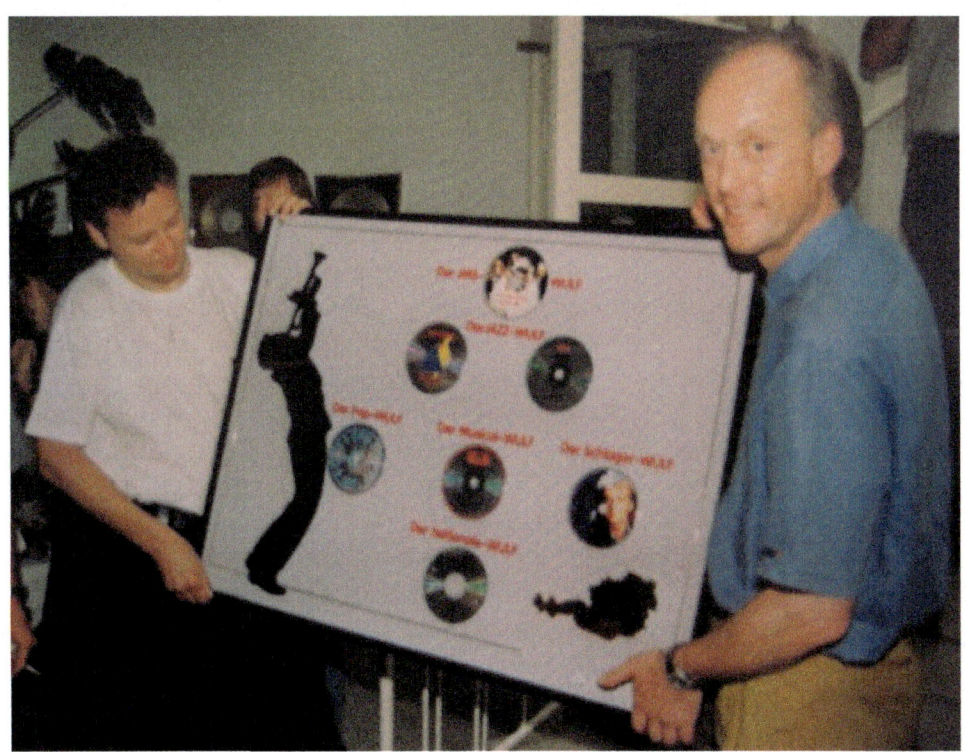

Farewell PolyGram Austria, with Chris Wemcken

I was kind of happy to leave for a new challenge as, meanwhile, my working relationship with Chris was getting worse, as I was pushing for the changes we discussed to be made and he wasn't able to make up his mind or decide on anything and others in PolyGram Austria used that for their own agenda, stepping into that vacuum. Not a pleasant situation for me. Eva and I had discussed the possibility to go to London and when it finally happened, we were ready to move. She didn't have a work permit, but until Austria would join the EU, she wanted to do English courses and continue with fine art photography, something she had started already in Vienna. Michael Golla, a colleague who had worked at International, but meanwhile had moved back to Germany, advised me to look for a flat in the Maida Vale area, mainly because it was well connected, quiet and had some good pubs. I found a small flat there and signed the rent. All set and on July 1st 1992 I started working at PolyGram International in London, but would continue, for the time being at least, working with my 'amadeo' jazz acts. The marketing director job in Vienna stayed in the family, as my brother Jürgen was appointed to that position.

London, Part 1
1992

The Yugoslav Wars continued with a siege of the city of Sarajevo by Serbian troops and Czechoslovakia broke up with the declaration of independence by Slovakia, which led president Vaclav Havel to resign. In Italy, the Mafia assassinated Judge Giovanni Falcone after him fighting against them all his professional life. In L.A. riots started after the police officers who had beaten Rodney King got acquitted in court. The violence, arson and looting left 63 people dead, over 2000 injured, 12.000 arrested and damage going into the billions. George W. Bush met Boris Yeltsin to finally declare the end of the Cold War and Denmark won the European Championship by beating Germany 2:0. The players of the Danish team had already been on holiday when they were called up to replace Yugoslavia, which was banned from the tournament for the war in its country.

Paul Simon was the first artist to tour South Africa after the cultural boycott ended. For the first time the CD had sold more units in the US than the music cassette, with the LP still being the most sold sound carrier. Before going to London, I had Elton John coming to Innsbruck for the biggest TV show in the German language countries: Wetten, dass…? He was performing his new single 'The One' and as usual with TV productions and performances there was lots of waiting time and we were sitting backstage talking. Good fun with Elton and his manager John Reid.

In my new job I had to make sure that we co-ordinated our various jazz A&R efforts, spread releases equally throughout the year and think about how to image the jazz activities within and outside the company. In my discussions with David Munns, we worked out that the US would continue using the Verve label and so would Polydor Japan, but the rest should release either via Emarcy or local labels, like JMT for the modern releases and the French Gitanes Jazz Label, sponsored by the cigarette brand of the same name. A&R should be done in a way that we would only sign new artists which we are 100% convinced about and committed to and give them at least two albums, if not three, to develop. This would stop the one album releases with the act being dropped right afterwards – for me not a way to do artist development. On my trips to the US, France and Japan I made it as well clear that we shouldn't get into bidding wars on the same artist – we had therefore regular A&R meetings or calls to make sure we wouldn't negotiate via two different departments with the same artist. We looked into arranging for regular global jazz marketing and product meetings, as well as key market meetings to discuss ideas for catalogue activities and marketing. And I started thinking about ways to create more awareness for our releases and artists. Local A&R was fine with me, if for the smaller markets it wasn't too much work and the artist or album had some international potential. We looked as well at ECM, which PolyGram distributed or licensed in most of the key markets, like the USA, Canada, Germany, France and Japan, plus a few smaller ones. I had some meetings with Manfred Eicher to discuss this when Keith Jarrett came in September 1992 to Vienna to hold a press conference at the Vienna Opera House. The live album from the concert there was released that month. Keith, Manfred, myself and our colleague from [...] Jobst, had a great dinner the day before the press conference, which w[...] the album.

Working with the most important jazz festivals in each market was anot[...] I asked Fritz Thom, friend and chief of LPS, the agency he ran with Heinz [...] various jazz festivals, including the one in Vienna, which they had started [...] the guys of the IJFO, International Jazz Festival Organisation, which at th[...] Vienne in France, Vienna, Molde, Vitoria, North Sea Jazz, Perugia, Mont[...] met first in November in New York and I got to talk to them and preser[...] how we could work better together and in one of the following meetings [...] special Verve events at the festivals. As they would book some of our [...] proposed to combine them with some of our new and upcoming artists, ca[...] would support it financially and with marketing. They obviously liked the i[...] into details, first with Montreux and North Sea, then some of the others followed swiftly. Meanwhile back In London I had found an assistant, Andrea Watson, who would help me to get all this done. Cees continued some of the catalogue re-issues and series and issuing the PolyGram Jazz release bulletin, while we started a proper monthly release schedule and made sure that, for the big releases, the local markets knew what marketing tools would be made available and when. As the International Marketing office, we were more to focus on the top releases and less on the smaller ones, making sure that the big releases got worked properly in every single country and that the repertoire owner would create and offer the markets tools to work these records. These, at the time, were posters and blow-ups of the album cover, shirts, interview discs or having the artist available to do promo in the key territories.

The 1992 top releases from PolyGram's various sources for jazz were: saxophone legend Joe Henderson's first Verve album 'Lush Life', a tribute to Billy Strayhorn, featuring Stephen Scott on piano, Christian McBride on bass and Gregory Hutchinson on drums as well as Wynton Marsalis on three tracks. The album won Joe a Grammy award and was generally well received; the Charlie Haden's Quartet West release 'Haunted Heart', his first album for the French company after Verve US had dropped him, an album that established the quartet as one of the leading jazz groups of its time; Shirley Horn's 'Here's To Life', Betty Carter's 'It's Not About The Melody', 'Abbey Lincoln's 'The Devil Got Your Tongue' and the John McLaughlin Trio release 'Qué Alegria'. Beside these I remember the first Art Porter album, the wonderful Stan Getz & Kenny Barron release 'People Time', as well as Marc Beacco and the JMT album by bass player Marc Johnson 'Right Brain Patrol'.

On 'amadeo' we released that year a live recording by the Vienna Art Orchestra titled 'Highlights 1977 – 1990, Live in Vienna' and a special project by members of the orchestra, Vienna Art Special, with the title 'Fe & Males', in which each instrument was covered by a female and a male musician performing Mathis Ruegg's compositions.

Austrian trombone player and label head Paul Zauner's PAO label licensed to 'amadeo' the Blue Brass Connection album 'Cool Affairs', which he had recorded with Graham Haynes, George Adams, Ron Burton, Cameron Brown and Ronnie Burrage, a truly grooving and cool affair.

In the US, the A&R guy for Antilles Records, Brian Bacchus, had signed singer Patricia B[...] decided to have Wolfgang Muthspiel on the recording. Brian did like Wolfgan[...] was open to all kinds of improvised music, as long as the quality was th[...] many of our records from Emarcy, like Wolfgang, Red Sun · SamulNor[...] didn't matter where the music came from, as long as it fitted his concept [...] artists like Shannon Jackson, Frank Morgan or Ben Neill. Barber's wonder[...] Love' came out in 1992 and Wolfgang sounds really great on it. Brian, who [...] music man, went on to produce numerous successful and timeless recording[...]

On the night when the L.A. riots started, the Lester Bowie Brass Fantasy played a concert in Switzerland, which was recorded live and later released under the title 'The Fire This Time', referring to the events in Los Angeles. For me, jazz is all about communicating emotions and, on this particular live album, they are laid bare as one can seldom hear it, especially on a recording. Their outstanding and extremely touching rendition of Billie Holiday's 'Strange Fruits' still gets me every time I listen to that album. The anger and sadness expressed has deep roots and was what the musicians felt when they played – conserved forever on this incredible disc.

Other jazz recording from 1992 that I still listen to include, of course, Miles' last album 'Doo-Bop'; Medeski, Martin & Wood's 'Notes From The Underground'; Bill Frisell's wonderful 'Have A Little Faith' and Chick Corea & Bobby McFerrin's 'Play'.

The year ended with my first PolyGram International Christmas Party – the difference, to what I was used to and what happened there, couldn't have been bigger – in Austria the event usually was a sober and festive affair, with great food, wine and some speeches, but nothing excessive. In the UK they had hired a place with a fun fair in it, with rides and everything, drinks everywhere and food. But it was just wild and everyone got really wasted, with two guys getting arrested later that night while trying to climb the Christmas tree in Trafalgar Square. I had fun, watching from the side, nursing my wine and chatting to people. This would be something to get used to – a different way of celebrating.

1993

'The Best Jazz Is Played With Verve' became our slogan to image the label and promote our artists at the 1993 jazz festivals. We created Verve logo boards with and without the slogan, t-shirts, banners, blow-up of album covers of touring artists and even Verve jackets. All these marketing tools needed to be designed and produced, ordered by the markets and finally sent, so they would be in the shops and festivals in time.

The best jazz is played with...

Cees every year had sent out a numerical list of all available jazz items and as much I thought this was helpful, I wanted to produce a real catalogue, with all records in alphabetical order and all covers printed. Andrea and I started to work on this for the summer festival season in 1994, as the first of these catalogues obviously was the most work. Therefore, we decided that Cees should continue, in cooperation with us, to make the PolyGram Jazz release magazine for another year, until we started doing it in London. This was also the year I started to go regularly to the summer festivals in Montreux, Umbria, North Sea and some of the others.

After the first trip to some festivals, I came back to London in mid-July and Eva and I got married. We had decided to do it quickly and quietly and without a big party or anything. Wolfgang Puschnig and Linda Sharrock were there as our witnesses, as well as an Italian friend of Eva, Giovanni, and his wife, when we said 'Yes' at the Marylebone registry and they all joined us for lunch. The reason for doing it low key, was that Eva was pregnant with our child and we had booked a short honeymoon right after. My family was happy for us, but disappointed to miss out on a real good party ….

1993, wedding day – with Linda Sharrock, Giovanni and his wife   Photo by Wolfgang Puschnig

The Maastricht Treaty, signed by 12 member states of the European Community laid the ground for the European Union and the way it works today. It announced "*a new stage in the process of European integration*", talked about European citizenship, a single currency, and, without too many details, about common foreign and security policies. Bill Clinton became the 42nd president of the United States, while the Waco siege was the headline for all news programs for over 2 months. Federal government forces and military suspected the leader of the sect Branch Davidians and some of its members of hoarding illegal weapons and came with a search warrant. When they tried to enter the farm, they were received by gunfire, which in the end cost four officers and six members of the sect their lives. The siege by the FBI lasted 51 days and ended in them storming the compound, where the main building quickly was engulfed in a fire which culminated in 76 dead people. Who started the fire was never really cleared and it could have either been from the FBI actions or from the sect themselves. Michael Jackson was accused for the first time of sexually abusing a young boy, but denied all allegations vehemently.

The PolyGram jazz division was in most markets part of the classical set up, except in France, the USA, where Verve stood on its own and in Germany, where it was part of Motor Music, a local pop label. In Japan it was still divided between Phonogram and Polydor, with both delivering product into the system. The rest of the world more or less had a jazz manager within the classical department. This is what I had asked all Managing Directors to do, so we had a person everywhere looking after our releases. As we were planning to celebrate Verve's 50th anniversary in 1994, I continued to discuss the idea of special Verve Nights with the festivals and had meetings with them in Cannes, where we had a wonderful dinner, I had invited to, but in the end couldn't pay as the restaurant didn't accept my credit card for whatever reason and Fritz Thom needed to step in and advance me the costs for the meals and drinks. Someone had invited Patrick Rains and this was the first time I met Pat, and we hit it off immediately. He was then managing Al Jarreau, but we would continue working on various acts from then onwards.

We were planning with our US colleagues to hold a special concert at Carnegie Hall for the celebration of Verve's 50th anniversary, which wasn't actually correct, as Verve, as a label, was only founded in 1956 by Norman Granz, when he signed Ella Fitzgerald and he then folded all his previous labels, Norgran and Clef into the new venture, which was named after a very cool art magazine from that time. What was actually celebrated, was the first recording by Norman made in 1944. I went to New York a few times to discuss with Richard Seidel ideas for the show and which artists should be there, as I had the feeling, left alone, the guys at Verve wouldn't invite many non-US signed artists. In the end, we found the right balance and they even gave in to my and Japan's request of inviting Yosuke Yamashita to perform. Meanwhile we found the title 'Carnegie Hall Salutes The Jazz Masters', which was referring to the past of the label as well as to a very successful mid-price CD series on Verve, called the Jazz Masters, which by that time already featured 30 volumes.

That year the main releases for PolyGram jazz were Joe Henderson's 'So Near, So Far', his wonderful Miles Davis tribute featuring ex Miles-sidemen John Scofield, Dave Holland and Al Foster; Shirley Horn's 'Light Out Of Darkness', a tribute to Ray Charles, featuring special guest Gary Bartz; Dee Dee Bridgewater's 'Keeping Tradition', her immaculate Standards recording; Abbey Lincoln & Hank Jones' 'When There Is Love,' an intimate and touching duo album; John McLaughlin's Bill Evans tribute 'Time Remembered' and 'Zappa's Universe', a deeply respectful take of Frank Zappa's music, arranged and coordinated by Virgil Blackwell and featuring a choir and an orchestra. Amazing stuff and one of my personal favourites from our releases of 1993.

We released as well the first album for PolyGram of the Rosenberg Trio, 'Live At North Sea Jazz', which Cees had brought to the Dutch company and whose previous record had sold just in that market over 40.000 LPs and CDs. Other releases that year came from Django Bates, Eric Reed, Yosuke Yamashita, Caetano Veloso, Mercedes Sosa, Cassandra Wilson and the Finnish Trio Toykeat, which stands for The Rotten Jazz Trio, featuring pianist extraordinaire Iiro Rantala. On 'amadeo' we released Wolfgang Muthspiel's new record 'In&Out', featuring Tom Harrell, Chris Cheek, Larry Grenadier and Jeff Ballard. This was the first album on 'amadeo' in which my brother and I acted as Executive Producers together. Wolfgang featured as well on the quartet recording 'Muthspiel – Peacock – Muthspiel – Motian', a great album with all compositions written by the brothers. The Vienna Art Orchestra delivered and toured 'Standing ... What?', one of the few VAO albums that didn't feature a composition of leader Mathias Ruegg, letting other band members take the spotlight this time. I had listened to a copy of the Mari Boine album 'Goaskinviellja' which Sonet Norway had released earlier in the year and was mesmerized by Mari's incredible voice and unusual compositions. When checking if we could release the album internationally, Harald Tømte said he would have to check with her as she had only signed a deal with Sonet for Scandinavia and in the end told me that she wanted to meet me before agreeing to an extension of territories in her deal. Harald and myself met in Oslo and flew up to the North of Norway and then had a rented car to go to Karasjok, Mari's home town, where she was to perform in the local sports hall. The show was incredible and she totally got me and afterwards we met and went for a typical dinner and later to a disco. When back home, Harald called and told me that she had agreed to the contract extension and was looking forward to work with me. The album, released on the Verve World label, did very well in Europe, with Mari touring in various markets and being very happy with Sonet and PolyGram International. ECM had too a very strong release schedule, including albums by Keith Jarrett, Carla Bley's Big Band featuring Wolfgang Puschnig, Jan Garbarek's wonderful and melodic '12 Moons', Eberhard Weber's classy solo bass recording 'Pendulum' and the first release on the label for Norwegian pianist and composer Ketil Bjørnstad, 'Water Stories', featuring Terje Rypdal on guitar.

In the cinemas 'Schindler's List' and 'The Piano' were making waves. The later as well through its stunning music by Michael Nyman, which was one of the top discs of the year. My favourites from other labels included Guru's 'Jazzamatazz, Vol. 1', US 3's 'Hand on The Torch', Bjørk's 'Debut' and James Blood Ulmers 'Harmolodic Guitar With Strings'. Joe Zawinul performed his symphonic work 'The Story Of The Danube' for the first time at the Klangwolke festival in Linz, Austria, in front of 80.000 people. The Symphony follows the river Danube through time from its source to its estuary, including political events and different cultures.

On November 7th our daughter Hannah was born at the St. Mary's hospital in London. There are no words to describe the feelings I had when holding this little human being in my hands for the first time. I was engulfed in happiness and love and couldn't take my tearful eyes off her ... her eyes wandering around, taking in colours and schemes of things, seemingly content.

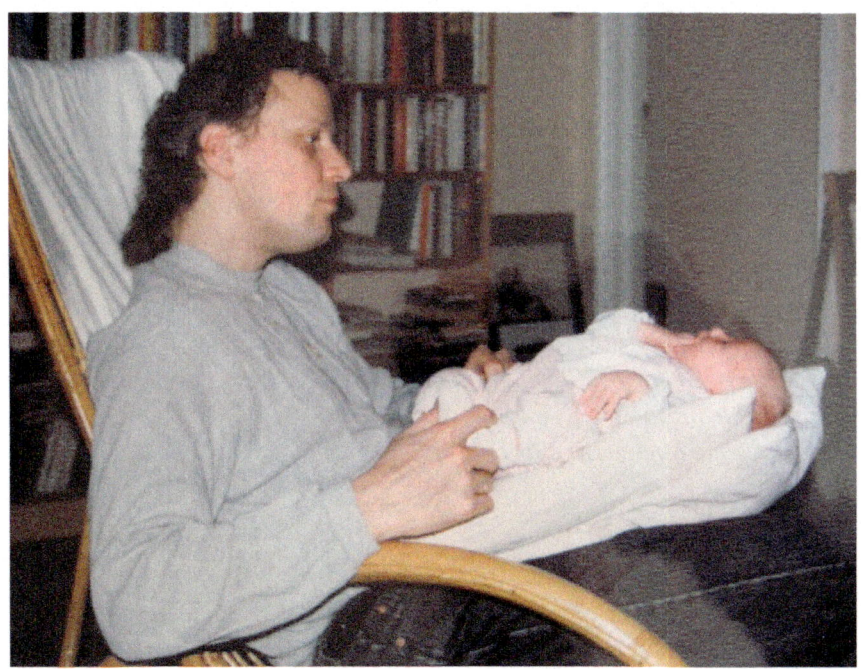

1993 with the wonder that is Hannah

I had thought about what it would mean to become a father, but as there are no manuals, one can only do what one thinks is correct and right for everyone. But I knew I would enjoy being a father and looking after my little beautiful princess, who came home with us the day after. But before that, I went out to buy the newspapers of the day, the # 1 book (Jung Chang 'Wild Swans') and the # 1 CD of that week, 'The Best of Kate Bush' and put them all in a box, to be given to Hannah at her 18th birthday. A few years later, Jürgen and myself bought 3 cases off a 1993 Rioja, as the godchild of his wife was born in the same year and we wanted to give them both a case each for their 18th birthday and have one case to check every so often, if the wine was still good. I had taken a week off and loved holding her and watching her checking out her surroundings, wide awake.

It was at that week that Ornette Coleman came to London to perform a concert with his group, including Don Cherry. As the French jazz division was talking to him concerning a possible contract, I had promised to be there, but had in advance discussed with David Munns that in case my daughter would be born around that time, that he had to go. And so, he did. When I came back to work, Munns called me into his office and told me *"Never do that again to me – it was awful"*, but he had of course gone backstage and talked to Ornette, telling him that he didn't like his music, but respected what he did (typical Munns) and had a real good chat with Ornette after that, ending with him promising Ornette a DCC player, which I had to send to him, plus some tapes. No problem there!

My father started to write letters to Hannah every year on her birthday and occasionally in between, if there was a good and important reason. In his first letter he wrote:

Dear Hannah   *7. November 1993*

It was 19:54:45 when your father called us, to let us know that you were born into this terribly beautiful wonderful world. Welcome!
You were born on a Sunday. In Denmark, the temperature was 6 ° C, the sky was overcast, the wind came from the east and it was raining. For a U.S. Dollar, we had to pay DKK 6.77 and for an English Pound DKK 10.03; the DEM - DKK 3.98, the ATS (Alpine dollar) cost DKK 0.57.
The news told of fighting in Bosnia - Croats against Muslims - Serbs against Croats - Muslims against Serbs. In Africa - Hunger - Revolution - Racism - civil war - everybody against everybody. In India - Pakistan - Philippine's disasters. Chaos in Russia; in the former Soviet Union: Civil War. That's the terrible side of this world.
But there is more.
There are the arts: painting - music - literature. Beyond all borders, races and continents.
There is sport, which is connecting people. That's the beautiful side of this world.
We have lakes, seas, mountains, landscapes full of charm and flowers, trees, animals.
There is peace to see and hear and to learn and find one's own individuality.
This is the wonderful part in this world.
But it is up to you to see it that way.
You are born into a young Europe, just 7 days older than you. And you have all the prerequisites to be a true European: Keep the charm of your Austrian mother, the will of your German father, the serenity of your English birth country!
We wish you a safe, long life guided by your parents!

We ask you:
To respect all human beings
To love animals
To appreciate nature
To always trust your parents
And more than anything else, to be tolerant of everything!

Your great-grandmother Bamler once wrote for a birthday of your great-grandfather:

Be a spendthrift of love, of warmth and kindness.
Be a miser with words, hard and loud spoken

Be wise in enjoyment
Then all your "wishes" will come true, if you do all your "have to's"

With warmest regards from,
Your grandparents

Hannah's grandparents, around 2000

1994

I am not sure if it was in 1993 or 1994 that I got a call from Charlie Haden, who was then recording for our French company. He was complaining that he and his band were not part of the various Verve Nights and events in Europe that summer and threatened to sue me for that. Patiently, I had to explain to him that first of all I considered him one of the most important acts on our artist roster and that secondly these events were supported by us, but not arranged by us, which meant the selection of the participating acts was up to the promoters of the festivals, who got a list of all touring artists from my office in advance. Of course, Charlie was part of that list and all confirmed and available dates were given, it just turned out that his dates didn't work out with any of the planned events. He calmed down a bit, but we surely had a bad start working together. I called his booking agent, Thomas Stöwsand, and explained the situation to him as well and told him to give me a call if I could help in any other form. Which he did a few weeks later – on Charlie's tour one or two festivals in the end didn't book him, as it happens occasionally with not yet confirmed dates, but these ones would have been essential in terms of income and without them the whole tour was in financial trouble. As Charlie had a new album out, we wanted him to tour, so I asked if I could help with some tour support and through that saved Charlie's European tour dates. When I saw him at the North Sea Jazz Festival later that year and introduced myself, he gave me a big hug and a *"Thank You"* and from then on, we worked pretty well together.

We had as well the first Asian regional meeting for Classic and Jazz that year, held in Seoul, Korea in March of 1994 and beside meeting all the product and marketing managers of the various countries, I took the chance to meet and hang out with my friends from the percussion group SamulNori.
I went to Vossa Jazz in Norway, as Mari Boine performed a commissioned composition which would be the base for her next album for us and as on the same festival Abbey Lincoln and Charlie Haden were booked, it made even more sense to go there. I sat next to Abbey during the opening concert of the festival by guitarist Knut Reiersrud, who performed the music of his 'Tramp' album and was, at one point, joined by the Five Blind Boys From Alabama and both Abbey and I loved the gospel and blues fuelled performance. Mari performed her new work the day after with her usual group and after the show we had the annual special gala dinner to honour the artist who had written new music to be premiered at the festival. There were two choices of food – sausages and smoked sheep's head, a local delicatesse, which was only eaten for special occasions. I choose the half sheep's head and so did Abbey. We both really liked the tender meet of the cheeks, but I didn't know what to do with the eyes ... Helge Norbakken, Mari's percussionist at the time, showed me and after having eaten my portion, I became an honourable member of the band. When driving back to the airport the day after, I shared a car with Abbey and as it was a two hours' drive, we had time to chat and exchange our views on this small but wonderful festival. Abbey was fun to be around – wise and enjoying life, her music and meeting people.

Later in the year, I went to Hamburg to coordinate some interviews with German media for Herbie Hancock, who just had released his first album with PolyGram, 'Dis Is Da Drum', which was on Mercury in the US but handled by Verve internationally. It was a great record with a nod to Acid Jazz and African percussion and featured beside Herbie, among many others, Wah Wah Watson, Wallace Roney and Bennie Maupin as well as rappers and DJ's. The concert was great and we were hanging out until late afterwards. Herbie did his Buddhist chanting in the morning and then all the interviews, despite the fact that we were both a bit hangover. Herbie has always been extremely professional – the moment an interview schedule was set, he would be there and do what was agreed upon. Once his flight to Japan was delayed for many hours and when he arrived the first thing he asked was if he had missed an interview and if yes, if they could re-schedule it. The Berlin gig and press event was the first time for me to meet Herbie and luckily many others would follow.

But the main focus of 1994 was on the 50th anniversary celebrations. The event, planned for April 6[th,] at one point, seemed to be off as the US seemingly had a problem with the budget. I got on a plane to New York and had a look at the numbers and discovered that the financial director there had forgotten to add the money we, at International, had promised to put into the concert. Once added, all was good and I was glad that I had come over, as otherwise the guys would have cancelled the show, just because their financial controller made a mistake. 'Carnegie Hall Salutes The Jazz Masters' was a major event, recorded and filmed and brought together the legends of improvised music, plus the next generation of jazz artists in an unforgettable 3-hour concert. The show was hosted by Vanessa Williams and Herbie Hancock, who both performed as well. There was so much great music in honour of Basie, Ella, Miles and many other jazz greats, that it is difficult to select a favourite performance, but for me it was Yosuke Yamashita's piano solo of Bud Powell's 'Parisian Thoroughfare'.

At the same time as the event, we had a worldwide jazz meeting in New York, hosted by Verve and the head of Classics and Jazz in the US, Chris Roberts. At the meeting, Stefan Winter, head of JMT records, after his presentation, handed out 36 pieces of a painting by Thom Argauer, which all together created a red filled in circle on white canvas. Each manager around the world had one and together we would as well have one big piece of art. A wonderful and unique idea.

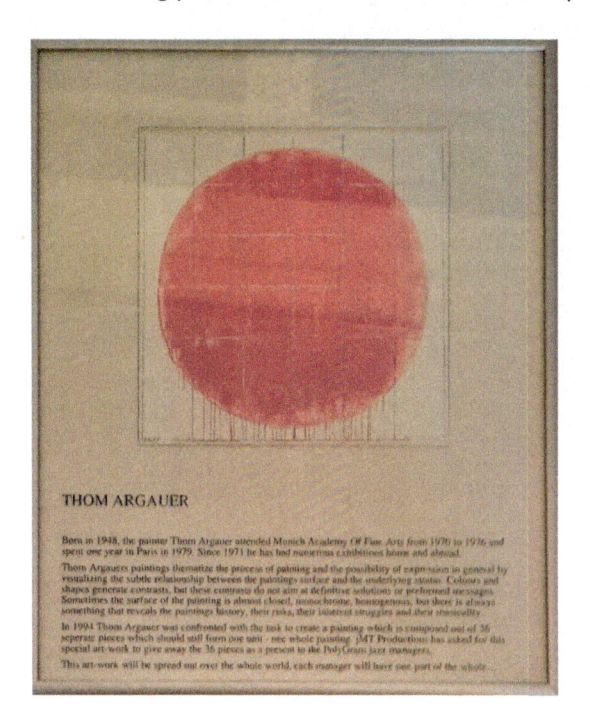

The 50th anniversary celebrations went on, with a special gift I had made for the Managing Directors meeting of that year, where every attendee got a waistcoat with the logo of the anniversary – the vests were not for sale and are rare and now collector's items. Within the various festivals that summer special events were held in Perugia and Verona, Italy; Glasgow and London, UK; Vienna, Austria; Vitoria, Spain; Aarhus, Denmark; Kongsberg, Norway; Hamburg, Germany and Pori, Finland. In Montreux, we had for 2 nights a stage just for our artists in a real Verve Night and at the North Sea Jazz Festival in The Hague, we had one stage for one night as well for our acts only. We had created tons of merchandise material and give-aways for competitions, including Verve watches and shirts and jackets and display material in all sizes, which looked great in the shops at the festivals, especially around our special events.
It was great to work with the guys at the various festivals, especially right from the start with Claude Nobs in Montreux and Theo van der Hoek and Paul Dankmeyer at North Sea Jazz. Carlo Pagnotta in Perugia and Iñaki Añua in Vitoria, Jacques Launier in Vienne, France, Andre Menard in Montreal, Rolf Bugge in Molde, Norway and Gorgun Taner in Istanbul, were part of the IJFO as well and we would have events in all of these places in the coming years. We had now started to produce the newly titled Verve Release Magazine in London, with a changed design and more overall info on our artists and labels. Verve won six Grammy awards that year and the Jazz Masters CD series was extended to 40 items. And in the summer of '94 we had as well the first ever International Jazz catalogue, 95 pages with all CD covers, track listing and list of participating musicians. The catalogue was

extremely well received globally and we got lots of requests for copies and even people writing or calling to point us to printing mistakes or misspellings.

Beside the CD and Video of the Carnegie Hall event, the main releases for PolyGram Jazz that year were Charlie Haden's Quartet West 'Always Say Goodbye'; John McLaughlin's 'Tokyo Live' with Joey DeFrancesco and Dennis Chambers; the Cees Schrama produced 'Caravan' by the Rosenberg Trio featuring Stephane Grappelli; Roy Hargrove's Verve debut 'With The Tenors Of Our Time'; Shirley Horn's live album 'I Love You, Paris' and my personal favourite, Bheki Mseleku's 'Meditation's', a wonderful and touching solo piano meditation. ECM released their first ever mid-price CD series with 'Works' plus the global successful recording by Jan Garbarek and The Hilliard Ensemble 'Officium', which became one of their bestselling albums ever. The stunning mix of medieval songs and Garbarek's saxophone made a very unique album, that, in Germany at least, was marketed to a younger audience as a kind of 'chill out' music. I had given as well Manfred Eicher the OK to record the next of the Red Sun • SamulNori album, as he liked 'amadeo's first album of this collaboration. Wolfgang Puschnig was fine with it too, so the musicians went to Korea to record there with Jan Erik Kongshaug, Manfred's preferred recording engineer from Oslo. Manfred didn't make it in the end, so Wolfgang had to advance all the costs for the studio, food etc. out of his own pocket and on their return, Jan Erik and him started mixing, with Manfred being around, but according to Wolfgang very busy on the phone for most of the time. Overall, not the best experience for Wolfgang. Linda Sharrock did the artwork and delivered it with all instructions … but when the finish product arrived (ECM didn't sent proves to check), the artwork was the wrong way round and Manfred had put himself as the producer, even so he wasn't in the studio, so Wolfgang asked that to be changed as well as the cover. ECM had to destroy all booklets, re-print them with the correct artwork, Wolfgang being named as producer and Manfred as Executive Producer and then they put the record out. A great album, but the last for Wolfgang on ECM.

Linda in the same year released her second album on 'amadeo', 'Like A River', recorded in London with producer Ashley Slater, who gave Linda's songs a modern sound. Christian Muthspiel's Octet

Ost released their second album 'II', featuring Thomas Stanko and Arkady Shilkloper among others. Herbert Joos, German trumpet and flugelhorn player and member of the Vienna Art Orchestra, was as well a wonderful painter and did many sketches of artists. He released three amazing books in a limited edition with sketches of his of Chet Baker, Miles Davis and Billie Holiday respectively. For the Billie Holiday book he had recorded an album with his takes of songs connected to Billie and this was inserted in the book and we decided to release it on Emarcy. Herbert did for many years design our Christmas cards, mainly with portraits of our acts, like Ella or Charlie Parker and later multiple current artists on one card.

Pat Metheny released his most controversial album, 'Zero Tolerance For Silence', solo electric guitar improvisations, which got really mixed reviews, ranging from 'masterpiece' to 'total rubbish'. For sure, an unusual Metheny record, one that required time to get used to.

While the world was stunned by the theft of the Edvard Munch painting 'The Scream' in Oslo, Barack Obama becoming the first Afro-American US President and Berlusconi being elected as Italian President, we moved into a slightly bigger flat just around the corner from our old one in Maida Vale, so we would not have stairs in the apartment and Hannah a bigger room to grow up in. She was doing really fine and was the sunshine of my days at home with her.

Munch's painting was found a few months after the theft, unharmed. The first passengers travelled by train through the Eurotunnel, connecting France and the UK. Woodstock celebrated its 25th anniversary and O.J. Simpson got arrested for being a suspect in the murder of his ex-wife and her boyfriend.

Kurt Cobain died of a self-inflicted gunshot wound and the Three Tenors entertained the world again at the football World Cup final in Los Angeles, which Brazil won against Italy.

As both of our parents adored our little energetic human bundle called Hannah, we spent our holidays and festive breaks either in Austria or Denmark, where my parents lived. Which was fine with me, as food was always great there … sometimes we rented a place close to my parent's actual house and stayed there, or in my younger brother Thomas's place on a small island.

1994, with Hannah

Hannah was growing fast and the communal garden in London was a blessing, as other kids where there and space to first crawl, then walk and finally run around in a safe environment. On one of my trips to New York I had bought her a charming children's book titled 'Charlie Parker Played Be Bop' by Chris Rashka and she loved me reading it to her, smiling especially on the sound of Be Bop! An early jazz education!

1995

I started to build up my relationships with the many artists, after whose recordings I looked in terms of promotion and global marketing, by seeing them as often as I could on tour and finding time to chat or dine with them. A good personal relationship always makes working together easier. In the same way I trusted the artists to deliver the best possible record at the time, I wanted them to trust me to come up with the best global marketing campaign under the given circumstances and to represent them internally in the best possible way in all global, regional or genre related conferences. In 1995 we released the first Ornette Coleman album via our French company, 'Tone Dialling' and I set up with my colleagues there the global promotion plan, which brought Ornette to a handful of countries just to give interviews. I travelled with him to a few of these and we built up a good rapport. It was fascinating to see him in interviews, humble and shy to an extent, but attentive and willing to talk about his music. When people asked strange questions, he always gave the right answer. One guy was asking if it was true that he never had a proper education on his instrument and his answer was simple and on the point: *"Children learn to talk without knowing the Grammar"*! I loved it! Honest journalists wrote afterwards that when he spoke about Harmolodics, his philosophical and musical concept, they had no clue what he was talking about. The few others pretended to have understood, but couldn't quite explain …

We had lots of meetings and conferences throughout the year within PolyGram, but the most important meeting every year for the company was the Managing Directors Conference. I remember the first one I attended, in Miami, when I did my first presentation to that audience. I started with the famous quote by Frank Zappa, whose music I love, *"Jazz Is Not Dead – It Just Smells Funny"* and then, after telling them that the smell wasn't actually that bad, stated what we had planned as the main releases for the coming year. It went down well and we had Jazz established at that level as well. I usually started to prepare a video which featured the most important releases and I did play this after saying a few words before, so that the repertoire had a face in some form. These presentation videos I made with a wonderful team, which was led by Barry Barnes and Paul Hussey and we became friends over the years and they did as well one or the other video clip and other necessary filming for me. But their ideas and enthusiasm for the videos we did together over the years will always be with me.

In 1995 we had the MD's conference in Sevilla, Spain and for the first time we were offered to have a live jazz act performing at one of the lunches. As Verve just had released the first Christian McBride album, Chris Roberts wanted him to be the one performing there. I thought about the audience and didn't think that a core jazz gig would do the trick with these guys – we needed to give them something they would be able to enjoy, being entertaining and classy, but as well accessible for them as mostly untrained listeners of jazz.
My obvious choice was Dee Dee Bridgewater, as I knew that she would swing and the MD's would love it. We had a long discussion and, in the end, Chris called David Munns, who then asked me what the problem was. I explained, gave my reasons and he simply said: *"You decide"*. When Dee Dee performed in Sevilla, she, as I expected, really got the guys going and everyone loved her short but intense show. Even Chris afterwards came by and said *"You were right to have her as the first act in such a meeting"*. Dee Dee, the band and myself had a great dinner afterwards in a wonderful traditional restaurant in town and then she was off and I went back to the meetings.
I think it was at the same conference that we had Ornette Coleman as the guest of honour for the jazz division at the gala dinner. There were pop stars from around the world, classical artists and Ornette. I remember especially a Portuguese funk and soul singer, Pedro Abrunhosa, who after he had met Ornette told me that we *"had made one of his dreams come true"* … that made my day too.

1995 was a very busy year for us in jazz, as we had planned for the summer and beyond a special campaign for the young artists, we had signed at the various repertoire centres: The Next Generation.
We had prepared 2 mid-price CD samplers with 16 tracks each, so including 32 artists from 12 countries in the campaign, the first ever global jazz campaign for new talent on such a scale. The campaign ran throughout the summer into October, with global concert events held on the 21st of that month in New York, Tokyo, Paris, Milan and Hamburg.
Various other items like t-shirts, display material and interview discs had been produced to drive the campaign in retail as well. All CDs of the participating artists had a sticker with the Next Generation logo on it *and "Special Next Generation events took place in The Hague's North Sea Jazz Festival where on Saturday Night Wolfgang Muthspiel, Graham Haynes, Linda Sharrock, Stephen Scott and Mark Whitfield entertained a packed house with their bands. Other special nights were arranged in Glasgow, Vitoria, and Pori, where we even had our own venue: The Verve Jazz Club."*, I wrote in the Verve Release magazine #3, 1995.

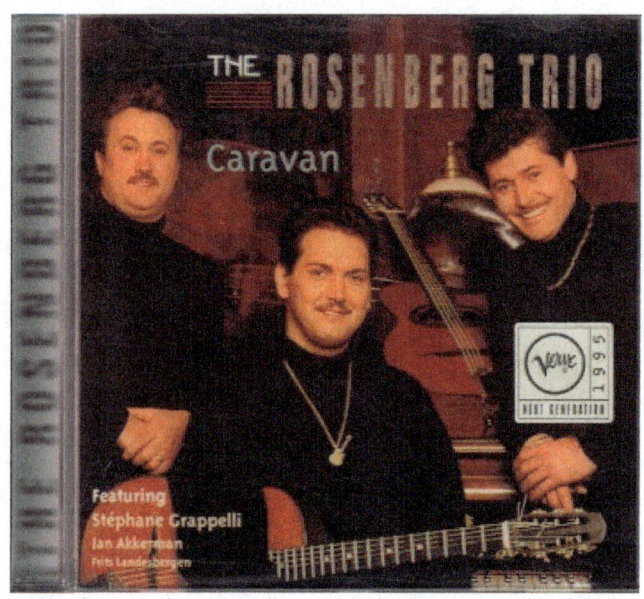

1995. The Rosenberg Trio album with the 'Next Generation' sticker

Linda Sharrock was supposed to play in Vitoria-Gasteiz that year and she and Wolfgang Puschnig came in from Vienna, but the band had to fly in from Philadelphia and got delayed for over a day and were not in Spain at the time the show was supposed to start. Instead of cancelling, Linda and Wolfgang asked percussionist Arto Tuncboyacian, who was there to perform with Joe Zawinul, if he would like to play with them before his show with Joe. Arto and Joe were fine with the idea, but it wasn't possible for Arto to take his instruments, as they needed to be set up on the bigger stage for the show with Zawinul, so he grabbed what he could – a small table from his hotel room, borrowed other percussion instruments from the festival and took an empty Coca Cola bottle. They had never played before in this set up, had only about an hour to rehearse and then went on stage and played a stunningly touching and intense concert, which luckily was recorded by a local radio station. The power of music making spontaneously!!! The recording was finally issued on 'amadeo' in 1997 as 'Live In Vitoria' and is one of Linda Sharrock's strongest albums overall.

Jimmy Smith, organist extraordinaire, had just released his latest album, 'Damn', on Verve, on which he was playing with some of the Next Generation artists, like Christian McBride, Mark Whitfield, Nicholas Payton and Roy Hargrove. Therefore, the US team decided to send them on tour in that formation and Larry Clothier, Roy's manager and booking agent, was to book the shows. As they started their tour in Europe, Jimmy played the first few gigs just with drums and guitar and hardly ever called the other young guys out on stage. We met and had a discussion about it, but Jimmy seemingly didn't care and after him doing so again, we decided to send him home and finish the tour with Roy leading the 'Next Generation' band, which was a huge success everywhere. Jimmy showed a few more times that he was a grumpy old man and no fun to be around. Pity, that such a great musician had to behave in such a way, at one point leaving one of my managers in Europe deeply frustrated and in tears.

The success of such major and global campaigns depends fully on the commitment of all markets. And I can only say, that the international team we had a that time was truly special. The key markets being on the forefront but the others equally important. In the UK we then had Richard Cook, revered journalist and jazz expert, who had signed trumpet player Guy Barker; In Spain we had Marta Grech and Javier Pouso and then later Alex Sanchez, who also started to do a bit of A&R; Pietro Paravella was our man in Italy, well connected and enthusiastic; Daniel Goodwin in Switzerland, always full of good ideas; Harry Gruber in Austria, who continued the 'amadeo' series for a while; Pjotr Rzeczycki in Poland, who brought us Anna Maria Jopek and others; Sten Nilsen in

Norway, who introduced us to Bugge Wesseltoft and was working closely with Yngve Naess, the local A&R guy; Goran Israelsson in Sweden, well established in the local scene, who signed Anders Widmark; Ole, whose family name I forgot, in Denmark, who signed NHØP for two projects; Paul Popma and his team in Holland, who still used Cees for jazz productions occasionally; Ken Druker in Canada, who would soon come to Verve in NY; Stelios Koniaris in Greece, thanks to whom we worked with Eleftheria Arvanitaki and Pete Song in Korea, as the second most important market in Asia, after Japan. Great personalities, great team players and wonderful individual human beings. All of them used the Verve Release magazine, now with full colour covers, and the catalogue, which we did again in 1995 to the orders of the markets. The Jazz Masters series of mid-price CDs was extended to 50 discs and Verve signed Wayne Shorter to a recording deal. In Germany Roy Hargrove won the Echo for best jazz album, then the only jazz category in the Echo awards and in the US, jazz won 3 Grammy's – 1 for the McCoy Tyner Big band album and 2 for the Ella Songbook Box Set.

The big records of the year for PolyGram Jazz came from Joe Henderson, whose 'Double Rainbow', a tribute to the music of Antonio Carlos Jobim, got amazing reviews and strong sales. Dee Dee Bridgewater's tribute to Horace Silver 'Love & Peace', featuring the master himself on two tracks; Ornette Coleman's 'Tone Dialing', recorded with his Prime Time group; Van Morrison's first jazz album titled 'How Long Has This Been Going On' and his first # 1 on the Billboard jazz charts as well;

plus new recordings by Wayne Shorter, Abbey Lincoln, Roy Hargrove and Charlie Haden with Hank Jones. Van, surprisingly, said that he would do some interviews in connection with this album, that as well featured Georgie Fame, so we set up some top interviews for him. German magazine Der Spiegel was one of them and the journalist was to fly in from Hamburg and then go to the studio where Van would do the interview. All journalists had been briefed that Van wanted to talk about this album and jazz in general, but not about his pop records of the past. Once the journalist had landed and was in the limo, we had ordered to get him to the studio I called him and he bluntly told me that he wouldn't keep his part of the agreement and would ask Van about his classic old recordings as well. As I had a few more interviews planned in the coming days, I couldn't afford Van to be pissed off right at the start of doing promo, so I called his manager at the time, a cool guy named Willie Richardson and told him about my problem and suggested that I would first talk to Germany, then the journalist again and if he wouldn't change his attitude and mind, I would ask the driver to turn around and drop the journalist at the airport again. After speaking to Christian Kellersmann in Germany and then to the journalist again, I called the driver and told him to go back to Heathrow immediately and drop his passenger there. Christian meanwhile had spoken to the magazine and this particular journalist didn't do any interviews for him again. Thankfully the rest was cool and got loads of coverage for the album. I had worked with Van's music for many years in Austria and whenever he came, I went to the gigs – he checked if the record company was there, but I didn't think we exchanged many words over the years. This album was different and I enjoyed working on it. For the US only, we even got a promo only live EP, 'Live At The Point', which helped to make the record a success there. So much, that at the Leverkusen Jazz Festival Willie, Van and I already talked about his next jazz recording.

Wolfgang Puschnig released that year his new album 'Mixed Metaphors', using at times a singer, poet and rapper in the same song, to showcase the various forms of using lyrics in musical contexts. Wolfgang Muthspiel's new recording was called 'Loaded, Like New' and was produced by JMT head Stefan Winter. And the Vienna Art Orchestra delivered their 'European Songbook', inspired by Verdi, Wagner and Schubert. Other non-Us artists that released albums that year included Maria Joao, Mari Boine, Monday Michiru, Barbara Dennerlein, The Rosenberg Trio, Courtney Pine and Mercedes Sosa. And ECM had top releases from John Surman, Keith Jarrett, Tomasz Stanko and Terje Rypdal.

This was the year Austria, Sweden and Finland joined the EU to enlarge this free trade and travel zone. The Aum Shinrikyo Sect attacked the Tokyo subway system with the nerve gas Sarin, which left 13 people dead and over 5000 injured and, in the US, the Oklahoma City bombing, by home grown terrorist Timothy McVeigh, killed 168 people and wounded over 650, while Radko Mladic and his Serbian troops massacred thousands of Bosnians. The war in former Yugoslavia continued and brought in NATO, which attacked some of the Bosnian Serbs positions, to end the atrocities. In a highly controversial verdict O.J. Simpson was cleared of murdering his ex-wife and her boyfriend. The court case was top news all around the world and it seemed that O.J. had gotten away with murder. But in a civil court in 1997 he was found guilty of wrongful deaths and the families of the victims were awarded $ 33.5 million in damages, most of which he hasn't paid.

DC Comics released in 1995 their Batman Special mini-series called 'Batman Jazz'. This Legend of the Dark Knight Special got mixed reviews from critics and fans, but are for me a valuable possession since I got them as a birthday present from my friend Hannes Schweiger, as is the book 'Poetic Reflections' by the Watts Prophets, which I got after a concert they gave in Vienna with Don Cherry. The jazz café 'miles smiles' did the catering for this event and I got to talk to the Prophets a bit and the concert, which as well featured singer and songwriter Dee Dee McNeil, was just divine in the combination of Cherry's music and their poetry. My copy of the book is a bit worn out and whenever I have a look at some of these wonderful and guiding poems, I simply can't believe that that book was once black-listed in America and neither properly published nor read on radio. Later I got some of their CD's as well, which are extremely powerful and timeless, just as the book is.

In May 1995 my father wrote to Hannah *"that the celebrations of the 50th Anniversary of the surrender of Germany are over.*
WAR from 1 September 1939 to 9 May 1945
The result: at least 55 million deaths
25 million of which were in the Soviet Union
6 million of Jews and millions of Poles, Gypsies and political prisoners killed in German concentration camps by an insane idea of race superiority.
Deaths, atrocities, torture, inhuman treatment which we must never forget and can never explain away.
During the war, soldiers of the Soviet Union, Englishmen, Frenchmen, Americans, Poles, Indians, Sri Lankans, Australians, Canadians, Italians, Germans, etc. died at the front
What for?
Why?
Today we have discussed whether the end of the war was defeat or liberation for Germany?
There are many opinions - the further away since the war's ending, the more it is believed it was, in fact, liberation.
Theodore Hess, the first president of the newly founded Federal Republic of Germany, said in 1949, that Germany has been redeemed and destroyed in one. Richard von Weiszacker said at the 40th Anniversary in 1985, liberation and defeat.
But right now, there are at least 6 veterans in the Bundestag who openly speak of defeat as well.
The Federal Chancellor Helmut Kohl, distinguished by the grace of late birth (he was born in 1935), speaks of the birth of freedom and says the right thing unintentionally.
So, let's say: the door to the future was thrown open.
It took me years to understand that the defeat was liberation. I never wanted to be a soldier again. Work – yes; build something - yes. Be productive.
I have mentioned before that 'Jews' was considered a despicable word. Racism is dangerous. Jews are members of a community of faith as Catholics, Protestants or Muslims. I love all people. I am neither interested in any religion, nor in skin colour. And not in politics.

*We should never forget what happened in World War II, we must never deny the Holocaust.
On the occasion of that 50th Anniversary I heard some things and names for the first time and I was ashamed of it."*

We had started a discussion with Claude Nobs concerning his tremendous archive of audio and video recordings from the Montreux Jazz Festival and on one of the trips I made there, this time with David Munns, we went out for lunch to Giradet's in Crissier, just outside Lausanne. Ossi Drechsler, then head of PolyGram in Switzerland, joined us as well. Fredy Giradet was then considered one of the best chefs in the world and Claude knew him well. Claude basically asked Fredy to improvise something for us and something different for Ossi, who had some allergies that were taken into consideration. Before the meal arrived, Claude simply called Fredy the *"Charlie Parker of the cuisine"* and he definitely proved to be worth that label when we tasted the food, which was absolutely divine. I find it as difficult to write about food as to write about music, as both are an individual experiences based on emotions and personal history. The combination of tastes and textures made me enjoy that meal more than any other before. I love food, but this was the first time I had been at a restaurant that was considered one of the best in the world and it definitely woke an appetite for top cuisine within me.

In between all of this I celebrated my 40th birthday in London. We had rented the upstairs of a local pub and asked them to do a buffet with mostly Indian food. Family and friends from all over Europe turned up and my parents made a rare visit to London to celebrate with us. Neighbours and colleagues were there and all together made this a memorable event. We had a wonderful time and Hannah especially enjoyed the attention she got from the guests. For me it has always been the best to celebrate with family and friends in a relaxed atmosphere.

In December that year, over 4 nights at the Knitting Factory in New York, JMT celebrated its 10th anniversary and most of the current artist roster performed there. It was at the end of the last day, that Stefan Winter announced that he had sold JMT earlier that year to PolyGram Japan and that they would close it down with the end of 1995. Somehow most artists thought that we would delete their JMT recordings from our catalogue, something no-one ever even considered at the time. Artists got upset and I had a bit of explaining to do and in the end, we didn't delete any recordings immediately and in the long run, licensed the 81 catalogue items back to Stefan Winter to be released on his new label Winter & Winter. Unfortunately, the truth was, that PolyGram Japan couldn't make it work financially and neither could Stefan Winter, as otherwise he wouldn't have sold the label to PolyGram. But the compromise to license the repertoire back to him and so guaranteed that the music would be still available, made sense to everyone. It was interesting to see how quickly the major label was accused of neglecting art and deleting the musician's history and whatever else there was. Strange, as I always experienced it the other way around: smaller labels in general gave much worse deals in the jazz world than majors – they paid less royalties, in most cases included the publishing rights and spend less on marketing and promotion. I have seen contracts I would never sign as an artist and would advise against, but as there weren't then and are now, not enough labels to release all the albums made, it is easier to accept a bad deal, but have at least a release, than having nothing at all.

John Scofield had released his then latest album 'Groove Elation' and was coming to Europe to tour this repertoire. Chris Roberts called me and said that they were talking to John about a possible deal and if I could do something on the tour that would swing John's decision in our favour. I called all the jazz managers in the touring markets and said that they should go to the gig and backstage afterwards to just say *"Hi"* and introduce themselves. As the last gig on the tour was in London I went as well and introduced myself to John and he was truly impressed that PolyGram showed up in every single market and his own record company only in a few. We had a great chat about our international structure and what we could do for him and a few weeks later Chris called to inform me that they had made the deal and that International was the issue that drove his decision. The first album for Verve came in 1996 and is for me one of the pearls in John's classy output. 'Quiet', is exactly that – relaxed and laid-back quality music. Influenced by the colours of sound of Gil Evans, John wrote and arranged beautiful brass-based music for this stunning album, that featured among others Wayne Shorter, Steve Swallow, Randy Brecker and Howard Johnson. 'Quiet' is so far the only Scofield album where he plays solely on acoustic guitar.

That year we lost two of jazz's most important improvisers and composers: saxophonist Julian Hemphill and unique trumpet player Don Cherry, whom I had the pleasure to see and hear many times over the previous two decades.

Don Cherry, 1936 - 1995

1996

It must have been late 1995 or early 1996 when we had a Classical & Jazz meeting for the Scandinavian region. This one was organised by the classical division, but I had been invited to come along, as in the region the two genres were housed in one division. Tim Harrold, the Head of Classics International at the time, had as well invited the labels Deutsche Gramophone, Decca and Philips Classics to do presentations and he spoke about the overall business. The meeting was to last 3 days and on the last evening we went out for a great dinner and I was hanging afterwards with some of the guys at the bar of the hotel. When I came back to my room about 3 am I had a message from David Munns telling me to call him no matter what the time was. I decided to wait until the morning and called him at 8 am my time, in that case 7 am his time, just before going to breakfast. He told me that he wanted me to know that Tim Harrold would announce his leaving of the position of Head of Classics International and that a new division would be created, officially titled PolyGram Classics & Jazz International and that this new department would be led by Chris Roberts and that I would be part of it. He didn't want me to hear this in the meeting, but be informed before, which I appreciated. I really had enjoyed working with David Munns, a true marketing man and amazing in dealing with people. The way he worked with me and guided me in my new job, made him the second mentor for me in the music business and someone I surely learned a lot from. As I knew Chris, I had no problem with the change and looked forward working closer with him. Chris set up the new department in the new building PolyGram International had moved into at St. James Square in central London and we were situated at the top floor – a division which then had classical marketing, jazz marketing, DVD, financial and administration people working for it. The Executive Committee for Classics & Jazz International consisted of Chris as the president, the three classical label presidents, the Verve president, the classical international marketing manager and myself for jazz. Chris had brought in a president for Verve after his move to the UK, which was Chuck Mitchell, a great guy, with incredible taste and knowledge, who was easy to work with and interesting to talk to. Of course, I knew the label heads from meetings before, but thereafter we were to work a bit closer.

I had actually brought a project to Philips Classic hat was finally released in 1996: Joe Zawinul's symphonic work 'Stories Of The Danube'. I had met Joe a few years before at one of the festivals and as we both spoke the same language, hit it off immediately. I went from then on to see his gigs whenever possible and we talked a lot – I went to his place in New York, when he was living there, and sat in the studio with him talking and drinking Austrian Schnaps and listening to some unreleased Weather Report tapes. He said he was looking for a label for the classical piece and I started to inquire with Philips, who were interested. I told Joe so in The Hague in 1995 and he was very happy and we had yet more Schnaps to move the deal forward. This piece in seven movements is a powerful trip through time and history and Joe's music is captivating and touching and perfectly played by the Czech State Philharmonic Orchestra Brno directed by Caspar Richter with special guests guitarist and singer Amit Chatterjee, percussionists and singers Burhan Öçal and Arto Tuncboyaciyan, as well as drummer Walter Grassmann. I always stayed in touch with Joe and we were talking about other ideas, some concerning string quartet pieces he was working on, but unfortunately, we never got to do them.

Dee Dee Bridgewater performed three sold out nights at the glamorous and legendary Paris venue L'Olympia, with new signing to Verve France, singer Jeffery Smith, opening for her. Dee Dee's show was spectacular and really established her as a star in France. She had young trumpet player Roy Hargrove and saxophonist David Sanchez as guests and finished each night backed up by a wonderful gospel choir. The French press called her 'The new Josephine Baker' and everyone was taking about her. Dee Dee was as well the main protagonist of another Philips Classics album from that year: 'Prelude To A Kiss – The Duke Ellington Album', which featured the Hollywood Bowl Orchestra conducted by John Mauceri. This Robert Sadin produced album included next to Dee Dee, who appears on eight of the twelve pieces, as well Bobby Watson, Charles McPherson, Ira Coleman, Jeff Hamilton, Cyro Baptista, Cyrus Chestnut, Steve Turre, Wynton Marsalis and Hassan Hakmoun. A classy tribute to one of the most important composers of our times.

PolyGram Brazil meanwhile had signed and recorded an album with legendary keyboarder Sergio Mendes, his first recording in four years and the first for PolyGram since recording for Philips between 1961 and 1967. 'Oceano' featured a host of great musicians and special guests, including Gilberto Gil, Caetano Veloso, Hermeto Pascoal and Zucchero. Sergio was doing promo for us for the album – that's when I met him for the first time and then he came on tour and I met him again at the airport in Geneva. I was travelling back from a visit to the Montreux Jazz Festival, while he was on the way there to perform, but first he said he would stop at Giradet's for a nice meal. Lucky guy, I thought.

Beside that record we had a bunch of really great and successful albums that year, first of all a new studio recording by the Guitar Trio of Paco de Lucia, Al Di Meola and John McLaughlin. They had recorded the new album at Real World Studios in England and I went to see them there. These are three band leaders and all of them got big egos and I knew them all from their own projects and liked them individually. But when I came to the studio it was already clear that there was tension in the air and while we took a photo shot it was becoming a bit silly, as we had to take the pictures with each of the three once in the middle, once on the left and once on the right … I wondered if they ever would agree on which photo to use … and in the end the cover had only their names on it … The day after I had been there Paco smashed one of his guitars on Al's head. Police came to the studio and Al left. Our French guys convinced him in the end to finish the album and they made up and went on tour, but each in a separate limo to be picked up and separate dressing rooms backstage …it was crazy, but very successful. A proposed live recording in Latin America unfortunately never happened, as by that time Paco and John finished the tour as a duo.

Herbie Hancock's 'The New Standard' was another big record for us that year – his jazzy interpretations of songs by Prince, Stevie Wonder, Peter Gabriel, Kurt Cobain and others opened up the American songbook to new standards. It helped that he had picked an all-star line-up for the recording, including Michael Brecker, John Scofield, Dave Holland and Don Alias. On the tour, I met personally for the first time Dave and Michael and it was great to see John again.

Ornette Coleman released two albums at the same time – 'Sound Museum: Three Women' and 'Sound Museum: Hidden Man'.

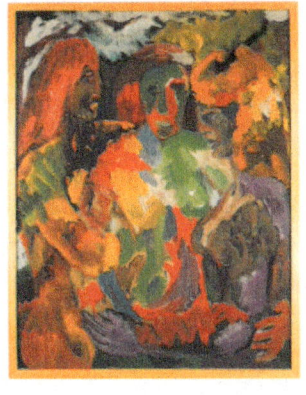

As Ornette explained: *"Sound Museum exists in two CD renditions of the same compositions played differently in each rendition. This concept was done to show music harmolodically. In the Harmolodic world the concept of space and time are not past or future but the present"*.

While working on these albums I met Ornette again and he gave me a wonderful silk shirt with musical motives as appreciation for the work I had done for him. That shirt I still have and value extremely.

When in New York I always tried to see him and Denardo, his son and drummer, for a chat over lunch or dinner. Ornette was always interesting to talk to, as he spoke a lot in symbolics or images and I needed to translate these for me into something more real in my world. Usually Ornette would say *"Yes, exactly"* or use different words to make me understand. Once we were sitting in his loft, just the two of us and having a nice bottle of red wine while talking. He tried to explain Harmolodics to me, his philosophical and musical system, but to no avail. I don't read music at all, so what he was trying to tell me was simply beyond my world, but still fascinating in his attempt to liberate music from all structural inequality. We went a few times to his favourite Thai in Manhattan, usually with Denardo, but once Denardo didn't make it and the two of us had the most incredible meal and a lot of fun. Ornette could be really funny when he told stories and I was cracking up a lot. One story was about the time when he had just released the 'Free Jazz' album in 1961 and he had gotten a gig somewhere. So, he called the band together for rehearsal and got ready. Then on the day before the show the promoter called and told Ornette that they hadn't sold one ticket and therefore he unfortunately had to cancel the concert. Ornette was really disappointed as he had to pay the band for the rehearsal without a chance to get any money in. The day after the cancelled show the same promoter called him again. *"You can't imagine what happened – there were hundreds of people here yesterday coming for the gig*". Ornette interrupted: "*But you told me that you hadn't sold one ticket?*". "*True*" the promoter replied, "*they all came expecting to get in for free, expecting free jazz*". Another time when in New York I had the afternoon free and went up to see him and Denardo at the studio they had for a time. Ornette was rehearsing a new bass player, as he wanted again use two in his group. I just sat there and watched and listened for hours and it was truly interesting to hear Ornette explaining what he wanted them to play, rehearse it and then at the end telling them to play whatever they heard. He gave them an idea what was on his mind, but as well the freedom to explore the music from their individual understanding.

'Red Hot + Rio', the ninth album for AIDS benefit, paid tribute to the music of Antonio Carlos Jobim and the rich tradition of Brazilian pop music from the 60's and 70's. The album featured a mixture of Brazilian legends and current pop stars like George Michael, Sting and Crystal Waters and charted around the world and MTV did a one-hour special on the record on world AIDS day that year. Singles and remixes drove radio and club play and I enjoyed meeting and working with Beco Dranoff and John Carlin.

The other top releases of 1996 came from Van Morrison, who together with Georgie Fame, Mose Allison and Ben Sidran recorded 'Tell Me Something', a wonderful tribute to the music of Mose Allison and another Billboard Jazz Chart # 1 for Van. Joe Henderson's Big Band recording, plus new albums by Betty Carter, Shirley Horn, Charlie Haden and Pharoah Sanders complete that list. 'Amadeo' released the new Red Sun SamulNori album 'Nanjang – A New Horizon', originally recorded and released in South Korea by SamulNori and we licensed it for European release. 'Perspective' was Wolfgang Muthspiel's last album for us before he started his own label Material Records to release his music and occasionally someone else's.

The ECM highlights of the year were the wonderful and percussive 'Visible World' by Jan Garbarek, featuring among others Mari Boine; a Dave Holland Quartet album and the Carla Bley Big Band recording 'Goes To Church', featuring Wolfgang Puschnig, who would record a total of four Big Band albums with her. This one was partly recorded at the Umbria Jazz Festival in Perugia that same year.

The summer of '96 was busy with Verve events at the festivals, especially in Montreux and The Hague. In Montreux we had for two days both stages in themed events: on July 8th the Verve Star Night and the Verve Blues Night and on July 16th the Verve Rockin' Night and the Verve Jazz Night. At North Sea Jazz we had Herbie, Mari Boine, Mark Whitfield, Pharoah Sanders and Art Porter in our event and many others throughout the festival. Of course, Roy Hargrove was there again as well. Roy would play North Sea every year with a different project or as a sideman with someone, but he was there for sure. And it was guaranteed that he would come to the sessions at the Bel Air hotel, blowing his horn all night long. More than once, I went to bed in the early hours of the morning after having listened to the jam sessions at the hotel and Roy was always at the centre of it – whether other jazz stars or legends were on stage with him or some newcomers, he just played and had fun. Some amazing musical moments happened there over the years. Roy was like that; he would always hang and talk to other musicians and play with them. Whether it was in New York late at night at the Zinc Bar or in The Hague or in Vitoria-Gasteiz in Spain.

There I saw a late-night jam session that ended in the most incredible trumpet battle I have been lucky enough to witness: the Eric Reed trio was playing, Mark Whitfield at the beginning as well, if I remember correctly, but then Nicholas Payton showed up and later Wynton and Roy. There were still about 75 people left at about 3 am and what they got to hear, they will remember forever: Wynton, Nicholas and Roy started a trumpet battle like they must have been in the old days – exchanging choruses and pushing each other to unheard heights. Wynton shone with his unparalleled technique, Nicholas with his tone and improvisational skills, but when Roy played it was all that plus baring his soul with every note. He had it all and on top of it he put all of himself and his emotions into his playing and so touched the audience in a very special way, which the two others couldn't match. This being Spain, shouts of "Olé" were heard when a solo reached its climax and at the end the musicians and the audience left happy, but exhausted. For me that was a moment in musical heaven I will never forget.

At the festival in Vitoria that summer we had as well a few acts performing, including the Carla Bley Big Band, the Herbie Hancock Quartet, Kenny Barron and the Wayne Shorter group. After the shows we all usually went with Iñaki and the musicians for a late dinner to the restaurant El Portalón and so we did that day. I was with one of our artists, possibly Herbie and his band, while in one of the other rooms were Wayne and band with Dahlia Ambach, his tour manager, so I went over there for a minute to say "Hi" and have a chat.

As the concerts were really great everyone was in a fantastic mood and the amazing food and wine helped as well. Wayne told us that he would tomorrow meet his wife and niece in Italy and was looking very much forward to it. After the meal we said our goodbyes and wished each other safe trips. When I went to breakfast late the next morning, I heard from some musicians the terrible news that Anna Maria Shorter and her niece Dalila had vanished when TWA flight 800 crashed into the Atlantic Ocean near New York, about 12 minutes after take-off. Cause of the break-up of the plane was supposedly an explosion of flammable fuel vapours in a fuel tank, most likely ignited by a short circuit. The accident must have happened just around the time we left the restaurant, abut 2:30 am our time.

Wayne had already left and was on his way back to New York, trying to come to terms with what had happened.

I think our big Managing Director's meeting that year was in Hong Kong and I can't recall if we had a jazz act performing there or not, but most likely not. I had put together with Chuck a presentation, the video as usual put into some great visual form by Barry and Paul and we did our little show there.

What I remember most from that meeting was the many acts that performed there from all the labels, especially the US and the UK. But the one act standing out from the crowd was German – the company there had released the year before the first album of their rock act Rammstein, 'Herzeleid' and now had brought the band to perform in Hong Kong, including all pyrotechnics and lights.

The jazz crew was sitting at one table that dinner, Chuck, Chris, myself and I can't recall who else and we loved the short and heavy show, seemingly the only table to go wild about them, which was appreciated by Tim Renner, head of Motor Music, the label that had signed the band and was as well responsible for looking after jazz in Germany. Rammstein became one of Germany's biggest rock acts, plus building a global fan base.

After the meeting finished, I stayed on for two more days, as I had arranged with my brother Jürgen to meet in Hong Kong and spent some time together there, before he would go off to Macau and myself either back to London or somewhere else in Asia. It was great to see him, have time to chat, walk around the city and have some nice meals. We didn't do that too often these days.

1996, In Eitzersthal with Hannah

Hannah had turned 3 and it was a wonder to watch her develop and grow. Every day something new happened, new words, new connections … amazing!! I missed some of these moments for business travel, but enjoyed the ones I had the more. We were playing around a lot, or when I put on a Miles Davis CD I always asked *"Who's playing the trumpet?"* and Hannah would answer *"Miles Davis"* … so cute!
I was promoted to Vice President International Marketing Jazz that year and was made responsible for all local jazz signings around the world. We wanted to make sure that the markets wouldn't sign too many acts and lose focus on the ones from Verve and as well that the signed acts possibly had international potential. That way I got to work with many outstanding and exciting international jazz and world music acts. Chris wasn't that big on hanging out with artists, which in the jazz world is essential in building relationships, so we made a deal, that he would take care of all the political issues that a big company like PolyGram brings with it internally and I had to hang out with the musicians – seemed like a great deal to me!
In the Yugoslav wars international arrest warrants were issued for Radovan Karadzic and Ratko Mladic for war crimes they were made responsible for. The IRA ended a ceasefire when they bombed the Docklands in London and later Manchester, which left in total 2 people dead and over 200 injured. The European football championship in England was won by Germany beating the Czech Republic 2:1. In the music world Tupac Shakur died six days after being shot in Las Vegas and in the movies, it was 'Shine' by Scott Hicks with the outstanding Geoffrey Rush playing pianist David Helfgott, that made the biggest impact. 'Fargo' by the Coen Brothers, featuring Frances McDormand and Tim Burton's hilarious 'Mars Attacks' are two more films I remember from that year.

In November 1996 Thailand celebrated the 50th anniversary of the reign of King Bhumipol and a jazz festival was part of the celebrations. The King was a jazz fan himself, so this was no surprise. As we had planned a regional jazz meeting anyway, we decided to hold that a few days after the festival, in Kuala Lumpur, Malaysia. David Mc Donagh, Verve US' head of international exploitation and myself went to Bangkok for the festival as we had a few acts performing there on a Verve Night – Sergio Mendes at the opening ceremony, which we didn't attend, Courtney Pine, Bheki Mseleku, Art Porter and a few more and we had a great time and heard some amazing music. The day after the Verve event David and myself went to Kuala Lumpur to make sure all was set up for the meeting, during which we had planned a small club gig of Art Porter for the attendees of the conference. At around 2 am in the night before the meeting was supposed to start, David called me and I could immediately hear that something bad had happened. He told me that he just got a call from Art Porter's manager and that Art, on his day off before coming to our meeting, had taken a boat trip with some people and that boat had capsized and Art had drowned. I just couldn't believe it … we had seen the guy perform just a day before … The rest of the night and the two days of meetings passed like in a trance and it took both of us a while to get over the shock, especially as Art's manager kind of made us responsible for having brought Art over to Asia. Art was not only a wonderful guy, but a musician who was starting to get worldwide recognition and one wonders what might have been … To help the family financially we released two years later 'For Art's Sake' a collection of unreleased recordings and some live tapes from North Sea Jazz, including a powerful 23-minute version of 'Lay Your Hands On Me'.

1997

For the 39th Grammy awards in 1997 we got 15 nominations and collected 3 Grammy's out of these, one each for Herbie Hancock, Wayne Shorter and James Cotton. Herbie and Wayne were as well the sole protagonists on one of our main releases for that year, the incredible duo recording '1 + 1', which they toured extensively.

I think I must have seen the two guys performing together about ten times that year, but the concert in London and one in Italy remain in my mind for their sheer musical beauty and deepness. The concert in Italy was to be held outdoors and the piano tuner came in the afternoon for the soundcheck to tune the piano, but as temperatures changed before the show started, he should have come back before the gig to check the piano again. Which he didn't and Herbie immediately got problems as some keys were out of tune. They tried to find and call the tuner, but couldn't locate him, so Herbie had to play on the discordant piano, which seemed to had sharpen his instincts, as he simplified his playing to tremendous effect and Wayne often checked on him with a smile. The concert lasted less than an hour and the piano was basically unplayable at that point.

After the show Herbie, Wayne, our guy in Italy, Pietro Paravella, the promoter of the show and myself went to have dinner in a local taberna, which was excellent. The wine was great too and so was the conversation. We spoke about religions and as Wayne and Herbie both are Buddhists, Wayne told a few stories about his belief. Like when one day Ike and Tina Turner had a major argument and Tina fled their home and came to Wayne's house to hide. But they expected Ike to figure out in the end where she would have gone and come to get her. Wayne suggested to sit down and meditate, pray and chant, and while they were doing so, outside a very thick fog settled over the neighbourhood. Ike, who was on the way to Wayne's house, got lost in the fog and never made it there.

Wayne truly believed that their prayers helped. He had more stories like that, truly amazing. For me Wayne is a guy who has a deeper understanding and feeling for human beings than anyone else I ever met. It is as if he can read people's emotions and feelings directly, connecting with them on a different level. Truly astonishing.

The other big record of the year was also a duo recording, this time by Pat Metheny and Charlie Haden and was called 'Beyond The Missouri Sky'. It was great to see and work with Pat again after the ECM years in Vienna and Charlie and I, meanwhile, got along very well too. As Pat was very busy working on a new project when this record was released, he could give us only two days for promo in Europe, so we decided to bring him and Charlie in via Concorde from New York, have an international press conference in Paris, plus a few important face-to-face interviews and then fly him back again and Charlie would continue doing more press and radio. Pat would do some more from New York via telephone and overall, we got some incredible coverage for this very unique and beautiful album. Roy Hargrove's Cuban project 'Crisol', Joe Henderson's take on 'Porgy & Bess' featuring Sting on one song and Dee Dee Bridgewater's love letter to Ella Fitzgerald, 'Dear Ella', were the rest of the big releases for that year.

Wolfgang Puschnig's new album was a live recording from the previous year, when he celebrated his 40th birthday with an impressive concert featuring various aspects of his illustrious career. Eva and I had been in Klagenfurt, Austria, when the concert was held and recorded and witnessed the unique power of Puschnig when performing with his friends. 'Roots And Fruits', the album title, featured Linda Sharrock, Jamaaladeen Tacuma, the SamulNori group, pianist Uli Scherer, the Amstettner Musikanten and many others and in the grand finale of the night Puschnig met the Austrian brass band and the Korean drummers for some outstanding music making. Something that never worked in the rehearsals, finally clicked perfectly on stage to create music from another universe! Werner Hascher, then the jazz guy at PolyGram Austria, invited me to write a few words for the liner notes, which I did with pleasure. Puschnig had become, and still remains, one of my best friends and writing a few sentences for his CD was an honour for me.

ECM's outstanding release of the year was without any doubt trumpet player Nils Petter Molvaer's 'Khmer', a groovy electronic and beat-laden modern jazz record, that kind of felt lost on the label. Molvaer mixed jazz with dance music, worked with remixes and had a very young audience. This, his first album as a leader, featured exceptional guitar player Eivind Aarset plus other Norwegian top musicians. Keith Jarrett's solo piano live recording 'La Scala' and the Ketil Bjørnstad/David Darling duo album 'The River' complete the highlights of ECM for that year. Not only Molvaer was into the 'Nu Jazz' thing from Norway, keyboarder Bugge Wesseltoft was to release his 'New Conception Of Jazz' album, which he had put out on his own label Jazzland Recordings, licensed by Sten Nilsen to PolyGram Norway. Bugge too used electronics and beats and grooves to create a new sound, danceable and club oriented, but with its base in jazz. His album included guest appearances by Molvaer and Aarseth as well as by singer Sidsel Endresen. That was the start of Jazzland Recordings, now one of Europe's most exciting and successful labels.

In the US, as they didn't have many big jazz festivals like in Europe, they started in January 1997 a tour event called 'The Verve Jazzfest'. The tour had 19 dates, all in different major cities in the US, from California to Texas, Washington and New York and also in Toronto, Canada and finished in Kansas City. The touring group included Joe Henderson with Al Foster and George Mraz; Charlie Haden Quartet West and the Kansas City All-Star Band featuring amongst others James Carter, Christian McBride, Nicholas Payton and Mark Whitfield. Based in the Verve tradition of 'Jazz at the Philharmonic', the Verve Jazzfest got enthusiastic reviews and standing ovations everywhere. The summer in Europe was busy as we had all of our main acts and some of the younger one's touring. Special Verve events were booked in Vienne, France; Umbria Jazz, Vitoria; North Sea and Vienna, where Wolfgang Muthspiel opened for Herbie Hancock's New Standard Band with a solo guitar show. While Roy Hargrove's Crisol, featuring pianist Chucho Valdez, played all major European festivals, only Montreal in Canada had Charlie Haden and Pat Metheny performing the music of 'Beyond The Missouri Sky', a touching and deeply emotional experience for me. The duo would not go on tour before 2003 and this concert remained one of the very few before that.

On a trip to Istanbul, for meetings with the local PolyGram team and the people from the jazz festival, I was invited by the A&R guys there to come with them to the studio where local star, singer Sezen Aksu was recording a new album. All songs on the record were compositions by Goran Bregovic, the successful composer and band leader, who became famous for his soundtracks to the films of Emir Kusturica. Sezen Aksu's new album of Goran's work with Turkish lyrics got the international title 'The Wedding And The Funeral' and I put it out later that year via Emarcy globally, with decent success. She is a strong and unique singer and the record is very good. Goran was in the studio when I went there and as he was then recording for PolyGram in France, I was familiar with his recordings and we talked a bit about his own albums, as well as Sezen doing his songs.

If I remember correctly the Managing Directors meeting that year took place in Vancouver, Canada, and we did our presentation there as every year and had our special guest at the gala dinner, which was Joe Henderson. I had met Joe on tour before and found him to be a very gentle, highly intelligent man, who was fun to be around. Joe had done some promo for us in connection with his albums on Verve and I was astonished to find out that he spoke several languages almost perfect. One of these languages was German, as he was stationed in Germany as a soldier after the war. At the time of the dinner in Vancouver Joe was managed by Edith Kiggen, but she couldn't attend, so she sent her son, John, who was working with her. I was sitting on a table with Chris Roberts, Joe, John and I can't remember who else, and at one point Joe started to speak in German to Chris and myself. Chris had studied and lived in Germany as well and Joe knew about that. He simply wanted to play a prank on his manager and have a conversation without being checked. John was lost and Joe had fun and all of us enjoyed the great food.

Haruki Murakami released the English translation of his epic master piece 'The Wind-Up Bird Chronicles', a multi-layered story about being human and the borders between reality and what is happening in one's mind. A theme Murakami often refers to in his books. The first of the Harry Potter books was published with a run of 5000 copies and got mixed reviews. But word of mouth was making a second print necessary soon after. In the UK Tony Blair was voted the new Prime Minister by winning the elections for Labour and IBM computer Deep Blue beat chess world champion Garry Kasparov in a match – the first time a computer had beaten a grand master.
Pat Metheny released his 'Imaginery Days' album and saxophonist David Liebman his outstanding recording 'The Elements: Water', featuring an all-star line-up with Billy Hart, Cecil McBee & Pat Metheny. And the Spice Girls, then Hannah's favourite group, released their first single, while Shania Twain ruled the airwaves in the USA.

We were in Austria that late summer with Hannah, staying with my brother Jürgen at his house in the country side and then with Eva's parents. While there, we went to a travelling circus, who had set up tent in a nearby town. First Hannah was fascinated, but when the clowns came out and being loud, she got scared and when they asked me to come and play with them, she couldn't be consoled until I was safely back next to her. Eva and I went to the jazz festival in Saalfelden for a day to see our friends from the Vienna Art Orchestra, leaving Hannah with her parents and after the concerts on the way back to the hotel, we heard of the car accident that killed Lady Diana in Paris. Kind of a shock, especially as immediately rumours started to spread about a possible assassination. The outpour of emotions, in the UK especially, was unheard of. When back in London after a few days, there was no escaping this event or the funeral, which was held a week later. That same year the singer of INXS, Michael Hutchence, passed away as well. I had met him once when working his records in Austria and they came to play in one of the stadiums. He seemed a nice guy. What a waste to die so young allegedly during a sex game that went wrong.

In his letter to Hannah, my father mentions Lady Di's accident as well and continues: *"Completely submerged in the turmoil surrounding Lady Di, was the death of a truly great woman, Mother Teresa. She was a nun from Slovakia, who had dedicated her entire life to serve the poor in India - Calcutta. She received the Nobel Peace Prize, and she deserved it like no other before or after her. India honoured her with a state funeral.*
Almost at the same time died Sir Georg Solti, one of the great conductors of this century."

1998

In May of 1998 Philips Electronics announced that they had come to an agreement with Canadian company Seagram on the sale of PolyGram for $ 10 billion. Seagram, originally a liquor company, already owned Universal Music, which was much smaller than PolyGram, who by far was the market leader in Europe. Chris Roberts moved back to the US to be closer to the top management and decision making and to figure out what Universal's plan was for us at Classics & Jazz. In June PolyGram President Alain Levy resigned and soon after David Munns followed. It would take months until the merger was completed in 1999 and sometimes one wondered if all decisions were based on the right motives … In Italy for example PolyGram was the market leader and Universal about 25 % of its size, but the top job in the combined company went to the Universal guy, despite the fact that he was close to retirement age and our managing director was one of the most respected executives in the Italian music business. Jørgen Larsen became the new head of International for Universal, which had a different structure than PolyGram. We used to have a global structure, but Universal had North America and International split and Jørgen was to run the world excluding the US and Canada out of London.

Max Hole became the new international head of marketing pop, basically replacing Munns. It was a pity to see David go, he was a strong marketing guy, a great boss from whom I learned a lot and an amazing character. He was and still is one of the main guys behind the Nordhoff Robbins Music Therapy charity and one day he invited me to go with him to a fundraising lunch and we were sitting next to Robert Plant, singer Gabrielle and some colleagues from the UK offices, and items musicians had donated were offered for sale to benefit the charity. It was a lot of fun and incredible to see the invited guests spending money for a good cause.

On the merger we didn't really know what exactly would happen and hadn't heard from Chris anything either, so we simply continued with what we were doing best: schedule the releases from the various repertoire sources and put the marketing tools and campaigns together in co-ordination with the repertoire owner and then communicate with the markets around the world to make these releases global successes. As we had more and more releases coming from other sources than Verve in the US and France, we re-designed the release magazine once more, giving it now a full colour real magazine feel. We went back to calling it PolyGram release magazine, as other labels like Emarcy, Jazzland or Antilles became more prominent. Marina Detienne joined my team as an assistant, as Andrea wanted to travel the world and we again did an updated jazz catalogue, this time with a numerical barcode section. The catalogue now had about 150 pages and had become an important part of every year's marketing efforts.

We had a great year at the Grammy's, winning seven altogether, with two going to Dee Dee for 'Dear Ella', one each to Doc Cheatham with Nicholas Payton, Charlie and Pat, Herbie & Wayne, the

Joe Henderson Big Band and Roy Hargrove's Cuban album 'Crisol'. And we had many artists touring that summer, of which 21 performed at the North Sea Jazz Festival, where we as well had again a special Verve Night, featuring Medeski, Scofield, Martin & Wood, Terry Callier, Nicholas Payton with Mark Whitfield, a tribute to Cal Tjader featuring Eddie Palmieri and Courtney Pine. Other Verve Nights were happening in Vitoria-Gasteiz and Perugia, at the Umbria Jazz Festival. They had booked Ornette Coleman for 3 nights. Doing a different program each of them and I flew in to see the second show, titled 'Global Expressions'. This program featured Ornette, Denardo on drums, Charnett Mofett on bass plus a male choir from Napoli, some Indian musicians and a Japanese singer. At one point, they were all on stage making music together, as if speaking with one voice, which was simply amazing!! I never had heard anything like it, but somehow it made total sense. Ornette standing there, his playing somehow keeping it all together and it was as if he was glowing! Another moment of music heaven I was lucky enough to experience. And in San Sebastian in Spain, they were talking about Abbey Lincoln, who performed with her trio a wonderful concert to which at the end she invited Randy Weston to join her on stage. Randy had played a solo show before and together they performed 'Blue Monk' and 'Hi-Fly' to a mesmerized audience.

John Scofield had jammed a few times with the groove masters Medeski, Martin & Wood and so it wasn't a major surprise when he asked them to record with him his new album 'A Go Go'. This funky record really did well and the gigs were stunning and fun to see. Herbie Hancock's 'Gershwin's World' is a respectful bow by the piano master to one of jazz's most important composers, George Gershwin. And Herbie was stretching out and recorded pieces by friends and contemporaries of George, like W. C. Handy, Maurice Ravel and Duke Ellington. Guest stars on this Robert Sadin produced and conceived album are Chick Corea, Wayne Shorter, Joni Mitchell and opera star Kathleen Battle. As this was a record that was difficult to tour, Herbie went out in the summer with his funk outlet The Headhunters, who had just released their 'The Return Of The Headhunters' album. Another tribute album to George and Ira Gershwin was the new Red Hot release for AIDS benefit 'Red Hot + Rhapsody', which featured Nathalie Merchant, Sinead O'Connor, Jovanotti and many more hot acts performing the brothers' music in modern versions. Gilles Peterson, legendary label head, journalist and DJ from London, brought singer and songwriter Terry Callier to Verve and his first album for them 'Time Peace' is a true timeless master piece and touchingly beautiful. I went to see Terry whenever he came to London and got to know him a bit – what a sweet and humble human being. But on stage a powerful and emotional performer and singer.

The output from the local markets of projects with a global sales potential increased year by year and 1998 was no exception, with artists coming from Norway (Mari Boine, Eivind Aarseth), India (Zakir Hussain), Italy (the wonderful drummer Paolo Vinaccia), South Africa (guitarist Jimmy Dludlu), Czechia (Peter Lipa), Mali (Amadou & Miriam), Denmark (Niels Henning Ørsted Pederson, Nils Lan Doky), Portugal (Maria Joao), Austria (Wolfgang Muthspiel), France (Akosh S.) and Germany (trumpet star Till Brönner) and that is only a selection from more than twenty releases. In most of these I had been involved in one form or the other and made the final decision whether to add them to the international release schedule or not. I always tried to work like a small indie label, but from within and with the advantage of a major record company. Personal involvement was important, managing expectations to the artists and internally, as well. We made our annual budgets with Chris, based on the expected releases and catalogue activities and had to reach these targets. No-one would bother us, if we stayed within our own expectations, which most of the time we fortunately did. That way we could fly under the radar and do things a bit differently.

ECM had a bunch of great releases that year too, above all the Jan Garbarek album 'Rites', featuring among others Bugge Wesseltoft. Bugge playing the accordion on their touching version of Don Cherry's composition 'Malinye', with Jan on sax and Marilyn Mazur on percussion. The Keith Jarrett Trio with Gary Peacock and Jack DeJohnette delivered another stunning live album with standards performed on the highest level. And Ketil Bjørnstad introduced his new group featuring cellist David Darling, guitarist Terje Rypdal and drummer Jon Christensen with the beautiful 'The Sea' album. Otherwise, I was listening to Lester Bowie's Brass Fantasy's 'The Odyssey Of Funk & Popular Music,

Vol. 1', which featured his takes on the music of the Spice Girls, Manson, Puccini and Cole Porter. Only Lester could make such a we... does!!! On my playlist also were Burhan Öcal & Jamaaladeen Tacuma's 'G... Tour', a powerful live album by the Zawinul Syndicate, featuring among othe... Brad Mehldau's second and third albums in 'The Art Of The Trio' series, titled ... respectively. Mehldau and his sidemen bassist Lenny Grenadier and drummer Jorge ... setting the level for all the younger players then. Lauren Hill's 'The Miseducation of …' a... Page & Robert Plant's rocking 'Walking Into Clarksdale' round up that list, which included as w... wonderfully weird album 'Hot Room', a selection of solo performances in an old tepidarium ... Vienna by accordion player Otto Lechner, Wolfgang Puschnig, bassist Achim Tang and Tunisian oud player and singer Dhafer Youssef. I had met Dhafer thanks to an introduction by Wolfgang Puschnig and really liked what he was doing and him as a person. When he got an offer to release his first album on 'enja' records and asked what I thought about that, I told him to go ahead, as I always liked Matthias Winckelmann and the music he released on his label. And then there was the 'Panthalassa' album, which was created by Bill Laswell and featured the music of Miles Davis in a *"modern mix translation and reconstruction in sound"*. Bill took four tracks from the 'In A Silent Way', 'On The Corner' and 'Get Up With It' and used the original multitrack masters for his modern mix. An interesting idea.

France became football World Champions by beating Brazil at home and Microsoft released their Windows '98 program, while the IRA called a ceasefire after they exploded a bomb in the city of Omagh, so finally ending 30 years of, so called, Troubles.

Hannah started nursery that year and she was ready for it … some of her friends in the communal garden went already and she wanted to go as well. Holidays now had to be taken when she was off, but that was fine. Hannah loved nursery, had no problem to be with new kids and overall was really happy and content and made friends easily.

Her grandfather wrote to her that year again with a bit of historical background: *"In June, we celebrated the 50th Anniversary of the beginning of the Berlin airlift. The Soviets had blocked all access routes to Berlin and the city's 2.5 million inhabitants, were supplied from the air with food, coal supplies and industrial goods. The airlift lasted 469 days with 270.000 flights, as well as, 78 deaths. It was the largest logistics performance to date, to guide planes in 5 levels through 3 corridors.*
I can still hear the voice of the Berlin Mayor Ernst Reuter: "People of the world, in the U.S., in the UK, in France, look upon this city …" Berlin became the symbol of resistance during the Cold War against the Soviet Union and the Warsaw Pact, and it has remained so until reunification in 1990.
In June the D-Mark has turned 50 years old as well. It had been a symbol of reconstruction, stability and prosperity in Germany. It is difficult for many, especially older people, to lose the D-Mark and to get used to the Euro".

The International Jazz Festival organization had every year, and most likely still has, a meeting in which they discussed the festivals of that year – what did work, what didn't, any problems with artists or managers, new trends and ideas for the coming year. In September 1998 that meeting was held in Vitoria-Gasteiz, Spain and I was invited by the festivals to be part of the meeting for some sessions, which I gladly accepted. The cooperation with the festivals did work well for the Verve Nights and I kept the guys informed about our releases and helped with other issues when asked or needed, as I did with Iñaki when he had a little problem with a manager of an artist who wasn't even ours, but as I knew the manager in question well, I could help by talking and making them understand. I assume that's was one of the reasons I was invited, another that with some of the managers of the festivals I really got friendly, like with Claude, Gorgun and Carlo. At one point at the meeting, they had a piano / bass duo performing for us and these youngsters were really great. The

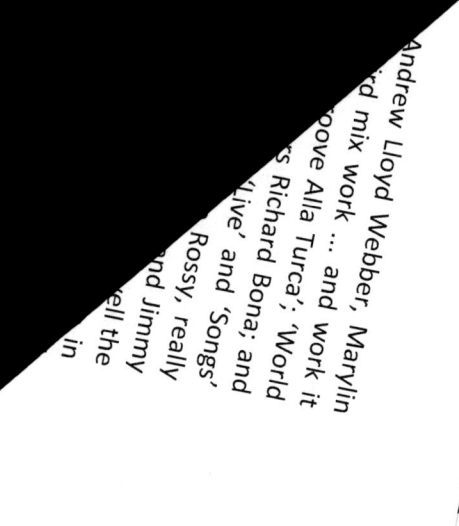

amazing and I got to chat with him a bit. Pablo Martin
ore spoke very well German, which helped. I can't recall
though it was Pablo with whom I stayed in touch. One
newly opened Guggenheim Museum and its exhibition on
saw some examples of the Terracotta Army and was blown
gures. Just imagining that there were at least 8,000 soldiers,
avalry horses made is simply mind boggling. Then we had a
st famous vineyards, Marques De Riscal, and tested some
s a long tradition of making excellent wines and when on the
he locals call the 'Cathedral', a cellar built into a hill, housing
to today, every year being represented. No one has access to
ard and the King of Spain … and Iñaki … as when the meal was
got a bottle of wine from the year of our birth. I had a 1955
e and I decided I would open it on the New Year's Eve when the

That same day, legendary singer Betty Carter passed away after a short illness. I always thought she was the strongest of the three singers of that generation I worked with – her, Abbey and Shirley Horn. And I really liked Betty's no-nonsense approach to life and her music and she was fun to be with. Whenever she came to London we went out for dinner before one of her shows at Ronnie Scott's, where she usually played. She would complain a lot about the US team, but in general was fine with International and the efforts made there for her recordings. I saw her perform many times all over the world and every single time I was mesmerized by her vocal abilities, impossible scatting and stage power. One of these great concerts in London was released as a CD, 'Feed The Fire', a stunningly powerful and captivating recording, that featured Geri Allen on piano, Dave Holland on bass and Jack DeJohnette on drums – it doesn't get much better than that!!!! Betty was an amazing educator and a lot of the top musicians of today went through the school of Betty Carter. She created a program called Jazz Ahead, featuring 20 selected students who could spend an entire week training and composing with her, but the real 'academy' was performing live with her on tour – she had no problem stopping a song right in the middle when she heard something she didn't like from one of her sidemen … told them what and why and then continued the song. The most amazing thing about this was, that the player in question wasn't embarrassed at all, just accepted that this was part of the learning process and that the standards Betty set were high. I experienced her doing so at a gig at Ronnie's and was impressed how cool everyone was about it and how straight, but positive, she handled the situation. I had a lot of respect for her and her loss for the music world was and still is immeasurable.

We had a regional Classics & Jazz meeting for Asia in Manila that year and David McDonagh and myself had decided to bring new signing Brazilian singer and guitarist, Badi Assad, there for a solo performance. Badi was travelling with her husband and producer, guitarist Jeff Young, known from his time with Megadeath, and was to perform songs from her recent album 'Chameleon'. As we prepared for the dinner at which she was to perform and set up the stage, my classical counterpart, Kevin Kleinman, came back from a walk through the city. As he hadn't brought a live act and didn't want to be outplayed, he had hired a choir he had heard performing on the street in the city to sing a few songs there as the 'classical' act. I couldn't believe it, but said "Fine, if that's what you want, OK with me, but if any of these guys just makes a step on our stage, you are in so much trouble, you can't even imagine". I had his choir perform first and it was ok, but Badi's show was incredible – I hadn't seen her perform before, I really liked the album, but live it was out of this world – stunning guitar technique, wonderful vocals and some body percussion combined with a sweet personality and the passion for her music, made this event unforgettable for everyone. And it was the beginning of a great friendship between Badi and myself.

Deutsche Grammophon was celebrating its 100th anniversary in 1998 with great releases, marketing campaigns, merchandising material and a big event in Hamburg, where the label had its headquarters then. As part of the Classics & Jazz Executive Committee, I was as well invited and enjoyed an evening of good food and exceptional musical performances. As my eldest sister Marlis was living in Hamburg, I took the opportunity to see her and have a dinner and few nice single malt whiskeys with her. Single malts had become my main hard drink since living in London and especially Springbank and Ardbeg I liked, as different as they are.

In Vienna they had a few changes at PolyGram: Chris Wemcken was let go and Vico Antippas, took charge of Austria as well as Switzerland, where he was already Managing Director. He wanted to bring in his own team and therefore my brother Jürgen was unfortunately let go in early 1999.

1999

It must have been around the end of 1998 or the beginning of 1999 that I got a call from Jørgen Larsen to come and see him. As we still hadn't heard anything from Chris, this could have meant either they wanted me to stay or the start of discussing my farewell package, which as I had heard from others, would be fair and generous.
I prepared myself to explain what we were doing in Jazz, took a printed catalogue and set out to meet the new boss. It shouldn't have surprised me that at one point in the meeting he started to speak German, as most Danish people do, but it did, but I recovered quickly and answered a bit in Danish, which in exchange took him by surprise. He basically asked me to continue in my position and that the overall Classics & Jazz structure might remain intact, with minor changes, which he wouldn't elaborate about. I was happy, as I really liked what I was doing and that my team was safe and we could continue and even add Universal's jazz releases to our overall schedule.

Shortly after that it became clear that Verve and Universal's GRP would be merged in the US and led by Tommy LiPuma and Ron Goldstein. That unfortunately meant that Chuck Mitchell, with whom I

really liked to work, had to leave his position as president of Verve Records. The new Verve Label Group was not reporting to Chris Roberts, but internationally I was looking after their top releases as before, in cooperation with David McDonagh, who remained on the label's team.
The classical structure was changing as well, as Philips Classics was integrated into Decca Records, with Costa Pilavachi heading this new unit. Philips Classics would have lost the right to the Philips name anyway as part of the deal when the electronics company sold PolyGram.

The International Classics & Jazz office in London was reduced further by the decision that all DVD and video should be handled by the labels directly and that Chris asked me to become Vice President International Marketing Classics & Jazz, which meant working the classical top releases the same way I would do for jazz and so I added another product manager to the team, Emma Perry, which would look after some of these, plus the few local ones on Emarcy Classics, which I had started as well.
We introduced a Priority Release system, in which all major releases from all labels would be handled through my office, always together with the repertoire owner's international manager, and I would send out marketing plan forms and requested the markets to fill them in and send them back. I would then look over these, afterwards discuss them with the repertoire centre in question and finally get back to the markets with comments or suggestions how to improve their plans. In that way we could guarantee that the global activities would be coordinated and hopefully led to a worldwide success.

We had the first European Universal Jazz Meeting in 1999 in Hamburg and both Tommy and Ron came. Tommy had called me before and told me that they had recorded a new Diana Krall album and that he believed that this was the one to break her and he wanted her trio to perform at the meeting, but as she was on tour in Europe, the dates didn't seem to allow that. I said I would look into it and called Burkhard Hopper, her European agent at the time and checked if there was any chance to move one of the dates or replace her with someone else.
We made a deal, which didn't cost us much, helped one of our acts to perform instead of her wherever it was she was supposed to be and got her to Hamburg to perform for her new international team. Tommy was happy and so was I and from then on, we talked often and made sure we had the success for the big records they deserved. I had heard some of Diana's music before and didn't really get the hype.
I saw her live once and I thought it was ok, but …. In Hamburg the performance was great, she showed more confidence, talked a bit to the audience and overall seemed stronger musically than the first time I had seen her. She was still shy in a sense, but open to chat and we got along well.

The 1998/1999 catalogue was still named PolyGram and hadn't included the new Universal/GRP repertoire yet, but we were already working on doing so for the next edition. But we did re-name our release magazine into Universal Jazz Magazine and immediately included all releases from the GRP labels as well (some of these would use the Verve brand, being the strongest label in the overall mix). That magazine would be issued three times a year and was full colour with 8 or 12 pages featuring short info on and covers of most releases and catalogue activities.

Germany had started two years earlier to release an annual low-price compilation called Verve Today and they would usually run some sort of new release campaign around it. This was one of Christian Kellersmann's ideas and seemed to work very well. In one of our meetings, he then came up with the idea to have some artists perform as part of the campaign and from there we developed together the idea for Verve Now, which was to be a fully subsidised developing artist touring program in Europe to give new and promising acts, who had recently released a new album, a first step into various European markets. We would deliver the artists to the markets and the local team had to invite retail, media, VIP's and via radio contests some fans. We were working with a booking agent to get these dates, Bremme-Hohensee if I remember correctly and Veit Bremme being my main contact there. A truly great guy to work with, straight and honest. We would always take one act coming from Verve in the US and one from somewhere else and for the first year we invited Bugge Wesseltoft and US-signed Brazilian singer and songwriter Vinicius Cantuaria to be part of Verve Now. A promo sampler was made with 2 tracks by each act plus one by guitarist Eivind Aarseth, who was playing in Bugge's band and had also released his first album in 1998.

The tour went to the following cities: Hamburg, Amsterdam, Cologne, Milano, Munich, Paris and London and was a big success and both artists did as well a lot of promotion while out on tour. Unfortunately, we didn't find a sponsor for the tour, as Heineken, the beer brand, first showed interest, but in the end didn't go for it.

The main releases, global priorities, for jazz that year were 'Remember Shakti' the new Indian group by John McLaughlin and tabla wizard Zakir Hussain, featuring Vikku Vinayakram and Hariprasad Chaurasia. A powerful and spiritual concept which did extremely well live – I saw them in Oslo and talked a bit to John and Zakir, who, strange enough, remembered me from Vienna and the concert he and L. Shankar had given at the jazz cafe 'miles smiles'. Diana Krall's beautiful 'When I Look In Your Eyes' was the next top release and with her working hard on promo and touring, this album became one of her biggest successes. Johnny Mandel's wonderful arrangements and her immaculate vocal delivery made this her break-out recording.

Michael Brecker's 'Time Is Of The Essence' was inspired by Breckers's appreciation of time – *"Where the notes are placed is as important as what the notes are"* – and featured among others Larry Goldings and Pat Metheny. I really loved Brecker's playing and would try to catch him live whenever possible to hear his music and have a chat.

Other great records came from Terry Callier, Horace Silver and Regina Carter, while Emarcy had another year of releases from all over the world with records by Eleftheria Arvanitaki (Greece), Sezen Aksu (Turkey), Michiel Borstlap (the Netherlands), Maria Joao (Portugal), Sadao Watanabe (Japan) and others from France, Austria, Norway and the UK.

Most of these artists were touring in the summer for the festivals, in which we had various Verve Nights again. This time in Vienna, Austria, Montreux, The Hague, and Vitoria-Gasteiz. In Perugia we had every night of the festival the 'Round Midnight Verve Series', which had Kenny Barron as artist in residence and featured as well some of the younger acts we had on the roster and overall was a great success.

My team in 1999 was consisting of two marketing managers, Marina Detienne and Emma Perry, plus Peggy Bonaventure as assistant and together we dealt with over 40 Emarcy and Emarcy Classics releases and I looked after all the priorities on top. Lots of work, but we enjoyed working together and had a lot of fun doing do. Chris stayed mostly in New York, working from there with his P.A. Wendy Life, a really efficient and very nice lady, with whom I always worked when I was over there for meetings or gigs. Overall, the headcounts had be reduced again, but so far, we could handle the

work without problems or neglecti[...]
ones, had their international managers [...]
me they would work the priority acts. That w[...]

At one point the former jazz manager of our Norwe[...]
me if he could send me some demos of a singer he sign[...]
working on. *"Sure"*, I said and when the cassette came, I list[...]
and a few very good originals by a singer called Silje Nergaard. [...]
and, as I had to go there for the MD's meeting that year anyway, I a[...]
more tracks and liked her unique voice, amazing control and song choice[...]
As we didn't sign artists then to our central office, I sent the music to Yn[...]
check what he thought. He told me that he knew of her, had heard some of [...]
that she hadn't had a new record in 4 years and that of course he would be intere[...]
especially as she had a fanbase at home already and some in Japan, where a song she [...]
Metheny in 1990, was kind of a hit. He made the deal and the first record came out in 200[...]
very well at home and in some other EU markets and she started to get a few concert dates ou[...]
of Norway as well.

ECM celebrated their 30th anniversary and 15 years of ECM New Series, their classical label. I went to their international meeting that year to celebrate the anniversaries and there I finally met Ketil Bjørnstad and we started talking and decided to stay in touch.
The top release for the label in 1999 was the wonderful solo piano studio album 'The Melody At Night With You' by Keith Jarrett, a selection of standards performed unbelievably beautiful and touching. Jan Garbarek released another stunning album with the Hilliard Ensemble titled 'Mnemosyne' and composer Arvo Pärt, who had recorded for ECM New Series since its initiation, his 'Alina'. Dave Holland released his quintet recording 'Prime Directive' featuring Chris Potter on saxophone.

The first classical priority releases I worked with either Marc Johnson (Decca) or Ruud De Sera (DG) in my new role as marketing VP Classics & Jazz were Cecilia Bartoli's 'The Vivaldi Album' and Anne - Sophie Mutter's 'Le Quattro Stagioni' with the Trondheim Soloists.
Bartoli really had studied all of Vivaldi's operas and found some beautiful and almost forgotten arias, which she recorded for this album. The release event took place in Venice and classical managers from around the world attended the little concert she gave. I had arrived in the morning of the event and had some time to kill, so I went for a stroll through Venice, a truly magical place. I passed a little shop which had some colourful hand painted jackets in the window and had a closer look. I went in and tried a jacket, which fitted perfectly. Black with golden hand painted ornaments ... very classy. Even so it wasn't cheap, I bought it and did wear it for the event, which caused a bit of a stir, as people were used to my more relaxed and funky jazz outfits.

...cilia Bartoli

...e of the most famous and successful ...this repertoire she truly had great ...n Krystian Zimerman, the outstanding ...especially seeing him perform Brahms ...ns and his dramatic performance were ...and 2, a highly recommendable album. ...Mischa Maisky's release of Shostakovich ...l year.

In the ... you are doing, in general and then as well specifically for ... dequate in a constantly changing world. With the internet becoming m... ces and at home, and with Napster starting as a file sharing platform in 1999, w... to find and download music files in the MP3 format, we had to think about the HOW an... e. Napster took the music industry by surprise, even so that shouldn't have been the case … but the industry didn't have many internet-savvy young people and therefore didn't see it coming … and when they saw it, they fought it instead of trying to embrace the new delivery systems. I wasn't an exception and didn't know enough about the internet then to fully understand its potential and dangers. But it was clear that the way music was going to be distributed and listened to would change dramatically. And as a marketeer I needed to be informed to use the new technologies.

Günter Grass, one of my favourite German language writers, released his book 'Mein Jahrhundert' (My Century), a biographical look back in time, with his own stunning illustrations. Grass was also given the Nobel Prize in Literature that year, for me a well-deserved honour. Boris Yeltsin resigned and so making it possible for Vladimir Putin to step in as acting president of Russia. In the Yugoslav war NATO launched air strikes against Yugoslav forces and finally pushed for a peace treaty. In Columbine, Colorado, USA, two students started a shooting at their high school, killing twelve pupils and one teacher and injuring another 24 students before committing suicide. There was a debate about gun control, but till today, unfortunately, nothing has changed. In Milan 'The Last Supper' by Leonardo Da Vinci was on public display again, after 22 years of restoration. One of mankind's most famous paintings could finally be seen again by a curious public.

Beside our releases I was listening that year to the debut album by Dhafer Youssef, 'Malak'. The record featured among others trumpet player Markus Stockhausen and guitarist Nguyên Lê and is deeply emotional and musical, mixing Arabic grooves with jazz expression and Dhafer's Sufi-based chants; singer and bass player Richard Bona's outstanding first album 'Scenes From My Life', plus Brad Mehldau and his Vol. 4 of the Art of the Trio series and Wolfgang Puschnig's 'Aspects', a captivating album he released on Paul Zauner's PAO Records, featuring Herbert Joos and a really emotional version of his composition 'Impermanence', which originally was recorded for the 'Mixed Metaphors' album in 1995.

At one point, while travelling and reading, I recognized that I was holding my book pretty far away and that my arms soon would be too short to be able to hold any book far enough to read. I was always the only one in the family who didn't have to wear glasses, but it seemed now was the time to have my eyesight checked and, at least for reading purposes, get some eyewear. And so I went to the optician and got some cool glasses and the problem of the length of the arms was solved quickly and reading while travelling became more comfortable again. That summer we did spend our holidays again in Greece, travelling via Athens, where we spent the night, before heading to Santorini the next day. We arrived in Athens on the night of the Champions League final between Manchester United and Bayern Munich and when I switched the TV on in the hotel it stood 1:0 for Bayern and there were only 5 minutes left to play. In injury time Manchester first scored an equaliser through Teddy Sheringham and then, unbelievably, the winning goal through Ole Gunnar Solksjaer. Hannah loved the sea and the little hotel we stayed in on Santorini and their pool, in which she learned how to swim. The hotel was run by a family and more or less had every year the same guests, which was kind of nice. Great food, good wines and time to read and relax – a perfect holiday!
Hannah started school proper as well, having turned 6 years old in 1999. She loved it, picked up things easily and made a lot of new friends. School wasn't that far away, so occasionally I dropped her off before going to the office.

I still was travelling a lot for the job and on one occasion I took the Eurostar train from London to Paris, going via the tunnel under the Channel. Hannah liked that so much that she did a little drawing for me ... one that I gave a place in my PolyGram office and that still has its space in my home.

In 1999 the jazz world mourned the loss of many great artists, including Edward Vesala, Grover Washington Jr, Art Farmer, Michel Petrucciani, singer Leon Thomas and the wonderful trumpet player Lester Bowie, whom I had seen many times with either the Art Ensemble of Chicago or his Brass Fantasy ensemble and some of whose ECM albums I worked in Austria. A true gentleman and unforgettable musician.

Lester Bowie, 1941 - 1999

We ended the year and started the new millennium with a nice meal with friends on New Year's Eve. Eva and I had gotten friendly with a neighbour family – Gilles Aufray, a French playwright and his wife Claire and son Oliver came over for dinner and we had great food and opened the 1955 Marques de Riscal - what a wine!!!!!! Full in body, a dark red colour and a taste I never had before or since. Perfect to start the year 2000! The so-called Millennium Bug did some damage in various networks and computers, but nothing as feared and the world continued to turn. The year 2000 was as well the first century leap year since 1600 adding February 29th to the calendar. The next time that will happen will be the year 2400.

2000

I was always a bit of a gadget freak and tried new technologies when I got a chance. I had in 1995 bought one of the first digital cameras from Casio, which was kind of cool, but the quality was not really there yet, nothing in comparison to what you get on an average smartphone today. More or less the same year I got my first mobile phone, a Motorola MP2, which was still a bit bulky, but great. I used it a lot later with the PSION PDA (Personal Digital Assistant) Series 3, which was a small handheld computer and a really cool tool to have before there were smartphones. The first of these I bought was the Nokia Communicator 9110, called 'The Brick', as it had almost the dimensions of one, housing a bigger screen and keyboard, visible only when the phone was opened. In 2000 the new model, the Communicator 9210, was a bit slimmer and had already a colour screen. I really liked these for the amazing features they had then and the keyboard, which for me made typing emails when travelling much easier. I, for sure, preferred these to the Blackberry's we got from Universal at a later stage. I had as well purchased a Creative Nomad Jukebox, one of the first MP3 players, that could store about 100 tracks. Great to have on trips and do presentations from it – no need to take CDs with me anymore. When it came to music players I stuck with Creative; they might not have been as well designed as the later arriving Apple ones, but in terms of quality they were ahead in every single aspect.

We released the first proper Universal Jazz catalogue that year, the 1999/2000 issue had 196 pages and included now the GRP and Blue Thumb recordings. I had asked Tommy LiPuma to write a few words as an introduction and he did and explained what the newly created Verve Music Group and their four labels, Verve, GRP, Blue Thumb and Impulse stood for. We did run two major campaigns that year: Brazil 500, worked with the Brazilian company and featuring the re-issue of 16 important albums plus a few new releases, of which the most important was the new Joao Gilberto album 'Joao Voz E Violão' and again Verve NOW, which that year featured German trumpet player Till Brönner and New York based Chilean singer Claudia Acuña. They both had just released new recordings, 'Chattin' With Chet' and 'Winds From The South' respectively and did play the following cities as part of the tour: London, Paris, Hamburg, Amsterdam, Vienna, Basel and Madrid. We did again a sampler with tracks from both records to be given away at the venues and in competitions and some display material for the record stores in the visited cities. The show in London, at Ronnie Scott's jazz club, was very well attended and really great, as were all the other gigs, from what I heard.

The main releases and priorities for the year 2000 in jazz were Al Jarreau's 'Tomorrow Today', John Scofield's groovy 'Bump', Dee Dee Bridgewater's 'Live At Yoshi's', a strong statement from the world's leading jazz singer, Courtney Pine's 'modern dance record 'Back In The Day' and George Benson's wonderful 'Absolute Benson' featuring the single 'The Ghetto' and produced by Tommy LiPuma. George is a real cool guy and worked a lot in terms of giving interviews for us. When he came to London for promo, we had a fun dinner at NOBU's and at one point towards the end of the meal he asked me who was playing at Ronnie Scott's that night. Checking my phone, I told him it was Roy Ayers. He asked us to quickly end the meal, went to his hotel room in the same building, got his guitar and off we went to Ronnie's. And then he jammed …. Another time I was in Montreux and had some time off and went for a walk along the lake. When getting back and coming closer to the hotel, I could hear a big band with a guitar player that sounded like George. Of course, I got curious and went to check the kid out, knowing that in the afternoon there were university big bands performing on the outdoors stage for free. As I got closer, I saw that it was indeed Benson who was playing with these kids – a big smile on his face. When I asked him later how it came to happen that he played with that big band, he told me that he heard them play in his hotel room and liked it and as he was in the mood for a bit of a jam, he simply went down with his guitar and joined them. Something neither these kids nor myself will ever forget. I really love Benson's guitar sound and my favourite albums are the CTI live recording 'In Concert – Carnegie Hall' from 1976, with his amazing versions of 'Take Five' and 'Summertime' and his collaboration with Al Jarreau 'Givin' It Up', which I had the pleasure to work on with the two guys in 2006.

Another really successful record that year came from Spain: film director Fernando Trueba's new label Lola Records had released a duo album by pianist Michel Camilo and flamenco guitar master Tomatito titled 'Spain' and the local Universal company had made a global distribution deal with them. We put the record out internationally and especially in Japan we did very well with it. I went to Madrid for the release concert and met Fernando, Michel and Tomatito there for the first time and heard the music live for the first time as well. Stunning and powerful, especially when they played Chick Corea's composition 'Spain', which gave the album its title. Corea himself had released that year two incredible solo piano recordings – 'Originals' and 'Standards', both among the best of his diverse and incredible output. Richard Bona released his second album 'Reverence', confirming his status as one of the best bass players around and a singer of huge potential. His African based music is touching and beautiful and the hype around him was more than justified. Otherwise, I was checking out the first album by singer Rebekka Bakken with Wolfgang Muthspiel, titled 'Daily Mirror' and featuring Chris Cheek on saxes, Scott Colley on bass and Brian Blade on drums. An album of surprising beauty and deep songs with lyrics by Rebekka and a strong first step in her coming career. Classical priorities included releases by Anne Sofie von Otter, 'Folksongs'; Valery Gergiev with Jean-Yves Thibaudet and their recording of the Grieg and Chopin Piano Concertos and Jessey Norman's 'I Was Born In Love With You', her take on the songs of Michel Legrand. Norman could do everything and had successful recordings of Spirituals, but could sing jazz too. And she was a very nice and down to earth lady, as far as I can say from having met her twice. For me personally, her best recording is the 1983 album with the Gewandhausorchester under Kurt Masur and their take on Richard Strauss' 'Four Last Songs'. I discovered that recording by recommendation of Ketil Bjørnstad's wife Catharina, who played it when I was at their home once for dinner and I was really taken by this sublime music. Ketil's new album with cellist David Darling, 'Epigraphs', was one of the highlights of ECM's releases in 2000. The other one was Nils Petter Molvaer's second release, 'Solid Ether', another captivating modern and electronic driven album and the Keith Jarrett Trio's 'Whisper Not', recorded live in Paris.

Looking at the marketing plans from the various countries was always interesting and boring at the same time. The plans had a general info part, including the status of the artist in question in the market and sales targets, an activity part, with details on the what, when, where and a financial part, with all the costs listed. For me it was mainly the second part I was interested in – what were they doing when in relation to the album release in what media. Of course, the financials are important as well, but I wanted to see some creativity in building awareness for a new record more than them spending tons of money. Some smaller markets seemed to think that they could get away with sending the same plan for all priorities, as they didn't have a lot of different media outlets to use, but that didn't mean one couldn't be creative in retail deco's, radio activities or endorsements from local VIPs. Having worked in a smaller market like Austria did actually help a lot to understand, as well as to motivate the local managers to come up with something special they could do for a new record. Usually, the key markets like Germany, France, the UK and the US were pretty good with their plans and often brought the artist to their countries for media events, retail visits and interviews. Something I always encouraged, as face-to-face interviews are better than by telephone and even for the marketing manager it is easier to work with a person, than just a disc. After looking through the plans, writing down my comments and recommendations, I generally had a chat with the responsible international manager in the label, went through the plans quickly with him or her and then send my email response to the various markets with comments, ideas and suggestions. And then I followed up via the sales reports I got every week. When I saw that someone was behind expectations, I was on the phone again, discuss reasons and what should be done to make up what was missing. Communicating with respect and understanding was the key. I wanted to be a positive force behind them, pushing them, but with a helping attitude. That was one of the reasons why I was travelling to the key markets at least twice a year for meetings with the teams and then having various other events, either regional or by genre or by label. A lot of lasting friendships were formed that way.

Singer Ute Lemper had her first record on Decca released in 1988 and over the years had worked with the label on many more and had built a great relationship with Decca's then president Roland Kommerell, a wonderful, intelligent and supportive label executive, whom I had the pleasure to meet a few times. His presentations at the big meetings were the stuff of legends – fun, on the point, clever and imaginative. When he left in 1996 and was replaced by Roger Lewis, a bit of style and culture left Decca as well. Lewis was a strange character with a love for flip-charts and was finally replaced by ex-Philips Classics president Costa Pilavachi, who was in charge in 2000 and had asked me to come to a studio in London to hear some tracks of the new Lemper album and Ute would be there too. I arrived a bit early and sat in the studio with Ute chatting and as we both speak German and showed each other respect, we hit it off immediately. The guys from Decca came a bit later and we were already having fun and I recognized that they were kind of stiff with her, as if they didn't know how to talk to her or deal with her. Ute is a strong woman and knows what she wants and doesn't take on everything the labels tells her, just because they think it's right and I am not sure if the Decca team could handle that. She played us a few songs from her forthcoming record 'The Punishing Kiss', which I thought was very cool, adult oriented music with a bunch of great songs. She had recorded compositions by Nick Cave, Elvis Costello, Philip Glass, Tom Waits and Scott Walker and used as producers Hal Wilner, Jon Jacobs and as well Scott Walker. I love when Ute sings Brecht/Weill and the old German songs, but this for me is one of her best recordings ever, for the song choices, arrangements and her powerful and touching vocal delivery. We did a lot of promotion for the record, Ute toured as she always does and gladly the album did reasonably well. Ute, who is a painter as well, gave Decca one of her paintings in a limited-edition print to be used for promo purposes, like competitions in radio or retail. One of these hangs at home in our flat in Madrid, always reminding me of this album and an exceptional artist, which whom I stayed in touch.
In a year when George W. Bush won the US election after a Florida recount and a Concorde aircraft crashed outside of Paris and with that initiated the end of supersonic travel, France won the European football championship which was held in Belgium and Holland with a 2:1 win over Italy in the final, which was decided by a golden goal by David Trezeguet. In Austria a tunnel fire killed 155 skiers and snow boarders in Kaprun, when a funicular train got stuck in the tunnel of the Gletscherbahn. I was reading Murakami's 'South of the Border, West of the Sun', the latest novel by the Japanese writer translated into English and went to the movies to see Ang Lee's 'Crouching Tiger, Hidden Dragon' and Steven Soderbergh's biopic 'Erin Brokovich', featuring a great Julia Roberts. And I saw with Hannah 'How The Grinch Stole Christmas' and we both loved it. I always liked to go and see these kinds of kid's movies with her, as she enjoyed them a lot and I had fun as well. We also went to the Millennium Dome in London to see the show to which Peter Gabriel had written the music.

In August 2000 my parents celebrated their Golden Wedding anniversary and family from all over Europe came to the party, as well as friends and neighbours. There was a lot of singing going on, as the Danes seem to like that when having a celebration. They take a famous song and re-write the lyrics to fit the occasion and then sing ... and sing ... and sing ... and need lots of beer and Aquavit afterwards. Even the local newspaper brought an article based on an interview they had done with my parents and mentioned all the countries people came from to their party. A wonderful celebration of their vows it was! In his letter to Hannah from the year before my father remembered the wedding as such: *"What a difference to a wedding today: 9 am at the registry office, 10 am champagne breakfast with grandparents and parents. Then, for the church wedding, in a car borrowed from the company, a Ford Taunus, to Nomberg/Ohm, a small town in northern Hessia. Only us and my parents. After the ceremony: lunch and then back via Hanover, Hamburg-Neustadt, Holstein - Lüneburg nach Höchst. The whole exercise in 3 days and always the four of us. It must not have cost much. As an operations assistant, a position that today doesn't really exist anymore, I had a starting salary of just 280, - DM a month."*

Family photo at my parents 50th wedding anniversary – in the centre my parents, Hannah and myself, on the right my uncle Hans Joachim Bamler and his wife Marianne

The summer holidays we spent as usual with family and in Santorini and in October we celebrated my, Eva's and Hannah's birthday in one go with our families. Unfortunately, the weather wasn't that great, as my father wrote to Hannah in the letter he sent when being back in Denmark:
*"Uschi and Jürgen also departed Sunday afternoon and arrived 1 1/2 hours late in Vienna.
Now the storm began - it was raining and the wind was so strong that you couldn't use an umbrella, or you would be blown away. It rained and stormed all night. London was flooded. Subway stations were closed, the airport express trains were not running, the highways were blocked or clogged with miles of traffic jams. We had to wait with your father at Victoria Station for over an hour for a taxi, only for the trip to Gatwick to take 3 hours. Your mother was going with your grandma Riegler and Diana to Heathrow and kept us informed via mobile what the situation was. The flight to Vienna, took off 3 hours late, but we have arrived with 8 hours of delay in Copenhagen. Tired and heavy on the legs we really wanted to stay for the night in Copenhagen. In the end we still found a way to use local trains (which stopped at every kennel) with 3 changes and finally get home by taxi.
It was difficult but is already forgotten and what remains are only the memories of happy days with you and much joy."*
For Christmas we stayed at home and had Gilles and his family over for a great meal once more. But before the year was over, I had to go to New York again and being there for some jazz business first of all, I got invited to the premiere of the Seussical, a musical based on the stories and characters from the Dr. Seuss books, which Hannah loved as well as many other kids around the world. The

music was ok, the musical well done, but nothing really special. Decca Broadway had the soundtrack rights and that's how Chris and myself and some other colleagues ended up there and at the party afterwards. The musical wasn't a success on Broadway, but a re-worked version spawned two US tours, a West End show and is still played in schools and local theatres around the world.

2001

Internally another wave of changes and re-structuring meant that Peggy would work more with the digital media side of things, Emma left to pursue other interests and we brought in Suzanna Reast, who previously had worked for the Norwegian company, but re-settled in London and immediately was a great addition to the team. Suzannah started to work with me on the new jazz catalogue, for which I wrote the introduction for the first time. We were both setting up the last of the Verve Now tours in 2001, as the US label really didn't sign any new acts that had a global appeal and the costs were getting a bit too much, even so we, for the first time that year, sold tickets to the shows.

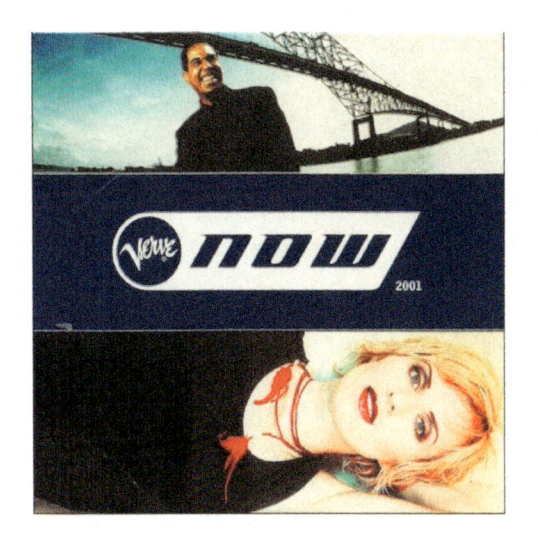

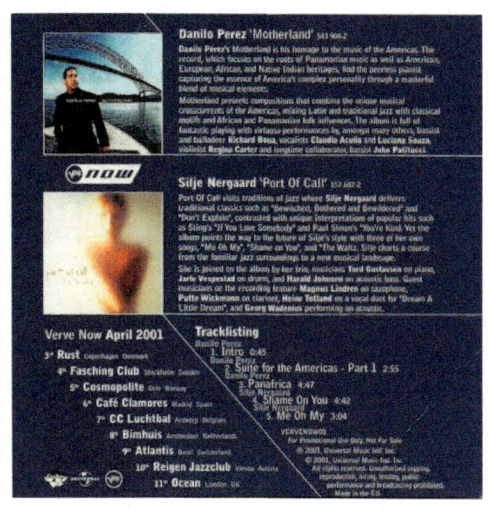

The Verve Now tour featured Danilo Perez and Silje Nergaard, who both had recently released new albums – Danilo his 'Motherland' and Silje the very successful 'Port Of Call', tracks of which were represented on the promotional sampler we did again. The tour brought that year the two artists to Copenhagen, Stockholm, Oslo, Madrid, Antwerp, Amsterdam, Basel, Vienna and London and was again a big success in getting awareness for these new acts. Silje especially could built on this tour for the future.

On the classical side, both Christian Kellersmann, meanwhile the head of the jazz department within Classics & Jazz Germany, and Ruud De Sera, head of international at Deutsche Grammophon, were thinking about how to attract a younger audience to classical music and at one meeting they discovered that they were both going in the same direction. Christian had the concept of a lounge event with classical music, live and DJ's and Ruud thought similar and based on the colour of DG had already come up with a name: Yellow Lounge! Christian's team set up the first YL in a bar in Hamburg, still trying to find the right mix and concept and then during a DG meeting in Vienna Ruud brought everyone to the Semper Depot in the 6th district.

The Semper Depot is a production shop and scenery depot for the Vienna Opera house and the Burgtheater and was built for that purpose between 1874 and 1877. Ruud had set up a Yellow Lounge in this amazing building with trapeze acts, live music by Mischa Maisky and others and special guest including Elvis Costello. A real cool event, which showed everyone what could be done, even so it didn't need to be on that grand a scale. Ruud also had a classical DJ, which if I remember correctly was Jonas Lönna, our man in Sweden and a DJ in his free time.

A promo CD by the same name was made with the subtitle 'The Classical Mix Album', which was then as well released commercially, with various more samplers and live CDs following over the years. From there the Yellow Lounge concept would be refined and the became a success globally, but especially in Germany and other European markets like Holland, Spain and Austria.

Semper Depot, Vienna, pr photo

On June 30th 2001 tenor sax master Joe Henderson passed away in San Francisco, aged 64. His legacy as a musician ranks among the greatest on his instrument, the early recordings on Blue Note as well as the late ones, there especially the two volumes of 'The State Of The Tenor' (with Ron Carter on bass and Al Foster on drums) and the Verve song book recordings, which brought him late fame and recognition. Joe was a great guy, down to earth and relaxed and a wonderful spirit. He made me feel at ease in his company, joked and always had this cheeky smile around his eyes.

As every year we had a few Verve Nights planned in the festivals around the world – North Sea Jazz had about twenty of our acts over the three days and a special night on Saturday; Montreux featured the Camilo/Tomatito duo and Remember Shakti in the Verve Night and in Perugia that year we had even two Verve events, while in Montreal Michael Brecker and Roy Hargrove were the artists in residence and performed five and four nights with different projects respectively.

That year Polish singer extraordinaire Anna Maria Jopek came to London for a show – she had released the album 'Bosa' in 2000 and we had taken it on and internationalised it and gotten some great response. Anna Maria is a very talented lady and a real nice person and we chatted a lot and stayed in touch.

Backstage at the Montreux Jazz Festival 2001 – Tomatito, his manager, Michel Camilo and Chick Corea

The key releases in jazz that year came from John Scofield, who after the more groove-oriented releases, decided to put out a straight jazz record again and recorded 'Works For Me' with an all-star cast featuring Kenny Garrett, Brad Mehldau, Christian McBride and Billy Higgins. Michael Brecker's touchingly beautiful 'The Nearness Of You – The Ballad Book' had a line-up as good as Scofield's with Herbie Hancock, Pat Metheny, Charlie Haden and Jack DeJohnette and special vocal guest James Taylor. Both recordings did extremely well and deservedly so. Diana Krall's 'The Look Of Love' rounded up the priority releases in jazz and was the most successful one – after having sold almost 2 million copies of her previous recording, this new album was highly anticipated. Some of the recording was done at London's Abbey Road studio, with Diana, producer Tommy LiPuma, legendary recording engineer Al Schmitt and arranger Claus Ogerman all being present. As I went there to say "*Hi*" on a nice June weekend, I took Hannah with me to the studio and she really enjoyed it a lot. Diana explained to her how the recording desk worked and who was doing what and that she was singing and playing the piano. And we got to hear some of the new music, which was extremely beautiful, as the strings added an emotional touch to the overall great arrangements. Most of Hannah's friends took piano lessons from one of our neighbours, but so far Hannah hadn't showed any interest, despite it being offered. After the visit to the studio and her chat with Diana she asked if she could check the lessons out and began to learn. She seemed to enjoy it for some time, but always was adamant not to take exams, as for her playing the piano was for fun. She had no problem performing for the parents once a year, just didn't want the pressure of exams spoiling the fun.

2001 was also the year we released the first Ketil Bjørnstad album on Emarcy. Ketil had been in touch and had send me the music of a concert he had given in Voss at the festival. He had written music to the love poems of John Donne and used Anneli Drecker and Bendik Hofseth as the voices for this project. I really liked what I heard, but didn't want to get into problems with Manfred Eicher, as we still distributed ECM in most key markets. I asked Ketil to have Manfred pass on the album in writing, as then I could talk to Yngve Naess at Universal Norway to take it on and I would release and work it internationally. Manfred sent the email and then I sent the music to Yngve, who loved it and we arranged a meeting – they would chat about the deal and I would join about the What, How and When after that. I flew to Oslo and we had the meeting and then I asked Ketil what he would like to have on the front cover of the album, as we in London would do the art for him in that case. He looked at me with surprise and then said that he hadn't heard that question for many years, as at ECM the cover art is always Manfred's decision and the artists are hardly involved. As Ketil was telling us what he imagined, a photo by my wife came to my mind and I told him that I would send him a photo, which I thought would be what he was looking for. And so it was. And for the next 5 Emarcy releases he used her pictures as well for his covers.

Nils Petter Molvaer's 'Recoloured – The Remix Album' was his first on his own label Sula Records, after he had left ECM. Nils had offers to license his new music from various labels, but decided to go with Universal Germany, as he knew the team there already (they were working the ECM repertoire) and liked Christian and Astrid. Having lost two artists to us didn't sit well with Manfred and he called Chris Roberts to complain about me poaching his artists from the label. Chris in turn called me and asked me what was going on ... and I explained: Nils would have left ECM anyway and before he would have gone to another company, Christian just made sure that he would stay with us, while the Ketil album was something Manfred had passed on, which I had in writing. There was no reason for ECM to be upset. He understood but asked me to call Manfred to set the record straight and get this off the table. Which I did. And calmly explained to Manfred that he couldn't complain that we put out a record he passed on and didn't want on his label and that Nils Petter was leaving, no matter what and therefore it made sense for us to keep him within the family, something from which the ECM recordings could only benefit as well. I knew he wasn't happy, but he understood that he hadn't any arguments anymore and therefore we left it at that. I would have gladly reacted if he would have taken Ketil back for his next album immediately, but he didn't and therefore I was lucky enough to work a bit closer with this wonderful artist. Initially, I wasn't aware that Ketil was a writer of novels and biographies as well, but soon after we met, I found out about it and started to read some of his books, which were available in German. 'Erling's Fall', 'Villa Europa' and 'Ballade in g-Moll: Edvard Grieg und Nina Hagerup', left a deep impression on me and, from then on, I got all of the books once a German or English translation was available.

British band US3 had been signed by Nathan Graves, who was the jazz man in the UK at that time and their album 'An Ordinary Day In An Unusual Place' with the hit single 'You Can't Hold Me Down' was fun to work on and did pretty well for us that year. Other records I really liked from our releases were Chris Potter's fabulous 'Gratitude' and the Wolfgang Puschnig / Uli Scherer duo recording 'Traces'. Both showcasing musical communication and expression on the highest level.

The classical year was focused on Luciano Pavarotti, as he was celebrating his 40th anniversary as a performing artist. On April 21st we gathered in Modena to celebrate with a spectacular concert event, featuring the maestro and a host of important classical performers, like Roberto Alagna and Angela Gheorghiu. A one-off event I remember fondly. Luciano released a special Recital recording for the anniversary and later in the year 'Amore – The Love Album', a 2-CD compilation, that did well for us. As the years before he held the Pavarotti & Friends event for children in need or in war areas wherever in the world. These events were then released and created funds to help charities like WAR CHILD or Children In Need. I had been at the concert the year before – an amazing spectacle with tens of thousands of spectators and an amazing line-up of guests, including Caetano Veloso, George Michael and the Eurythmics. We had a wonderful dinner afterwards and everyone enjoyed the concert for a good cause. I had met Chris when we went to the show and he was shocked of seeing me in a linen suit with a green t-shirt underneath, which had some cool black pattern on it and green shoes. He couldn't get over the green shoes, something he would never consider to wear, but for me a bit of colour was something I always liked when dressing for an event and still do. Overall Pavarotti between 1992 and 2003 held 10 of these special concerts, which were all filmed and recorded and released on CD and DVD and made millions for these charities. Something I have a lot of respect for. Cecilia Bartoli's 'Italian Arias' was the other big record for that year and the release event took place in Rome this time. Anne Sophie von Otter's new album was 'For The Stars – Anne Sofie Von Otter Meets Elvis Costello', opening up new repertoire for this wonderful singer. And Portuguese pianist Maria Joao Pires released her take on the 'Beethoven Sonatas' and DG arranged their release event and an international meeting in Lisboa and at her place in Belgais, which was really beautiful and relaxed. Michael Lang, who had been the head of catalogue for Verve Records and won a few Grammy awards there with his amazing box sets, had been made General manager of DG and was running the meeting there together with Ruud de Sera, his international guy and they presented all the new records for the coming months and a wonderful performance by Maria Joao Pires.

Belgais

The Keith Jarrett Trio's 'Inside Out' is a captivating live recording from the Trio's performance in London the year before. I was at the concert and remember the stunning free improvisations the three musicians created then. The musical communication and reaction to each other was second to none and deserved a release. Swiss singer Susanne Abbuehl's debut recording for ECM 'April' was another highlight for the label that year, as well as Charles Lloyd's 'Hyperion With Higgins' featuring Billy Higgins on drums, pianist Brad Mehdau, bassist Larry Grenadier and John Abercrombie on guitar.

2001 saw as well the launch of iTunes and later that year the sale of the first iPods. Wikipedia was launched, while Berlusconi won another election in Italy and became PM for the second time. Proving once more that money and media access, with the right populistic message, can win political power. The Taliban destroyed the Bamiyan Buddhas, two historically and culturally irreplaceable statues from the 6th century. The madness of extreme beliefs, as shown again and again over the centuries by all leading religions of the world. It seems that mankind never learns. Palestinian group Hamas bombed a discotheque in Tel Aviv, killing 21 teenagers who just wanted to have a good time. In this ongoing conflict there seems to be no interest from either party to find real peace. A conflict that still is raging and killing people to the day of me writing this account, that is political convenient for some on both sides, who only care about their own power and not about their people. I can't and won't take side for either of them, as they are both guilty and responsible for what has happened and is happening today.

Brazilian singer Zizi Possi came to London to record parts of her new album 'Bossa' there and Hannah and I went to see her in the studio and listened to some of the music. Zizi had the year before released her touching 'Puro Prazer', which I had made available internationally and which is my favourite of her albums. We spent our Easter break with my parents in Denmark and the summer holidays in Santorini. Hannah and I went to the movies a few times to see 'Monster, Inc.' and 'Shrek' among others. The piano lessons showed progress and school was fun for her. The school had organised a school walk in Regent's Park for charity and we took part in that as well. Gladly it was a sunny day!

We were working with Jazzland Recordings now successfully for a few years and Sten Nilsen, who originally had signed the license deal with them via the Norwegian company, was now partner in the label with Bugge Wesseltoft. But we hadn't managed to get a proper release in the US, or a strategy to introduce the label there, despite the fact that Bugge and Eivind Aarseth had played in the US and Canada at festivals already. I had a long discussion with Verve and finally it was decided that Sten and myself would fly over to do a presentation for the team there and the date was set with September 10, 2001. Sten and I met in our NY hotel close to the Verve offices on the 9th, went through our presentation again and were ready to go. On the 10th we took our time, explained the European success story, the future plans for the label and forthcoming releases. We played music and videos and after a few hours with the Verve team they were positive and promised to send a concept and schedule for the first releases in the coming two weeks. Sten and I were extremely happy and decided to go out that evening/night to celebrate. At the Cornelia Street Café Wolfgang Muthspiel was playing a show with Chris Cheek, if I remember correctly, Brian Blade and Wolfgang's girlfriend, singer Rebekka Bakken. Sten and I had a problem to get a cab to go down to the venue, but a guy saw us trying and as he was waiting for his boss, who was in a meeting, he offered to drive us down there for $ 20 – in a stretch limo!!! We thought the day deserved it and got in, drove down and got out at the corner, as the limo couldn't get into Cornelia Street ... it was simply too small. The show was great, the beer cold and we had a good time, which we extended by going with Wolfgang and Rebekka to their place for a few more drinks and some chatting. Their flat was close to the twin towers and we could see them when we got there. About two in the morning, we left them and headed back to our hotel. The next morning, we had agreed to meet at a given time for breakfast and when going down to the breakfast room I saw in the elevator, which had a little TV screen, a fire in one of the Twin Towers and then saw that obviously a plane had crashed into the tower. Arriving at breakfast there was a tense atmosphere and the news told that other planes seemed to be highjacked. I couldn't believe it. The thoughts of having breakfast disappeared quickly and we went back to our rooms. There I saw the second flight crashing into the second tower and heard about the other crashed flights as well. By speaking to Sten I knew that he had tried to call home too, but hadn't got through – the phone lines were completely overloaded. I had a meeting with Chris planned anyway, so I headed over in that direction and from his office we could see the towers burning and everyone was in shock. I finally got hold of my office in London and asked them to call Eva and tell her I was OK and that I would try to call later. I tried numerous times to get in touch with Wolfgang and Rebekka, knowing how close they were. They in the end told me they got out of their flat around the time the second tower was hit and were shaken, but fine. Then the towers collapsed. Images I will never forget. New York was declared no-fly zone and the city was to be closed off. Many people had already or were leaving town. All flights were cancelled and all we could do for the time being was to tell our travel offices to get us out as soon as flights would resume. No food came into town for a few days. Restaurants and bars and clubs were closed and there were no people on the streets. New York had turned into a ghost city, with Sten and myself some of the few people out for a walk. All in all, the Al-Qaeda organized attacks left almost 3000 people dead and about 25.000 injured. This was terror on an unimaginable scale, religious fanatism at its worst. I couldn't get my head around it. Sten and I were sitting in the Universal Classics offices, talking to our families and trying to get confirmation to fly out, but it took time. Slowly people returned, places opened up again and some shows were announced for a week after the attacks. We decided to go out to one of the first shows, having had a choice between Chares Lloyd and Michael Brecker, we picked Brecker at the Iridium club on Broadway. Michael played with Joey Calderazzo on piano, Chris Minh-Doky on bass and drummer Jeff 'Tain' Watts, but he is the one I am least sure about. The music was powerful, angry, hurt and made us all cry, as he and his musicians displayed the same vulnerability we showed and amplified through their music and emotions what we felt. A day or two later we both got flights back home on the same day, Sten from JFK airport and myself from La Guardia. The security check didn't seem much more than before to me, which surprised me a lot and made me a bit nervous going on the flight. Back home all the stress and shock came out and while I was sitting on the sofa in the living room and saw the news and some of the images again and broke down and cried ... and let it all out. I spoke to Sten a few days later and he told me that the same more or less happened to him.

Silje Nergaard and Mari Boine, Oslo, 2001

In the fall of 2001, the first movie in the Harry Potter series was released and Hannah and myself went to see it, as we both loved the book. The first movie in The Lord Of The Rings trilogy 'The Fellowship Of The Ring' was also released that fall and being a fan of Tolkien's stories, I went to see it and loved the way they portrayed the characters, told the story and created the images. They were really close to what I had imagined when reading the books many times over. I was listening to Dhafer Youssef's second album 'Electric Sufi', integrating electronics into his music and having as a guest our common friend Wolfgang Muthspiel. Murakami's 'Sputnik Sweetheart' was a fantastic book, but the read of the year for me was the imaginative homage to books and libraries 'The Shadow Of The Wind' by Carlos Ruiz Zafón. Before the year came to an end, while George W. Bush launched his 'War On Terror', we paid a visit to Vienna to celebrate 20 years of 'miles smiles' and it was great to see old friends again.

And in December I went to Oslo to see Sten and ran an international jazz meeting around the Jazzland Sessions, a live event of two nights at the Blå Club. We had invited as well the jazz festival promoters and showcased the best of Jazzland. It was great to end that dramatic year with some really incredible music.

2002

The team in London for Classics & Jazz International in 2002 consisted of Susannah Reast as marketing and product manager, Peggy Bonnaventure as content manager, working more closely with Jonathan Gruber, our head of digital, Jo Clarke, who worked with Chris when he was over, but supported the rest of team as well and Eamon Sullivan, our financial controller. I really liked the way Jo was relaxed, but extremely efficient and helpful and could step in any time when needed. She had been with Universal at different departments before and brought a lot of experience with her. Eamon had become a friend and we were socialising outside the office occasionally and the trips we did together to the various countries to sit down with the teams there and check their budgets for the coming year, were always fun, besides having been tough work.

Suzannah and I prepared as every year the new catalogue, which for the first time was divided in a jazz and a world music section. Lists of which artists would go into which section were to be found at the beginning of the catalogue, to make searching easier. This was the result of more and more repertoire that had a world music base and of requests from the people who wrote to us about the catalogue from the previous year. We too ran, for the first time, a competition in the Jazz Release Magazine to win a catalogue, so collecting mail and email addresses for direct marketing activities.

The real big news of the year was the introduction of the Euro as a single currency for initially 12 countries, the Eurozone, replacing their old currencies. For someone who was travelling a lot in Europe and always had to carry some local money with him, this was a blessing and made taking a bit of money on the road much easier.

Chris and I had seen a decline in releases from Verve in the US, but as we had teams around the world that needed repertoire beside the local signings on Emarcy, we decided that we would carefully sign artists to International to give the managers around the world more repertoire to work with. While we were looking for some names, we would of course look into promising new acts as well.
The A&R for these would be my responsibility and so I started to look around and put the word out to some of my contacts. I have been asked a few times in the lectures to young musicians I do, what is it I am looking for in an artist – the answer is not a simple one, but in general I look for individuality, originality, personality and of course quality. But the most important for me is, that an artist is able to touch me emotionally, whether be it in a concert situation or on record. For me pure technique is not enough, as I need to feel the music and when that's the case, I will go for the artist.
Once that is done, the next steps in A&R (Artists and Repertoire) are to talk about ideas, concepts, which means what kind of record are we going to make and when and with whom and where. I like to listen to the many ideas artists usually have for their next record and try to filter out which one I think would make the most sense to do. Then we go into details of the idea, turn it into songs, either existing or new and think about which players would be good to record this music, these compositions, songs. Once all that is clear, the rest is booking a studio, an engineer and a producer, if necessary, as not every artist needs a producer to record what they do envision for their album.
For me A&R is simply to make the best possible record the artist in question can do at that point in his/her career. It is not about what is in fashion musically or what radio plays, it is about making an artistic statement in time. Only once the music is done, I will start thinking about how to market it. The artist has to be comfortable throughout the whole process to achieve that goal, because only when we have a great record, which everyone is proud of, the artist will be able to do his/her best in promoting this new music.

The first album I signed on in 2002 was Tuck & Patti's 'Chocolate Moment', a wonderful and touching recording. Someone told me that they were looking for a new deal and as I had been a fan of them since their 1988 'Tears Of Joy' album, which features a classic rendition of Cindy Lauper's 'Time After Time', I got in touch with them and we made the deal quickly, got the record out in time for their tour in Europe.

They came to London to perform at the Union Chapel and I went to see them and Nathan Graves, our UK jazz manager, told me to check out the local guy who was opening for them. I went and really liked the first act, thought maybe the flow of the concert was not the best, but otherwise I enjoyed his songs and covers and the way he performed standards. This was the first time I saw Jamie Cullum and seeing Nathan's enthusiasm for this act, I was sure it wouldn't be the last time. Tuck and Patti did a wonderful show and we had a great chat afterwards. I really like these two warm and extremely sweet and caring people and I was happy to work with them and that the album did get great reviews and sold well. The deal was a license deal, which meant that they would own their music and we would distribute it, do marketing and promotion, in this case for Europe only. License deals were becoming more common and I had no problem with that, as I didn't believe the record company needed to own the music they work with. Times were changing and artists started more and more to own their music and find a partner to work with on getting this music out.

Meanwhile Mary Ann Topper, who at that time already was a legend in the jazz business and whom I had met a few times before, got in touch as she was in discussion with the French office regarding her client Richard Bona. I pushed a bit on her request so the colleagues in Paris would sign him, which they did in the end. Mary Ann had worked either as a manager or as a producer with some of our time's best known jazz stars and helped them on their way, including Diana Krall, Jane Monheit, Christian McBride and Joshua Redman. She had discovered numerous of the jazz stars and brought them into the spotlight and did produce some of their albums. We got along very well and I always enjoyed meeting her when going to New York or at festivals – she always had a new act to look at and gave hints whom one should sign. For me it was clear: when Mary Ann called, you listened and checked out the artists she was talking about. She did send me a live recording of Bona to listen to, but I loved the guy anyway already and when Daniel Richard signed him, I was very happy to get to know Richard and to work with him on future releases.

In a referendum Gibraltar voted to stay British and rejected Spain, while in The Hague Slobodan Milosevic's trial for war crimes started and in June the FIFA football world cup was won by Brazil, who beat Germany in the final 2:0, with both goals scored by Ronaldo. The event was held jointly by South Korea and Japan. In the summer, after having our holidays in June in Santorini, this time with my sister Barbara and her two foster kids Ulla and Masanti, so Hannah had someone to play with and I had some time with Barbara, whom I didn't see that often, I was doing my annual festival trip, visiting some of the Verve Nights. I started in Montreal, where I did an interview for a local paper about jazz in general, Universal at the festival and in the end the guy asked me whom I would recommend for him to go and see and I said: *"check out guitarist Eivind Aarset, as he is one of the best around today, but still not as known as he should be*". I ran into Scofield there as well and we had a nice chat and I told him that I would leave his gig a bit earlier, as I wanted to see Eivind and he was: "*Eivind is playing? Where?*". I gave him all the details and we said that we would see each other later. I was standing in the venue and checked out Eivind's show, which was really powerful guitar music with ambient and groovy bits, when in the middle of the set a sweating John Scofield entered the small venue, guitar on his back, coming straight from his own gig. He smiled and greeted me with a nod of his head, checking out Eivind. Shortly before the end of the show he left. After they finished with an encore, I went backstage to say "*Hi*" and there I found Scofield in deep discussion with Eivind, talking about sounds and pedals and whatnot. Eivind, a real nice and humble guy, couldn't believe that John had come to check him out and then asked questions about some of his gear. The following day the guy from the newspaper wrote about Eivind's concert, stating that he had seen the Jimi Hendrix of jazz!

Next stop was The Hague for the North Sea Jazz Festival where we had a Verve Night as well as a Jazzland Night, featuring Bugge, Wibutee, Beady Belle and Eivind Aarset. A strong statement from the young label.

I hadn't been to the festival in Vitoria-Gasteiz in Spain for a few years, as it often collided date-wise with North Sea, but in 2002 I went as we had a Verve Night there featuring Silje Nergaard and 'Directions In Music' by Herbie, Michael Brecker, Roy Hargrove and featuring bass player John Patitucci and drummer Brian Blade.

While sitting in the lounge of the hotel, chatting with my Spanish colleagues Javier and Alex I had at one point the unexplainable urge to turn around. And when I did, I saw this beautiful woman talking to Blanca Sanz, the lady of the festival working with Iñaki. I got up and went over, hoping to be introduced, but Blanca didn't. Later that evening I saw her again backstage at the venue and took the chance to introduce myself. Her name was Yolanda Chalmeta and she was a volunteer for the festival for a few years then and a good friend of Blanca. We talked and later met again after the show at the hotel where the jam sessions were and again sat and talked a lot. In the early hours of the morning, I walked her to where she was staying and we kissed. She was so down to earth, straight and amazing to talk to. I got her phone number the next morning before she left to go back to Madrid, where she was based. I was emotionally touched and thought about her a lot in the coming weeks. We stayed in touch via email and calls and then I had a meeting in Madrid and saw her for a drink, which was really great and when I had to come back for the budget meetings a few weeks later, I made sure that I had more time to spend with her. She took me on a little trip to Pedraza and Segovia with more great conversations and wonderful food. I felt relaxed around her, at ease. I had fallen for her, but didn't admit it to myself. And when we met in September in Amsterdam, where I had to go for a Decca meeting and she was visiting a friend and attending a KLM course, it was obvious that this was more special and deeper than I allowed myself to think.

The key releases in jazz for 2002 were the outstanding African album 'Mouffou' by Salif Keita, whom the French press called 'the African Caruso'; John Scofield's rocky and groovy 'Uberjam', which was fascinating live and an album Scofield thought Miles would have enjoyed. Silje Nergaard's 'At First Light' became one of the biggest jazz albums ever in Norway and did well all-around Europe. Hancock, Brecker and Hargrove's 'Directions In Music – Live at Massey Hall' is a spectacular jazz album, which won two Grammy awards and another one went for the 'Live In Paris' album by Diana Krall. Verve started the Verve Remix series, a successful and modern compilation series with re-mixes from the Verve catalogue by some of the most important DJ's and producers. Harry Gruber in Vienna started the Austrian Jazz Art series, which included some re-issues from records I had made in the late 1980's. Strange to see these records coming out again and being put into a historical context. Nils Petter released his 'NP3', a grand album with little melodies and funky grooves and Puschnig his '3+4 – Austrian Songs', which was his small group take on Austrian traditional music. Releases by Wayne Shorter, Dee Dee Bridgewater, Charlie Haden with Michael Brecker and Natalie Cole rounded up a strong release schedule. Natalie was fun to work with – she came to Europe to do promo and I saw her in London and we had a nice dinner with her and the UK team. Once we were finished eating and got for the drinks, she simply ordered I can't remember what and took out of her bag all ingredients for her favourite long drink. She mixed it herself and told us that she never gets it done right, so she started to carry all she needed with her and usually mixed the drink herself, knowing it would be good. Cool!

We had a bunch of international meetings that year as well – a classical meeting in Paris, a regional meeting in Taipei, an Eastern European meeting in Dubrovnik plus a regional meeting in Mexico City. It was a truly interesting experience to go to Mexico and have a meeting there with all the Latin American countries and only be a small part of the meeting, as this was for all genres of music, so in the end mainly run by the pop labels. They presented tons of projects and artists and it was fast and loud and I thought that it was just too much to remember anything. So, I changed my presentation and went in the complete opposite direction: slow and quiet and contemplative. I spoke briefly about the classical priorities, one maybe two more jazz albums and then focused on Diana Krall and played one full track from her 'Live In Paris' album – Joni Mitchell's 'A Case Of You', all six minutes and fifty seconds of this touching and emotional performance, which left everyone in the room kind of speechless, jazz manager or not. Exactly what I wanted, they would all remember that one song from this meeting and of course some of the live shows. For me, the one I remember is from an artist I hadn't heard of before and whose short show I really enjoyed: Juanes. He was presenting music from his third album 'Un Día Normal', including the memorable single 'A Dios Le Pido'. The album was produced by Gustavo Santaolalla, whom I met there as well and who was the mastermind of the tango-electronic band Bajofondo Tango Club, who had also released their first album that year and were a grooving, powerful live band. As we had the last afternoon off, some of the guys there did a trip to Teotihuacan, an ancient mysterious city built around 100 BC and is thought to have been one of the biggest cities in the world at its peak, housing 125.000 or more people. The weather on the day was bad, but after we drove the 40 km from Mexico City and entered the old site, clouds opened up and for two hours we had sun. Walking around I kind of felt the history of the place, the many unknowns and mysteries, but the importance as well. It was really special to be there.

2002, Teotihuacan

I am not hundred percent sure if it was that year, but I think the meeting of UMe I was invited to in Barcelona might have been. UMe is the department for Special Projects and catalogue exploitation and usually we didn't really work a lot with them, as we controlled our catalogues in the labels, while in pop all catalogue went via UMe. Of course, they would have loved to take care of our catalogue activities as well, but we had so far resisted and took a careful approach in terms of working with them. But they had a few activities we could benefit from and therefore Chris asked me to go to this meeting, which was a pretty relaxed affair, with even a room set up for jam sessions. I attended two of these, as a listener, and found that our jazz man in Poland, Pjotr Rzeczycki, who was also the UMe guy there, was a mean violin player. The one activity I discussed with the teams there was Kiosk packages. We were very open for them to make deals with local or regional companies to exploit our repertoire that way – the Best Of Verve on CD, etc., as long as it would be done together with the classical or jazz guys. Javier Pouso in Spain and Mirko Gratton in Italy were extremely great with these campaigns and did a lot with Verve, at one time a very successful jazz DVD series via Kiosks. They would combine many different labels to give the series the best product possible or just highlight a label or a genre, like Blues. In that sense the meeting was good for me to be there and we got a few activities out of it.

Hannah turned nine years in 2002 and with each year it was different and exciting to see how she was developing and learning and always trying to understand. She was good at school still, nice with people and made me proud to be her dad. We had a fun trip to Disneyland near Paris together that year and spend time in Austria at her grandparents, as well as at Jürgen's place. My brother was then doing some horse-carriage racing, actually as the second man on the carriage he became Austrian champion and took part at the European championships as well, and when we had a chance, we went to one of the races. That was pretty cool to watch and a fun day out and as Hannah loved all animals, she was in heaven around all the dogs and horses there. I had been in London now for 10 years and it was interesting to realise that only a handful of people, beside family, really had made an effort to stay in touch over the years. When I had expected some of the guys from the 'miles smiles' team or from PolyGram, it was in fact Heinz Krassnitzer with whom I stayed in touch by mutually being active to do so. Rainer, my friend with whom I had started 'Jazz Live', was another one who regularly checked in or we met when I was in Vienna or he came to London. His new digital photographs were amazing and he won a few awards with these and one outstanding shot of Joe Henderson. Heinz, on the other hand, continued to run with Fritz the Vienna Jazz festival and concerts in Austria and always was on the know – when he called and asked me to check an artist out, I always would do so and he was the first to point me to Gregory Porter, at a time he wasn't known at all. And then there was Wolfgang Puschnig, with whom I would chat, listen to and comment on his new music and tried to meet whenever I could, which in the end wasn't very often.

2002 in my office

On the classical side we worked the 'Sacred Songs' by Placido Domingo, Chinese pianist Yundi Li's 'Chopin', the new Pavarotti and friends for the children in Bosnia and crossover acts tenor Russel Watson, called 'the people's tenor' in the UK and girl group Bond, the string quartet with a twist.
ECM had a bunch of great releases by the Keith Jarrett Trio, this time live from Japan and with Jarrett's own compositions; Charles Lloyd's wonderful 'Lift Every Voice' featuring the pianist Geri Allen and Jan Garbarek's new album 'Wayfarer', this time with Bill Frisell. Rebekka Bakken and Wolfgang Muthspiel followed up their 2000 album 'Daily Mirror' with 'Beloved', another musical gem. Rebekka had gotten an offer to record for ACT Music, as she had done another album there singing for Julia Hülsmann and they really liked her. I wanted her to sign to Universal, as I thought that she was a special talent, besides being a great human being. When she sent me the deal, they offered her, I simply said that I never would sign such an agreement and asked her to check with Universal in Vienna, as she was living there, and told her to go to Harry Gruber, our extremely capable guy. I had spoken to Harry and he was interested in signing her and I would take the record international. They made the deal, one much better than the contract offered by the small label and immediately started to record her first album. Beside that Bakken/Muthspiel album I listened in 2002 to Anna Maria Jopek and Pat Metheny's 'Upojenie', a wonderful collaboration of two very special artists; Brad Mehldau's 'Largo' was another one that I played a lot that year as well as Branford Marsalis' 'Footsteps Of Our Fathers'.
I was reading Terry Pratchett's Discworld novels and had fun doing so. Very clever, amusing, but humanistic stories. Henning Mankell and his Wallander were on the reading menu as well and in the movies, I saw the second instalment of 'The Lord Of The Rings', 'Magic River' by Sean Penn and Sofia Coppola's wonderful 'Lost In Translation'. And with Hannah I saw the 'Pirates Of Caribbean' and 'Finding Nemo', which I actually both liked ... and so did she.

Before the year was over, I went again in December to the Jazzland Sessions in Oslo and we had invited the jazz managers from around the world and the festival promoters again. I had promised John Scofield at one point to make it happen that he would play with Bugge and this was the chance – I flew John into Oslo, the guys had an afternoon to talk about what they would do and, in the evening, they played together ... and wow, how they did!! This was funky, danceable, groovy music with tons of freedom to improvise and let it fly! John loved it and so did the rest of the band, Bugge and of course the audience. It was as always great to have a dinner with all Norwegian artists around the table chatting and having a good time.

John Scofield, Silje Nergaard and Nils Petter Molvaer at our dinner in Oslo, 2002

I also went to the Rainbow Studio to see Ketil, who was working with Anneli Drecker, singer of the group Bel Canto, on new music. This sounded really interesting and I was looking forward to hear the final mix soon.

In November 2002 an outbreak of severe acute respiratory syndrome started in China's Guangdong province and spread fast through Asia and a few cases came as well to Canada and Europe. This SARS epidemic was brought upon by a coronavirus which in the end spread to 29 countries and infected thousands of people. The outbreak continued into 2003, until it was finally declared over in 2004. But it left many feeling extremely vulnerable and thinking about what would happen if a more contagious virus would spread.

Meanwhile, Yolanda and I had stayed in touch, as we both had started to feel strongly for each other, and when I had to go for a meeting with DG to Hamburg, I asked her to join me to see where the relationship was taking us. Hamburg in December was freezing cold, but we still had a wonderful time together.

Despite the question marks over my relationship with Eva, we celebrated New Year's Eve with Wolfgang Puschnig, his partner Gabi and his son Samo and some friends in London, with lots of great food and wine.

2003

I started 2003 with a trip to Toronto. The International Association of Jazz Educators had invited me to their first ever conference outside of the US. I took part in a panel discussion with the title 'Jazz Is A Universal Language', hosted by writer Ashley Kahn and featuring beside me Francois Zalacain of Sunnyside Records, a great NY indie label for jazz; Derek Andrews, who booked the Toronto JVC Festival and my friend and producer, A&R man Brian Bacchus. It was a good conference, like the ones I had attended before in NYC and one always ran into musicians, agents and managers. Here pianist and jazz legend Oscar Peterson was to be honoured in a gala and black-tie event. Scott Morin, our man in Canada, had just started to work with Oscar for a CD and DVD project titled 'A Night In Vienna' and asked me if I could attend. I had 5 hours to get a suit and went immediately to buy one, had it shortened and got to pick it up half an hour before I had to leave for the event. It all worked out fine and I got to meet Oscar, whose music I always liked, especially the 'Exclusively For My Friends' recordings for MPS and whom I had seen a few times in concert before.

Next up on the list of meetings was a regional Classics and Jazz conference in Shanghai. As Yolanda was working for KLM in the cargo division, it was easy for her to travel and so we arranged to fly out to Shanghai together and spend the weekend there before my meetings would start. We had a few great days and most of the time were out and about to see parts of this amazing city. It was wonderful to see her again and feel her close to me and simply talk and walk. Even so I still didn't allow myself to admit to what was obvious, that I had fallen in love with her and that she was given me so much more than my current relationship ever had, I kind of felt that I had to do something.

In my following indecisiveness I created more pain for everyone involved by starting an ill-fated attempt to see if there was something to salvage from my relationship to Eva, but in the end, it just made it clearer, that we had drifted apart to an extend that wasn't fixable. I had spoken to Hannah before about problems her parents had and now, I had to tell her that I would be moving out, but live close by, so I could still take her to school as usual in the mornings and see her as often as possible. I knew she would be sad and it would be difficult for her, with an age of 10 years, to understand, but I was sure in a few years' time, she would. I found a small flat in the middle between her apartment and her school and moved in there. Despite me messing things up, Yolanda had stuck with me and we met in May in Madrid and did a little trip to Toledo, which was sublime, as there was no weight on my shoulders and we could be relaxed and start our relationship proper.

This was the year the Iraq war started and Saddam Hussain was captured; when the Concorde made its last flights and referendums were held in seven states about joining the European Union, which all were approved by the respective people. Suzannah and I worked again on the jazz catalogue, this time with the support and help of Jo Clarke. We, as every year, worked this catalogue with our co-ordinator in Holland, Frits Doornenbal, who had from the beginning worked with me on it, as he had the experience doing the catalogue for Philips Classics for many years and knew exactly what was needed and when. As we printed in Holland anyway, he oversaw this for many years for us. A great guy on top of everything, Frits was irreplaceable for us. The catalogue again was split into jazz and world music sections, plus a numerical section with all barcodes and, as in the last few years, I wrote a few words as an introduction.

That year we also produced the final two issues of our release magazine, as orders from the various markets got lower and lower and it simply didn't make any sense anymore to produce such an elaborate magazine. Music sales generally were not as good as in the years before, as file sharing hampered the business and legal digital downloads didn't create as much money as sales of CD's. Everyone had therefore less marketing money and such a general tool as a release magazine didn't fit into the times anymore. We therefore built websites, especially for Emarcy to give information on all new releases and our artists and for some time did the release magazine in a digital form as a PDF file that could be distributed by email to people who had subscribed to this form of information in the various markets.

Before going to the festivals in July, Hannah and myself made a trip to Denmark to celebrate my mother's 75th birthday. My parents had bought a house with garden close to Rødby when my father retired, so he had work to do outside and inside. From Rødby a ferry was going to Puttgarden in Germany, therefore it was easy for them to shop all the food they liked from their home country. The whole family descended on the little house for the celebrations and most of us had to sleep in tents, which was cool with Hannah and OK for me. Riegers came from Berlin, all six kids and their kids plus friends and neighbours. A truly special event. We put up a marquee tent for the dinner, roasted a piglet and had a great time as all of us only came together every few years, living apart from each other, spread-out all-over Europe.

Even so that year, some of us met again a few weeks later in Mallorca, this time to celebrate my sister Christine's 50th birthday, which had actually been the year before, but we couldn't find a date to celebrate then. Christine and her family had booked a holiday there and Hannah, Juergen, Barbara and her kids and myself joined them for a long weekend.

2003, My parents, my brother Thomas and Hannah at my mother's 75th birthday party

The festival season brought me to various festivals, but most of all I remember North Sea Jazz, as it was the first time that Yolanda and myself went together to The Hague, as she shares my passion for music, with a similar stylistic openness. It was great to have someone to share the music with and we saw a lot of great shows there, especially Roy Hargrove's RH Factor, Richard Bona, Marcus Miller and Lizz Wright. We also went to Vitoria for the festival, the first time as a couple, back to the place where it all began. The Verve Night there had Bona and RH Factor and we saw Lizz Wright again. It was amazing to see how easy-going Yolanda was around and with people. All the musicians immediately took to and opened up to her. I was really happy.
We went for a day to San Sebastian for a swim and with the weather being amazing, we really enjoyed the little break.

That summer we had the first proper European tour for Charlie Haden & Pat Metheny in support of their 'Beyond The Missouri Sky' duo album from 1997 and for this reason we released the album in a limited 'European Tour Special Edition' that included a DVD with 2 live songs from the Montreal Jazz Festival 1997 and a short EPK with interviews with both musicians. At the beginning of this little film one can see yours truly, together with Daniel Richard, picking up the guys at the airport in Paris, when they originally came to promote the album. Great to see some more known faces in that little movie. Good memories!

I came back to Madrid in early August to celebrate Yolanda's 40th birthday with her friends and family and kind of being introduced to them. A cool party on the terrace of her apartment with a bunch of really nice people. Later that month I spent some time with Hannah in Austria. We were in Vienna first, then went out to the country side with my brother and his wife Uschi to one of his horse carriage races and finally spent a few days in Eitzersthal, in their little house there, which got a pool and a huge garden. Important quality time with my daughter.

Yolanda and myself at her 40th birthday

The main jazz releases of the year were the soulful and funky RH Factor album 'Hard Groove', which featured a host of special guests like Common, D'Angelo, Erykah Badu and Q-Tip and included the track 'Forget Regret', which still is Yolanda's and my favourite from this record. Lizz Wright's debut album 'Salt' was a major statement of an unknown artist. Her song writing and singing is excellent and very unique. And live she was too extremely powerful and captivating. Wayne Shorter's 'Alegria', David Sanborn's 'Time Again' and John Scofield's groovy 'Up All Night' completed the list of Verve's big records for the year. Ken Druker, the head of catalogue at Verve, gave us re-issues and series of compilations, that at a lower price level, did very well globally. Ken had been our jazz man in Canada before coming to New York and run the catalogue side for Verve and did a wonderful job with constantly coming up with new ideas and listening to what the key markets needed.

By then I had done more jazz A&R, therefore Chris promoted me to VP International Marketing and A&R and in 2003 the first bigger releases came through on Emarcy, especially the Chick Corea album 'Rendezvous In New York'. Chick and I had started to talk a bit about what to do with his Universal owned catalogue and threw a few ideas around. We met a few times and then he said that he had recorded three weeks of gigs at the Blue Note in New York, featuring a lot of his old sidemen and that he had done so with the help of Philipps Electronics and all recordings were in surround sound. Philips was promoting the Super Audio CD and therefore wanted these recordings to be made available. As Chick had already in 1992 started his own label, Stretch Records, he was able to license any record to whomever he wanted and I gladly picked up the option to release this outstanding album. The list of artists featured over the three weeks residency at the Blue Note is too long to include here, but Bobby McFerrin, Gonzalo Rubalcaba, Michael Brecker and Gary Burton were among them. I remember Chick as a wonderful, humble and kind person. Generous and open, always listening to ideas and checking out what was going on. The hybrid multichannel SACD/CD did well internationally and was a good start for my Emarcy A&R activities. Another of these was the release of jazz DVD's from concerts at the Montreal Jazz Festival, the first batch featuring Carla Bley, Charlie Haden and the Liberation Music Orchestra, Dizzy and John Lee Hooker among others. DVD's were still good business then and there weren't that many in jazz, so this was a good series for us.

Ketil's new album with Anneli Drecker came out that year as well and was called 'The Nest' and was music written to the poetry of Hart Crane. Another outstanding album of lyrical jazz and European classical music mixed into a very personal and touching musical experience. Other Emarcy releases from around the world included Portuguese singer extraordinaire Cristina Branco, Japanese pianist Makoto Ozone and Bugge Wesseltoft's New Conceptions Of Jazz 'Live' album. Our French company released 'Munia – The Tale', the new album by bassist and singer Richard Bona. Like the two albums before, I really liked this one for its beauty and African feel. It was great to get to know Richard a bit, as he is a wonderful and kind human being, besides being a groovy and funky keyboard player, composer and producer Peter Wolf, who played with Fra the Jefferson Starship hit 'We built this city', came to me with a cool jazz r and released on Emarcy. I had heard an early solo piano album by Peter and he is a truly nice guy, whom I met again that year at the North Sea Ja Jamie Cullum's first Universal album 'Twentysomething' became anothe for him. Jamie is a real cool guy, with a great sense of humour and sor He is a great entertainer who mixes his jazz influences with pop writi really different and special. Another noteworthy debut album that year came whose 'The Art Of How To Fall' was very successful in Austria and Germany, p recognition in a few other markets. I was happy that in the end she had signed with Har Vienna and this first album was with us. In Austria she achieved the rare award of a golden jazz which at that time meant sales over 15.000 units just there. Impressive!!!

Dhafer Youssef released his third album 'Divine Prophecy', cementing his status as one of the most unique voices in a jazz/world music context. His live shows were and are still always something special, as the purity of his voice when chanting always gets me and his expressed emotions are deep and touching.

In September we were invited to Jo Clarke's wedding and met up there with some of my colleagues and had a great time at the celebrations.
Yolanda and myself flew back and forth between London and Madrid to see each other, or went to other places for a short break together, like Paris and Denmark, where I introduced her to my parents and sisters. Both my father and mother took an immediate liking to her, even so they hardly could communicate. But my dad simply took her hand when we went shopping and so made clear what he thought. A gesture I witnessed from walking behind them and that took me by surprise and I loved that little emotional clear signal.

2003, introducing Yolanda to my family – here with my sisters Christine and Marlis

With Hannah I did spend most of the weekends going to the movies, to parks, fairs and generally trying to have a good time together, despite having to do homework as well. We celebrated her tenth birthday together with her mom and a bunch of her friends were coming over for a little party, which was good fun. It was important that she understood that the separation of her parents had nothing to do with her and that they tried to deal with the situation in an amicable way.

The classical priorities from Deutsche Grammophon and Decca Classics respectively for 2003 were Chinese pianist Yundi Li's 'Liszt' recording; new classical star singer Anna Netrebko's 'Opera Arias'; Elvis Costello's 'North', a modern classical and slightly jazzy album; Pavarotti's 'Te Adoro', which was a classical crossover album and his final recording and Cecilia Bartoli's 'The Salieri Album', which had its presentation in the theatre of Vienna's Schloss Schönbrunn. The last of the lavish and expensive album presentations for Decca. It was actually really educational to work with Elvis, as he called some meetings to discuss marketing and promotion ideas for the record, making sure everyone understood what he had in mind when making the album and getting the right message out. He was very involved and knowledgeable and did as well listen to what we had to say. A really good experience, as usually artists are not that much involved.
DG meanwhile had brought in Bogdan Roscic as their #2. Bogdan had been the head of the national pop radio station when I was still in Austria and I had met him once or twice then. He then took over as boss of Universal Austria between 2001 and his change to DG. An interesting and intellectual guy, but down to earth and cool to talk to.
ECM had as highlights a new Carla Bley big band album with Wolfgang Puschnig titled 'Looking For America'; the outstanding debut by pianist Tord Gustavsen, featuring Harald Johnsen on bass and Jarle Vespestad on drums. This trio was for a while the backup band of Silje Nergaard and made some wonderful recordings with her. But this first album, 'Changing Places', put them immediately on the jazz map as one of the trios to look out for. 2003 was as well the year Amy Winehouse released her first album 'Frank' and I really liked what she did. Beside that I was listening to Branford Marsalis' new quartet album 'Romare Bearden Revealed', featuring most of his family, guitarist Doug Wamble and Harry Connick Jr. as special guests.

While I started reading the books by Michael Conolly in his Hieronymus Bosch crime noir series, which features some jazz, as Harry, short for Hieronymus, is an avid jazz fan, I went to see Clint Eastwood's 'Mystic River' and loved that movie and of course had to go to see the third instalment of the 'Lord Of The Rings' trilogy 'The Return Of The King'. Epic!

In December Yolanda and I did a little trip to Vienna, staying with my brother for a few days and visiting the Christmas markets, drinking mulled wine. When going to the jazz club Porgy & Bess we met Rainer and Rudi and Rebekka Bakken took this photo of the original 'Jazz Live' team.

2003, with Rainer Rygalyk and Rudi Staeger

Before the year was over, Michael Jackson got arrested on child molestation charges and I travelled to Madrid to spend New Year's Eve with Yolanda and her family after celebrating a relaxed Christmas with Hannah in our little flat before that.

London, Part 2
2004

The year 2004 started with a trip to New York to attend the IAJE conference to network and have meetings with the Verve team and managers and agents. This was one of the last big conferences as the IAJE went bankrupt about 2 years later. Seems like they wanted too much, too fast. It took six years until a replacement came, The Jazz Connect Conference, which started as part of APAP, in January and in New York. Then I was off to a meeting in Hong Kong, followed by a trip to Tokyo, the most important market in the region.

Hannah had met Yolanda and we had started to do a few things together, despite Eva thinking it was too early for Hannah to meet her. I am sure this wasn't easy at all for Hannah, but she tried her best. And for Yolanda too, as she didn't want to start of wrongly with Hannah either. In April that year we did our first trip together to Madrid, a city Hannah immediately fell in love with and where she met Yolanda's family and friends. In May I went with Hannah to the Parc Asterix outside of Paris – a fun weekend for both of us, with lots of scary (for me, not my daughter) rides, entertaining shows and food and drink.

Yolanda had won at the Christmas party of KLM a pair of flight-tickets and invited me to go with her to a destination we could pick and we chose Cuba, which was simply an amazing trip. Incredible to see together the decay of the city next to some modernity, all the wonderful old cars and friendly people. Music seemed to come out of every bar and Havana was a cool place. We both loved it and enjoyed this trip a lot. Yolanda had as well asked at KLM to let her know in case a position would open up at their cargo offices in London and then it really happened and from June 19th that same year we started living together. It was a hell of a trip for Yolanda every morning to go by tube and bus from St. John's Wood to the cargo building outside of Heathrow airport and therefore we decided to buy a car. She only needed a day or so to get used to drive on the 'wrong' side of the street, but the distance to the office was still a problem. As the flat I had rented was too small anyway for two, let alone for three, which we were sometimes at the weekend, we started to look around for something new and more in the direction of the airport. Yolanda is much better with money than I ever was or will be, therefore she convinced me that the best option was to buy and so we checked out a lot of flats in West London.

Every year in March or April the festival promoters came to London for the ILMC (International Live Music Convention) and for some years I had the tradition of inviting them to Matsuri, a great Japanese Teppan-Yaki restaurant where we had the rule not to talk but business, but just have fun and eat and drink well. Sometimes I invited a manager or an artist along, but in general it was the festival organizers and me. For the summer we, as always, had a lot of acts touring, but as far as I can recall we only had a special Verve Night in The Hague, where on the Saturday Night we had the rooftop terrace for our acts, Chris Potter, Kenny Barron, Silje Nergaard and Eivind Aarset, plus Michael Brecker as artist in residence, who performed with a different band on a different stage each of the three nights.

March 2004 will be unforgotten because of the horrendous events that took place in Madrid on the 11th – the detonations of 10 explosives on four commuter trains going from Alcala de Henares to Madrid Atocha. The 'Cercanías' trains exploded in and close to Atocha and two other stations and left 193 people dead and over 2000 injured. The suicide bombers were radical Muslims with contacts
Qaeda. Yolanda and I were watching the morning news in London when we heard about the
ities and got really nervous, as this was all happening on the train line her mother Maria took
day to go to work. Only after she got her mother on her mobile phone and talked to her, we
breathe a bit more relaxed. Her mother actually had been on the train that got to Atocha
e the one that exploded there. This was one of the worst attacks on innocent civilians by

religious fanatics in Europe and was initially attributed by the conservative government to the Basque nationalist and terrorist organization ETA. The handling of the bombings by the government made it lose the General Elections, held only three days after the events and gave power to the PSOE, the socialist party in Spain, under new prime minister José Luis Rodríguez Zapatero.

At work, we were still doing the printed jazz catalogue and Suzannah and Jo helped a lot with that. Unfortunately, Suzannah left Universal that year and I had to bring in someone new. Sascha Kilias had been working with the production team for a bit already and therefore knew what was expected when creating artwork and putting a project into the system and he loved jazz, thus he was an easy pick and he was a great guy, so he started right after the summer. I had been asked to have a look at the Fantasy catalogue, which included then the labels Fantasy, Milestone, Prestige, Riverside and Pablo, and evaluate the package. These are wonderful catalogues with some historic recordings, but a few of the important ones were soon falling out of copyright in Europe and were, therefore, of less value and I thought that if we were to buy these catalogues, we shouldn't pay more than $ 45 million, which the owners thought wasn't enough. Pity. On the other hand, just a little bit later Concord Records would pay them an estimated $ 83 million for it. Concord had that year as well made a deal with Universal to distribute and market their repertoire in the US and International, which gave us a ton of new releases to look at and catalogue to work with.
At the same time Decca had started to work loosely with Rounder Records and had a kind of first look deal with them and occasionally they would send music my way, when it was jazzier or world music oriented. Through that deal, one day an advance CD landed on my desk with new music by singer Madeleine Peyroux, whose first album four years earlier had been reasonably successful. I listened to the wonderful production, song choices and arrangements and really liked the recording. Shortly after I had finished my phone rang and Christian Kellersmann from Germany was on the line, asking if I had heard exactly that advance CD. He wanted me to sign this album to Emarcy immediately. With my boss, Chris Roberts, I had the agreement that I would only sign acts which at least one of the key markets would support actively. In this case, having Germany behind me, I went ahead to talk to Rounder and made the deal for the international rights for Madeleine's next three albums for a very reasonable advance. Madeleine's 'Careless Love' was a huge success for Universal and Rounder, us selling more than 700.000 copies of the album outside the US and Canada.

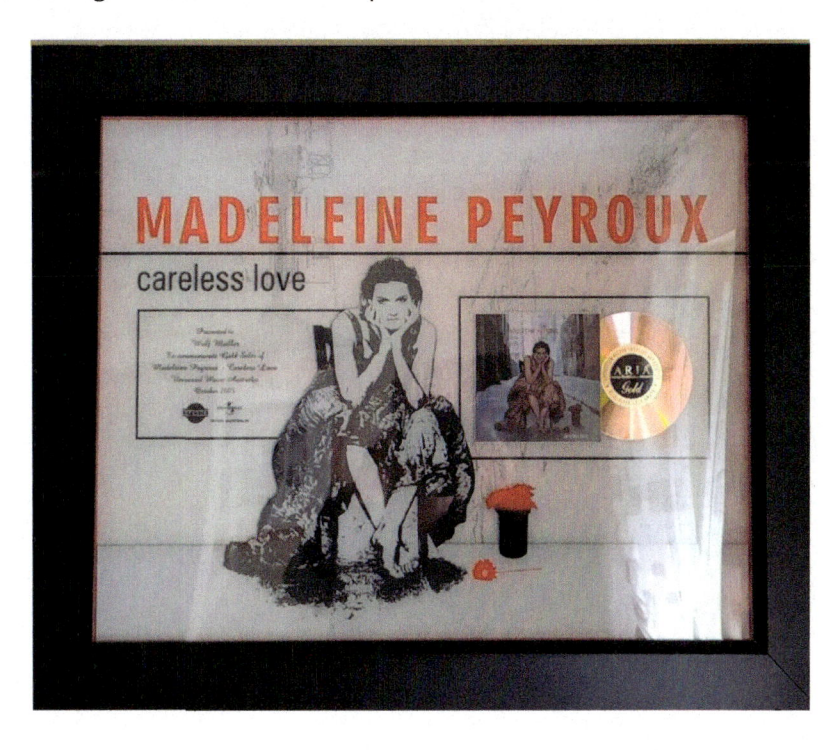

ine supported the record with promo and touring, but in the UK, they thought a great story
'ed to push the record into bigger numbers and so they came up with the story that she had
 ..d, couldn't be reached for PR and gigs, which they 'sold' to all big daily newspapers. And
 .e I knew about it, I had her manager on the phone asking what this was and where it came
from. I thought it was a silly made up story, as in a way, it was damaging her reputation and festival and concert promoters started calling me, checking whether she would show up for her concert ... When I spoke to the responsible two guys at Classics & Jazz in London about this and mentioned that I now had an artist relation problem on my hand, they simply said that this was my problem not theirs, they had to sell records and the story did so. They couldn't care less about the artist being pissed off, as long as the record sold. They were the kind of people that could sell socks instead of music ... they had no understanding of and nothing to do with artists or artist relations and in the few cases they did sign an act directly, it never lasted because of exactly that problem. I sorted things out with Madeleine and Cynthia Herbst, her wonderfully competent and understanding manager and from there onwards it was smooth sailing with both of them.

Another album I signed on that year was the new Matt Bianco recording 'Matt's Mood', featuring the original three members Mark Reilly, Basia Trzetrzelewska and Danny White and it was a pure pleasure to work with these guys and their manager, business legend Carl Leighton-Pope. While working together on the new album and tour, Carl and I discovered not only our passions for music, but for football as well and as he was a Chelsea fan and this was my club of choice in England when moving there, we had a lot to talk about. Carl and his family held 4 season tickets for Stamford Bridge, the Chelsea stadium and as European manager and agent of Bryan Adams, he had access to two more when Bryan was touring. Because his two sons were in the agency business as well, he happened to have one or more tickets available almost every weekend and called once in a while to check if Hannah, Yolanda or myself would be interested to come and join him or pick the tickets up at his office in case he couldn't make it himself and then return them again the next Monday. And so it came that over the coming years we, all three of us together or two at a time, were able to see a lot of Chelsea's home games in the Premier League. 'Matt's Mood' is a wonderful album with great tracks and did OK, but once they started touring, we did fine with the album. In Poland, where Basia is from originally, we even got a Gold Disc Award for excellent sales and we did fine in the US as well.

Watching a Chelsea football game with Hannah and Yolanda

And then there was the new Terry Callier album I signed on for Europe, excluding the UK, 'Lookin' Out'. Terry had been dropped by the Verve team and as I really liked the new songs, especially 'Jazz,

My Rhythm And Blues', 'What About Me' and 'Blues For Billie Holiday' and France was backing me up in this case, I made the deal. Terry came to tour in Europe and we got some incredible reviews – sales were low, but reasonable and we met again when he was playing at London's JazzCafe. What a great guy!! Andreas Vollenweider's 'Vox' was another signing I did in 2004 and I released as well, via Norway's deal, Ketil Bjørnstad's latest recording 'Seafarer's Song', talking in music and lyrics about the drama of immigration into Europe. Ketil wrote his own lyrics, based on articles in the Guardian on the subject and used texts by Homer, Shakespeare, Oscar Wilde and many more to create a sobering and deeply meaningful album, that in the years since it was released unfortunately hasn't lost any of its actuality and shocking truth. Singer Kristin Asbjørnsen delivered the tough lyrics with emotion and warmth, anger when needed and the rest of the band, including Nils Petter Molvaer and Eivind Aarset performed incredibly well. Ketil used an El País newspaper article by Spanish writer Juan Jose Millas for the liner notes, which Yolanda had suggested to him and translated into English. This album is for me a European jazz classic – for the music, the message and the honesty of it all. At the same time, I was also reading Ketil's book 'Der Tanz Des Lebens', a fascinating story of an ageing man and how he is losing the grip on his world. The list of my A&R releases for Emarcy is complete with the second album by Tuck & Patti, 'A Gift Of Love', for which we had rights for Europe and which featured some wonderful songs, this time not just performed by the two of them, but adding strings and keyboards. I always looked forward to see these two wonderful people and their shows.

Verve gave us that year a new album by Diana Krall titled 'The Girl In The Other Room' and it is a very different Diana Krall album altogether, as for the first time Diana wrote music to seven of the tracks and her husband Elvis Costello lyrics to six of them; the rest were songs by Tom Waits, Mose Allison, Bonnie Raitt, Joni Mitchell and Arthur Herzog. This therefore was by far the most personal album Diana had recorded and one could hear that. As much as I like Diana as an interpreter of standards or covers, these songs are deeper and emotionally extremely strong. Her 'Almost Blue' and the Elvis/Krall songs 'Narrow Daylight', 'The Girl In The Other Room' and 'Departure Bay' are outstanding and especially 'Narrow Daylight' has become a song other female singers are interpreting. Diana came to Madrid to do promotion for the album – first a press day, then more interviews and a short showcase. At the end of the first day we, Diana and band, management, the Spanish team, Yolanda and myself, went for a Spanish dinner in a very cool restaurant. After a wonderful meal with some great wines, I think it was Marta who suggested to have some typical Spanish digestives, Orujo, the Spanish version of Grappa or Pacharán, a dark berry liqueur. As in Spanish tradition they serve you a glass but leave the bottle on the table, we re-filled a few times and drank the whole lot. The next day when we arrived for the showcase, sitting in the first row, close to the stage, Diana, before starting the showcase, with a smile looked down at us and asked: *"And how are you guys feeling today?"* We smiled back to an artist who obviously had suffered a bit of a hangover as the result of our fun dinner and smiled as well *"Not too bad"*!

The other important releases coming from Verve were John Scofield's live recording 'En Route'; George Benson's 'Irreplicable'; Al Jarreu's 'Accentuate the Positive' and the groovy RH Factor 6-track EP 'Strength'. The first releases we got from Concord were singer Peter Cincotti's 'On The Moon', Karrin Alyson's 'Wild For You' and Chick Corea's 'To The Stars', inspired by the book of the same name by Ron L. Hubbard, the founder of Scientology, of which Chick was a supporter, but without trying to convince everyone around him. I had talked to Chick about releasing the album, but as Concord came to Universal that year anyway, it wouldn't have made any difference to whom he licensed the album, except that possibly Concord paid him a higher advance. Concord's head of international and my direct partner to work these records was Peter Holden, a great and efficient guy, who would, from then on, represent Concord in our international meetings. Paco De Lucia released his stunning new album 'Cositas Buenas' and for once agreed to do interviews in his then home in Toledo. We had journalists from all over the world coming and a German TV crew walked with him through the city he was living in then. In-between interviews I spent some time with him at his house, which had a great covered patio to sit in and a little studio in the cellar. The house was right in the centre of old Toledo, opposite a church that had some 'El Greco' paintings displayed. The new album did well and Paco went out to tour in Europe and of course played the festivals as well. As usual he was happy to see me around, calling me '*Hombre*' and couldn't believe that after all the years I was still working with the same company.

The classical priorities of the year were releases by Anna Netrebko, Lang Lang, the soundtrack to the movie 'Gladiator' by Hans Zimmer, Ludovico Einaudi's 'Una Mattina' and UK tenor Russel Watson's 'Amore Musica', which included a version of the song 'You Raise Me Up', originally recorded and written by Norwegian band Secret Garden. Keith Jarrett and Jan Garbarek were both releasing new albums on ECM, but for me their album of the year was vocal group Trio Mediaeval's 'Soir, Dit-Elle', a touchingly beautiful record, their second after their stunning 2001 debut 'Words Of The Angel'. There were many releases from other labels, but none seems to stick out for me now, maybe except the Petra Haden / Bill Frisell album and the live recordings by Brad Mehldau and Patricia Barber.

In a year when George W. Bush had been re-elected president of the USA, armed robbers stole a few Edvard Munch paintings from the Munch Museum in Oslo, including 'Madonna' and 'The Scream' and Greece won surprisingly the Euro 2004 final against hosts Portugal, Hannah, her friend Edie and myself went to Austria to stay at Jürgen's place for a bit, where the girls had fun in the pool and going out to ride on horses. Then just Hannah and myself went to Denmark to see her grandparents and Christine and her son Sander with his family. In November I did a quick trip to Vienna to celebrate my brother Jürgen's 50th birthday with friends and colleagues. A relaxed and cool event.

And then luck struck – Yolanda spotted a small apartment for sale in Fulham and I put in an offer and by December we were owners of a flat!!! There was some work to be done in what was once a Victorian house, that in the sixties or so was converted cheaply into two flats and we had the top one, which strange enough was on three levels. A charming place that needed refurbishment, especially in the bathrooms and living room. Through a work contact Yolanda got in touch with a Polish worker, Wacek, who brought his crew and did all the work exemplary and more than that. When working in the bathroom and taking down the old tiles, a wall collapsed, as it was really only a bit of wood planks and he set it all up again and made it solid. We saved tons of money that way – Yolanda did most of the work, searching for the right ideas and parts and came up with the best concepts – she would have been a great interior designer. We got rid of the fake fireplace in the living room and so saved space and converted one small room next to the kitchen into a walk-in wardrobe. Eva's attitude towards an amicable separation changed and she decided to bring in the lawyers. I had left her everything in the flat except my personal belongings, shared all savings and income equally, agreed to share additional costs for Hannah equally as well, but she wanted more, especially future bonuses and pay rises, which I refused. Pity that it always ends up to be about money.

Meanwhile, Hannah and I continued to read the Harry Potter saga, this year with book six and I read as well Yann Mantel's captivating 'Life Of Pi' and went to the movies with Yolanda to see Clint Eastwood's 'Million Dollar Baby', with an outstanding performance by Hilary Swank, and Martin Scorsese's 'The Aviator', featuring Leonardo Di Caprio.
Early December Yolanda and myself went to Oslo for the Jazzland Sessions again – too cold for a Spaniard who is used to warmer climate, but a wonderful trip nevertheless. We were staying with our friends Yngve and Cecilie and went out to see the city, its museums and of course the gigs at the Blå Club, this time featuring among others Eivind, Sidsel Endresen, Mari Boine and Tore Eriksen. Heinz Krassnitzer came as well from Vienna to check out the new groups from Jazzland and see an old friend. While in Oslo we also met our friend Ketil for a nice meal.

with Ketil Bjørnstad in Oslo, 2004

We celebrated Christmas with Hannah in the old flat on December 23rd, as on the 24th we flew out to Vienna to celebrate my father's 80th birthday. Hannah stayed in London to have another Christmas party with her mother and friends. Vienna was fun – Barbara and Patrick came with Ulla and Masanti, my parents were obviously there and Goran, who was one of Jürgen's best friends and a family friend of many years. The parents of Uschi, my brother's wife, had joined us as well for a wonderful dinner and we spent some time to see the city and had a little trip to a farm of one of Jürgen's friends and horse carriage race partner.

On December 26th a powerful earthquake in Sumatra released a wave of tsunamis which, with waves of up to 30 meters height rolled onto the beaches of Indonesia, India, Sri Lanka and Thailand and caused unimaginable damage to people and property. It is estimated that more than 227.000 people vanished in the destruction the tsunamis caused all around Asia. Many tourists lost their lives while enjoying a break away from home and I remember knowing that Silje Nergaard and her family were in the region as well, but thankfully unharmed. This was one of the deadliest natural disasters ever and the world was shocked by the force of nature once again.

Yolanda and myself saw the year out in Madrid with Yolanda's family, celebrating with her aunt and uncle and their kids and families with tons of incredible food the aunt had prepared.

2005

The new year started with a European Classics & Jazz meeting in Berlin, set up by Christian and his team, that now featured as well Per Hauber and Peggy Schmidt for Classical and Astrid Kieselbach und Matthias Künnecke for Jazz. There we had a chance to go to one of the new versions of the Yellow Lounge, which was now more a chill out event with classical music, live and with DJ, and was already very popular in Berlin.

2005, Meeting in Berlin

Jo and myself finished the 2004/2005 jazz catalogue, which we had started with Suzanna the year before. We changed from hard cover to soft cover to save some costs, but in the end, it was an antiquated tool and too expensive and that year's catalogue was to be the last. Information on the various catalogues we were distributing was now spread over the various websites of the labels. Overall, the sales numbers in the music business were going down. Legal digital downloads in 2004 were at 160 million tracks, and the number for illegal was manyfold of this. Jazz and Classical fortunately were not that much affected by the illegal downloads yet, but the decline in overall sales could be felt there as well. People spent their entertainment dollars on mobile phones, DVD's and video games, plus on more traditional activities as going to the movies, buying books and last but not yet least, buying music, but each of these had a smaller share than before the ascent of mobile phones and video games. TV shows like Pop Idol and X-Factor created short-lived careers (with a very few exceptions) but thanks to their TV exposure sold lots of records quickly, in that case first compilations of songs from the show and in the end the records of the winner or finalists. Jazz more or less disappeared from the TV screen or was simply aired late at night and then mainly recordings from a local jazz festival. YouTube, which was launched in 2005, would change that and make thousands of historic and new jazz movies, documentaries and live concerts available to everyone who was interested. Not that they paid or are paying much to the right holders, but the small income might be better than having the footage gather dust in some archive.

We moved into our new flat in early 2005 and loved the place. Fulham is a well-connected location with lots of bars and restaurants in the area. There were two amazing Thai places – one the classy and really good Blue Elephant and the other the small and extremely good Sukho, both just around different corners. Hannah learned to take the bus and metro from her place to us and after some early hesitation got really confident and relaxed about it. Growing up in the city! We went all three of us together to Denmark for Easter and met there with Barbara, Ulla and Masanti, Marlis and her son Karsten with his family, Christine, Patrick, Sander and their families for a week of fun and good food. In April we spent a weekend in Paris, going together with a friend of Hannah's we had invited, to the Parc Asterix again. Rides and shows and great weather helped to make these enjoyable three days. That April we had the final ruling on our divorce and Eva just got a tiny bit more from my Pension Fund, but none of what she had hoped for in terms of future extra payments. We were divorced, but the discussion about money didn't stop, despite the papers stating that all additional costs for Hannah needed to be shared equally. We had shared parental and financial responsibilities from then on, which made me ask Eva to urgently try to find some income on her own and save some money, as the music industry every year reduced their workforce and I was sure that at one point it would be my turn to be made redundant and then what? I had to warn her and make sure that in such a case she would be still be able to fulfil her responsibilities towards Hannah.

It was announced that the rock group Cream with the original members Eric Clapton, Jack Bruce and Ginger Baker would play four nights at the Royal Albert Hall in May 2005. Tickets would go on sale on a Monday from 9 o'clock onwards. As exactly that Monday in late January, I was on a flight to Asia, I asked Carl Leighton-Pope to get me four tickets for one of the nights. Carl, with his connections delivered the tickets and I was very grateful, as all four shows were sold out in just under one hour. We had tickets for the second day, if I remember correctly, and my brother Jürgen and his friend Goran came from Vienna to join us for the concert. The show was incredible: the music a bit less rock and a bit more bluesy, but they played all the hits and some cool old blues. All three musicians were in top form and seemingly enjoyed this reunion. From the four shows later a double CD and a DVD would be released. After the high of the concert, we went home, had something to eat and opened some wine and watched the DVD from the Royal Albert Hall concert in 1968, their last proper show before 2005.

2005, Cream reunion, London

For the last of the four concerts Claude Nobs, the owner and manager of the Montreux Jazz Festival came to London and told me about it. After speaking to Yolanda, we invited him and his friend to come to our place after the show for some Spanish tapas and wine and he agreed to do so. We had everything prepared when Claude came and had some good Rioja and chatted about the shows and music in general. I showed Claude my three limited edition books by Herbert Joos, featuring his drawings of Miles Davis, Billie Holiday and Chet Baker respectively and he really loved these. I had seen some of Miles' paintings hanging in Claude's chalet in Montreux – amazing stuff and nothing in comparison to the print of a Miles drawing I had.

As Chelsea had won the English league that season, Hannah and I went to the victory parade through our neighbourhood, as we now only lived 4 minutes from the stadium and thanks to Carl, we had seen a few games in this successful season. This was Chelsea's first title in 50 years and a good reason to celebrate. Back in Madrid, Yolanda's friend Patricia, took us to a Corrida, a bull fight. I had never seen one before and was truly impressed with the colours and the choreographed rituals at the beginning. And the atmosphere was really amazing too. Bullfighting in Spain has a very long tradition and is part of the culture there. I watched this one and I was happy that I had seen one, but so far, we haven't been to another. Patricia is a real connoisseur of the art of the bull fight, knowing the various rituals and steps and when it was a good fight or not. I just loved the spectacle and getting to know a bit more of the culture of Yolanda's country.

While I was in Madrid on July 7th, in London four suicide attacks on the Underground and on buses killed 52 people and injured about 700. Yolanda was fine as she took the car to work, but we were all shocked. Flights back to London were suspended for a few hours until it was clear that most likely wouldn't be any more attacks. This was another reminder how dangerous any form of extremism is, whether it be religious or political. When hate stops dialogue, people will suffer.

I visited the jazz festival in Antibes, Juan Les Pins, as Dee Dee was performing there. The French company hadn't renewed her contract, but had asked me if I could sign her, which was fine with me. Dee Dee always was one of my favourite artists, straight like an arrow, no bullshit. She had her opinion on things and didn't hold back, but she always listened and was open for discussion. I trusted her musical instincts completely and offered her a new deal for three albums on Emarcy. Her daughter Tulani, who was and still is running DDB Productions and managing her, and I go back many years as well and therefore we knew what we got ourselves into. We discussed some ideas for the first album and Dee Dee really wanted to do a 'French' album, which I agreed to, as this was something she had told me about a while ago. She wanted to say *"Thanks"* in some form to her new home, Paris and what better way than to do so with music. Afterwards I was off to Perugia to see Al Jarreau and then, together with Yolanda and her friends Yusef and Cati we went to North Sea Jazz in The Hague and enjoyed tons of great music, were hanging out with Michel Camilo and his wife and manager Sandra, were backstage with Roy Hargrove and legendary saxophonist Johnny Griffin, who was as funny as he always was.

Al Jarreau, Perugia, 2005

Johny Griffin, North Sea Jazz, 2005

August brought us, together with Hannah, to Eitzersthal and Vienna. Unfortunately, we had really bad weather, so instead of chilling at Jürgen's pool, we saw a few museums in Vienna. In August we spent some time in Madrid with Hannah and Yolanda's brother Jorge. We went to the zoo, had dinners with friends and once Hannah's friend Edie joined us, we went for a little trip to Toledo and spent time on the pool in the block of flats Yolanda and her mother Maria have their apartments. Upon our return to London, Hannah started secondary school at the St. Marylebone School for girls. Initially they had refused her entry, as she wasn't connected to any religion, but once they had another look at her school reports over the years, they changed their minds and she got thankfully in. A great school that looked after her progress and guided the girls well and having some of her friends going there already made the change easier for her and she quickly made a lot of new ones anyway.

August 2005 was the month when hurricane Katrina hit the US with its full force and caused unimaginable damage in Louisiana, Mississippi and Alabama, but the worst affected area was the city of New Orleans. The levees, a flood protection system with fatal engineering flaws, broke and flooded 80% of the city. Despite the area having been evacuated, many people stayed in their homes, afraid of letting everything behind. The loss of life was reportedly in Louisiana alone around 2000 and Katrina displaced over one million people, who temporarily or permanently searched for new homes all over the USA. Re-building New Orleans took time and a lot of support came from local musicians and their fundraising activities, like Branford Marsalis and Harry Connick Jr.'s 'Musicians Village', created with the local 'Habitat For Humanity' organization.

I had that year made a deal with Ann Marie Wilkins, Branford's manager, and Branford to license the new releases and catalogue of Marsalis Music, the label for Branford's own releases and some artists he liked or produced. We had a label launch event in London with Branford and some of the artists he had signed, including Harry Connick, Jr, who released his instrumental albums via Marsalis Music and guitarist Doug Wamble, performing a few songs at an international press conference. The other releases I brought to Emarcy that year were the Tuck & Patti DVD/CD package 'Live in Holland', featuring, beside the concert, a documentary about the two on the DVD. Another DVD we did was for Terry Callier, whose concert in Berlin was filmed by a local company and we licensed the material for release. A really great show by Terry and his band. Dee Dee's first album under her new deal with Emarcy was the 'J'ai Deux Amours' recording, in which Dee Dee was interpreting famous French songs, most of which had a successful English version as well and so she could switch languages within the songs to stunning effect. The album got her a Grammy nomination and worldwide critical acclaim. Ketil Bjørnstad's new album came about when he, Yngve Naess and myself were having dinner in Oslo, talking about the next Emarcy album and, as Ketil correctly remembers in his liner notes to the recording, I asked him to make an album in a traditional piano trio setting, as he had never done so before. He hesitated, not wanting to let go of his melodic approach, being afraid that without other lead instruments he would play too much. I simply thought it could be a chance to show how to play differently as a trio, staying within the melody and not putting ornaments and endless improvisations into the music.

2005, cover photo for Ketil's promo single

Ketil agreed and began to look forward to the challenge and then went into the studio with bass player Palle Danielsson and percussionist Marilyn Mazur and recorded 'Floating', a wonderful and melodic collection of his compositions that did very well. For the promo single 'Ray Of Light' we used a photo that I had taken in Richmond Park and I thought it was just perfect for this little jewel of music. Meanwhile Veit Bremme had started to book Ketil in Europe with exception of Norway, where Kjell Kalleklev did that job, and we had therefore more things to talk about and work together on, which, with Veit and Peter, always was a pleasure.

Verve Records in New York had a few strong releases as well in 2005, including the new John Scofield album 'That's What I Say', in which John is paying tribute to Ray Charles with a host of special guests including John Mayer, Dr. John, Aaron Neville and Mavis Staples. The third album in the Verve Remixed series did good business and brought the old recordings to a new audience. Wayne Shorter's 'Beyond The Sound Barrier' is a further classic in the saxophonists output and Diana Krall gave us a swinging Christmas album, recorded with the Clayton/Hamilton Jazz Orchestra. Kurt Rosenwinkel delivered with 'Deep Song' one of the best recordings of his career and was at the time managed by Anders Chan-Tideman, who had been Joe Henderson's road-manager and who slowly grew into a friend, whom I always like to see when going to New York.

Yolanda and I got as well friendly with Pat Rains, then manager of Verve artist David Sanborn, and his wife singer Jonatha Brooke, whose music we both love. Emarcy releases coming from local signings included wonderful Japanese pianist Chihiro Yamanaka, Cristina Branco, Wolfgang Puschnig with Indian percussionist Jatinder Thakur and Dhafer Youssef, Niels Petter Molvaer, Spanish Tom Waits-influenced band Marlango with singer/actress Leonor Watling leading the group, and singers Noa, Hedvig Hanson and Rebekka Bakken, to name just a few. Overall, we dealt with about 40 albums on Emarcy that year and while most of them came from one of our affiliated companies and we got music finished and artwork too, we had to create all that for our own signings and thanks to Matt Reid, our in-house designer, we always had great looking covers for our product. Matt understood his brief, often excelled and surpassed our expectations.

Jazzland had a wonderful album by pianist Maria Kannegard titled 'Quiet Joy', plus releases from Beady Belle, Torun Eriksen and Eivind Aarset and Concord's release schedule that year included Soulive, Tim Ries, Dave Samuels and the Rippingtons plus we were feeding their immense catalogue into our systems. ECM introduced us to the wonderful Marcin Wasilewski Trio and had another outstanding release from Tord Gustavsen, plus albums by Keith Jarrett and Many Katché. Arild Andersen's 'Elektra', originally composed for the performance 'Electra' by the 'Spring Theatre' in Athens, is a wonderful and touching album based on the classic tale. Arild had send me the music as it was recorded and I had sequenced it, as I was hearing it as a play, with the chorus introducing each new scene. I really liked my sequence and so did Arild, but when Manfred at ECM finally decided that he would release the album, he did his own sequence, which for me is very good too and proves, that you can hear things in a certain form and someone else will hear the same album different, feeling a different flow and storyline. Which means that not only is the performance of music something individual, but the listening as well and both actions are informed by the person's experiences and history. In any case, this is an album definitely worth checking out.

Classical had a good release schedule in 2005 with albums by Roberto Alagna, Lang Lang, Anne-Sophie Mutter, Cecilia Bartoli and crossover releases from Hayley Westenra and Renee Fleming, whose 'Haunted Heart' album features Fred Hersch on piano and Bill Frisell on guitar and the eclectic repertoire ranges from Standards via Joni Mitchell to Berg and Mahler. A fascinating recording. Deutsche Grammophon had started to use the sub-label eDGe for more world music or jazzy projects and I was happy that with a little bit of my help, Brazilian guitarist, singer and friend of mine, Badi Assad had landed there with her new album 'Verde'. Badi had divorced from her husband Jeff Young and then had some health issues that prevented her from playing for almost a year. We had stayed in touch and when she had new music, I spoke to Hartmut Bender at eDGe and he liked what he heard. Badi did some Promo in Europe and we did interviews in Paris and afterwards went to the Buddha Bar for dinner, a cool place run by the guy who did all the Buddha Bar CD compilations, Claude Challe. The album did well for her and got great reviews around Europe and in Brazil.

John Cumming and his Serious Productions started an educational program for young jazz artists in 2005 called 'Take Five' in which the selected participants would, for a week, receive tutoring and lectures on all aspects of the music business and work on their stage presence and make music together as well. I couldn't go to the first issue to which John had invited me to lecture about the major record companies, but I did send Sascha Kilias and he did it then for two or three times until I had time and took over. And I really liked talking to these young musicians, answering their questions or simply giving them advise for their careers. With quite a few of them I stayed in touch over the years and saw their careers bloom. It was always great to see and chat or hang with John in any case and see John Surman there every year too, as he was the one working with the youngsters on some music performances. I always tried to stay overnight, so I had a chance to listen to some music performed by the participants and never was disappointed.

I think it was that year that Ketil Bjørnstad's book 'The Story Of Edvard Munch' was released in its English translation, to coincide with a major Edvard Munch exhibition at the Royal Academy in London. The book was basically put together by Ketil from Munch's own words in letters and diaries in an extremely detailed and work intense fashion and tells the tale of his doubts, illnesses and successes in a wonderful and personal way. Ketil came to London and did some promotion for the book and for one evening was reading in the Royal Academy and playing solo piano in-between the selections, he read. A very memorable and touching event, to which Ketil had invited Yolanda and myself.
'Kafka On The Shore' is the other outstanding book of that year – Haruki Murakami at his best: weird and philosophical, straight and full of fantasy with a great narrative. Ang Lee's 'Brokeback Mountain' and James Mangold's 'Walk The Line' were my movies of a year, when Danish newspaper Jyllands Posten published the controversial drawings of Muhammad, which enraged radical Muslims around the world. In the year the trial of Saddam Hussain began and Angela Merkel assumed office as the first female Chancellor of Germany, I turned fifty years old.

We had decided to have the celebrations in Madrid and everyone we spoke to, loved the idea. Thanks to Yolanda's mother Maria and her brother Jorge, we had a place reserved in time. As Yolanda had won once again two free international business class tickets at the Christmas raffle of KLM from the previous year, we decided to go to Aruba for a week in early October. Yolanda had also booked the KLM staff hotel there and it was simply incredible – they had a boat going from the lobby of the hotel via a short tunnel out to sea, to a small private island, which had a restaurant, bar, gym and tennis courts and wonderful beaches with flamingos and leguaans roaming freely. One of the best holidays ever, with a bit of snorkelling, good food, walking around and reading on the beach with a drink next to us. What else can you ask for? When we checked out, we saw that they hadn't charged us for the breakfasts, which we every day had as the most important meal for us, but, when pointing out the mistake, the guy behind the reception simply said: *"This must be your lucky day then!"* Lucky indeed.

When getting back to London we heard that for unknown reasons the place we had booked for the birthday party had cancelled on us. We had to start from scratch again, but luckily found a nice place to rent called Mi Bodega, in the centre of Madrid. Thanks to Jorge, who knew someone who did catering for events, we quickly had that sorted too and all could go ahead as planned on my birthday. Family and friends came from all across Europe to celebrate with us. My parents didn't make it, as travelling got too exhausting for my father, Hannah flew in and my sisters and brothers came with their partners, with the exception of Marlis, who wasn't free that time. Yolanda's family was there via her aunt and uncle and of course her mother and brother and from Vienna came Wolfgang Puschnig, Heinz Krassnitzer, Rainer Rygalyk with Andrea and representing the gang from 'miles smiles' were Christian, Monika, Tom and Freja. Yngve and Cecilie as well as Ketil came all the way from Oslo and the rest of the more or less 50 people were locals – friends of Yolanda whom I knew meanwhile and liked and my friends form Universal in Madrid.
We had a really great party with wonderful food (especially the Jamon Ibérico got great reviews!!!) and good wine and the best company one could ask for.

at my 50th birthday party with Ketil, Wolfgang Puschnig and Heinz Krassnitzer

Yolanda was the perfect host, making sure people mingled and had a good time and Hannah running around, taking photos and smiling at everyone. Once the party was over, Patricia took Puschnig and a few others to a Flamenco bar to end the night with music. My nephew Sander had asked if we could get him tickets for a Real Madrid game when he was in town for my birthday. We tried, but without success. I then asked Javier Pouso, the head of Classics & Jazz for Universal in Madrid if he could help and he said he would check on it ... and indeed he came back with two tickets for Sander and Poul and they were for the VIP Lounge, where the guys got snacks and beer served during the match. Despite Real losing to Valencia, they had a great time. Hanging out with my family in Madrid was a lot of fun and only reminded us that we should do that more often.

2006

The year 2006 started with the usual trip to Asia for local meetings and talks about the bigger releases for the forthcoming year. Back in London Hannah told me that her friend Maeve was a big Jamie Cullum fan and that she had her birthday the day of his concert at the Hammersmith Apollo and if I could get us tickets to go. We would invite her for a sleepover and then go to the gig, without her knowing. I called Marc Connor, Jamie's manager and got the tickets as well as a short meet & greet before the show. All was set up and we went on the big day and Maeve was extremely happy to, not only have seen the show, but to have met Jamie personally as well and having a bit of a chat with him. The two girls brought their school teddy bear with them, who would every weekend stay with someone different from class and then they had to report on Monday what the activities and experiences of the teddy were. I am sure going to a gig and meeting the artist wasn't happening too often.

a school bear's outing …

After that Yolanda and myself took off for a few days in New York – I had to attend an international Verve meeting and then we were recording the second Michel Camilo & Tomatito album, for which I had made the deal for Emarcy.

The Verve meeting was good fun and it was great to see all the guys and ladies again in one spot and Tommy presented us with the new recordings for the year: Diana Krall's 'From This Moment On', wonderful interpretations of standards with the Clayton/Hamilton Jazz Orchestra and Gerald Clayton on piano on a few tracks; new music from Roy Hargrove, who had been busy recording with the RH Factor their new funky album ' Distractions' featuring D'Angelo and a straight ahead jazz album called 'Nothing Serious'. We had a little showcase of Elvis Costello together with Allen Toussaint, introducing us to the music of their Joe Henry-produced album 'The River In Reverse', a great New Orleans influenced recording. After the meeting was over Yolanda and myself met up with Sandra, Michel and Tomatito and went to the rehearsals for the recording. These were done in the cellar of the Steinway building in NYC and it was great to see the two masters go through some of the music. At one point someone called Juan Luis Guerra was about to join us. I didn't know then who he was, but when I told Yolanda, she was very excited about it and told me how great a singer he was. The next day we went into the studio and the recording was quick and amazing and Yolanda was right, Juan Luis did an amazing job on the one song he was guesting on.

Michel Camilo and Tomatito in the studio, 2006

When it comes to Latin and Spanish music Yolanda knows much more than I do and she has introduced me to a lot of other groups and artists as well, in the same way I introduced her to some jazz artists she hadn't known before. When we talked about the cover of the new Camilo/Tomatito album, Michel thought it would be best to continue with the theme of the first album 'Spain', which was a drawing of the two and as the new album was to be called 'Spain Again', it made sense. Yolanda's brother, Jorge, was an art teacher and did a lot of drawings and paintings and photography, therefore I asked him if he would like to come up with a cover idea for the record and he immediately said "*Sí*". The artwork he delivered was stunning and both artists loved it and Matt Read put it all into a beautiful album package, ready for release.

Easter, I spent with Hannah in Denmark, seeing Barbara, Christine, Sander, Dorthe and all the kids attached to them. A few days of fun with my parents, who always loved a full house.
Beside the Camilo & Tomatito album, for which we had a release concert in Madrid and some promo work while they were touring, we were setting up a few other records I had done the A&R for or I signed already made and one of them was the Randy Crawford & Joe Sample album 'Feeling Good'. Pat Rains, as well David Sanborn's manager, came to me with this album, produced by Tommy LiPuma and I loved what I heard from the first to the last song. Not a filler on that record and Randy sang so beautiful, with Joe's tasteful accompaniment filling spaces and giving colour to the songs.

We had the rights for the world excluding North America and Japan and we did very well with the album, as they toured as well in Europe. We did a bunch of interviews while on the road and it was always fun to hang with Pat, Joe and Randy. The first time we went out in London we went in Marylebone, close to their hotel, to a restaurant called Fishworks. They sold fresh fish as well and had cooking classes in the restaurant in the off hours. We always ate well there and drank Albariño, the great Spanish white wine from Galicia that goes perfect with fish. As a digestive we had Orujo, the Spanish version of grappa and Joe loved it! From then onwards, whenever they came to London, we ended up at Fishworks. I even bought Joe the cookbook with their recipes. Once they were performing at the Hammersmith Apollo and Hannah came with us for the concert, which was amazing. At one point, when they played 'Imagine', I think half of the audience was in tears over Randy's emotional take of the song. We went backstage afterwards and had a drink with Pat and the group and Joe offered the next time when in London he would give Hannah a piano lesson. What a wonderful guy he was! Always a smile on his face, generous, gentle and understanding and an outstanding pianist and composer.

Another release that year was the second album on Emarcy for Madeleine Peyroux, 'Half The Perfect World', a record of originals and wonderful covers sung in the unique style of Madeleine. She did a lot of press and TV for the album and it did well globally and allowed her to tour internationally as well. At one point she had trumpet player Ron Miles in her band, who gave the music a jazzy edge and wonderful colours.

I had heard that Sonny Rollins had started his own label Doxy Records for his future releases and thought that he would need someone distributing these recordings and that someone should be me. I sent an email to his media person for many years, Terri Hinte, and told her to let him know that I was very interested in distributing his label, all artistic freedom given. And I told her that I could come and see him while on tour in Europe in July, preferably at the Vitoria-Gasteiz Jazz Festival. Terri came back to me after a few hours and told me that Sonny was happy to talk to me after the show in Vitoria and was looking forward to meet me there. And so was I. I, of course, was familiar with Sonny's music for many, many years, but I never had met the 'Saxophone Colossus' and the chance to work with him was too good to pass on. Yolanda and myself had planned anyway to go to Vitoria, as Michel & Tomatito were to play there as well and we had a CD signing arranged with Javier and Alex for them after the show. On the same night flamenco singer Enrique Morente performed with his group and we all went for a wonderful late dinner together, talking music and enjoying the amazing food and the great Rioja wines of the restaurant El Portalón. And I had helped the festival to make a little jazz cover exhibition, by sending them a few from old Verve and Emarcy LP's.

Dinner in Vitoria. Yolanda with Tomatito and Enrique Morente, 2006

The show Sonny played was really amazing and he had so much energy, hardly ever taking the saxophone down. We went after the show to say *"Hi"* and he was surprised that I had reacted so quickly and wanted to distribute his music and after I explained what I was doing and how I saw a possible deal being structured, he simply told me to get in touch with his lawyer in New York, Peter Shukat, a legend in the music business for his work with Jimi Hendrix, Miles Davis, Bob Marley and John Lennon amongst many others. And so I went to New York and sat down with Peter to talk business and within two hours we were done and had a deal. After all I had heard about Peter, I couldn't believe it. I didn't think I had overpaid or gave away too much, just got a fair deal. Peter was friendly and straight and cool and I had the impression that he was happy with the deal too. The first album in the agreement, a new studio recording titled 'Sonny, Please' was ready to go and we released it in the fall of 2006. The album got a Grammy nomination the following year in the Best Jazz Instrumental Album, Individual or Group category, which in the end was won by Chick Corea's Concord release 'The Ultimate Adventure'.

Normally I would have waited with the release, but this was Sonny Rollins, so we didn't really need to introduce the artist to anyone. The usual way to set up a record for me was to talk to the artist and/or manager and see when the master would be ready, once that was established, we would set up the schedule for long lead magazine interviews, creation of tools, release date, more promo and then tour. The key is the release date. Once that is set you work backwards four or five months to send out music to all marketing managers around the world, so they could, in turn, send it to long lead magazines they were targeting with the album. At the same time, you started to create marketing tools, like videos, video interviews, interview discs, display material for shops and concert sales, merchandise like t-shirts for competitions or send journalists somewhere to see him perform and for interviews. Closer to the release date there would be more interviews for radio and weekly or daily newspapers and the same would appear after the release. Then the tour would start about six weeks after the release and these dates would give the artist another wave of promo opportunities or just concert reviews. Of course, not always one could hang on to this time frame, as recordings were delayed for one or the other reason, and then we had to rush to get the album out in time for the tour, which had been booked a year in advance already. I always thought it is better to rush the album than not having it for sale when the tour starts, as a great concert is still the best promotion for any new record. You like the gig; you buy the album on the way out because you want to relive the emotions of the show.

Sonny is such a wonderful, gentle and caring human being, working with him has been one of the highlights of my professional career. Over the coming years we talked a lot about ideas and concepts and started to chat once every two or three weeks, a pattern that would last for many years. At one point I called Sonny, just after the had come back from some dates in Japan and he told me had had been very close to play what he heard inside of himself and he was very happy about it. Another time I called and he was practising some licks on the sax and just said *"Hold on for a minute"* and I could hear him in the background running through this one phrase over and over again, until he was happy and then we could talk. A fascinating and deeply spiritual person, who seemed to enjoy his chats with his record company executive and believe me, so did I and I learned a lot on the way as well.

I had licensed the new project by pianist and composer Ketil Bjørnstad, a three CD set of solo piano recordings. Norwegian master sound engineer Jan Erik Kongshaug had decided to move his famous Rainbow Studio to a new location and Ketil had come up with the idea to record on the last day of the old studio and then again on the first day when the new studio would be open and had prepared two discs worth of material. That in the end, it would be a three CD set had to do with the fact that a benefactor asked Ketil to pick a Steinway piano for the new studio and he was the first to record on that instrument. 'The Rainbow Sessions' is a collection of melodic and beautiful solo piano miniatures, all written by Ketil with the exception of a piece by Brahms and a traditional Christmas song. I helped a bit with the sequencing of the three CDs and came up with the concept for the cover, which, as usual, Matt Read executed into a wonderful overall design. I love these miniatures and listen to this music a lot, always having it with me and especially on air-travels it has been my audio companion ever since.

The Esbjørn Svensson Trio was one of the hottest groups in Europe and doing very good business for their label ACT Music, owned and run by music biz veteran Siggi Loch. But they were not as successful in the rest of the world as they were in Europe and so I took the chance when offered and made a deal for the America's and Asia and the first album that I worked with was 'Tuesday Wonderland', with the outstanding track 'Goldwrap' on it. I flew to Stockholm to the live presentation of the album and after the gig I hung out a bit with the trio and their manager, Burkhard Hopper, who as well was their agent and whom I knew for many years. Pianist Esbjørn, bass player Dan Berglund and drummer Magnus Öström had this incredible tight understanding and their communication on stage was impressive, intuitive. I really liked their music and they were developing a very unique and recognisable style. All three of them seemed to be very nice guys on top of it, which makes working together much easier.

Other releases on Emarcy, coming from all over the world, included that year the 50th birthday special edition 3 CD box set of Wolfgang Puschnig called 'Things Change', some cool remixes of Nils Petter Molvaer's music, a new Chris Potter titled 'Underground', a great new album by Rebekka Bakken, as well as, releases from Richard Bona, Bajofondo Tango Club, Japanese pianist Makoto Ozone, Mari Boine, Marlango and Silje Nergaard. These and more kept us busy and made sure the jazz guys in the markets had enough repertoire to deal with.

2006, us by Jorge Chalmeta

The North Sea Jazz Festival decided to move from The Hague to Rotterdam, as one venue in the complex in The Hague needed to be demolished to make place for something else and Rotterdam's Ahoy Arena was big enough to deliver a similar feel and atmosphere. It was difficult at the beginning to find my way from venue to venue and to the respective backstage areas, but once I had my shortcuts sorted, I enjoyed Rotterdam a lot, as it definitely had a bit more space. We had stopped doing Verve Nights, as we didn't have the marketing funds anymore to do so and Verve had less and less new acts to present. Paul Dankmeyer had left the festival and there was a new team of bookers, Michelle Kuypers and Sander Grande, working with Theo. Both Sander and Michelle are extremely open and knowledgeable and we had many good discussions about new acts and ways how to present legacy artists within the festivals.

One of Yolanda's neighbours has a flat in Benicassim, two minutes from the beach, and they offered the flat to us for two weeks that August. We gladly accepted and flew in with Hannah to spend time on the beach, eat Paella and overall have a relaxed time. For the second week Maria and Jorge joined us and we went for a little trip to Morella, located too in the Community of Valencia. In Morella they celebrate the Sexenni every six years since the seventeenth century as a remembrance of overcoming The Plague. There are processions and dances in the honour of the Virgin Mary and the city is decorated with paper artworks, created over years before the festivities. The year we visited one street was decorated with artwork based on the paintings by Keith Haring, another inspired by Disney. It was impressive to see these artworks and all the colours and processions. A very special event and we all enjoyed having seen it. We had found a place to stay the night a bit outside of Morella in a very small village, where the school had closed as there were not enough kids anymore to go there and, in the restaurant, you needed to book dinner in advance, so they knew for how many people to cook. There was no menu, they cooked and you ate. We booked a table and came for dinner, which was heavy food with sausages and so on, but really excellent. The place was packed, even a group of Germans had found their way there. I was full and tired and when we got to our house to sleep, we all crawled into our beds quickly. The church tower then started to ring its bells every 15 minutes. I couldn't believe it, as during the day and dinner we hadn't heard it, but now it was clear and loud. After finally drifting off, we heard a big bang downstairs. Jorge had fallen off his small bed! Back in our bedroom we heard Maria stumbling over a heater and cursing. Then, having falling asleep again, I had a nightmare and lashed out around me and hitting Yolanda unintentionally. She woke me up and that was it concerning sleep that night – the church tower kept me awake until we had to leave. A strange night in the 'haunted house', but something to remember forever.

2006, Morella

In 2006 legal digital downloads reached 795 million tracks and a staggering 1 bn on iTunes since its inception. Spotify was funded in Stockholm that year, immediately changing the streaming market in Sweden from an illegal to a legal one. Google bought YouTube for over $ 1.6 bn and integrated it into its portfolio. The football World Cup in Germany was won by Italy against France after a penalty shoot-out. Serbia and Montenegro became independent states, ending an 88-year lasting union. I was reading Haruki Murakami's collection of short stories 'Blind Willow, Sleeping Woman' and Ketil's 'To Music', which became his biggest international success as a writer. Günter Grass's first part of his memoir, 'Peeling The Onion' was another captivating read that year, in which I went to the movies with Hannah and Yolanda to see films like the second part of the 'Pirates of Caribbean' series or

'Borat' by the incredible Sasha Baron Cohen. We still travelled between Madrid and London a lot, to see Yolanda's family and friends and relax with good food for a few days. And we went to Vienna for some hot wine and visiting the Christmas market with my brother Jürgen and his wife Uschi.

Concord had a strong year in terms of releases in 2006, above all the new Sergio Mendes album 'Timeless' featuring the Black Eyed Peas in a new version of Sergio's old hit 'Más Que Nada'. Sportwear company Nike decided to use that song globally in all their advertising around the football World Cup, which gave us a lot of exposure of the song. When Sergio heard that we would be working together he sent me a short note and a signed photo saying *'Great to know that we are working together'*. We planned a European interview tour for Sergio and he always told me in advance in which hotels he would like to stay and in what restaurants he would like to eat. He knows his food and wine like no-one else. When he was in London for promo, I had invited him and his wife and singer Gracinha Leporace for lunch after he had an interview at the BBC.

I can't remember the name of the restaurant, but when Sergio arrived, he knew already which wine he would order and what to eat, as he had checked the menu before online. He loved his food and always went to the best places. Once he had invited Hannah and myself for lunch at an Italian restaurant, but unfortunately the whole block had no electricity, even so for Sergio and us they still managed to create some incredible food. 'Timeless' did well for Sergio and Concord and put Sergio back on the map again in a big way. 'Más Que Nada' was already a huge hit for Sergio in 1966, recorded for his debut album with his band Brasil '66 on A&M Records. The song is originally from Jorge Ben, but Sergio's version is, by far, the best known globally. Sergio always liked to have the sounds of the time in his recordings, therefore re-doing that song in a new and updated version made a lot of sense. And the Black Eyed Peas were the best choice for doing so. The other two outstanding releases by Concord were the George Benson / Al Jarreau album 'Givin' It Up' and Chick Corea's 'The Ultimate Adventure'.

Our friend Jonatha Brooke released a 'Careful What You Wish For' album, which we both liked a lot and we went to see her in Milton Keynes perform music from that album. Unknown singer Melody Gardot self-released her first album 'Worrisome Heart', which started a bidding war of sorts between Decca UK and Verve Records, with Decca signing her in the end. They would put 'Worrisome Heart' out globally in early 2008. Melody had a horrific accident when riding her bike at age 19, being run over by a car, which left her seriously injured. She used music as therapy, writing songs while at the same time learning to walk again. She would struggle for many years to come from the sustained injuries.

Dhafer Youssef had played over the last few months a lot with Norwegian musicians, including Bugge and Eivind Aarset. He finally recorded with some of them in Bugge's studio and then decided to give the album to Jazzland Recordings to release. 'Divine Shadows' is a very strong album, mixing Sufi chants with jazz and electronica, ambient sounds and driving beats. On top of all of those soars the clear and touching voice of Dhafer, full of soul and emotions. He can get me every single time I go to hear him live – his voice is so pure, his chants the simplest and at the same time deepest expression of emotions, transporting, while not having words, no fixed meaning, but lots of emotions that can reach deep into the listener. Torun Eriksen, violinist Ola Kvernberg and the Mungolian Jet Set were further interesting releases from Jazzland. ECM released the outstanding 'Vossabryg' by Terje Rypdal, a live recording from Vossa Jazz 2003, inspired by Miles Davis' 'Bitches Brew' and featuring Terje's son Marius as a composer and on electronics, samplers and turntables. Singer Susanne Abbuehl's second album 'Compass' was another highlight on their release schedule, as were Keith Jarrett's incredible solo show from 2005 'The Carnegie Hall Concert' and Charles Lloyd's 'Sangam'.

In a year in which the jazz world lost percussionist Don Alias, whom I had met when he was performing with Wolfgang Puschnig, as well as mourned sax player Dewey Redman and Austrian jazz legend, trumpeter Oscar Klein, I was listening to Charles Tolliver's big band album 'To Love', wonderfully produced by Michael Cuscuna and the Pat Metheny / Brad Mehldau duo album. 'Back To Black' was the stunning second album by singer Amy Winehouse, which Yolanda and I still hadn't managed to catch in concert, as the one time we had tickets, she cancelled the show.

Deutsche Grammophon tried to move into a more contemporary classical world and released the beautiful album 'Songs From The Labyrinth' by singer Sting together with lutist Edin Karamazov. This record of the music by John Dowland was the start of a series of four records Sting did with DG and which I was working internationally. Another modern release was the second Elvis Costello album, this time live at North Sea Jazz 2004 with the Metropole Orkest and performing classical arrangements of his songs. The second CD in the set included the music for a ballet Elvis wrote, recorded at Abbey Road. The rest were typical DG albums by Anna Netrebko, Krystian Zimmerman and Lang Lang. Decca had moved strongly into releasing soundtracks and did pretty well with these, but the big albums of the year were Andrea Bocelli's 'Amore' and Ludovico Einaudi's 'Divenire'. They also had the second album by Canadian crooner Matt Dusk. I remember being invited to an industry showcase for him and I liked his voice, but thought it was all too much Frank Sinatra and not enough Matt Dusk. I told the Decca UK guys that and mentioned that I would never sign him, as every country has at least one singer of this kind and quality, so it would be hard to sell internationally. They signed him nevertheless. The first album didn't do much and neither did the second outside of Canada, which is where he is doing well, but hardly anywhere else. Decca Records had a change in management that year, with Bogdan Roscic coming from DG to run the UK based label and Costa leaving the company. The jazz division had moved to Chiswick into the Decca building and was now sitting at the same floor as Bogdan, so we had more time to chat and work on some marketing and other ideas together.

For Christmas Maria and Jorge came to visit and we spent together with Hannah a few great days and a wonderful Christmas in our little flat and walking around in London. Jorge took tons of pictures and tried a few new techniques with beautiful results. He really had a good eye for photography.

Portrait of Hannah by Jorge Chalmeta

I ended 2006 and started the new year the way I like to do it: with family. Christmas at home with Hannah and Yolanda and New Year's Eve in Madrid with Yolanda and her family or in Denmark with my family. A few quiet days at home, focused on people I love and without thinking too much about work. My work is very important to me, but I never defined myself through it, but through who I am as a human being, my personal history. As much as I liked what I did then, there was always more to life than the job. Family first of all. I had seen, when at PolyGram in Austria, how the financial director of many, many years had a heart attack when he was told that he had reached the age of retirement, as he had nothing beside his job. He was defined through his work and once that was gone, there was nothing left. That I wanted to avoid, because I knew that when this work would be gone, me as a person with other interests, could be as happy as working a job I really liked. I knew I would find something to do that I would enjoy, surely something to do with music in some form, even if it would only be to finally listen to some of my old LPs and CDs again. And there are so many books to read, movies to see and friendships to maintain.

2007

Business started with a trip to Tokyo for the regional Classics and Jazz Meeting, as usual with all labels and their international representatives, including Concord. We had violinist David Garrett doing a little showcase of his first crossover album 'Free'. Then I was off to Paris, as we had John Medeski, John Scofield and Billy Martin doing international press there for the new MSMW album 'Out Louder', which I had signed on for Emarcy. Alex Sanchez/Universal Spain had come with a few journalists and it was good to see him again and chat a bit. John was as well working on a new album and as Verve had not renewed his contract, I stepped in and signed him for three future recordings. 'This Meets That' was the first album in our deal and it was John's Trio with Steve Swallow on bass and Bill Stewart on drums plus 4 horn players. All music was arranged by John and with the exception of three songs, composed as well. This is a real great record with some of John's best writing, like 'Heck Of A Job' and 'Pretty Out' and some outstanding playing by all involved, including Bill Frisell on a wonderful 'House Of The Rising Sun'.

I was back in Paris a month later, this time with Yolanda, to see Dee Dee Bridgewater's new project live for the first time. 'Red Earth – A Malian Journey' was released later that year to critical acclaim around the world and garnered another Grammy nomination for Dee Dee. The combination of jazz and Malian roots music worked extremely well and Dee Dee standing out with some of her best vocal work ever. Having Malian musicians recording this journey back in history made it even more exciting for her and authentic for the audience. The show was not only a musical delight, but a visual one as well, with colourful costumes and lights. That's Dee Dee: whatever she decides to do, it will have style and class. She might bring in a co-producer for certain elements she isn't an expert in, as here with Cheick Tidiane Seck, but she knows what she wants and how to achieve it. Not much to do as an A&R guy here, but still rewarding to be part of the journey making this album with her. For the initial release in Europe, we did a limited edition 2 CD set, which included a DVD of the 'Motherland' Documentary, filmed when Dee Dee was in Mali to record the album. These limited editions usually sold out fast, so helping to get higher into the (jazz)charts and giving the core fans something extra. I think we did about 10.000 units of this edition and they were gone quickly. Till today, this is one of our favourite Dee Dee Bridgewater albums, among the many great recordings she did.

I always had been a fan of The Bad Plus, the wonderful and quirky trio that took pop and rock songs and played them like jazz tunes and their own compositions had this unpredictability and fun in them, that made the group a favourite with a younger audience. Their manager at the time, Darryl Pitt, whom I knew from working on the Verve albums by Michael Brecker, who was his client as well, asked me if I was interested in signing them for Europe and of course I was. 'Prog' their first album for us is an eclectic mix of their own music and songs by Tears For Fears, David Bowie and Burt Bacharach. All three guys in the band are really nice and cool and we got on extremely well and the album did good for us too, with the guys working hard and touring a lot. Darryl and I spoke about Michael Brecker, who wasn't doing that well at the time. Michael was diagnosed in 2005 with the blood disorder myelodysplastic syndrome (MDS) and was globally searching for a stem cell donor without success. In August 2006 he felt strong enough to go into the studio to record a new album. At that time Michael was looking into the music of the Balkan region and I had sent him some CDs to research and listen, like the Bulgarian Voices or Goran Bregovic's recordings. But he hadn't gotten deep enough into that yet to record something with that influence and therefore he called some of the best jazz musicians around to record with him his new music: Herbie Hancock and Brad Mehldau on piano; Pat Metheny on guitar; John Patitucci on bass and Jack DeJohnette on drums. Despite being seriously ill, Michael sounds powerful and clear. Six months later, on January 13th, 2007

Michael Brecker passed away in New York. The album 'Pilgrimage' went on to win international awards and 2 Grammy's. It was posthumously released in May 2007 on Emarcy in Europe and Asia and in North America on Heads Up. I really liked Michael, a very kind and humble human being, always interested in new sounds and ideas. He always was asking me what was going on in Europe and I sent him some music from Nils Petter Molvaer, Bugge Wesseltoft and others, so he could hear the new sounds we were working with. I was glad I got involved in this album after Verve didn't renew his contract and I will never forget this outstanding musician and friendly man. His death hit us all in the jazz community pretty hard.

I had been talking to Larry Clothier, Roy Hargrove's manager, to sign Roy to Emarcy, as again, Verve didn't seem interested in continuing with him. In the end we did a deal via Groovin' High Records, run by a friend of Larry's, Jacques Muyal, and included Italian singer Roberta Gambarini in the deal. We had to wait a bit longer for Roy's first album, but Roberta delivered, as her Emarcy debut, a duo recording with the wonderful Hank Jones, titled 'You Are There'. In Japan the album was released by my friend and ex-colleague Hiroshi Itsuno on his own label and was called 'Lush Life' and had a slightly different track listing. Roberta is a top jazz singer with great taste and feel for the standards. In combination with Hank, this becomes a dream team and outstanding music. I had spoken a few times over the last few months with Ketil Bjornstad about the next album for Emarcy and told him that I could hear a bass clarinet with his compositions and that I thought that Wolfgang Puschnig, whom he had met at my 50th birthday party, would be the perfect player for and with him. Ketil thought about it, then asked me to get the two of them in touch, which I did and then he went on to record his new compositions with Wolfgang, Arild Andersen on bass and Alex Riel on drums. Wolfgang plays not only alto sax and bass clarinet on the album, but as well various flutes. I liked the idea to have a suite as the centre piece of the album and Ketil's three part 'Suite: Dance Of Life (After Edvard Munch)' is the paintings main colours white, red and black, set to music, expressing the themes of Munch's art: Mortality, Desire, Anxiety and Isolation. Only someone who really had studied the painter's life could transform paint into notes as Ketil does here.

Easter, we spend as usual with my parents in Denmark. They loved to see us and Hannah loved to be there and see Ulla and Masanti and Barbara and the rest of the gang, whoever made it there any given year. I knew that the time with Hannah would be rarer in the future anyway. She was growing up, being a teenager and became of course more interested in spending time with her friends than her dad, but we still did our trips and had a good time, whether it was in Austria, Spain or Denmark.

2007, Hannah and her grandpa

Yolanda and myself had decided to get married and do so in Madrid. She claims that she asked me, but I have a slightly different memory about that. Unfortunately, normally she has the better memory and is usually accurate in her accounts, so it might be wishful thinking on my part that it was me who proposed.

I spoke to Hannah about it and she was fine with it, wanting me to be happy, even so I am sure inside it wasn't all that great for her, as she still somehow might have wanted her parents to get together again. But our decision was made and we therefore went to the Spanish Embassy in London to get the ball rolling. They would collect all the necessary papers and then pass them on to the registry.

Maria, Yolanda's mum, had helped us with that and booked a date on July 7th, 2007 in San Sebastian de los Reyes, Madrid. We didn't even ask for that 07/07/07 date, but it was for sure one to remember. While the Spanish Embassy basically got all the documents together for Yolanda, my Embassy didn't do anything and therefore I had to get all papers myself, so much for German efficiency.

Starting with a birth certificate from Hünfeld, which then had to be sent to Kassel to get the The Hague stamp. It took me a bit to convince the lady in my birth place that it would be best if she could send the document to Kassel and not to London, only for me to send it back to Germany. In the end, she did, but as a favour, not because that's the way to do it.

Once we got it back from Kassel and passed it on to the Spanish authorities, they told me that the 7 language EU version wasn't what they wanted, but the German original version, as it had the religion of the parents mentioned as well. One wonders why there is a European Union and European forms for certain things …. Back to Hünfeld and asking for the right certificate, again begging it to be sent directly to Kassel for the stamp and when I finally had it in London it needed to be translated into Spanish by an approved translator!!! Unreal!

Next was a certificate from the police of the last German city I lived in to confirm that I was allowed to marry. Calls to Berlin Lichterfelde and Steglitz until I got to the right place. Then again asking if they could send it directly to wherever in Berlin they would put the The Hague stamp on it.

Issuing one of these documents cost about € 10, but the money transfer from London to Germany was almost double that. Welcome to Europe. It was simply a bureaucratic nightmare and we almost gave up and were close to get married in London, where you only needed your passport, a copy of your birth certificate and a utility bill or bank statement with your name and address on it.

But we got everything together just in time for the Spanish Embassy to send it to the registry in the north of Madrid.

07-07-07, wedding day in Madrid

Meanwhile we made the list of invitees and send the invitations out and checked the restaurant of a friend of Jorge, which is located in the neighbourhood of their flats in Vallecas. Paco, the chief, cooked a few things for us to try out and we tested a bunch of wines as well. The place was new, Paco a great guy and the food excellent, so we booked the restaurant for our wedding dinner. Then a week before the wedding we got call from Maria saying that the registry hadn't received the papers yet and time was running out. Yolanda checked with the Embassy and they confirmed that they had indeed sent them. After pressing them a bit more they recognized that they had sent the papers to the wrong San Sebastian – while the papers where in the Basque country, we were to be married in Madrid. They promised to make sure that the papers would be there in time and if not, we decided that we would have the celebration anyway. As the big day drew closer, people from all over the world came to Madrid to celebrate with us. From my family it was of course Hannah and then Jürgen and Barbara who attended, as we had planned a family party in Denmark for later that month anyway.

Friends from Australia (Tim & Tina) came, as well as Esther & Bill from London, Puschnig representing Austria, Yngve and Cecilie Norway, Dhafer Youssef came from Paris to join us and Yolanda's mother, her brother, grandmother, uncle and aunt and all cousins with spouses. And all our close friends from Madrid joined us as well (Amparo, Cristina, Patricia, Claudia, Jose & Inma, Yusef & Cati, Toño & Ofe, Javier & Luci, Nicole & Gerry and many more). First, we had the official ceremony with a smaller group of guests, followed by a drink in a local place around the registry.

The big event was the dinner at Paco's place and he had decorated the tables perfectly and did food that was beyond expectations. At one point Alex Sanchez came over to me and asked: *"Is this El Buli, or what?"*. We had told my sister and others that we didn't want any speeches, as we just wanted everyone to enjoy the dinner and time afterwards, but Cecilie did one anyway and it was great fun and ended with Yolanda and myself on chairs kissing, every single time she made a noise with her fork on her plate.

The atmosphere there was simply amazing. I have never before and never since experienced such a great feeling within a room of people who didn't know each other, but all having a great time. Yolanda's grandmother chatting with everyone who spoke Spanish and everyone who didn't! She had a ball and Dhafer was sitting next to her talking to her and holding her hand. The vibe was really special.

In the afternoon, before the dinner I had checked my emails and there were tons of well-wishing ones, but the one from Chick Corea stood out, as he had attached a little song, recorded in a hotel room on the road and titled 'Wulf's Wedding Song'. Yolanda and myself were in tears when listening, as we never had expected such a wonderful gift from Chick. I hoped the night would never end, but it did and we all went home in the early hours of the day after, happy, tired and grateful.

2007, wedding dinner

As it is custom on weddings in Spain, the couple gives a little farewell present to its guests and we had put together a CD with some of our favourite songs, called 'Music Affair' and featuring all great music by friends and artists we knew or liked. And it was something that made sense for us: we met at a jazz festival, both were passionate about music and so could pass a bit of that on to everyone at the dinner. While our guests made their way home, Yolanda and I went to Olmedo for a few days to relax in a Spa. Fully deserved after all the excitement of the wedding.

MUSIC AFFAIR

01) The Bait - Ketil Bjornstad
02) Pale Blue Eyes - Marisa Monte
03) Cover Me With Snow - Rebekka Bakken
04) Careful What You Wish For - Jonatha Brooke
05) Until You Come Back To Me - Hil St. Soul
06) The Truth - India.Arie
07) Forget Regret - The RH Factor
08) Feeling Good - Randy Crawford & Joe Sample
09) Bad Spirits - Dee Dee Bridgewater
10) Dipita - Richard Bona
11) Doce Nao Entendeu Nada - Badi Assad
12) Soul Rewind - Puschnig/Thakur/Youssef
13) Spain - Michel Camilo & Tomatito
14) Lagrimas Negras - Bebo & Cigala
15) Volar - Paco de Lucia
16) Familia Habichuela - Pitingo
17) As de Corazones - Chambao
18) Fuego - Las Ninas
19) Amor de Conuco - Camilo/Tomatito/Guerra
20) Yolanda - Pablo Milanes
21) Time After Time - Miles Davis

A week later we were at North Sea Jazz in Rotterdam, listening to great music once more and meeting friends. There we had a chance to say *"Thanks"* to Chick for the song he had sent us and got to hear Ketil and Wolfgang perform the music of the new album together with Arild and Alex. Ketil then dedicated in the concert the song 'Devotion' to us newly married couple, which I thought was extremely nice and touching.

Ornette was there and so was Dee Dee with the powerful 'Red Earth' show and Dave Holland, Roberta Gambarini, Nils Petter and many more. It was a great weekend of shared fantastic music.

Ornette Coleman and Chick Corea, backstage at North Sea Jazz, 2007

Three weeks after the wedding we went to Denmark to celebrate my sister Barbara's 50th birthday and again, with the rest of the family, our wedding and as Barbara and Yolanda share the same day for their birthdays, we celebrated Yolanda's birthday as well.

Hannah, Maria and Jorge had come with us for the party and all my brothers and sisters with their kids and friends of the family were there as well. The kids had tents to sleep in the garden and the adults stayed in the few hotels in Rødby. A Goulash was cooked on an open fire for one evening, a party tent set up and the catering service brought the food for the big event. Jorge was the official photographer and gave us so many wonderful captured memories.

As every time when all of us come together, we took a photo of the parents, then one of them with their kids, one with the kids and partners, with the kids and their kids and then one with everyone, this time about 40 people. What a party and all documented by Jorge's great photos!

2007, the complete family plus close friends

As a family, with everyone living somewhere else all over Europe, we don't come together that often, but when we do, it is like we had only yesterday seen each other for the last time. We have a lot of fun, as we are enjoying each other's company, laugh a lot and joke around. We have as well individual chats about the things in our life's, but as a group it is truly hilarious and some of our kids, like Alexander, Patrick and Hannah have grown over the years to become part of the circle. A great family!

At the end of August and in early September I travelled with Hannah to Vienna and Eitzersthal for a few days to see Jürgen and Uschi. My brother took us to the album presentation of 'Neuer Morgen', the new album by the group STS – just three singers with their guitars and occasionally some extra instruments. Together they had a long and successful career in Austria and Germany and it was great to see them again after some years. Ludwig Hirsch was there as well, another special artist with lyrics and songs that were unique.

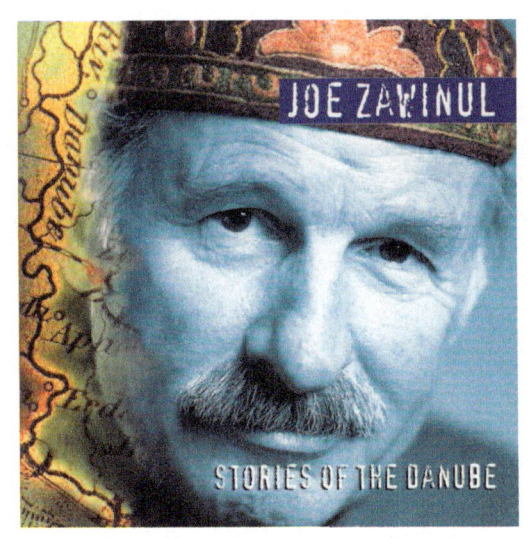

Peter Kokoefer, a friend from Austrian TV, told me at that event that Joe Zawinul was in Vienna in the hospital and not doing well. I had heard that he was ill, but didn't know that he was doing badly. Joe passed away on September 11th and it was for me as if he had given up, wanted to be re-united with his wife, who had died earlier that year. Joe just had finished his tour, had celebrated his 75th birthday on our wedding day and then gave up the fight. I will remember Joe and his typical Viennese sense of humour for ever.

In October I went to Vienna for his funeral, a touching celebration of his life and music. Austrian violinist and friend of Joe, Toni Stricker, played a really emotional homage and when we left there was no dry eye around. In the evening there was a reception with food and drink in Joe's club Birdland in Vienna – all the Viennese food Joe loved was served as well as a special Schnaps, that carried his name. Joe's three sons were there and we spoke briefly as I knew them from before. Heinz, Wolfgang and Harry Gruber paid their respects along with many other musicians I knew.

Jo Clarke had unfortunately moved to a different position within Universal and therefore we needed a new assistant for our marketing and production activities. I looked at a few and, in the end, we brought in Lucie Cooper to assist me and Sascha and to be there when Chris was in town to assist him as well. Beside our own signings we again had a lot of international artists to deal with on Emarcy. There were four recordings coming from Austria, Harry Gruber enjoying a good run with some really great records, a handful from France, Japan and Norway, plus recordings from Germany, Belgium, Spain, Poland and so on. It was pretty amazing to be able to work with so many amazing artists from all over the world and constantly to listen to new exciting music. By releasing and working local albums outside of their home markets, we surely unlocked some doors for a more European openness and music exchange. While it was rare to have European artists at a jazz festival in the past, by 2007 it was something normal and we at Emarcy, together with labels like ECM, enja, ACT and others did help to make that happen. Jazzland Recordings continued to release great albums, that year by Bugge Wesseltoft, Eivind Aarset and Hakon Kornstad among others and ECM contributed Tord Gustavsen's 'Being There', a new Keith Jarrett Trio live recording from Montreux and the beautiful 'Folk Songs' by the Trio Mediaeval. Concord's main releases came from young and exciting trumpeter Christian Scott, whose first album on a big label was a pleasant and modern surprise; Chick Corea, whose duo album with Bela Fleck 'The Enchantment' did very well in the US and fine everywhere else; singer Curtis Stigers jazzy 'Real Emotional' and 'Supermoon' by Zap Mama. Verve continued to release less core jazz recordings, but their incredible 'River: The Joni Letters' by Herbie Hancock was a real hit. Herbie had invited various singers, including Joni herself, to work with him on Joni's music and lyrics. The guests included Norah Jones, Tina Turner, Corinne Bailey Rae, Luciana Souza and Leonard Cohen. The album is deep musically and shows Mitchell's art in a new light, but remains accessible and beautiful to listen to. Herbie came to London to promote the new album and did a TV show called 'Live From Abbey Road', filmed at the famous studios. There his guests included Corinne and Melody Gardot, who did a great job singing Joni's songs the way Herbie heard them. This was great for Melody especially, getting to play with Herbie for this show even before her first album came out. Verve's other bigger releases from that year included Queen Latifah's 'Travelin' Light' and Luciana Souza's touching 'The New Bossa Nova'. Meanwhile I was listening to the new Metheny / Mehldau Quartet album and the stunning Wolfgang Muthspiel / Dhafer Youssef collaboration 'Glow', as well as Dutch singer Trijntje Oosterhuis' album with the Metropole Orkest and Vince Mendoza, 'The Look Of Love'.

Apple Corp. released the first iPhone in the US and later in the year in six other countries, so finally starting the age of the smartphone. Bulgaria and Romania joined the EU and Slovenia became part of the Eurozone. In Blacksburg, Virginia, student Seung-Hui Cho went on a campus killing spree, leaving 32 people dead and wounding another 17, before committing suicide. As usual a short-lived discussion about American gun laws followed, but, again as usual, without any results. I never understood the gun philosophy in the USA: the right to carry or own a gun for me implicates the right to use it. The easy access to weapons in that country has cost so many lives and nothing ever seems to change, as the gun industry keeps hammering into people's heads, their 'right' to weapons. Is it therefore a surprise that many police actions end in a shooting? If, as an officer, you have to expect that you will be facing someone carrying a gun, it will always be about who shoots first. I am not approving police brutality, far from it, but I am trying to put myself into their shoes and if I have to defend my life, because any person I encounter can or could carry a gun, what would I do to survive? Gun culture and racism are the major problems in the US and it seems over the years nothing has changed.

I was reading Murakami's 'After Dark' and Stieg Larsson's captivating third part of the Millennium Trilogy 'The Girl Who Kicked The Hornets' Nest', as well as the funny and truly human 'Making Money' by Terry Pratchett, whose Discworld series with that book stood at 36 volumes and I had, to my delight, read all of them. In the movies we saw the Coen Brothers 'No Country For Old Men' with the outstanding Javier Bardem and John Carney's wonderful 'Once' with Glen Hansard and Marketa Irglova and some really great music and Marion Cotillard as Edith Piaf in 'La Vie En Rose'.

Yolanda got from our friend Bill two tickets for one of the 21 nights Prince performed in London and happily we went. Bill is a true Prince fan and went seven times and told us that the song list was different for every single show. And what a show it was!!! We both had a great time and simply loved the man and his band. Another act we really got into that year was Imelda May, whose album 'Love Tattoo' is great and rocky and we went to see her live a few times, once Jeff Beck coming on stage to perform with her. Out of the song 'Big Handsome Man' I made a ringtone for her phone, which Yolanda still is using for my calls to her!

Ryanair in November offered really cheap flights from London to Jerez in the South of Spain and we spontaneously decided to go to Cadiz for a long weekend, booked the flights and off we went.

2007, on our first trip to Cadiz

From Jerez we had to take the train, which was easy and when we arrived in Cadiz, I was mesmerized – the weather was amazing, people still going out for a swim. The old city, located on a narrow stretch of land surrounded by the sea, is the oldest documented and still inhabited city in Europe and is wonderful with its narrow alleys, parks and the old market. Cadiz immediately became one of our favourite places and we have tried to go back there almost every year. The people are friendly, there is so much history and sensationally great food.
We ended the year with a relaxed Christmas celebration with Hannah in our flat and then went to Madrid to see Yolanda's family and friends for further festivities and dinners.

2008

The year 2008 started with Yolanda having to go through a big dental operation including rebuilding of some parts of the jaw, a lengthy and painful procedure. She had decided to have this done in Madrid, as her family could look after her much better than her always busy husband and the whole procedure was ten times cheaper than in London. I had the day after she came home to go to Asia for the annual meeting and therefore, I was glad that she was with her mother, caring for her needs. And the day before I had ordered a bunch of red roses to be delivered to her while I was flying to Hong Kong for the Classics & Jazz regional meeting, feeling a bit guilty leaving her there without me. Hannah and I went to Denmark in March for a few days to celebrate Easter with my parents. My father did fine, but was more tired and quiet than I had remembered and my mother told me that he had a heart problem bothering him over the last few months. He was 83 years old by then and his age showed more, than the years before. Christine came as well and we enjoyed the time in our parents' house. Back in London Jorge and Maria visited and we went out to see Dee Dee Bridgewater perform at the Barbican. I think it was still the 'Red Earth' program she did there and Jorge and Maria, as well as friends we invited, Esther and Bill, loved the show. Sascha was there with us too and we all had a good time backstage after the show with Dee Dee. Jorge got inspired by Dee Dee's concert to create a piece of art in a very old technique, which he gave me to my birthday later that year. I simply love it, as technique and expression just come together to celebrate the wonderful artist and human being that Dee Dee is.

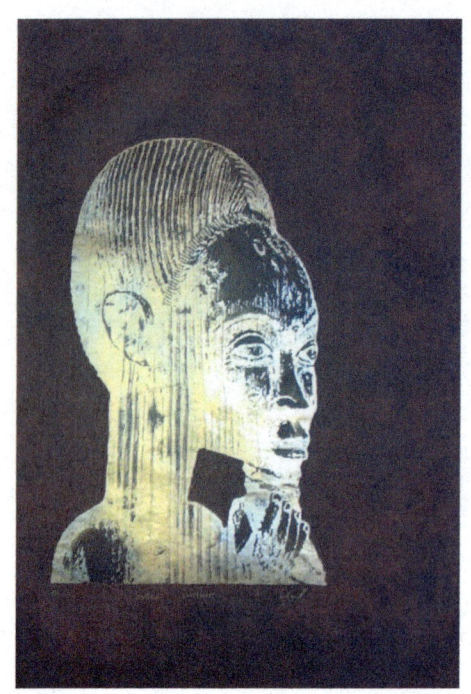

2008, Jorge's artwork inspired by Dee Dee Bridgewater

The father of one of Hannah's best friends is kind of a songwriter, even so earning his living as a travel agent, and he wrote a song for his two daughters and two friends, one of which was Hannah, and got them into a studio to record his composition. They had some photos taken and a cover made and some CDs burned and so they had their own single. I can't really recall the song, but the girls had a lot of fun doing it and learned a bit about the music business on the way. The group was called HUGGS, but it never got beyond that one song, done for fun.
At Emarcy we had another busy year with tons of releases, first of all our own signings, of which we had twelve that year. The first of these was the all-standard recording 'I Remember You' by Tuck & Patti, another masterpiece of duo conversations, vocal control and sensitive accompaniment. Randy Crawford and Joe Sample delivered another outstanding Tommy LiPuma produced album with 'No Regrets', a wonderful mixture of modern tunes and some blues. Randy and Joe were just so amazing together, especially live it was a true jazzy dream team. And again, we saw each other a few times and surely ended up at Fishworks for some delicious food and wine.
'Bare Bones', the new album by Madeleine Peyroux, was the first record with all songs written or co-written by her. There are a few gems in there, like the title track and the touching 'Our Lady Of Pigalle'. Madeleine, as usual, worked hard for the album, which was one really close to her heart and toured around the globe. By now, she was established as a recording artist and live act.
Sonny Rollins had started to dig into his archive of live recordings and started the 'Road Shows' series. Volume 1 featured performances from the years 1980 up to 2007 in different line-ups. Sonny is extremely critical about his work, so selecting the songs for the album had been a long process, but in the end, he was happy with the picked tracks and gave us the master for release. A little bit after that, we released a DVD from a concert in Vienne, France. Sonny was then playing with his nephew Clifton Anderson on trombone, Bobby Bloom on guitar, Bob Cranshaw on bass, Victor Lewis on drums and Kimati Dinizulu on percussion and the show was definitely a great one!! Clifton released on Emarcy, via Sonny's label, that year an album titled 'Decade', as it came ten years after his first recording. A wonderful straight ahead jazz record with some great playing. The new Bad Plus record was a special one in many ways – when they first mentioned they would do a vocal album, I didn't quite believe it, but when they delivered the music, it was just perfect. The trio had invited singer Wendy Lewis to be part of the recording and following tour and they covered songs by Kurt Cobain, the Bee Gees, Roger Miller and, for my taste the outstanding ones, Pink Floyd and Yes. I saw

them perform in London together and it was just amazing. Their usual quirkiness, but with words, the powerful and unique way Wendy played with the melodies and lyrics and as a surprise Reid Anderson as well singing ... and not bad at all!

The rest of the releases came from new signings to Emarcy and one of them was Charlie Haden. I had agreed to sign Charlie when the French ended their relationship, as Charlie was a global bestseller for us. When we did the contract, things got a bit complicated as it was done in the US, with me being in London and usually I like to be close to the legal people, so I could explain why I wanted for jazz a different kind of deal they were used to make. It was usually a much simpler agreement, as some pop related concepts had to go. In the US they weren't used to me doing it that way, so we had endless conversations and at one point Charlie called me at home, complaining about a new draft he got. I was listening to him going on about for almost two hours and explained that I would make sure he got the deal we discussed. Yolanda, who was at home with me, just was amazed how patient I could be, even when Charlie raised his voice. In the end we got the deal done, everyone was happy and Charlie delivered the first album in the agreement, the Americana influenced, biographical 'Rambling Boy', featuring family and friends. This was Charlie looking back to his early years, his parents and the music of that time. A very personal record that finishes with Charlie singing 'Oh Shenandoah' in a very beautiful and touching way. The number of friends on the record is too long to list here, but they all gave something to the timelessness of this album.

Roy Hargrove finally had gone into the studio to record a new album, his first for Emarcy and when his manager Larry send me the music, I couldn't believe it – there were thirty tracks to choose from! And all were amazing! I made my pick, sequenced it and sent it to Larry. It was slightly different to Roy's, but we both at least had picked the outstanding Hargrove composition on the record 'Strasbourg / St. Denis', which became an immediate jazz standard. In the end we put 13 tracks on the record, in a sequence everyone was happy with. This is still my favourite Roy album, not because I was involved in it, but because of the great music, the amazing band he had put together for the recording and touring, featuring Gerald Clayton on piano, Justin Robinson on alto, Danton Boller on bass and Montez Coleman on drums. That same group had recorded as well a show with most of the music from the new record, live at the New Morning in Paris and we also released that gig as a DVD. Both, the album and DVD did very well and Roy was on the height of his career.

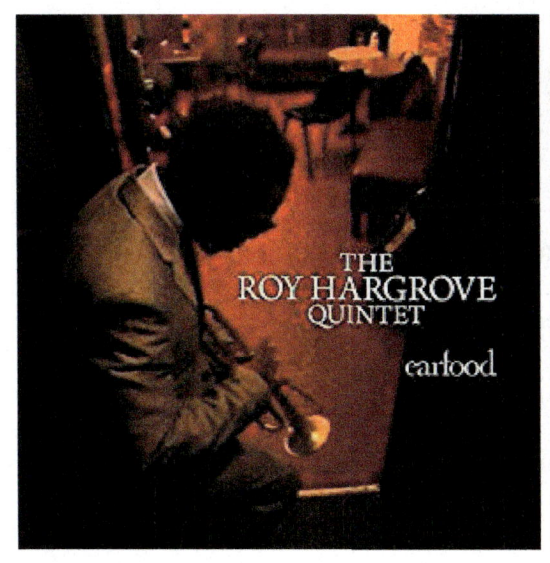

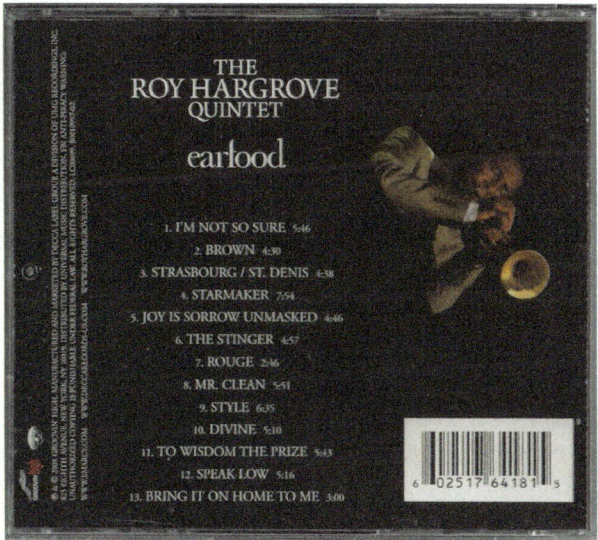

Whenever I met Larry and Roy, we talked a lot about ideas for the next album and one of Roy's ideas was to do some kind of jazz-rock album. In a way something like Miles' 'Tribute To Jack Johnson', but modern, now. Roy had some ideas, like using the Red Hot Chili Peppers' Flea on bass, Mike Stern on guitar and I joked *"and Lars Ulrich on drums"* and he kind of liked the idea of using a real heavy rock drummer. But that record unfortunately never happened. Would sure have been cool! Roy came to

London as special guest of Johnny Griffin's band for a few days of performances at Ronnie Scott's and I went there to say *"Hi"*. Griff was amazing as always and full of great and funny stories. Roy was in top form and there were too Griffin's agent Gaby Kleinschmidt, her husband, writer Mike Hennessey, who just had released a book on Johnny Griffin, which I bought right there ... and had it signed by both, Griff and Mike. A great book! Gaby's son, Frank, who runs the label In&Out Records, was also there and as we knew each other from before, we had a great chat about music.

Soenke Lohse, manager and booking agent from Germany, called me to ask if I would be interested in Italian guitar player and producer Nicola Conte's new album 'Rituals', featuring new songs by Nicola and a host of great guests. Nicola had always a thing for great voices and on this album, he featured Italian singer Chiara Civello, Jose James, Kim Sanders, Philipp Weis and Alice Ricciardi. Other guests included Till Brönner, Greg Osby and Timo Lassy. This is a groovy and swinging modern album, that was also great on stage and Nicola went out to play a bunch of festivals that and the following year.
I always wanted to work with Bill Frisell, of course because of the 'miles smiles' gig and his great recordings. The closest I came to that was by releasing a soundtrack he had recorded for a low budget Canadian film titled 'All Hat'. A cool record with little miniatures and sound clips, which can stand on their own and don't necessarily need the images.
Sax player James Carter was another great artist I had signed. He was managed by Cynthia Herbst and being with good management always helps. James is a great guy and wonderful player, fierce and energetic. He has a technique on his horn, that allows him to play anything, there seem to be no limits for this guy. When I heard him first, I always thought that he was packing too much into every song, kind of showing off what he could do. Over the years he got better and used his technique to improve the song and the improvisation and that was what I wanted. I had heard an album by the Charles Tolliver Big Band 'With Love', that was produced by Michael Cuscuna, a legendary producer and re-issue specialist in the jazz world and I thought he would be great to have to make the album James needed to do. I met with Michael, he said *"Yes"* and after instructing him that we want James' outstanding technique to enhance the songs, but not be the centre of the album, they started to work. 'Present Tense', so the title of James' first album for Emarcy is a truly great record and when the first reviews came in, they were fabulous and incredibly positive. Michael and James had delivered big time!!!

The Grammy awards that year brought a few surprises, one was that Michael Brecker with his album 'Pilgrimage' won two awards posthumously for best instrumental jazz album and best instrumental solo and the real big one was that Herbie Hancock's 'River: The Joni Letters' won not only best contemporary jazz album, but as well the overall category of best album of the year!!! Only once before a jazz album had won this award in the history of the Grammys: in 1965 the album 'Getz/Gilberto' by saxophonist Stan Getz with Brazilian icon Joao Gilberto. This was really special and we all were extremely happy. When I saw Herbie a few months later in London at the Classical Brits in the Royal Albert Hall, where he was performing 'Rhapsody in Blue' with classical pianist Lang Lang, we had a great chat. And when I asked him *"What is going to be the next project"*, he looked at me and said: *"Oh, you don't know! Verve has forgotten to take the option in the contract, so I am free to go with the next record wherever I want!"* I couldn't believe my ears, but when checking with Verve the next day they had to admit, that they had let pass the deadline of the option and therefore lost Herbie. Right after the artist had won the biggest prize available for any album in the US, our guys at Verve forgot to look at the option calendar, if they had one, and because of that we lost one of our biggest jazz acts. It was hard to believe and I didn't blame Tommy, as he was there for the music, not to administer the deals, which was on Ron Goldstein's side of responsibilities. But what had happened, happened and we would have to bid for Herbie's next album, as anyone else who would want to put that out.

The international releases again came from many different markets and covered all facets of improvised music. The big one here, approved to be released on the Verve label, was Melody Gardot's 'Worrisome Heart', a stunning album of amazing songs and vocal performances. And of course, Till Brönner's 'Rio', featuring Sergio Mendes, Annie Lennox and Melody Gardot, which did exceptionally well in Germany. A Richard Bona live album, plus records from Dave Holland, Jef Neve and many others rounded up the release schedule.

Earlier in the year I had gotten a call from my colleague Javier Pouso in Madrid, asking if I knew a good Gospel choir in London and I recommended the London Community Gospel Choir and asked why he would need that info. A young flamenco singer by the name of Pitingo wanted to use a choir for his new album. Shortly after, Pitingo, who didn't speak much English, and Javier plus management came to London to record at the Townhouse Studios, which I had recommended as well. I went to check it out and it was amazing to see how Pitingo basically sang to the choir what he wanted them to do and the recording moved pretty fast that way. We released the resulting album 'Souleria' as well in 2008. The album is a mix of Soul and Flamenco, Pop songs treated in a new way and when one hears his 'Killing Me Softly With This Song', featuring the Gospel Choir, it is simply incredible. And so is his version of 'I Will Survive'. The limited edition came with a DVD featuring a live concert, which is fantastic as well.

Once that year agent Veit Bremme came to London with his wife and I invited them for dinner. Yolanda and I liked a little Thai in our area, Sukho, and I asked him if this was okay and he mentioned that they loved Thai food. Actually, which he had told me was that they were going every year to Thailand and had cooking classes there too. I was a bit nervous about the place we liked and how it would compare, but they loved the food, thought it was authentic and extremely well done. After the meal we went to our place for a night cap and I put the DVD with Pitingo on. They both loved the show and Veit said he would discuss internally and see, maybe they could book Pitingo.

Polish singer Anna Maria Jopek was working on a new album, when she called me and said she would need a special voice for one or two of the songs. I asked her a bit more about the music and then told her to check out Dhafer Youssef and if she liked the voice, I would talk to him and get them in touch with each other. She called a few days later and asked for Dhafer's details, which I sent to her, after having checked with Dhafer and explained him who she is and what she wanted. After a few months passed without anything, one evening while I was still in the office, she called and told me, in tears, that she was in Paris in the studio with Dhafer and that his voice moved her so much and that she was extremely thankful for the recommendation. The album 'Jo & Co' features as well percussion master Mino Cinelu and Richard Bona as guests and is for me one of Anna Maria Jopek's best.

I was at home with Yolanda on Saturday, June 14th 2008 when I heard the sound of an incoming text message on my mobile phone. I got the phone to check and couldn't believe my eyes. The message was form Pino Brönner, Till's brother and manager at the time, and he wanted to let me know that Esbjørn Svensson had had a diving accident and had died that day aged 43. That was a true shock and I immediately went online to seek confirmation, even so I knew if Pino had sent this message, he would have checked as well before. The trio had just delivered a new album, 'Leucocyte', which now was to be released posthumously. The European jazz world had lost one of its brightest and most creative spirits and the void would be felt for some time to come.

When on the morning of July 3rd my office phone rang, I picked up and on the line was my mother. My parents more or less every year for a week or two in the summer rented a house somewhere on the Danish coast for a relaxed vacation. Often, they would go to a place called Hvide Sande on Mid Jutland, at the Ringkøbing Fjord. They had planned for this year to do so as well, but while on the way there, my father's health problems made him collapse and he had to be brought to the hospital.

As he wasn't improving, he knew that his life would come to an end soon and therefore had asked my mother to call all his kids to come visit and say Goodbye. My sisters and brother living in Denmark went immediately. After speaking to my mother, I called Jürgen and we arranged to meet later that afternoon in Hamburg. I called Yolanda and told her what was going on, went to the airport with just a few promo t-shirts and an airline washbag that I had in the office and flew to Hamburg. From there we drove to Hvide Sande, where we met Barbara, Thomas, Marlis, my mother and the kids of my brother and sister, who had come for my father, but as well to celebrate the birthday of my mother, her 80th, on July 5th.

In the afternoon of July 4th, Jürgen, my mother and myself went to see my father in the hospital, who was happy that we had come. Even so he was physically in a bad shape, his mind was clear. The doctors asked us if we wanted to have my father put on life-saving machinery and both Jürgen and I answered *"No"*, as this was my father's wish. All kids and my mother had given them the same answer and they were impressed how everyone in the family respected our father's wishes. He chatted a bit more with us, happy that we all together had some great times, had fun, good food and drink. He was content and, in some way, ready to move on. Which was kind of really good to see, but heart-breaking on the other hand. When he told my mother that he was ready, she simply said that *"it was now the time to channel his energy not into living, but to pass on"*. We left him there, he smiled at us and the same evening we got the call around 10 pm that he had passed away.

He left the day before my mother's birthday, not to spoil the day for her forever. It was obvious that my parents had spoken about him passing and somehow, they found the spiritual depth to deal with this in a realistic way. My mother never showed her deepest feelings directly, but I am sure when alone she struggled and suffered more than all of us. Especially when she went to say her last goodbye, seeing his body before cremation. She asked me if I wanted to go inside as well, but I simply couldn't and didn't want to blemish the memory of the last time I saw him in the hospital, smiling. It all had happened so fast, there was hardly any time to process what had happened and we were on our way back home. My father had left my mother a folder with all information she would need to deal with his death. Phone numbers, contact details and so on. He even instructed her through this, which hymns to sing in the memorial service and what food to eat when the family came together to celebrate his life. The funeral service was set for 2 weeks after his passing in a small church close to where they did live at the time.

one of the last photos I took of my father, March 2008

In the meantime, I went to the North Sea Jazz Festival, as I couldn't just sit at home and think about what happened. I was looking forward to see my family in a weeks' time and celebrate my father's life, but I needed to go out and be distracted. We had a lot of artists playing there and no-one knew about the passing of my father, as I usually keep these private things to myself. Melody Gardot did a wonderful show in which at one point a mobile phone started ringing and she reacted to it in a cool way, joking around, so making the person who hadn't switched it off, see his or her mistake without being called out in front of many people. After the show I went for a drink with her to a wine bar, open to the general public and she enjoyed having selfies taken with her from a grateful audience. I like Melody, as I always got along very well with her and see her as a down to earth, warm human being. A bit later during the festival, when I went backstage to say "*Hello*" to Wayne Shorter, he, before I could say anything, asked me: "*Why are you so sad?*". I was surprised and relieved at the same time, as I now could tell someone and Wayne, who had felt me dealing with the loss of my father, listened. Wayne, like no-one else I know, feels people, receives their vibes on a much deeper human level and therefore can react to them better than anyone. When I left his little room in the backstage area, I was still in a kind of shock of what just happened and came across Danilo Perez, Wayne's pianist and a good friend of mine and I told him the story. "*Oh*", he replied, "*Wayne is doing this all the time. When I was told by my wife that we were expecting our first child and went to Wayne to tell him and share my happiness, but before I started talking, he already had said 'Congratulations'. He is so deep, man*".

It is difficult to write about music, as it is all about an individual reaction on the emotional content of the composition or performance, but writing about feelings is even more of a challenge, as how can one put into words what the soul experiences? Feeling is the physical component of emotions that come straight from the inner depths, the core of any human being. Individual, subjective and indescribable, at least for me. I can't seem to find the right words to explain the loss of my father for me, maybe because I don't know myself or I am just not good enough in expressing myself. Other writers might be able to, but I struggle with that. My father's funeral, or better the burying of his ashes, and the family-come-together were planned as follows: first we had the ceremony in the church, short, touching and, for me at least, another way to say "*Goodbye*". All of us had tears in our eyes, when the ashes went into the unmarked grave, feeling the end of a chapter in all our lives. Whether as father, grandfather, grand-grandfather or father-in-law, he was a role model for all of us in some way. For me it was his openness and willingness to learn, trying to understand and to accept what his kids' decisions were in their lives, even so he might not always have had the same opinion.

The small Danish church, where my father's ashes are buried

Former colleagues and neighbours liked and respected him and all came to the church service, which was followed by everyone having a drink and some food together in a nearby place. After that it was only family in my parents' house. Everyone was there, all children and their kids and my mother's brother with his wife. We had typical food from Hessia, the region my father was from in Germany

and drank apple wine, also from there. And we told stories, endless and funny and we remembered together all the good times we had, laughing a lot. A true celebration of his life, parts of which we are all carrying within us.
In August we went with Hannah to Madrid to spend some time in the sun and at the pool in the house were Maria and Yolanda have their flats. We did a few little trips in the area around Madrid and had some fun, including a great barbeque at Jorge's place with a handful of friends. And we were of course watching the Euro 2008 in Austria and Switzerland, which was won by Spain in Vienna with a 1:0 victory over Germany. Yolanda was, of course, over the moon!

The year saw the stock market crash as the mortgage crisis hit the financial world, followed by the bankruptcy of the Lehmann Brothers financial services. Cyprus and Malta joined the Eurozone and the Kosovo declared its independence from Serbia. The Google Chrome browser was released for the first time and the Android system introduced for mobile phones, quickly becoming the dominant software in this field. In Sichuan, China an extremely powerful earthquake shook the region and killed an estimated 87.000 people and, in the USA, Barack Obama was elected the 44th president and the first Afro-American! A sign of hope! A fire at Universal Studios in Los Angeles resulted in the destruction of some attractions and about 40,000 to 50,000 archived digital video and film copies, according to Universal. Only through an article in the New York Times Magazine in 2019 the full disaster of this fire became known: up to 175.000 audio masters belonging to Universal Music, some of them the originals that hadn't been digitised yet, had disappeared in the incident. Universal tried to deny, but was later forced to confirm the loss of many irreplaceable master tapes. The list published by the New York Times Magazine is endless and includes among many others jazz artists like John Coltrane, Dave Brubeck, Terry Callier, Louis Armstrong and Earl Hines. One would think that a label would be looking a bit better after their most valuable assets!

Verve had a slow year and after all the excitement and shock with Herbie and the forgotten option, they simply released a compilation with most of his biggest hits, the fourth instalment of the Verve Remixed series, the David Sanborn album 'Here And Gone' and Brian Blade's 'Season Of Changes'. Concord put our another cool Sergio Mendes album with 'Encanto', co-produced by Will.I.Am and featuring a ton of special guests, including Italian singer Jovanotti, Ledisi, Fergie and Natalie Cole. Sergio again worked a lot for the album, toured Europe and Asia. In Japan we had some promo, followed by an outstanding dinner in which Sergio gave the colleagues from the Japanese company a lecture in Sake. Wines and food are his passion beside music and family and he knows so much, but this was a real surprise for everyone. One time, when he was playing in Rotterdam at the North Sea Jazz Festival, Sergio invited Yolanda and myself to dinner on the Friday evening. As we only had one act performing that night, we gladly accepted and met Sergio at his hotel and then drove by car to the restaurant, a Michelin star place outside of Rotterdam, directly at one of the many canals. Gracinha joined us a bit later, as her flight was arriving after Sergio's. They never fly together when on tour, as in case of an accident, their kids would always have one parent surviving. The food in that restaurant was outstanding and Sergio ordered some incredible wines. At one point he didn't agree with the young sommelier on a certain year from a certain French vineyard. He took out his phone, called the owner of the vineyard and passed the mobile to a perplexed sommelier. Normal for Sergio, but something truly special for the young guy. And Sergio always paid. Even when I said it would be on the account of Universal. He loves being the host and seeing people enjoy great food and drink with him. The other Concord album that stood out that year was the Chick Corea / Hiromi 'Duet' album, a musical communication between two wonderful artists, recorded live at the Blue Note in Tokyo the previous year.
Jazzland gave us the groovy new Beady Belle album 'Belvedere', and the New Conceptions Of Jazz box set, while Marsalis Music released via Emarcy the outstanding Miguel Zenon recording 'Awake', produced by Branford Marsalis. ECM had a strong year with many great releases, but for me the outstanding one was the Ketil Bjørnstad / Terje Rypdal duo album 'Live In Leipzig', a dynamic and

powerful recording of two masters of their instruments, which at times sounds much fuller than just a duo. In a year when jazz celebrated the 50th anniversary of the release of Miles Davis' 'Kind Of Blue' with a special edition box set, the jazz world lost, beside Esbjørn Svensson, the extremely talented and truly wonderful person and pianist Bheki Mseleku; trumpet player extraordinaire Freddie Hubbard and composer, clarinettist, saxophonist Jimmy Giuffre.

I was listening to Musiq Soulchild's 'OnMyRadio', the Roots, the new Metallica album 'Death Magnetic' and the incredible new album by our friend, singer Jonatha Brooke, 'The Works'. Jonatha had gotten access to the texts, letters and lyrics of Woody Guthrie, picked a few and set them to music. Then recorded these new songs with an all-star band featuring Joe Sample, Christian McBride and Steve Gadd, added a few special guests and had a record that I truly love and still often listen to. 'Madonna On The Curb' and 'My Sweet And Bitter Bowl' are just two of the many incredible songs on the album. She came to England for a few shows and we of course met up and saw her perform, which was a truly wonderful experience.

There weren't too many classical priority releases, but the most successful one was Andrea Bocelli's 'Incanto', featuring his version of 'Santa Lucia'. Core classical releases came from Renee Fleming, Placido Domingo and Helene Grimaud, to name a few, but it was the album 'Raising Sand' by singers Robert Plant and Alison Krauss, that stood out for me. Originally released in the US on Rounder Records, Decca took the international rights and this blues oriented, country rock album became a huge hit – and deservedly so. Produced by T. Bone Burnett and featuring Marc Ribot on guitar, this collection of songs is simply out of this world, especially 'Please Read The Letter', on which Krauss as well plays the fiddle.

Carlos Ruiz Zafon's captivating 'The Angels Game' was my book of the year and in the movies, we went to see 'Mamma Mia', a charming story based on the music of ABBA and Danny Boyle's 'Slumdog Millionaire' with the wonderful Dev Patel.

When in late 2008 I got a call from Ted Kurland and he was talking about a 'kid' he was managing and I definitely should listen to, I had no idea what I was going into. I asked him to send me the music and meanwhile I googled a bit on Julian Lage, as this was the 'kid', found the documentary Ted was talking about, 'Jules at Eight' and other stuff and was intrigued. Then I got the music he just had recorded with a great band, including among others Taylor Eigsti on piano, Bela Fleck and Chris Thile. The songs were mostly his own compositions and showed an artist mature beyond his age. He was 20 years old then. I called Ted and said that I wanted to be part of this story and agreed, which was unusual at the time for a completely unknown artist, to license the new album and put it out on Emarcy. When I met Julian the same year, I encountered a humble, smart, charismatic and intelligent young man, who knew what he wanted. I always liked talking with him about music or whatever, as he is following what is going on in the world, not only in terms of music. We did actually pretty well in terms of global sales for the first album, which we released in 2009, having in mind that not many people had heard of Julian before the release of 'Sounding Point'. We were all really enthusiastic at Emarcy and as he toured a lot, he continued to build a profile globally. And meanwhile I was looking at another new and young artist for a debut in the coming year.

Hannah turned 15, was still really good at school, spend a lot of time with her friends and in general was a normal teenager. I didn't see much of her daily life and behaviour, as she was living with her mother, to whom I still said often that she should try to stand on her own feet, as I might be losing my job one day, as so many others had over the last few years in our department and the music business in general. And then what? Telling her, reminding her and outlining the consequences was all I could do. Hannah came over for the weekends when she wasn't with friends and for holidays, which she enjoyed with us either in Madrid or sometimes in Austria or Denmark.

Before the year was over, I quickly went to Berlin to see Sonny Rollins perform at the Philharmonie. It was, as always, a wonderful and amazing concert, with Sonny improvising on the highest level, continually throwing little references to other songs into his music. The audience went really wild there and loved the show. Afterwards we were backstage, together with the German team, led by

Christian Kellersmann. Sonny was happy with the show and to see me to discuss the second Volume of his Road Show series.

with Sonny Rollins and Christian Kellersmann in Berlin, 2008. Photo by John Abbott

I flew back the following day, after meetings with the German team, ready for a holiday. Christmas, we spent as usual together with Hannah on the 24th in our place and had some great food, opened presents and had a relaxed time together. For New Year's Eve Yolanda and I had travelled to Lisbon, Maria and Jorge with us, to see the city and celebrate with Yngve, Cecilie, Alex and Estefania at Paulo Ochoa's place, which was a lot of fun and a really great way to finish the old and start the new year!

2008, New Year's at Lisbon

184

2009

At the 2009 Grammy awards, 'Raising Sand' was the big winner, with 5 Grammys, including Record and Album of the Year!! We had as well had a nomination each for John McLaughlin and Till Brönner, but unfortunately, they didn't win. In another move to cut costs I had to let Lucie go and from then on it was just Sascha and myself in the department, plus the digital team, which got smaller as well. Wendy Life thankfully offered to help when necessary and came occasionally over with Chris to look after him when he was in town.

In March Yolanda's family from Colombia visited and we went together to see their son Pierluigi, who was living in Milton Keynes with his family and working for the Red Bull Formula 1 racing team. We got a tour through their premises and it was really interesting and cool to see all the cars from the past and present. After the death of my father my mother decided to travel a bit more again and visit her kids. She came to London in late March and we showed her around London, went to exhibitions (she especially liked the Egypt exhibition at the British Museum) and shopping and had dinner at the Blue Elephant. I think she really had a great time with the three of us. We then spent Easter at home in London with Hannah, just taking it easy.

Sightseeing in London with the three women in my life

My mother was still living in the same house, which now was too big for her to maintain, she therefore was thinking of getting a smaller one in the region, as she had some friends there. But that move didn't materialize and she finally decided, as we had suggested, to move closer to where Barbara lived at the time, to be nearer to one of her children.

My A&R work yielded seven records in 2009, very different projects, but all great music. For me, what I was doing at Emarcy was simply to 'collect' artists I liked and make it possible for them to record the albums they wanted under the best possible circumstances. I am not a music producer, but I can help the artists to make the best record they can do at a certain time in their career. Running a little label like Emarcy was for me like being an art collector, with the artist in the centre of all activities. The new acts we had that year were Julian Lage and the pianist in Roy Hargrove's band, Gerald Clayton. Gerald, managed by the wonderful and extremely professional Gail Boyd, had financed the recording of his first album via artistshare and was looking for a label. Gail called me, sent me the music and as I knew Gerald from Roy's band and performances and the quality of his playing, I signed him to the Emarcy roster. His first album 'two-shade' is a wonderful trio recording with bass player Joe Sanders and Justin Brown on drums and brought Gerald his first Grammy nomination, something he shared that year with new label mate Julian Lage. Roy Hargrove's Big Band album 'Emergence', a powerful statement by the trumpet star, got another Grammy nomination for us and so did the new Roberta Gambarini album 'So In Love' featuring James Moody and Roy as special guests. I had signed the Medeski, Martin & Wood box set 'Radiolarens: The Evolutionary Set' for the world excluding North America. This amazing limited-edition set included 2 LPs, 5 CDs and a DVD and sold pretty OK for such a big and expansive set. John Scofield went to New Orleans to record his latest album 'Piety Street' with a bunch of local musicians, including George Porter Jr, John Boutté and John Cleary. I went to Amsterdam to see this band perform at the Paradiso, the perfect venue for them and I really enjoyed the New Orleans grooves, Cleary's voice and of course John's wailing guitar. A truly great recording and groovy live band. As the limited edition of the Ketil Bjornstad three CD set 'The Rainbow Sessions' had run out, we decided to release a single disc compilation from the sessions, titled 'The Rainbow'. Ketil did the sequence, but I helped a bit and asked him to use the same composition as the first and the last song, but from different sessions, so the whole album was like a circle, starting and ending with 'Solace'. Despite being a compilation, I think this album stands on its own and has a wonderful flow and atmosphere. In many ways it feels like a rainbow converted to sounds.

In April, the UNESCO launched their World Digital Library to promote international and intercultural understanding. The digital library is open to the general public and hosts important historical documents, photos and films, dating back over 8000 years. Slovakia joined the Eurozone and the Czech Republic the EU, while the H1N1 influenza strain caused a global pandemic called the 'swine flu', being found in over 200 countries and causing the death of about 8000 people.

Spotify started in the UK and in June the world's biggest selling entertainer Michael Jackson passed away at the age of 50. Two weeks before his show 'This Is it' was about to start in London, he died from a heart attack. As a musician he leaves a legacy of outstanding and timeless songs, as a human being, with all the child abuse allegations being part of his life, he has failed to be the role model he wanted to be. The jazz world lost Hank Crawford, Charlie Mariano, whom I had met with German singer Konstantin Wecker, Blossom Dearie, the wonderful singer and really kind lady, who once showed up at my office while in London and playing at Ronnie Scott's to talk about re-issuing some of her old Verve recordings and Ian Carr, the trumpet player, composer, journalist, educator, writer and TV producer. I had first heard of Ian when listening to Nucleus, his unique jazz rock formation of the 70s. Then I heard and saw him with the United Jazz & Rock Ensemble and got introduced to him while in London at a gig at one point and we then stayed in touch. He was an interesting and intelligent guy to talk to and wrote a great biography of Keith Jarrett, but the one he wrote about Miles Davis, 'The Definite Biography', is by far the best of the many I have read over the years. Ian also worked on TV specials about Keith and Miles, which both are outstanding. He has been a true gentleman; a humble and kind human being and his death diminished the UK jazz scene tremendously.

Before going to the jazz festival in Vitoria-Gasteiz, Yolanda and I went for a few days to the La Rioja region to relax and enjoy some great wine. Iñaki had arranged for us a private tour through the Marques de Riscal vineyard, including a wine tasting. Beside their wonderful reds, we discovered that they were doing some refreshing and fruity whites in the neighbouring Rueda region. They are made from the Verdejo grape and really tasted amazing. At Vitoria we had Madeleine Peyroux, Dee

Dee Bridgewater, featuring James Carter, previewing her tribute to Billie Holiday program, and Gerald Clayton, who played at the hotel and provided with his trio the band for the late-night jam sessions, which Dee Dee and James joined in the early morning hours and brought to boiling point.

Dee Dee in Vitoria, with Ira Coleman and James Carter, 2009

My friend Ken Drucker, who had left Verve and was now working with the Jazz At Lincoln Centre Orchestra, had come to Vitoria as well to conclude a deal we wanted to make for an album recorded in Vitoria and featuring the orchestra plus Wynton Marsalis and Paco de Lucia. Thankfully everything went smoothly, the deal was signed and we had a wonderful lunch at one of our favourite restaurants in Vitoria, Sagartoki, which not only makes the best Tortilla in Spain, but some incredible and very unique Pintxos.

After checking out the concert of the group SMV, which stands for Stanley Clarke, Marcus Miller & Victor Bailey, and therefore for heavy and groovy bass lines, we made it back to London. But for me only for a few days and then I went to Rotterdam for the North Sea Jazz Festival, where we had as usual a lot of artists performing. This year they included the Roy Hargrove Big Band, Silje, Melody, Charlie Haden with Brad Mehldau, John Scofield and the Piety Street band and new signing Gerald Clayton, whose trio played an outstanding set for their North Sea debut.

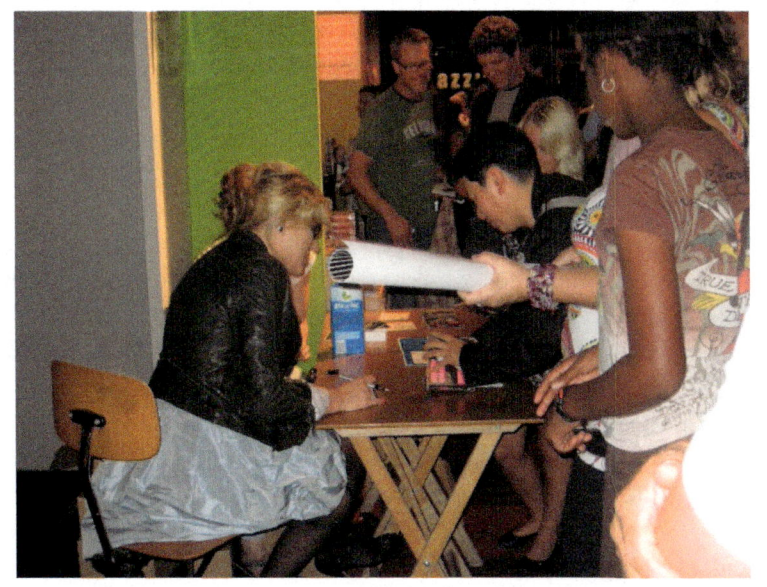

2009, Melody Gardot signing CDs after her show at North Sea Jazz

Of the artists signed to one of our local companies, Melody Gardot, an UK signing, became the biggest seller. Her new recording 'My One And Only Thrill', featuring with the exception of one standard all her compositions and lyrics, had been sent to me in advance, after the first mix. I immediately called the guys in the UK and told them in the final mix to put the strings more in the background, as they were too heavy and sweet so upfront. Luckily Melody heard it the same way as I did and the second mix rectified this problem and the album then sounded fantastic. Produced by Larry Klein, with the strings arranged by Vince Mendoza, this is Melody pure: a bit rough on the edges, but melodic and very cool. An outstanding and timeless record that both Yolanda and I still listen to very often.

Rebekka Bakken had signed a new deal with Universal, but this time in Germany and not in Austria. The German company had more power and connections and so it was a sensible next step. Her first release in the new agreement was 'Morning Hours', a collection of great new songs, produced by Craig Street and featuring her outstanding version of 'Ghost In This House' by Hugh Prestwood, first released by US group Shenandoah. Other releases came from France: Salif Keita, Richard Bona, Lucky Peterson; Germany – Nils Petter Molvaer; Norway – Mari Boine, Kristin Asbjørnsen; Japan – Chihiro Yamanaka and many other countries, including South Korea, (via a deal in Tokyo) which brought us the really incredible album 'Songs Of Coloured Love' by the group Winterplay. Frontwoman Haewon Moon is a strong and at the same time delicate singer, here doing originals and some great covers, like 'Billie Jean' and 'Moon Over Bourbon Street'.
Spain signed the new album by Israelian singer Noa, a collaboration with Mira Awad, a singer with Arabian roots and they both performed together at the Eurovision Song Contest the title song of the album 'There Must Be Another Way'. Noa and Mira showed, as artists should, that we humans are all the same and there is never a real reason for hate and violence. For this alone, they should have won the contest!!

Verve Records in New York gave us another wonderful Diana Krall album titled 'Quiet Nights' and the sticker on the album pointed out that these were *"ballads and bossa novas with quartet and orchestra"*. Diana produced the album together with Tommy Lipuma, Al Schmitt was the recording engineer and Claus Ogerman the arranger – it can't really get any better than that! They did as well a special limited deluxe edition of this release, featuring a DVD with 7 songs recorded live at O.R.C.A.M.'s auditorium in Madrid on May 29th and one song of Diana with Elvis Costello and Elton John. New recordings by Bebel Gilberto and Teddy Thompson did well for Verve, beside some more US oriented albums. Bugge Wesseltoft released his album 'Playing', a solo effort of touching beauty and captivating music. ECM released a live double CD by Jan Garbarek called 'Dresden (In Concert)', which is for sure worth listening to, plus new releases by the Keith Jarrett Trio, Miroslav Vitous's 'Remembering Weather Report' and a new album by the FLY trio, featuring Mark Turner, Larry Grenadier and Jeff Ballad, titled 'Sky & Country', featuring all new and impressive compositions by the three members. Live as well this band was amazingly tight, open and fluid in their music making. The same must be said about the Branford Marsalis Quartet, one of the best bands in jazz and one whose line-up hadn't changed since 1999. Their new album 'Metamorphosen' is powerful proof that better understanding between musicians would lead to better performances. On his label he also released the wonderful Miguel Zenon recording 'Esta Plena', which got 2 Grammy nominations and a new album by Chilean singer Claudia Acuña, 'En Este Momento', which, if I remember correctly, he produced as well beside guesting on one song.
And Concord released George Bensons' 'Songs & Stories', a clever and cool mix of soul, funk, jazz, led by George's voice and guitar. This recording features Marcus Miller, Toninho Horta and Steve Lukather among others. Miller was also the producer of the album, which did very well and George was out touring as usual. Chick Corea and John McLaughlin had recorded their Five Peace Band live and released a rocking and fresh double CD. Beside the headliners the band featured Kenny Garrett,

Christian McBride and Vinnie Colaiuta, plus Herbie Hancock as a guest on the outstanding 20-minute 'In A Silent Way / It's About That Time'.

Hannah and I were reading and watching the Harry Potter saga and we both loved the books and movies. Something we enjoyed together, like our trips. Besides that, she lived in her own world, gave short answers and I had to look back often and remember how I was at that age. Sure, every generation is different, is a product of its time and the values of that time. Another difference was that my generation, the one right after the war, didn't have that much, whereas her generation, or at least a lot of them, grew up with having access to almost everything. And as we, when we were teenagers, they as well wanted to be different than their parents. When Jürgen and I had earrings and long hair in the late 60s and seventies, Hannah's generation had a nose ring or one in the belly button. As every phase in her life, I watched, tried to understand and enjoyed seeing her growing up, being independent and having a great circle of friends, which whom she liked to spend time. Yolanda and I watched the Guy Ritchie movie 'Sherlock Holmes' with Robert Downey Jr and started to read the Scarpetta crime novels by Patricia Cornwell, as well as continuing the Millennium stories by Stieg Larsson, whose second and third part were released in English that year. We both preferred the books to the movies but if we went for the later, then the Swedish original and not the US remake. Larsson wanted to write 10 books about journalist Mikael Blomquist, but unfortunately died in 2004, after having written only three novels in the series. On TV we saw finally 'The Wire', a realistic and captivating series about crimes and policing in Baltimore and one of the best TV series ever made. During over sixty episodes in five seasons, you were left guessing who was really bad or good and it was never clearly divided between criminals and police officers. Like it is in real life. We got the DVD collection of the full series from Suzannah Reast, who meanwhile had become the marketing director for Europe for HBO – what a treat! This show made many careers and most of the actors from it are popping continuously up in new series or movies.

Max Hole, the head of Universal International by now, had asked that I should be part of the international marketing managers meeting, where they were discussing the various pop priorities and their progress. I wasn't so sure that was a good idea, as the overall numbers of our top releases hardly ever got anywhere near to what the pop records could do, but it wasn't my call and so I was sitting there every week feeling kind of weird, but reported on the progress of our big releases in classical and jazz. When I spoke first to Max and when I told him what I was actually doing over there in the other building, he had no clue about all the jazz acts we had signed to International and how we handled the local jazz releases by giving them an international chance. But if he wanted to get more involved, fine with me.

Despite the fact that the classical labels still were producing and releasing core classical repertoire, to attract new audiences and sell records they had to move into what is called crossover, a mix of classical and pop in most cases. Deutsche Grammophon therefore signed Sting and released in 2009 the wonderful album 'If On A Winter's Night', a collection of seasonal songs based on compositions by Bach, Purcell, Schubert and others, plus some originals. It was great to work with Sting and his team on the marketing of the album, for which he did a lot of press and TV. This is a true record for the cold season, touchingly arranged and produced by Robert Sadin and the album did extremely well and sold alone in Germany over 100.000 CDs, which was a Gold Award at the time. Sadin released his own album as well that year on DG, next to core releases from Lang Land and Roberto Alagna and a special campaign for the 111th anniversary.

Decca's big releases were coming from Dutch violinist Andre Rieu, whom I had met a few times before and seen in concert. He usually had a hand-picked orchestra, flew them on his own Boing 747 to all the gigs, designed the costumes for the show and was generally involved in every aspect of it. I saw them once at the sold-out Waldbühne in Berlin. That meant 22.000 tickets sold! They had a really amazing light show and at the grand finale 100 back pipe players turned up …. Pretty impressive. Not really my cup of tea music wise, but extremely professionally done. They released as well albums by singer Rufus Wainwright and pianist, composer Ryuichi Sakamoto. Core releases came from Cecilia Bartoli and Renee Fleming, among others.

Decca head Bogdan Roscic left the company to run and re-built Sony Classical worldwide out of Berlin and Paul Moseley took over.

I was listening a lot to the outstanding album '75' by Joe Zawinul & The Joe Zawinul Syndicate that year. The recording was made on Joe's 75th birthday in Lugano with the exception of the track 'In A Silent Way', which was recorded on August 2nd that year in Hungary and features a touching guest appearance by Wayne Shorter. This was one of Joe's last concerts and the last time he and Wayne would perform together.

The other record that came out that year and I didn't work on, but I was listening to a lot was the Kurt Elling album 'Dedicated To You' on which he sings the music of Coltrane & Hartman. This is an individual and stunning tribute to a timeless original. Only Elling could pull this one off. He is such a classy singer and on this record pianist Laurence Hobgood and sax player Ernie Watts shine next to him.

with Dhafer Youssef in Madrid, 2009

We let the year run its course by meeting with Dhafer Youssef in Madrid in October and taking a short break in November in Sharm El Sheik. British Airways had started again to fly there regularly and at the beginning had a fantastic offer of around £ 500 per person for flights and hotel plus meals for one week. We took that chance and had an unforgettable, relaxed and lazy week together with a bit of snorkelling, massages and reading on the beach, with a cold drink at our side. Perfect! We celebrated Christmas with Hannah and New Year's Eve with Pier and his wife Ariana in a Spanish restaurant we liked, close to where we lived in Fulham. The party at the 'La Rueda' restaurant was fun, had great food and wine and so we slipped into 2010 in good company and with a glass of excellent Cava.

2010

The year 2010 started with heavy snow in London, which made me walk to the office once, as the Underground didn't run – it took about an hour, but was kind of fun in the fresh snow. In Haiti a powerful earthquake hit the city of Port-au-Prince and devasted the surroundings and the city, leaving over 300.000 dead behind. It would take years to rebuilt this city in one of the poorest nations of the region. I went to New York for meetings and when I returned Sascha told me that he and his wife Naomi had decided to move to Munich, from where he is originally, to live close to his parents. That was a tough one, as he really knew how we worked and what to do and training someone new would take time. Glady, I found a replacement quickly in Jennifer Ewbank, who stepped into Sascha's shoes as if it was a simple task. She is a quick learner, enthusiastic about music and a real nice young lady. I was very lucky to get her on board.

For Easter my mother made the trip to Madrid and Hannah came as well and we went to see Sara Baras and her flamenco dance troupe, made a little trip to Toledo, went to one of the Easter processions and ate lots of great food. She especially liked the 'Huevos Rotos' in the restaurant 'En Busca Del Tiempo', so we went there twice! It was great to have my mother and Hannah together in Madrid and to see how much both of them liked these few days together.

2010, my mother with Hannah and us in Madrid

Herbie Hancock had finished his new album, 'The Imagine Project', used many guest artists on it, had various producers and created an album, that was a bit like a patchwork: some pieces excellent, some less so, but together they all made kind of sense. Max Hole had heard that the album was done and called me to tell me to *"get this record"*. Of course, I got in touch with Herbie and Melinda and we started talking. I knew that Sony was in the game too and we pushed each other up in terms of advances. Once we reached a certain and high number, I told Max that we should walk away from the bidding, as we wouldn't make any money on the album, according to my sales expectation. He didn't want to hear any of it. He wanted us to get the album and not Sony. This was the *'we are the # 1 and Sony is # 2, so we get it'* mentality of competition. It didn't make any sense to me, but OK, I continued, but was in the end happy when we didn't get the record and it ended up with Sony. They must have paid more than double the amount on which I wanted originally to stop, but they had over 30 Herbie Hancock albums in their catalogue and with a good campaign, this can make up for a lot of the advanced money on the new record. Some you win, some you lose.

It must have been early May, when I had been called to a meeting with Andrew Kronfeld, the head of international marketing, who was running the meetings I was attending. I thought it was about the usual formality to tell me that my deal was renewed for another two years, as it has been the case since 1992. But this time it wasn't. On the contrary he told me that my deal wouldn't be extended and with June 30th I would stop being an employee of Universal International. It came a bit as a surprise, but not as a shock, as I always knew that one day it would happen. But I wasn't really prepared for it to happen that day, as I hadn't heard a word of warning or anything from Chris Roberts, who was still my boss. So, I called him in New York and he explained to me that he was negotiating his goodbye on Universal's demand and therefore couldn't protect me. A word in advance would have been great, but.... Shortly after that conversation Max Hole called and said he was sorry, they were re-structuring, but would take care of me and I should talk to someone in HR to sort my exit out. Overall, Universal treated me fairly under the circumstances. They immediately agreed to extend my deal until September 30th to give me time for the change and we started to discuss some kind of consultancy for me. Yolanda was shocked as well, but then immediately practical and we started planning for the time after Universal. I informed as well my ex-wife and told her that I wouldn't be able to pay the same amounts in the future, as I wouldn't have the same income. Inevitably, I couldn't tell her how much I would be able to pay, as I had no idea yet, what my future earnings would be. Despite all my warnings over the last few years, she wasn't prepared for this.

While discussing the new agreement with HR, I continued to release the new albums we had prepared for the year. Charlie Haden's second album in the deal I made with him was 'Sophisticated Ladies', the Quartet West with a selection of some of the best female singers around then, including Cassandra Wilson, Diana Krall, Renee Fleming, Norah Jones and Melody Gardot. Charlie's wife Ruth Cameron also sang one track. The album was produced by Jean-Philippe Allard, whom I had asked to do so after speaking to Charlie and he happily agreed. As he had a long-lasting friendship with Charlie and Ruth, it made a lot of sense and the album is truly special and did very well for us, despite not being cheap to make.

The Metropole Orkest in Holland is one of the leading ensembles that can play all kinds of music and they had worked with Vince Mendoza, composer and arranger, on a program featuring John Scofield and his music. They offered me the chance to make and release this recording and I took it immediately, as Vince's arrangements were cool and powerful, reaching the essence of John's compositions and Scofield's playing was outstanding as always. The album '54' was premiered at the North Sea Jazz Festival and is still one of my favourite Sco recordings. I had signed an artist whom I always loved and who just released a record once in a while: Bobby McFerrin. Linda Goldstein, his manager and producer, came to me with the new music almost done and I really loved what I heard. This was Bobby pure, but with a twist: he was using up to 50 singers per song and so created a kind of powerful vocal album that stands out through its layers of vocal tracks and sparse instrumentation. Titled 'Vocabularies' Bobby, when touring, used local singers to re-create the songs on stage to wonderful effects. Once in Germany he performed two songs from the album in a stadium with 50.000 singers from various choirs. Unreal!!

'Never Stop' was the new album by the Bad Plus and as usual we had the rights ex North America, where they were with eOne Music, run by my old friend Chuck Mitchell. The new record featured all new compositions by the members of the trio and is as surprising, fun and musically deep as you would expect from them.

Jane Monheit, now managed by my friend Cynthia Herbst, released her first Emarcy album 'Home' to critical acclaim, but unfortunately didn't tour as much in Europe as I had hoped, so sales stayed OK, but not as expected.

Gerald Clayton released his second trio album 'Bond: The Paris Sessions' and started touring a lot, performing in clubs and festivals all over the world, which helped to build his name. He got as well another Grammy Nomination for the new album, making it two out of two – not bad for a young musician!

And then we had Dee Dee Bridgewater's tribute to Billie Holiday 'Eleonara Fagan (1915-1959): To Billie With Love', featuring James Carter and Christian McBride amongst others. As we had the recording and video from the concert in Vitoria from the previous year, we did a limited edition set with the DVD and marketed the album that way. The limited edition of 10.000 units was gone fast and the album sold very well around the globe. It got Dee Dee another Grammy Nomination for best jazz vocal album and I sincerely hoped that this time she would get it. The show was a great success as well, as the band with James Carter was amazing and perfect for performing this repertoire.

with Dee Dee Bridgewater after her London show, 2010

Dave Holland had released via a deal with Alex Sanchez at Universal Spain, the album 'Hands', an unusual collaboration with flamenco guitarists Pepe Habichuela and his son Josemi Carmona. The Habichuela family had taken Dave into their fold when, while working on the album, Dave's wife passed away, which helped him immensely to get through this difficult time. Dave had to learn how to play flamenco to record this album and Pepe was the best teacher he could have asked for. The album is a wonderful and captivating mix of compositions by the family's members and Dave and on tour, supported by Juan Carmona and Bandolero on percussion, this project reached incredible musical heights and captivated audiences around Europe. I had seen them in Cheltenham together with Yolanda and we both loved the show and had some great fun with the guys and then saw them again on various occasions, recognizing how they got tighter and tighter as a band.

After my brother Jürgen and his wife Uschi visited us in May and we saw Michel Camilo performing the 'Rhapsody In Blue' in Madrid, I went to the North Sea Jazz Festival in Rotterdam. We had almost twenty artists or groups there, a lot of running around, saying *"Hi"* and hardly listening to anything in full. But that's North Sea, always busy and networking and chatting. I had a talk with Herbie after missing out on the new album, but no hard feelings there. Dee Dee delivered a stunning show with her Billie Holiday tribute and new acts Julian Lage and Christian Scott really did well. Ornette was the artist in residence and did 3 different shows, all amazing, whether it was with Charlie Haden or James Blood Ulmer. Randy Crawford and Joe Sample did as well a wonderful and touching show and so did both Sonny Rollins and Diana Krall. After Sonny's show I was sitting backstage with him, talking about his planned 80th birthday celebration in New York, where he was promoting himself a show at the Beacon Theatre with some special guests. I told him to record the concert, but he hesitated saying that sideman fees would be too high if the show would be recorded. To which I replied that he could tell all sidemen that the show would be recorded and that they would get paid additionally in case the recording would ever be released. In that case he would have a recording and if it was any good, we could put it out and if not, then he had it for his own pleasure. He looked at me, smiled and said that he would think about it. Gladly, in the end he decided to take that route. He was getting ready to leave and I was going to see if I could say "*Hello*" to Diana, who was about to play next. When I saw her, she quickly said "*Hi*" and then asked if I knew where Sonny was, as she wanted to meet him, something she hadn't had the pleasure yet. I showed her where he was and she went over and started talking to him. I got a beer from the fridge in the backstage area and sat down to enjoy the cold drink. About half an hour later Diana came back and gave me a hug, said "*Thanks*" in tears, happy to have met Sonny and had the chance to talk to him. It really meant that much to her, which made me happy too.

This was the day the football World Cup final was being played between Spain and The Netherlands in Johannesburg, South Africa, and exactly at the time of the match, Dave Holland and his Spanish musicians were supposed to be on stage. They had a TV set installed at the mixing desk, right next to the stage, as sometimes not the full band would play and the musician not in action could check on the game. The crew at the same time had set up a little space outside the venue where they had as well a TV set and could watch the game. After 90 minutes the match was still standing 0:0 and Dave, Pepe, Josemi, Juan and Bandolero had finished their show. They rushed backstage, got a seat in the outside area and watched the extra time, with me hanging around there too. When Andres Iniesta scored for Spain in the 116th minute, the Dutch went silent, but the four Spaniards and myself started a fiesta! Four minutes later it was all over and Spain had won. World Champions for the first time! From somewhere a bottle of whiskey made the rounds and the Dutch showed themselves as fair sportsmen and congratulated the Spanish musicians. Back at the hotel later that night, it was unusual quiet for the last night of the festival, the only people one could hear celebrating were four Spaniards in the shirts of their national football team and a smiling German.

Watching the game with Pepe Habichuela, Josemi and Juan Carmona, Bandolero and some stage hands, backstage at the North Sea Jazz Festival, 2010

In July we went to Madrid with Hannah, who more and more grew into a confident young lady. She loved Madrid, so coming here was always fun and we met people and went out a lot and met with

Yolanda's half-brother Rene and his family. Hannah had brought her friend Rosie and she showed her around a bit and together they enjoyed the city and the pool a lot.

I was still discussing with Universal the details of the consultancy agreement for jazz, basically only continuing what I was doing for Emarcy as an A&R man and the term would be two years. Even so we hadn't come to an agreement yet on the payment for this, I knew that it would be dramatically less than I used to earn before. In a meeting with my ex, I explained to her that I was still negotiating and didn't know what our financial situation would be in the future, nor how much I would be able to pay for her or Hannah. I stressed as well that our top priority was trying to stay in London and maintain our home, as this flat was supposed to be Hannah's at one point. She didn't say much, but a few weeks later I had her answer: via a court order she had frozen all my assets, as she, for whatever reasons, had assumed that I would move our money to Spain. That I was surprised would be an understatement: we had separated with a full financial agreement and now what??? And that move meant I had to pay the same monthly amounts to her as before, until the case was judged, which resulted in me having, for months, much more outgoing money than incoming. Under these circumstances, we had no alternative but to start the process of selling our flat in Fulham and were hoping for a good offer. Yolanda was realistic enough to see that we couldn't maintain our lifestyle with a negative income in London. We were therefore forced into considering a move to Madrid, even if it meant for her to quit her job at Heathrow Airport, or never finding a new job in Madrid due to the Global Economic Crisis. Her flat in Madrid was rented out, so she had in the end to inform the tenants that she wanted to use the flat for us. Renting laws in Spain are a bit odd, but we were lucky and they agreed to leave as long as we would pay for the air-conditioner that they put into the flat without asking.

In August, for Yolanda's birthday, we flew from London to Paris. The thing about it was, that we could fly on the brand-new Airbus A380, normally used for long haul flights, but as Air France had to train the crew on the new aircraft, they introduced for some weeks this flight to Paris and we both were curious about the plane and booked the weekend away. The aircraft was truly amazing: spacious and almost noiseless, with cameras outside so one could look at the flight path, which is amazing at taking off or landing. We loved it! In Paris we went to the restaurant ´Le Procope´ to celebrate Yolanda's birthday and had a wonderful meal in the oldest restaurant in town, going back to 1686.

Yolanda and I had started to register a company in Madrid, as by then we knew that with the income from the consultancy and having to pay my ex the same amounts as in the past, we couldn't make it in London. I was earning about 1/3 of my previous income and that gave us no chance than to move to the cheaper Madrid. The company would make the deal with Universal for two years and within these two years we had to build some clients in whatever form to be able to make it after that Universal deal was over. After a lot of back-and-forth going discussions, Yolanda came up with the name of our company: All-In-Music Service (AIMS).

Our company logo – designed by Jorge Chalmeta

I had kept Hannah informed on the situation and when I told her that Yolanda and myself had for financial reasons to move to Madrid, she wasn't too surprised. I am sure she didn't like it much, but on the other hand she was probably as well more worried what all that would mean to her and the way she and her mother were living. I had hoped to have a job until Hannah was finished with school, but that was obviously not to be. I had to make sure she would be able to continue the last two years where she was, but wasn't sure yet how. Based on her mother's actions, we later in the year had a mediation meeting with a judge, to possibly come to an agreement and avoid another court ruling and the female judge in that meeting said at one point: *"this looks like someone wants another bite of the cherry"*. I had nevertheless agreed to make an offer, but she rejected it, obviously wanting more. During the process of discovery, or whatever it is called, it came to light that over the years she hadn't saved a penny, not for her nor for Hannah. The court date was set for June 2011, but meanwhile I had to pay the same amount of support as before, even so my income from October was about a third of before. As if losing your job of 28 years wasn't hard enough ….

While dealing with all that Yolanda and I flew to New York to attend Sonny Rollins' 80th birthday event on the 10th of September. We went to the Bacon Theatre, looking forward to the show, of which I had a good idea who the special guests would be. Sonny had told me in advance that Roy Hargrove, Christian McBride, Roy Haynes and Jim Hall would be there, but the last guest he didn't reveal to me. Then, when he, McBride and Haynes had started as a trio to play 'Sonnymoon For Two', Ornette Coleman walked on stage and the two titans of the modern jazz saxophone played for the first and only time together. Jazz heaven!!! The whole show was musically outstanding with all guest contributions sensational, but this was the peak, the ultimate dream of many jazz fans and here we were and could experience it! Unbelievable! And I was really happy that the tapes were rolling that night and the we had recorded the whole show.

Finally, in October, we got an offer for the flat that was serious and good, but the guy wanted to have the apartment within a week. We started packing, arranged for the pick-up and transport of our stuff to Spain, where it would be stored in Jorge's garage until the people were out of the flat in Madrid and all renovations done. We gave the furniture from our place in Fulham to a friend and had the apartment empty within six days and finalised the deal. Until we would go to Madrid, we had to rent a smaller and cheaper place, closer to the airport in Hounslow. Not a great area, but it had to do. As Universal had allowed me to keep the office for a while, I could go there to work and Yolanda was as well still working, so we didn't spend much time in the flat, which was small, lived in and a bit smelly of all the Indian food cooked in the house.

Branford's manager, Ann Marie Wilkins, called me out of the blue one day and asked what I would do after Universal. I explained that I had been given a two-year consultancy as a cushion, but was thinking further ahead already, but not yet made up my mind. She asked if I would be interested in booking Branford's jazz gigs with the quartet and the duo with Joey Calderazzo. I answered that I would need a day or two to talk to Yolanda about it and that I would get back to her then. We had a relatively short discussion and then I called Ann Marie and said *"Yes"*. I knew many agents and promoters and could set up a team of sub-agents in all major countries relatively quick and so soon was ready to start booking Branford, an artist I really enjoyed working with on his records, but then as well as his European agent.

That was the year Greece and Ireland needed a Eurozone and IMF bailout due to their faltering economies, something which had a negative effect on the global standing of the Euro. And it was the most active year for Wikileaks, releasing almost half a million secret documents in relation to the US wars in Afghanistan and Iraq.

Jennifer and I were working the big releases from all associated labels, at least for me until the end of the year, then I was only responsible for Emarcy A&R and initially helping the smaller markets to release their approved jazz records internationally. The big record beside my own signings came from Concord that year and was Sergio Mendes' 'Bom Tempo', a groovy and danceable modern Brazilian album, featuring beside his wife Gracinha Leporace, Milton Nascimento, Seu Jorge and Katie Hampton as vocalists. It is always great to see Sergio and Gracinha and have a relaxed chat and maybe a dinner or a drink. They are amazing people and always made me and Yolanda feel like we were part of the family.

Verve didn't have much to offer that year and Emarcy had, as usual, a lot of great records, the Dave Holland & Pepe Habichuela album 'Hands' being the outstanding one next to the 'Vitoria Suite' with the Jazz At Lincoln Centre Orchestra, Wynton and Paco, for which we did a version with a little documentary on DVD. Great album that one! Jazzland released their first album with Dhafer Youssef, the wonderful 'Ábu Nawas Rhapsody', featuring Tigran Hamasyan on piano, Chris Jennings on bass and Mark Giuliana and drums. I really liked Tigran as a person and as a pianist and talked to him about possibly signing him. He told me that the French guys were already in touch with him and so I gave them a call, telling them that I would support the signing with pushing it from International. They made the deal in the end and I was happy that he was part of the Universal family. Dhafer had signed with Jazzland as he was at that time working a lot with Bugge and Eivind and it seemed a natural step then, so it was great to have him in the house as well.

Paolo Vinaccia, Italian drummer with residence in Norway had just been given the green light from his doctors after having had chemotherapy for a while and therefore he released a live 6 CD box set titled 'Very Much Alive', featuring Terje Rypdal on guitar, Ståle Storløkken on keyboards and special guests Palle Mikkelborg and Bugge Wesseltoft, to celebrate this news. Paolo was a fighter and a great human being and friend and everyone was so pleased for him. New albums from Eivind Aarset, Beady Belle, Atomic and Torun Erikson completed a strong year for Jazzland. The Marsalis Family released the outstanding 'Music Redeems' album, a live recording to benefit the Ellis Marsalis Center for music. Make no mistake: That family can swing!!

The main releases from ECM that year came from the duo of Keith Jarrett and Charlie Haden. Their album 'Jasmine' is beauty in sound! Jan Garbarek and the Hilliard Ensemble did 'Officium Novum' and touched the hearts of many people with that recording.

In 2010 we unfortunately lost many great jazz artists like James Moody, whom we had met when he was out playing with Roy's Big Band and Roberta Gambarini; Marion Brown, whose early recordings I liked a lot, especially the 1973 'Geechee Recollections'; the wonderful Abbey Lincoln, with whom I had the pleasure to work and chat and hang and whom Dee Dee Bridgewater had promised to look after her music, which is still played a lot today and her 'Throw It Away' became kind of a jazz standard meanwhile and last, but not least, Hank Jones, with whom we had recorded in February that year his last ever session, in a duo with Charlie Haden. We had decided not to release the album in 2010, as Charlie had the record with Keith out on ECM, so Hank's last recording had to wait until the coming year to be heard.

On the classical side I was working on the Sting album 'Symphonicities', a kind of best of, recorded with band and orchestra. Yolanda and I went to see one of the shows and it was simply incredible to hear in one concert how many great songs Sting had written over the years and how great they sounded in the new arrangements. And, as always, it was great to see Ira Coleman again. Especially the arrangements for 'I Hung My Head', originally written for Johnny Cash and 'We Work The Black Seam' I thought were amazing. The concert in Berlin was filmed and recorded and released as a DVD / CD set. Working on the promotional set-up and the marketing with Sting's team was always great and professional and I really liked working with his European PR Lucy-Maxwell-Stewart, for her relaxed ways and efficiency. As expected, the album did very well and so did the tour. Core releases that year at Deutsche Grammophon came among others from Anna Netrebko, Martha Argerich and Patricia Petibon. Decca had a few core releases, but the bigger albums came from crossover, led by David Garrett and Ludovico Einaudi.

While we saw in the movies 'The King's Speech' by Tom Hoper, with an incredible performance by Colin Firth and 'Black Swan' by Darren Aronofsky with an equal impressive showing by Natalie Portman, I was reading 'Der Fluss' by Ketil Bjørnstad, the follow up to 'Vinding's Spiel / To Music'. Here the story continues of Axel growing up and we are following his development through the years. Madeleine Peyroux came to London to write songs with Bill Wyman and seemed to enjoy the experience. We met up and Yolanda and I took her out for dinner once, which was a lot of fun and really interesting when she described the way how she and Bill were working on songs. She was preparing the recording of a new album and was now in the process of co-writing with various people, including, beside Bill, our friend Jonatha Brooke, violinist Jenny Scheinmann and David Batteau. In November Yolanda and I went to the Tennis Masters in London on invitation of their sponsor Barclays Bank, which we had done before, but this time we were lucky to get VIP tickets. In the VIP section there was food and drinks and we rubbed shoulders with Boris Becker and other tennis greats and could see some of the best players in the world perform. What a treat! By then we went back and forth between London and Madrid a bit more often. I was invited by Javier Limon to go with him to Barcelona and see Buika, whose producer he was. I gladly accepted, as I wanted to get to know more people in the Spanish music scene and I liked Buika anyway. After celebrating Christmas as usual with Hannah in London, we went back to Madrid to celebrate New Year's Eve with Yngve, Cecilie, Rachel, Alex, Estefania, Josemi, Sandra, Paulo, his partner and Maria. A great party indeed!!

Portrait by David Sinclair, London 2010

MADRID
2011

In early 2011 we were still going back and forth a lot between London and Madrid, seeing Sten and his family in England and then went to a concert by Javier Limon and his 'Mujeres' project in Madrid. And we went to New York for some work-related meetings and the recording of the new Michel Camilo album 'Mano A Mano'. This was a trio album featuring master percussionist Giovanni Hidalgo and bass player Charles Flores, both great guys and wonderful musicians. We were in the studio when they recorded the album, swift and easy, except for one crazy bass line Michel had written and Charles initially struggled with. We had flown in a few days earlier and really were lucky, as when our plane approached New York it had started to snow like crazy and our flight was the last one to touch down. They had to close down the airport and, in the blizzard, it took us almost an hour to reach our gate – but we had made it. New York with a lot of snow is actually quite beautiful, but once it starts to melt it's a major mess.

Like with Gerald Clayton, James Carter and Julian Lage, I had asked my friend Ingrid Hertfelder to come and take some shots of Michel and the guys for the cover and as always, she delivered stunning and top-class work. We met Dee Dee Bridgewater and her daughter and manager Tulani in

New York for dinner. We had decided to go to Nobu's and had as well invited Wendy Life, who was still with Universal, but with an unclear future. Dee Dee and her had become friends and so it was easy to add her to the dinner list. We had a wonderful meal, talking about ideas and projects, and at one point Dee Dee asked me what I was listening to at the moment, what cool record was upcoming. I told her I was having the new and yet unreleased Kurt Elling album 'The Gate' on my phone to listen to. The album was produced by Don Was and is simply divine. Just the opener of the album, King Crimson's 'Matte Kudasai' was and still is amazing. I put the song on for Dee Dee and while we were waiting for the desert, she was listening and soon started to tear up. She smiled and I said "Only Kurt can do that" and she agreed. For me he was then, and still is today, the most outstanding male jazz singer. Period.

My sister Marlis had her 60th birthday in December of 2010, but only celebrated in April, so we went to Hamburg to party with her. Jürgen and Uschi came from Vienna, Barbara and our mother from Denmark together with Søren and Skipper, friends of the family. At the airport I bought Metro tickets for everyone and we went to the trains to get where the hotel was. There were no barriers or machines you needed to put your ticket in. Yolanda was surprised and stated that "*in Madrid no-one would pay if you can just walk freely to the train*", but in Germany they religiously do, making sure the system works. For all of us eight Marlis had booked a hotel and when arriving there we were all shocked. This was by far the worst place I ever stayed in and beside Marlis saying it would be close to where she lived, we had to take a bus. After we had drunk some of the whiskey we had brought for the party, even this hotel wasn't that bad anymore ... We had a fun evening with Marlis, her family and friends, stayed another day to explore Hamburg and then went back home. Meanwhile work in the flat in Madrid progressed well and on April 19th we finally made the last trip in our fully loaded car, taking the overnight ferry to Santander and then having a stop in Vitoria. I was ready for a new chapter in my life, and so was Yolanda, happy being back in Madrid.

While talking to Branford's manager again, Ann Marie told me that she had no objection in changing agents in the various markets, but insisted especially on a change in Germany, as they hadn't played there for a while. They wanted to come to Europe in the summer, so I started working as an agent with the major jazz festivals directly and as well asked Amparo Tebar, with whom they had worked for Spain and Portugal before, to see if she could get some dates. Amparo is a real cool character and a very good agent and we had known each other from before, but now really worked together and well. She is part of the amazing group of female managers and agents (and close friends), featuring as well Gail Boyd, Karen Kennedy and Ina Dittke. I love to work with each of them and like to hang with all of them as they are great human beings and a lot of fun. While getting the first dates for Branford, I helped as well Sandra Camilo to get some festival dates for Michel, so the agency got off to a busy start. And while doing all this, Yolanda's cousins took me to my first match in the Bernabeu stadium, seeing Real Madrid beating Getafe. What an amazing atmosphere!!! I had loved going to see Chelsea in their 40.000 capacity stadium, but being one of almost 100.000 enthusiastic fans, definitely beats that!

On May 15th the Spanish youth all over the country started to protest against high unemployment, economic conditions, welfare cuts and political corruption, with a focus on Madrid's Puerta Del Sol, where the 'Indignados' built a camp. Inspired by their dire circumstances and Stephane Hessel's manifesto 'Time For Outrage', the youth were protesting peacefully and many citizens of Madrid came by to deliver food and water. The camp lasted until early August and was the initiation of the Podemos party, a left populist and anti-corruption movement. Hannah came to Madrid and we spend some days together, as usual going out, eating well and relaxing.

2011, Puerta Del Sol, Madrid

Shortly after that Yolanda and I went back to England for the court date. We met with my solicitor and went to see the judge, who was clearly overwhelmed by the load of paper he had to look up before. My guy was doing well, making it clear that my ex-wife had been asked to do something to stand on her own feet many times, as the job loss was predictable. But all the judge saw, was, that on one side there was money and on the other there wasn't. And despite our clear financial split in the original divorce, he awarded her a substantial sum of the savings I had made over the years, mostly thanks to Yolanda and her skills in dealing with money. This didn't make any sense! We had saved money for our future and Hannah's and my ex hadn't saved a penny and I was the one being penalised for being responsible! I wouldn't call that justice. My ex got lucky with the judge and I lost a lot of money. Back in Spain we went with Maria to Almeria, as Jorge had moved there and we spent a few days with him and on the beach, which surely helped to calm my nerves.

Working from home was a bit of a change than going to an office every day and it took me some time to find my own rhythm. Yolanda did all the work with the Spanish authorities and taxes and whatever was needed in bookkeeping and I was doing the work with the artists for Emarcy and the booking. Yolanda helped when it came to co-ordinate promotion for our releases and artists and a lot of times we travelled together to gigs and festivals. The agreement with Universal had a clause that I needed to request the OK for travels to recordings, meetings, festivals, and for this year I had the approval for Montreux, North Sea, Vitoria and San Sebastian, as we had some of our artists playing in all of these. But before we started the festival circuit we went to the Madrid Gay Parade, the biggest in Europe and a simple party of colours and people having a good time being themselves. The parade in the centre of Madrid was visited by over 1 million people, us included. And in the summer heat people were throwing buckets of water from their balconies on the audience and participants, which was more than welcome. Yolanda and I got soaked at one point, but we loved every minute of the event. Great people, great music.

My first festival stop was Montreux. Tommy LiPuma had invited me to come to see his 75th birthday concert, which he had arranged with Claude Nobs. Some of the artists Tommy had produced over the years came and it was a sensational event featuring, more or less in order of appearance, Lee Ritenour, Dave Grusin, Dan Hicks, Joe Sample, David Sanborn, Randy Crawford, Leon Russell, Diana Krall, Dr. John and George Benson. They all played their part and then jammed together, joined by other musicians, like Trombone Shorty and took the roof off the house! Claude was the perfect host backstage with finger food and drinks, making announcements and when the music was really great screamed *"Unbelibable"*, a word he often used, but never could pronounce correctly. After the show we crossed the road to go for a few drinks and Tommy was a happy and content guy. Who wouldn't be with these guests at your party!

Tommy LiPuma celebrating his 75th birthday in Montreux, 2011

Next stop was North Sea in Rotterdam, where I saw Chick and Madeleine, Sergio and Scofield, Gerald and many more. Great music, wonderful chats and good Dutch beer. Branford performed there as well as Michel, two of the first few shows we had booked as an agency. Vitoria was next on the list and Yolanda joined me there, as Michel Camilo was performing the music of 'Mano A Mano' with Giovanni Hidalgo and bassist Anthony Jackson, as Charles Flores, the bass player on the record, unfortunately struggled with serious health problems. A great concert, a wonderful weekend among friends (Alex had joined us there and Yolanda knew everyone anyway from her time working and living in that city). After the show we went to a hotel for some drinks and I saw that Gerald Clayton was playing there and went to say "Hi". Michel Camilo is a friend of Juan Muga, producer of the great Muga wines from the Rioja region and he and his partner joined us. In the end, we had a few bottles of the excellent Muga, paid for by the owner of the vineyard, who seemed to enjoy the evening and his own wine as much as we did. Music brings people together. The last stop for us both was San Sebastian Jazz Festival. San Sebastian is a beautiful city with the best food one can buy for money. That is the reason why our Norwegian friends Yngve and Cecilie go there almost every year and so did Alex and Estefania. I had a few acts performing, but for whatever reason, the guy running the festival didn't allow me to get a backstage pass, not even for the artists I had signed. Which made work a bit more complicated, but that had never stopped me to see and meet my acts. In this case, I simply had to call the road managers and they came and opened the doors for me. When the guy running the festival then saw me backstage talking to the artists, he hardly could say anything, but didn't look too pleased. I couldn't care less.

On July 22nd a detonating bomb killed eight people in central Oslo, followed by the killing of 69 young people in a summer camp on the island of Utøya. Responsible for both attacks was the domestic terrorist Anders Breivik, arrested on the island and later found guilty in court. All of us were shocked when the news of the attacks came through and with many Norwegians there with us, it was emotional and tough. The next day singer Kristin Asbjørnsen was supposed to perform and she was considering to cancel her show, being emotionally completely overwhelmed by what had happened at home. In the end she decided to do the concert and her band supported that decision. Her performance that night, singing spirituals, carried the sadness and loss, expressed the mourning and shock in an extremely touching way. We all sat there crying, as she touched our souls and helped us to understand and heal. Only music and great musicians can do that.

The following day it was time for the John Scofield Quartet, performing music from his new Emarcy album 'A Moment's Peace', but with a slightly different line-up than on the record. The show featured Mulgrew Miller on piano, Scott Colley on bass and Bill Stewart on drums and it was a great and swinging open air gig, which we all truly enjoyed. After the show John did a CD signing session with FNAC Records, at the venue. I looked thought the CDs on offer and found a bootleg and when someone bought it and wanted it signed, I pointed that out to John and he wrote on the CD *'this is an illegal recording'* and signed it for the guy, who probably had no idea that it wasn't a legal product when he bought the music.

July ended with a visit from my sister Barbara and her adopted son Masanti, who both loved Madrid and our little trip to Toledo, where, when we were having lunch, the waiter thought that Masanti was Neymar Jr., the footballer, and asked for an autograph. We had a good laugh about that for a while. Barbara had brought us one of her paintings for the new flat, which we both really like and put up immediately.

2011, painting by my sister Barbara

This was as well the year in which the Arab Spring started in Tunisia, spreading in the region to Egypt, Syria and Libya with long lasting consequences for the freedom of the people in these countries. Bin Laden was killed by US forces and they finally declared that the war with Iraq had ended. ETA, the Basque terrorist and separatist movement responsible for over 800 deaths, ended all violence after 43 years of terror. A 9.0 Richter scale measured undersea earthquake hit Japan, followed by a massive tsunami and killed over 20.000 people and caused meltdowns of three reactors at the Fukushima Daini Nuclear Power Plant. Because of that the region needed to be evacuated, affecting hundreds of thousands of residents. When nature is let loose, nothing can stand in its way and mankind doesn't still seem to have understood that. The radioactive waters from the incident will over the years be dumped into the Pacific Ocean, spreading the fallout around the globe. A decision hard to understand.

Reinhold Ernst, who is part of my father's family and one of the few who had been, over the years, in touch with him and my mother, lives in Germany, but has a house in Javea, Spain, where he drives to in his old BMW every summer. He meanwhile was in his 80's and when he came to Spain that year, he told my mother that he would like to invite me to come and visit him. I hadn't met him before, or at least I can't remember, but Hannah and I decided to go and see him for a few days when she came in August. We took the bus from Madrid and Reinhold picked us up and we drove to his house. A nice place, with enough space for us and a small but fine swimming pool. We went to a German restaurant, as most people living in that area were either German or English, where the food was basic, but great. We spent a few days going to the beach or checking the area and generally had a great time, before returning to Madrid and Hannah staying with us for a few more days.

I had nine records to release in 2011 as a direct result of my A&R work, plus the ones coming from the various markets. I had helped to sign Madeleine Peyroux directly to Universal after her three-album deal with Rounder Records expired and the first album under the new agreement was 'Standing On The Rooftop', in which she had written or co-written all songs except the usual covers she does on her records, this time by Lennon/McCartney, Bob Dylan and Robert Johnson. A great album with great tracks that did well for Madeleine and Emarcy. As always it was a pleasure to work with Cynthia and Madeleine on promotion for the album. Michel Camilo's 'Mano A Mano' featured beside his new compositions a really groovy version of Lee Morgan's 'Sidewinder' and a very touching 'Alfonsina Y El Mar', which got huge applause in Vitoria, when performed live at the festival. Sonny Rollins' 'Road Shows, Vol. 2' had two tracks recorded in Japan in October 2010 and four tracks from his 80th birthday concert in New York. 'In A Sentimental Mood' featuring Jim Hall is a gem from that show and so are the tracks 'I Can't Get Started' and 'Rain Check', both featuring an outstanding Roy Hargrove. But the true highlight is the over 21-minute long 'Sonnymoon For Two' when Ornette Coleman joined the trio of Sonny, McBride and Haynes. I was so happy that the show was recorded and that I had this historic moment in jazz on an album, which got 2 Grammy nominations ... and deservedly so!!! John Scofield's 'A Moment's Peace' was the last album in the existing deal and I had started to talk to him about a new contract, the details of which I then handed over to Verve, in case they would want to sign him after my departure. The album was recorded with Larry Goldings, Scott Coley and Brian Blade and I had originally planned to go to the recording session in New York, but then John told me that he didn't like anyone to simply hang around in the studio when he was working and that was fine with me. Artists are very different in that respect: some don't mind at all to have people in the studio at the recording, others only want certain people and John preferred no-one who wasn't producing or playing. Fair enough! They recorded a really touching version of Abbey Lincoln's 'Throw It Away', which belongs to my favourite takes of that song.

Saxophonist James Carter even had two releases that year, something I normally wouldn't do, but the two records were so different, that an exception could be made. Cynthia Herbst, James' manager was at the time as well the manager of classical composer Roberto Sierra, who had written a 'Concerto For Saxophones And Orchestra' especially for James and, after having it performed a few times, they wanted to record it. They picked another of Roberto's composition 'Caribbean Rhapsody' and with a Tenor Interlude and a Soprano Interlude the repertoire for the album was done. A real cool record of modern classical music with some wonderful soloing by James. Where the Concerto includes a full orchestra, the Rhapsody uses a string quartet and special guest violinist (and James' cousin) Regina Carter. Produced by Michael Cuscuna, this record got wonderful reviews and did fine under the circumstances, meaning he could only do the odd performance once in a while and not tour it as a jazz record would be toured. For that we had album number two, a recording by his Organ Trio, featuring Gerard Gibbs on organ and Leonard King Jr on drums, both amazing musicians and wonderful guys. The stand out track for me on this record is 'The Hard Blues' by Julius Hamphill, which they performed powerful and inventive in their improvisations, with the right groove and freeness.

Julian Lage's second Emarcy album 'Gladwell', was a more of a group effort and showed Julian's skills as a composer. He toured that album and initial sales seemed to be fine, indicating a step forward. Therefore, I hoped that Universal would keep Julian and make the third album I wanted to do, but soon it became clear that they wouldn't fill my position and that there wasn't much interest in me really doing anything, beside putting the records out which had already recorded or were contractually obliged to make. I had signed American singer Nailah Porter, who had been recommended to me by Gilles Peterson and Nicola Conte. Her album 'ConJazzNess' is a true spiritual beauty, deep and full of great originals. Nailah is a wonderful and warm human being and an inspired performer. Her song 'Beautiful Anyway' was my song of the year and I played it a lot at home and when travelling. Nailah was managed by Guy Eckstine, the former Verve A&R man and good to work with, as we knew each other from then.

with Nailah Porter

Finally, we could as well release the last recorded music of Hank Jones, the duo album with Charlie Haden titled 'Come Sunday', a wonderful take on gospels and spirituals. What we didn't know at that time, was, that this would be as well Charlie Haden's last studio recording. All the albums coming out after 2011 were recorded before 'Come Sunday', except a live recording by the Liberation Music Orchestra, 'Time/Life (Song For The Whales And Other Beings)', on which two songs dated from a performance from August 15, 2011 at the Jazz Middelheim Festival in Antwerp, Belgium. Charlie started to suffer from post-polio syndrome and unfortunately soon wasn't able to perform anymore.

Sergio Mendes had asked me if I could compile a kind of Best Of for him and so I started digging deep into his music. Universal and Concord were holding most of his albums anyway, so it was a rich field to pick from. I wanted to do it chronologically, so people could hear the development of his sound, follow his musical journey. I listened a lot to the early recordings, went through most of what I didn't know already and then sent the track list for the 2 CD set to Sergio for approval. He changed two songs and was happy with the rest. 'Celebration – A Musical Journey' was released with a great booklet featuring historical photos of Sergio with everyone from Frank Sinatra to Pele and got some really great reviews for covering the artists career from his first recordings in 1962 to 2011. And it was fun to put it together.

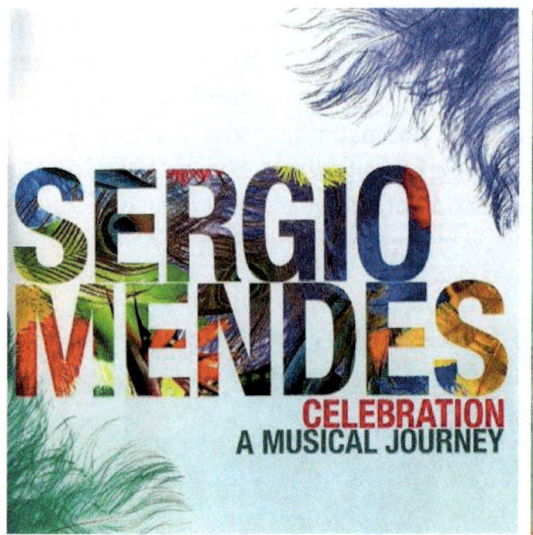

2011 was another year in which we lost many great jazz musicians, including George Shearing, a pianist I always liked; Ray Bryant with whom I briefly worked when he was recording for Mercury in Japan; Danish swing legend Papa Bue, a favourite of my father; Paul Motion and Sam Rivers, both artists I had the pleasure to see live. But the biggest shock was the passing of singer Amy Winehouse at the age of 27 from alcohol poisoning. Both Yolanda and I love her records and we tried a few times to see her in concert, but never got to see her. Twice she cancelled the show we had tickets for and the third time we had tickets, we gave them to Carlo and Annika, our friends from Perugia, when they were in London and asked if I could get them tickets. A nice gesture though that show was cancelled too. Her two albums 'Frank' and Back To Black' are essential listening, whereas on the other hand the documentary 'Amy' (2015), is good but one cannot oversee that the record company seems to get away with praise for their conduct, only to find out that the same company produced the film. A troubled character indeed, whose pains and uncontrolled life style was reflected in her music.

I was still in touch with Tommy LiPuma occasionally and during one of our chats he told me that he was talking to Sting and his management to do a jazz album. I knew that Sting had recorded tracks with other jazz musicians over the years and told Tommy that I would put a compilation together for him, as a guidance. I picked a lot of the songs Sting had recorded as a sideman and there was as well a really touching version of 'Strange Fruit', which he had done for an Amnesty International album called 'Conspiracy Of Hope' in 1986. But I opened the compilation with 'My Funny Valentine' from a Japanese movie, featuring Herbie Hancock. Tommy really liked the compilation I had done, but unfortunately due to other commitments in that period, the Sting jazz album never happened.

My book of the year was without any doubt Haruki Murakami's '1Q84', his personal and unique tribute to '1984' by George Orwell. The new book was released first in Japan in three volumes and had sold over one million copies in less than a month. For me one of the best Murakami novels, captivating and imaginative as only he can be. Ketil Bjørnstad's 'Die Frau Im Tal' ends the trilogy of the story of Aksel Vinding and again takes the reader into the music world of the young pianist and sees him further grow up and develop. Ketil would release an album on ECM to go with the books: 'Vinding's Music', featuring him on solo piano and then some classical pieces he is referring to in the books. 'The Prisoner Of Heaven' by Carlos Ruiz Zafón was another of my favourite books that year. What a storyteller he was!!! Hannah and I went to see the last of the Harry Potter movies and with Yolanda I saw 'The Artist' the wonderful black and white film by Michael Hazanavicus, as well as 'Tinker Taylor Soldier Spy' with Gary Oldman.
Musically my highlights were coming from Chick Corea and Stefano Bollani and their duo disc 'Orvieto' and Kurt Elling with his masterpiece 'The Gate'. And our friend Ketil released an album with

cellist Svante Henryson called 'Night Song', which I really like. Branford Marsalis and Joey Calderazzo put out their beautiful duo album 'Songs of Mirth And Melancholy', with amazing new compositions by both musicians plus a piece each by Wayne Shorter and Johannes Brahms. The best albums on Emarcy came from Rebekka Bakken, Cristina Branco and Solveig Slettahjell, whose 'Antologie' is a great album of covers, including 'Wild Horses' and 'The Winner Takes It all'. Bugge Wesseltoft had recorded a few jazz standards on his solo piano album 'Songs', which got fantastic reviews and is among my favourite albums by this outstanding artist. As an agency we hadn't booked any fall shows, which gave me time to complete the set-up of sub-agents in the most important markets and I managed to get my friend John Cumming and his company Serious in the UK on board, as well as Matthias Wendl and Jolanda Vujasinovic in Germany. Immediately we got started to look into concert dates for 2012.

Hannah turned 18 that year. A young, confident lady. Focused on her school work, respected in her circle of friends, she made and still makes me proud every day. My father started the tradition to give every one of the kids at their 18th birthday a ring with their initials and a rune, which is connected to his name. As I was about to get my father's ring from my mother, I had mine changed to Hannah's initials and she got that one, so in a way coming directly from her grandfather via her father's finger to her. A-levels were coming up and she started to think about what to do after them. University, travelling, work experience. Too many options!

In October, Bugge had invited Josemi Carmona to be the special guest at the Jazzland Sessions in Oslo, as they had met via Alex Sanchez asking Bugge to be on Josemi's album. As neither Josemi nor his wife Sandra, who was travelling with us, could speak a word of English then, they asked me if I could come with them and so we took a flight from Madrid to Frankfurt, and changed planes there to go to Oslo. We had to rush to get the other flight and just after we stepped into the plane the doors closed and then someone shouted *"Wulf!?!"* and I turned around and there was Dee Dee Bridgewater, smiling at me, surprised. I introduced her to Josemi and Sandra, then sat down next to her and explained what we were about to do in Oslo and that if she had time, I would love to invite her to the show with Josemi, which was to happen the next evening at the Victoria club. She was going to Oslo to rehearse for a few Christmas-shows she would do in December with an orchestra and the wonderful composer and arranger Kjetil Bjerkestrand. She actually made it to the show the following day, bringing Kjetil with her. The concert was truly amazing. Dee Dee loved how Bugge deconstructed some of the jazz standards and then put them together again, but different. Violinist Ola Kvernberg and saxophonist Hakon Kornstad were amazing and so was guitar player and singer Knut Reiersrud. Josemi came on and played a solo piece that was surprising in many ways: for many people flamenco is about playing fast and spectacular, but his piece was slow and touching and all about atmosphere and emotions. Then he played with the rest of the gang, had some wonderful interplay with Ola and Hakon and Bugge. Music is a global language, this again was proof of that, as these guys couldn't communicate as they didn't speak the same languages, but when playing, it really didn't make a difference!

Next, I went to Paris to see James Carter performing with his Organ Trio at the New Morning club. I always met with the local Universal guy when going somewhere, as I still needed them to work my releases and some of them actually had become friends over the years, like Pascal Bod in Paris. The opening act for James there was singer Gregory Porter, who had been recommended to me by my friend, concert and festival promoter Heinz Krassnitzer and I was looking forward to see him live for the first time. He just had released his really promising first album 'Water' and was promoting it through this tour. Great show as well! But James really rocked the house with his trio and I was happy that I made the trip.

The last show of the year for me happened in Barcelona and it was the final show of the tour of Dave Holland and Pepe Habichuela, featuring Josemi, Bandolero and Juan as well. It was amazing to hear how much this group of musicians had grown into a band, a unit, that made music so tight and intense, but with love and passion. For me that was the best show I had seen them play and I hoped they would get together again for another album and tour, as this music was truly special.

2011, Dave Holland, Pepe Habichuela and group in Barcelona

In November I started as well to write a little blog about music, that is concerts and releases and other things, mainly for me, but for a few readers I collected along the way as well. From this blog at Wordpress, I decided to occasionally integrate what was written then to add more detail to what I am writing in this book.

I got the news that Tommy LiPuma had left Verve. For me that was the end of an era at the label. I spoke to Tommy and we agreed to stay in touch, which we did and I was looking forward to see what he would do, as there always were artists to produce or guide. But for Verve, as a jazz label, things changed and they became more crossover and mainstream oriented. Universal didn't seem to see the value of that brand, something we had built up again since I started at International. It was a pity to see acts like Andrea Bocelli to release albums on Verve. Don't misunderstand me: Bocelli is great and has his audience, but why destroy the image of Verve to have albums like his and other crossover acts on that label? Usually, it is in a big company like Universal to please someone's ego and in this case, they had signed top producer David Foster and gave him Verve to run. As said before, Universal didn't understand the value of the label in the jazz world or didn't care, as jazz was then maybe 2 % of their total business. A real pity!

Spotify opened their app and streaming service in the US in 2011 and that was the beginning of the success of streaming globally, with it soon becoming the most important source of income for the big record companies. A service that is definitely pop oriented and had not much interest in niche genres like jazz and classical, which are both represented badly, as a lot of the information the jazz and classical listener wants was not given at the service. Pop rules, as for Spotify Jazz and Classical each only represent about 1% of their turnover. Thankfully, for the time being at least, CDs did still sell pretty well for these genres, but unfortunately that as well was about to change slowly.

Before the year was over Yolanda and I did a trip to Sevilla with Blanca, our friend from Vitoria, to see the Davis Cup Final between Spain and Argentina. Spain, with Rafael Nadal, David Ferrer,

Feliciano López and Fernando Verdasco, won to our delight 3:1 and became Davis Cup champions that year.

2011, Spain winning the Davies Cup, Sevilla

We let the year run out with a Christmas party at the flat of Yolanda's aunt and uncle and celebrated New Year's Eve with Hannah at Maria's place, having the famous midnight grapes, when you have to eat one with each of the twelve times the bell tolls to ring in the new year. Supposedly it will bring you luck if you manage to eat them all and not choke! We did.

2012

We started the year with work on the summer tour for our act Branford Marsalis and we had now James Carter as well to book for Europe, which kept us busy. To introduce our company a bit into the Spanish market and to see some friends, we decided to have an 'All In Music Service' dinner at Paco's restaurant and invited Alex and Estefania, Javier and Luci, Josemi and Sandra plus Josemi's manager Morgan and his wife, as well as singer La Shica, with whom we became friendly after meeting her via Javier Limon, bass player Pablo Martin Caminero and Dhafer, who was in town as well. We had a great dinner, amazing food prepared by Paco and lots of fun.

The day after the dinner Dhafer, Yolanda and myself went to see Josemi at his house in Madrid and the two musicians almost immediately started playing around – Dhafer had brought his studio oud and after a few minutes the tape was running – and out of an idea a song was brought to life in an instant. It was pure magic to see these guys communicate musically with so much respect for each other, but as well with the sensibility to follow or to lead and to play together. One take, one song! After 2 more hours, sketches to more music were recorded and everyone had a smile on their faces. Later we went to see Pablo perform in a small club, in a duo with a guitarist and really enjoyed what they were doing. As he hadn't brought the right oud for a concert, Dhafer didn't take up the invitation from Pablo to join them – he would do that on his next visit.

the first AIMS dinner, 2012

I went to England to be part of a new version of Take Five – Take Five: Europe, *'a scheme in the UK designed for emerging jazz musicians who want to significantly develop their international careers. Participants are given the unique opportunity to take 'time out' to increase their profile, improve their performance skills and expand their professional networks. Ten talented emerging artists (two per country per year – from France, the Netherlands, Norway, Poland and the UK) take part in a specially devised programme of events, including an inspiring week-long residency where they can strengthen all aspects of their professional future. In addition to motivating creative and business sessions, the artists will take part in special showcases across European jazz festivals.'* The artists selected for the first edition were Benjamin Flament, Bram Stadhouders, Maciej Garbowski, Celine Bonacina, Fraser Fifield, Gard Nilssen, Maciej Obara, Oene van Gaal, Ole Morton Vagan and Tom Arthurs. A shining collection of talents. I did my usual presentation and talked about the music business and labels. Over the years I had done it with various guys running indie labels, from David Stapleton to Siggi Loch, with whom I did it in 2012 and who spent more time talking about his biography, than about what these young musicians might need. In the end he even told them not to send him any music, as he was finding the artists, he wanted to work with himself and that in a few years there wouldn't be any jazz business left anyway. Very encouraging! I set the record straight and asked them to send music any time and, in any form, and I would listen and get back to them and that the way I saw the business, was that it will be tough, but people will always listen to jazz, no doubt about that. There is actually a really cool photo taken by Emile Holba of me rolling my eyes in a *"I can't believe what he is saying right now"* way. From the group of participating musicians, the two Norwegians, bass player Ole Morten and drummer Gard Nilssen and Polish alto sax player Maciej Obara would become the Maciej Obara Quartet (with the addition of pianist Dominik Wania) and record some fabulous albums for ECM. And Sony Poland signed on my recommendation the group RGG, featuring founder member and bass player Maciej Garbowski, as well participating in this event. John Surman as usual guided the youngsters through the music sessions, which were really great to listen to.

2012, Take Five with John Surman on the right

Branford was in Europe for a classical concert and I took advantage of that and set up some promo for the forthcoming album 'Four MF's Playing Tunes', the best quartet album he had delivered so far. Impressive how much understanding and outstanding communication is happening within his group when they play and this album captured that perfectly on record. We did some promo in Vienna, where I went with him to discuss the next steps for Marsalis Music and for himself. The dinners and times off, when we could chat, were for me the most interesting part, as he is a very clever and conscious man, with his own set of strong views about the music and the world. As he is a teacher as well as a musician, he deals a lot with young players and it took me bit by surprise when he mentioned that a lot of the young musicians he met when teaching, think that the history of the music is not important any more, as long as they have their own 'concept'. They know who Bird (Charlie Parker) is, but don't consider him relevant. As an educator and performer, Branford knows that evolution comes from the knowledge of the past and taking it into a new age – whatever form of art you are talking about. If you get stuck in your 'thing' or 'concept', you might stay there forever. What is needed to move forward is curiosity, but a lot of the youngsters don't have it – like in many different ways in our times, in music as well, all is centred around the ego and oneself.

A word on Branford – it has always been a pleasure to work with him, as he is truly one of the most professional guys in the business. Within three days in Vienna, he did 23 interviews with media from all over Europe – each at least 40 minutes long! Never tired of talking about his music, the way the band approaches a recording or concert, his philosophy. An example in many more ways than musically. The promotion Harry Gruber had set up was really amazing and, in the end, when the album came out, it entered to Austrian Pop charts, not very high, but …!!! A first for Branford for sure.

Meanwhile Universal was telling all my artists that they wouldn't continue making records with them, either with immediate effect or when the last agreed album was released. Branford's label deal was also not to be renewed. It was kind of sad to see the dismantling of Emarcy in such a short time as well as the changes in Verve. Tough times for jazz indeed!

Beside the Branford album, another record that came out from an act signed by me, was 'Made Possible' by the Bad Plus, another great album with compositions from all three members of the trio.

In my consultancy agreement with Universal it said that at the end of the two-year period I wasn't allowed to work for another label for 6 months. As I didn't want to wait in case an offer came up, I asked them to waive this clause, which they agreed to do and confirmed this via an email. Good! Now I just had to find a new company that needed a jazz A&R guy with some of the best connections in the business.

Herbie Hancock, in his role as UNESCO ambassador for the promotion of Intercultural Dialogue, announced, that April 30th 2012 would be the first International Jazz Day and that concert performances would take place in New Orleans, Paris and New York besides other cities. He himself would perform on that day in New Orleans, as well as New York. What's the point? Maybe they really need such an annual event in the US to re-focus their attention on their biggest cultural contribution to the world, but internationally? There are more jazz clubs and radio station/programs for this music outside the US than inside – most American jazz artists make a living from touring Europe and Asia and less from performing in their home country and record sales, which used to be for the genre 65% in the US are now about 70% outside that market. Herbie is quoted saying: *"I'm really excited about International Jazz Day because so many artists from various countries and genres have a connection to jazz and will be able to honour this music that has had a profound effect on them, I hope that this day spreads the joy of spontaneous creation that exists in this music. Jazz has been the voice of freedom for so many countries over the past half century,"* he added and that the *"international diplomatic aspect of jazz"* will be celebrated that day. There is no doubt, that Jazz can use all promotion it gets and there is no doubt as well that it is a universal language, a way to communicate without words. Improvisation doesn't know cultural background, as it is the vehicle to express oneself on a common ground with other musicians. Let's just hope that all involved in jazz will take this opportunity and make the best out of it – promoters, artists, labels, venues – if all work together it could actually be a worthwhile and great annual celebration of what we all love: improvised music, or simply said something that is more than that: Jazz.

On March 8th I gave a presentation to the International Jazz Festival Organisation, hoping that they would hire me as a consultant to work with them in building a better communication between their festivals, artists, managers, labels and agencies. The objective was clear: only together we could create Specials for the festivals, like All-Star Bands or tributes or special collaborations and develop the next jazz stars, by having a long-term plan for the selected artists. They liked the ideas I presented, but it never got further than that, for that they were still too much looking at their own festival instead of the bigger picture. Only a few years later, on initiative of the young bookers from North Sea, Sander Grande and Michelle Kuypers, they got into a system to develop a few new artists over a longer period together by booking them every year over a five-year period, either as sideman or with their own projects.

In April my mother came to visit and we did the usual little trips, ate well at Paco's and generally had some great days together. Unfortunately, this time without Hannah, as she was preparing for her A-Levels. I saw her less, but we either used Skype or phones to stay in touch. Living apart changes the relationship, as one has less experiences together, but that didn't change that we love each other. She was growing up, started to live her own life, with her circle of friends, her dreams and hopes and as a parent I have to respect that, accept it and support her. We were both extremely happy when Chelsea won the Champions League that year against Bayern Munich. In June Spain won the Euro 2012 with a 4:0 win over Italy and Andres Iniesta was voted best player of the tournament. A classy player, with incredible ball control and vision for the game.

2012, with my mother in Madrid

Universal Music was finalising the purchase of EMI and in 2012 all hurdles had been passed. They got EU and US approval to buy, but had to sell almost 1/3 of the combined assets and therefore got rid of Chrysalis Records, EMI Classics, Mute Records and a few others, including the German MPS jazz catalogue and their share in Jazzland Recordings in Oslo. Sten and Bugge bought back the shares Universal held and were from then on running the label as an Indie, looking for distribution partners around the world. MPS was bought by Edel Records, and slowly started to work on the catalogue, but only really got into releasing box sets and new recordings, when Christian Kellersmann joined them in 2014.

I didn't have many records to release in 2012, as there were hardly any acts left to work with. I had signed singer and daughter of Dee Dee Bridgewater and host of a music show on MTV France, China Moses. She had released one jazz album before, a wonderful tribute to Dinah Washington and the new recording was continuing that concept with a tribute to the early Blues singers. 'Crazy Blues' definitely helped China to build her career further, but unfortunately, when I left, they wanted to give the deal to the French company, now with the guys with whom she had worked on the album before, as they were integrated into the jazz team at Universal after the purchase of EMI, which included the US and French Blue Note operations. So, we only had that one album and it fell kind of between the chairs, still doing fine and getting some great reviews. Then Max Hole gave me call one afternoon and told me to make a jazz record with Chinese singer Karen Mok, who was a superstar at home and wanted to do an international album and Max thought it should be jazz. I said I would go ahead immediately. We agreed not to record in the US, as this is what everyone else would do, but record in China and try to use local traditional instruments and players from the region. But for me the first question was: who is the producer going to be? I asked for all CDs and DVDs of Karen to be send to me and checked her out. I hadn't known her before, but she was for sure a great singer and, as I found out later, a great actress too. Her music is more pop oriented and modern, so a more traditional leaning producer wouldn't do. I send a few things to Bugge to check his interest and he did like what he heard. I got the two in touch with each other, then they met and started to work on some ideas. And from there onwards we planned the recording. Bugge was great to work with and extremely efficient.

At the same time Sergio Mendes had asked me to help a bit with an album he was doing for Universal Japan, using local singers for the re-makes of some of his old hits. He wanted to know if there were any other singers in the region he should consider and I mentioned Karen Mok. Sergio checked her out and, in the end, she did one song on the album 'Rendez-Vous', a really cool and fun version of 'Killing Me Softly With This Song'.

Our agency had nine shows for Branford in April in Europe and three more for James Carter, for whom we also got six shows in Europe in the fall. Slowly, we got into a rhythm there and we were hoping to see more shows coming in the following year, when we didn't have a label yet lined up for additional income. I went to Rotterdam to see the young musicians from Take Five: Europe perform, as well as Michel Camilo. When backstage with him Japanese pianist Hiromi popped by and we all had a little chat. I recognized that she was wearing a pair of trainers with a piano keyboard design, and as I had the same shoes at home, I told her so. She then explained to me that these were actually designed by her husband for her and then Puma, the sportswear company, bought the rights to do a limited edition. Cool, or what?

Michel Camilo and Hiromi, backstage NSJF 2012

James Carter was as well performing at North Sea and so were The Bad Plus with Joshua Redman, a cool combination and great show. In Vitoria we had Sonny Rollins performing a great concert, especially the first set was incredible – he was flying over the swinging music of his band, soaring!! That was some of the best playing I had heard from Sonny ever! Truly amazing! He signed CDs after the show for almost 2 hours. What a guy!

Hannah came to Madrid in July and we went together to the victory parade of the Spanish football team, following their success at the Euros. She had been in Vienna and Eitzersthal before, traveling with EuroRail and we had some really good days together, going to Alcalá de Henares for a little trip, eating tapas. In August Yolanda and I took a little break in Almeria again, taking it easy with Maria and Jorge, relaxing at the various beaches of the area and going out to see Josemi perform as well. Meanwhile Hannah had gotten her A-Level results and she hadn't made the necessary grades. She was extremely surprised and devastated as all the mock exams had been fine. She had to re-sit the exams early the following year, which would mean plans for university or whatever else were all on hold. She thought the overall marking was much lower than before, but that didn't change the fact, that she hadn't passed. Therefore, she had to take an intense September to January re-take course and had to focus on that only.

That same year Barack Obama was re-elected as president of the USA: Greece needed another financial bail-out from the Eurozone countries and the never-ending conflict between Israel and

Palestine started up once again. In Newtown, Connecticut, 20-year-old Adam Lanza killed 26 people, mainly children, in an elementary school, after having shot his mother earlier the same day. When police arrived at the scene, he shot himself. As usual there was a short and intense debate about gun control in the US, leading to nothing.

The year was a good one for jazz in terms of top-quality releases, with new albums by Diana Krall, Till Brönner, Madeleine Peyroux, Tord Gustavsen, José James and Gregory Porter, whose 'Be Good' is a sensational record of great new songs. But my album of the year was 'Saltash Bells' by John Surman, which somehow took me back to his 'Amazing Adventures of Simon Simon' album, which he recorded with Jack De Johnette in 1981– layers of saxophones and electronics combine to a sound so unique and touching, with small melodies floating around. John credits his son Pablo Benjamin with some of the sound design – he obviously listened to his dad's past creations and intentions and together they created a typical Surman album of lasting quality. Just listen to 'On Staddon Heights' and the title track 'Saltash Bells' and you will be under John's spell as well.

Besides many others, the jazz world lost that year Portuguese pianist Bernardo Sassetti, whom I had met when he was in Guy Barkers group; Austrian pianist and jazz legend Fritz Pauer; Dave Brubeck, whom I had fortunately seen perform as well and bass player Charles Flores, whom we met when recording with Michel Camilo. He was only 41 years old, having played with Michel for 10 years, after leaving Cuba. An immensely talented musician and a quiet and charming person. At the age of 67 Terry Callier, the great singer and songwriter from Chicago, passed away in 2012 as well. His songs have been performed by many, but he was for sure underrated as a musician and performer. I met him around 1998 when he released 'Timepiece', one of his most successful recordings and then worked with him as Executive Producer on the 'Lookin' Out' album and 'Live in Berlin' DVD. What a great, warm and humble human being. We met and talked a few times; I saw him perform in London often and he always captured me emotionally with his warm voice and deep lyrics. His last recording was 'Hidden Conversations' (2009), a collaboration with Massive Attack and a superb album by any standard.

And then the call I was waiting for came. Bogdan Roscic had been for three years running Sony Classical worldwide, had it made profitable and efficient again and was ready to add jazz to his portfolio, as within Sony no other department was doing it. I flew to Berlin, where he had his global marketing office and the repertoire centre for core classical, whereas in the US they had with Masterworks an open label for more adult oriented music, crossover and soundtracks. We had a great chat and I accepted to get them back into jazz and started thinking about strategy and possible signings. I had checked before going to Berlin which jazz labels they owned and I really liked the idea of using OKeh Records for what we wanted to do. The main reason was that it was founded in 1918 by a German immigrant by the name of Otto K. Heinemann and that he had had an open mind as to what music to record and release. He not only did jazz recordings, but as well a lot of folk music from European countries to be sold to immigrants in the US. On OKeh are too the first recordings of an Afro-American female blues singer, Mamie Smith and of course the most important small group recordings in the history of jazz: Louis Armstrong's Hot Five and Hot Seven. Duke Ellington, Bix Beiderbecke and many more are part of that history as well. What I wanted to do was pretty simple: stay in the history, but make important records for our days. Start with some good names, then add a bunch of new talents to the roster and in phase three bring in some top acts.

OKeh

As I couldn't do anything before October 1st, because the Universal deal ended September 30th and as they had been generous and good to me, I didn't want to do anything to break that deal and our good relationship, I had to wait speaking to artists or managers. But finally on October 1st I could send an email to all my contacts, letting them know what I was about to start. At the same time, I was in Berlin at the global Sony marketing managers meeting for classical music and was presented there and did present my concepts and ideas for what we wanted OKeh to be. It was easy, as there were a few faces I knew from Universal, like Per Hauber, who was running the core classical A&R department, or Liam Toner, who was running the UK offices and a few more. My main contact would be Alexander Boesch, the global head of marketing and someone who knew his jazz, having signed Nils Petter Molvaer and Silje Nergaard to Sony Germany before moving to International. Sony did send out an announcement, that read as follows:

Berlin/New York, October 1, 2012
"Sony Classical announces the appointment of Wulf Müller as an exclusive Jazz A&R consultant. Working with the Sony Classical teams in Berlin and New York, he will be bringing new and established artists to the company, overseeing product development and supporting the international marketing of the releases.
Wulf Müller has 29 years of experience in the music business, most of them in jazz marketing and A&R for PolyGram and later Universal Music International in London where he has been responsible for all signings on the Emarcy label. He has been Executive Producer on countless recordings, including albums by Michael Brecker, Dee Dee Bridgewater, John Scofield, James Carter, Jane Monheit and Charlie Haden and has worked closely with or signed artists like Sonny Rollins, Madeleine Peyroux and Sergio Mendes.
Bogdan Roscic, President Sony Classical, said: "Wulf is one of the most experienced and respected executives in the jazz world and I have wanted to bring him to Sony for a long time. As the Sony Classical labels steadily broaden their scope in terms of musical genres, he will contribute to the depth of the roster and projects that we deliver. The last years have shown how many great opportunities the many facets of today's jazz present – it's a great time for Wulf to be joining our team."
Wulf Müller commented on the appointment: "I am honoured and excited to be asked to start jazz activities within Sony Classical and look forward to working with the Sony teams on some of the greatest artists in today's music world."
The appointment is effective immediately. Mr. Müller will remain based in Madrid where in 2010 he founded All-In Music Service, an independent company whose core business is international consulting for artists, sponsors, touring agents, music festivals and managements in the world of Jazz and related music genres."

For the first A&R meeting with Bogdan I had put together a list of possible signings and releases for the coming year, that included Bob James & David Sanborn, Sonny Rollins, Bobby McFerrin, Jeff Ballard, Craig Handy, RGG, Theo Croker, Charlie Watts and the Danish Radio Big Band, Tuck & Patti and it had as well some long term options like Michel Camilo, Denardo Coleman with his own group and some unreleased Ornette material, James Carter, Sergio Mendes, Julian Lage, Charlie Haden, who unfortunately wouldn't record anything new anymore, Dave Holland, Dhafer Youssef and Ute Lemper, among others and some we did sign in the end and others we didn't, but it was a good list to start with. And when Bogdan shortly after bringing me on announced that he had hired my old friend Chuck Mitchell to run the US Masterworks operations, the set up was perfect. Chuck and I had worked together extremely well while he was at Verve, then again shared some artists between e-one and Emarcy and now we would be working on OKeh together again. It was great to know that I had someone in the US who would understand what I was doing and knew the music and artists. Within a week from sending out my email about my new job, I got some really interesting answers. The first one came from Lee Townsend, Bill Frisell's producer and manager and he was not only delighted for me, but as well interested in working together. And the second one came from keyboarder John Medeski, who informed me that he had some unreleased solo piano recordings and if I would be interested in these? Sure, I was. It was time to get some artists signed, as I wanted to have the first recordings out in April 2013. I went to Barcelona to see Sonny Rollins performing there. He had told me that Don Was had called him a few times, asking if he would want to record for Blue Note. I asked what did you tell him and Sonny said, that he wasn't sure about it and wanted to talk to me first. He said *"I know you and like to work with you, so if you can, make me an offer"*, which I gladly did. Sonny was in great form in Barcelona, even at the sound check. After the check was done and all the other musicians had left the stage, Sonny was standing there alone, improvising. I was blown away. This was absolutely incredible! I spoke with his sound man Richard Corsello and he told me that he had recorded all of it and that they had hours of Sonny doing solo improvisations at sound checks in their archive. Really something to think about.

Sonny Rollins, Barcelona, Palau de Musica, 2012

2012 was truly a busy year in which I had seen the first part of 'The Hobbit' in the movies, as well as Ben Affleck's 'Argo', the amazing documentary 'Searching For Sugar Man' and the wonderful 'Le Havre' by Aki Kaurismaki. I read the first two books in the Department Q series by Jussi Adler-Olsen, thanks to a recommendation by my sister Barbara and Gillian Flynn's 'Gone Girl'. We finished off the year as always – with Yolanda's family and great food. Ready for more action and back doing A&R.

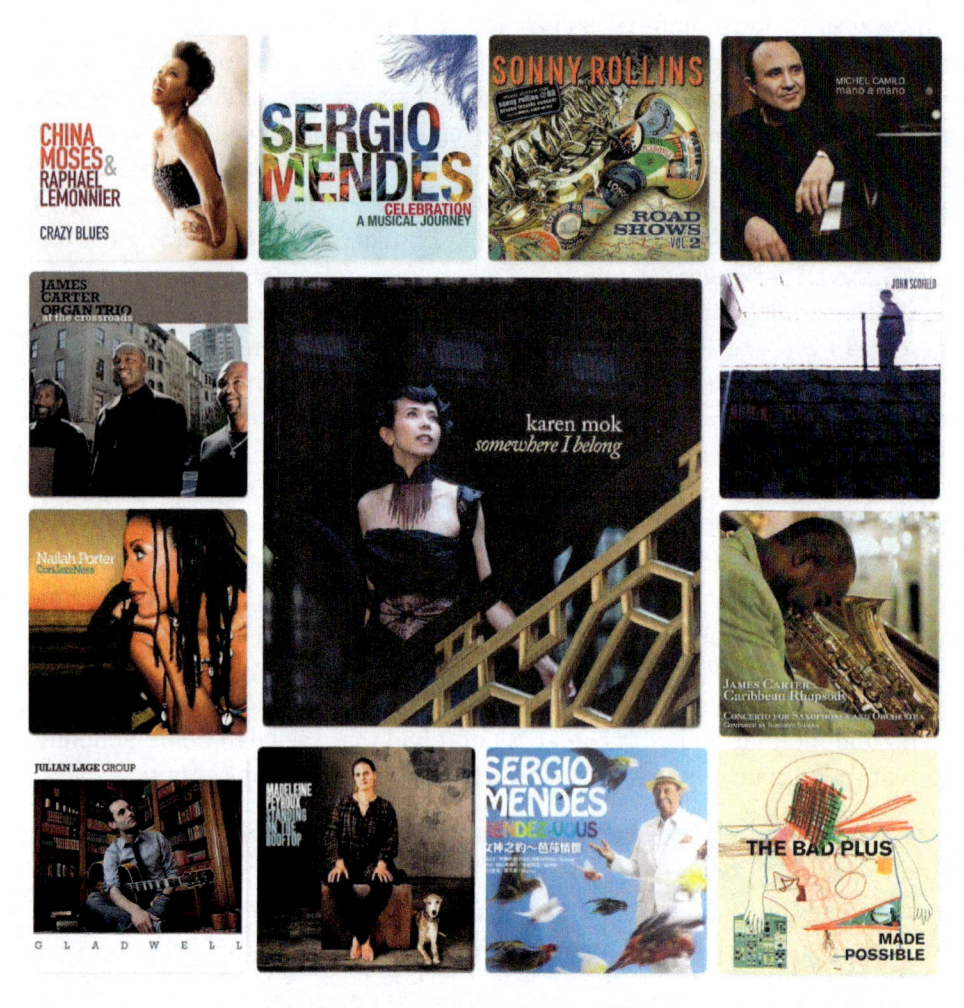

last Emarcy releases, 2011 to 2013

2013

On January 10th 2013 Sony Masterworks, via the US jazz PR company they used, DL Media, sent out another info on the re-launch of Okeh Records and the appointment of Chuck and myself. This text as well included the first three records to be released: John Medeski´s 'A Different Time', Bob James & David Sanborn's 'Quartette Humaine' and Bill Frisell's 'Big Sur'. It also mentioned that a further five to seven records would come out later that year. In the end, we had seven releases overall, as some didn't get finished in time and for others the deals weren't done fast enough. But it was a good package of records to get started with. Except for Nicholas Payton, who, on his blog, wrote that it was unacceptable that the re-launch of OKeh was with white artists only, as this was a label important to Afro-American music. I really couldn't care less about what Nic was writing on his blog, unresearched and without fact-checking. OKeh's history is so much more than just that one, even so important, aspect, not forgetting to mention that OKeh was actually founded by a German immigrant. It's OK for Nicholas to write whatever he wants, but if a journalist is repeating that same message in an important newspaper, it gets a bit too far. And that's what John Murph did. It would have been easy to reach me or Chuck to get a statement or a release plan, which would have set the record straight, but that didn't happen. We had to complain to his editor for unprofessional conduct when writing his piece and in the end, he had to correct it and apologise. I didn't know John then, but when I met him at a later point, I thought he was a kind and reasonable guy. We put this episode behind us quickly and stayed in touch from then on and I started to send him info on our releases, so he was always up to date. These accusations were weird and really pissed me off, as everyone who knows me would confirm that this is not the way I think. I put records out that have quality and are relevant to our times (at least that's what I am trying) and race is of no importance for me when picking an artist or project and never has been, as my professional record shows. Nicholas knew Chuck and myself from the times when we put out his Verve albums, so a call would have been really easy, to check what the long-term plan was for the label. A little unnecessary storm that blew over quickly, as the release schedule became, as planned, as diverse as it should be and as international, as we wanted it to be.

I went to New York for meetings around the Jazz Connect Convention, which for the first time was to be held as part of APAP, the live music convention. Jazz Connect was created by Peter Gordon of the Jazz Forward Coalition and Lee Mergner, JazzTimes, plus some help by Don Lucoff, the PR guy we used as well. Workshops and panels were the main ingredients of the convention and I was invited to hold a panel about an international jazz market – over the years I did, Norway, Germany, Australia, Turkey and others. Really interesting. Music could be heard at the Winter Jazz Festival which ran at the same time in the area around their main venue, Le Poisson Rouge. The two most amazing shows for me were Julian Lage & Nels Cline: extraordinary guitar improvisations by the masters of two generations. I knew how good both individually are, but together they just blew me away with the deep understanding and always interesting improvisations they delivered, usually with a big smile on their faces; and Bugge Wesseltoft and friends with Erik Truffaz on trumpet, plus percussions, sax, drums and bass. Musicians from all over the world performing together in the typical free funk of Bugge and creating beautiful ambient sounds and powerful rhythms for the soloists to go crazy over.

After New York it was the UK for me again and Take Five: Europe II, this time with Airelle Besson (tp) and Guillaume Perret (sax) from France; Marcos Baggiani (dr) and David Kweksilber (cl) from Holland; Per Zanussi (bass) and Daniel Herskedal (tuba) from Norway; Piotr Damasiewicz (tp) and Marcin Masecki (p) from Poland plus Arun Ghosh (cl) and Chris Sharkey (git) from the UK. John Surman as usually supervised the music sessions, which for me were the best I heard in all the Take Five programs I had been part of. I was looking forward to see them perform a full concert at North Sea the coming summer.

2013, Take Five: Europe

UNESCO released the location for the 2013 International Jazz Day Concert: Istanbul and some of the most important musicians of the genre were to perform there, including Terri Lyne Carrington, George Duke, James Genus, Robert Glasper, Herbie Hancock, Abdullah Ibrahim, Al Jarreau, John McLaughlin, Marcus Miller, Dianne Reeves, Lee Ritenour, Christian Scott and Wayne Shorter. With other concerts to be held around the globe, International Jazz Day really became an important event in the calendar.

Montreux Jazz Festival empresario and friend Claude Nobs passed away on January 10th, after a skiing accident that left him in a coma for over two weeks. Claude was a larger-than-life character and a tireless worker for the cause of music and jazz especially. A great harmonica player and a fun-loving, kind human being. It was Claude who introduced me to Quincy Jones. I was at the festival in Montreux a few years back when Claude asked me to come with him and he led me to an area where Quincy was sitting, having a drink. He introduced us and then left. I told Quincy what I was doing and that I was honoured to run Emarcy at that time, holding the same job more or less he had in the late 1950's when he ran the label and produced for them. He seemed genuinely interested in what we were doing at Emarcy and we had a great and amicable chat. I will always be thankful to Claude for having made this possible. Switzerland lost shortly after Claude another great jazz man with Kurt S. Weil, musician, journalist, label man: he did it all and always with a smile. I had met him a few times and always liked his level-headed approach to things.

For Easter Yolanda and I went to Granada to see the Alhambra and some processions for the holidays. Jorge and Maria were with us and, despite the weather being bad, we had a great time in this beautiful place.
Meanwhile Hannah had sat her A-Levels again and this time did pass with flying colours! Shortly after the exams she did a trip to Sri Lanka for four months to work there for a charity as an English teacher for young people. It was the first time she was away from home for such a long spell on her own, but she thoroughly enjoyed the experience, the people there and her work with kids. The country offered a lot as well and on her days off she explored Sri Lanka a bit. I think it was an important step into her being completely independent and set her up well for studying in Nottingham, where she was accepted for History and German. She had already dealt with all student loans and housing and was ready to go. The initial A-Level setback seemed just to have made her more determined and stronger. Way to go!
Yolanda and I went to the Madrid Tennis Masters and enjoyed a day out, watching top class tennis, which was what you got when you have Serena Williams, Roger Federer and Andy Murray on your program.

In March I went back to London for TAKE FIVE UK VIII and it was great to talk and discuss with these eager and interested to learn young musicians. Good to see Gwyneth Herbert in the group, who I really like and had the pleasure of working with a few years back. Unfortunately, my schedule didn't allow me to listen to the group rehearsing and performing, which I usually liked to do. As always it was good to see John Surman again and having another chat about music with him and John Cumming.

In April Yolanda and I went to 'jazzahead', the jazz fair in Bremen, which over the years had developed from a German event via a European to a global meeting of all things jazz. 'Jazzahead' is more about individual meetings and business than the panel-oriented Jazz Connect and it has a wonderful and always interesting schedule of 40-minute showcases.
We checked out the technically incredible pianist Omer Klein, the really great Zoe Rahman quartet and some of the Motema 10th Anniversary showcase featuring a solo bass performance by Charnett Moffett and a solo piano set by Marc Cary performing the music of Abbey Lincoln and then Charnett

together with label founder and singer/songwriter Jana Herzen. The two solo performances were for me some of the best of its kind! For Yolanda these three days were interesting, but too much talk about music. We took some time to walk through Bremen, but between meetings and showcases, it wasn't much.

In April we had as well the first concerts of the year for Branford in Europe, with six duo dates for him and Joey and then we had 12 dates for July with the quartet, including the Love Supreme Festival in the UK, Umbria Jazz, North Sea and Vitoria. We also had three dates in Europe for James in July and started to look after Jane Monheit as well, booking the first dates for her in the fall.

Then I went for another Take Five, this time Switzerland, as they asked John Cumming and his team to organize one for them.
The participants were this time drummer Florian Arbenz, singer Elina Duni, trombone player Samuel Blaser, pianist Marc Perrenoud, violinist Tobias Preisig, pianist Stefan Rusconi, singer Andreas Schaerer and pianist Leo Tardin.
The schedule looked a bit different to the previous ones for Europe, as it was adapted to the needs of these musicians – and therefore focused more on to learn about other EU countries and regions and their jazz scene, as means to make it easier to get into these markets. Their music sessions were with Norwegian Jan Bang, who improvised with these musicians based on sounds and samples he used and they partly created some astonishing music, just improvising and listening to each other. Each of these artists could perform and improvise on a very high level and one piece especially was truly exceptional for a spontaneous composition and left us all deeply impressed. I stayed in touch with most of these guys over the following years and it was interesting to see how they developed.

2013, Jan Bang working with the participants of Take Five Switzerland

April 2013 was the month the first new OKeh album was released: John Medeski's 'A Different Time', which was recorded on a 1924 Gaveau piano, the predecessor of the modern piano and sounded beautiful. It was the right album to start the new version of the label: it was by an established artist, but him doing something different and a bit surprising, but maintaining top quality. A kind of statement for the label's objective. I went with John to Berlin and Paris to do interviews in advance of the release and we had a great time, finding many hours to chat, something we never had the time to do before, when we only met before or after a gig or at a festival.

The second release was the Bob James & David Sanborn re-union album 'Quartette Humaine', featuring James Genus and Steve Gadd. Bob and Dave had released a very successful smooth jazz album in 1986 and this was now the acoustic follow up and a real cool album, that Dave's manager Pat Rains brought to me. That album was # 1 in Billboard and Jazzweek and the single 'Deep In The Weeds' as well # 1 and reviews were extremely great. I was happy, as we got a lot of attention because of that and who doesn't want to have a # 1 jazz album as a label?

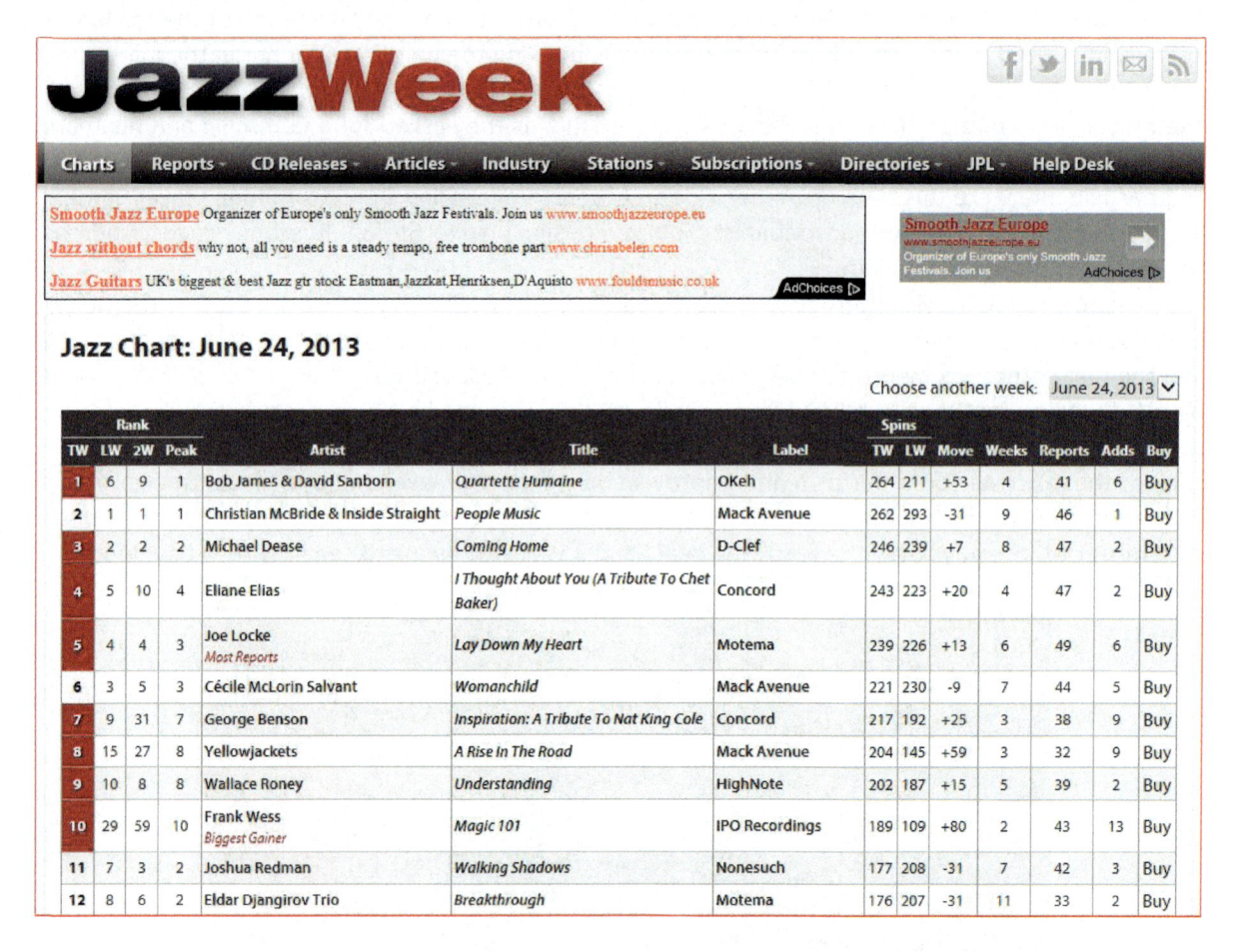

JazzWeek

Jazz Chart: June 24, 2013

Rank TW	LW	2W	Peak	Artist	Title	Label	Spins TW	LW	Move	Weeks	Reports	Adds	Buy
1	6	9	1	Bob James & David Sanborn	Quartette Humaine	OKeh	264	211	+53	4	41	6	Buy
2	1	1	1	Christian McBride & Inside Straight	People Music	Mack Avenue	262	293	-31	9	46	1	Buy
3	2	2	2	Michael Dease	Coming Home	D-Clef	246	239	+7	8	47	2	Buy
4	5	10	4	Eliane Elias	I Thought About You (A Tribute To Chet Baker)	Concord	243	223	+20	4	47	2	Buy
5	4	4	3	Joe Locke *Most Reports*	Lay Down My Heart	Motema	239	226	+13	6	49	6	Buy
6	3	5	3	Cécile McLorin Salvant	Womanchild	Mack Avenue	221	230	-9	7	44	5	Buy
7	9	31	7	George Benson	Inspiration: A Tribute To Nat King Cole	Concord	217	192	+25	3	38	9	Buy
8	15	27	8	Yellowjackets	A Rise In The Road	Mack Avenue	204	145	+59	3	32	9	Buy
9	10	8	8	Wallace Roney	Understanding	HighNote	202	187	+15	5	39	2	Buy
10	29	59	10	Frank Wess *Biggest Gainer*	Magic 101	IPO Recordings	189	109	+80	2	43	13	Buy
11	7	3	2	Joshua Redman	Walking Shadows	Nonesuch	177	208	-31	7	42	3	Buy
12	8	6	2	Eldar Djangirov Trio	Breakthrough	Motema	176	207	-31	11	33	2	Buy

Bill Frisell's opus 'Big Sur' was next in line for a release. An album that showcases some of Bill's best writing in a mix of folk, jazz, country and world music only Bill can produce. Contemplative and touching. And another one that got great reviews around the globe.

I had gotten an email from Brian Bacchus, producer of Gregory Porter and many others and a good friend since our days together at PolyGram. He had sent me a few tracks by Somi, an American singer and songwriter, whose original music is directly influenced by her Ugandan and Rwandan heritage and he highly recommended her to me. Both Yolanda and myself really liked what we heard and I got in touch with her and arranged to meet her in Paris, where she was doing two shows at the Duc Des Lombards club. I thought the show was great, she had personality and stage presence and we started to talk about her possibly signing to OKeh, as one of the new acts for 2014.

I had taken Michel Camilo with me from Universal, as he is an artist I really like and both he and his wife and manager Sandra, became friends of Yolanda and myself. The new album 'What's Up?' was a solo piano recording, re-visiting some of Michel's classics, plus new compositions and four standards, the most outstanding on an overall great record being his version of Paul Desmond's 'Take Five'! Technically this is almost impossible to play, but Michel manages and how! Chuck wanted to sign singer Kat Edmonson and as she was performing in London, I went to see her. Kat is a truly talented performer, who captures your attention and doesn't let go throughout the concert – her stage presence is strong, her vocal delivery without fault. Her songs are clever little stories and she is a great story teller. A recognisable voice, with hints of Blossom Dearie or Silje Nergaard, but all her own in her way of singing and phrasing. And the record, which she had self-released already in the US, sounded really great as well. 'Way Down Low', which shows what an amazing song writer she is, included the single 'Lucky', a wonderful little tune that got a lot of radio plays.

I had started to talk to Sergio Mendes about putting out his next record on OKeh and he kind of liked the idea. As he was in Paris in June, as always staying at the George V Hotel, Yolanda and I went to Paris to finalise the deal. Work on the deal was done relatively quickly and the rest was about eating well. Sergio took us to a Chinese who used to have a Michelin star and still was impressive and then one day to a Brasserie with outstanding oysters and fish dishes. What a treat! And his selection of wines was always incredible. I am not sure if it was at this trip or another, but once he took us to a restaurant called 'L'Ami Louis' and explained that he went there for the first time with Norman Granz, the founder of Verve Records, in the 60's. We arrived a bit before Gracinha and Sergio and were guided to the table Sergio had booked, but when sitting down we were told that the side of the table with view into the restaurant was usually where Sergio and Gracinha would sit. We changed, of course. The food was excellent, the wines Sergio selected outstanding and at one point Chico Buarque plus a group of ten friends entered the restaurant, to celebrate his birthday. That was fun! Sergio had a bottle of wine delivered to his table and we continued our incredible meal. Sergio is a real generous guy and I learned a lot about food and wine from him.

Dinner with Gracinha and Sergio, Paris 2013

After that little trip we went to Denmark to celebrate my mother's 85th birthday in Hvide Sande and all her kids and their partners and kids and friends of the family came to party with her. Barbeques and beer, a bit of swimming in the cold North Sea and generally having fun. Hannah, just back from Sri Lanka, came as well to celebrate with us and we got the first stories from her trip abroad. And share her excitement of starting to study in Nottingham soon.

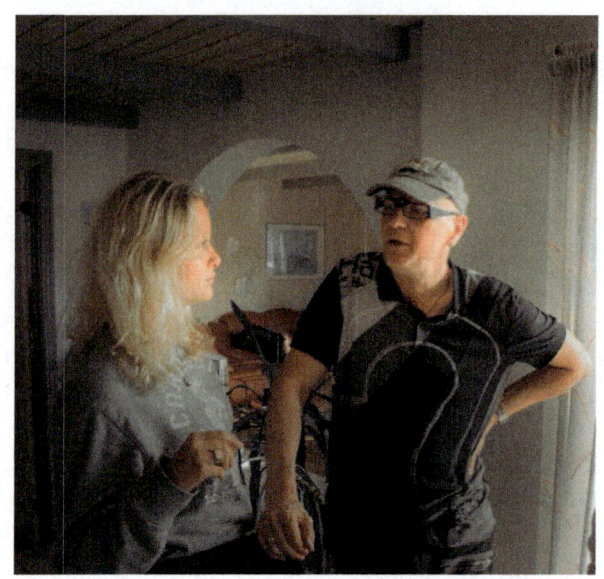

with Hannah at my mother's 85th birthday, 2013

Then we were off to North Sea Jazz in Rotterdam, where we had with our Dutch team set up a lot of promotion for Kat Edmonson and John Medeski. They had hired indie PR lady Sabina Vissers, who did a great job, as both acts were busy with interviews, radio performances and CD signings. Bob James & David Sanborn performed a wonderful show at the festival and so did the young musicians from Take Five: Europe II, were especially the composition by trumpet player Airelle Besson stood out for its melodic beauty and emotional content. Michel Camilo and Tomatito played one of their amazing duo concerts, which the audience, plus Yolanda and myself, loved. We had booked Branford too into the festival and saw a great show, plus had a chance to say *"Hi"* to Diana Krall, Chick Corea, Roy Hargrove and his manager Larry Clothier, as well as Jamie Cullum and Dee Dee Bridgewater, who played a rare concert with Ramsey Lewis.

with Bob James and David Sanborn in Rotterdam, 2013

From Rotterdam, via Madrid to change clothes, we went to Vitoria, as we had Branford performing there as well with the quartet and Bill Frisell with 'The Big Sur'. Chick was in Vitoria too and so was Paco de Lucia, who played an incredible gig, joined at the end by Chick and then they really got the audience going. Something special was happening, as always when these two amazing musicians came together. Melody Gardot gave a stunning show, making everyone in the audience feel as if she would sing just for him or her.

Later in July, on his way to his holidays on the Canary Islands, Tord Gustavsen stopped in Madrid for a solo concert at the Club Clamores. Over the years I have seen or been involved in many solo piano concerts or recordings, but few have been so touching and spiritual as this one by Tord. I knew him since his time with Silje Nergaard and had followed his music ever since, as I believe that he is one of the most unique and talented pianists around (together with Jef Neve, Tigran and a few others). He opened the evening with a suite based on 'Tears Transforming', which he originally recorded with his trio on his second ECM album, 'The Ground'. And this suite immediately showed what Tord is all about: a pianist of subtle tones and great imagination and a composer, whose main influences from the European tradition seem to be hymns and from outside of Europe gospel songs and blues. He followed that with an unnamed piece of the same qualities and a bit more tempo, then went into 'Where we went', which was followed by a beautiful version of a Norwegian hymn. 'Right There' was a new piece which he had just recorded for a forthcoming ECM quartet album and it was a beautiful and deep meditation with all the qualities that make Tord such a different and amazing musician. 'Silent Spaces' and a Norwegian lullaby closed the evening before an up-tempo encore that made everyone smile with its uplifting theme. Such great music performed by a very nice, intelligent and soft-spoken man, only disrupted by a bartender who constantly made noises while the performer gave his best. It shows a lack of respect for the artist and the music if you can't wait to prepare the bar for the next event and distract the audience from the pleasure of listening. A club with the tradition of the Clamores should have known better!!!

Bugge had done a real great job with the Karen Mok album, and when 'Somewhere I Belong' was released, it got some wonderful reviews. Barry Barnes, my video guy for many years, did a bunch of great videos for her, which helped to sell the album. Universal even did a Deluxe Edition, with a bonus DVD featuring the 'Making of ...' documentary. This was the last album to come out on Emarcy I was directly involved in and one I am actually quite proud of.

Hannah came to visit in August and for the first time she brought a boyfriend with her! In a way I thought that was cool and could see that she was happy and that's all I really care about. We got tickets to an Atletico Madrid game and had fun watching them win. They had a good time in Madrid, as by then Hannah could show him around. I am always happy when my daughter is in town and we can all spend some time together.

For the second half of the year, I had three albums to release: the rocky and powerful 'Prism' by Dave Holland, featuring Kevin Eubanks, Craig Taborn and Eric Harland; Dhafer Youssef's masterpiece 'Birds Requiem', featuring among others Turkish clarinettist Hüsnü Şenlendirici, Eivind Aarset, Nils Petter Molvaer, Phil Donkin and Kristjan Randalu. A truly spiritual and touching album, with one of the best covers I had on OKeh, with all the stunning photos taken by Dhafer's partner Shiraz; and saxophonist Craig Handy's '2ND Line Smith', his New Orleans inspired take of the music by Jimmy Smith, featuring guest appearances by Wynton Marsalis and Dee Dee Bridgewater. My friend Ingrid Hertfelder did some of the photography for this album and as I always liked to work with her, she would do a few more for OKeh in the coming years.

Completely unexpected my friend of over 30 years, a great human being and jazz concert promoter, Heinz Krassnitzer passed away that September, being just 60 years old. When I moved from Vienna to London Heinz was one of the true friends who always stayed in touch, had time for a chat about music, sent recommendations. And he came to visit. Heinz for me was one of the 'unsung heroes' of the Austrian jazz scene. By bringing a lot of international acts to Austria, he and Fritz Thom gave the local scene a strong injection of ideas and concepts and then by booking local acts into the festivals they were programming, they put the Austrian musicians up next to the international ones, helping them in terms of gaining status and recognition. He was the guy behind the scenes, with a passion for the music we call jazz. We had talked about that year meeting to celebrate Christmas together on the Canary Islands, where he went for a short break every year in December. Unfortunately, this was to remain a plan forever ….

Heinz Krassnitzer, 1953 – 2013

I had done an update on my A&R activities for Bogdan and Chuck highlighting what was already out and what was in preparation for release for the rest of this and the first half of the following year. And I had as well updated the list of possible signings, which were under review or discussion. This list included then Branford Marsalis, MSMW, a Chick Corea solo album, John Scofield, Roy Hargrove, Kenny Garrett, Julian Lage, Kurt Elling, Madeleine Peyroux, whose Universal deal had only an option left, Till Brönner, Sachal Vasandani, Ute Lemper and Gretchen Parlato and a few others. The third section on that update was a list of projects that had been offered to me either by the artists themselves or by a manager or agent. This list included then among others Randy Crawford, Raul Midon, David Sanchez, Pat Martino, Avishai Cohen, Magos Herrera & Javier Limon and Jacob Collier, whom I met in London on recommendation by Tommy LiPuma and who was then a very interesting young man, to whom I suggested to go out and play with some friends and continue to develop what he was doing. And lastly there was a list for the local releases for which we had the use of the OKeh label approved, that included Nils Petter Molvaer, Silje Nergaard, Robin McKelle and a few more. The changes on the list to the previous year was a reflection of the A&R work and negotiations – some deals were made, others not, for a variety of reasons. These lists, which I did provide to my bosses every once in a while, constantly changed with names dropping out and new ones coming in, artists shifting from one section into another, once a deal was done or getting closer being finalised.

While speaking to Sonny as usual, he told me that he was having respiratory problems and wasn't able to perform for a while. The problems continued for most part of the year and slowly Sonny, who was hopeful to perform again, got to think about that this might not happen. He still 'heard' a lot of music in his head, but couldn't play it, which was very hard for him. To keep himself busy, he started working with Richard Corsello, his sound engineer for many decades, on a list of the live recordings they have in Sonny's archive. I then spoke to him about an idea I had concerning the solo improvisations they had recorded over the years at sound checks. I thought that he should listen to them and pick ten segments of four to six minutes that made sense musically and then we would discuss these pieces and send eight of them to various musicians, like Herbie Hancock, Dave Holland, Brian Blade, Robert Glasper or Bugge Wesseltoft and so on, to play with him on these. The other two would as solo pieces open and close the album. In that way we would have a new Sonny album, which would be essential Sonny, but at the same time a tribute to him as well by some of the most important jazz musicians of our time. He really liked the idea and was going to think about it a bit more before moving forward with it.

Meanwhile I had received an email to my All-In Music Service account from a young sax player by the name of James Brandon Lewis. I hadn't heard of him before, so I checked him out a bit online and listened to the songs he had sent. Wow! The quality and fire of his music really took me by surprise. Free, but controlled, emotional and spiritual. Really deep! I wrote back to him asking if he got more and he did send me the full album he had recorded and for which he was looking for a label. Incredible stuff, featuring top jazz musicians William Parker on bass and Gerald Cleaver on drums. Music in the tradition of Sonny, Coltrane, Shepp and Sanders, but taken into our times. As I had some meetings in New York planned for October anyway, I arranged to meet with him and talk about a deal for this and future albums. When Yolanda and I went to New York that month we had meetings with Sony, saw Wendy Life and I met James, who didn't have a manager or agent and his sax needed an urgent repair. But we made the deal nevertheless and I asked Sony as well to have the sax fixed on top of a reasonable deal. James is a very charming and intelligent, deeply spiritual person and I was glad to be able to help him find a manager in Cynthia Herbst, who aided him to get organized.

For one afternoon Yolanda and I got an invitation to a music salon held in a private apartment with students of the Berklee School of Music performing with their teacher, Javier Limon, giving a focus on artists and the music from the Mediterranean region, plus musically related countries such as India. Those students were Shilpa Narayanan (voice, India), Eleni Arapoglou (voice, Greece), Tali Rubenstein (recorder, Israel), Tal Even-Tzur (piano, Israel), and Layth Sidiq (violin, Iraq/Jordan) and their music was inspiring and beautiful and crossed borders culturally and musically and proved once more that music is truly a global language. Back in Spain and another encounter with Berklee – this time at the Valencia campus: bass player and educator Eddie Gomez was given an honorary doctorate, the first the new campus ever awarded, in a ceremony that highlighted the career and music of Eddie as well as showcasing him with teachers and pupils of the school in a beautiful concert. Impressive the quality of the young musicians, coming to Berklee in Valencia from all over the world. Great to see how eager they were to learn from a master like Eddie Gomez, who showed all the improvisational skills that made him such a force in the Bill Evans trio and with all the other musicians he played with.

I had started as well to pick up locally signed artists and their albums for international releases via OKeh. The first one came from Italy and was a tribute album to Lucio Dalla made by some stars of the Italian jazz scene. Kat Edmonson was signed to Masterworks, but we used OKeh as a label for her internationally and I had taken on Taiwanese pianist Jo-Yu Chen and French signing Robin McKelle and from Sony Germany I would release new albums by my friends Nils Petter Molvaer and Silje Nergaard.

'That's OKeh' is a compilation album I made for November to highlight the new releases on OKeh and as well showcasing songs from forthcoming albums in 2014. All 2013 albums were featured as well as music from albums by drummer Jeff Ballard, whom I had signed after a great talk in Rotterdam and after he had sent me some incredible music; guitarist Nir Felder, who was brought to me by David Passick, his manager; Jo-Yu Chen, Robin McKelle, Somi, the singer I had finally signed; sax player James Brandon Lewis and young trumpet player Theo Croker, whom Dee Dee Bridgewater had signed to her label and brought to me. There were two versions of the sampler: a free one with about 2 minutes 30 seconds of each song, and a sales version at a very low price with the full songs. We ran some campaigns around the sampler and really got a lot of attention for the signings we had done and the albums that would come out in the following year. In the US they had changed the music on the sampler and called the campaign 'The Sound Of Next', focusing only on the forthcoming releases and it created quite a buzz there.

Japanese article on the re-launch of OKeh Records, 2013

Yolanda and I were watching 'La Vie De Adele' by Abdellatif Kechiche in the movies, as well as 'The Butler' by Lee Daniels and starring Forest Whitaker. Both movies are amazing and telling globally valid human stories extremely well. Of course, I saw 'The Hobbit' part 2 and with Yolanda as well the Woody Allen film 'Blue Jasmine' with a wonderful performance by Cate Blanchett. My favourite books of the year were Jonas Jonasson's fantastic, funny, clever and odd 'The Hundred-Year-Old Man Who Climbed Out the Window and Disappeared' and 'Gone Girl' by Gillian Flynn, a story with an interesting twist.

It was this year that Hannah started to study History and German and the Nottingham University and she seemed to have settled into student life fast and easy. Croatia became the 28th member of the European Union and Edward Snowdon leaked classified NSA documents, which brought him charges of espionage in the US. Only in 2020 an US federal court ruled that the mass surveillance program exposed by Snowden was illegal and possibly unconstitutional.

In October I went to Berlin for meetings with Bogdan and Alexander Boesch and while being in town, I went to see John Scofield perform at the Jazz Festival with his Uberjam Deux band, playing in Europe in support of the album with the same name, which was the follow up to 'Uberjam', which caused a stir about 10 years earlier when it was released. The new band had one member who was as well in the original line up – Avi Bortnick (guitar and electronics), the rhythm section of Andy Hess (bass) and Louis Cato (drums) was new, but not bad at all. Hess was a great time keeper and pushing the guys to GO, and Louis Cato was simply amazing and brought the audience up from their seats, but it was Avi and especially John who played absolutely amazing – Scofield's guitar with a beautiful sound, dancing, rocking and expressing the joys of life, but with the occasional scream of pain and sadness, which unfortunately is part of life as well. A true jam band that doesn't care how long the songs ran for, as long as they have something to say, find a new way to move over a groove and express themselves.

A quick trip to Paris to see Dhafer perform at Les Bouffes du Nord with his incredible band. France was his best market and the album was doing extremely well there and in some other markets, like Austria, Germany and Turkey.

November brought Madeleine Peyroux to Madrid for a touching show, as well as Kat Edmonson, who opened for Jamie Cullum, just with a guitar player and after two songs really got the audience. We had some great time afterwards going out in Madrid to eat and drink with Alvaro Bouso, our OKeh/Sony man in Spain.

2013, hanging out with Kat Edmonson, Madrid

I had regularly been in touch with German booking agent and friend Veit Bremme since a few months earlier when I had called his office and they told me that I could only reach him at home. When I rang him at his house, he explained to me that he was seriously ill and didn't know how long he still had to live. I had had no idea, and he told me no-one had, as I was then the only one, beside the people in the office, to know. From then on, we spoke every one or two weeks and I could hear how he got weaker over time. When I was with Yolanda in Cordoba for a few relaxed days in early December, he called me and we had a chat and even so he didn't say it, it seemed like he wanted to say 'Goodbye'. Two days later I tried to call him back, being in Madrid again, but he was too weak to talk. A day later he had passed away. We had spoken about life and death in the months and weeks before his passing, the most unusual conversations, honest and fearless from his side. Like Heinz Krassnitzer and Claude Nobs, he was one of the driving forces of the European jazz business. One of the many who were not in the spotlight but without whom nothing would have worked. Losing three wonderful human beings and friends in a year was tough to swallow.

Musicians who left us that year included Alvin Lee, the guitar hero of my youth and leader of the group Ten Years After; modern drummer Ronald Shannon Jackson, whom I had seen a few times, but I will never forget the power of the trio he had with James 'Blood' Ulmer and Jamaaladeen Tacuma; Bebo Valdes and Jim Hall and many more incredible human beings.

We ended the year with Hannah coming to Madrid for Christmas, us going to the Christmas market and for dinner to Paco's restaurant, talking about our times as a student, Yolanda and me from memory and Hannah from recent experiences. Then, with Yolanda's family, we relaxedly glided into the new year, which we knew would be a busy one.

2014

Over the previous few months, I had been in negotiations with Brice Rosenbloom, who was running the Winter Jazz Festival in New York City, to have a special showcase for the new OKeh acts within the festival. We managed to agree that we would have the Groove club for our night, but under the same deal for the artists as the festival would offer. We looked at many of our acts to perform, but in some cases, like Dhafer, we couldn't make it work for the dates and in the end, we had the following line-up for January 11th: James Brandon Lewis, Theo Croker, Jeff Ballard Trio, Nir Felder, Somi and finally Craig Handy and his 2nd Line Smith band.

James Brandon Lewis opened the night with a powerful set of improvisations: *"What I did hear in that time slot was a calmly smouldering performance by James Brandon Lewis, a tenor saxophonist originally from Buffalo, just barely in his 30s. Working with a pair of experienced partners, the bassist William Parker and the drummer Gerald Cleaver, Mr. Lewis dug in hard, accessing the sacramental side of 1960s free jazz. 'Wading Child in the Motherless Water,' his imploring hybrid of two foundational spirituals, was especially captivating business. I chose to see Mr. Lewis because I knew so little about him, and that small risk brought its bigger reward."*, wrote the New York Times.

He was followed by trumpeter Theo Croker, whose energetic set brought the temperature in the room up and when Dee Dee Bridgwater joined him on stage for a song, the crowd went wild. Theo therefore was the second surprise, as he was as well a newcomer just starting to build his reputation.

The Jeff Ballard Trio followed this set with a master class in improvisation. Tim Wilkins on a blog supreme: *"My 'peak musical moment' was the Jeff Ballard Trio with Lionel Loueke and Miguel Zenon, on a tiny stage at Groove. Three superb improvisers at the height of their powers, having so much fun!"* Three great musicians listening and reacting and seemingly creating great music from that. Jeff then was hanging around until late in the night and had a good chat with his new label mates.

Guitarist Nir Felder entertained his audience with his unique blend of jazz and rock and built his set to a fantastic climax, showing his incredible skills as composer and player in the same way. His band went through the repertoire of his debut album 'Golden Age'. Some of the European Jazz Festival promoters, which I had all invited, picked his set as their favourite one from the night. He was a real surprise for them.

OKeh jam session at the Groove with (among others) Theo Croker, Nir Felder and Craig Handy

Somi is such a rare singer and storyteller and her songs are deep and musically extremely interesting and that night she showed that live as well she was a force to reckon with: a great band that played her material with passion and dedication, allowing her to let her vocals flow over the music and touch everyone in the room. She is a singer and composer in the spirit of Nina Simone, but taking the music into the future with her special blend of African influences, jazz and R&B.

The evening was finished off in style by Craig Handy & 2nd Line Smith. The crowd started dancing after the first few bars and didn't stop until the end and was rewarded with some extraordinary sax soli by Mr. Handy and some hard grooves by his fellow musicians.

After a short intermission Craig and his group re-joined and opened a 40-minute jam session, to which Theo Croker and Nir Felder and more guests joined the band and had a lot of fun ... and so had the audience! And we had made our point: OKeh Records will be all about outstanding new and established talent in the world of improvised music.

Next on my schedule was the OKeh promo tour in Europe: five new artists on OKeh did interviews in Berlin and Paris, two days in each city with journalists from Italy and Switzerland participating as well. I had thought that bringing over five new acts in a package would create more media interest than having each of them coming individually and thankfully I was right. Jo-Yu Chen, Nir Felder, Somi, James Brandon Lewis and Theo Croker made the trip from the US to answer questions on their music in Europe and set the ball rolling for their respective releases, which were going to happen from January to the end of April. The resonance to this unusual package of artists was very positive and reviews of the albums in questions and bigger pieces followed soon.

Theo, Jo-Yu, Somi, Nir and James Brandon in Berlin

The initial releases for 2014 were therefore mainly from this group of musicians: James Brandon Lewis and his 'Divine Travels', for which once again Ingrid Hertfelder did the cover photo. Then we had Nir Felder's 'Golden Age', Jeff Ballard's 'Time's Tales', his debut album as a leader at the age of 50, but one, that left a deep impression. Then came Theo Croker's 'AfroPhysicist', a modern groove album produced by Dee Dee Bridgewater and featuring her on three songs, as well as having guest appearances by Roy Hargrove (as a singer) and Stefon Harris and Somi's wonderful 'The Lagos Music Salon', featuring the outstanding song 'When Rivers Cry,' which had rapper Common as a special guest. Pianist Jo-Yu Chen's 'Stranger' album came via Taiwan, but fitted perfectly into our objective of documenting 'Global Expressions In Jazz'. A line I borrowed from Ornette Coleman, explaining clearly what we wanted to do.

The A&R update for January of 2014 included the records just released and some that were in preparation for release, including new signing Magos & Limon. The 'in discussion as possible signings' list had Sachal Vasandani, Branford Marsalis, MSMW and Bill Charlap on it, whereas the long-term possibilities had now a new album by David Sanborn listed, which was to be produced by Marcus Miller. I also looked closely into the possibility to record an album with Stefano Bollani and Caetano Veloso, a likely live recording at Umbria Jazz. Names added to be discussed as probable targets for us were Christian Scott, Kurt Rosenwinkel, Jane Monheit, Aaron Goldberg and Marc Ribot. From this list none happened in the end, but I would have loved at least Christian to be with us. The Okeh artist roster looked as follows that year:

Direct OKeh signings:
John Medeski
Michel Camilo
Bill Frisell
David Sanborn   Ex Japan
Craig Handy
Dhafer Youssef
Dave Holland   Ex USA
Jeff Ballard
Nir Felder
Somi
Theo Croker
James Brandon Lewis
Sonny Rollins
Sergio Mendes
Magos & Limon
Sachal Vasandani

MASTERWORKS signings on OKeh:
Kat Edmonson
Regina Carter
The Bad Plus
Jazz and the Philharmonic

LOCAL signings:
Robin McKelle - France
Jo-Yu Chen - Taiwan
Nils Petter Molvaer - Germany
Silje Nergaard - Germany
Monika Borzym - Poland

Beside the A&R work, which is finding the artists, listening to them, talking about projects, discussing the basics of the deal and when signed, continuing to have contact and communication with them on updates of current projects and future ones, we also compiled a release schedule for OKeh, which included the local signings I had picked for international release, beside the ones we had delivered. And we compiled a complete artist's tour list with all dates in every country, so the product managers always would know when an artist would be in their market. Were necessary we worked on the promotion for our acts in the various countries they visited and co-ordinated these efforts with the repertoire owners or New York and Berlin. Communication with Alexander Boesch in Berlin was excellent and with his team great overall. Chuck was the man in New York and his support and understanding was the basis of my A&R work. I worked too with the artists and the inhouse teams in Berlin or New York on the cover art and overall design of the packages for our CDs and LPs and on the creation of the marketing tools, such as filmed materials, promo singles, bonus tracks, posters etc... And we updated the OKeh Facebook page regularly with info and photos and sent to the team in Berlin all relevant info to post on the OKeh website. All that kept Yolanda and me busy, her as well doing all the admin and finances for our little company.

On 25th of February 2014 it was announced that master guitarist Paco de Lucia had passed away at the age of 66. He had suffered a fatal heart attack while on holiday with his family in Mexico. I was introduced to his music via the 'Friday Night in San Francisco' album, which he played on with John McLaughlin and Al Di Meola and then started listening to his own music as well. I met him for the first time in Vienna in the mid-1980s, shortly after having started working for Polygram and had the pleasure to work with his music and meet him occasionally for almost thirty years after that initial meeting. His concerts were always something special: his technical ability just outstanding and unmatched and his music touching and full of emotions and every time performed with the best musicians the Spanish scene had to offer. I was involved in the 1996 re-union of the Guitar Trio and the album and then again with Paco's consequent releases for Universal up to his last studio album 'Cositas Buenas' and then to the 'Vitoria Suite', on which he performed with Wynton Marsalis and the Jazz at Lincoln Centre Orchestra. Always searching, trying to improve, even so he was considered the best guitar player of his generation by many. A great human being, who called me 'hombre' with a smile whenever we met and a fantastic artist, who left a major legacy to music, not only to flamenco.

In February it was off to Bore Place for another of the educational series Take Five – this time UK IX. As always it was a pleasure meeting the team and John Surman again and then there were the young UK musicians for this edition: Alex Roth, Shama Rahman, Laura Jurd, James Mainwaring, Peter Edwards, Dan Nicholls, Nick Malcolm and George Crowley. For me surprising how clear each of them had an idea of what would be there next career step and beyond – what the vision was for their music and how to present it. Very refreshing to see for young musicians like these and a joy to listen to them as well, when they performed their own music with John Surman. A truly talented bunch. John Cumming had started to do my presentation in the form of a two-man show: he would ask the questions and guide me through what the musicians needed to know and then we had usually short face-to-face sessions to answer to individual queries. These discussions with John were really fun, but as well informative and we both had a great time doing them and having a drink afterwards.

Back in Madrid we had a series of good concerts to attend: Pablo Martin and band, Josemi, the Brad Mehldau Trio featuring Jeff Ballard and The Bad Plus. And we spent a wonderful weekend in Pamplona, a beautiful place with great food and this time my friend Badi Assad performing as well. We took a bunch of friends from Madrid and went together to enjoy the music and the city. Badi's solo performances are amazing: she not only is a truly great guitar player (which obviously runs in the family with the Brothers Assad being her actual brothers), but she is an inventive and amazing singer and her vocal acrobatics are unparalleled, never simply for the effect, but in support of her music.

May brought Richard Bona to Spain to perform with a group of Spanish musicians, including singers Sandra Carrasco and Israel Fernandez, as well as guitarist Antonio Rey. The combination of the African grooves and lyrics with the flamenco feel and singing was an experience in itself and musically it worked extremely well. Guitarist Antonio Rey was the outstanding musician beside Bona and the singers. The first concert showed how much Africa there is in Flamenco and that this project has a lot to look forward to, surely growing the more they will perform.

2014, Badi Assad in Pamplona

'Dawn' was the first collaboration of Mexican singer Magos Hererra and Spanish guitarist, composer and producer Javier Limon and I am proud to have been able to sign them to the OKeh label. The duo created such an intimate atmosphere and simplicity in music that it was a pleasure to listen to them, whether they play jazz standards, Spanish and Mexican traditional compositions or their own songs. Magos has this magic in her voice that draws you into the music and makes you listen and Javier simply supports her with his guitar and some flamenco touches that creates the musical path for Magos to walk on. What worked incredible on the 2014 record was even better in concert: Magos captured your attention with her impeccable delivery of the vocals, her dramatic movements within the music and her smile when Javier played something unexpected, but supportive and giving her a direction to go and scat or simply introduce a different idea into the song. Jazz and Flamenco in perfect harmony and when they introduced at the end of their concert in Madrid's Teatro Galileo the harmonica player Antonio Serrano into the mix, it became something truly special. For me, he is one of the best in the world on his instrument, with a warm and touching tone.

'Jazzahead' in Bremen is every year again a great place to meet old and new friends and collaborators in jazz in all levels of the business: musicians, managers, agents, labels and all sorts of media and of course just the fan. I arrived on Friday, April 25th and dived right into a series of meetings and the few showcases I really wanted to check out. I managed to hear Shai Maestro, Avishai Cohen's ex–pianist who performed with his trio and so introduced me to his new album 'The Road To Ithaca', a brilliant and dynamic complex record of improvised music based on jazz and pop. Then off to the bar and to some music talk and wine! The next day, without hangover, more meetings and chats and encounters with journalists and musicians and then off to see Belgian pianist Jef Neve doing a solo concert at the Focke Museum. For me Jef is one of the most exciting European pianists and this solo show just confirmed that view: from an emotional and touching 'Lush Life' to some of his own pieces, the 40 minutes were gone too fast and the desire to hear more lingered on. After that and a quick bite at the Bremen fun fair that was placed right in front of the Congress Centre, I went to see and hear young Dutch guitar master Bram Stadhouders' 'Henosis', a project I had seen already in Rotterdam at North Sea 2012, but that again was pretty amazing and of a haunting and atmospheric beauty and really touching in the best moments of Choir and guitar interplay. Then off to the Schlachthof to catch some music there, but I ran into writer Stuart Nicholson and over 2 beers we discussed the status of jazz in the world ... very interesting indeed.

Then a bit of Elephant 9 with Reine Fiske, which was pretty amazing and off to have a drink with some friends from Vienna. Just a breakfast meeting on Sunday and then back home, with lots of work and ideas to follow through on. And being a bit exhausted and tired, but that is part of coming back from 'jazzahead', which seems to still grow and becoming more important; a fact that will see 'jazzahead' move next year to bigger premises within the Congress Centre.

As every year Yolanda and I went to the Madrid Tennis Masters and enjoyed, this time, seeing Rafa Nadal playing, amongst others. A day off with great sport and sun. We just had released the new Somi album, but while we were preparing the release, she dropped not only management, but agency as well and for some time we had nothing to support the album release in Europe. Working as an agent anyway, I stepped in and got her 3 club dates in Europe: Paris, Berlin and London and as the fees were low, the label had to put some money up for the dates as well. But it was worth it: her triumphant mix of jazz/African/soul and R&B was amazing and the stunning control of her voice and deep-felt emotions gave meaning to lyrics telling stories of the everyday African life.

I was hoping to maybe being able to sign Madeleine Peyroux to OKeh, therefore I went to London to see her perform at Ronnie Scott's. Madeleine, vocals and guitar, with Jon Herington, guitar and Barak Mori, bass, a trio that has been part of some of Madeleine's previous groups since 2006 and therefore had a great understanding and communication between them. The intimate setting suited Madeleine well, even so she had more focus on her vocal delivery, she seemed more relaxed in the small group and had the full support of both musicians, which added sounds and filled spaces with ease. Herington is an excellent guitar player with a jazzy sound, who played with Steely Dan among others, his little soli showing great touch and feeling and Mori a solid anchor in the songs with beautiful solo efforts, which were surprising and musically good. They performed together songs from all of Madeleine's records, the odd standard and all sounded great and personal, as if she was singing just for you. The small venue surely helped, but I have been told that she did extremely well with the same set up at the Norwich festival in front of 1500 people.

After the London trip I went for a short visit to New York, had meetings with Sony and then went to see Michel Camilo perform solo at the Blue Note. What a show! His first OKeh album 'What's Up?' had just won a Latin Grammy for best jazz album and he played most of the repertoire from this solo album to an enthusiastic audience, which especially loved his rendition of 'Take Five'!

A few weeks after my trip to New York, Yolanda and I went to Berlin to see Sergio Mendes and had him meet the Sony Classics & Jazz International team. We just had released his new album 'Magic' and Sergio was on tour to promote the release. 'Magic' is for me one of the best records Sergio has made: a truly danceable top-quality recording, featuring Will.I.Am, John Legend and among others, Carlinhos Brown, with whom Sergio had recorded the song 'One Nation', with one eye on the FIFA World Cup in Brazil (which was won by Germany), as this would have been a great official song for the event. We got a lot of radio play around the World Cup for this song, but didn't manage to get it to be the main song for the tournament in any country.

Fortunately, we had the song included on the official World Cup album, which sold very well and helped us recoup our investment in the recording. While finishing the album, Sergio sent me a picture he thought would be good for the cover, but I didn't quite like it. It was a cool painting, but not good for the cover of such a positive and fun record. So, I had to look around for alternatives and browsing the internet for contemporary Brazilian artists I came upon Claudio Souza Pinto and his painting 'Pianist' and it was perfect. I sent a photo of it to Sergio and thankfully he loved it too. We quickly made a deal with Claudio and the cover is wonderful and truly reflects what's inside.

I thought that the song 'Don't Say Goodbye' featuring John Legend had the potential to get us some great airplay around the world and therefore I asked Mark Cavell in the US to check if we could release it officially as a single to push it further than the good radio play it already got from the album. But they didn't want to call a favour from Columbia, John's label and simply weren't interested. They as well quickly dropped the ball on the Sergio album and it didn't do what we had expected in the US, but did fine in Europe and the rest of the world, but not great, which it could have done with a further bigger push with the single. It nevertheless garnered Sergio a deserved Grammy Nomination!

While in Berlin I showed Yolanda the places I used to live and went to school when in Berlin in the 60's as a kid. A trip down memory lane. We were also invited to see the concert of Dolly Parton: not usually an act I have on my list to see live, but the opportunity presented itself and we took it and we enjoyed it immensely! Yolanda always loved her songs and she is a true entertainer, engaging with the audience via stories of her life, performing with a great band and still has an amazing voice to perform all of her hits, and there are many. And some covers, like a gospel-ish version of Bon Jovi's 'Lay Your Hands On Me'!

The other records I released on OKeh that year were Medeski Scofield Martin & Wood's groovy new album 'Juice'. Which, beside a few amazing originals, had a bunch of covers by Cream, The Doors and Bob Dylan, which are simply powerful and rocky. These four guys were meanwhile so tight and seemed to have a lot of fun when playing. Then there was another album of covers and originals: Bill Frisell's stunning 'Guitar In The Space Age', on which he is performing songs by the Beach Boys, The Kinks, Pete Seeger, Lee Hazelwood and others. The album got a Grammy Nomination and did very well, as the little film we did to introduce it, was really cool. Bill did some promo for the album in Europe and I travelled with him from Berlin to Paris for the interviews. We first had met in Vienna when he was playing at the opening night of the 'miles smiles' club and now, over 30 years later, we for the first time, had time to chat. I really like Bill, a great and humble human being, with a deep kindness and a good sense of humour.

Sonny Rollin's 'Road Shows, Vol 3' has live recordings from the years between 2001 and 2012, when he performed live for the last time and is another proof of what an exceptional improviser he was. We had a bit of a discussion about the cover, as he insisted that they should be all the same in the series, just with tiny variations in the colours. We compromised on the same style, but a bit different. Not enough for me, but acceptable and Sonny was happy as well. Branford Marsalis' first OKeh album was the solo live recording titled 'In My Solitude: Live At Grace Cathedral', which had been recorded in San Francisco in October 2012. A truly contemplative album, in which he is using the reverb of the cathedral to incredible effect and is performing originals, standards and classical pieces. When talking to him about it, he explained that he needed to adjust the repertoire depending on the sound of the church or cathedral he was playing in, as not every song fits every venue. I started to look for some EU dates for him as a soloist, as I wanted to hear this live.

All of the OKeh releases that year were out also on vinyl, as LPs had become good business again, as younger people bought them as well now. And we could all do with a thousand or more additional sales, in times when CD sales were declining even in jazz. Not as much as in the pop world, but still enough to make the LP sales relevant in our business. Streaming in jazz hadn't taken off properly yet, but was becoming important as well.

July and festivals: in 2014 for me it was the North Sea Jazz Festival again to see our few acts there and to check out potential new signings, as we were still looking for acts for the next phase of the re-launch of OKeh: phase three was to sign some bigger names, like Branford, whom we already had and Sergio, whose first record was just out. But I was looking and talking to a few more and some of them would be at North Sea, so it would be a good opportunity to chat a bit more and try to move deals forward a bit. As usual I was running around, checking acts out and occasionally saw a full show, as with John Scofield's Uberjam Band. John is just incredible: every single time I hear him he really gets me with his amazing playing and the guys in this band were just pushing him further and further. Playing the recordings from the two Uberjam albums live is a treat and, on the night, John was in amazing form and improvised and let rock like only he can! He is for sure one of the best jazz guitarists of our time: versatile and constantly exploring new avenues of expression. He was one artist on my list for future signings, as we got along very well and he is a class act.

2014, John Scofield at the North Sea Jazz Festival

Then I had a bit of a dilemma: both OKeh acts for that day performed at the same time: Dave Holland's Prism with Craig Taborn, Kevin Eubanks and Eric Harland and Nir Felder 4, the group of our young guitarist. I had a chat with Nir and the guys before the show and listened to them for around 40 minutes performing tracks from the 'Golden Age' album Nir had released earlier that year. The audience in the packed room was truly amazed and, as well as I, glad that we had heard at least some of this show. Prism was one of the hottest groups around then and they showed again why: jazzy improvisations on rock grooves and fantastic interplay made this group so special. They played mainly tunes from their first album, but were looking forward to record again the following year and

I couldn't wait to hear this new music. I heard a bit of singer Sachal Vasandani's guest appearance with Ian Shaw and really liked it. Sachal was one to look at as a possible signing. Back to the Hotel to have a drink with Dave Holland, I just arrived in time to see the second half of extra time in the World Cup final … Germany won (as I had expected and hoped, as they had been the most impressive team overall in the tournament) with a great goal and we all celebrated a bit afterwards. While I was at the North Sea Jazz Festival, messages came in from various sources on various social networks: Charlie Haden had passed away age 76. This was hard to believe, even so the great man had been struggling with health problems over the last few years and hardly having performed anymore. I started working, in different functions, with Charlie in the early 1990's. He was then signed to Verve US with the Quartet West, then moved his contract to Universal France and finally I signed him directly to Emarcy, all of these labels being part of Universal Music. I always had loved Charlie's music – his beautiful and full sound on the bass, the way he could tell you any story on his instrument, the clearness of his music and the deep emotional content he offered to his listeners. I had listened to him on record and live in Keith Jarrett's American quartet, in the group Old And New Dreams with Don Cherry and many other combinations. I love the Quartet West and Charlie's work with John Taylor and of course The Liberation Music Orchestra. Charlie was a man with many faces, as a human being as well as a musician, but the talks we had about music and movies I will always remember, as well as signing him to Emarcy/Decca and being involved in some of the last recordings he made under his own name: 'Rambling Boy', 'Sophisticated Ladies' and the second duo album with Hank Jones,' Come Sunday'.

Charlie Haden, 1937 - 2014

Just two weeks after that shocking message, we lost another jazz master: one of the greatest groove drummers of his time, Idris Muhammad (born Leo Morris). Not only did he support almost all jazz greats of today at one time or another, but he did as well some amazing albums under his own name, first of all the evergreen 'Power of Soul' on the KUDU label in 1974. As a sideman he worked among others with George Benson, Lou Donaldson, Pharoah Sanders, Randy Weston and over the last few years with Ahmad Jamal, giving them the backbone for their performances and recordings. I met Idris when he was living in Austria and then again on many festivals and had the pleasure to hear him in Vienna and as well with Ahmad. I will always remember Idris as a warm and kind human being, with a great sense of humour and many music stories to tell, as one can check out in his 2012 book 'Inside The Music: The Life of Idris Muhammad', which he wrote with his friend Britt Alexander. As almost every year Yolanda and I visited the jazz festival in Vitoria-Gasteiz to listen to great music, eat well (at the amazing Sagartoki, which has been voted three years in a row as having the best Tortilla de Patatas in Spain and their Huevos Fritos alone are worth a trip up there) and generally have a good time in the company of the great people who are running the festival. Our first day opened with a performance of pianist Chano Dominguez and guitarist Niño Josele. This was their first duo concert and a world premiere of the album 'Chano & Josele', which was to be released via Sony Spain's deal with Fernando Trueba's new label. A deep musical understanding of the two artists made this concert special from the first minute, exchanging improvisations, playing with the tunes and seemingly enjoying this show. Some of the songs just worked perfect, like John Lewis' 'Django', one of the most amazing tracks on the record, here performed with many new ideas and twists and full of feeling for the essence of the song. A deserved standing ovation from an enthusiastic audience that asked for two encores ended that amazing concert. Israelian singer Noa had a great concert as well and so had singer Miguel Poveda, one of Spain's most impressive voices. He is a very emotional and expressive singer of Coplas and Flamenco, who performed from a really small more flamenco-based group to up to an octet with horns and in every format, he was truly comfortable and musically at home. The audience definitely loved it and showed their appreciation with shouts of "*Olé*" and standing ovations after some of the songs.

Hannah came with a friend to visit late July and early August, which for me is always something special. It is simply great to have her around, even so she was for sure living her own life by then. We met our friends here in Spain, some of Yolanda's family and had some great days together, with her showing Madrid to her friend, who was visiting the city for the first time. Then we went with Yolanda's family from Colombia for a short vacation in the south of Spain, Vera in Almeria, to be precise. We all had a relaxed and fun time there together, but got all a bit of a stomach upset. Might have been the water, we thought. After a few days we all were fine again, except for Yolanda's brother Jorge, who continued the whole week and beyond complaining about stomach aches.

In a year in which Latvia became the 18th member of the Eurozone and the UN judged the Arctic whaling program of the Japanese as commercial and not scientific and forbade further permits to do so, an international military operation against IS began in Syria and the Iraq, with the objective to defeat the Caliphate. I was reading Haruki Murakami's 'Colorless Tsukuru Tazaki And His Years Of Pilgrimage', a puzzling and captivating read, as I would expect from a new Murakami novel. Maybe not as great as '1Q84', but very good. And Jonas Jonasson's 'The Girl who saved the King of Sweden' another great human and fun story by this writer. The records I was listening to included, next to all OKeh releases, Chick Corea's 'Portraits', Paco de Lucia's final and posthumously released work 'Canción Andaluza', Gretchen Parlato's 'Live In New York', Bugge Wesseltoft's 'OK World' featuring Josemi Carmona, bass player and singer Ellen Andrea Wang's first opus 'Diving' and Rebekka Bakken's new album 'A Little Drop Of Poison', her outstanding Tom Waits recording. Except for three, all Waits songs had been arranged wonderfully by Jörg Achim Keller and Rebekka sang through these with ease and feeling.

For the agency it was a quiet summer. We had a few days for Branford, but having played the bigger festivals the two years before, we couldn't make it work. But we had a small run in the fall, including a solo show in Hamburg in November.

On September 12th I got the news that composer, pianist and keyboarder Joe Sample had passed away. I first met Joe in 2006, when we were preparing the release of the album he recorded with Randy Crawford 'Feeling Good' and they came to London to record an EPK. And then we met various times over the years, as after that I released on Emarcy their follow-up album 'No Regrets' and saw them a few times while touring that album around Europe. Joe was always smiling, enjoying life and searching for more and new music inside him. A great sense of humour and a remarkable talent for telling stories made him the perfect companion. Most people will remember him for the work with the Crusaders and the hits he wrote: from 'Street Life' via 'One Day I'll Fly Away' to 'Rainbow Seeker' and many others, but his trio recordings, like the Sonet album 'Fancy Dance' or 'The Three' with Ray Brown and Shelly Manne are definitely worth listening to, as is the beautiful solo album 'Soul Shadows'. Joe was also a highly requested studio musician, having recorded on the following albums: Marvin Gaye's "What's Going On," Joni Mitchell's "Court and Spark" and "The Hissing of Summer Lawns," Tina Turner's "Private Dancer," Steely Dan's "Aja" and "Gaucho," and on a few recordings by B. B. King. The year 2012 saw his last two recordings coming out in Europe: 'LIVE', a great concert recording with Randy Crawford, Joe's son Nicklas on bass and Steve Gadd and 'Children of the Sun', an outstanding recording with the NDR Big Band performing his music and Joe on piano and keyboards. I still have a copy of an unreleased recording he did, titled 'Creole Joe' and I hope that someone someday will release that album. I heard as well a recording from a concert he played with George Duke, just two pianos. Each of them would play a tune and explain why this tune meant something to them and then they would play something together. Musically a dream and truly educational. Not released yet either and in the hands of Joe's long-time manager and friend Pat Rains.

That year we lost as well pianist and composer Horace Silver and clarinettist Mr. Acker Bilk, one of my fathers' favourites, who loved especially his instrumental hit 'Stranger on the Shore'. Pete Seeger and Jack Bruce, bass player and singer of Cream and occasional bass player with Carla Bley, both passed away as well in 2014.

September brought me a trip to Scotland to take part in Air Time: Jazz CDP Scotland, the Scottish version of Take Five, that year featuring Alan Benzie (piano), Lauren Sarah Hayes (piano and electronics), Sue McKenzie (saxophone), Phil O'Malley (trombone) and Simon Thacker (guitar). John Cumming and I did our usual little show and then had face-to-face time with each of the five musicians. I did enjoy talking to them a lot, as they asked the right questions and I was happy to advise and help out.

From October 30th to November 6th the first Montreux Academy happened in Montreux, Switzerland: an educational week for young jazz musicians from all over the world, who in the past two years had participated in one of the Montreux competitions: guitar, piano or vocal. They were on guitar: Andres Corredor (Columbia), Yoav Eshed (Israel), Alexander Goodman (Canada) and Leandro Pellegrino (Brazil). On Piano: Lorenz Kellhuber (Germany), Mathis Pecard (France) and Jerry Leonide (Mauritius). And on vocals: Myriam Bouk Mouin (France), Alita Moses (USA), Patrick Rouiller (Switzerland), Woiciech Myrczek (Poland) and Paula Grande (Spain). Mentor of these musicians through the music sessions of the week was the great Lee Ritenour, as well as some guests, some of them being part of the concert at the last evening of the Academy. I knew Lee from our Verve days and it was really great to see him again and in work with these youngsters. I had the pleasure doing a session with these young musicians on the music business, especially how agencies, managers and local promoters as well as labels can work together to help the artists to develop their careers. An interesting two hours of presentation, discussions and Q&A, which showed the desire of the group to know and understand, to learn. The evening before our session I went with the musicians to dinner and afterwards to a relaxed and playful session, just for me to see some of them in action. Even so the jams never show the true art of a musician, it can show a lot of other things especially in terms of improvising. They all did great that night and I enjoyed the music a lot.

After coming back to Madrid, I had James Brandon Lewis in town for the first time, featuring Max Johnson on bass and Dominic Fragman on drums. The club Clamores was the venue and as James was truly a new artist, I didn't expect too many people there, but in the end about 200 enthusiastic fans showed up and had a great night! James and the guys started with 'Divine', one of the key tracks on his OKeh Records debut album, 'Divine Travels' and with it set the tone for the night: free flowing improvisations on little melodies, deep spiritual expressions on all instruments, led by an immaculate James, whose ideas never seemed to run out or showed repetition, who was dismantling melodies and putting them together again upside down and it all made sense and sounded great! A song he wrote as a tribute to Charlie Haden had the trio at its best in performing an improvised ballad with a hauntingly beautiful theme that they knitted into the song in a communication of respect for the late bass player. More music from the great album 'Divine Travels', including the amazing 'Wading Child in the Motherless Water' rounded up the night. This is accessible deep, improvised music, free jazz with melodies if you want, but made by a bunch of great guys, who love to express their fun in life that way.

Hannah turned 21 that month. A strong young woman now and having a great party with her friends. Unfortunately, without me, having been in Switzerland at the time and then having the Madrid Jazz Festival going on, with a few OKeh artists performing. Hannah understood this, even so sometimes I am sure she would have loved it for me to be there. But we had agreed to meet in Vienna later in the month, when my brother Jürgen celebrated his 60th birthday and the whole family would come together. We had so much fun these few days, with walking around Vienna, drinking hot wine and laughing our heads off. The party was great as well and everyone was happy, especially Jürgen, as he saw what a good time everyone had.

2014, Vienna ... the family having fun ....
From left to right: Christine, Patrick, Avi, Alexander, Hannah, Barbara, Jürgen, our mother and myself

Yolanda's brother Jorge continued to have problems with his stomach, after we all had a bout in the summer. He went to see some doctors and finally they found a huge cancerous growth in his stomach, which they couldn't operate on, but hoped to be able to reduce the size via chemotherapy, which he was starting at the end of that year. From that day onwards he came more often to Madrid, as presumably the health system is better here than in Almeria and of course here he had his mother Maria and us to support him through the process.

After our trip to Vienna Yolanda and myself went to Barcelona for the Jazz Festival to see and meet Branford, who performed a great gig with his quartet. Branford presented new drummer Evan Sherman, as Justin Faulkner couldn't make that trip, who with his 21 years got plenty to learn, but overall did a great job and fitted well into the musical adventures the rest of the group got themselves into. Joey Calderazzo, as ever, was full of ideas and with powerful and impressing solo work and Eric Revis was keeping the beat and telling little stories. Branford let them go, listening, reacting and played absolutely amazing, always keeping the melody in mind and at the centre of his improvisations.

2014, Branford Marsalis solo, Hamburg, Kulturkirche

The Branford solo concert in the beautiful Kulturkirche Altona in Hamburg, which I saw shortly after Barcelona, was a completely different beast: this was only the second time Branford actually did a solo concert: the first being the concert which was recorded for the album and then Hamburg. More or less, he played the same repertoire in Hamburg as what you can find on the album, notable exceptions were that he played 'Body & Soul', 'On the sunny side of the street' and 'Bach's Allemande', from the Cello Suites No 1, which was for me one of the highlights of the evening. Twice more or less 45 minutes plus an encore! Branford used the space and sound of the church to its best, changed between soprano and tenor and kept the audience mesmerized. It is difficult to explain the beauty of the sound in this place, the melodic inventiveness of Branford's soli and the beauty of the selected repertoire, as not every song works in that setting. The two concerts I was lucky to see that month simply confirmed that Branford Marsalis is not only one of the leading sax players of our time, but he is as well still open to take risks, to move into areas unknown and be able to make a valid musical statement there.

And immediately after coming home, the local jazz festival continued for me with a gig by MSM&W at the Conde Duque. Playing mainly repertoire from their latest album 'Juice', the quartet moved from jazz to funk and rock without letting the audience feel musical borders. Scofield made his guitar scream and swing, cry and tell stories, each played emotion mirrored by facial expressions, simply showing how deep he dug into himself to perform these incredible soli. But this is a band project, not a Scofield solo show, and Medeski, Martin & Wood again proved why they are such an amazing trio, with free-flowing improvisations, groovy tunes and incredible musicianship all around. Adding Scofield to the mix is simply taking them to a different planet. John Medeski showed why he had been riding high in all keyboard and organ polls and added some great piano soli too, while Chris Wood and Billy Martin gave the music a solid carpet and heartbeat, with a few amazing irregularities! Constant changes in the music kept them and the listeners alert, once you think they settled in a groove, they are just taking it apart, flowing freely around, only to get back to the initial rhythm again. A great example of this was 'Sunshine of your love', even more spaced out than on the album, groovy, even when they went into a free improvisation and only the inherited groove kept things moving, before they got back into their own time again and finished the song as they started it: lose, but tight on the beat. When they finished the night's concert with The Doors' 'Light

My Fire' the audience jumped up and gave them an immediate standing ovation and only left after an encore that closed the evening on a quiet note: Bob Dylan's 'The Times They are A Changing'. A great concert with a great band: almost two hours of music and not one dull moment.

2014, Medeski, Scofield, Martin & Wood, Madrid

Dee Dee Bridgewater came to Madrid next and she used her protégée's band as her backing group: Theo Croker's DVRK FUNK. Theo had arranged most of the music for Dee Dee and gave standards like 'Love For Sale' a different edge, a more modern and darker vibe. Same is true for a gorgeous arrangement of Abbey Lincoln's 'Music Is The Magic', which moved from hauntingly beauty to a sinister dark place and back! Dee Dee still is one of the best performers out there, her voice immaculate and her control second to none. It was fantastic to see her energised by these young players and the great arrangements they came up with for her music.

After a great show by Pablo Martin Caminero and his group, the live season for us was over for 2014 and we took it a bit easy and celebrated Christmas and New Year's Eve with Maria and Jorge and Yolanda's aunt and uncle.

2015

As most of the previous years, 2015 started with a trip to New York, where I attended the Jazz Connect Conference, which for the first time was not part of APAP, but ran independently for two days of panels, discussions and speeches at Saint Peter's Church. Interesting aspects of all parts of the jazz world being discussed and presented by some of the key artists of the genre and people in the business. I conducted the panel on Canada and together with my panellists, singer Kellylee Evans; Jean-Pierre Leduc (Lunched Management & Booking); Ross Porter (JAZZFM91) and Jim West (Justin Time Records/Wild West Artist Management) we informed the audience of the situation in Canada's jazz market. Just walking around the venue of the event after the panel was quite amazing with so many familiar faces and great artists being around, talking, doing interviews and generally having a good exchange on topics of jazz. It is great that the annual Winter Jazz Festival is always at the same time, so there is a lot to see and hear whenever I come for the conference. As I had a lot of meetings that year, I had to be selective to which gig I would go and picked to see Taylor Eigsti's Free Agency featuring Gretchen Parlato, Becca Stevens and Alan Hampton on vocals, Eric Harland on drums, Harish Ragavan on bass and James Francies on more keyboards. A very sophisticated vocal project with beautiful written harmonies for the singers. Sometimes it reminded me of Carla Bley's 'Escalator Over The Hill' and at other times of 'Grace', the John Donne project by Ketil Bjørnstad, but overall, it was very much its own music.

After that I walked in freezing temperatures from the Subculture to 55 Bar to see Nir Felder and his band performing to a full house. Nir is a truly gifted young guitar player with a good ear for a tune and his compositions are part rock, pop and jazz and are appealing and catchy, but musically full of surprises and deepness. Could have listened all night, instead of two intensive sets only. The next day, after having a great lunch with Theo Croker, James Brandon Lewis and Somi, I went in the evening to see Sachal (Vasandani) perform his new music at the Rockwood Music Hall. Unfortunately, the singer who was on stage before him didn't know when to stop, so everyone had to wait outside in the cold, which didn't make the act a lot of friends. But once inside and immediately after Sachal had started, that was forgotten: Sachal sang the new tunes perfectly, with fitting movements (on a small stage) and a very good band behind him, featuring Taylor Eigsti on one of the keyboards. Songs like 'No More Tears' and 'Cover The Water' came across extremely well and the rest of the new songs simply caught everyone's ear. As Sachal started late and we had a drink together after the show, I missed Theo Croker's DVRK FUNK. I had seen them with Dee Dee Bridgewater in Madrid and was looking forward to hear them playing some new songs live.

Later in January, singer Paula Grande, whom I had met at the Montreux Academy, came to Madrid to perform in a small club and informed me about it. We went with young actress and film-maker Olga Alamán to see Paula showcase her amazing talent by putting some vocal snippets into her loop machine, then a second layer, creating a beautiful groove and then starting to sing on top of these loops, constructing captivating atmospheres and showing what a great singer she is. Originals, standards (like a great version of Nat King Cole's 'Calypso Blues') and covers in English, Spanish or Catalan, she makes it all her own, doesn't seem to be bothered by limits and genres, enjoying the moment of music making and sharing this joy with her audience.

Flamenco pianist Ariadna Castellanos and Josemi Carmona were the other local acts we went to see in February.

In March, first Kurt Elling and then our friend Rebekka Bakken came to Madrid for concerts. No doubt, Kurt Elling is the most amazing jazz singer around today, he can not only interpret the standards like only a few, but his way of vocalising soli from known songs and artists is second to none. In the concert at the Auditorium Nacional in Madrid on March 7th he proved again that he is in a class of its own: starting the show with an unaccompanied solo and then moving into 'Come Fly With Me', only to go afterwards straight into the Marc Johnson song he wrote lyrics over the guitar soli of the original, 'Samurai Cowboy'. This was followed by U2's 'Where The Streets Have No Name' - a weird mix in any book, but with Kurt Elling it all makes sense, as it was driven by his musical understanding of a song and his very personal take of it. He then went into the music of his latest album, 'Passion World', a collection of love songs from various countries, sung in English, German, Spanish and Polish. 'Where Love Is', a song based on a poem by James Joyce, is a true gem in this collection. And in Madrid, obviously, the Spanish one did get a great reception. A happy and enthusiastic audience was rewarded with 2 encores.

I hadn't seen Rebekka live for quite a while and I was truly surprised having forgotten how great a performer and songwriter she is. Rebekka performed with a quartet she hadn't played with for about 2 years, but still the musicians Børge Pedersen–Øverleir (guitar), Rune Arnesen (drums) and Lars Danielsson (bass) seemingly enjoyed the evening and playing together again. Arnesen, known for his work with Nils Petter Molvaer among others, is a drummer for all emotions, Pedersen-Øverleir a guitarist who can play anything and rocks amazingly when needed, all given a steady and intelligent heartbeat by Swedish bass player Lars Danielsson and Rebekka was holding all this together with her amazing voice and confident stage performance.

2015, Rebekka Bakken in Madrid

She played mainly her own songs, as her latest record of Tom Waits tunes is a Big Band album, but she still performed three powerful tracks from that recording, including the title track 'Little Drop Of Poison'. The rest came from her other five discs, released over the course of 12 years since her amazing first album 'The Art Of How To Fall' (2003) and two songs that were new at the time. What was truly incredible that she jumped from Tom Waits to her own material and from a quiet and touching ballad into a rocker like 'Powder Room Collapse', reminiscent in groove and power of performance of Janis Joplin, to a hauntingly beautiful Norwegian song; starting alone, then building up with sounds created by all musicians and ending in something Pink Floyd would have been proud of. Sometimes starting a song simply accompanying herself on piano, which she actually plays very well, then the rest of the band coming in and taking the song where it should go emotionally. With the incredible range of her voice and the control she displays, it is no wonder that she can make you smile or cry or just listen in awe about what she is able to do with her instrument. Is what she does jazz and is she a jazz singer? Who honestly cares? She is a great singer and songwriter. Period!

I had a few meetings to do in Berlin with the Sony guys, talking A&R, new signings and marketing, and while in town I went out to see Jeff Ballard's new group Fairground at the A-Trane club. A band that consisted of Ballard on drums, Lionel Loueke on guitar, Kevin Hays on keyboards and Reid Anderson on electronics couldn't do much wrong and even on their first night out as a group, they sounded amazing: careful sonic explorations with Ballard's sensitive percussion driving the music forward, little themes popping up and disappearing, searching what this band could sound like. Loueke sometimes added just sounds to the soundscapes of Hays and especially Anderson, whose occasional beats drove the exploring further into rhythmic territories, with a smiling Ballard following happily. It seemed the band was working from kind of sketch sheets, developing the music while playing and coming up with new ideas, going around unexpected corners. There were some freer elements, which you would expect by musicians of this calibre improvising, but there were great beautiful melodic parts and a wonderful tune sang by Kevin Hays. This was the project that Jeff asked me to release next and he recorded all dates of the tour to edit some cool music together for the first Fairground album.

2015, Jeff Ballard's Fairground, Berlin, A-Trane

I think it was that year when I got a call from Melody Gardot, telling me that she would have a stop-over in Madrid, while coming back from a holiday she had spent with her mother in celebration of her mother's 50th birthday. And on their way back, the mother to the US and Melody to Portugal, they would stay in Madrid and if we had time we could go out for dinner. Yolanda booked a table at Casa Alberto; I sent her the details and then we had a fantastic meal with some great wine and good fun. We had as well bought for her mom a typical little Spanish hand fan, colourful and great when it's hot, which her mother really liked.

For the first half of 2015 we had the following releases planned: Sachal's OKeh debut 'Slow Motion Miracles', produced by Michael Leonhart. When I proposed to the team and Chuck that I wanted to sign Sachal, they were very enthusiastic about it and asked if I would be OK if they would do the A&R for the album, as he was at that time mainly known in the US, bits outside, but not that much yet. As I liked the idea of Michael producing and making a more modern sounding album, with Sachals's songs instead of standards, I agreed. Unfortunately, in the middle of the making of this record the Masterworks A&R lady Cathleen Murphy left the company and the project fell aside a bit. I still think the resulting album is very good, some of the songs really strong, but overall, the step from who Sachal was before this album and what he did on it, was maybe too radical and his fans didn't immediately follow him. The album didn't get much support in the US, had some good airplay, but nothing what I expected.

Meanwhile I had worked with James Brandon Lewis on his next album for OKeh 'Days Of Freeman', a four chapter look back into the music he grew up with. When discussing the music being funky and groovy, hip-hop beats with the sax as the rapper so to speak, he didn't know which bass player would be good for this, so I recommended him to check out Jamaaladeen Tacuma and he really liked the idea and so we got Jamaal and then drummer Rudy Royston on the record. In one of the many discussions about music we had, I had made James aware of the wonderful Don Cherry album 'Home Boy Sister Out', from which in the end he took the song 'Bamako Love' and featured it on the new album as the only cover. It turned out to be a really great album and helped James to make a few strides forward in his career, even so sales weren't very good, especially in the US, his home market.

Overall, sales in the US for jazz were going down in the last few years. When I started in jazz, 60% of all worldwide jazz sales were in the US, now it was the other way round, probably even higher for international. Markets like France, Germany or Japan could easily outsell the US in direct comparisons by certain artists. Catalogue sold better in Europe and Asia than at home and international artists could sell big numbers everywhere, except in the USA. One example from that year shows that perfectly: Gregory Porter's first album for Universal 'Liquid Spirit', produced by Brian Bacchus. This album sold in the first year of release around the world a staggering 1 million units, mostly in France, Germany and the UK, as Universal put tons of marketing money behind it. In the US the album sold in the same period 35.000 copies! There are a few jazz singers that can sell in the millions – Diana Krall, Madeleine Peyroux, Melody Gardot, Norah Jones, Tony Bennett and now Gregory. All these are accessible jazz singers, but they don't have single hits, it is the quality of the songs overall and the album as such, that makes them sell, plus personality and hard work. Diana, Norah and Tony sell better in the US than the rest, but would still have good sales outside too.

David Sanborn had brought us a new album, produced by Marcus Miller, who also played bass on 'Time And The River'. The album features a guest appearance by Randy Crawford on a sublime version of 'Windmills Of Your Mind'. A cool record that did well for us and Dave, who as always was supporting the release with many tour dates. Dee Dee Bridgewater had sent me the music she had recorded with trumpeter Irving Mayfield and his New Orleans Jazz Orchestra, short NOJO, 'Dee Dee's Feather's', a cool and funky New Orleans album that had lots of groove, blues and swing. And Dee Dee was as usual immaculate and powerful. Of course, I had to say "*Yes*" to this: she is a star and I know her and like her a lot and as an artist she is really special. And this project was fun and cool and everything she stands for.
Michel Camilo had asked me if I would be interested in the soundtrack to a documentary titled 'Playing Lecuona', in which he took part next to Gonzalo Rubalcaba and Chucho Valdes. I had a chat with the guy who produced the little film and as he told me that they would go theatrical and the music was really good, I made the deal. Unfortunately, the documentary never made it to the movie theatres and the showing in a handful of international film festivals didn't sell the music. Soundtracks usually sell well in case the movie does well, or there is a unique hit single attached. Otherwise, it will sell as a jazz album, which is usually not a big number in comparison to pop or other genres. Jazz records sell via marketing and touring and promotion and they sell over longer periods. As the film business is completely different to the music business, the producer of the film and soundtrack didn't see my point that I needed the theatrical release to really do something out of the norm to push the record.

Germany gave us a new album by Silje Nergaard, 'Chain Of Days' on which she is singing a wonderful duet with Kurt Elling on one of her songs, 'The Dance Floor' and I was more than happy that I could help her to make this happen, as I spoke to Kurt and had sent him the song and asked him to sing it with her, which he gladly did. The song 'Morgenstemmning' was arranged by Vince Mendoza and is one of the highlights of this recording. Other local releases I worked on that year came from Polish trio RGG, whose album 'Aura' got some good press in Europe. Unfortunately, as the guys didn't have a booking agent and no dates, there wasn't much happening with the record outside of Poland.

Magos & Limon recorded a live album in Mexico, that the local Sony released and I picked up internationally, 'He For She', in support of the UN program for gender equality of the same name. The beautiful music had guest stars like Sachal, wonderful clarinettist Oran Etkin, Gregoire Maret and others and was filmed as well. Italy gave us for international the new Mario Biondi album 'Beyond', which did extremely well at home and fine in Germany and a few other markets. Biondi came as well to Madrid on tour and performed a funky and cool show.
And from France we got two albums that year: singer Hugh Coltman's Nat King Cole tribute 'Shadows' and Stacey Kent's touching 'Tenderly', recorded with Roberto Menescal. For the second half of the year, we had only the 'Branford Marsalis Quartet Performs Coltrane's A Love Supreme, Live in Amsterdam' re-issue. A cool and musically valid DVD and CD set, plus a digital only EP by Theo Croker titled 'DVRK FUNK', which was to lead into the next album by the young trumpet player.

I had met sound engineer Fraser Kennedy the first time in Montreux when I was there with Wolfgang Muthspiel and he offered me the possibility to have a professional recording of the gig, as this was his job there. I said *"No"* at the time, but whenever I saw him there again in later years, we always had a good chat. After he left the festival and went back to England we stayed in touch and often met while I was living in London. Then he became part of the team that produced the TV program 'Live From Abbey Road' and I met him there on the few occasions we had an artist on the show. Now he had started his own program, this time from the Metropolis Studio in Chiswick. And for one of the first shows of 'Jazz @ Metropolis' he wanted to interview me. I flew to London and did the interview, which covered my background and my work at Universal and OKeh. The series focused on history, interviews with musicians and other people in the jazz business and live music. Unfortunately, there wasn't much international interest in such a TV series and they only did a few programs before closing it down.

In April Rainer Rygalyk, my friend from Austria came to Spain for a course in fine art photography and on the way back stopped in Madrid and we met and went out. As it was just around Easter, we had already the traditional Catholic processions going on in town and I took him to see one. I had a seen a few of these and they are spectacular in colour and atmosphere and I had taken a lot of photos, but never really captured what it was all about. Rainer, an award-winning jazz photographer, took a few and showed them to me. Astonishing!!! We went to have dinner and a few beers and talked about the time we did the ''Jazz Live'' magazine together.

Photo by Rainer Rygalyk, 2015, Madrid

Shortly after Rainer's visit, Hannah came by for a week and told us that her studies were going very well and that she was going to live in Vienna for almost a year, as part of the foreign language exchange program during her German studies. Vienna, of course, as she had family there from both parents' sides. I knew she would love it and gave her names and addresses of places I used to hang, especially of course the 'miles smiles' jazz café. In the end, she actually found a shared apartment close to the club and for sure visited it occasionally. She had gotten it right, the way she was doing her studies: work hard, party hard!!

'Jazzahead' in Bremen had truly become the most important international jazz meeting of the year, together with Jazz Connect in New York. That year's edition had moved into a bigger hall, therefore giving additional space for more exhibitors and guests to meet and talk and listen. The 2015 participants were: 929 exhibiting companies and over 3000 industry attendees from 55 countries. And it worked perfectly by having two great venues in the main building to showcase new talents and another hall where gigs were played, within two minutes walking distance. I arrived on Friday early afternoon and basically ran from one meeting to another, which was cool in a way, as it was always only a few steps to the next place, but even then, you usually ran into someone unexpectedly and your schedule for the day was messed up pretty quickly! After dinner I went to see my first live act of jazzahead 2015: Canadian singer Kellylee Evans, who I had the pleasure to meet (but not hear) at Jazz Connect earlier in the year and I did enjoy her show. Kelleylee mixes her jazz with a big portion of Soul and HipHop and is not afraid to improvise or scat over an Eminem song and make that her own. The band she played with didn't knock me out, but was good enough in this showcase to let her talent and individuality shine. A beer at the bar with some old friends, chatting and then off to the SACEM Night, which was part of the French focus of 'jazzahead' that year, to see trumpet player Airelle Besson, whose project 'Prelude', a duo with guitarist Nelson Veras, I adore. There she premiered her new project: the Airelle Besson Quartet, featuring Isabel Sorling (voc), Benjamin Moussay (p, keyb) and Fabrice Moreau (dr) and it was as impressive in terms of song writing and performance as the first album is. Airelle has a beautiful sound on her instrument and wrote some cool tracks for this bass-less band to perform. Great too was singer Isabel Sorling, whose voice mainly added wordless colours to the music, intensifying the emotions and supporting the overall feel.

2015, jazzahead, Airelle Besson

Saturday: meetings and running into Sten Nilsen, my friend from Jazzland Recordings in Oslo, which was a great surprise, as I didn't know he was coming and we both then talked to our ex-colleague Christian Kellersmann, who then managed 'edel:kultur' and through that the MPS label. This was followed by the first music of the day: Franz von Chossy Quintet, led by the pianist himself and featuring the slightly unusual line-up of clarinet, violin, bass and drums. A few people had previously mentioned Franz to me and I could understand why: his music was an eclectic mix of jazz, classical and European folk music, often wandering into Balkan grooves and sounds. Next: Come Shine, the Norwegian band fronted by the amazing singer Live Maria Roggen with Erlend Skomsvoll on piano, Sondre Meisfjord on bass and Hakon Mjaset Johansen on drums, a true band with a unique sound and a captivating way of playing with the American Songbook. The opener, a strangely grooving, but slow 'Caravan' was sublime, their version of 'Dock of the Bay' was really cool and the song the band took their name from, 'Come Rain Or Come Shine' was the icing on the cake with sublime vocals and overall improvisations. Later that night I checked a bit of the Arkady Shilkloper & Vadim Neselovskyi duo: dreamlike sounds and beautiful playing by French horn and flugel horn player Shilkloper and young pianist Neselovskyi and beside a great music statement this was as well a political one: a Russian and a Ukrainian creating beauty together – no problems when it comes to music! Then I was hanging with above mentioned friends for a few beers at the hotel bar and continued the music talk. The big International Jazz Day concert was held in 2015 in Paris and as usual was featuring Herbie Hancock and a host of great jazz musicians, including OKeh's Dee Dee Bridgewater and Dhafer Youssef, plus Till Brönner, Wayne Shorter and Al Jarreau. For the first time Herbie told the audience that they would perform John Lennon's 'Imagine' at the end of the show and would do so from then on, every year. When it came to play that song Herbie played a little intro, then obviously waited for the first vocalist to start the song, which was Dhafer. He started to chant and one could see how all the musicians were looking in his direction to figure out where this beautiful sound came from. He got them all, most had never heard of him before, but would remember him from then on. Dhafer told me that Wayne and Herbie and the rest came to him afterwards to congratulate him on his singing and that Herbie even offered to do something at one point together. When Dhafer chants, it is the purest form of human expression. Beauty in sound, emotion in notes!

Within a few days in May 2015 three very important people in the music business passed away: first guitarist and singer B. B. King, whose music I heard first through an album my father had, the 1965 'Live At The Regal'. Later I really liked his 'Deuces Wild' and the album he did with Eric Clapton, 'Riding With The King'.

Then Bruce Lundvall, who had been one of my role models in the music business: a label guy, A&R man, business executive, all in one. And with a tremendous passion for music in general and jazz specifically. He built a great jazz roster at Columbia, afterwards at Electra Musician, where he signed an unknown singer by the name of Bobby McFerrin. And finally, he brought Blue Note back and gave them with Norah Jones one of their biggest acts ever. And on top of it all, he was a real gentleman, a kind and warm human being who cared. I will never forget the few meetings we had and how much his career has influenced me in a positive way.

At the age of 58, only one day after Bruce Lundvall, American saxophonist, arranger, composer, bandleader, and producer Bob Belden died of a heart attack in New York. I had met Bob first at one of the Jazz Connect Conferences and since then we had occasionally exchanged emails about his projects and jazz in general. His recordings 'Black Dahlia' and 'Miles From India', an album of Miles's tunes with Indian musicians and some old sidemen of the trumpeter, stand out of his exceptional legacy. Just a few days before his death he had come back from a concert trip with his band ANIMATION in Iran. He was the first American musician to perform there in 35 years and told me in an email, how incredible this trip had been and how enthusiastic the audience had received them: *"It was amazing! Beyond my wildest dreams"*.

I had continued to speak with Sonny Rollins every two or three weeks, to see how he was doing. It was tough for him not being able to play his sax, but it was even more difficult to finally realise that he might not be able to ever perform again. The initial hope was soon replaced by a kind of fear and ultimately by acceptance of the fact, that live performances were a thing of the past. The idea for a record I had come up with and discussed with Sonny, by using his solo sound check recordings, didn't materialize either, as he was tiring too fast to listen to hours and hours of material, which was a pity, but reality. Sonny lived his life secluded and mostly at home, but since many years tried to follow The Golden Rule: 'Do not treat others in ways that you would not like to be treated'. We spoke a lot about that, his desire to become a better person every day and that he believed in re-incarnation. Of course, we spoke about music as well and I occasionally sent him some CDs, like the Branford solo album or the James Brandon Lewis recordings, which he liked a lot and he even mentioned James and J.D. Allen in an interview as the two young sax players he liked to listen to. In

2015 Sonny got the lifetime achievement award from the Jazz Foundation Of America, a well-deserved honour.

In May we went to Barcelona for a few days to see Yolanda's family again and spent some time with them. Back in Madrid we did our annual pilgrimage to the Casa Mágica to see some of the world's top tennis stars, this time Maria Sharapova and Fernando Verdasco, among others.

As an agency we had a few spring gigs for Branford: he was going to do a rehearsal and then two shows with the HR Big Band in Germany, followed by a solo show just outside of Berlin, in Neuhardenberg and then two masterclasses for young musicians in Berlin and Cologne, respectively. The focus on Germany for Branford started slowly to bear fruits with more shows and better fees. For July we had his quartet in Europe again for the festivals, including North Sea Jazz, where he was also booked to perform a solo show in the local church. But first we went to see Madeleine Peyroux again in Madrid's MADgarden festival … with the same small group setting I had seen her early last year in London, Barak Mori on bass, but with a new Brazilian guitar player instead of Jon Herington. Not much of a difference (Guillermo Montero maybe being a bit softer in his playing), the simplicity of the group helps to focus on Madeleine's unique voice and her constantly improving singing and obviously her very individual phrasing. While going through all her famous songs extremely relaxed and letting the music flow, she created a special intimate atmosphere in the open-air arena and, in a concert full of highlights, her version of Randy Newman's 'Guilty' was really special. At the same festival we saw Imelda May, a powerful singer of rockabilly, with a fantastic voice. One of Yolanda's favourites and I like her as well a lot. She is simply the best in that area and the audience in the almost full garden of the Complutense University was with her from the first note to the last! Imelda was backed by a great band, having fun and giving her the groove needed to rock the house. From her many hits to Sonny Bono's 'Bang Bang', she kept the good times rolling!

On June 11th, 2015 the music world lost one of its foremost thinkers and creative forces: Ornette Coleman, composer, performer, philosophic musician and great human being! There is no end to the list of artists in various fields he has influenced, no end to the musicians that took his message on and so moved improvised music in a new and different ways.

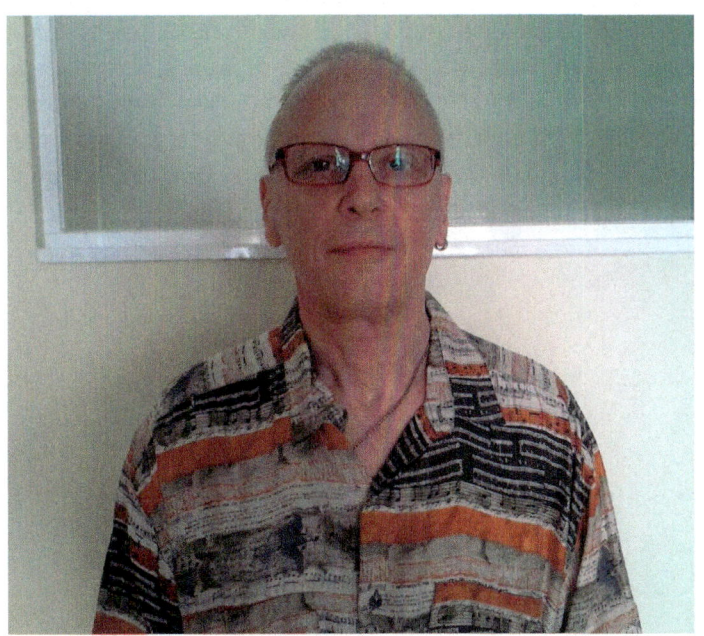

2015, wearing the shirt Ornette Coleman gave to me a few years back

I was lucky enough to work with Ornette for a few years when he released his Harmolodic albums via Universal France and stayed in touch with him and his son Denardo ever after. Unforgettable the moments of simple chat (even so, simple it never was when talking to Ornette: he was always challenging your perceptions, even in a little chat), his incredible storytelling and his warm personality.

He told me to grab an instrument and play, no matter if I knew anything about it, just to express myself. We exchanged some philosophical books at the time, he gave me and his label contact in France, Jean–Philippe Allard, a silk shirt each, printed with musical motifs. I was once sitting in the Harmolodic Studios a whole afternoon, just watching him rehearse the two bass players for his new band – there was so much wisdom in these teachings and talks between the three and when he tried to explain to me Harmolodics, the all-round philosophy of his music and life and I thought I got it, only not to understand anything half an hour later. And then there were the shows with him, I was lucky enough to witness over the years: from the indescribable beauty of the Umbria Jazz event called 'Global Expressions' to the Meltdown Festival in London which he curated and performed in, including one of the most magical moments I ever experienced when listening to music: Ornette, Denardo and Charlie Haden performing a 15-minute rendition of Ornette's most known composition, 'Lonely Women' ... pure jazz heaven. He surely made the world a better place.

Two further amazing artists, pianist John Taylor, with his light and beautiful touch and Natalie Cole with her tender voice, passed away in 2015 as well and I was lucky to have seen them both perform at least once.

My friend, bass player Pablo Martin Caminero, had called me to ask me to come and see a singer he was working with and he really wanted me to hear her. As Pablo hardly ever before had recommended someone to me with that passion, Yolanda and I agreed to meet up with Ganavya Doraiswamy, especially after hearing some of her new music.

A young Indian singer, born in the US but raised in South India, who studied at Berklee Valencia, where she met Pablo. Together with him, Moises Sanchez on piano and drummer Michael Olivera Garcia, she performed at the club Bogui. A truly unique singer with her own identity and idea about what to do: mixing her Indian tradition and jazz. So is the intro into 'Summertime', sung in her native language Tamil and then switched to English in the middle of the song and it seems to make a lot of sense. And when she does traditional Indian songs which are hundreds of years old in a new jazzy way, they all sound fresh and captivating. This great band surely helped to make that night special as Moises is a great piano player with tons of ideas and lots of feeling and he made her smile in wonder a few times by his inventiveness and Pablo Martin Caminero was the anchor of all that, guiding and encouraging while Garcia filled the spaces and kept the beat going. But it was the voice and control of Ganavya that was truly remarkable and her stage presence, mature, but shy. We both loved what we heard and talked a lot to Ganavya after the show.

2015, Ganavya and Pablo at Bogui

Right afterwards we were off to the Festival International de Jazz in Alicante, which was programmed then by our friend and agent for Spain, Amparo Tebar. We met Amparo and had a great paella lunch together, before going to see Dee Dee Bridgewater, Irvin Mayfield, Jr. and the New Orleans 7 to perform music from their recent OKeh release 'Dee Dee's Feathers'. And like the record they opened the show with Harry Connick Jr's 'One Fine Thing' and all musicians were on top form from the first note: Dee Dee is just such an amazing singer, she can do anything, is the best when it comes to scat and extremely sensitive to ballads, as she showed in Ellington's 'Come Sunday' and the Irvin Mayfield Jr. original 'C'Est Ici Que Je T'Aime', but can go deep into the blues as she did in 'St. James Infirmary' and groove, as needed in 'Big Chief'.

2015, Dee Dee Bridgewater & The New Orleans Seven, Alicante

Perfectly supported by the band with leader, arranger and trumpeter Irvin Mayfield Jr: emotional in 'What A Wonderful World', powerful in the groovy material and full of surprising ideas with musical depth, firmly rooted in the New Orleans tradition. And the rest: all great players within the ensemble and remarkable when asked to step forward and take the lead, like in a great duet by trombonist Michael Watson with Dee Dee, which was one of the many highlights of the show; others came from pianist Viktor Atkins and sax player Ricardo Pascal, all set on the tremendous rhythm work by Jason Weaver on bass and Adonis Rose on drums. A great project with the big band, a great show with the smaller version: they all got New Orleans within themselves and brought a piece of that city to Alicante! And it was fun to hang with Dee Dee after the show and chat about new ideas and projects. We stayed another day to see and hear Marcus Miller, which was a really cool show as well and a chance to chat with Marcus and his percussionist Mino Cinelu

Vitoria Jazz was the next stop on our annual festival round trip. Anat Cohen and Estrella Morente with Niño Josele were the acts we saw the first night there and then the following day, the James Brandon Lewis Trio with Luke Stewart on bass and Warren 'Trae' Crudup on drums. About 500 people made it to the Teatro Principal for the show in which the band went straight into the grooves of the new record and turned the heat up! James was fully in command of the directions the music went, leading from the front and directing his companions with short movements by his hand. They went with a hard rock feel into 'Lament for JLew', then into the beautiful ballad that is Don Cherry's 'Bamako Love' and last but not least into the straighter hip-hop grooves of 'Boom Bap Bop', at one point slightly going into some Latin rhythms within that song, only to hit the audience even harder when getting back into the original tempo. The audience loved every minute of it and came back for an encore and later for a CD signing session with James. The festival was closed by a duo performance by Chick Corea and Herbie Hancock and if you knew their two live records, released 1978 and 1979, then expectations were probably high. But the two piano and keyboard giants didn't go out and simply repeated what they did in the late 70's, they added some keyboards to the mix and actually integrated these into some of the numbers as reflections on careers which had more to offer than great piano playing. Even so most of the keyboard improvisations were a bit too flat and ambient for me, when they simply played the two acoustic pianos then standards like 'I'll Remember April' or 'Milestones' became fresh and exciting and at times surprising. Of course, there were some of the hits as well: 'Maiden Voyage', 'La Fiesta' (the only tracks they performed as well in the late 70's) and 'Cantaloupe Island' and with them they brought the audience to a standing ovation. I like both guys individually and as a duo when on pianos, that's when they shine and show their class.

The 40th anniversary edition of the North Sea Jazz Festival was a truly great one. As always, I tried to arrange my program in a way that I could see my acts (OKeh recording artists, of which 9 were performing this year) and then some others I personally knew or wanted to discover. The Friday already gave me a dilemma: at the same time Sergio Mendes performed there was as well as a tribute to Paco de Lucia. I went to say *"Hi"* to Sergio and Gracinha and listened a bit to the great show with his new band, as always, a summer party on the highest musical level!

2015, backstage at NSJF: José James and Sergio Mendes

Then I rushed over to the other stage to see a bit of the guys doing the Paco de Lucia tribute with members of the various incarnations of his band, led and kept together by Jorge Pardo, who as well told many touching stories of the great man, supported by short video snippets and of course the music. I had come to Amsterdam on the same flight from Madrid as harmonica player Antonio Serrano and, as we knew each other from the Magos & Limon concert, we chatted a bit and then he invited me to go with him in the limo that was picking him up to take him to Rotterdam, which I gladly accepted. I would most likely have arrived in Rotterdam faster by taking the train, but having the chance to chat a bit with Antonio on the way was worth the delay. Then I was off to see Jose James, who was simply amazing: his Billie Holiday tribute album was by far the best of all the ones I have heard that year and live it was touching, engaging and powerful. Jose can sing anything and his jazz singing has become something truly special. After that I walked to the next stage and sat down to enjoy the trio of Bugge Wesseltoft, Dan Berglund and Henrik Schwarz. What on the album is more of an ambient affair, turned live into a groovy and still at times contemplative performance. Given that it was past midnight, probably the right move.

The second day of the festival started for me at 2 pm in the Sint-Laurenskerk with a fantastic solo performance by Branford Marsalis, who was using the room almost as a second instrument, this concert was even better than the first I heard live in Hamburg the previous year, with beautiful melodies, perfectly played on his various saxes and the pick of the repertoire as usual spot on. From the pieces I hadn't heard him doing before, 'The Peacocks' by Jimmy Rowles stood out: melodic birdlike calling, sound travelling through the huge church, hugging everyone! Branford really liked the sound of that church and said, that if he were to do another solo recording, he would surely do it there. Back at the venue I heard David Sanborn doing the repertoire of his new OKeh album and then Dee Dee with the NOJO giving a powerful performance. Somi and Theo both did wonderful gigs and so did the last band for me on the night: The Bad Plus Joshua Redman. The reason that there is no & between the group name and Joshua's is that they are a unit and not the Plus + and whoever wasn't clear about that at the beginning, was surely convinced very quickly: these guys played so tight and communicated so well, performing music from each member of the group and got the audience screaming and giving a standing ovation.

Sunday late morning I went with Branford to a laundromat close to the hotel. He needed to wash some clothes while on tour and preferred to do it that way than overpaying in a hotel. And it gave us time to chat about ideas for the next album. While the washing was in the machine we went for an Italian lunch and he told me that he would like to do an album with the quartet and a singer. But the singer shouldn't be a guest, but a fifth member of the group and he could only think of one artist who would be able to do that: Kurt Elling. I was immediately excited by that idea and asked him to move forward with it, as he had loosely talked to Kurt already. Soon after they started to exchange ideas for songs and their arrangements. And it was Kurt who was the first artist I saw that evening, for me confirming that he was the perfect partner for Branford.

2015, NSJF, Kurt Elling

Then Bill Frisell played in a packed venue his outstanding 'Guitar in the Space Age program', songs from the 60s, The Byrds, Beach Boys, The Kinks, to a knowing audience, which enjoyed every single tone. Branford's quartet started right at the end of the Frisell set, so off I was and couldn't get into the venue, too many people were already queuing. I went in via the back stage area and listening from the side of the stage (with a cold beer) wasn't too bad, but the excitement in the room told me that they had the power and intensity of this improvisational performance full force. Then off to Melody Gardot, another of the great jazz singers performing at this festival and as usual she created a tight and intimate atmosphere, drawing people into her songs and make them feel she was singing for them alone. 'Currency of Man', her then latest album, is full of great songs and she had a great band to do them justice. I closed the evening and the festival with Roy Hargrove and his band, one of the favourites of the North Sea Jazz crowd and he gave them what they wanted: hot jazz with great soli and good grooves.

In August Hannah, who had spent the month before in New Zealand, visiting her old primary school teacher and seeing the set of the Lord Of the Rings film, including the Hobbit village, came to visit with her new boyfriend Luke, a nice guy who really enjoyed being in Madrid with her. We made a little trip to Alcalá de Henares with them and then went to see Real Madrid playing Galatasaray Istanbul in a friendly at the Bernabeu Stadium. Before the kick off, while walking around outside of the stadium, the two got interviewed for a small tv channel. They loved it. After they left and

Hannah had started her exchange year in Vienna, Ganavya came to stay a few days with us and we talked a lot about music and her studies and the record she was about to work on with Pablo while in town.

2015 was the year Lithuania became the 19th member of the Eurozone and Greece missed a debt payment to the IMF, continuing their economic crisis. Cuba and the US re-established full diplomatic relations, after 54 years of political enmities. A suicidal German co-pilot crashed an Airbus in the French Alps on his flight from Barcelona to Düsseldorf, killing all 150 passengers and crew on board and a stampede in Mecca killed over 2000 pilgrims, while IS demolished the ancient city sites of Nimrud and Dur-Sharrukin in Iraq, so destroying part of humanity's heritage. The 2015 United Nations Climate Change Conference was held in Paris and was the 21st of its kind. It resulted in the Paris Agreement, which was adopted by consensus by the 195 UNFCCC participating member states and the European Union. There was finally hope that mankind was a step closer in dealing with climate change at a time, when the worst effects still could be reversed.

I was reading the new book in the Millennium series, which David Lagercrantz was allowed to continue with the captivating 'The Girl In The Spiders Web'. Anthony Doerr's touching novel 'All The Light We Can Not See' I read on recommendation of Kurt Elling and I loved every word of it and recommended it to Hannah and some friends. Leonard Padura's 'Der Mann, der Hunde liebte' (The man who loved dogs) was a birthday present from Christian Kellersmann and a fantastic book, which I truly enjoyed. In the movies we saw among others 'The Danish Girl' by Tom Hooper with an outstanding Eddie Redmayne and Bill Condon's charming 'Mr. Holmes', starring Ian McKellen as a retired Sherlock Holmes. When it came to listen to new recordings that year, I favoured Eberhard Weber's 'Encore', Tigran's wonderful work with choir 'Luys I Luso', Hakon Kornstad's impressive and unique 'Tenor Battle' between his voice and his sax, Gregory Porter's successful and captivating 'Liquid Spirit' and Jose James' outstanding 'Yesterday I had The Blues: The Music Of Billie Holiday', an album that proves again what a great jazz singer Jose is. I remember seeing him once at Ronnie Scott's doing a project titled 'Facing East: The Music Of John Coltrane' featuring that night pianist Jef Neve and sax player Michael Campagna and others I don't remember, but it was simply divine what these guys did with Coltrane's music. Jose gave me a live recording from a festival and I still have this one and listen to it occasionally, as the music is so deep and spiritual and full of respect and emotion. And whenever I meet Jose, I tell him to finally record this project, as I think it is truly worth to be heard by many people.

In September my A&R update for management included the final recording of Jimmy Scott, a touching album with a bunch of guest stars. In the last minute the producer got cold feet and we didn't make the deal and he released via an indie. Fair enough! Gretchen Parlato was still on the list, but had extended her maternity leave, so I just kept in touch with Karen Kennedy, her manager, to see when there would be new music to check out. Youn Sun Nah was a big seller in France and Germany and her deal with ACT had only one album left, but the next one was available for the US, where she wasn't known that much. A good starting point, if expectations could be managed. I had added as well China Moses and Ganavya as possible signings, which should be discussed internally.
We looked at each signed artist's overall performance in terms of sales, touring, management, etc. every year at least once and then decided how to move forward. Nir Felder unfortunately hadn't toured his album at all, except for three shows in Holland, and therefore, as no improvement on this situation was to be expected, we had to tell his manager that we couldn't go forward with another album. This is always tough, especially when you like an artist, but reality is, that each of the artists signed need to be able to tour and so support their releases.
As Somi had new management and agency, we decided thankfully to go ahead with the second album, but with Michel Camilo we were stuck in a discussion about advances. We saw what the sales of the previous album had brought in and based our offer on that and he saw his status as a live act

in the market and based it on that. No way we could come together. This happens in business, but it gladly didn't affect our friendship.

September brough Gregory Porter to Madrid for a show at the Nuevo Teatro Alcala and Amparo Tebar invited us to the show. He started the night with one of my favourites of his songs: 'Painting on Canvas' and that's what he did the rest of the show: painting scenes of everyday life on an imaginary canvas: scenes of horror and sadness, but as well of humanity and love. They went through the repertoire of his three previous albums: 'Water', 'Be Good' and 'Liquid Spirit'. Porter is as good a song writer as he is a performer – expressive and powerful, laying his emotions bare for us, the audience, to take them on and experience what music can do in a positive sense. And when he sang 'Hey Laura' or 'Musical Genocide' or the powerful '1960 What?', he got us all. Then he jumped into a simple but captivating version of 'Papa Was a Rolling Stone', his voice as always impeccable, his singing strong and without fault, pushing the message on a lyrical and emotional level. His band supported him perfectly and added some deep jazz moments to the show, especially pianist Chip Crawford and saxophonist Yosuke Sato delivering some impressive solo work.

2015, Gregory Porter & Band, Madrid

From October 5th to 11th for the second time the Montreux Jazz Artists Foundation, under Stephanie-Aloysia Moretti, organised a week of education for young jazz musicians, who were part of their annual competitions – all in all 10 musicians from the finals of the vocal, guitar and piano competitions gathered in Montreux for an intensive residential arts program. That year's participants were: On Guitar: Hector Quintana Ferreiro – Cuba / Pedro Martins – Brazil / Sebastian Böhlen – Germany; Vocals: Alina Engibaryan – Russia / Yumi Ito – Japan/Poland/Switzerland / Vuyo Sotashe – South Africa / Amiyna Farouque – Sri Lanka; And on Piano: A Bu – China / Yakir Arbib – Israel / Krisztian Olah – Hungary.
I went to see them on Saturday night performing at the Session in Funky Claude's Bar and was positively surprised by the quality of what I heard, even so one has to have in mind that the music they performed was not what they might usually do, one could hear the individuality and quality of their performances: all three guitar players with great sound and technique, good expression and especially Sebastian with some surprising soli, full of unexpected twists and turns, while at the same time staying with the song. Same for the pianists: all three were very good and interesting, but the show, when I was there, was stolen by a ten-minute solo performance from Yakir Arbib, powerful and energetic and full of references and musical statements and for once the noisy audience stopped talking and listened. The vocalists were more difficult to judge: great control from all of them and they performed the standards on display very well. Alina and Vuyo doing most of the work that night, Yumi sounded great too and so did Amiya when she did a very personal take on 'Feeling Good'. Their musical mentors during this week were Yaron Herman, Al Jarreau, Ziv Ravitz, Joe Sanders, Kurt Rosenwinkel and Nils Petter Molvaer. And beside the workshops and the jam sessions

(and the final concert) they had lectures concerning matters such as social media, composing and arranging for films, International Tax Aspects of Music, Branding Yourself and Understand the Music Business, in which I shared the panel with friends from festivals around Europe and TSF radio in Paris. A great panel and discussion which we ended talking through lunch in the garden of the villa where the musicians stayed for the week.

Chuck Mitchell had hired that month Matt Pierson as a consultant for Masterworks, who as well could do some producing. The idea was to have me with an international perspective for OKeh and Matt for jazzy crossover product coming from the US, with the possibility of bringing one or the other jazz act to OKeh as well. I had only met Pierson once before, years ago at the Montreal Jazz Festival and didn't know the guy, except for some of his production work with Brad Mehldau, early in Brad's career.

Later that month I celebrated my 60th birthday with family and friends at Paco's restaurant. Hannah and Luke had come over for this event, and so had my mother, my three sisters Marlis, Christine and Barbara and my brother Jürgen with his wife Uschi. Then there were Yolanda's family, represented by Maria and Jorge and her aunt Luisa and her uncle Luis. From Norway we had Yngve, Cecilie, Sten and Ann Katrin, plus old colleagues and friends Suzannah Reast, Paulo Ochoa, Christian Kellersmann and his wife Cristina, Sophia Robb and her husband Simon, Dhafer Youssef and his partner Shiraz, Rainer Rygalyk and his wife Andrea, Goran Gartner and Katharina, Søren and Skipper, plus over 20 friends from Madrid, including Alex and Estefania, Inma and Jose, Patricia, Claudia and Cristina.

At my 60th birthday, 2015
left to right: myself, Hannah, Yolanda, Christine, our mother, Jürgen, Marlis, Barbara and Uschi

We had a wonderful time together (Yolanda and I even had time to go out and help my sister Marlis to buy a Spanish guitar, a beautiful and great sounding instrument) and a great party, with tons of drinks and the wonderful food that Paco had prepared for us, especially the Paella. 60! When one is 18, 60 seems really old and far away and when you once hit that mark it is actually feeling just like another birthday, but overall, I didn't feel old at all. Seems that the music and my family and friends are keeping me young.

For me the JazzMadrid15 festival started November 9th with the John Scofield / Joe Lovano Quartet, featuring Ben Street on bass and Bill Stewart on drums. The music they performed came mostly from

John Scofield's latest recording 'PAST PRESENT' and took that very personal album to new heights on stage. Great tracks like 'Mr. Puffy' and the title track were live extremely powerful and intense and the soloing of both main artists was immaculate! Deep musical exchanges of ideas, powerful statements about the artist in their time and their emotions, made this concert a very special one. I am a big fan of Sco and have followed his career with pleasure and still can hear that he is getting better and better, digging deeper into himself to reveal his inner thoughts through his writing and playing. Next up was Marc Ribot with the Young Philadelphians, which consisted of Mary Halvorson on guitar, my old friend Jamaaladeen Tacuma on bass and Calvin Weston on drums. The music was described to me, before I heard this concert, as 70's Philly Soul meets Ornette Coleman and that's what it was: powerful grooves with free-flowing guitar improvisations and cool sounds, created with the help of three local string players, which did extremely well to create the amazing overall sound and power of this music. Marc and Mary were tremendous and inspired and the groove section as you would expect from these legendary guys.

While sitting backstage after the concert, chatting with Jamaal and Marc, we heard the first news of the Paris attacks and they got worse by the minute. Attacks outside the Stade de France during a football match and inside the music venue Bataclan left 130 people dead and over 400 injured. The fanatical Islamists of IS took responsibility for this senseless act of violence. What a crazy world we are living in – there is no respect and no tolerance any more.

November 15th and it was time to see Kurt Elling again. After some emotional and touching words and a minute of silence for the victims of the attacks in Paris, Kurt opened the evening with 'La vie en rose', a fitting tribute. He then went through the songs of his latest album 'Passion World' and brought the audience exactly that: a world of passion. His immaculate voice carried these songs, plus a few from earlier recordings, like the amazing 'Samurai Cowboy' from the album 'The Gate', into messages of love and harmony and understanding. The storyteller trying to heal the world with his words and emotions. Kurt was supported by a great group of musicians featuring John McLean on guitar, Clark Sommers on bass, Ulysses Owens Jr on drums and the new member of the team, the very talented Stu Mindeman on piano and Hammond B3.

Branford had booked a studio in New Orleans to finally record the album with his quartet and Kurt Elling and, as they hadn't played together before, they were doing four nights with two shows each night at the Snug Harbour club. The best way to get into the repertoire was by playing it. As neither Yolanda nor myself had been to New Orleans before and always wanted to go, we decided that the recording was as good a reason as any and booked our flights. The cradle of jazz is still a place full of music: in almost every bar, at the corners of the streets in the French Quarter and of course in the many jazz venues, there were bands playing and most of them on a pretty high level of musicianship. From big bands to solo performances, the streets and plazas of New Orleans cover it all. We didn't go to hear Branford and the guys immediately, but went to show three out of eight and the wide spectrum of the repertoire they were working with was a real positive surprise, including songs from Nat King Cole, Jobim and Sting. Not all songs were yet 'there', but one could hear what the possibilities were! It was fun to chat with the guys and Bryan Farina, Kurt's manager and hang a bit with them. On show 8, the second one we watched, it all came together and this show was full of promise and excitement for a great recording to be made. On top of a great performance by the quartet (Branford, Joey Calderazzo, Eric Revis and Justin Faulkner), who started the evening with an amazing rendition of Keith Jarrett's 'The Windup', fast and powerful in all soli and interplay, Kurt's immaculate singing, especially in Sting's 'Practical Arrangement', a beauty of a song, made that show unforgettable. The night came to an unexpected and incredible end with Dee Dee Bridgewater and Irvin Mayfield, as well as Delfeayo Marsalis joining the guys on stage for some amazing music and fun. Something really special was happening in front of our ears and eyes …. magic!

2015, The Branford Marsalis Quartet jamming with Kurt Elling, Dee Dee Bridgewater and Irving Mayfield

While walking home that night we passed a wedding procession, swinging and dancing! The next few days we explored the amazing city, had a little cruise on a steamboat on the Mississippi, did some tours to learn more about New Orleans and its history, but stayed mostly Riverside and didn't venture further into the city, there is too much to discover in a few days!

And we visited the New Orleans Jazz Market, home of Irvin Mayfield's New Orleans Jazz Orchestra, which was rehearsing for its Christmas shows, with guest Dee Dee Bridgewater. A truly great place with a community program, lots of music and a great hall to perform. While being there Irvin mentioned that his drummer Adonis Rose would play his club on Bourbon Street, The Irvin Mayfield Jazz Playhouse, that night and so we decided to spend the last night of our trip with some more music. And music we got! We were there a bit early and sat down on our table having a drink. There were maybe another 10 people in the club. Just as the band started to play Irvin and Dee Dee and her manager/daughter Tulani walked in and came to our table: what company to have, which only got better when Joey Calderazzo and his wife joined the group and then the stage – Dee Dee and Irvin were having fun with Adonis' band and Joey joined in as well before leaving and then Branford walked in as well and sat down with us, but didn't play, as he was at a friend's house before and didn't bring his horn. What a night: great company and great music again!! We also enjoyed the food in New Orleans, even so it was a bit on the heavy side – the best meal was at Antoine's!!

When leaving even at the airport a band was playing, which made me understand the song 'You don't know what it means to miss New Orleans' a little better.

We rounded up the year with a relaxed Christmas party for the family at the house of Yolanda's aunt and a laid-back New Year's Eve celebration at her mother's flat, for which we were joined by Jorge, Yolanda's half-brother René with family and Ganavya, who was in town, staying with us for a few days and who was singing for all of us a touching traditional song from home.

2015 / 16, at home with Ganavya

2016

2016, as the years before, started with a trip to New York for Jazz Connect and Winter Jazz. I arrived on Wednesday afternoon and after a long flight, all I needed was some cool music and Kurt Elling at Birdland was the one to deliver that. He is always great listening to and never have I heard a dull concert when he performs and Birdland was no exception: mostly repertoire from his amazing catalogue, with a new song in the repertoire by Carla Bley, for which he wrote lyrics. I had invited Madeleine Peyroux and her manager Cynthia to the show and we all really enjoyed the gig and had a good chat with Kurt afterwards.

The next day meetings from morning to evening … then gladly a dinner with friends and business partners (best combination) and off to the next gig: the new Joshua Redman band at the Jazz Standard. They call themselves 'Still Dreaming' and are a tribute to the group 'Old And New Dreams', which Dewey Redman founded with Don Cherry, Charlie Haden and Ed Blackwell as a tribute to the music of Ornette Coleman, in the mid 1970's.

2016, NYC, Still Dreaming

I was lucky enough to have seen the original band perform in the late 70's and always was a fan of the music of this group, therefore I was pleasantly surprised to see Joshua with Ron Miles, Scott Colley and Brian Blade slipping easily into the spirit of the original band and playing music on an immense level and with deep intensity. They performed their own compositions as well as songs from 'Old And New Dreams' and of course compositions of Ornette – all perfectly done. This quartet is like a re-incarnation of the original, taking the music into today. When they finished their set with Ornette's composition 'Happy House' I was simply in jazz heaven!!

On January 15th the festival had the first day of the 'jazz marathon' and after another day of meetings and a panel at the Jazz Connect Conference, I was looking forward to see a few gigs that day, starting with James Brandon Lewis, who performed at the Zinc Bar with his trio. What makes James so special is that he is powerful and imaginative, but within the essence of the songs he performs – mostly from his recent OKeh album 'Days Of FreeMan', touching and full of rough emotions. Next was Korean singer Youn Sun Nah, who had already made a name in most of Europe, but not yet in the US and as I like her records, but never had seen her perform, I was looking forward to it and it was simply impressive: partly alone, partly with the incredible guitarist Ulf Wakenius, her simple approach to the song material was stunning and effective – from standards to Randy Newman to Korean folk songs – her voice and personality carried the performance! I had met her manager and we were looking into maybe signing her, but that was still in discussion at the time.

Then I went to hear young trumpet player Theo Croker performing material from his forthcoming OKeh record 'Escape Velocity'. Theo's band DVRK FUNK featuring Kassa Overall on drums, Anthony Ware, saxes; Michael King, keys; Eric Wheeler, bass and Ben Munson on guitar, was on fire: the new songs were great and modern, swing and rock and the ballad 'Because of You' was simply incredible. The Bitter End club was packed – a young and hip crowd came to check Theo out – and they got something they enjoyed: intense music, great grooves and beautiful melodies, some hot trumpet playing by the leader, who is on the way to become a true star. No problem to hang around until 3 am with music that cool!

Day 2 of the 'marathon' started with warming up in the afternoon at the Gail Boyd Mgmt. and Karen Kennedy 24Seven Artist Development showcases: young violinist Scott Texier impressed with a beautiful sound and a great performance; Jen Shyu's show was deep and powerful, but for me in the wrong place, as it was very theatrical in visual and musical terms and the venue just didn't do her justice; Tillery the trio of Becca Stevens, Gretchen Parlato and Rebecca Martin performed four songs from their new and upcoming album and it was pure magic! Vocal harmonies and beautiful melodies, simplicity with a focus on the voices, touching, emotional and truly special. I hoped to sign that project to OKeh, as it was simply the best vocal group I had heard in ages. I then had a chat with Karen Kennedy concerning the signing of that album and wanted to know if the girls would be able to tour together, as all three were having their own careers. The answer was "Yes" and therefore I presented the music, which I really liked, to Sony. I truly could hear some potential there, for festivals of all kinds, jazz, world music, folk, as all these elements are present in their music. The guys in the US didn't hear it and Matt Pierson even said that the production wasn't good, which I couldn't understand at all, as I thought the sound and the mix were clear and crisp, as I would like it for such an album. But he seemed to have his own idea how things should be mixed, which was fine by me, but that didn't mean everything had to sound that way. I found that comment strange, to say the least.

Sax player J.D. Allen just did one song with his group: enough to make it clear that he is one of the most talented improvisers around and for me together with James Brandon Lewis the future of this instrument. And finally, Somi, who as always did a great show, singing impeccably with great support from her band. She is just such a personality on stage, powerful, but at the same time vulnerable when she is singing about the fate of African women. The songs of this showcase came all from 'The Lagos Music Salon', as the new material she was working on for her coming record was not yet ready to be performed, but I just couldn't wait any longer to hear the new songs.

Dinner and then off to see Becca Stevens at Rockwood 3. She brought her band and some special guests. I never had seen her doing her own material, just saw her opening the London Jazz festival with a few songs by others, or with Taylor Eigsti, so this was it and how good it was! She is a star in the making: a great voice, great performance and great compositions. Beautiful the song she performed with Jacob Collier and perfect the rest! I loved every minute of it! To end these crazy days of amazing music, I went to see Julian Lage with his trio featuring Scott Colley on bass and Kenny Wollesen on drums. Amazing playing from all three guys with Julian leading the way with jazz and rock-tinged licks, backed up by one of the best rhythm sections around. The many musicians in the venue enjoyed the gig as much as I did, as screaming and endless applause confirmed.

For the second time PRO HELVETIA sponsored the Take Five Switzerland event, arranged for and ran by Serious Productions in London, this time featuring 7 young Swiss jazz musicians plus one young man from South Africa. The participants this year were: Julie Campiche – harp / Yilian Canizares – violin, vocals / Yeal Miller – vocals / Nils Fischer – sax, cl / Joel Graf – sax / Christoph Irniger – sax / Manuel Troller – guitar and from South Africa Mandla Mlangeni – tp. The event was held, as in the past, at Bore Place, outside of London and lasted a full week. I arrived on Thursday around midday and had my general session, together with agent and manager Mike Bindraban and concert promoter Jan Ole Otnæs, both good friends, talking more general how the music business works and how labels, managers, agents and concert promoters (festivals and clubs and other venues) need to work together in the long run to create awareness for new artists and built careers. After that initial session we had that evening and all of Friday morning for one-to-one discussions, so we could talk about topics individually important to each musician and maybe provide advice and guidance. These face-to-face sessions proved to be extremely valuable and interesting, not only for the musicians (at least I hope that was the case) but as well for me, as it is interesting to get to know these young artists a bit better and, as this is an exchange, to learn something in the process. It was great to see John Cumming again, as he came by for a chat and a glass of wine.

Hannah came to visit in March and we had, as always, some good days together, with lots of talks, walks and little trips, like the one when the two of us went to El Escorial for a day or when we went with Yolanda, Maria and Jorge to Manzanares El Real and then we all went to some Easter processions in Madrid. What a colourful and amazing event, with people singing or shouting in excitement and everyone appreciating the tradition.

with Hannah, 2016

That month Yolanda and I saw a few shows in Madrid: our friend Pablo Martin Caminero premiered his new album 'Salto Al Vacio' with his band at the Bogui club. Ariel Bringuez (sax), Toni Belenguer (tb), Moises P. Sanchez (p), Borja Barrueta (dr) and new member Cepoillo on cajon, jumped right into the new music, which was again a great mixture of flamenco rhythms and jazz phrases and was full of surprising (and musically challenging) changes. Probably some of the best music Pablo had composed so far and played on the highest level by these incredible musicians, with Pablo and especially Moises standing out in an excellent group. A few days later it was Cecile McLorin Salvant at the Clamores club. Her band, Renee Rosnes on piano, Rodney Whittaker on bass and Lewis Nash on drums, was perfect for her – especially Rosnes did some fantastic soli taking the music to a higher level. Cecile is an incredible talent as a singer, but for me too often was showing off what she can do technically instead of using her technical skills to enhance the performance of the songs. She is young and I am sure she will get there, but that concert was a promise of what might be, but not yet a great show.

I hadn't seen Geri Allen for some time and then I heard that she would play in Madrid and of course I had to see and hear her and it was everything one could expect from a piano solo concert: sheer beauty in expression, melodic improvisations and adventurous excursions into the inner most places of a song. Detroit, Allen's hometown, stood in the centre of the concert and she was performing songs from composers somehow connected to the city (a bit of Motown thrown in of course), from Alice Coltrane to Michael Jackson and Stevie Wonder, Marcus Belgrave, Monk and others; a true trip through the city and its music. The repertoire can be heard on her wonderful and critically acclaimed 2013 Motema album 'Grand River Crossing'.

Last but not least back to the Bogui for a concert of the Eric Revis Trio featuring Kris Davis on piano and John Betsch on drums. Revis, whom I have seen many times with the Branford Marsalis Quartet, took a slightly freer approach to his music with this trio and explored the essence of the compositions, moving from a beautiful melody to a free improvisation only to go back to the beauty of the song, as if to say: there is more to life than beauty and we need to explore it, as it will lead us back to beauty, but with a different understanding of it. Revis is a great bass player and he showed that not only in his soli, but as well in the collective trio improvisations and Kris performed with such sensibility and understanding of the music, that all her playing seemed to make perfect sense. John Betsch, a historic figure in his own right, played at times with such minimalist use of his drums, but still driving the music forward. Outstanding music by a tight-knitted trio.

In terms of A&R, I brought 7 records to the label in 2016. Bill Frisell had the previous year played a concert at the Lincoln Center, which was filmed and that was the program he wanted to record for his third OKeh album. I watched the video and really liked what he and Petra Haden did, as she was the singer on this project. 'When You Wish Upon A Star', which also featured Eyvind Kang, Thomas Morgan and Rudy Royston, is a collection of songs from film and TV and for 'record store day' we released a limited edition single with two tracks which weren't on the album. This record got Bill another Grammy nomination, as well as a nomination for the German Echo awards and he won the Dutch Edison for it. Dhafer Youssef's second OKeh recording 'Diwan Of Beauty And Odd' was recorded with an all-American group, featuring Ambrose Akinmusire, Aaron Parks, Ben Williams and Mark Giuliana. It is a powerful and amazing album, but we had some discussions about the cover, as I didn't think that it was as good as the previous one. In the end, we compromised midway and got the record out, but despite him touring (with Justin Faulkner on drums instead of Mark) the album didn't do as well as 'Birds Requiem', which might have to do that in France especially he expected more in terms of marketing around the big show he had in Paris. The album got a nomination for the German Echo and won the Dutch Edison in the following year.

Another Echo nominee was Theo Croker's second OKeh recording 'Escape Velocity', a modern and cool jazz album recorded with his working band and having Dee Dee Bridgewater as a guest on one song. Neither CD nor LP of this release had any printed text on the cover, just a sticker on the shrink-wrap so people knew what they bought. Theo had asked for it and I am always happy to do something different and it actually looked really great as the photo of him is amazing.

'Holding The Stage' is the fourth volume of Sonny Rollins' 'Road Shows' series and features live recordings from 1979 to 2012, his last year on the road. I finally managed to convince Sonny to make a proper cover for the release and get away from the same style design we had in the past and we gave it a proper title as well. With the photos by John Abbott and the liner notes by Ted Panken, we had a great product altogether. Sonny's playing has been truly amazing over the years and it was great to close the disc with 'Don't Stop The Carnival', as he always ended his shows with that song. Sonny did a bunch of interviews and phoners and the album was globally very well received.

The Branford Marsalis Quartet and Kurt Elling had, after the eight shows at the Snug Harbour in New Orleans, recorded the album in two days, but as they had another day of the studio, they fooled around a bit and tried out things and songs and some actually made it on the album 'Upward Spiral', released in June 2016. There is so much great music on this recording, but my personal favourite is 'From One Island To Another' by Chris Whitley and Yolanda's is 'Practical Arrangement' by Rob Mathes and Sting. I just love the combination of Branford and Kurt and the rest of the guys and what they can do with and within a song.

Right after re-launching OKeh, I had started to talk to Till Brönner and his brother Pino about signing Till and then Bogdan and Per got involved, as they were all based in Berlin, which made communicating directly much easier. We made the deal and Till released his first OKeh album 'The Good Life', produced by Dutch legend Ruud Jacobs, in September. Larry Goldings was on piano and the rest was basically Diana Kralls's band: Anthony Wilson, John Clayton and Jeff Hamilton and they were perfect for Till's trumpet and voice and the standards they recorded. We also made a deluxe edition of this release featuring a double LP, the CD and a photo book with shots of Till and from the recording session by Andreas Bitesnich. The record sold extremely well in Germany, Austria and surrounding countries and relatively ok in France, Spain and Japan.

I had always wanted to work with Kurt Elling and that year I even had two records with him: the one with Branford and his first Christmas album titled 'The Beautiful Day'. When Kurt and his manager Bryan Farina told me that they would love to put a Christmas record out, I wasn't too excited initially, as these mainly sell in the US and personally, I hardly ever listen to one, except for the Singers Unlimited or Ella. But his album changed that and added a third one to my short list. It is touching and accessible, deep and moving and simply great music. Kurt did a few gigs in the US with this program and during a wonderful dinner we had in New York and to which I had invited Till, who was in town, he actually asked Till if he wanted to come out with him for these few Christmas dates and Till said *"Yes"*. Which was really great, as it gave us at least something to work with in the US for Till's album.

The US released albums by The Bad Plus and Bria Skonberg, France one by Baptiste Trotignon – Minino Garay and Germany released the great Nils Petter Molvaer album 'Buoyancy', on which I worked internationally.

The A&R list in 2016 included still the artists we were watching for possible signing after their deals were fulfilled with their current label. To this list I had added Melody Gardot, as she had only one album left in her deal. Madeleine was still there, so was Cecile McLorin Salvant, even so her manager said he didn't want to sign to a major, Youn Sun Nah and Robert Glasper. I had as well been in touch with the manager of Gregory Porter, directly with Jose James, Becca Stevens and her manager and Gretchen Parlato. Sometimes one needs to build relationships in advance, so when the moment comes and the artist is available, you are in a good position. But, as jazz is a small business, most people know each other anyway. I brought also a lot of European artists for discussion and a few we did sign. The most important aspect overall was, that we had acts with global appeal and potential.

In April Josemi Carmona, guitarist extraordinaire and Javier Colina, Spanish bass master presented, with the help of percussionist Bandolero, their new album 'De Cerca'. From wonderful originals played as a duo or trio to some tracks with guest vocalist Antonio Montoya or with special guest Jorge Pardo on flute, this was all about beauty and melody. Josemi can of course do the fast runs on the guitar, but in general he is a flamenco player with a jazz feel that is based in melodic playing with rhythmic undertones; their beautiful version of 'You And The Night And The Music' is an amazing example of that approach. Colina not standing much behind with some of his soli being impressive in terms of ideas and expression and Bandolero has grown into a full flamenco drummer from the cajon player of early, sensitive in his support of the two masters.

2016, De Cerca

Dhafer Youssef, friend and oud master and singer, performed with his band at the Theatre du Chatelet in Paris on Thursday, April 7th. The venue (sold out with around 2000 people) was the perfect place for him, carrying his incredible voice in every corner of the hall, giving the audience the goosebumps. The band featured the young pianist Isfar Sarabski, Phil Donkin on bass and Ferenc Nemeth drums and long-time collaborator Eivind Aarset on guitar and they grooved when necessary or supported melody and performed ambient sounds when requested. Besides the incredible painter of sounds Aarset, especially new pianist Isfar Sarabski was a bit of a surprise with his almost classical touch in the ballads and his powerful sounds when pushing the rhythm. Beautiful as well in a haunting ballad that Dhafer just performed with him and Phil on bass, here the voice was just riding over the two other instruments in clarity and emotions carrying beauty, which is hard to describe. Not many voices can carry so much message without words, can touch by simply expressing emotions and always ending in an uplifting tone. The two hours show and hanging with Dhafer afterwards were surely worth the trip to Paris.

Then I was off to ´jazzahead´ again, which that year included companies from Asia and Cuba besides the European and American presence the fair already had and stood under the sign of Switzerland. And artists from this partner country had a strong presence at the festival – the opening night on Thursday, April 21 presented the Colin Vallon Trio, Weird Beard, Christoph Irniger's Pilgrim, Elina Duni, Julian Sartorius, Plaistow, Pommelhorse and Luca Sisera Roofer. Beside the focus on the partner country, the festival had three more lines of programming: German Jazz Expo, European Jazz Meeting and Overseas Night. I didn't manage to see any of the German acts (guess in the end I simply had to many meetings scheduled), but went instead to check out some of the Overseas Night acts like Canadian singer Laila Biali, whose simplistic version of 'Nature Boy' was amazing to listen to and showed her immense talent and voice control, or the Aaron Diehl Trio, which used changing dynamics to a great result, keeping the listeners drawn in the music, surprising constantly and communicating on the highest musical level. Great too was trumpeter Amir Elsaffar and his Two Rivers Ensemble, whose blend of Arabic music and jazz reminded me of Dhafer Youssef and Ibrahim Maalouf, but still had something individual to offer, as well as Kevin Hays' New Day Trio. Here Hays focused on his piano playing and occasional singing and created a relaxed atmosphere for the trio to dwell in.

2016, jazzahead – with Wolfgang Puschnig and John Cumming

The European Jazz meeting opened with the Trondheim Jazz Orchestra & Ole Morten Vagan and it started therefore powerful and bassist Vagan's compositions got the best out of this remarkable orchestra, featuring as well violinist extraordinaire Ola Kvernberg. Modern Big Band Jazz at its best! A bit annoying was, that while the band played the announced last piece of the show, on the side of the stage some stage-hand held up a sign YOUR TIME IS UP and as they tried to finish the song the sign, a minute or so later, changed to STOP NOW!!! For a jazz meeting and concert this was slightly out of place, even when a tight schedule of shows needed to be preserved.
After more meetings on that Saturday, I went to see the 20th anniversary celebration concert of the Norwegian Jazzland label at the NDR Sendesaal. I had the pleasure of working with Bugge Wesseltoft and Sten Nilsen, the two forces behind the label, for many years and I am still a great fan of the music these guys put out every year. Celebrations started with Beady Belle introducing the audience to some new material of her forthcoming record – with Gregory Hutchinson on drums, Bugge

Wesseltoft on piano and Ole Marius Sandberg on bass. The new songs were really great and the band performed extremely well and, not surprising, Bugge ahead of everyone else with some incredible piano work. Then one of my favourite Jazzland acts took the stage: Hakon Kornstad with his ensemble performing music from his album 'tenor battle', which sees his tenor sax battle with his tenor voice!!! He is one of the most interesting young sax players in Europe, studied operatic singing for three years and now combines the two worlds he is living in musically to something utterly unique and touching, as the audience in Bremen experienced first-hand. Most of them didn't know what to expect and were moved to tears by the simple beauty of these melodies and Hakons performance and the acoustic sound fitted the venue perfectly! Then followed Bugge Wesseltoft's New Conception Of Jazz (Anniversary Edition) and some awesome grooves and improvisations. The new band (Marthe Lea on saxes; Oddrun Lilja Jonsdottir on guitar; Sanskriti Shrestha on tabla and Siv Øyun Kjenstad on drums) did extremely well for only playing their second gig together, supporting the master keyboarder perfectly! The evening ended with a short set by Moksha, a new group on Jazzland Recordings, featuring Jonsdottir and Shrestha plus percussionist Tore Fladjord. A beautiful finale to a very special night! A great celebration of one of Europe's most unique labels.

Our agency had a few gigs for Branford set up for March and April. These quartet shows were mainly in Germany, Austria and one in Luxembourg, followed by a run of three solo shows in the UK. The first one was in Bath, then Union Chapel in London and finally Norwich. These were the last days we booked, as work on the OKeh A&R and releases were becoming a bit too much and we couldn't really focus on the touring side of things anymore. Ann Marie suggested a change and I agreed and so we passed on our history with Branford to Katherine McVicker, who just a year before had started her own agency, after working for many years with Scott Southard's IMN, which as well acts as management for some artists, including Brad Mehldau.

In Madrid, Yolanda and myself went to see the concert of Chinese super star Karen Mok, with whom I had worked on her English jazz album in 2013. Karen was the first female Chinese pop star coming to Spain and the Chinese community went out to see her show, which was attended by about 2500 people.

2016, with Karen Mok, after her Madrid show

They sang along to all songs and we had a great time. Karen did as well two songs from the 'Somewhere I Belong' album I had worked on, which was really special. The day before, we had had a wonderful lunch with her and her German husband and went to say "Hi" after the show and thanked them again for inviting us. We must have been two of only a handful non-Chinese fans in the audience.

FLY is a trio consisting of Mark Turner on saxophones, Larry Grenadier on bass and OKeh recording artist Jeff Ballard on drums and they have recorded three albums since their debut in 2004. The repertoire of the show at Madrid's Bogui Club was mainly repertoire from these recordings: opening the first set with Ballard's 'Lady B' (written for his mother) from 'Sky & Country'. These three guys can play! Not only were they very tight as a group, their interplay and communication almost perfect, but they were as well outstanding soloists in their own rights, knowing when to let go and have one of the others take the spotlight and knowing when to step forward and take it themselves! Next on the set list was Mark Turners 'Brothersister' from the ECM album 'Year of the Snake'. After that they played another Ballard composition 'Perla Morena' and 'Super Sister' by Turner, both from 'Sky & Country'. The last tune opened with an unaccompanied tenor sax solo of the highest order: melodic and inventive and touching. The second set had another four songs and Turner started it off with a change to the soprano sax for a beautiful song called 'Come with me Miss B', which was followed by a Larry Grenadier composition dedicated to Oscar Pettiford. Larry was throughout playing incredible and some of his soli had the audience in the packed club screaming: a powerful, but emotional and sensitive performance. 'Lone' (Ballard) from the 2014 album 'Fly' led into the final piece of the evening that had the house go crazy; a deserved standing ovation and a beautiful encore rounded up a night to remember. And of course, it was great to see Jeff again and find a bit of time to chat and have a laugh.

2016, the FLY trio in Madrid

Paula Grande came a few days later to the same club and presented her new album' Viatge Interstel:lar'. She started the show solo and with the help of some loops with Nat King Cole's 'Calypso Women', simply stunning and showing her amazing vocal skills. Then the band joined her and they went on a global tour of music: from her own compositions to America, Brazil, Colombia and Australia and musically from Nat King Cole to Hiatus Kaiyote, whose two songs 'Swamp Thing' and 'Nakamarra' she made completely her own and that was what made her concert so special: no matter what source she uses, it is always something personal she can add to the existing song and her own compositions are on the same level as the covers or standards she picks.
May was also the month for the Madrid Tennis Masters and we ended up seeing Novak Djokovic, Fernando Lopez and Roberto Bautista playing on the day of our attendance.
2016 was as well the year when radical Islamists bombed the airport and a metro station in Brussels, leaving behind 35 dead and over 300 injured. The Panama papers caused an uproar in the financial and high-income world, laying bare who had off-shore accounts to circumvent paying taxes. In June, Portugal won the Euro 2016 in France and the UK voted to leave the EU in what was called the

Brexit. A terror attack in Nice saw a truck running over people in the city while celebrating Bastille Day, killing 86 and injuring a further 400. The attack was claimed by the Islamic State (IS) and was one of the worst of Islamic terrorism in Europe. The result was an intensification of French air strikes on IS in Syria and Iraq. A never-ending spiral of violence!

And Real Madrid won under new coach Zinedine Zidane the Champions League final in a dramatic penalty shoot-out. This was their eleventh European champions title and, like the tenth title in 2014, it came against their neighbours Atletico Madrid.

The festival season of 2016 started for Yolanda and myself with ViJazz, which stands for Vilafranca del Penedes and 'Vino y Jazz', a truly sensible combination. While you walk around the city, sampling the various local wines, you could enjoy some of the free concerts in the square in front of the church or go to one of the proper and guided wine tastings, obviously promoting the local whites and Cava. This festival was then booked by our friend Amparo Tebar, who arranged for us to go to a wine tasting, which we both enjoyed. For me a tasty surprise was the Cosmic by the Pares Balta Winery, a great mix of Sauvignon Blanc and Xarello (the local grape in the region). And of course, the music: the beautiful setting in the square helped to create a good atmosphere, but once you got Dee Dee Bridgewater on stage, supported musically by young trumpeter Theo Croker and his gang, the already hot square got to boiling temperatures! Dee Dee was so energetic and the young band was pushing her limits, and she accepted the challenge with a smile. Whether it was her repertoire or music from the two Theo Croker recordings and of course the music of New Orleans, Dee Dee and the band delivered in musical terms and in terms of entertainment. No wonder she was named Jazz Master by the NEA a few weeks earlier! The second day in Vilafranca offered more good wine and music by GoGo Penguin, reminiscent a bit of e.s.t. in the more powerful and driven moments, but still their own and making a few waves around Europe. This UK piano trio was really strong and deserved the great applause it got before making way for Richard Bona and his Mandekan Cubano project: cool rhythms and all that is great about Bona: good songs, great vocals and unreal bass acrobatics!!

Next on the list of summer jazz festivals was North Sea Jazz in Rotterdam. I kept it relaxed that year, started the Friday with a bit of Snarky Puppy, which was fine, but didn't blew me away; tried to listen to Diana Krall, but didn't have the right wrist band to see her as this was one of the few bonus concerts, where you have to pay extra, but was happy enough to go backstage and say "*Hi*" to her; off to see Kamasi Washington with the Metropole Orkest, conducted by Jules Buckley, and the ZO! Gospel Choir. Great music, really powerful stuff, but unfortunately the sound in the venue didn't transport that power as much as I would have liked; sometimes the orchestra sounded thin, the choir too much in the background and the group with Kamasi too dominant, but one could hear still how good everyone on stage was, how beautiful the band and orchestra fitted together and how the choir gave a different dimension to the compositions. Christian Scott is a wonderful player, with cool and captivating compositions and a fantastic live band and he proved again that he can capture his audiences and give them a good time. As I wanted to see Ibrahim Maalouf with his 'Kalthoum' band, I left Christian after a while and moved to the next venue to see Maalouf performing with Mark Turner on saxophone, Frank Woeste on piano, Scott Colley on bass and Clarence Penn on drums. 'Khartoum' is a homage to the Egyptian singer and composer Baligh Hamidi and her work 'Alf Leila Wa Leila', which was presented as a jazz suite and all players were in the mood to stretch and improvise and give this music something special.

I started the Saturday with a young man, whom I had met a few years back when he was just an internet phenomenon and who had developed his musical ideas into his first record: Jacob Collier. As on the album, the show featured only Jacob on all instruments, loops and samples. He even looped some of the videos he had running in the background, so even visually you could see him playing three or four instruments at the same time ... but let's take away the gimmicks for a moment and then the young man showed quite a lot of talent: between his own songs and his covers of standards or more modern songs, not only can he play, but he is as well a fantastic singer and has lots of great ideas on improvisation and the use of his tools. When he performed a song just with acoustic guitar and singing beautifully, one got the real picture. The 'I do it all' is part of his story and the new album and the show strengthens that, but there is more to him than that and once he has developed fully and has his own band, this could be an interesting (jazz) singer who doesn't seem to know borders – what for anyway?

OKeh artist James Brandon Lewis played a free-flowing melodic funk jazz set based on JBL's latest album 'Days Of FreeMan' and the audience really got into it and screamed and gave standing ovations within the set, as the hip hop based grooves and Lewis' impressive improvisations were simply stunning and local media mentioned the gig as one of the highlights of this year's festival. Got to listen a bit to Cyrille Aimee after that. She is a great singer with incredible control but sometimes I am not so sure about the repertoire choices, but the girl can sing! Then I had to go and see the Branford Marsalis Quartet featuring special guest Kurt Elling, now that their record was out. They have grown together as a unit since I saw them in December in New Orleans and were able to do almost anything with the songs they performed, mostly from their recently released disc 'Upward Spiral'. A pleasure of interactivity between all musicians, surprising changes and smiles all around. The guys surely had fun and it was reflected in the audience's enthusiastic response.

2016, collage NSJF

Sunday, I started with seeing a few old friends: composer and trumpet player Michael Mantler performed The Jazz Composers Orchestra Update with the Austrian Big Band Nouvelle Cuisine, conducted by Christoph Cech and in the band, as soloist next to Mantler was my friend Wolfgang Puschnig, alto sax player, composer and Harry Sokal, tenor sax player and another of Austria's greats. They all performed a captivating show of incredible big band music – doesn't get much deeper and better than that! And yes, the radio.string.quartet was part of that gig as well. I ran into

Christian McBride and Chick Corea, who was celebrating his 75th b
to his heroes – with a great band that featured beside McBride,
Marcus Gilmore. Totally amazing the other legends, I went to
Pharoah Sanders. Lloyd performing with Jason Moran, Reuben
could go wrong here. These guys played so well together, suppo
laying the ground for his improvisations. I was just sitting there
go away when Pharoah Sanders came on. The trio was compl
and the excellent Trilok Gurtu on percussion and they suppor
and with lots of feeling and intuition. And last on Sunday nigh
Mehldau and Mark Giuliana, with really funky grooves and the

The jazz festival in Vitoria-Gasteiz in the north of Spain,
anniversary and they put a very good program together, w
Friday and Saturday, July 15th and 16th. We have a lot of frie...
back to this festival and enjoy the impressive music too! Friday started with the
Holland duo, which I didn't see in Rotterdam, as I knew I would have the chance to see them
Vitoria and they were simply incredible. 'The Art Of Conversation' was the album most of the music came from and the title made truly sense when these two world class musicians were talking to each other via their instruments, as if one single mind spoke and improvised, together searching for new ideas or melodies within a song, constantly challenging each other without showing off. Then Jamie Cullum, who, every time I see him, has become an even better pianist. His just piano and voice version of 'Blackbird' was absolutely outstanding! And he still can make every song he touches his own: 'Love For Sale' was cool and modern and still the same great song, but that night it was Jamie's and so it was with the rest and especially his 'And The Wind Cries May' by Jimi Hendrix.
Saturday was the end of the festival and started with the Pat Metheny & Ron Carter duo, which I really enjoyed, but in comparison to the day before with Barron/Holland, this was a less connected affair. Great soli by both, but less communication and deeper understanding. Great their version of Sonny Rollins 'St. Thomas', surely one of the outstanding tunes of the show. Cecile McLorin Salvant closed the festival, once again showcasing her undeniable talent and control. She is a star in the making, but as I have said before, there was still too much technique and not enough emotions for me. She tried too hard to show what she could do and didn't let the song decide what it needed, except when she sang at the end of the show 'Alfonsia Y El Mar' in Spanish, then the audience was touched, as she concentrated on the beauty of the song (and most likely the Spanish pronunciation) instead of unleashing a technical firework. Incredible as well Aaron Diehl on the piano, who really made her sound even better and got the loudest screams and applause of the show for one amazing and breath-taking solo.

What better way to end our jazz festival summer than going to see Melody Gardot in the Noches Del Botanico in Madrid: an open-air show on a hot summer night and amazing music from one of my favourite singers. Melody is a natural performer, reaching to her audience with her songs and little stories once in a while and with her outstanding band (featuring sax player Irwin Hall) she can do whatever she wants, slow and quiet as in the beautiful and touching 'Baby I'm A Fool' or powerful and engaging as in 'Preacher Man' or 'She Don't Know' from her latest CD 'Currency Of Man'. She is an artist who can touch me deeply, as she did with her incredible rendition of 'Morning Sun' from the same album and a simple, but extremely powerful 'See-Line Woman', the iconic song by Nina Simone, which she made completely her own in a version full of respect for the original, but still being able to add something special to it. The Madrid audience was fully behind her and sang with her creating some extremely beautiful moments. Melody Gardot and her band were in great form that night and delivered what easily could be one of the best concerts of the year. We had a quick chat after the show with Melody, before she went out to sign CDs and LPs for a grateful audience.

2016, Melody Gardot, Madrid

In August it was time for a break and we decided to visit our friends Sophia and Simon in their house in the country, Horcajo de la Sierra, to be precise. A small place in the middle of nowhere, quiet and relaxed and perfect for his bike tours and for her running. We had, as so often, a great meal together and chatted for hours about music and other interesting topics. Hannah and Maria then went with us to visit Jorge, who did spend most of his time between treatments in Almeria, where he had his flat and friends. A few days on the beach, with breakfast at a brasserie and little trips into the surroundings, like Níjar, made this an enjoyable trip. Back in Madrid we went to see the Hieronymus Bosch: The 5th Century Exhibition, an excellent showing of this outstanding artist's work.

At the end of the month, Yolanda and I flew to Tunisia to attend Dhafer and Shiraz's wedding. The celebrations were split into two parts: first the traditional wedding in a colourful tent with all traditions and music by a local band, that was really good. Traditional food was served, but no alcohol, just sweet drinks. There was family from both sides, friends local and international, some of them friends of us as well, like Rebekka Bakken, Anna Lauvergnac, Nils Petter Molvaer, Wolfgang Muthspiel and many more from several countries, all dancing through the night.

2016, Dhafer and Shiraz dancing at their wedding

The next day we travelled to the north of Tunis, where Dhafer has a house close to the beach and where the second part of the celebrations was set to be held. There was a little stage set up in the garden and with all the musicians around it didn't take too long for a beautiful session to be running.

Meanwhile food was served, as well as beer and wine, actually a good Tunisian Syrah, named Kaprice. We had brought some top Spanish Jamón Ibérico and had that served too, to the pleasure of the guests. It was a wonderful and memorable night with old and new friends, great music and very happy newlyweds.

Back in Spain, I went to see 'Miles Ahead', the movie and my verdict was: the music won over the images by a clear count. I am not sure what the film wanted to be: a film about Miles Davis or an action movie with Miles Davis in it, but then there are scenes that are drawing you into the music making, as the one with Gil Evans, and they make up for most of the rest. The great soundtrack is mostly from Davis' catalogue and some from Robert Glasper and at the end from a cool live concert with Don Cheadle, who plays Miles in the film, that featured among others Herbie Hancock, Wayne Shorter, Robert Glasper and Esperanza Spalding. I am sure Miles' life had enough bad, good and crazy moments to make a captivating film from, so why this??

A business trip to New York is always a good opportunity to hear some music and meet some friends and artists. This time was no different and the first we went to hear was David Sanborn, who performed for one week at the Blue Note, introducing a brand-new band. I had never heard of the pianist Andy Ezrin before, but throughout the show I did enjoy his playing on piano and organ, of course I knew Wycliffe Gordon, but had never seen him performing and loved every second of it, especially when he performed on the soprano trombone, which sounded almost like a slide trumpet. The rest of the gang beside the amazing Sanborn were Ben Williams on bass and Billy Kilson on drums and both don't need further introduction. This was the first night this group ever played together and they were smoking from the first note! They started the set with a powerful rendition of Michael Brecker's 'Tumbleweed' and with that made a statement of intent: this was going to be a hard hitting and swinging modern jazz band! They continued with two more Brecker compositions, 'Half Moon Lane' and 'Night Blooming Jasmine'; both showcasing the amazing talents of this band, led by Sanborn, who was in the best possible mood and inventive and inspired in his soli, followed by Wycliffe, who pushed his sidemen to deeper musical levels. This was followed by two of Sanborn's own compositions, 'Maputo' and 'Sofia', here given a hard swinging and grooving treatment and the D'Angelo/Roy Hargrove tune 'Spanish Joint', featuring more impressive soli. They ended the set with Gordon's 'On The Spot' and smiles all around.

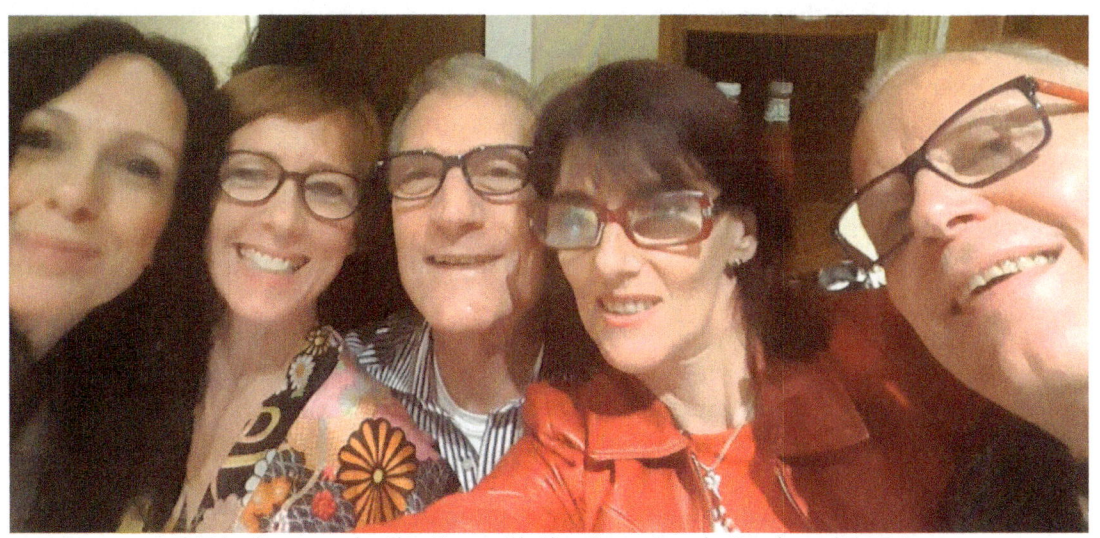

2016 backstage at the Blue Note, with Alice Soyer, Jonatha Brooke and Pat Rains

After days of meetings and dinners and a great walk through her neighbourhood with singer Kat Edmonson, we finally had another show to attend: Dee Dee Bridgewater – 'Songs We Love', at the

Jazz at Lincoln Center. Supported by a group of 10 musicians, led by trumpeter Riley Mulherkar, Dee Dee and the band went through the American Songbook and who is better than she to do so? Starting off with 'St. James Infirmary', she showed total control, was inventive in her soli while always pushing the song and its emotional content. She is an amazing performer, but never puts the show before the song.

On the night she had two guests working with the same group of musicians – singers Vuyo Sotashe and Brianna Thomas. Young South African Vuyo, I had met in October the previous year at the Montreux Academy and it was a pleasure to see how confident and really good he performed his own pieces and especially his duet with Dee Dee on 'Miss Brown To You'. Brianna Thomas is a delightful singer with a great voice, obviously trained while on the road with The Legendary Count Basie Orchestra and truly beautiful in ballads.

Dee Dee as always was the best, but the guests showed a lot of promise and it was good to see Dee Dee nurturing new talent that way.

2016, Dee Dee Bridgewater and Vuyo Sotashe swinging in New York

The autumn of music in Madrid started for me with the concert of the Bill Frisell group performing his latest album 'When You Wish Upon A Star' on October 27th at the Auditorio Nacional. The program was based on the music of the record, with slight variations and focused therefore on movie and film themes. Petra Haden, the singer on the record and in the show, was unfortunately suffering from a cold and therefore kept her performance to just three songs, which on the other hand gave Bill and his bass player Thomas Morgan and drummer Rudy Royston more space to explore the inner secrets of these compositions! Bill's beautiful explorative melodic lines, clear and captivating and full of twists and turns, kept the listeners attention, supported by his rhythm section perfectly. Especially in 'You Only Live Twice' the improvisations of the trio were amazing and a spectacular exchange of ideas from all three musicians. Whatever Frisell is taking on in terms of repertoire, he always is making it his own, adding depth and personality to the music he performs.

Becca Stevens' show on November 1st at Clamores in Madrid was just in a trio with her on vocals, guitar and other string instruments and with Chris Tordini on bass (with added backing vocals) and Jordan Perlson on drums. She performed repertoire from her marvellous 'Perfect Animal' album, as well as songs from her forthcoming new song cycle 'Regina'. Becca is an amazing singer with perfect control of her voice and her writing is challenging and needs the listener to pay attention to capture the subtleties and beauty of her music and lyrics.

I was interested in signing her to OKeh, as I truly believe that she is a special artist, but the colleagues in New York again didn't hear what I heard and even called the new songs "too arty", whatever that means. So, I had to let that opportunity pass ... Like so many others since Matt Pierson had joined and was part of the decision making. His musical vision didn't go further than the US border and staying conservative, like asking that David Sanborn should do another Standards album, preferably with strings. Dave didn't want to hear about it and rightly so, as he had done that many

years ago and had moved on from it. Now i[...]
once they had a few new tunes written for [...]
Dave directly on this, which really pissed me [...]
isn't mine. Not enough with pissing me off like [...]
not accept such behaviour, it got even worse: a [...]
remain un-named, had come to me with a ne[...]
presented it in the A&R meeting and made sure [...]
our past work and that I would move this forward [...]
guy and wanted to run the project. The musician [...]
made and then I got a call from the artist's manage[...]
supposedly harassed the musician's wife on the stre[...]
enough and called Chuck to have a word with Matt to [...]
create problems constantly. Which he thankfully did [...]
end, as according to Matt it wasn't the artist's b[...]
International at Masterworks, who as well was part o[...]
artist didn't have a history of streaming and therefore w[...]
simple: the indie label he was on until then hadn't pu[...]
services yet, making it impossible to have a streaming hi[...]
well ongoing discussions with the US team about the re[...]
'streamable' product. I had two answers to that: 1. I try to n[...] given artist at that time of his or her career and only when the musi[...] start thinking about marketing. The music will fit into some playlists for sure, b[...] will not be produced for them. I prefer to be in the right playlist, than in one that has a lot of subscribers, but doesn't lead to any follow-up. My second answer is, that I reminded them that in the 70's in the US smooth jazz radio was the dominant format and actually then did sell records. Until everyone started to produce records for the radio format and everything started to sound exactly the same and sales dropped completely off. But they didn't remember these times or didn't want to hear and were repeating the mantras of the bosses: streaming, streaming, streaming, which kind of made sense for pop, but not for jazz or classical music. And when Chuck announced that he was to retire with early 2017, I wondered who would control Matt for me, as I really didn't need these constant additional distractions.

The US were electing a new president between Hilary Clinton and outsider, business and show man as well as right wing populist, Donald Trump. When Yolanda and I went to bed that night in November it all looked as if Hilary would win, which was surely better than Trump and his social media driven extreme conservative and nationalist agenda. But when we woke up the next day and checked the news, Donald Trump had been elected as the 45th president of the USA. I always said that each country deserved the leader they elected, but I wasn't so sure on that one.
In the movies we saw 'Lion' with Dev Partel, a truly touching story and 'La La Land', as it supposedly was bringing jazz to a wider audience. I really didn't think so, but the film was charming and entertaining.

My favourite non-Okeh jazz records of the year were:
    Vijay Iyer & Wadada Leo Smith – 'a cosmic rhythm with each stroke'
    Julian Lage – 'Arclight'
    Bugge Wesseltoft – 'somewhere in between'
    GoGo Penguin – 'Man Made Object'
    David Bowie – 'Black Star'
    Wolfgang Muthspiel – 'Rising Grace'
    Wolfgang Puschnig – 'Faces And Stories'
    Robert Glasper – 'ArtScience'

ATMOSPHERES'

passing of too many jazz greats, including Toots Thielemans, Claus
Allison, Bob Cranshaw and Nana Vasconcelos, to only mention the
to meet and hear perform.
musically, like Keith Emerson and Greg Lake, both part of ELP and Rick Parfitt,
ock group Status Quo, as well passed away that year. I remember very well having
Alexander over for a visit and we went to a gig of Status Quo in Vienna and then
them to another gig, which happened to be at a lake side venue and the guys came to the
by boat. Sander and myself had been backstage in Vienna, were backstage at the second gig
o where Rick and Francis greeted him as if he was an old friend, which he was really proud of. He
got his CD and LP signed and is still valuing that memory of his two gigs with Status Quo.

This year most of the concerts of the Jazz Madrid festival were happening either at the Conde Duque, a nice little venue for about 320 guests or the Teatro Fernán Gómez, which is more or less double that size. Our first gig was the new Dave Holland project AZIZA at Conde Duque.

2016, with Louise and Dave Holland

The band, featuring Chris Potter on tenor and soprano saxes, Lionel Loueke on guitar and Eric Harland on drums, just had released their first record, as well called AZIZA. And they opened the show the same way that great album does, with Loueke's 'Aziza Dance', a groovy little number showcasing all the musicians plus the groups fantastic interplay and understanding. These musicians can go wherever they want – from swinging jazz to rock riffs and grooves, to freer explorations of a theme to beautiful ballads and it all makes sense, as the artistry on display is just tremendous. Holland keeping the pulse going, Harland pushing the beats, changing accentuations, always keeping time perfectly and Potter and Loueke improvising jointly or individually on the highest level!

Singer and OKeh recording artist Somi opened her intimate show at the Teatro Fernán Gómez with a beautiful rendition of her own 'Ankara Sunday'. Like this song, most of the performed music came from her 'The Lagos Music Salon' album, but she also sang a few new songs: 'They are like Ghosts' and 'I remember Harlem (Like Dakar)' stood out as extremely beautiful and catchy. To perform just with piano and bass put the spotlight surely on her, but with her sublime vocal skills this was no problem at all – probably a benefit for the audience, as the intimate atmosphere got every listener deeper into the songs. Pianist Jerry Leonide supported Somi incredibly, filing spaces perfectly and bass player Michael Olatuja pushed when necessary and otherwise was the heartbeat to Somi's soul. Outstanding, as well, their renditions of 'Brown Round Things' and 'Last Song'.The next gig we saw must surely count as one of the concerts of the year: the Dhafer Youssef Quartet delivered not only a powerful and spiritual show but they also managed to keep the listeners on their toes, holding attention and giving suspense, before grooving again – until the audience got up as one to dance. Simply incredible how Dhafer's voice touched everyone, Aaron Parks on the piano played some beautiful soli based on Dhafer's melodies, Ben Williams kept the odd rhythms going and put in some powerful bass soli and Justin Faulkner drummed as if his life was depending on it, with a smile on top of that incredible energy. This was a band of top players, having fun with complex music which compelled their audiences to dance and scream!

2016, Somi

Singer Kristin Asbjørnsen has a voice that would fit a rock singer – slightly rough, but with immense control and power. Her previous records were based on songs from the Afro-American culture: gospels, work songs and spirituals and she sang them surprisingly well for a small girl from Norway! Supported by guitarist Olav Torget and Gjermund Silset on bass, she glided through these songs with ease and made them her own. A beautiful first concert for her in Madrid.

Next on the list of shows was the ever amazing and surprising John Scofield. 'Country For Old Man' was the title of his recent release and the program for this fantastic show. As usual John had assembled an amazing group to work with him: Larry Goldings on piano and Hammond organ, Steve Swallow on bass and Bill Stewart on drum. Outstanding in their collection of country songs were their versions of Shania Twain's 'You're Still The One' and Jack Clements's 'Just A Girl I Used To Know', where Scofield's soli were simply beyond: inventive, melodic and full of emotions. Goldings, when on the piano (my preferred instrument for him in that show), was subtle and beautiful and on organ powerful and seemingly having fun. Both Swallow and Stewart were at their best – a group of masters at work.

When Sly & Robbie, the veteran Jamaican rhythm group of drummer Sly Dunbar and bass player Robbie Shakespeare, met up with Norwegian trumpet player Nils Petter Molvaer one thing was certain: the music would definitively groove!!! Add to that mix the genius of guitar player and sound creator Eivind Aarset and the electronic percussion of Vladislav Delay and you got some truly cool music, hip and beautiful, sometimes ambient, but with a steady pulse. Molvaer is such an interesting trumpet player with his little melodies and haunting sound. It was a perfect mix of musicians and ideas and the concert was extremely enjoyable, even so it was a bit too loudly mixed, which took away some of the fun. These guys were in the middle of recording an album together and I couldn't wait to hear it. I was hoping to release it on OKeh, working with managements and the German team on a deal already.

The next concert showcased three European jazz legends in one gig: Norwegian guitar hero Terje Rypdal, Danish trumpet player Palle Mikkelborg and my friend Italian drummer Paolo Vinaccia, who added young keyboarder Rune Tylden to the mix and performed music from the 'Skywards' album from 1997. Rypdal's sound is so personal, longing and still kind of uplifting, is easily recognisable since his early recordings in the 70s and Mikkelborg is one of the greats as a composer and trumpet player and he showed again why: from Miles influenced muted ballad playing to powerful moments he did it all in perfection and Paolo Vinaccia powered all this energy from his drums, culminating in a fascinating solo over a dialog from the movie 'The Godfather' (at least I think it was from that film). The keyboards filled the sound gaps, made the music complete and so it became a concert to remember for a while.

Terje Rypdal, Rune Tylden, Palle Mikkelborg and Paolo Vinaccia

Theo Croker had a great band that feels at home in all kinds of music, as long as they can play it like jazz. The show in Madrid consisted of material from his latest OKeh album 'Escape Velocity' and he built up the concert beautifully, giving his band members space to show their skills, but maintaining an ensemble feel at the same time – a standing ovation at the end and a furiously great 'Because of You' as an encore had everyone going home with a smile.

I really like Madeleine Peyroux a lot, as a person and as a singer, her way of phrasing and playing with the melody of a song. The repertoire of the concert in a full Teatro Fernán Gómez was based on her latest release 'Secular Hymns', but included some of her previous well-known covers and songs and a heartfelt version of 'Bird on a wire' as a tribute to the late Leonard Cohen. Madeleine seemed to have fun on stage, she successfully made most of her announcements in Spanish, which the audience really appreciated.

The last show of the festival for us came from the amazing Gregory Porter, performing the songs of his latest album 'Take Me To The Alley', but as well singing his previous hits like the gorgeous 'Hey Laura' and even going into a cool version of 'Papa Was A Rolling Stone'. The band was very good, especially his longstanding pianist Chip Crawford was in great form, bassist Jahmal Nichols surprised with a reference to 'Smoke On The Water' in his bass solo and sax player Tivon Pennicott and drummer Emanuel Harrold did also an amazing job. Gregory is such a huge personality, his voice and control of it is tremendous and his own songs are truly great. Some people asked: Is this really Jazz? Who cares, it is great music, presented well, giving the audience a great time!!

Then, outside of the Festival, I went to see Harold Lopez-Nussa, a young Cuban pianist who played with his trio in the Clamores Club. Ted Kurland had recommended me to go and see him and I had heard some of his music before and live I really enjoyed his melodic playing. His focus is on the essence of the song, using rhythms, but not having them overpower the melody. He played an absolutely beautiful solo piece as part of the show, which left the small, but dedicated, audience speechless. Definitely a player to watch for the future.

I had gotten a call from Jordy Freed, whom I knew from DL Media and who then was working for the Blue Note group of jazz clubs and they were in negotiation with the Only You Hotel in Madrid Atocha to create a temporary Blue Note Jazz Club there. They would provide the occasional big name to perform, but the rest would be filled by a local piano trio and he was checking if I could recommend someone. They weren't paying much for the three weekly gigs, but it would be a good exercise for the band and they would do PR for the pop-up club. I checked with young pianist Juan Sebastian Vazquez, a talented young man whom I had met via Theo Croker, and he liked the idea. Therefore, I got him and Jordy in contact and they made a deal. Jordy came over to check on things and we went out together with Yolanda, showing him the city a bit. For the opening night they had Bill Charlap playing solo piano. It was a truly beautiful set and I had a great chat with Bill, whom I hadn't met before. And as long as the club lasted, Juan Sebastian played there with his trio and the occasional guest.

2016, Bill Charlap opening the temporary Blue Note club in Madrid

Early December I saw that Kurt Elling was performing at Guy Barker's Christmas show at the Royal Albert Hall in London and checked if Hannah would be interested to see that. Once she said *"Yes"*, I called Bryan Farina (Kurt's manager) and asked him for two complimentary tickets, which he provided immediately. Hannah really liked the show, Barker's jazzy arrangements and the guest vocalists, mainly of course Kurt Elling. To let the year run its course, Yolanda and I had a quiet holiday season, celebrating with Jorge, Maria and great food.

2017

New York in January 2017 was really cold and with tons of snow. I came into town for lots of meetings and to moderate the panel at Jazz Connect on Israel – an introduction into this market and its musicians – one of the international aspects of the Conference, which I covered since a few years. It was always great to meet friends and colleagues at Jazz Connect and that year was no difference, and then of course, it was always great to go out and hear some music, as long as the weather didn't get too crazy. Choice is the word if you want to describe New York and what you get when you want to go out to hear some jazz, especially during Winter Jazz. I arrived on the 4th and took it easy, but on the 5th, I had to hear some music: originally, I wanted to see Jonatha Brooke performing new material at the City Winery, but in the end, as the dinner I had with Kurt Elling and his wife Jennifer took a bit longer than expected, Kurt and I decided to go and see John Beasley's MONK'estra at Dizzy's: great arrangements of Monk's tunes performed by an amazing big band and some guests, which that night included harmonica player Gregoire Maret and the wonderful Dianne Reeves. I listened to a few tracks of young singer Vuyo Sotashe, who followed the orchestra on stage and he again proved to be a unique talent with lots of control and great songs.

The so-called 'jazz marathon' started on January 6th and the first gig I went to, on invitation of my friend Anders Chan-Tiedeman, was the Rachel Z and Omar Hakim band, performing at the Zinc Bar, one of the many venues in the Bleecker Street area hosting the festival. Sandro Albert on guitar and Jonathan Toscan on e-bass completed the band, which played some new tracks of contemporary fusion, with power and beautiful little melodies.
From there I took a quick trip up to the Jazz Standard to see Regina Carter with her band playing songs connected to Ella Fitzgerald – some of the famous, some lesser known, but incredibly beautiful ones, like Artie Glenn's 'Crying In The Chapel'. Regina is a master on her instrument and these great songs were perfect material for her improvising skills.
Next up was SOMI, who presented some of her new songs at a packed Subculture. As I arrived early, I had a chance to hear a bit of the group before her Jacob Garchik's Ye Olde, featuring Jacob on trombone, Ava Mendoza, Mary Halvorson and Jonathan Goldberger on guitars and Vinnie Sperrazza on drums – jazz and rock and power and subtle playing all perfectly done. Unusual and really great!! Then Somi came on stage and presented her new songs, from the album 'Petite Afrique'. Somi is the essential story teller and these beautiful songs were no exception and the band played them wonderful, carrying the emotions and stories she wants to communicate perfectly.
After a short walk through the wintery and freezing cold NYC, I arrived at The Bitter End just in time to see Nir Felder starting his set. The young guitar player was accompanied by Matt Penman on bass and Jimmy MacBride on drums and for me the set was really amazing. Nir seemed to be much more relaxed and less focused on the song format and more on the essence of the song and simply let fly with incredible technique and power. Since I saw him the last time about a year ago, this young man definitely had improved a lot.
Day 2 of the jazz marathon started for me with the Michael Leonhart Orchestra. Michael had asked me to come and see his orchestra and I had no idea what to expect: he had 26 musicians on the stage of the Poisson Rouge and used these musicians to create some very impressive music!

2017, Winter Jazz NYC, Michael Leonhart Orchestra

There was no limit to what these guys were able to do under Leonhart's direction, from arrangements of music to Charlie Browns Christmas to a newly arranged Wu Tang Clan song. He seemed to have the whole history of Big Band jazz within the orchestra, but at the same time was very unique thanks to his compelling arrangements: powerful, deep, thoughtful and emotional at the same time. A very impressive orchestra, under an immensely creative leader.
From there it was a short walk in the snow to the Zinc Bar for Claudia Acuña's set. She performed with her Chilean Connection band and as usual she was best when singing in Spanish. Claudia is a great singer and I always enjoyed listening to her – this show was no exception to that. At the same venue I listened then to The Baylor Project, as I had heard some good things about them and I wasn't disappointed: Jean Baylor and Marcus Baylor together with Shedrick Mitchell on piano and organ, Yasushi Nakamura on bass, Keith Loftis on saxes and Freddie Hendrix on trumpet and flugelhorn delivered a grooving set, supporting the beautiful vocals of Jean Baylor perfectly. Outstanding their rendition of Leonard Cohen's 'Hallelujah'. Next, I went to see the duo of Bill Frisell and bass player Thomas Morgan: another gig that was much too short for my liking, but it gave the audience a taste of their forthcoming album: touching communication on beautiful themes and impressive improvisations from both artists. I intended to end the night with Marc Ribot and the Young Philadelphians, featuring my friend Jamaaladeen Tacuma. I had seen this project already in Madrid the previous year, but enjoyed it so much that I wanted to hear them again. Unfortunately, quite a few people had the same idea and the SOB's was packed to the limit and waiting outside in the snow at – 9 degrees Celsius wasn't really what I had in mind. So, I just had a little malt whiskey at the hotel bar and then got some sleep.
I had some meetings while in New York with Sony's Legacy department, as they were responsible for all catalogues within Sony Music, except classical. In 2018 OKeh would celebrate its 100th anniversary and I had a few ideas and had started to work on a 2 CD set about the history of the label plus a bunch of compilations and album re-issues. As at the beginning OKeh mainly released singles and only later full albums, I tried to get the history right with the re-issue program by doing a mix of artist compilations and original albums, which would represent the story of OKeh. The Legacy guys seemed to be interested and so I continued working on these, while thinking about a few other activities for the anniversary, like an album of newly recorded versions of some of OKeh's most important songs or maybe even a concert (here I checked with JALC, but in the end they weren't interested) or tour. I thought anyway that we should control the OKeh catalogue, as it would give us easier access to our history and as well give the label a bit of extra income from working this catalogue, which Legacy didn't really do, with exception of the Louis Armstrong recordings. But neither Bogdan nor Mark were interested to start a fight for the catalogue, so I had to deal with

Legacy. The problem with that was, as Mark at one point told me, that if we were to release any of the compilations and re-issues, all revenues would go to Legacy and not to us. As this didn't make much sense to me, I asked him to have a word with the guys at Legacy and see if there was anything that could be done to make this worthwhile for everyone … and hoped for the best.

Madrid in February was in terms of concerts a bit quiet; I just went out to see Seamus Blake with his French trio, featuring the pianist Tony Tixier, who was the actual reason for me to go and see this band – he is a very interesting young man, who as well leads his own trio and, even so this wasn't his music, left his mark on the performance. And we went to see our friend La Shica with her new program and as usual she just nailed it: perfect vocal performances and cool song selection make her concerts every single time a special and enjoyable event.

The third Montreux Academy was held in Lausanne, and this year HEMU, the jazz school there, stepped in as the host of the week-long event. 10 young musicians participated this year – the 3 finalists from the Montreux piano, guitar and vocal competitions and one musician picked by the HEMU to represent them in the mix. Guitar: from the UK Rob Luft and from Finland, but living in New York, Olli Hirvonen. Piano: Estaban Castro, from New York, was with 14 years the youngest Academy invitee so far; Guy MIntus, Israel-born but living as well in NYC and Casimir Liberski from Belgium. Vocals: Arta Jekabsone, Latvian who studied in New York; Cristina Tanase, Rumanian who studied law first before focusing on her singing career; Fabio Giacalone a global citizen being an Italian born in Brazil, who studied in NYC; German Erik Leuthäuser, the vocalise expert and Belgian Imelda Gabs, who was chosen by her university to participate in the Academy. The event started with a lecture on film and TV music by John Altman, very interesting and captivating. After that it was all about setting up the jam session for after dinner and that where the musicians showcased their abilities and talent.

2017, Montreux Academy, guitarist Rob Luft in action

Guy Mintus was selected to run the show and he did a great job to keep the music flowing, adding some really good moments on piano to the overall great mix. From all the talent displayed, in an environment that is not musically what they usually do on their own, Guy, Rob and the vocalists stood out, especially Imelda and Erik, who closed the session with a beautiful 'Body & Soul', just with Rob on guitar and a little help from Guy at the end. The following day I had with my colleagues to lecture these 10 young artists about the music business: in four hours we tried to cover all aspects of our industry, including rights issues, working with promoters, agents and clubs well as what to expect from labels. These young musicians were extremely well prepared and had great questions and I simply hope we gave them something for their future careers. It has been, as always, a pleasure and honour for me to be there. Over the following few days these young artists had more lectures and did more sessions and worked with some great mentors on their musical development, including Trilok Gurtu, Yaron Herman, Elina Duni, Marcus Miller, Kurt Rosenwinkel and Ziv Ravitz.

On March 13 Tommy Lipuma, outstanding producer, record executive and great human being, passed away at the age of 80. He was not just one of the best producers of our time; he was a man living music. Ever fibre in his body was swinging and when talking to him it always ended up being about music, as this was what made him tick. I first met Tommy when Universal bought PolyGram in 1998 and we started merging the two companies; in our case the jazz activities around the world. For me he became kind of a role model, together with Bruce Lundvall: one the producer with a passion and love for the music and artists and the other the executive with equal passion and understanding of the creative being. They were the guys to learn from and to look up to. When Tommy was running the Verve Music Group and we had meetings it was always a pleasure to hear him talk about music and artists. He let the business part be done by someone else, his mind was in making great records and he did exactly that over all these years. And all the stories he could tell! I never got tired of listening to him and gladly stayed in touch after we both had left Universal; and he produced for PRA/Emarcy the two studio albums Randy Crawford did with Joe Sample, which I released outside the US. I was invited to go to Montreux for his 75th birthday celebration: a star-studded affair which only he could manage to get on one stage. We had a great time there with music and good food and wine, another of his passions. The last time we spoke, he advised me to get a DAC player to improve the sound of compressed digital files. Music and sound were always on his mind. Tommy will be with me forever – as he will be with many people for the rest of their lives. He and the music he created with his artists touched many people and will continue to do so for a very long time.

That year's event in Bremen was the 12th edition of 'jazzahead' and had the most exhibitors and visitors so far and, as always, it was good to see old and new friends, having meetings and chats about the state of the jazz business and discuss promising talent and exciting new releases. But the showcases were, as every year, the main draw and some of them this time were simply spectacular. After long day of meetings and chats I needed some music and decided to check out sax player Eli Degibri, whom I had met during my panel in New York at Jazz Connect – his quartet ran through some originals showcasing the incredible technique Degibri has. Wonderful his sound on the soprano and powerful his soli on this instrument. After some very interesting dinner conversations at the Karsten Jahnke / Enjoy Jazz dinner on Friday, I had to hear the new project by Marilyn Mazur SHAMANIA. I always liked her compositions and her performances and recordings, since the time I saw her first with Miles Davis. Her 40-minute late night set was pure power: two percussionists, drums, piano, bass, vocals and horns made up her all-female ensemble – great grooves, really good soli by all musicians and fantastic interplay. It got rhythm and space to improvise, nice little melodies and amazing energy. Her bass player was then Ellen Andrea Wang, a very unique artist, who beside playing her instrument is as well a great singer. I met Ellen the following morning as I wanted to start talking to her about possibly coming to OKeh with her next record.

Saturday was less meetings and more music, starting with German pianist Lorenz Kellhuber, whom I had met at the first Montreux Academy and always wanted to see him live – 30 minutes is never enough if the show is good and his was – a great and inspired trio performance of originals and extended improvisations. Next up was Gilad Hekselman, a young guitar player who was making waves in the jazz scene and rightly so as his melodic compositions are timeless and beautiful and his playing ranks with the top on his instrument. The trio with Rick Rosato on bass and Jonathan Pinson on drums was tight and showed great understanding and communication. He is an artist Matt Pierson wanted to sign, but I thought if we went for a young guitar player, it had to be Julian Lage, as I believed his musical potential was much bigger. I had heard Camilla Meza in New York about 2 years earlier, thanks to a recommendation by a Spanish friend of mine (Fernando Ortiz de Urbina), and really enjoyed her show. She had certainly developed well and her set in Bremen was interestingly diverse with great guitar work by her and some astonishing vocals. Her music was reflecting the two cultures she lives in: her Chilean roots and her New York influence. Effortless she moved between these two worlds, sometimes expressing them together, sometimes keeping them apart. Her guitar playing was very good and she reminded me a bit of George Benson when she sang along to her soli. Her version of 'Cucurrucucu Paloma' was unique and very touching. She had been offered to me to sign for OKeh, but the only problem I had with her album, was that her own compositions were absolutely fine but not great and she needed to co-write with someone to improve in that area. I saved the best for last: the Julian Lage Trio, with Julian on guitar, Jorge Roeder on bass and Eric Doob on drums, played a perfect and incredible 40-minute set of Julian's music from his recent release 'Arclight' and from a new and forthcoming album. Julian had grown musically year after year, his compositions were stylish and accessible, even so the trio's improvisations left space to wander and let go. His sound was beautiful and clear and his playing left you asking for more. Not yet thirty years old at the time and he had become the one guitar player everyone was talking about and he deserved it, as he seemed to be at home in any musical environment. As far as I remember, he had then one more record in his current deal and afterwards I hoped to sign him to OKeh. 'Jazzahead' 2017: for three days Bremen became the jazz centre of the world and showed that, even so the jazz record business was having a tough time, the music was alive and kicking!

2017, Julian Lage

After Chuck's departure it was announced that Mark Cavell would head the US Masterworks division next to his job as Chief Financial Officer for Sony Classics worldwide. He would bring in an A&R guy for Masterworks and would himself be hands on with soundtracks and Broadway, together with some A&R for crossover acts. These are areas where he is really good. Core classical and jazz, on the other hand, are not his forte nor interest. He had decided, with Bogdan's blessing, that going forward there would be changes in the way we dealt with OKeh. He promoted Josh Lerman to kind of Head of OKeh and he would deal with immediate effect with most of the stuff I did before: release schedule, tour schedule (which would be integrated in an overall classics & jazz one), social media, website, packaging and tools and pr co-ordination. That left me to do A&R for the acts we had on the roster and the new ones I wanted to sign. Concerning A&R he decided that Josh, Matt and I would have regular calls on A&R and all decisions would be made by the three of us together. Which didn't sound great to me but I had to give it a chance. Josh actually is a nice guy, a numbers man with a good overview on the business, but not an A&R man at all. And Matt is a producer and US oriented A&R guy with a tendency to professional jealousy, which sometimes clouds his judgements.

That year I only delivered 2 albums to OKeh, Somi's second recording for us 'Petite Afrique' and Dee Dee Bridgewater's wonderful 'Memphis ... Yes, I'm Ready'. I still think that Somi's album is truly amazing in terms of song writing and performance. She actually used Sting's song, 'Englishman in New York' as the base for 'Alien' and changed the original lyrics a bit to fit her African in New York theme. As I had worked with Sting and knew his manager Martin Kierszenbaum, I sent them the song and asked for permission to release this new version and they gladly said *"Yes"*. And when I asked, on Somi's insistence, if they would give her a small part of the publishing, they actually agreed, which really surprised me, as it was very unusual. Just before the release of the album, Somi had, once more, decided to change management and agency, so all we got, in terms of touring, were a handful of dates in Spain. When Somi, after these dates, stayed in our flat for one night, she complained about the tour, the food, the hotels – nothing seemed to have been good enough. I am not sure she understood when I explained that all these costs needed to be within the budget of the tour, as she was only starting to build a profile and not getting big fees yet. After her return to the US, the agency for these dates, our friend Amparo, pulled out and we again were left without a booking agent. Somi is an extremely talented woman, but her sense of her place in the music business was lacking back then a connection to reality. But her new record was voted NAACP Jazz Album of 2017, which didn't sell any additional units, but was a great award to get.

I was extremely happy that I was working with Dee Dee again on an outstanding record, which her Memphis tribute surely is. Her jazzy soul songs and spirituals are showcasing her vocal artistry and she gives known songs like Norman Whitfield's 'I Can't Get Next To You' or Elvis' 'Don't Be Cruel' a new lease of life and shines in all the other ones from Isaac Hayes to Pops Staples. And then she worked her socks off on promotion and toured constantly and above all is a very cool lady and a lot of fun. That album got her a nomination for the German Echo award and brought in much better streaming numbers than her previous OKeh album.

It was the international schedule that initially kept me busy in 2017 with five records coming from Germany alone, including trumpet player and composer Markus Stockhausen's 'For The Stars'. Markus, who got my contact details from Dhafer, had given me a call out of the blue and asked if I might be interested in his new recording. I asked him to send me the music and really liked what I heard, having known his music from some ECM albums. I wanted to know why this one would not be coming out on ECM and he informed me that Manfred Eicher had told him that he would only be able to release this record in two years, as he had such a backlog of productions needing to come out. No artist wants to wait that long for a release, especially as in that time they are musically already somewhere else. I asked the German team if they were interested, as that was by far his biggest market and they made the deal in the end.

Silje Nergaard released 'For You A Thousand Times', a real beautiful record with the song 'Coco Bello', which got some really good airplay around Europe. Silje as well toured a lot, especially in Germany and Norway and sales and streams were satisfactory. France had four albums coming out under Herve Defranoux, a very nice guy and very capable A&R man. The biggest of these was the new Stacey Kent album 'I Know I Dream: The Orchestral Sessions', which did extremely well physical and online and despite it being hard to tour, she did a few dates with orchestras and they were received very well. I met her while working on her previous OKeh France album 'Tenderly' and really

liked her concerts and personality. The other big record from France was '1970' by bass player and singer Avishai Cohen. An interesting record, even so I prefer his instrumental work to his singing, but that's just me. Expectations from the artist and management were a bit too high and therefore unfulfilled and unfortunately this was the only record we did with Avishai.
The US had two local signings on OKeh, the great Regina Carter's stunning 'Ella – Accentuate The Positive', her personal tribute to the first lady of jazz and Bria Skonberg's 'With A Twist', a Matt Pierson production.

We had planned as well to release a new Dhafer Youssef album that year, featuring tabla master Zakir Hussain plus Eivind Aarset and Turkish clarinet player Husnu Senlendirici. But in the end, I asked the guys in New York to let him go without insisting on the third contractual album. Dhafer wasn't happy with the French team and there was nothing I could do about it. He wanted to work with a smaller and more focused local French label, expecting better marketing. If an artist doesn't feel at home with us and wants to leave, I personally think it is better in most cases to let him or her go, as working under such conditions doesn't really produce any good results. And as we were OK in terms of finances on the two records we had released, Mark Cavell agreed to let him go. My friendship with Dhafer wasn't affected at all and we continued working together.
We actually had already started to think about his next record and he wanted to have Brad Mehldau on it, next to Dave Holland. Therefore, I got in touch with Brad's manager, Scott Southard on this, but didn't hear back. As I know Brad's wife, singer Fleurine, with whom I worked around 2000 when we had her album 'Close Enough For Love' on Emarcy, I spoke to her and then sent her Dhafer's OKeh CDs. She came back a few weeks later saying that Brad would be interested and I now should talk to management again, which I did. They came back to me asking for an outrageous amount of money for him to play on the album. Which really pissed me off. By then, I knew Scott for many years and we were both no novices in the business, but asking for as much as the total cost of most jazz albums would be, just for Brad to appear on the record, was an insult. He could have easily told me that he as the manager didn't think his client should do that and I would have said *"Fine"* and moved on. No-one is paying such money for a full album sideman job. And so, Dhafer and I moved on. To Herbie Hancock!
On Dhafer's behalf I wrote an email to Herbie reminding him of the Paris International Jazz Day Concert they played together and asked if he would like to be on Dhafer's next album. Herbie wrote back to me within three hours and confirmed that he would love to be part of the recording, but under one condition: Dhafer would need in exchange to be on Herbie's next album as well. No problem at all with that request!

Sonny Rollins and I still spoke every two weeks, more or less, and he told me before it was officially announced that he was to donate his personal archive to the Schomburg Center for Research in Black Culture, one of the research centres of the New York Public Library. I am not sure what it all included, but he spoke about written music, posters and other stuff he held on to for a very long time. Later that year, he started the "Sonny Rollins Jazz Ensemble Fund" at Oberlin College, *in "recognition of the institution's long legacy of access and social justice advocacy"*. As Sonny said to me, he wanted to give some youngsters something back of what music gave to him. Not being able to perform any more was still tough, but he was dedicating himself to other things now and these two activities were the result of that.

While Hannah was writing her final essays in Nottingham, I went to a few gigs in Madrid: I had been a fan of boundary pushing trumpet player Christian Scott for a while and went to see/hear him whenever I get a chance. When he came to Madrid again and performed at Clamores, I was of course there. He had as usual a great group of young musicians to support him and the powerful mix of old and new tunes and his impressive stage presence and trumpet playing made a full house and enthusiastic audience enjoy the show. Tracks from his latest, very modern and exciting album 'Ruler

Rebel' made a big part of the set list, but as well classics and some of his own compositions from earlier records. Great to hear him again and have a little chat after the show.

Guy Mintus, whom I had met at the Montreux Academy earlier that year, is a young man of immense talent, who performed a self-booked gig in Madrid and presented some of his own compositions and some standards, solo on the piano, just using the occasional loop to add some clapping or vocal bits to the piano improvisations. His own pieces are full of beautiful little melodies and surprising changes and allow the listener to fall into the music easily; his improvisations on known themes like 'All Of You' are full of ideas and understanding and are going to the essence of the song. He occasionally started to sing as well, something he was experimenting with, but for me wasn't half as good as his piano playing.

2017, Guy Mintus solo, in Madrid

Luciano Supervielle is an accomplished pianist, keyboarder, who has performed with Jorge Drexler and is a prominent member of Bajofondo (formerly known as Bajofondo Tango Club) and he also performed solo in Madrid … piano, keyboards, samples, beats and turntables were at his disposal to create solo pieces that could be modern classical music with beautiful melodies and simplicity or grooving modern tracks with cool beats and tasteful selected samples and piano work, even including the powerful 'Perfume', from the first Bajofondo Tango Club album. The show was truly amazing – his use of all the tools he had always enhanced the song, which was performed perfectly on the great sounding piano in the Café Berlin. Luciano was slowly stepping out of the shadow of Bajofondo and building himself a reputation as a composer and performer.

Yolanda and I again went to the Madrid Tennis Masters and enjoyed the best of the best playing their sport. That year we were lucky enough to see Simone Halep and Andy Murray among others. Then Ganavya came to stay a few days with us and to perform again in Madrid with her project and as a guest of saxophonist and singer Antonio Lizana.
Hannah had finished her studies and we had already booked our tickets to the UK to see her and celebrate her graduation with her. She made me immensely proud by successfully concluding her studies of History and German, being independent and strong minded. We were both looking forward to go to Nottingham for the event. As that year was as well our 10th wedding anniversary, Yolanda and myself had decided that we wouldn't go to the North Sea Jazz Festival nor to Vitoria, but instead would stay home and celebrate with a great meal in a fantastic restaurant, which was exactly what we did.

But of course, there is no summer without music and we went to see a few shows in Madrid: first was Lee Ritenour, who, with Dave Grusin and Tom Kennedy on bass and Wesley Ritenour on drums gave a rare club concert and a master class in elegant guitar playing. And elegant is the right word for Ritenour's style of playing: even when he rocks (and did he rock sometimes that night!) it was with style and a smile on his face, watching his son and Kennedy pushing him into further explosive soli. Keyboarder Grusin was the perfect partner for Ritenour, but also a great pianist in his own right, which his incredible solo performance over one of his film themes showed. Ritenour is a musician who is at home in all possible styles, from smooth to swinging jazz, into rock and a touch of Brazil and it all makes sense and comes natural and elegant! After not having seen Lee for a while, it was great to hear 'Captain Fingers' again and catch up a bit between the two shows, one of which had a short live broadcast on local TV station TeleMadrid!!

2017, Lee Ritenour and Dave Grusin live on TeleMadrid TV

The day after Lee, Julian Lage stopped by in the same club and had a sold-out show. This time he showcased a new trio, featuring Chris Lightcap on bass and Eric Doob on drums: both great musicians and fitting sidemen for this extremely talented young artist, whose flow of ideas was surprising and never ending and his expression one of joy and deep-felt emotions, stated in a groovy melodic way.

Then it was Theo Croker at the Bogui Club with the Juan Sebastian Vazquez trio, featuring bassist Francisco Manuel Lopez and drummer Daniel Garcia Bruno. The Trio started of each of the two sets we saw with music from its latest release 'tribute'. After these strong introductions into each set, Theo came on and they played some Miles, Gershwin, Shorter and the title track of the Juan Sebastian Trio album, as well as the Croker composition 'Meditations', from his 'Escape Velocity' album – all performed to the highest standards, especially from Croker and Vazquez, who showed inspired and melodic improvisation skills. Played acoustic, the Croker tune, on the album in a more modern sound bed, showed what a great composition it is and held its place beside the other great standards the group performed. Celia Krull, a local jazz singer, joined the band for two beautiful songs, perfectly executed.

The summer open air show by Madeleine Peyroux we saw, was based on her latest release 'Secular Hymns'. The trio with her on acoustic guitar, Jon Herington on electric guitar and Barak Mori on bass, was even more tight and together and seemed to thoroughly enjoy the concert, as did the audience, despite temperatures of more than thirty degrees Celsius at 9 pm. They were tasteful in ballads, swinging when needed to and maintained an overall high musical standard and Madeleine's singing was still full of melodic invention.

Madeleine was followed on the stage by singer Jose James and his band, featuring James Francies on piano and keyboards, Nate Smith on drums and Josh Hari on bass. I hadn't seen Jose in a while and it was good to hook up a bit before the show and then he went on and it was pretty cool: strong songs with heavy grooves, plus a few ballads of sheer beauty. This was more the R&B leaning James than the jazzy guy, but nevertheless, this stuff was funky and had its roots in jazz in any case. A great band with an outstanding singer, who in his gorgeous version of 'Lean On Me' sang immaculate and James Francies played a solo on the e-piano that was reminiscent of Les McCann, but still modern and all his own. There is not much more to say about the qualities of drummer Nate Smith that hasn't be said and written in other places – he was just the driving force in this music and Josh Hari was the solid anchor they all needed. Jose James favourites like 'Trouble' sounded fresh and powerful and everyone left with a smile after his final encore of 'Ain't No Sunshine'.

John Scofield's Uberjam is one of my favourites of his various projects: having been started in 2002 with their first release, simply called 'Uberjam', they came to Madrid with the updated band and this time the drummer was Dennis Chambers! The repertoire was taken from both of their albums and they gave each song a lot of space to improvise and second guitarist Avi Bortnick and especially Scofield made the best use of that space with some incredible soli, sitting on top of some astonishing grooves by Chambers and bass player Andy Hess.

And last but not least, we saw Michel Camilo and Tomatito at the Teatro Real. This venue seemed to be the perfect place for them in terms of atmosphere, sound and style. I have seen the two perform in many different venues, but none of them felt so right for this duo than the Teatro Real. Playing material from all three releases in their Spain Trilogy ('Spain', 'Spain Again', 'Spain Forever') it was clear right from the start that they had grown even closer musically, to the point that sometimes one could only hear one sound, as piano and guitar melted into one by being played perfectly together. From 'Libertango' to Charlie Haden's 'Our Spanish Love Song', via Eric Satie to Chick Corea or some originals, everything sounded as if composed for this duo. This was the best of the many shows I have seen by them and got a deserved standing ovation after two encores.

2017, Michel Camilo & Tomatito, Madrid, Teatro Real

Then it was time to head to Nottingham to celebrate Hannah's academic achievements. We met the day before and she showed us around the city, which had been her home for a few years now. We had a drink in England's oldest pub and general enjoyed being there with her. The next morning, we went to the celebrations and I can't express how proud I was about my daughter walking up there on the stage, with her robe and graduation cap. We stayed around for a bit, took photos, met people, including her new boyfriend Oliver, who had studied with her. Then we were off to change and meet again for lunch, which included her mother and was relaxed and in celebration of Hannah. While we were heading back to London, Hannah prepared herself for a night of well-deserved partying. In London we met friends and had a walk in our old neighbourhood, before heading back to Madrid.

2017, Graduation Day for Hannah and her boyfriend Oliver

Early August we were travelling again, this time to Bornholm to celebrate my sister Barbara's 60th birthday and as it is on the same day as Yolanda's, we celebrated hers as well and Hannah's graduation, this time with the full family being around. Of our siblings only Marlis and Thomas didn't make it, but Patrick and Alexander brought their families, Hannah flew in, Jürgen and Uschi drove all the way from Vienna, bringing Goran with them and Søren and Skipper plus local friends of Barbara joined in as well. Our mother had a great time and the party was really amazing and a lot of fun. Barbara had for Hannah arranged a game, where she had six different bottles of alcohol in front of her and six pieces of paper with countries and six pieces of papers with dates or years on them. Having studied History, she had to put in front of each bottle the right country and year or period it was created to win the game. If wrong, she had to have one drink from that bottle.

celebrating Barbara's 60th birthday

For Yolanda and me she had as well come up with a game where she would ask questions about the other and we had to answer correctly, which brought a huge round of laughter when she asked Yolanda the name of the place I was born and she answered "Chickenfield", which was a kind of correct but totally unusual translation of Hünfeld and came completely unexpected. We had a wonderful time there with the whole gang, as we usually have.

Hannah and Oliver then came to visit us in Madrid and we spent a lot of time showing him the city, went out to have meals with Maria and Jorge and took it easy. While thinking about her next steps, Hannah would stay for a while with her mother and see what would come up jobwise, while Oliver went to China for a few months to improve his Mandarin. And Jorge was unfortunately still receiving treatment, but the doctors hadn't been able to stop the activity of his cancer and they needed to find a new and better treatment. Jorge was fighting and being positive and a real example of how to deal with such a challenging illness. Always joking and full of ideas and positive energy.

The September A&R update I had prepared for Bogdan, Mark, Josh and Matt had under 'in discussion as possible signings' singer and pianist Sarah McKenzie, who I thought had a lot of potential and had with Burkhard Hopper good management and booking. Sarah writes her own songs, which are easily accessible and cool. At one point, I got a few demos from Burkhard and shared these with Matt and Josh. Matt's answer was a respectless *"NO"*, basically saying that she wasn't a good singer and her songs were not great. Sure, one can be of different opinion about that, but what Matt didn't tell me nor Josh, was, as I found out later, that he knew Sarah and was supposed (and wanted) to produce her first album for ABC Records a few years back. For whatever reason the Australian Broadcast Company and their label changed their minds and brought in another producer. These things happen, they are not pleasant, but not unusual either. His answer therefore was personally motivated and not honest about the artist nor the music. Other acts on that list included The Bad Plus in their new version with pianist Orrin Evans and it would have been a good continuation of the work we had done with the original line up of the band, but their sales and streaming figures weren't that great and therefore I had no chance. I loved these guys and had no argument against low streaming numbers, beside the quality of the music and that's not what Sony wanted to hear. Helen Sung and Belgian group TaxiWars were on that list as well, but didn't make it either. Gretchen Parlato was ongoing; Herbie Hancock was working on new material and would need a label once finished, so I stayed in touch with him and his team; Roy Hargrove was ready, after ei[ght] years, to record again and I was in touch with his manager Larry to see what the idea was. Andrea Wang had finished her record and it was really good, but as she wanted to have September and I couldn't turn around an album by a new artist that fast, we agreed tha[t] release this one via our common friends at Jazzland and we then would look at her n[ext] really needed more time to prepare a release, introduce the artist to the guys i[n] everything up in the systems and prepare marketing tools and promotion co[verage] finished music to release in a perfect world, I would like to have six mo[nths] possible set up, followed by a release and tour. That hadn't changed, stre[aming] case, but better do it that way, than fail with a new act, because I di[d] the release. And of course, I put Ganavya on that list, as she is a very special talent and I hoped to be able to work with her in the future. The same was true for the Michael Leonhart Orchestra, but again, the US didn't think that was a project for us. Then I had to focus on the preparation of the releases for the following year, which were thankfully quite a few.

Unfortunately, the global madness of terror attacks continued to devastating effects: shootings and bombings in Istanbul, Manchester (at an Ariana Grande concert), Las Vegas and many other places left hundreds of people dead and thousand injured and there was no end in sight. Again, it seemed that mankind really hadn't learned anything from history. The same was true for Europe's political move to the right, where in some Eastern countries the rights for minorities of any form were slowly getting abolished. The UK started the complicated negotiations of the Brexit, which would drag on for years and Donald Trump, within his 'America First' policies, withdraw from the Paris Climate Agreement, even going so far to bluntly stating that the climate crisis was *"Fake News"*, like anything else that didn't agree with his picture of the world.

The Champions League Final was played in Cardiff between Juventus of Turin and Real Madrid. Coach Zinedine Zidane's Madrid team won 4:1, with two goals scored by Cristiano Ronaldo. Real was with this win the first team ever to defend their Champions League title, something that really would be difficult to be repeated in the near future. An illegal referendum in Catalunya ended with the, as well illegal, declaration of independence, but nothing really came off it, except that a lot of local politicians were either arrested or fled. As in many cases this was not only about nationalism but about money. Catalunya wants a different system of how contributions to the national funds are done and how the money is then re-distributed, being after Madrid the second biggest contributor and so supporting the poorer south of the country. As the conservative Spanish government didn't want to talk about more power (or money) for Catalunya, it came to a head and the situation escalated. And in the rest of the world more documents on off-shore banking accounts for companies, politicians, footballers and many more, were published, resulting in hundreds of court cases for fraud and tax evasion.

We saw in the movies 'Three Billboards Outside Ebbing, Missouri' by Martin McDonagh, with the incredible Frances McDormand in the lead. Guillermo del Toro's 'The Shape Of Water' I really enjoyed it, as it was a wonderful, but different tale of love. And I continued reading the Harry Bosch series by Michael Connelly, as well as the Department Q series of crime novels by Danish writer Jussi Adler-Olsen. And I read the wonderful novel by Carlos Ruiz Zafon 'The Labyrinth Of Spirits' plus 'Good Things Happen Slowly' by pianist and composer Fred Hersch. As Hersch and I were born in the was describing. I never knew much of his music, but I tely the duo album with Julian Lage and the Trio album endously. His story was interesting in many ways and on iew, the gay man's experiences and the health issues he ther) and it is well told – the highs as well as the many t in the end, it is all about the music, the will to create, Captivating and educational at the same time.

Geri Allen, 1957 - 2017

That year the jazz world lost many great artists, among them a few I had been fortunate to see or work with or get to know a bit: Al Jarreau, the versatile singer and wonderful human being; blues master James Cotton, whom I met when he recorded for Verve France; Geri Allen, whose concert with Betty Carter in London will always be with me; Danish legend Sven Asmussen, Larry Coryell, Alphonse Mouzon and Arthur Blythe, who I saw performing live and journalist and writer Mike Hennessey, whose wonderful book on Johnny Griffin I got signed by him and Griff.

In October, we saw two shows we really liked and they were completely different: Mario Biondi is a star in his native Italy and known around Europe, but not yet on the same level as at home. His rare visit to Madrid therefore was something special and a good chance to see a singer whose records I enjoyed. The repertoire for this show came mainly from his previous two albums 'Sun' and 'Beyond' and the audience happily sang along to the great performance – a top band that got the groove and Mario singing absolutely wonderful. Live he showed what a great singer he actually is and what control he has and that there is much more to him than having a voice like Barry White.

Pepe Habichuela is a master of the flamenco guitar and he celebrated 60 years of performing live over three days at the Teatro Circo Price in Madrid, with most of his family and friends, who travelled all or part of this journey with him. We went on the third day when dancer Israel Galvan, Miguel Poveda, Silvia Perez Cruz, Javier Colina, Jorge Pardo and the rest of the Familia Habichuela ended the celebrations in style! The show opened with a spectacular solo dance by Galvan, which was not only amazing in terms of body movements, but as well a treat rhythmically as his feed created a firework of percussive sounds. Miguel Poveda, either with Pepe or his own group showed again what an amazing and emotional singer he is and the same can be said of Silvia Perez Cruz, who from solo, via duos with bass player Colina to a trio with Pepe and Colina simply got everyone screaming "*Olé!*"

2017, Pepe Habichuela celebrating with his friends and family ...

Then Josemi Carmona, Pepe's son and fellow guitar player, who acted as musical director for all three days, played a new composition dedicated to his father: a beautiful and touching song full of love for life and music. After a wonderful flute solo by Pardo the family came on stage and all played together – danced together – sang together! Even Tomatito joined in for that part of the show again. A great end to a concert that as such will be long remembered and will be impossible to do again – it was like being invited to the Mount Olympus of Flamenco and watching the gods having a ball.

Our guys in Berlin had signed singer Thomas Quasthoff to a recording deal and he wanted to record a jazz album before even considering a classical one. He had done one already in 2007, which was produced by Till Brönner, and now wanted to have another go. The idea was to record with an orchestra, but keep the arrangements jazzy and not to 'sweet'. He wanted to do the album with the Orchester Der Vereinigten Bühnen in Vienna and I suggested Jörg Achim Keller as the arranger, as I really liked his work with Rebekka Bakken and others. We came together in Berlin for a meeting and had a talk through what we wanted to achieve. Keller got the message of Gil Evans-like arrangements with colours and edges and not too many strings and the orchestra guys told me they could do all of that. Now I just needed a budget from the orchestra and when that arrived, I was shocked: just the costs for the orchestra would be much higher than what Sony had given me as a budget for the whole recording and I would have to add arrangements, sideman from Thomas' trio and hotels, transportation, food etc. I had to react and got in touch with some of the German radio big bands and orchestras to see if they would be interested and under what conditions. Between the WDR, BR and NDR, the last one had the best offer and a very good reputation and Jörg had worked with them before, which was a true advantage, as he knew the studios and the musicians. Quasthoff was fine with the change of orchestra and we set the recording date for January 2018.

Comes fall, comes the Jazz Festival season and in Madrid the festival of 2017 started on November 2nd but just before the festival got under way I went to the concert of the Norwegian World Orchestra, which performed for two days in town. Lead by Javid Afsari Rad this ten-piece orchestra was a reflection of our world: ten musicians from four continents; eight countries and their cultures mixed into one sound, one idea of expression. Here music showed what politics is missing: communication on a human level, common expression for the love of life and compromise and understanding. The orchestra featured beside Rad, who plays the santur, saxophonist Trygve Seim, violinists Harpreet Bansal and Sara Ovinge, Andres Maurette O'Brien on viola, Adrian Fiskum Myhr on double bass, Solo Cissokho on cora and vocals, Aissa Tobi on sinter, rabab and vocals, Jai Shankhar on tablas and Habib Meftah Boushehri on percussion. Each musician and instrument contributed to the universal sound and beauty of the music, which had a flow and lightness to it that was difficult to achieve. From duos to the full orchestra playing, the music never stopped to cross borders and engage the listener – global expressions of the highest kind and a flicker of true humanity in a crazy world.

Gilad Hekselman is one of the leading young guitarists around today and his trio with Rick Rosato on bass and Jonathan Pinson on drums, a great band to hear live. Add to that the amazing saxophone of Mark Turner and you are in for a night of great jazz. Hekselman's compositions were beautiful and clear, as was his playing and his understanding with Turner, who added some deepness to an already great band. The communication between the sax and the guitar was truly special, as was the support the bass and drums were providing. The musicians seemed to have fun on stage and the audience enjoyed the show as well, as a standing ovation highlighted. 'Clap Clap' was not only the name of one of Gilad's great compositions performed that night, but as well the sound of the audience after each song.

Becca Stevens´ show in Madrid, featuring Alicyn Yaffee on bass and backing vocals and Jordan Perlson on drums, featured songs from her album 'Perfect Animal' and of course of her latest release 'Regina' and again showed what an excellent singer she is. Her songs are not simple pop songs, but compositions of fine art and touching and with excellent lyrics. And even when she performed someone else's songs (like Stevie Wonder's 'Always') it sounded like it was one of hers, she made them completely her own with her phrasing and arrangements. The audience had a great time listening, sometimes singing along and in the end asking for two encores!

One of the shows I was looking forward to within the excellent program of that year's festival was Bill Frisell: Music For Strings. Frisell, in musical partnership with long time collaborators Jenny Scheinman on violin, Eyvind Kang on viola and Hank Roberts on cello, revisited gems from his own catalogue plus other compositions, notably Burt Bacharach's and the theme to the TV show 'Bonanza', which ended the concert as second encore. The four musicians drifted between arrangements that felt more Americana and others that felt more like contemporary classical pieces, never forgetting the beauty of the basic melody in each tune.

2017, Bill Frisell – Music For Strings, Madrid

The concert of John Medeski's Mad Skillet on Sunday, November 12th, could be described as 'Sun Ra visits New Orleans', as the quartet with Medeski on piano and organ, Will Bernard on guitar, Kirk Joseph on tuba and Julian Addison on drums, grooved their way through some impressive originals that the band has recorded for their forthcoming new album, as well as 'Golden Lady' by Sun Ra, which completely fitted in with the rest of this psychedelic groove gig. Medeski is a master on the Hammond B3 and the rest of the gang did some great soloing and were extremely tight as a group. Couldn't keep my feet still!!

After New Orleans, the next gig took us to Memphis, birth place of the unique singer Dee Dee Bridgewater. Dee Dee brought the Memphis Soulphony with her to perform songs from her latest album 'Memphis…Yes, I am ready' and did so in style! Dee Dee proved again that she is one of the greatest singers of our time – whether she does Jazz, Soul or Blues – it doesn't matter – she makes the songs her own and delivers without fail. This project was a trip back into her teenage years and the music she listened to back then, but putting her own stamp on these compositions. One of the many highlights of the two hours show was Pops Staples 'Why (Am I Treated So Bad)' with an explanation of the roots of this song and a performance that was full of emotion and power.

Dee Dee's former saxophonist James Carter hadn't performed in Madrid for a while and as I had been working with him on his Emarcy records, I was looking forward to see him again and with a new project titled 'Elektrik Outlet'. This new group featured keyboarder Gerard Gibbs, who had so effectively played the organ in James' previous trio, Ralphe Armstrong on bass and Alex White on drums. This show was only the second gig of this group, which used electronic effects to enhance their sounds and grooves, as this was truly a more funk-based project that any other James did before. These guys could definitely groove – Carter blowing so hard that at one point he lost the mic on the soprano sax and just stepped closer to the audience and continued to play and we could still hear him well over the infectious bass grooves and drum shots. James has this incredible technical ability and uses it perfectly to fit the songs, with the grooves of the trio behind him he could showcase his incredible circular breathing and spectacular sax runs.

The Fred Hersch Trio with Hersch on piano, John Hebert on bass and Eric McPherson on drums had been playing together for many years and had developed an almost telepathic way to communicate while playing together, which made the music-making look and feel very easy and light, despite the difficulty of the compositions presented there. The majority of these were by Fred Hersch, from which for me the tribute he composed for British pianist John Taylor was the most touching. Like on their last trio album 'Sunday Night At The Vanguard', the guys performed Paul McCartneys 'For No One' and Monks 'We See' perfectly. The Trio's playing almost felt understated, there was no showing off in any form and maybe because of that, the music was so emotional and touching. The solo encore Hersch gave the thankful audience, alone would have been worth attending this show: a beautiful ballad whose emotional content brought tears to the eyes of the people sitting next to me. If music can create such strong emotions, it is at its best.

Saxophonist Melissa Aldana was growing in stature in the jazz world and rightly so: the show with her quartet featuring Sam Harris on piano, Pablo Menares on bass and Craig Weinrib on drums was energetic, intense and a great example in modern jazz improvising, as the group perfectly supported Aldana in her sax excursions with free playing, but always checking what her leader was up to, so musical context could be created. Outstanding her solo intro to 'I Loves You Porgy', which then the group performed beautifully. All in all, a great show, which could have even been better if the drums wouldn't have been too much upfront in the mix, making it sometimes hard to hear the exciting piano runs by Sam Harris.

Last but not least I heard a real power trio: Chris Potter on saxes, sounds, samples, loops and electronics, Reuben Rogers on electric bass and Eric Harland on drums! To start their show with an extended version of The Police's 'Synchronicity' was a statement as such: this is modern jazz and we can take any starting point and then move freely around in the song to express what we want to communicate to our audience! Potter, using electronics and loops to empower his sound and using different colours within each song, played with a seldom heard intensity and bass and drums powered him to further impressive soloing when needed, or simply and sensitively supported his ideas. Five compositions performed in a show of over 90 minutes. This was freedom to play around within a song, to go to new places and find new expressions as a group was an important part of this music, which only could be achieved by true masters of their instruments and musicians with an understanding for each other.

These were a lot of shows for one month, but with the quality so high of the music I heard, I had no problem to go to a gig every other night. And I wasn't done yet for November: Outside the jazz festival there were as well a few interesting gigs in town and Cristina Branco in the Auditorio Nacional was one of them. Cristina is blessed with a voice and a control that is very unique and her place as one of the most impressive Fado singers is undisputed. The repertoire for this incredible show came mainly from her latest album 'Menina' and the rest from her extensive catalogue. The simplicity in the instrumentation, just piano, bass and Portuguese guitar, gave her voice focus and musical support, without drowning her in sound. A great artist, with style and taste, in the tradition of the Fado, but as well bringing the music into our times.

On the 28th of November was the show of the Dave Holland Trio, which should have played the Teatro Fernán Gómez and not the Clamores ... but sometimes with all the shows going on during the festival, the better room is unfortunately not available... Nevertheless, the Trio, featuring beside Dave guitarist Kevin Eubanks and drummer Obed Calvaire, delivered a show that was a mixture of powerful jazz, blues and rock elements, that only musicians of this calibre can create! Despite some memorable soloing by Eubanks, this was first of all a group effort and without the different individuals it wouldn't have worked the way it did. They included the whole history of jazz somehow, from blues to Miles (especially 'Tribute to Jack Johnson') plus a bit of the Band of Gypsies.

Just a day later another highlight of the festival, the solo piano concert of Tigran Hamasyan. I have known Tigran and his music for many years and met him first when he was playing in the group of Dhafer Youssef. He has developed a unique voice on the piano and it shows best when working solo – from 'a fable', his first solo piano album from 2010 to the new solo recording 'An Ancient Observer', he has made various steps into becoming one of the most celebrated composers and performers today and the show in Madrid, in front of a very young audience, just showed that his music doesn't know borders and attracts an audience that is not necessarily jazz, classical or world music oriented – they came to simply hear great music – and that's what they got in abundance!

Another artist who wasn't part of the festival, but surely worth checking out was China Moses, who performed on Friday, December 1st with her band in the smaller room of the Auditorio Nacional.

2017, China Moses and band

China's captivating soul, jazz and R&B mix didn't really fit into the venue, which is more for acoustic music and therefore the sound wasn't too good – unfortunately the drums drowned a lot of what else was going on. The really good band did their best and China worked hard to get her audience going, which in the end happened and they sang along and got up and danced. The music of the concert came from China's latest album 'Nightintales', which, as the live show, I really like.

In terms of non-OKeh albums from that year, here is the list of my personal favourites:
1 Hudson / Hudson
2 various artists / Celebrate Ornette
3 Ellen Andrea Wang / Blank Out
4 Ron Miles / I am a man
5 Fred Hersch / Open Book
6 Bill Frisell, Thomas Morgan / Small Town
7 Café Drechsler / and now …. boogie!
8 Silvia Perez Cruz / Vestida de nit
9 Rohey / a million things
10 Jef Neve / Spirit Control

While we met with Mexican singer Magos Herrera in Madrid for a relaxed lunch, my 89-year-old mother had a fall at home in Bornholm and injured her shoulder and got a black eye, but thankfully nothing was broken or a lasting problem. She was lucky and for a few weeks had someone to look after her, did some cooking, until my mother was able to move her arm again, almost as before. The doctors were surprised by the fast healing of the injury and for her it was as if it never happened. We spent a relaxed Christmas at home with Jorge and Maria and Claudia and then New Year's Eve with some neighbours and very good food and drink.

2017, with singer Magos Herrera

2018

Jazz Connect 2018 called me back to New York for holding my panel, this time on Turkey, if I remember correctly and it was the first time that the event was held at the Jazz At Lincoln Centre premises. This meant more space for meetings and open discussions, smaller and bigger panels. Wednesday, January 10th was the first day of the Winter Jazz Fest with a showcase of new British talent, hosted by Gilles Peterson and featuring Terry Callier-influenced singer, guitar player and composer Oscar Jerome, young trumpet player Yazz Ahmed, who musically sits somewhere between Nils Petter Molvaer and Ibrahim Maalouf, saxophonist Nubya Garcia and last, but not least, one of saxman Shabaka Hutchings bands, The Comet is Coming – a powerful trio of Sanders-inspired saxophone, electronics and drums. Some amazing talent on display, with the first three acts still kind of work in progress and Shabaka showing again his incredible potential. No surprise that one of his other bands, Sons of Kemet, was signed to the new version of the legendary Impulse! label.

Thursday off to a dinner with Pat Rains, the manager of David Sanborn and then getting back to Le Poisson Rouge, the main venue of the fest, this time just to see Jose James celebrating Bill Withers. Jose took Bill's songs and made them his own, from 'Lean On Me' to 'Ain't No Sunshine' and 'Hello Before' (featuring the wonderful Jean Baylor). He showed respect to the originals, but put his stamp on these songs as well, making them modern, cool and a pleasure to listen to in this form. Supported by an exceptional band, featuring pianist Sullivan Fortner, guitarist Brad Allen Williams, Ben Williams on bass and Nate Smith on drums, plus Markus Strickland as a special guest, the soul and jazz grooves on the music got top treatment and carried James to new heights.

Friday was the first day of the 'Jazz Marathon' and I started at 6 pm at 55 Bar to see Tessa Souter, whose then unreleased new record I had listened to already and enjoyed. The gig was just her with bass and guitar, an intimate affair, perfect to support her voice. The new songs sounded good live as well and I thoroughly enjoyed that set. Next for me was David Sanborn at B B King's. With his new jazz band Sanborn seemed to be rejuvenated and full of energy: even so, the band wasn't that new, as I had already seen them late 2016 and they performed more or less the same repertoire: three compositions by Michael Brecker, some Sanborn classics and other jazz standards, but they seemed to be tighter and more powerful. Andy Ezrin on piano, Wycliffe Gordon on trombone, Ben Williams on bass and Billy Kilson on drums developed into a group that was starting to have its own sound. As I was hanging at Dave's gig and liked it so much that I didn't leave in time for my next show, I simply missed James Brandon Lewis, the young sax player I worked with the past few years, who was finally getting some recognition and was too part of Marc Ribot's project 'Songs Of Resistance'.

The 'Jazz Marathon' continued on Saturday, but my first showcase was at 11:30 am and was by The Baylor Project, whose self-released debut album garnered 2 Grammy nominations. The group of singer Jean Baylor and drummer husband Marcus are blending Soul, R&B and jazz in a perfect way, carried by Jean's incredible vocal skills. A Saturday morning couldn't start better than with their mix of gospel, jazz and deep musical expression.

The first show of the evening was the Theo Croker Big Brother Big Band, combining his usual working band with some of New York's most amazing talents. Croker led a big band only for the second time and surprised the capacity audience in the Poisson Rouge with a mix of standards and own compositions. Opening the show with 'Moten Swing', 'Milestones' and Bobby Timmons 'Moanin'' in the arrangement by Quincy Jones, was his way to pay his dues to the great composers and arrangers in the jazz history and the big band played these arrangements with fire and passion that made the young audience jump!

Next up were Norwegian neo-soul band ROHEY at the Nublu and the packed venue seemed to have turned into a music business meeting: at least three label representatives, a few managers, some artists and media were gathered to see the US debut of one of Europe's most acclaimed new groups and Rohey Taalah on vocals, Ivan Blomqvist on keys, Kristian Jacobsen on bass and Henrik Lodoen on drums delivered big way! As much as I like the album, that show was simply impressive: powerful vocals over grooving synth sounds and danceable rhythms got the audience going beginning to end. Not only a very strong US debut, but already one gig to be remembered for a while in the young new year.

Last, but not least I was on my way to see my old friend Jamaaladeen Tacuma, whose project Brotherzone ended the festival for me with a musical, political and socially relevant show. Powerful grooves over spoken words from Wadud Ahmad and Abiodun Oyewole (of The Last Poets). A perfect ending to my Winter Jazz Fest.

Sunday morning, on the way to my traditional brunch meeting with manager and friend Cynthia Herbst and sitting tired, but happy in the Metro, the doors opened and five gentlemen came in and started singing a simply wonderful vocal arrangement of 'My Girl' …. Smiles all around and we gladly gave a few bucks for this uplifting performance …

While in town I had a few more meetings with Sony on the OKeh 100 concepts and ideas, but neither Legacy nor Masterworks showed much enthusiasm. I had prepared a 2 CD set on the history of the label and even written a 20-page story about it for the booklet and I had prepared 23 artist-oriented releases and 3 genre-oriented ones, for a series of mid-price CDs and digital offerings, called 'The Legacy Of Okeh'. Through the title I wanted Legacy to be more drawn in and it made sense anyway.

my design for the OKeh 100 mid-price series

The list of possible releases featured:

Louis Armstrong	single CD selection from OKeh box set, chronological
Bix Beiderbecke	from the 'Bix Beiderbecke Story' and 'Bix And Tram'
Cab Calloway	complete OKeh recordings based on 'Are You Hip To The Jive'
The Dorsey Brothers	based on 'The Faboulous Dorseys in Hi-Fi'
Champion Jack Dupree	single album compilation based on 'New Orleans Barrelhouse Boogie'
Duke Ellington	single CD compilation based on OKeh Ellington 2 CD set
Benny Goodman	complete OKeh recordings, based on 'Dance Parade' & 'BG with Peggy Lee'
Billie Holiday	complete OKeh recordings
Mississippi John Hurt	based on 'Avalon Blues – The complete 1928 OKeh recordings'
Gene Krupa	single CD compilation based on 'GK with Anita O'Day and Roy Eldridge'
King Oliver	single CD compilation based on 'West End Blues' and 'OKeh Sessions 1923'
Mamie Smith	single CD compilation
Frankie Trumbauer	single CD compilation
Joe Venuti	based on Original Recordings 1926 to 1931 featuring Eddie Lang
Count Basie	complete OKeh recordings
Big Maybelle	from 'The Complete OKeh Sessions 1952 to 1955'
Dr. Feelgood	'Dr. Feelgood And The Interns' album plus OKeh singles
Screaming Jay Hawkins	single CD compilation based on 'I Put A Spell On You … Best Of.'
Little Richard	single CD compilation based on 'The OKeh Sessions'
Walter Jackson	based on Greatest Hits
Major Lance	single CD compilation based on Best Of …
Johnny 'Guitar' Watson	single CD compilation based on 'Bad' plus 'Play Fats Waller' plus 'Two For The Price Of One' featuring Larry Wiiliams
Larry Williams	single CD compilation based on Greatest Hits plus 'Two For The Price Of One'
Western Swing	based on a compilation with this title from 1989 – featuring among others Bob Wills and His Texas Playboys
50's Jazz	compilation featuring the 6 Ahmad Jamal tracks plus Johnny Griffin, Arnett Cobb, Red Rodney, Wild Bill Davis and Mary Ann McCall – based on existing 1992 compilation
New Blues	single CD compilation from this period, based on a 1995 sampler, featuring G. Love and Special Sauce, Keb' Mo, Little Axe, Poppa Chubby, Anders Osborne and Alvin Youngblood Hart.

But none of these happened, neither the 2 CD History Of OKeh set, nor anything at all. Sony simply wasn't interested in spending any buck on this. Masterworks declined, as they wouldn't get the income from any activity including the catalogue and Legacy, because they had bigger fish to fry. One of the most influential and important jazz labels in the history of recorded music had its 100th Anniversary and no-one even mentioned it. No TV documentary, no merchandise with the logo, no new music, nor old music. Nothing. It was hard to believe for me, but true. With even a small campaign we could have increased awareness for the label and its history many-fold. It just showed how deep the interest in Sony Classical for jazz really was. Since Chuck had left, I hadn't gotten the approval to sign one new act. Everything I brought, was stopped by Matt and Josh and it became more and more frustrating. Whether it was US based acts or Europeans, they were never interesting enough, didn't have enough streams or sales or both, no matter what the new project was.

We had to let a few acts go, which is what every label needs to do every once in a while. I usually like to look at an artist after three albums and see if there was any development in terms of sales and touring and then discuss what the next steps might be and based on that information would then decide to either let an act go or stay on the label. We had to let go Nir, as his touring wasn't happening; Somi, as her constant change of management and agency didn't help either, even so personally I would have tried to keep her on the label, as she is, without any doubt, incredibly talented. Michel Camilo wasn't happy with our offer for a new album and John Medeski we worked with as part of MSMW. Overall, we did actually pretty OK. Matt had signed guitarist Pasquale Grasso, which I had warned against. My stand on him was that he was technically impressive, but the music didn't touch me and that's what people want from music. They signed him to Masterworks and not OKeh, so it wasn't about my opinion anyway and recorded tons of standards with him solo. They were only released digitally and unfortunately didn't do anything, as I had expected. Pasquale didn't tour, there was no marketing behind the releases and playlists didn't happen either as expected.

Back in Europe Yolanda and I saw a wonderful show by Stacey Kent in Madrid and then we went to see Goran Bregovic and his band doing a funky Balkan groove night and finally I headed off to Hamburg for the recording of the Thomas Quasthoff album with the NDR Big Band and strings, Frank Chastenier on piano, Dieter Ilg on bass and Wolfgang Haffner on drums. Jörg Achim Keller had the music already rehearsed with the big band and the strings and everything was ready to go, including Till Brönner, who would guest on two tracks. Beside a few little hiccups, the recording went pretty well and we were all happy with what we got. Now it was for the NDR to get the first mix to us to see how it sounded.

In February Yolanda and I did a trip to Oslo, or better Drammen, just outside of Norway's capital, to celebrate with Cecilie and Yngve and friends her 50th birthday. Before heading to Drammen, we stayed a few days in Oslo and enjoyed the beautiful, but freezing cold city and had a fun dinner with Nils Petter Molvaer and Silje Nergaard. We also met with Ketil Bjørnstad, who was writing his six-part biography and had a lunch with Rebekka Bakken and her husband Rune Arnesen, during which I promised her to check with the German Sony, if they would be interested in releasing her newly recorded album. Cecilie's party was a lot of fun and our friends from Madrid Alex and Estefania were there as well as some old friends from Universal Norway and singer Solveig Slettahjell, guitarist and singer Unni Wilhelmsen, both whom I had met before and like a lot as artists.

While in Oslo we had seen that the group GURLS would play at the National Jazz Scene and asked Sten if he could get us tickets to the sold-out show, which he did. GURLS is the group of sax player and singer Hanna Paulsberg and features as well singer and bass player Ellen Andrea Wang and singer Rohey Taalah and they celebrated the release of their first album 'run boy, run'. All three musicians have their own projects and this was one they did for the fun of it and it seemed to develop into something bigger than expected – opening slots for the Oslo shows of Norwegian stars

A-HA and a tour were just the beginning, deservedly great reviews for the album and shows pushed things further.

2018, Gurls in Oslo

The show featured the songs from the album, which are about boys, all written by Hanna Paulsberg and performed to perfection. Cool tracks, jazzy, poppy where necessary and in general not giving a damn about genres, all flowed, was deep and sometimes funny. Rohey is simply an amazing performer and she made Hanna's songs her own in a very special way, but GURLS was the combination of three amazingly talented artists, who seemed to have tremendous fun with what they were doing. Songs like 'Pork Chop Lover' or 'Dis Boy' stood out. Live they had a drummer for a few songs, on the album they all played percussions as well. The show in Oslo ended spectacularly with twelve more female musicians entering the stage, either singing or playing brass instruments to give the finale the grandness it deserved.

Paolo Vinaccia, Italian drummer living in Norway, came to Madrid to buy jamón ibérico, wine and cheese and asked if we could meet. Paolo was coming with his wife Trude Semb, a well-known painter, whom he had proposed to while playing a concert and he had a minister ready backstage to come on and do the ceremony right there in front of the audience. Trude, of course, said *"Yes"* and five minutes later they were married and the show continued. Paolo had a few years back been given the all-clear after having had cancer, but now it had come back and he was in treatment again. He seemed in good shape when we met and had some tapas and wine and a great chat. There he invited Yolanda and myself to a festival he was helping with some ideas for the programming in Bran, Romania in August. From what he told us, this festival was a lot of fun and we looked at each other and then both nodded our heads – we were on! We started to plan the trip immediately and arranged to meet up in Bucharest, stay there for a night and then travel together to Bran.

Then it was time to head again to one of the TAKE FIVE sessions for young English jazz musicians which Serious set up every year. I always enjoyed passing on a bit of experience to young artists and answering their questions. And I always loved to see John Cumming and do my session with him and have a chat about the state of the jazz world and also to see John Surman working with the youngsters. This time the musicians selected were: Al MacSween – piano / Ant Law – guitar / Camilla George – alto sax / Helen Papaioannou – saxes / Jonathan Silk – drums / Nubya Garcia – saxes / Rob Luft – guitar and Scott Flanigan – piano. After my talk for and with the young jazz musicians I was happy to hear them play a composition by Nubya Garcia, which was extremely cool and beautiful and the musicians executed the music with passion and amazing skills. A lot of talent there, without a doubt. I had met Rob Luft before at the Montreux Academy, a similar venture, and did enjoy his debut album 'Riser' a lot and I had seen Nubya in New York at Winter Jazz with a very good show!! Jazz is in good hands with these young artists.

2018, Take Five with John Surman on the right

In early 2018 unfortunately Jorge's health got much worse and he had to spend a lot of time in the hospital. Still, he was positive and joking around and making plans and dealing with his tough situation in an exemplary way. By March the doctors told his mother that there was nothing they could do for him anymore and a few days before his 51st birthday he passed away peacefully, with Maria being at his side. There are no words to describe the pain one could see written in his mother's face, the loss and the emptiness. I can't even start to imagine what it means to have to bury your own child. Yolanda, as always, was there for her mother and supported her the best way she could, hardly having any time to mourn herself. I'll remember Jorge as a guy full of life and ideas and as a wonderful photographer, visual artist and music lover. A great guy to hang out with, who always had a joke on his lips.

Jorge Chalmeta, 1967 -2018

306

Meanwhile we had gotten the first mix of the Quasthoff album from the NDR to give our comments on, but unfortunately that mix was so bad, that we had no other choice but to bring in another sound engineer to mix the album properly. Klaus Genuit did a fantastic job and the album sounded as it should: crisp and dynamic, transparent and clear, so all details could be heard. The additional costs for the mix the NDR had to share, as they were supposed to deliver a satisfying mix to us and they did reluctantly agree to do so in the end. And we had the album ready in time for the planned May release.

April, time to go to Bremen to network and see some young musicians perform. Jazzahead is the global meeting for the jazz industry and as every year has been inspiring and extremely interesting thanks to the presented music. Inspiring because the mood throughout the convention was very upbeat and positive, despite all the problems that have arisen with music delivery going to the streaming world in a rapid tempo, a change the jazz consumer wasn't participating in as fast as we would need. Positive, as this situation was seen as a challenge to question old and now dysfunctional models in the industry and to come up with valid answers – a period of transition in many aspects. And a period of great music from all corners of the globe.

This year's country focus was on Poland, a country that historically has a lively and unique jazz scene and still produces amazingly talented musicians today; young pianist and composer Kasia Pietrzko (who didn't perform at the showcases the country had to offer) being only one very good example. I missed the Polish night showcases on Thursday night, simply sitting outside the venue talking to other label heads about the state of the business and enjoying a warm spring night and a cold beer. The first act I squeezed in between meetings on Friday was by Swedish singer Emilia Martensson and her band. A powerful and in her Swedish-roots based jazz singer with a very unique style and a group that perfectly supported her. Next was new group LASSEN, featuring musicians from Belgium and Norway and performing a straight and highly individual jazz set, reminiscent of early and edgy Jan Garbarek, but still modern and accessible. The group consisted of Harald Lassen on sax, Bram de Looze on piano, Stian Anderson on bass and Tore Flatjord on drums and had their first album out on Jazzland recordings. After that I heard a bit of the concert by Adam Baldych with the Helge Lien Trio – sitting outside to watch the gig on a big screen and enjoying a drink … not bad at all, especially as violinist Baldych and Lien delivered a concert of great music between classical and jazz, with swing and room for explorations. The last show for me on Friday night was by the Finnish Pauli Lyytinen Magnetia Orkestri, featuring beside Lyytinen on sax the amazing trumpet player Verneri Pohjola, Mika Kallio on drums and Eero Tikkanen on bass. The first thought that came up when listening to their music was: Edvard Vesala! The Magnetia Orkestri had the same playfulness, power and melodic approach as some of Vesala's music. Fresh and exciting and played on the highest level.

2018, jazzahead, watching a show outside …

Saturday's showcases started for me with German sax player Paul Heller, who grouped with Dutch jazz legend and keyboarder Jasper Van't Hof, Martin Gjakonovski on bass and Bodek Janke on drums to deliver a jazz and fusion show of top quality. After that it was OKeh recording artist Markus Stockhausen, who presented his latest album 'Far Into The Stars' live to an enthusiastic audience. His band Quadrivium, with Angelo Comisso on keyboards, Joerg Brinkmann on cello and Christian Tomé on drums, created beautiful sounds and grooves for Stockhausen to lay his enchanting trumpet melodies on top. Live and on record this is special music by a very special composer and performer. Petros Klampanis, the Greek bassist who lives in New York, and his group performed a wonderful set based on Klampanis' compositions, which took the listener to melodic excursions between jazz and classical music – dreamlike, accessible and beautiful. And with the immensely talented pianist Kristian Randalu, who had just released his first album on ECM, Bodek Janke on drums and a string section consisting of Olga Holdorff and Sofia Baltatzi on violin, Sara Rilling on viola and Gregor Furhmann on cello, he had the band to perform his music to perfection. I wanted to see Jazzmeia Horn a bit later, but didn't make it into the venue, so full was the place – instead I watched the performance on TV and did enjoy her show a lot.

Pianist Gregory Privat really got his audience in his showcase with Chris Jennings on bass and Laurent-Emmanuel Tilo Bertholo on drums. Rhythms from Martinique and a general influence from Caribbean music are informing his very personal style of jazz. A great musical understanding within the trio helped to make this a remarkable set. On recommendation I went to see the show of the ACA SECA trio, which started 20 past midnight, but left after 2 songs as the sound in the room was simply unbearably bad and one couldn't really enjoy the music.

Jazzahead is a celebration of jazz, of improvised music in all its forms. It is not an industry event for clapping each other on the shoulder, but an exchange of necessary ideas for changing the way our music is distributed, marketed and brought to a wider audience. Streaming as such is not the real problem, the problem is to get the jazz audience to switch to the new form of listening to music and they will, once the streaming services present this music (and classical music as well) in a way the consumer wants it to be.

Before the International Jazz Day of 2018, there were already concerts and events all over the world leading up to the big show in St. Petersburg, having a week of jazz focused activities with a bit more than the usual mainstream media attention. When celebrating the International Jazz Day, we should not forget what we also celebrate: freedom of expression, global respect and understanding and individual as well as group communication, as all this is an integral part of the music we call Jazz, which is reflecting humanity at its best.

I went to see the Pablo Martin Caminero Trio at club Clamores in Madrid, featuring the wonderful pianist Moises P. Sanchez and Michael Olivera on drums.

2018, Pablo Martin Caminero

The Trio performed music from Pablo's latest albums 'Salto al Vacio' and 'OFNI' and was a slightly jazzier affair than his bigger ensemble was, but without neglecting the flamenco touches which are part of his compositions and musical heritage. Sanchez is one of the leading Spanish pianists of the younger generation and performed some captivating and excellent soli, with Olivera keeping time immaculately. Pablo is one artist I love to hear, with his full sound and amazing improvisations – one who never disappoints.

The Nels Cline 4 had just released an album on Blue Note titled 'currents, constellations' which features beside Cline guitar player Julian Lage, Scott Colley on bass and Tom Rainey on drums. The quartet, with Jorge Roeder on bass instead of Colley, came to Madrid's Clamores for two shows, in support of the album release. I was lucky enough a few years back to see Nels and Julian as a duo at Winter Jazz in New York and therefore was looking forward to the quartet show and wasn't disappointed at all. The interplay and communication between the two guitar players were second to none, ideas flowing freely to be picked up and transformed, answers given to questions that hadn't been asked, smiles all around and a stunned and excited audience. The music ranged from Robert Johnson to Metallica, if I may mention two extremes of influences. Blues informed jazz segments were followed by rock riffs any heavy band would be proud of, then moving on to a free sequence just to break into a swing phrase right after and Rainey and Roeder at the heart of things, making these musical excursions of Cline and Lage safe.

My friend and jazz critic / researcher Fernando Ortiz de Urbina gave in Madrid's jazz record shop 'Jazz y Mas' a very interesting lecture on the Miles Davis album 'Miles Ahead', with details on Miles, arranger Gil Evans and producer George Avakian, which overall told the story of a complicated, but extremely successful album production. Even a Miles Davis fan like me could learn a few new and interesting facts here. And at a relaxed dinner afterwards we had a chance to chat a bit more about Miles and jazz in general. Fernando is one of the guys I have a lot of respect for, as his knowledge of our music is amazing and he is constantly checking things, old and new. And on top of that he is a truly great guy.

Conciertos Mini was the name of a series of concerts, presenting old and new in an interesting mix of thirty minutes shows, two per evening. Over two nights and four concerts in May, pianist Sebastian Knauer, vibraphonist Pascal Schumacher and the Orquesta Nacional de España were exploring Johann Sebastian Bach and compositions by Arash Safaian, whose works for 'ÜberBach' are based on pieces by Bach as well. The schedule was simple: first a Bach original, then the Safaian composition, which wanted us to hear Bach without listening to one of his works. Knauer is a versatile musician and played his Bach with emotion and understanding and together with Schumacher he played the 'ÜberBach' with verve and power. The combination of the vibraphone with the piano sounded extremely strong and the strings just added to the beauty of this mix. Something really unique and interesting, which we were lucky enough to further explore over a dinner with the musicians after the show.

My old colleague and friend Piotr Rzeczycki, who was then still running the Polish Classics & Jazz department for Universal, called me to tell me that he was coming to Madrid for an international jazz meeting. This was the first of its kind for Universal in a while and he asked if we could meet for a chat, which of course I wanted. Shortly after that I got a call from Ken Druker, who was now back at Verve Records, telling me that he and his wife would be in town a few days before the meeting and if we wanted to meet. We had a great time together, showed them around a bit and had a fun meal at Casa Alberto. Then Ken asked me to come to another dinner, this time with the Canadian guys, including now David McDonagh, who had re-joined them as well. Almost like in the gold old PolyGram days. And he had booked Casa Alberto again, as he really liked the food there. The day after I went to the hotel where they had the meeting to see Piotr and of course ran into a bunch of other friends from my Universal time, some of whom I had stayed in touch with.

And of course, Yolanda and I went to see some tennis again at the Madrid Masters. That year we had in our schedule Rafael Nadal, Karolina Wozniacki, Simona Halep, Petra Kvitova and Fernando Verdasco. The weather wasn't that great and they had at one point to close the roof of the venue, which was a new experience for us. In June we went to Cadiz again, as we can't stay away from that beautiful city for more than a year. As always, we had a great time just walking around, having great food at the tapas bar of the El Faro restaurant and other amazing places. This time we did as well a little trip by water boat to Puerto De Santa Maria and did a tour through the famous Osborne sherry bodega, which ended drunken after a lengthy sherry tasting.

Yolanda's close friend for many years, Claudia invited us to her 60th birthday party, which was held in a Mexican restaurant, with great food and traditional music. That was one fun party with lots of tequila!! Hannah, who had visited Oliver in China and really enjoyed that trip, had through a woman she knew in Hastings, where she was living for the time being at her mother's place, been offered a job. The friend had various businesses and asked Hannah to help her out with different things. A great way to learn by being involved in different jobs, from running and booking an art festival to working on the marketing for an app and other stuff. She took it, as it sounded interesting and was close to home.

A drink (Tinto de Verano) and football ... life is good!

Real Madrid did the impossible that year by winning the Champions League for the third time in a row. Finalists Liverpool did what they could in Kyiev, but it wasn't enough to beat Zidane's record-breaking team, which won 3 : 1 with two goals by Gareth Bale and one by Karim Bezema. France won the FIFA world Cup in Russia that year with 4 : 2 against a strong Croatian team.

For 2018 I had delivered the following records to OKeh: Bill Frisell's outstanding solo guitar recording 'Music IS', which gave him a # 1 album at the Billboard jazz charts and globally enthusiastic reviews. All compositions by Bill, old and new, are done in a very personal and touching way, with the occasional overdub, to enhance one or the other track.

Then there was Kurt Elling's 'The Questions', a Branford Marsalis co-produced album of highest quality. We had much more songs recorded than were on the final album and while making the choices of which tracks would end up on the record, it showed, more unintentionally than anything else, that these were mostly songs with critical lyrics and texts dealing with the big questions in life. Therefore, the title became what it is. His re-recording of Paul Simon's 'American Tune' is simply incredible and his 'Washing Of the Water' by Peter Gabriel another highlight of a very strong album. The album got Kurt another, well deserved, Grammy nomination as best jazz vocal album.

Till Brönner and bass player Dieter Ilg delivered with 'Nightfall' a beautiful duo album, with compositions ranking from originals to Leonard Cohen, Ornette Coleman, Johann Sebastian Bach and Lennon-McCartney, among others. Simplicity and emotions and incredible musicianship.

Thomas Quasthoff's 'Nice 'N' Easy', with the NDR Big Band had a good start in Germany and then Thomas went out to tour with his trio and came as well to Madrid for a show at the Auditorio Nacional, but the smaller room. Quasthoff and his trusted sidemen Frank Chastenier on piano, Dieter Ilg on bass and Wolfgang Haffner on drums, all band leaders in their own right, performed mainly the repertoire from the new record, arranged for the trio and as powerful and swinging as the album with the NDR big band is. Incredible vocal skills and great feeling, especially in the ballads, as well as some beautiful soli by the three musicians, made that evening a very enjoyable one, with John Lennon's 'Imagine' one of the highlights of the concert.

Of the records coming from the local markets, I had been involved in two from Germany: I helped the team there to sign Rebekka Bakken, who, with her new album 'Things You Leave Behind', released one of her strongest recordings ever. Her songs 'Closer', 'True North' and 'Charlie' are exceptional and the rest is pretty amazing too and then there is her version of Cyndi Lauper's 'Time After Time': slow, deep and personal. The other one was the album 'Nordub', released under Sly & Robbie Meet Nils Petter Molvær Feat. Eivind Aarset And Vladislav Delay. This Jan Bang produced reggae, dub, ambient and electronica mix is astonishing and really cool. Robbie Shakespeare not only playing a groovy bass, but as well singing on two tracks. Sly Dunbar giving the cool rhythms and the rest floats over these and are creating sounds and little melodies and wonderful music. From all the releases I looked after on OKeh, this was the one that sold the most LPs, despite the fact that it was a double vinyl. But it had a bonus track, which wasn't on the CD and the Sly & Robbie fans (and Reggae fans in general) like their LPs. Two more German releases came from singer Lyambiko and Markus Stockhausen. France had a great record by vocal sensation Camille Bertault, produced by Michael Leonhart and showcasing her incredible abilities. Hugh Coltman and Lisa Ekdahl also delivered albums for the French company.

My contract with Sony had been changed a while back into a rolling one and needed to be cancelled, in case they didn't want to renew, before July 1st every year. In all honesty, I didn't think Sony would renew that year, as I still hadn't signed a new act and was only working the acts I already had or some of the local ones, where I got involved to a degree. For me, working with Josh and Matt was a pain in the neck and I had told Bogdan so, as they didn't understand what was going on outside of the US in Matt's case or were too much looking into numbers and streams than listening to the music, as in Josh's case. And Matt's tendency to display professional jealousy didn't help either, nor his arrogant and respectless comments on some of the European music I proposed to release. Under the circumstances I was really surprised that they did re-new the deal for another year, but when I was told that Bogdan would leave to run the Vienna Opera House in about a year and a half's time, I knew my time with OKeh would most likely be over then. Bogdan brought me to Sony and, together with Chuck, backed me up and helped to get OKeh off the ground. Mark couldn't care less about jazz and with him running part of the show at least, jazz wouldn't survive. No bad feelings, that's just reality, as all activities in any major record company depend on the people and if the guys at the top change, then everything changes in one way or the other. That happened at Universal and would happen at Sony as well. But for now, I still had some work to do and records to prepare for the coming year.

Early July Yolanda, Maria and myself flew to Hamburg to meet my brother Jürgen there and stay for a day, before driving into Denmark, to my sister Marlis' place in Højer. As Maria hadn't been in Hamburg before, we showed her the harbour, city centre and St. Pauli and had a great dinner then in a restaurant where Gerhard Schröder and Vladimir Putin once dined as well. The following day we were off to Denmark to celebrate my mother's 90th birthday. We set up the tent for the dinner in Marlis' garden and had a few beers while doing so. All six kids attended the party, plus grandchildren and friends of the family. Hannah unfortunately couldn't make it, as she just had started her new job. We had as always, a lot of fun, but for Yolanda and Maria it was a bit too cold in the Danish summer and as most guys spoke either German or Danish, there wasn't much to listen to in the conversations either. Nevertheless, we all celebrated our mother, who was enjoying the party immensely. With her 90 years she was amazingly fit, physically and mentally and was up with us into the early morning hours.

Our mother celebrating her 90th birthday with her six kids

After that great hang, it was time to get ready to travel to Rotterdam once again. I was really looking forward to this year's edition of North Sea Jazz, as the program really looked promising in its annual mix of established acts and new ones to discover.

Arriving Friday afternoon in Rotterdam to get ready for the first event on my individual program, which was the blind fold test Kurt Elling did for Downbeat's Dan Quellette before his Quintet show with special guest Marquis Hill. Elling's gig, with John Mclean on guitar, Stuart Mindeman on piano and organ, Clark Summers on bass and Adonis Rose on drums, was simply incredible: the band was so tight and had the new repertoire mastered fully and gave Elling the security to deliver his vocal artistry, following each turn the masters voice was taking. Hill fitted in perfectly in terms of sound and imagination and was a perfect partner for Elling. What a great start to the festival – all you wanted from a gig: great artists performances, improvisation of the highest level and tons of emotions expressed via music!

After that it was a bit running to a gig that wasn't actually planned: Carla Bley, unfortunately, had to cancel her tour for health reasons and the festival decided to put on stage Bill Frisell (who already had played that night with Charles Lloyd) together with John Surman. A duo both artists had been talking about doing for a while and then it finally happened – with half an hour to prepare! The result was simply stunning: explorations on themes by Surman or Frisell, improvisations and a music dialogue of rare quality! Surman on either bass clarinet or soprano and Frisell exchanged ideas, showed mutual respect and listened, so they could 'answer' each other in the best musical way! This was something I hoped they would follow up on with a recording!

Off then to catch a bit of Roy Hargrove, whose band included Justin Robinson on alto saxophone, Tadataka Unno on piano, Ameen Saleem on bass and Quincy Philips on drums. Roy sounded strong and powerful and all the guys seemed to have a great time playing most songs from Roy's extensive catalogue. He still got it!

2018, NSJF, Roy Hargrove

Last on my list for Friday was the great NuSoul band from Norway ROHEY - Powerful songs and an incredible voice make this something special! Rohey is a singer of amazing talent and always shows her emotions and puts her soul into each song ... a dancing and enthusiastic audience appreciated it!

Saturday, July 14: Day 2 I started with the wonderful singer Deva Mahal. Just a few songs were enough to confirm what a great artist she is – the record is good, but live: she nailed it!! Quickly running over to see and say "*Hi*" to Nubya Garcia and listen a bit to her powerful show. Her improvisational skills and her sense for melody were outstanding and she proved, with her grooving band, why she is one of the most exciting new acts in the current UK jazz scene. Next was David Sanborn, who brought his new acoustic band for the first time to North Sea Jazz. Performing with him were Michael Dease on trombone, Andy Ezrin on piano, Ben Williams on bass and Billy Kilson on drums and they got the audience going right from the start, with a powerful reading of Michael Brecker's 'Tumbleweed'. The rest of the amazing show was a made of Sanborn originals, standards and covers and the audience loved the way Sanborn and the band treated these compositions and

Sanborn's sound and emotional way of playing. We sat for a while backstage chatting and talking about the next album.

I had missed most of the Pat Metheny concert, but gladly heard a few bits and really enjoyed that new band he got with Gwilym Simcock on piano, Linda Oh on bass and Antonio Sanchez on drums and was lucky enough to have a long chat with Pat after his show, refreshing memories of when we worked together with Charlie Haden and Michael Brecker and a bit about some new and exciting acts of today. I checked about half of the 'Jazz Loves Disney' show, which I truly enjoyed. The four voices used for the concert were really well picked and, in their diversity, made the program work extremely well. Hugh Coltman, Sarah McKenzie, China Moses and Myles Sanko gave the show the emotions and class which was needed to take it beyond a collection of songs. To finish off the second night at North Sea I went to hear and see the Sons Of Kemet – maybe not the best idea if you want to sleep after that: this was full power music with Theon Cross on tuba, drummers Eddie Hick and Tom Skinner, as well as sax player Shabaka Hutchings. Improvisations over grooves that pushed Hutchings forward in his soli and melodic excursions.

2018, NSJF Myles Sanko

Sunday, I started with the Maciej Obara quartet, as I had wanted to see this group for a while and I really enjoyed their music. Dominik Wania on piano, Ole Morton Vagan on bass and Gard Nilssen on drums had such a great understanding with alto player Obara, that the music flowed like a chat between friends, moving to different places quickly and they always were responsive while listening what the other musicians had to 'say'. I just heard a bit of trumpet player Mathias Eick's concert before getting ready for HUDSON – Jack DeJohnette, John Scofield, John Medeski and Scott Colley performed the music of the first album of this group and took the songs to a different level. Outstanding their version of Hendrix's 'Castle Made Of Sand' with Scofield playing sensationally and the rest of the gang just kicking in … Wow!!! These guys were really something else!! Next was Keyon Harrold, whose album I like and the live show was even more exciting, pushing borders and him and guitarist Nir Felder played some deep and interesting soli. A truly great band, a charismatic leader and some great tunes! After that it was Avishai Cohen (the bass player) who presented his latest album '1970' live. Next to Avishai there were Karen Malka on vocals, Marc Kakon on guitar, Shai Bacher on keys and Noam David on drums and together they created Avishai's signature sound of various influences from around the globe and performed his new, more vocal oriented material, very well. I wanted to check out Ramon Valle a bit too, but there were so many people queuing, that it was unfortunately impossible to get into the venue, which was a pity, as I like his playing, especially with the trio. Therefore, I decided to end the Sunday and the festival with another super group in jazz – the Billy Hart quartet featuring special guest Joshua Redman, Ethan Iverson and Ben Street. Drummer Hart has excellent taste in his sidemen and this band was no exception: Iverson and Redman delivered blistering and thoughtful improvisations, based on Street's and Hart's rhythms, laid out for them to walk upon. Stunning interplay and communication and four musicians who obviously had a lot of fun playing together. The perfect ending for an exhausting, but wonderful festival.

After the great music at North Sea Jazz, I had the chance to see and hear a few more concerts in Madrid and Alicante: Julian Lage, in a trio with Jorge Roeder on bass and Eric Doob on drums, played as usual on the highest level of musicianship on his instrument and both Roeder and Doob were perfect sidemen for him, working well as a group. Most of the music came from the album 'Modern Lore', but from earlier in his career as well. Yolanda and I went to Alicante to see Dhafer Youssef, singer and oud player extraordinaire performing 'Diwan of Beauty and Odd' with Aaron Parks, Matt Brewer on bass and Ferenc Nemeth on drums and it was a powerful and beautiful show full of wonderful singing by the master, whose musical relationship with pianist Parks seemed to grow and grow. It's always great to hear Dhafer and then to chat a bit and have a drink together and Alicante was no exception.

We stayed a day longer to see and hear the incredible singer and performer Ute Lemper.

2018, Alicante, Ute Lemper

I know Ute since her 2000 album 'Punishing Kiss' and have seen and heard her many times over the years. But it had been a few years then since I last saw her perform and I was looking forward to her concert 'Songs from the broken heart', as it promised to be a voyage through her career and best songs from her catalogue. Vana Gierig on piano; Victor Hugo Villena on bandoneon and Romain Lecuyer on bass, gave Ute Lemper the support and sound she needed for the variety of songs she performed. From tunes connected to Marlene Dietrich (a new project, based on a 3-hour telephone conversation between Dietrich and Lemper) to Leo Ferrer, Brel, Reich, Dylan and of course Brecht/Weill, the trio made it all sound right and Lemper, with her energetic performance and vocal skills, made these songs hers and so kept the overall sound and quality of the show going. Especially Pete Seeger's 'Where have all the flowers gone'/'Sag mir wo die Blumen sind', which in the German version was done by Dietrich and which Lemper did in both languages, was stunning in terms of delivery and emotional content and for me a song I hadn't heard in years, but one I had a connection to in the late 60's and early 70's. Ute Lemper is without a doubt one of the great singers and performers of our time and she can't really be placed in any category, she seems to have created her own.

Early August we went with Maria for a few days to Valencia to quietly celebrate Yolanda's birthday. Valencia is a beautiful place, with a great beach and some amazing food from which we sampled some: an amazing black paella close to the beach one day and a fantastic seafood lunch at the restaurant Civera on her birthday, for example. We spent a lot of time walking thought the city or, even better, at the hotel pool with a Gin & Tonic. Time flies when you are having fun!

What better way to end the summer jazz festival season than by going to a new and exciting place and hear good music? To listen to jazz played in the original Dracula castle seemed exciting and cool and to hang with Paolo Vinaccia and Trude, his wife, makes any travel worth the effort. We met our friends in Bucharest and had a wonderful dinner together, before going to Bran Castle the next day. The trip from Bucharest was long, as traffic was horrific, but once we saw the beautiful small town and an inviting mountainous landscape and of course the legendary castle, we were happy to be there.

2018, Bran Castle

The festival was opened by the Omar Sosa Trio, featuring beside Sosa on piano and keyboards, Seckou Keita on kora and Gustavo Ovalles on drums. The trio's mixture of Latin and African rhythms was captivating and the flow of the group improvisations changed the music constantly. The sound created by the piano and kora was extremely beautiful and fitted the flowing compositions perfectly. The 200 strong audience (the court of the castle doesn't hold more) enjoyed the music immensely and honoured the trio with a standing ovation.
Paolo had invited us to the artist lounge, which served wonderful wines from around the world and some incredible and tasty food, so waiting for Lars Danielsson to set up for his show was very enjoyable and time flew very fast. 'Liberetto III' was the program Danielsson brought to the castle and this band included beside him on bass, John Parricelli on guitar, Gregory Privat on piano and Magnus Østrom on drums. Beautiful melodies brought to life by an excellent band. Privat, who replaced the original pianist Tigran, was the perfect choice, as his inspired improvisations, based on Danielson's compositions, gave the rest of the band something to smile upon and a direction for their own melodic explorations of the music they created together.
Saturday started at lunch time with a concert in a nearby church by the Duo Medieval and Arve Henriksen. This was scheduled as a Trio Medieval concert with trumpeter Henriksen, but unfortunately one of the singers of the trio, Jorun Lovise Husan, fell ill and couldn't make the trip. So, it was up to Anna Maria Friman and Linn Andrea Fuglseth to perform with trumpeter and singer Henriksen in an acoustic concert in the church and if one wouldn't have known, it didn't seem to

make a difference: their voices floated around the space and Henriksen added various trumpets and flutes to them, creating hauntingly beautiful sounds between medieval religious music and folk songs from Scandinavia. They too opened the evening show in the castle court yard and the music, this time with the addition of Paolo on percussion and drums, was simply perfect for the environment and left the audience asking for more. The soaring voices filling the castle, supported by simple but effective percussion to enhance the rhythm and Henriksen's sounds and immaculate trumpet playing, left no-one untouched. Next up on Saturday night was supposed to be a duo of Enrico Rava and Stefano Bollani, but unfortunately Rava had a fall at home and couldn't make it, so Bollani decided to play a piano solo show instead. He is an artist who doesn't know borders or genres and his solo show had therefore moments of classical music, known themes and standards, free improvisations and as always, a good sense of humour. All on a very high musical level and built up nicely, so the audience kept following him throughout.

The Saturday finished with a concert by my friend, trumpet player Nils Petter Molvaer, with Jo Berger Myhre on bass and Erland Dahlen on drums. They played the music from Molvaer's latest album 'Buoyancy', a mix of ambient sounds, jazz improvisations and rock elements that was perfect to close the night with its moving sound patterns and sometimes heavy grooves over which Molvaer laid his trumpet improvisations.

That was for us the end of the festival, as we had to go back on Sunday, when our wonderful host Paolo made a guest appearance in the show of Daniele Di Bonnaventura, before Rabih Abou-Khalil closed the 6th edition of Jazz at Bran Castle. Truly a weekend to remember: for the beautiful time we spend with Paolo and Trude, for the great music we heard and the wonderful hospitality we were shown by the team of the festival.

2018, Bran Castle, backstage with Gregory Private, Paolo Vinaccia and Nils Petter Molvaer

In September we went to see sax player Eli Degibri at the Café Central. I had seen him once before, at a show case in Bremen and was looking forward to hear him again, as I really enjoyed his sound and playing then and hoped a full show would be even more engaging than the 40 minutes in Bremen – and it was exactly as I expected: Degibri on saxes and his sidemen Tom Oren on piano, Tamir Shmerling on bass and Eviatar Slivnik on drums were cooking at Café Central in the centre of Madrid. Starting off with music from his latest album, 'Cliff Hangin', the quartet pushed the limits right from the start. Eli's sound is deep and beautiful and perfect for powerful outbursts, with him shouting to himself and encouraging him and the others to go even deeper into the music and express themselves. One of the highlights was his playing on the soprano sax in the wonderful 'The Unknown Neighbour'! His band was tight and they seemed to have a great understanding and communication. After playing some more cool compositions from Eli's catalogue the band went into their new release, 'Soul Station / A Tribute To Hank Mobley', which is basically a re-make of the original Mobley album by the same name plus one new composition by Degibri – 'Dear Hank'. To re-make a full album is an unusual statement, saying *"this is where I come from, what I like and what influenced me and this is as well what I can do with it now"*. And he totally makes the compositions his own … 'Soul Station' grooves and swings hard and 'If I Lose You' is a touching ballad with some beautiful playing on the night by Eli and Tom Oren.

Early October Christian Kellersmann and his wife Cristina stayed at our place for a few days to explore Madrid and spent some time with us, before going on a longer trip to the US. We had some wonderful days with lots of music chat and good food and wine and some music. We had bought in advance of their visit some tickets for the concert of flamenco singer Sandra Carrasco with 'El Amir' John Haddad, the oud, bouzouki and guitar player of Radio Tarifa for many years. A match made in heaven: Carrasco sang in a traditional flamenco style, but didn't restrict her repertoire to songs from that genre only and El Amir is a versatile multi-instrumentalist, who used sounds and loops to improve the soundscape of the performed composition. Together they created music of beauty and deep-felt emotions, expressed through their instruments and enthusiastically taken on board by the audience in the small venue of the AC Recoletos Hotel.

2018, Sandra Carrasco

That October I was as well celebrating 35 years in the music business. I had been lucky enough to turn my passion for jazz into a job that I truly enjoyed all the years. The celebration consisted of a great meal and bottle of good wine with Yolanda and then we continued doing what we normally do and went to see a few concerts that month in Madrid. Myles Sanko, Soul singer, came to Madrid for a sold-out show at the club Clamores and he and his band got the all standing audience going from the first song until deep into the night. Sanko has a beautiful voice, perfect for the grooves of his modern, but set in the tradition of the genre, soul and for the ballads he performs touchingly. The repertoire came from his catalogue of three albums, mostly from the recent release 'Just Being Me', and confirmed his incredible song writing skills. The band was perfect in supporting him, as only a band one is working with for a longer period, can do – intuitively knowing where the singer is going next. A powerful show, which had the audience singing along to his songs and the few, incredibly well-done, Soul covers! Myles is an artist I would have really liked to sign to OKeh, as he personifies all the label was about. I had met with him for lunch before the show and we had a great discussion and agreed to stay in touch and talk about the possibility to put the next album out on OKeh. Afterwards, I sent his manager, Soehnke Lohse, an update on our chat and he was as well interested to possibly sign with us. Then I just needed to convince the Americans, but for that I had to wait for new songs from Myles, which would be ready in a few months.

It is always a pleasure to have a chat with Madeleine Peyroux and to hear her live. She presented the songs of her new album 'Anthem', plus some of her older successes, in Madrid's Auditorio Nacional with Aram Bajakian (guitar/voc), Andy Ezrin (keyboards/voc), Paul Frazier (bass/voc) and Graham Hawthorne (drums/voc) to an attentive and thankful audience. Her phrasing is so unique and special and the band kept themselves in the background most of the time, to give the voice the ambience to shine. Outstanding her little solo medley – just her and her acoustic guitar doing a song in Spanish, then going into 'J'ai Deux Amours', before drifting into a Blues and a Spiritual … intimate, beautiful and touching, as only she can be. The month for concerts ended with a show by pianist Ethan Iverson of The Bad Plus fame and saxophonist Mark Turner, a member of the amazing FLY trio. The duo had just released their first record 'Temporary Kings' and were on tour in Europe to promote the album. This was an intimate musical communication between friends, performing standards like Coltrane's 'Giant Steps' or 'Chelsea Bridge' on an extremely high musical level, powerful, but as well full of emotions. Their own compositions for the duo were showing understanding and respect for each other and were touchingly beautiful. Both explored wisely the freedom the duo setting gave them and in the end the music and the audience benefited from that!

The cowardly terror attacks and shootings around the world continued in 2018 with trucks being driven into pedestrians in Münster, Germany and Toronto, Canada and a school shooting in Parkland, Florida which left 17 pupils and teachers dead and many injured. This shooting led to the so-called National School Walkout in favour of changes in the US gun laws, but in the end, as usual, nothing happened. The gun lobby is simply too strong and powerful and knows how to defend and increase their deadly business. The USA made a few more headlines that year, thanks to their President Trump, who withdraw from the UN Human Rights Council, started to set import tariffs for thousands of Chinese & EU goods and had to go through a government shutdown over the budget for Trump's wall to Mexico. While the initially peaceful yellow vest movement in France, which was fighting for economic equality and justice, as well as for political reforms, ended in the worst civil unrest since 1968, in Brazil the right populist Jair Bolsonaro was elected president and portraited himself, as Donald Trump did, as an outsider and family man. Schoolgirl Greta Thurnberg, aged 15, started her StayOutOfSchool days outside the Swedish parliament to call for stronger climate change action and gained global attention and popularity with it. And in Spain, Pedro Sanchez, leader of the social democrat party, became the new prime minister after a successful vote of confidence against reigning PM Mariano Rajoy, leader of the conservative people party. Sanchez built a coalition with the left populists Podemos, the united left party and got the support of some of the regional nationalist parties as well. He was at the time one of the very few socialist leaders of government in Europe.

I was reading that year the new Haruki Murakami novel 'Killing Commendatore', which in Japan originally was released in two volumes – 'The Idea Made Visible' and 'The Shifting Metaphor', but the English translation was released as a single book. This is definitely another masterpiece by the Japanese writer, taking us on a trip through ideas and metaphors and how to deal with and enjoy them. I just love the way he writes, moving between reality and his characters' fantasies. Hannah recommended me to read Sally Rooney's 'Normal People' and I did and I loved the simplicity and directness of the book in telling the tale of two people and their relationship. And then I got per mail from Germany the first part of the Ketil Bjornstad biography 'Die Welt Die Meine War – Die Sechziger Jahre'. In English that could be translated into 'The World I Used To Know' and he had started the series in the sixties and had dedicated one book to each decade. The first one, only

available in Norwegian and German so far, tells of the beginnings, the classical music education and his family. As he is only three years older than I am, it was interesting to read how he saw certain events in our youth, living in a big city like Oslo, in comparison of me being in Hünfeld.
Composer, arranger and pianist Monika Herzig, who is as well a jazz educator and writer, had released a very captivating and interesting book – 'EXPERIENCING CHICK COREA, A listener's companion', which is at the same time a worthy introduction as well as a guide to Chick Corea's music and vast output. Yolanda and I went to the movies to see 'A Star Is Born' and we both enjoyed the film and its music, with both Bradley Cooper and Lady Gaga acting great. Alfonso Cuarón's 'Roma' is an amazing and touching film, that deservedly won the Golden Lion at the Venice International film Festival, as well as three Academy Awards, including the one for Best Foreign Language Film, being the first Mexican film to win this award. We watched the new Netflix documentary QUINCY, which is an interesting and touching portrait of a great music man and human being! Quincy Jones is, by all means, one of the most important music creators, producers, composers and arrangers of our time and the documentary tells the story and portraits the essence of the man perfectly. I had the pleasure to meet Quincy Jones in the early 2000's in Montreux once and got to talk to him for a bit … about music of course … a really nice man, open and ready to talk, to listen and still showing great passion for music … and all that is manifested throughout his career, as the documentary perfectly shows.

In 2018 I was listening to many great records, but the most outstanding for me were:
Wayne Shorter / 'Emanon'
Michael Leonhart Orchestra / 'The Painted Lady Suite'
Ketil Bjornstad & Anneli Drecker / 'A Suite Of Poems'
Wolfgang Muthspiel / 'Where the river goes'
Kat Edmonson/' Old Fashioned Gal'
Tord Gustavsen Trio /' The Other Side'
Madeleine Peyroux / 'Anthem'
Piotr Schmidt / 'Tribute to Tomasz Stanko'
Paolo Vinaccia / 'Dommedag ifølge Paulus' and 'Mystery Man'
Dhafer Youssef / 'Sounds of Mirrors'

Before the 2018 Madrid International Jazz Festival took off on November 6th, I got to see two very impressive and groovy shows in town – at Bogui Jazz the James Carter Organ Trio and the wonderful Combo 66 by John Scofield at Clamores. Carter's organ trio, featuring Gerald Gibbs on Hammond B3 and Alex White on drums, was a powerhouse of grooves and heavy beats, but wonderful as well on delicate ballads. James is one of the most accomplished saxophonists of his generation and his horn gives him an outlet to scream, howl, tell you a story or whisper something into your ears. His range of expression on his instrument seems endless, from powerful wails to simple and beautiful melodic excursions, always given context by the sounds of the organ. John Scofield performed mostly the music of his new album, 'Combo 66', titled the same as his new band, featuring Gerald Clayton on keyboards, Vicente Archer on bass and trusted companion of many years, Bill Stewart on drums. This was more of a straight jazz band than some of the other Scofield groups, but they still grooved and rocked when asked for! Clayton has become an even better pianist since the days when I released his first albums and fitted perfectly into the musical world of Sco.

The news of the untimely passing of trumpeter Roy Hargrove at the age of 49 years have been a shock to the jazz world and to me personally. Roy had been a companion in my professional life since 1994, when he released his first Verve album 'With The Tenors Of Our Time' for which I coordinated the international marketing and promotion efforts. I worked with him on most of the follow up albums to that, including such masterpieces as 'Family', 'Moment To Moment' and the wonderful 'Habana', which won him a Grammy. Roy opened the doors for all the young musicians

playing modern jazz by including R&B and Soul into the mix; his RH Factor rec
with D'Angelo, Common and others are outstanding testimony to that. Lat
Emarcy label and we released his last two studio recordings: the amazing
and a big band recording titled 'Emergence'. I was then discussing wit
possible release of an early 2018 recording session Roy had done with
remember Roy as the man who made the late-night jam sessions at th
something truly special – the place to be during the North Sea Jazz Fe
playing with such energy, power and passion. Once in Vitoria-Gasteiz at th
doing a trumpet battle in the early hours with Wynton and Nicholas, supported
… unforgettable!!! Roy battled most of his life with his personal demons and then w
problems, but when he went on stage, he was pure focus and pure music! When I hear
him in Rotterdam in July that year, he sounded great and played wonderful soli to a grateful
enthusiastic audience. Roy Hargrove will always be remembered as a great musician, innovator,
improviser and fantastic composer and will be missed by many, including me.

Bill Frisell did a workshop and a rare solo concert as part of the 50th Voll-Damm Festival Internacional de Jazz de Barcelona. The concert confirmed Frisell's status as a unique story-teller on his instruments – with the help of some loops and sounds he 'told' the audience his stories in the tradition of the ancient storytellers, the same in content, but different in the wording, every time. A true narrator lives his stories and puts emotion into the description of the world the stories play in … Frisell is a master in this and solo he can focus on how he wants to express himself even more than in a group setting.

2018, Bill Frisell solo, Barcelona

Two days later trumpet player Nils Petter Molvaer visited Madrid as part of JazzMadrid 18 and brought his amazing group featuring Johan Lindstrøm on guitar and pedal steel guitar, Jo Berger Myhre on bass and Erland Dahlen on drums with him to perform the music of 'Buoyancy'. Molvaers music can make you feel like you are floating in a sea of notes, being thrown around by the different strengths of the sounds, the waves coming in a rhythm and move you as if dancing on the surface … then a tsunami of sounds washes over you and takes you up, only to let you land on your feet again, carried by the crystal-clear sound of the trumpet. There is no genre to this, it is just great music, powerful and touching.

...was time for Michel Camilo performing in Madrid a solo concert in support of his latest ..., a solo live recording from London, which, after he left OKeh, he self-released. Camilo is a ...erful performer with an incredible left hand and again showcased his amazing technical abilities ...his instrument ... starting with a groovy 'Island Beat', which immediately got the audience going. ...ut Michel is not only a power player, his sensitive touch in the ballads, like in his own 'Sandra Serenade', was beautiful and drew the audience deep into the song. The highlights in his show were the faster compositions and for me one of these was his incredible solo version of Paul Desmond's 'Take Five', which he originally recorded for the 'What's Up?' album.

How better to end this amazing week of great music than with singer Stacey Kent and her band, featuring husband, saxophonist, flautist and composer Jim Tomlinson, Graham Harvey on piano, Jeremy Brown on bass and Josh Morrison on drums. Despite some difficult travel on the performance day and Stacey battling a bit of a cold and a cough, she performed beautifully and the band, especially Tomlinson and Harvey, laid down wonderful support for her voice, as well as playing some touching soli. To keep the voice safe, the repertoire of the evening was mostly ballads and mid-tempo songs, from Brazil or France ... compositions by Jobim, Valle, Gainsbourg, Ferrer and others. A very laid back, but musically captivating concert.

John Surman with his 'Invisible Threads' Trio at the Conde Duque: beautiful little melodies performed by three masters of their genre: Surman on bass clarinet and soprano saxophone, Nelson Ayres on piano and Rob Waring on vibraphone and marimba. John Surman is a European Jazz Legend as a composer as well as a performer and creative improviser and in the concert his compositions, as well as the ones of the other members of the trio, gave the musicians space to develop ideas around the melodies, to follow the mood of the moment and create new music on the spot. The combination of the vibraphone with the piano sounded powerful and supportive to the main improviser, but the vibes, on the other hand, added a percussive element to the music. A wonderful, contemplative musical experience by a trio that revelled in its togetherness.

2018, Madrid, John Surman Trio

Violinist Regina Carter hadn't performed in Madrid very often and a visit was always a chance to enjoy her unparalleled playing and have a little chat with her. Her group featured Xavier Davis on piano, Chris Lightcap on bass and Alvester Garnett on drums dug deep into the repertoire of her latest album 'Ella .. Accentuate The Positive' and delivered a memorable concert mainly of compositions connected to the great singer. Carter is an outstanding improviser, swinging through these songs with ease, and occasionally she also sang, for example in a song by bass player and vocalist Richard Bona. Her band perfectly supported her with Davis outstanding in filling spaces and his melodic improvisations.

The wonderful pianist Tigran Hamasyan followed up his previous year's impressive solo concert with another delightful performance, showing his improvisational skills, using his own compositions from his two recent solo albums 'An Ancient Observer' and 'For Gyumri' as a base for his musical excursions. Floating between jazz parts, Armenian folk music elements and classical themes, Tigran combined his various musical influences into one single and unique voice on the piano.

Drummer Antonio Sanchez and his band Migration ended for me JazzMadrid18 with a captivating show. Sanchez made it clear that his music has a political and human message to it, by not only dedicating the concert, but as well the new album 'Lines in the sand', to migrants all over the world. He especially pointed to the situation on the borders between the US and Mexico and the music of this amazing group reflected all the despair and suffering, but as well all the hope and joy of these migrants. The group Migration featured beside the leader, vocalist Thana Alexa, Chais Baird on sax and EWI, John Escreet on piano and Orlando de Fleming on bass, all leaders in their own right and they created a powerful sound as a unit, being able to express all emotions together. No matter whether it was a beautiful little melody or a free-flowing soundscape they performed everything as a group and got a deserved standing ovation from the enthusiastic crowd. A powerful statement in many ways!

I had some meetings in Berlin at the end of November and took the chance to go to my favourite club there, the A-Trane to see Leona Berlin (that's really her name). I had heard and read about her before and was simply curious to see her perform … that time to present her first album live and she had put a decent band together with Gustav Anders on keyboards, Richard Müller on bass and electronics and Mathis Grossmann on drums. The repertoire came from the new album, with the exception of a brand-new song, performed there for the first time. Some of the songs from the album and concert, like 'Feel The Love' and 'Thinking About You' as well as 'Make Me Wanna' were really good and groovy and came across well. It seemed the band and her leader need a bit more time to gel, but that was only normal. She did a few songs on her own with loops and sounds and sounded really strong doing so. A great talent in terms of her vocals, not a jazz singer, but very much soul and modern R&B. She got still some way to go, but this first step was more than promising.

Back in Madrid I finally got a chance to hear young singer and Flügelhorn player Andrea Motis performing as a trio with Joan Chamorro on bass and saxophone and Josep Traver on guitars. An intimate setting in a beautiful theatre and laid-back music performed on top level. Motis is a good player and a great singer, working her ways through the great American songbook and a bunch of Brazilian classics, plus a few originals. Her sidemen did a great job in creating beautiful grooves and sounds for her to sing on and excelled in some pretty amazing soli.

The A&R update for the Sony Classical management I sent out in December 2018 included new info on the existing acts, as well as lots of the same from previous updates, as sometimes the process of signing an artist is a slow one. We had decided, on Matt's suggestion, to have Theo Croker's new album mixed by Bob Powers, one of the best soul and R&B mixers around and he did a great job. Originally Theo liked the idea, but didn't have money left from the budget to do so, but we could convince Mark to add this to the costs, as we believed that it would bring in more credibility and a more coherent NuSoul sound. Branford had as well recorded a new quartet album in Australia and was then mixing the tapes for an early 2019 release. I had added Myles Sanko to the list of possible releases, next to Ellen Andrea Wang, Butcher Brown, FORQ and Thana Alexa. On most of these, we were waiting for demos or newly recorded tracks to form an opinion. And then there was the following part, that as well hadn't changed that much from the last update:

"LONG TERM TARGETS

Herbie Hancock – still putting final touches to new album – I am in touch with his manager and Herbie as well. Expect Verve records to bid for that one too…

Julian Lage – The outstanding guitar player of his generation. Trio album getting lots of international awareness – has one album left in his current deal, which will most likely be a solo guitar recording. In touch with him and will see him again in the fall to discuss ideas.

Melody Gardot – She has one more album to deliver to Universal – would be a license deal, as she got that at Universal as well – I am in touch with management.

Madeleine Peyroux – last album in her deal was released in August – I am in constant touch with her manager. Let's see how the new album ANTHEM performs digitally and we take it from there. Will meet her in January in NYC.

John Scofield – last in his deal was released in September – will continue to talk to him and his manager. One idea is to record an album with Bugge Wesseltoft, as they always wanted to do so.

Ganavya – young Indian / American singer, studying at Harvard with Vijay Iyer, Wadada Leo Smith … finished her debut album for a self-release digitally – standards done in South Indian singing style with lyrics in Tamil and English … getting some hype in Europe and got herself an agent here as well … started to compose songs and write lyrics for her next recording .. Monitoring her progress and are in touch with her."

In 2018 we lost many great jazz artists and people behind the scenes again. Austrian pianist and composer Uli Scherer, life-long musical partner of Wolfgang Puschnig and co-founder of the Vienna Art Orchestra and a really great and spiritual guy, passed away that year as well as: Cecil Taylor, whom I had the pleasure seeing two or three times live, one of these an amazing solo show, in which he was dancing around the piano at one point; Charles Neville whom I had the pleasure to see with the Neville Brothers; Jon Hiseman, drummer of Colosseum and husband of sax player Barbara Thompson, a really nice guy; Tomas Stanko, Polish trumpet legend, who recorded on 'amadeo' with Christian Muthspiel's band Octet Ost; Randy Weston, the gentle giant of jazz piano and a wonderful and generous human being whose invitation to Marrakesh I unfortunately never took up; Austrian Erich Kleinschuster, one of the fathers of Austrian jazz; Jerry Gonzalez, whom I had heard a few times in Madrid and exceptional musicians like Hamiett Bluiett and Sonny Fortune, both I was lucky enough as well to see perform.

As December is usually a bit quieter, we spent time with friends and went out for meals and drinks a bit. On one walk through the city centre, we even found a stall who was selling "mulled" wine, as they would around that time of the year in Vienna. Not bad at all! We spent Christmas with Maria at our place and had decided to go to Malaga for New Year's Eve.

2018, with Yngve Naess in Malaga

And then we heard that Yngve, Cecilie and some friends would be there as well, so we arranged to have lunch on the 30th together in Malaga. It was really great to see them again, have a great chat and some wonderful food and wine, plus an Orujo to digest the lunch. The last evening of the year we spent together with Maria in the hotel and had a very relaxed end to an extremely tough and busy year.

2019

2019's early January trip to New York was not only because of the Jazz Congress, some meetings and to see and hear some music as usual, but as well about attending the memorial concert for Roy Hargrove, which was held at JALC's Rose Theatre on January 9th. Christian McBride, the MC of the night, was amazing in the choice of his words, in his jokes, that explained what kind of man Roy was, in his praise for the human being, composer, trumpeter und occasional singer – full of love and respect for a fellow musician with whom he played early in his career. Musical proceedings started with the Lincoln Centre Jazz Orchestra and Wynton Marsalis playing a joyful second line walking through the audience onto the stage. This was followed by the Roy Hargrove Big Band, whose sole album 'Emergence' I had released in 2009 on Emarcy, and they performed with trumpeters Theo Croker and Giveton Gelin songs from that record. A variety of quintets originally led by Hargrove followed and featured an array of new and big names and legends, all performing Roy's compositions, including the famous 'Strasbourg/Saint Denis' from the album 'earfood', this one featuring pianist Gerald Clayton, who as well performed it on the record. Before the night was over, we heard many great trumpet players, featuring, beside others, Jon Faddis, Freddie Hendrix, Jeremy Pelt and Terence Blanchard. Singers Dee Dee Bridgewater, Roberta Gambarini and Norah Jones left us speechless and touched, especially Gambarini's version of 'I Remember Clifford', which, with new lyrics, became the theme of the night: 'I Remember Hargrove'! There were over 200 musicians participating and paying their tributes, including his Grammy-winning band Crisol, the Dizzy Gillespie All-Star Orchestra and of course the celebrated soul outfit RH Factor, which performed some of their hits, featuring rapper Common, singer Stephanie McKay on the wonderful "Forget Regret" and, of course, Renee Neufville the original vocalist of that band. This celebration of the life and work of Roy Hargrove was surely an unforgettable event in many ways: five hours of music for one of the leading musicians of our time, a celebration of his compositions and collaborations. But also, a celebration of the music genre we call jazz, a powerful statement of its validity in these times and of its strength and importance. And afterwards at Dizzy's we danced the night away with a great jam session based on Roy's music. Dee Dee was there, as were many other musicians, talking, dancing, playing and remembering that shooting star that passed through our lives.

CELEBRATING THE LIFE AND WORK OF roy hargrove

Tuesday, January 8, 2019
ROSE THEATER IN JAZZ AT LINCOLN CENTER'S FREDERICK P. ROSE HALL
Broadway at 60th Street / New York, NY

DOORS WILL OPEN AT 6:30PM / EVENT WILL BEGIN PROMPTLY AT 7PM

The celebration will be open to the public and the general seating area will become available on a first come, first served basis. Seating in Rose Theater is limited, and Jazz at Lincoln Center reserves the right to close admission based on capacity. Additional seating will be available for simulcast viewing in Jazz at Lincoln Center's The Appel Room, Mica and Ahmet Ertegun Atrium and Ertegun Jazz Hall of Fame.

Photo: Courtesy of Universal Music Group

In terms of music, New York is always rewarding and so it was as well for this trip – starting with the incredible Kurt Elling performing at Birdland a program he calls 'Heroes', which pays tribute to some of the most important singers and those influential to him: Jon Hendricks, Oscar Brown, Jr and many others. With a band featuring Stu Mindeman on piano, Clark Sommers on bass, Ulysses Owens on drums and special guests from Australia James Morrison on both trumpet and trombone and Troy Roberts on sax, he ran through the classics with humour and style, always being himself and performing on the highest level. Fully deserving the standing ovation of the packed house.

On Sunday I had three shows on my list, starting in the afternoon with a showcase at the Rizzoli Bookstore by the Michael Leonhart Orchestra. What an amazing and powerful performance! This has become my favourite Big Band for many reasons: Leonhart is not only a great writer, but a fantastic arranger as well, as the show pointed out again: a mix of his own compositions (from 'The Painted Lady Suite' debut album of the band) to arrangements of songs from Spinal Tap and the Wu Tang Clan, to name a few … performed with an energy and fun, that is second to none! Great soloist rounded up the overall strong performance. Great to see too my friend Christian Kellersmann and his wife Cristina in the crowd there. Magos Herrera & Brooklyn Rider performed as part of the Global Fest music from their latest record 'Dreamers', a Grammy nominated beauty of an album. Singer Herrera and her fellow musicians, Johnny Gandelsman, Colin Jacobsen on violin; Nicholas Cords on viola and Michael Nicolas on cello, with some help from percussionist Mathias Kunzli, dug deep into the Latin American songbook and performed outstanding versions of 'Balderrama' and 'La Aurora de Nueva York' amongst many others. Herrera was in top form, with vocals that cut right into the emotions of the listener.

2019, Magos Herrera & Brooklyn Rider, NYC

Last on Sunday was Chilean singer and guitarist Camila Meza's late show at the Jazz Standard. The music mainly came from her new album 'Ambar' and was an eclectic mix of Latin standards, own compositions and covers. The Nectar Orchestra featured beside the singer and guitar player Meza Edin Ladin on piano, Noam Wiesenberg on bass and as arranger of the strings, Ofri Nehemya on drums, as well as Tomoko Omura, Fung Chern Hwei on violin; Karen Waltuch on viola and Brian Sanders on cello. Highlight of the second set for me was her rendition of 'This Is Not America', with a classy guitar solo and a powerful overall sound by the band.

Back at home we went to see our friend and bass player Pablo Martin again at the Bogui club, playing new music from the new album 'Bost' and then at the same place we went to the 27th birthday gig by pianist Juan Sebastian Vazquez, featuring his band plus guest trumpet player Raynald Colon and the Lyra string quartet – a deep and touching celebration.

The British magazine Jazzwise printed in their February 2019 issue an article by writer Stuart Nicholson about digital streaming, titled 'Stream Machine'. Nicholson asked a valid question with *"how long are streaming services going to hang on to music that's not generating revenue"*, meaning the underuse of millions of tracks from niche genres and pointing out in comparison, that Netflix did cut its content of films made before 1950 to just 25, because of the same problem. With streaming being song oriented, so argues Nicholson, jazz and related niche genres are falling through the system. If you add to that the bad presentation of jazz on most streaming services, one could think Nicholson might be right and one should for sure be worried. But there was, in my opinion, another possible scenario: all streaming services are constantly fighting for growth by adding subscribers, but slowly the pop subscriptions will be or already did then slow down and in the fight for additional income the services might start to look into the smaller genres like classical music, jazz, folk etc. Once that music is presented in a way the jazz consumer wants (more relevant information on sidemen, recording dates, etc and artists with the same name separated by instrument or date of birth ...) and in better sound quality (here amazon made the first move already) than there is a good chance that jazz fans will migrate to streaming services faster and subscribe. And with that, make the niche repertoire for the streaming services worth having within their businesses. Of course, it will as well depend on what the stand of the big record companies will be on that ... they are not only holding the biggest jazz catalogues, but also a share in some of the streaming services, but for all of them Jazz is only about 1% of their overall business and therefore not high on the priority list ... Interesting times indeed!! And maybe the time to think about genre oriented streaming services for niche repertoire like Jazz and Classical music featuring all labels, majors and indies alike has come ...

I only had two records to put out in 2019: the new Theo Croker 'StarPeopleNation', a real modern soul-influenced and R&B leaning jazz record, which got him a Grammy nomination and an album award in France. The second record was 'The Secret Between The Shadow And The Soul', the new recording by the Branford Marsalis Quartet. An outstanding jazz album of one of the best groups of our time, which got not only 2 Grammy Nominations, but as well was the # 1 Jazzalbum 2019 for the UK magazine Jazzwise, was also the JJA (Jazz Journalists Association) Jazz Record of the year and then got a nomination for the German JazzPreis 2020. That was it, only Germany and France released a few local acts that year too, including a great triosence album titled 'Scorpio Rising'.

In March, Yolanda and I went to Sevilla to have two days off in this beautiful city and to see the concert by the Branford Marsalis quartet at the Teatro Lope de Vega, part of the European tour to promote their new album. The show started, as the album does, with the Eric Revis composition 'Dance of the evil toys', a multifaceted piece that kind of stands for everything this band is about: powerful improvisations in a free space, but always with a focus on the melodic side of the songs. And despite some problems with his horns (a cab driver in Holland had dropped them the day before) Branford and his band members Joey Calderazzo on piano, Eric Revis on bass and Justin Faulkner on drums, took off into jazzy spheres not many musicians have been.

2019, The Branford Marsalis Quartet, Sevilla

The dreamlike understanding between the four artists was astonishing, the challenges they threw at each other amazing and the reactions, if one of them played something new and unexpected, rewarding for the performing musicians as well as for the audience. The quartet then played through the repertoire of the new album, touching the listener with the melodic and emotional beauty of the Joey Calderazzo ballad 'Conversation Among The Ruins', making everyone smile. Another highlight of the concert was their version of Keith Jarrett's 'The Windup', a powerful and fast played composition in which all four musicians excelled, but especially Calderazzo, whose solo brought cheers from his musical companions. A night, which ended with a wonderful version of W.C. Handy's 'St. Louis Blues', was all what one would expect from a jazz concert ... and so much more! This is probably one of the top three working bands in jazz around these days and whatever they perform it will always be the past and present of the music we call jazz, with an eye on the future and melody at its core.

A week later the Julian Lage Trio performed in Madrid, presenting new music from the recently released and highly recommended album 'Love Hurts'. As on the album, the bass player in the trio was Jorge Roeder, a long-time musical companion of Julian, but whereas on the album the drums seat is occupied by Dave King, on tour it was Eric Doob delivering the beat. I have seen this trio before and think they had grown a lot as a unit, delivering guitarist Lage's composition with understanding and a deeper sense for the melodies of their leader. They started the show with 'Love Hurts' the Nazareth hit from 1975 and continued to rock through Lage's 'Atlantic Limited' to arrive at Ornette Coleman and some blues. Lage and his impeccable sidemen played with power and emotional content and made the seemingly wild mix of songs work perfectly.

The 14th edition of TAKE FIVE UK took place that year between February 23rd and March 2nd at the usual venue in England. Serious, the music production company that organises the event, picked eight young and upcoming musicians to teach them about the music business in all its aspects – from performance coaching, to finance, funding, marketing, legal and film making. All this loosened up by music sessions. I have since many years had the honour to talk about the music business, labels, international career building etc. at these events and found that year a bunch of open and interested artists.

The participants were:

Abel Selaocoe – cello and vocals;
Cherise Adams-Burnett – vocals and flute;
Chris Ryan – drums and vocals;
Daniel Casimir – double bass and bass guitar;
Emma-Jean Thackray – trumpet, vocals and electronics;
Faye McCalman – saxophone and clarinet;
Jonathan Chung – saxophone and
Sam Healey – saxophone and electronics.

Most of these young artists were covering musically more than just jazz... from classical to world music and electronic music, everything included ... no borders, all individually had their way to express themselves. I was lucky enough to hear during their jam sessions that they performed with a confidence betraying their young age and with some wonderful ideas. They started the session with Roy Hargrove's composition 'Strasbourg/St. Denis' and let it flow and gave space to improvisations that enhanced the melody of this beautiful song.

All eight musicians were carefully listening to each other, following an idea, letting the other go ahead to solo, still adding something to the overall sound and the feel of the improvised piece. Lots of talent there and lots of acts to see how they will develop in the coming years. Especially, singer Cherise was someone I was particular impressed with.

After I had finished Take Five for that year, I had some time left and took the train to London to have lunch with Hannah, whom I hadn't seen for a while. She meanwhile had moved back to London and she had a new job at the Centre For Counselling, Psychology, Education in Maida Vale. She was the first stop for everyone coming through the door of that charitable centre, assessing and then sending them to one of the professionals for help. She really enjoyed that job.

I had Hannah promised tickets for Dhafer's show at the Barbican and Dhafer put them aside for her. She really loved the show and went backstage afterwards to say *"Hi"* to him and Shiraz.

2019, Hannah and Dhafer, London

Later that month Yolanda and myself went to the massive demo for women's rights and equality in Madrid and then with some friends to the match of Atletico Madrid against Barcelona, which set a new record of attendance for a women's football game with over 60.000 paying fans, which saw a great game of football, which unfortunately Atletico lost against the Spanish champions.

If you ever go to see a band at Ronnie Scott's in London, don't miss the chance to have a closer look at the jazz portraits which decorate the room. Most of these stunning photographs have been taken over the years by photographer extraordinaire David Sinclair, who passed away in March 2019. David was part of Ronnie's in many ways, taking a lot of his over 5000 artist portraits there, but he could as well be found at jazz concerts in other venues like the Barbican, where he took a picture of me in 2010, backstage at a gig by Dee Dee Bridgewater. As we had done so often during the years I was living in London, we had a chat about the music we passionately were involved in and unknowingly to me, he had a bit later taken this photo. A few days after the concert a letter from David arrived at my office, with the picture in it – a wonderful gesture by a truly kind gentleman. He will be missed, but his outstanding portraits of the jazz artists of our time will be a witness of his art for many years to come.

Kiyoshi Koyama, who as well passed away that month, was one of the leading Japanese jazz writers and led the world-famous magazine Swing Journal for many years. Beside that he was a radio DJ and an excellent researcher and compiler, even producer of jazz recordings. His outstanding work for Mercury, putting together substantial box sets, especially of Dinah Washington, gave him the nickname 'Boxman'. I had the pleasure of meeting this humble man on a trip to Japan in the early 90's and was amazed by his passion for and knowledge of jazz. He played a very important role in making jazz known in Japan and in bringing some historical recordings to a wider audience.

Even so it seemed clear to me, that Sony wouldn't renew my contract for another year, I went to `jazzahead`, as it was the best place to get a feel about what was going on in the jazz world and maybe one or the other idea or opportunity would come up in all the meetings I was to have. And to start talking to others labels not just about myself, but as well about some of the OKeh artists, who would need new homes. `Jazzahead´ 2019 was bigger and better than the ones before for various reasons: first of all, it had become a true international event for the jazz business, with plenty of music. Secondly that year's partner country Norway was a more active than many others before, with concerts, showcases and events, well prepared information on the market and its artists and by sending writer and poet Lars Saabye Christensen to do the opening speech, talking about jazz as only a poet could: *"Jazz is something that does not yet exist, that hasn't happened, that still hasn't been played. Jazz is movement, as indeed all music is. ... Jazz is always putting something behind us, without forgetting it, mark you, without forgetting it. In jazz, memory is the theme that creeps up on you or to which you return. In jazz, memory is forward looking ..."*.

2019, jazzahead, Lars Saabye Christensen

Overall, the mood at the fair/conference was very positive despite the jazz record market going through a rough time as audiences were not changing to streaming services as fast as they needed to with rapidly declining CD sales. Nevertheless, the indie sector (and that's what you found in Bremen and what was driving our business then) was picking up what the major labels were not able or willing to do anymore and most of them were thriving. All change, all challenge, but no panic!! As Lars Saabye Christensen said: *"We know where we are going, but not how to get there. That's jazz."*
In terms of showcases I saw four of the Norwegian ones and a few others, all of which I will describe in short words as follows: the first short concert was a duo by European jazz legends Karin Krog and John Surman. Krog had been the first Norwegian jazz musician who found in the mid 1960's success internationally and opened many doors for the generations after her. Her delicate duo with Surman was full of beautiful moments in their communication, so creating jazz as well as using Norwegian folk music as inspiration. A wonderful bow by the partner country to its own history and at the same time a reminder that jazz is ageless. Then off to Thomas Strønen's ´Time Is A Blind Guide´, a quintet performing chamber music like compositions based on influences ranging from folk songs to contemporary works. The musicians Hakon Aase on violin, Ole Morten Vågan on bass, Ayumi Tanaka on piano, Leo Svensson Sander on cello and Strønen on drums, played a wonderful and melodic set with a very unique ensemble sound. Musically open and sometimes adventurous, this was beautiful music that needed the listeners attention to fully enjoy the deepness and variety of their performance. There is a reason why Acoustic Unity, the trio led by drummer Gard Nilssen, featuring Andre Roligheten on saxes and Ole Morten Vågan on bass, was considered one of the most exciting jazz bands in Europe back then: first of all, these three musicians are some of the best improvisers of the Norwegian jazz scene and secondly, they work extremely well as a group: listening, reacting, driving the compositions through tons of space to a delightful conclusion. This was as energetic a group as you might find – the power was incredible and the trio delivered on each of their songs with a smile on their faces. Fascinating, challenging, but extremely rewarding for the listener. For

Frode Haltli the name of his band is the program as well: Avant Folk. The outstanding accordion players ten-piece band, featured instruments from the traditional fiddle of Norwegian folk music to electric guitar, performed his compositions with verve and perfection. The often-cinematic sounds of the pieces led them into free spaces and back into delicate melodies, touching and making one smile. I finished the Norwegian showcase night with Kristin Asbjørnsen, the wonderful singer I used to work with in the past. There she presented her then new music, solely performed with Olav Torget on electric guitar and Suntou Susso on kora and additional vocals. This was an incredible mix of gospels, African influences and vocal improvisations. With the additional vocals and some loops, they sounded sometimes like a full ensemble performing ... with the unique voice of Asbjørnsen leading the way.

2019, jazzahead, Kristin Asbjørnsen

On the second day of ´jazzahead´ I went to see another four showcases between or after the good meetings I had, starting with AKSHAM, a project featuring Elina Duni on vocals, Marc Perrenoud on piano, David Enhco on trumpet, Florent Nisse on bass and Fred Pasqua on drums. Duni provided all the lyrics for the compositions of her band members and performed those songs with feeling and quality – musically Perrenoud and Enhco were the perfect lyrical partners for Elina and Nisse and Pasqua laid the carpet everyone was walking on rhythmically. The Lisbon Underground Ensemble was next on my list, as I had heard about them and was curious what composer and pianist Marco Barroso would perform with his 15-piece band. In the mid 80's Frank Zappa had asked *"Does humour belong in music?"* And Barraso gave a clear answer with his band: *"YES!"* Incredible changes from free parts to swing elements, wonderful soli and some hilarious snippets from prepared tapes, gave this powerful performance some funny twists, without minimising the musicality and individual contributions. Impressive from start to finish! Elliot Galvin was next with a freely improvised solo piano show. Galvin is one of the new musicians in the UK that was creating a buzz. A unique piano player and composer with a feel for little melodies and flowing improvisations. Immaculate technique and inventiveness made the solo show a captivating experience, especially when he prepared the piano to get different sounds and therefore extended his possibilities to create new colours! Last but not least that evening, I listened to MDCIII, a project led by Belgian sax player and loop master Mattias De Craene with drummers Lennart Jacobs and Simon Segers, who as well used electronics. This music was all about sounds and grooves, samples and powerful sax lines. Spacy and ambient and then building a rhythm one could dance to. Modern and exciting music played in a cloud of colourful smoke ... perfect for a late-night gig!

Day three brought even more meetings with labels, agents, managers and artists – all really interesting and good, but I had to take a break in the afternoon to go and hear singer Simin Tander and cellist Jörg Brinkmann performing as a duo. This show was absolutely amazing, it's simplicity and beauty beyond words and the careful use of electronics only to enhance the songs, was very impressive. Tander is a wonderful singer with amazing control and expression and Brinkmann a sensitive companion to her. The mix of repertoire from early music songs to today was eclectic and extremely well done. Last for me was Matthew Whitacker, the then 18-year-old Hammond B3 player and pianist with his band, featuring Marcos Robinson on guitar, Karim Hutton on bass and Isaiah Johnson on drums. The perfect end of a busy day … organ grooves and piano fire works! Nothing really new, but extremely well done, down to his version of the Michel Camilo composition 'Caribe'. The tired-out audience loved it and danced along to his funky grooves.

In April we went with Yolanda's half-brother Rene and his wife Carmen to Jaen, where she had family, and spend a few days there, in unfortunately not the best weather. But it was fun anyway. Michel Camilo came to Madrid to perform a classical concert and as usual we met up and had a great dinner. This time at the wonderful fish restaurant Portobello, where there is a photo of Michel with Tomatito and Sandra hanging on the wall. The house photographer came by our table and took one of us four, disappeared and at the end of our meal, they were already hanging this picture close to the other with Michel and gave us a copy of the photo as well.

2019, with Michel and Sandra Camilo at the restaurant Portobello, Madrid, photo courtesy of Portobello

The Bad Plus were in Madrid to perform 2 shows at the Café Berlin … a sold out 9 pm concert and a second one at 11 pm. David King, the trio's drummer, had invited me to the first show and I went there with our friend José, who had purchased a ticket. Dave, Bassist Reid Anderson and new pianist Orrin Evans started the first show on time with mostly music from their first record together 'NEVER STOP II'. I had heard the album and really love it, but couldn't convince the US to release it on OKeh, so the band put it out themselves. Live this is something beyond, even so they knew each other from before and had performed together, by then the new trio was very tight, as the constant touring was paying off. Evans was incredible with his powerful, sometimes orchestral way of playing, then moving into beautiful and touching little melodies, always perfectly supported by Anderson and

King. These two wonderful musicians are responsible (as in the past) for most of the compositions of the trio, which keeps the expected edgy quirkiness to their music. We loved every minute of this set and in the break went to say *"Hi"* and then made our way to the exit as the club was emptied to make way for the new audience, but the manager of the club, having seen us backstage with the guys, invited us for the second set, which wasn't fully sold out and we were happy to stay – as the second set, without any repetition in repertoire, was even better than the first. Beside the amazing interplay between the three musicians, each of them delivered some outstanding solo work, with Anderson at one point calling up memories of Charlie Haden in the sheer beauty of his solo and by playing not one unnecessary note. Evans and King as well performed at the top of their game to prove that the group was still one to count with.

In May we paid our traditional visit to the Madrid Masters and were lucky to see again Rafael Nadal in action. And we saw promising Canadian youngster Felix Auger-Aliassime, as well as Simona Halep and Naomi Osaka.

2019, Rafa Nadal at the Madrid Tennis Open

Then Dhafer came for a visit with Shiraz and their little daughter Layan and we spent some great time together, eating and chatting. Hannah had finally found a new flat to live in together with Oliver, who had returned from his stay in China. The new place was just 2 minutes away from her work and in the neighbourhood where she grew up in London. They got a good deal and shared the flat with a friend from Uni.

My mentor and friend Cees Schrama passed away on May 22nd that year. Jazz icon, promotor of jazz music in the Netherlands and beyond, music producer, keyboard player, record industry executive and a wonderful person. From the beginnings when I started in the music industry and we both worked at PolyGram in the mid/late eighties and then with him being part of the North Sea Jazz Festival, which I visited and took every chance to see and chat with him, he played a big part in my professional life. As a successful jazz pianist, he always had stories to tell, running as well a radio show for jazz in the Netherlands for over 30 years added to the pool of stories about music or musicians. The albums he produced with artists like Toots Thielemans, Rosenberg Trio, Monty Alexander (Live in Holland), Tony Scott, Flairck and many other local Dutch acts, plus many re-issues from the PolyGram vaults, are proof of his tireless work in and for music, jazz above all other genres. Not many people know that he played as well on one of the biggest international hits coming out of Holland: Shocking Blue's 'Venus'. His passion for music is described perfectly in his 2007 autobiography 'It Don't Mean A Thing: Leven Met Jazz' and some of the anecdotes are told there as well. He helped me to set up a jazz structure within PolyGram International in the early nineties, having global meetings and co-ordinated release schedules, still working as a producer and radio and festival presenter on the side. His knowledge about jazz was second to none and I surely learned a lot from him in every aspect. Jazz had lost one of its biggest and friendliest advocates.

Saxophonist Eli Degibri started his 4-night residency at the Café Central in Madrid on May 23rd with his trusted sidemen Tom Oren on piano, Tamir Shmerling on bass and Evitar Slivnik on drums and a full house. The expressive sax player went through his own compositions from earlier records, plus a few new compositions, which would be on a forthcoming album. Not new in a sense was the standard 'Like someone in love', which Eli recorded already on his second album, but his new version was really different, as the group imagined how J. S. Bach might have played that song … to wondrous results: beautiful and melodic with an astonishing piano solo by Oren, that had Bach and Ella in it combined in a unique and breath-taking new way. 'Bach', the working title of another new song, was a composition by Degibri, as well inspired by Bach and similar powerful and captivating.

A week later we had Marcus Miller in town to perform at the Teatro Nuevo Apolo with his incredible band featuring Marquis Hill on trumpet, Alex Han on sax, Brett Williams on keys and Alex Bailey on drums, plus the master himself on various electric basses and bass clarinet. They mostly performed the music from his latest album 'Laid Black', with the outstanding tracks 'Sublimity' and 'Trip Trap', which had Miller performing a solo of unreal quality and funk power! Another highlight of the evening was 'Hylife' from the 'Afrodeezia' album and of course his nods to Miles Davis, this time with a wonderful and authentic version of 'Bitches Brew', as well as with his own compositions for the late trumpet legend, 'Amandla' and 'Tutu'. Han and especially Hill did extremely well in these numbers, with incredible solo performances and ensemble play. A great band seemingly having fun on stage and enjoying the enthusiastic response from an audience that started dancing and singing at the end of the show to the performance of the Beatles song 'Come Together'! Thanks to Marcus' manager and European agent Bernard Dulau, we had a chat with Marcus before the show, which I truly enjoyed.

2019, with Wolfgang Puschnig, Vienna

In June I made the trip to Vienna to hold one of my lectures on the jazz music business, having been invited by my friend Wolfgang Puschnig, head of the jazz department at the Musik Akademie in Vienna. Unfortunately, I had to do that on the hottest day that year in Austria and a lot of the students who had put themselves forward to attend preferred to go for a swim or have a cold beer somewhere. There were still a few people in the room so and I did what I could, to make it worthwhile for them. By that time, I had been officially told as well by Sony that they wouldn't renew my deal beyond September 2019 and I had to think about what the next chapter for me could be. There was still time, but it was crucial to start talking and looking around. But first I enjoyed Vienna, stayed at my brother's place and we went out a bit, had a reunion with our college class of 1975, which was fun and strange at the same time. Some of them didn't seem to have changed at all, some felt more mature. I guess it was just too long ago and too many things happened since I had been in touch with them.

The Champions League Final of that year was held in Madrid between Tottenham and Liverpool and the city was vibrating with British tourists and fans. No chance to get a ticket via the normal channels and outside of these the prices were just ridiculous. So, Yolanda and myself just went into town in the afternoon before the game to get some of the atmosphere, which was fun as well. Then we watched the game at home and saw Liverpool deservedly win. In July we attended the gay parade, called ´ORGULLO´, with its colourful parades and decorations all over town, while Hannah had a relaxed holiday on a boat in Greece with some of her friends. The images she sent looked amazing, and as the boat was owned by a friend of theirs, the whole trip wasn't really expensive at all, but seemed to have been a lot of fun for everyone.

Paolo Vinaccia had lost his battle with cancer on July 5th 2019. Words cannot describe the greatness of the man, not only as a musician, but as well as a humorous, gentle and caring human being. I have never met a man with such an appetite and love for life, a generous and always supportive gentleman. Musically there were no rhythms this drummer extraordinaire couldn't find within himself and/or a song; having been the driving force on numerous recordings of all genres of music, always serving the composition and performance, never putting himself forward when it wasn't his time. I met Paolo the first time in 1997, when I made his first album ''Mbara Boom' available internationally after its initial Norwegian release. We stayed in touch after that, me as well working his amazing box set 'Very Much Alive', a series of live recordings in a trio format with Terje Rypdal on guitar, Ståle Storløkken on keyboards and special guest appearances by bassist Marius Reksjø, Bugge Wesseltoft on keyboards, Jonas Lønnå for Sounds, Vinyl and samples and trumpeter Palle Mikkelborg, released on Jazzland Recordings in 2010. By this time, he was already the drummer in a trio with saxophonist Tommy Smith and bass legend Arild Andersen, which released three critically acclaimed recordings on ECM. Despite his ongoing battle with cancer, Paolo tireless toured with the trio and found time to record and produce more of his own music.

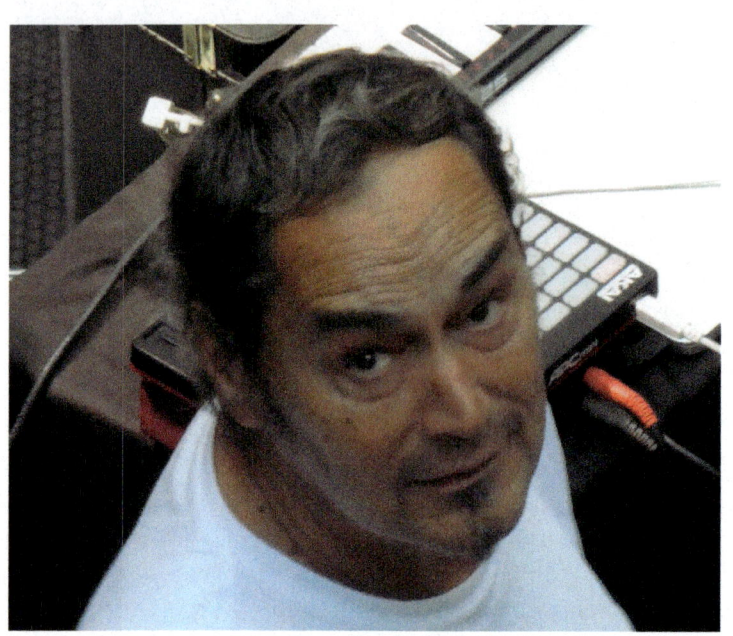

Paolo Vinaccia, 1954 – 2019

The touching and heartfelt music of 'Dommedag Ifølge Paulus', composed by Paolo with Audun Aschim Steffensen, is a document of his love for life, a reminder of the struggle of many people with this illness and a prayer for all of them. Performed with the Norske Solistkor under Grete Pedersen and Eivind Aarset on guitar next to Paolo on percussion, this recording and video is a lasting reminder of a great composer and performer.

I feel honoured that Paolo called me his friend, that we had a musical connection and one as human being. In 2018 Yolanda and I travelled with Paolo and his wife Trude to the festival Jazz at Bran Castle in Rumania, as Paolo was helping with the program of the festival. We had some truly wonderful days together, enjoying each other's company and the music on offer, good food and wine. With his smile and easy-going attitude, his willingness to help, Paolo made everyone relax. Over the last half year, he sent me some music he had worked on and mixed over the last few months. First a recording with Makoto Ozone, Tommy Smith and Arild Anderson, recorded and titled' Live in Japan' and wonderful, an extension of the ECM trio with pianist Ozone and immaculate as a recording. The other one was a WAV master of a live concert in Arendal with Bugge Wesseltoft and bassist Shri, an amazing musical adventure, with space for improvisations, light and driving rhythms and magical communication between all three musicians. Hopefully these recordings will be made available once. His legendary status as one of Europe's most important drummers will last forever and for those who met him, he will be an unforgettable person, who has touched them with his kindness and all-embracing humanity.

The loss of friends, family members, important musicians is always difficult to deal with and hard to move on from … beside Paolo, the music world also lost in the following few weeks: Karlheinz Miklin, the amazing Austrian saxophonist and flautist, whose musical expeditions reached as far as Argentina and Brazil and who was a respected and loved educator. Miklin was the first jazz musician I ever signed, and we released three recordings together between 1986 and 1989, classics of European Jazz like 'Echoes of Ilyria', which was re-issued in 2001. Charlie, as we called him, had played at the `miles smiles' jazz café many times and had been a very close friend of Rainer, with whom I founded the JazzLive magazine.

It feels sometimes out of place to say 'the show must go on', but it is the harsh reality, as exactly that will happen and so, we went out to see and hear local sax player and singer Antonio Lizana with top pianist Arturo O'Farrill plus bassist Yarel Hernandez and drummer Shayan Fathi at the Bogui Jazz Club in central Madrid. Three times Grammy winner O'Farrill is a powerful pianist with incredible technique, and he felt straight at home in Lizana's flamenco infused compositions, with Fathi and Hernandez pushing the two soloists into amazing performances. Lizana showed what an incredible sax player he is and what control and emotional power he has as a singer; O'Farrill got the audience going with fast and melodic soli and beautiful support of Lizana's voice. A sensational combination of international talent.

If I remembered correctly, the 2019 festival was probably my 25th time at the North Sea Jazz Festival and as always it was difficult to make sure that Yolanda and myself could see and hear all the artists and music we wanted. We started the Friday with a backstage visit to John Zorn's Bagatelles Marathon, a 4-hour event of adventurous music, featuring many wonderful artists, including Julian Lage and John Medeski, whom I came to say "Hi" to. Then off to Rymden, the amazing trio of Bugge Wesseltoft on piano and keyboards, Dan Berglund on bass and Magnus Öström on drums. Their set was modern jazz with rock elements, ambient sounds and groovy moments. Impressive ensemble-play as well as outstanding individual performances made this concert one of the highlights of the festival for me. The repertoire was mainly from their first album, but has developed a lot during their extensive tour and was more open for improvisation and collective excursions by then.

2019, NSJF Bugge Wesseltoft

Next on was James Brandon Lewis, the saxophonist with whom I did two albums on OKeh and who came with his new group to present the music of his latest album 'An Unruly Manifesto'. In the group he had the trusted sidemen from his trio, Luke Stewart on bass and Warren 'Trae' Crudup III on drums, plus the amazing Jaimie Branch on trumpet and the equally incredible Ava Mendoza on guitar. James Brandon is a very powerful and fiery player, exploring with his group the melodic side of free jazz – always open to improvise and lead the group to new musical territory, but never without a melodic anchor. His sidemen and -women were some of the best young musicians around and perfect to bring his compositions to life. Powerful next to Lewis were Branch with some incredible soli and Mendoza with a heavy guitar display, fitting perfectly into the overall sound. Challenging, wild and wonderful!

Saturday we had arranged to meet up with Yolanda´s Dutch friend Nicole and her husband Gerry and together started the evening with beauty in sound: Becca Stevens, Camila Meza and Lizz Wright, together with the Dutch Metropole Orkest, under Miho Hazama performing songs from all three singers' latest recordings. Camila Meza started proceedings with a song from 'Ambar' her latest album and her vocal delivery and guitar skills were impressive. Then the two other ladies joined to perform 'Old Man' with Lizz Wright. This song came from her album 'Dreaming Wide Awake' and 'Grace', the title song of her latest recording, were sublime and Wright sang her heart out … Becca performed a few songs from her album 'Regina', especially 'Mercury' stood out here. Meza did another 2 songs from 'Ambar' singing during her performances in English, Portuguese and Spanish and adding some colourful guitar to the rest of the concert. What a great and emotional tribute to the art of song by three very different and exceptional vocalists. Next on was Dee Dee Bridgewater, revisiting her 2005 Emarcy album 'J'ai Deux Amours', with the original band of that recording, featuring Marc Berthoumieux on accordion, Louis Winsberg on guitar, Ira Coleman, her musical director on this project, on bass and Minino Garay on drums. Dee Dee is such a force of nature, such an energetic performer, that it really doesn't matter what she does, as she will always give 100 % … and this show was not different: her singing immaculate, the communication with her musicians perfect and the stories in between excellent – and the audience had a wonderful time ... and so had we hearing this repertoire again after so many years. Songs like 'La Mer (Beyond The Sea)' or 'Mon

Homme (My Man)' sounded fresh and done in two languages more interesting and 'Ne Me Quitte Pas' or 'Avec Le Temps' were done brilliantly and touching.

This was the night of seeing and hearing good friends, as next on was Michel Camilo with the horns of the Dutch New Cool Collective performing music from Camilo's new big band album 'Essence'. The horns of NCC, under Camilo's direction, grooved amazingly and got all the Latin rhythms and fireworks going throughout a burning set, that included Camilo classics as well as lesser-known compositions like the wonderful 'Mongo's Blues'. And hanging with Michel and Sandra afterwards was as much fun as always.

Sunday had a slow, but beautiful start with Abdullah Ibrahim & Ekaya, performing new music from the recently released album 'The Balance'. Opening his show with a gorgeous piano solo which had a taste of South Africa in it, the band then got into his new compositions, which seem to be influenced by Duke Ellington's jazz writing. Beautiful melodies perfectly performed, swinging or grooving or balladesque. He surely got the balance right! Off to hear a bit of Kamasi Washington then, who performed to a capacity crowd in the big Maas Hall. Unfortunately, the sound in the venue was so bad, that all one could hear were the two bass drums and the bass, swallowing up the rest of the band. Pity, as the band seemed to really get into their version of 'Truth', a multi-layered melodically interesting piece, but the finer side of the music was simply drowned in the bad mix. So, we left ….

Next on was Chick Corea with his Spanish Heart Band featuring Jorge Pardo on saxophone and flute, Michael Rodriguez on trumpet, Steve Davis on trombone, Niño Josele on guitar, Carlitos Del Puerto on bass, Marcus Gilmore on drums and dancer Nino de los Reyes. 'Antidote' was the new album and it provided most of the repertoire for the concert, with Chick and the band in incredible form – Josele with some impressive solo guitar work, Jorge Pardo especially on the sax and dancer De los Reyes with astonishing energy and movements. The band paid with the song 'Zyryab' a tribute to the great Paco de Lucia, with whom Chick and of course Jorge and Josele had worked for many years. Overall, a wonderful concert, with a clear and well-balanced sound and outstanding performances from all musicians. Chick never failed to impress!

2019, NSJF, Chick Corea's Spanish Heart Band

Then we listened a bit to artist in residence Robert Glasper and his tribute to Miles Davis, 'Everything Is Beautiful', featuring the wonderful singer Ledisi. Music from and in the spirit of Miles – you couldn't go wrong with that! But, as I wanted to see Still Dreaming, I rushed to get to the next stage to hear them perform. Joshua Redman's tribute to the band Old And New Dreams featured Ron Miles on trumpet, Scott Colley on bass and now Dave King on drums, replacing Brian Blade. The music was a great mix of captivating originals and music Old And New Dreams used to play – mainly Ornette Coleman's compositions. King brought a different rhythm concept to the band, more rooted and so pushing the other guys to new highs. Redman and Miles communicating wonderfully and Colley keeping it all together. A great band, amazing musicianship and the perfect way to end that year's North Sea Jazz Festival!!!

After that I went to Berlin for some final meetings, had a dinner with my friend Christian Kellersmann and took the chance as well to see GURLS, the wonderful group featuring Ellen Andrea Wang, with whom I had met before the show. I had spoken to Ellen Andrea for a few months to possibly sign her next project to OKeh, but then had to let her know that this wasn't an option anymore, as Sony just had let me go and I didn't expect them to continue producing jazz records, which my meetings with Sony in Berlin confirmed. I told Ellen that, once her album would be ready, I would gladly help her to find a label, which she was happy about. She just didn't want to sign again in Norway, as she needed someone with a bigger perspective. The Gurls show that evening was great and their 45-minute set too drew mainly from their first record. The power of the group lies in the extremely different personalities, their impressive understanding and their musicality. Hanna Paulsberg is a controlled and powerful sax player, Rohey an incredible singer with astonishing technique and a cool sense of humour when performing and Wang is a delicate and wonderful bass player, with a deep sense for melody and a great singer to add a different voice to the songs. The combination is captivating and full of surprises and fun. Songs about boys, presented with a smile and amazing musicianship.

Madrid in July is a city full of music – various festivals and events are held, and incredible music heard. One of these series of concerts are the Noches Del Botanico, which had on the night of July 22nd José James and Melody Gardot on the program. José went out first, at 9 pm and at 35 degrees Celsius and he still managed to make everyone move. His unique mix of soul, R&B, jazz with a shot of funk and rock made us forget the heat. The band, consisting of James on vocal and guitar, Marcus Machado on guitar, Aneesa Almusawwir on electric bass and vocals and Aaron Steele on drums was much more funk and rock oriented than previous groups which played his wonderful tribute to Bill Withers, 'Leon On Me', but sounded fabulous to me. Machado with an incredible solo in typical Hendrix-style, including playing the guitar with his teeth, and the driving bass and hard-hitting drums made this heavier than the previous shows I have seen, but musically extremely interesting. Jose's singing was immaculate and powerful as ever and he seemed to have a lot of fun, including running into the audience and singing from between his fans.

Melody Gardot came with a group that included a string quartet supported her performing songs from her catalogue and a few new compositions. Gone is the heavy jazz band with powerful brass; this was soft, wonderful arranged music to listen to and to fall into. *"More feminine"* as she said to me after the concert. Her band was extremely well picked and got the best of their leader. Melody on vocals, piano and guitar was performing with Mitchell Long on guitar, Sam Minai on bass, Charles Staab on drums, Artyom Manukyan on cello, Astghik Gazhoyan, Astghik Vartanyan and Gohar Papayan on violin and they created some wonderful and magic moments with songs like 'Who Will Comfort Me?', 'Our Love Is Easy' and especially 'Morning Sun', which turned into a 10-minute prayer-like beauty of a song – touching and full of emotions! The new songs felt right at place within her compositions and sounded very promising, as well as her English rendition, partly spoken, partly sung, of the poem 'Caminante No Hay Camino' by Antonio Machado. The show ended long past midnight and then she came out to sign CD's and LPs. The audience loved her for both!

Lyon, France, July 27th – Les Nuits de Fourviere: double bill of Richard Bona and Dhafer Youssef. Dhafer, being a long-time friend, invited me to come and have a chat and see the show, which I gladly did. Bona opened the evening with a captivating show with Spanish Flamenco musicians (of which I didn't see and hear much but had seen a few years back in Madrid) and then Dhafer got to the stage. His latest release on a small French indie label, 'Sounds of Mirrors' gave the repertoire for this show, performed with Youssef on the oud and vocals, Eivind Aarseth on guitar, Raffaele Casarano on sax, Nicolas Viccaro on drums and Adriano Dd on percussion. During the second song heavy rain began to fall, after an initial drizzle, but the almost full arena saw not many people leaving, so much were they under the spell of his voice and music. His compositions are a mix of Arabic tradition with jazz and the band went through the songs with lots of energy and emotions. The ballads were extremely touching, and the melodies keep coming back in your mind. Eivind Aarseth had been playing with Dhafer for many years then and his ideas, sounds and overall play was perfect together with Youssef's voice and oud – Casarano fitted wonderfully into the musical mix, soaring over the beats and joining the voice as if they were one – drums and percussion were driving the music with power and finesse and Dhafer's voice was pure and magic in many ways – in Lyon he made the audience smile and forget the rain. I was truly happy to have been there to hear this show.

2019, Eivind Aarset

We talked a bit about future plans and what to do with the recordings he had made the year before with Dave Holland and Herbie Hancock, as well as Vinnie, Marcus and Ambrose, which needed to be mixed and put into a proper sequence. He was in no rush to do so and I agreed – music is ready, when it is ready: you can't force it.

Hannah came to visit in August and we did another little trip into the surroundings of Madrid, this time to Pedraza, a beautiful and old, small village, which is great to walk around and check the castle and the very good local food. Hannah knew Madrid pretty well by then, so these little trips were a welcome change of scenery. We heard a bit about the job she was doing and how living with Oliver was for her. I just love it, when she is around and we can chat or just go for a walk.
A bit later in August we had Anders Chan-Tidemann and his wife Stephanie in town and went out for a really nice meal at Casa Alberto. I know Anders since the times he was the road manager for Joe Henderson and then we crossed paths again later when he had his own management and agency company, looking after Kurt Rosenwinkel and others. He is a great guy and fun to have around and full of great stories about artists and managers. Whenever I come to New York for Jazz Connect or Winter jazz I try to hook up with him and I was glad that he called while being in town to have a bit of a chat and some Spanish Vermouth together.

Sound Out was a professional development and mentoring platform for creative musicians who challenge normal categorisation and was produced by Martel Ollerenshaw as an initiative of the Europe Jazz Network. The first event took place in Sokolowsko, Poland from 25th to 31st of August 2019 and had as *"objective to eradicate limiting factors which hold the artists back, such as insufficient industry awareness, lack of access to relationships within the music industry, limited cross border activities and communication".* The musicians taking part in this first edition of Sound Out were: Aviva Endean – clarinet, sound artist, performance creator (Australia) / Benedikt Wieland – electric bass, electronics, composition (Switzerland) / Inge Thomson – vocals, accordion, electronics (Scotland) / Joanna Duda – piano, electronics, composition (Poland) / Karolina Rec – cello, vocals, electronics, composition (Poland) / Lucia Cadotsch – vocals, composition (Switzerland) / Morris Kliphuis – horn, composition (Netherlands) and Ramon Landolt – synths, composition (Switzerland). Throughout the week the musicians had various workshops and guest speakers coming from all over Europe to participate and share their knowledge with this group of exciting artists. I had the pleasure of sharing a session on the recorded music business with my friend and Edition Records founder Dave Stapleton, which I thought was one of the best I had ever done, as the questions of the group were well thought through and challenging. This session was followed by 20-minute face-to-face meetings and discussions, which touched on some of the individual needs and questions the musicians had. Coming in on the end of the week, it was interesting to see how much the eight musicians had bonded and grown into a group, open to communicate within the group and beyond. While preparing for the session and listening to music from all participants, I was overwhelmed with the individual strength of each artist and the music and performances they created. The musical diversity within the group ranged from folk, to electronics, to jazz, to free improvisations and included other art forms in wonderful collaborations. Especially the various projects by singer Cadotsch were to my liking. When invited I was a bit surprised having to go to a small village in the middle of nowhere in Poland … but once there I came to understand why Sokolowsko was the perfect place for this kind of event: The local hosts were the Contemporary Art Foundation, headed by Bozenna Biskupska, Zuzanna Fogtt and Gerard Lebik, which were responsible for many activities in the village, including art festivals, exhibitions and restoring the old Sanatorium into a wonderful place for the arts. Sokolowsko is also home of the Krzysztof Kieślowski film festival and his archive and through the work of the foundation has become a small island for the arts in an ever more conservative and right-wing Poland. The first Edition of Sound Out felt to me an overwhelming success and I hope that many other editions would follow … there are many deserving artists out there and many experienced people working in the arts, willing to pass on some knowledge.

2019, Sound Out, Sokolowsko, photo courtesy of Sound Out

We took a few days off to have a short break with our friends José and Inma, walking and talking and eating excellent food. The two of them are constant travellers, knowing all regions of Spain very well and always have a great recommendation for a restaurant or hotel and they are both really nice people, with José being an eclectic music lover, which includes jazz as well. Then I went to London for the weekend to see Hannah and stay at her new flat in Maida Vale. We had a wonderful walk through the old neighbourhood and a great chat and she showed me where she was working and told me how much she enjoyed that new challenge. And of course, we had as well a great dinner with Oliver and visited a pub for a few drinks together.

I then had a meeting with Burkhard Hopper and AIR management and booking, talking about the possibility to join them in some function in the near future. The idea was to develop projects and concepts for the summer festivals – exclusive packages that we would sell to them, who always wanted something new, but with name power. The meeting went well and when I got home, I wrote to Burkhard that I was interested and we should move this further, while attaching a few ideas already. With the end of September, the OKeh / Sony deal was finished and looking around for a new challenge started in earnest and meeting Burkhard was a promising beginning. I spoke to many labels and managers, some with ideas, others with projects, but none with a fixed job. But I had still a bit of time. Meanwhile I was helping my OKeh acts, of which only Theo Croker seemed to remain with Sony, to find new homes by talking to labels and when interest was signalled to get them in touch with each other.

The Bad Plus signed with Edition Records and released 'Activate Infinity' in October that year. Jeff Ballard's amazing new album 'Fairground', which I helped to sequence (and I told Jeff, a drummer, that drum soli are for live shows but not for albums … and he took it off and the song was much tighter and more captivating for it), came out on Edition and I opened the door for David there to sign Kurt Elling as well.

Early October Yolanda and I went to Cadiz again, stayed as usual in the Hotel Senator and walked around the city a lot. This time we did a little boat trip to Rota and had a wonderful meal there. In Cadiz we discovered a new restaurant we really liked: La Curiosidad De Mauro Barreiro, which had some excellent and inventive food, plus a great wine list. Next to El Faro, this was the best we had eaten in Cadiz.

2019, Cadiz sunset

I saw singer and multi-instrumentalist Julia Biel in a great and diverse show when back in Madrid, showcasing her song writing and performance talents with a real good band behind her. Then it was the trio of Javier Colina / Josemi Carmona / Bandolero, known as well as the *De Cerca Trio*, which performed at the AC Hotel Recoletos, as part of a Colina residence. Both records of the trio are fantastic in the way they mix jazz and flamenco and the same is true for their shows … from Carmona compositions to flamenco and jazz standards they played everything in their own special way. They get better and better and this time their version of 'Moon River' was absolutely divine.

The last gig in October I went to was Sara Gazarek, who came for the first time to Spain for five concerts, three of them in Madrid's Café Central, where I saw her performing with Julian Shore on piano, Alex Boneham on double bass and Ferenc Nemeth on drums. Ferenc, who is a friend of Dhafer and had been at the wedding in Tunisia we attended, was surprised and happy to see me there. Gazarek is an immaculate singer with incredible control and technique and gave all chosen material her own stamp – as on the night the audience could hear her doing so with compositions from the Beatles, Brad Mehldau, Miles and many others, as well as her own songs. Her truly wonderful album 'Thirsty Ghost' provided most of the material, exceptionally performed by her band. Outstanding on the night her own 'Easy Love', co-written with Larry Goldings and a very powerful and touching rendition of Leonard Cohen's 'Hallelujah'.

2019 was as well the year we saw again deadly terrorist attacks around the world: from Christchurch in New Zealand to Sri Lanka and more fatal shootings in the USA and Mexico. The cowardly false heroism of the terrorists is hard to understand and even more difficult to prevent. The constant shootings in the US are a disgrace for a nation where gun purchase and use has spiralled out of control and no politician has the guts to take on the gun industry and change the laws. Same sex marriage finally became legal in Austria, while Vladimir Putin signed a law to better 'monitor' the internet. The last of the most successful car of all time, the Volkswagen Beetle, was produced in a factory in Mexico and Boris Johnson became the Prime Minister of the UK. At least he then had to sort out the Brexit, for which he was partly responsible. And unfortunately, for reasons of commercialisation, the rainforest in Brazil was allowed to burn down and be destroyed at a pace unseen so far, despite international protests.

November – as in the last few years, was the time for the International Jazz Festival in Madrid, which that year started on October 28th and ran until November 30th … and the first show I attended was Charles Tolliver presenting 'Paper Man @ 50'. The original album featured besides the leader and trumpeter Tolliver, Herbie Hancock, Gary Bartz, Ron Carter and Joe Chambers and was recorded at Town Sound Studios, Englewood, New Jersey on 2nd July 1968. The modern versions of these compositions were performed by Tolliver and Jesse Davis on alto sax, Keith Brown on piano, Buster Williams on bass and Lennie White on drums. Tolliver's music sounded modern and fresh and his and everyone else's playing was impressive and captivating. Brown and Davis were wonderful soloists next to Tolliver and his amazing rhythm section.
The second gig I attended was that of young saxophonist Nubya Garcia, whom I had seen before in Rotterdam and had enjoyed her show. This one was as good as the first I saw, and she and her band were giving the mostly standing Madrid audience in a packed Conde Duque groovy jazz to dance to. Excellent musicians who gave her the support and groove to improvise freely and with verve and lots of ideas. This was modern and adventurous jazz, deeply rooted in the tradition of Coltrane or Sanders. Powerful, groovy and melodic improvised music that reached a younger audience.
After these two great shows, the next gig for me was one of top Fusion: guitarist Mike Stern with keyboarder Jeff Lorber, Jimmy Haslip on bass and top drummer Dennis Chambers, with special guest guitarist Leni Stern rounding up the impressive line-up. Most of the repertoire came from their then latest album 'Eleven' and were compositions by Stern and Lorber – powerful rock and funk influenced melodic pieces, which gave lots of space for Mike and Jeff to improvise and both musicians delivered some extraordinary soli on their respective instruments. Stern, whom I first saw with Miles Davis in 1982, still had the same clear sound on his guitar and is surely one of the best guitarists of our time. His rock, jazz and blues informed playing was delivered with passion and fire … his wife Leni added some wonderful playing herself and touched everyone with a heartfelt vocal performance in the opening song. Lorber as well showed why he is one of the leading keyboard players and a master of the genre. Sidemen Haslip and Chambers drove the two main guys to amazing heights.

The concert of American singer Stacey Kent and her excellent band, featuring Jim Tomlinson on saxes and flutes, Graham Harvey on piano and fender rhodes, Jeremy Brown on bass and Joah Morrison on bass was next for us and one I was looking forward to, as I like the lush and relaxed way this amazing singer is performing. Her mix of repertoire ranged from originals (written by Tomlinson, her husband and musical director) via standards to some classy Brazilian repertoire and a French song. Whether she sang in English or French or Portuguese, she made the songs work and the audience gladly went with her on this rewarding musical journey. Kent's vocal control was outstanding and her delivery full of emotions. Tomlinson kept the band tight behind her and added some top improvisations to the mix. Harvey was an attentive and impressively supporting pianist, whose soli were as well serving the songs and were delicate and beautiful.

On November 19th it was trumpet star Christian Scott aTunde Adjuah, who performed with his stellar band in Madrid's Teatro Fernán Gómez. At only 36 years of age, Scott was already a veteran leading his own bands, having started around 15 years earlier, but had with this band probably the best so far, as his sidemen for this tour in Europe were alto sax player Logan Richardson, pianist Lawrence Fields, bass player Max Mucha, drummer Corey Fonville and percussionist Weedie Braiham and they made Scott's compositions groove and swing and ... whatever the song needed! Scott couldn't hide that he comes from New Orleans, as the rhythms gave it away, but then his music, a mix of jazz in the past, present and future, needs that groove. He bowed to Miles Davis with a powerful rendition of 'Guinnevere' in which Richardson and Scott performed impressively, played music from his own recordings as well as a stunningly beautiful new composition titled 'Songs she has never heard'. Beside the outstanding improvisations by Scott, especially Richardson and Fields impressed with their abilities and imagination. Polish bass player Mucha and Braiham and Fonville were exceptional in keeping the guys going.

2019, Christian Scott in action

Three days later it was time to go and hear John Scofield in a duo setting with singer and pianist Jon Cleary, with whom John recorded his 2009 album 'Piety Street' together with the cream of New Orleans' musicians; an album I released at the time on Emarcy Records. Scofield and New Orleans resident Cleary performed repertoire that had its roots in the Crescent City and was a mix of well-known songs as well as compositions of lesser-known musicians. Cleary is a wonderful pianist in the New Orleans tradition and an emotional singer, who brought life into these songs. Scofield in this set-up is not only an outstanding soloist but supported Cleary perfectly and brought out the essence of the songs. His solo in 'Fever' was out of this world, disjointed to a degree, but making total musical sense. Same has to be said for Cleary's piano solo in 'My Baby Is In Love With Another Man':

powerful and captivating. Their performance of 'Stardust' was another highlight of the gig, as well as a beautiful rendition of 'Talk To Me', another gem unearthed by Cleary. One could feel the fun the guys had playing as a duo and performing this repertoire – Scofield was his usual magnificent self and Cleary right up there with him. An outstanding concert in many ways, that got the packed house going right from the start. Uplifting and fun, rough and touching - a wonderful show by two great artists! I went out with the two guys for dinner and we had a great chat, before they had to go back to the likewise sold-out second show of the night.

2019, Selfie with John Scofield, Madrid

I hadn't seen Patricia Barber in a long while and therefore was curious about her concert in Madrid on November 23rd, because I hadn't heard her latest album 'Higher', from which most of the repertoire of the performance came. Barber is a singer of songs mixing jazz and pop and soul into something unique and as these are her own compositions and lyrics in most cases, she therefore brings emotional content directly into the pieces. She is moreover an accomplished pianist, in Madrid supported by Larry Kohut on bass and Jon Deitemyer on drums. Barber is a wonderful singer with unusual phrasing that makes her music unique and individual. Beside her own compositions she performed a captivating version of 'The In Crowd', as well as an encore 'You Are My Sunshine', which left the audience asking for more. Her sidemen were solid and incredible in reacting to all nuances and changes of her piano playing and together formed a special trio, instrumental or when Patricia was singing. It is a kind gesture to have your sidemen perform soli within the show ... but whether it is necessary to have a bass and/or drum solo in every song, in my opinion, is debatable. In most cases, it stretches the song unnecessary and by that losing intensity and the essence of the composition. Nevertheless, a performance of top quality and musicianship.

2019, The Bad Plus in Madrid

The Bad Plus were next in town on November 26th, performing at the packed to capacity Clamores Club. They opened the concert with two compositions by bass player Reid Anderson from their 2nd album, 2003's 'These Are The Vistas', 'Everywhere You Turn' and 'Big Eater', before running through some of their back catalogue, focusing on the first and second album of the new Plus, 'Never Stop II' and then recently released 'Activate Infinity'. What makes the Bad Plus so special is their quirkiness, their rhythmic power and openness to explore the essence of any song they perform. They can fall from a swinging moment easily into a free exploration of a theme, only to go back to a simple and stunning melody. Pianist Orrin Evans fits like a glove into the concept and the music mainly composed by Anderson and drummer Dave King, even so two of Evans' contributions to the evening as a composer, 'Commitment' and 'The Red Door' were amazing and touching. All three musicians had their incredible moments in the spotlight, but their tightness as a trio was simply astonishing and at times got the audience into shouts of wonder and encouragement. I have been working with the group(s) for almost 15 years and never heard/seen a show that didn't get me.

Unknowingly we kept the best for last: Norwegian singer and occasional pianist and friend for many years, Rebekka Bakken, performed a powerful and emotional show, bending genres and delivered a concert of pure class at the Teatro Fernan Gomes. Rebekka is an amazing singer, with a fantastic range and total control of her voice – she can be the rock singer one moment, a delicate and emotional singer of ballads next and all seems natural and easy. Her band, consisting of Kjetil Bjerkestrand on organ and piano, Johan Lindstroem on guitars, Tor Egil Kreken on bass and drummers Rune Arnesen and Pal Hausken, was for me the best she ever had and followed responsively each of her musical steps, pushing her, holding back when needed and, together with her, formed a compact unit, having fun playing together. There was not a dull moment throughout the 90-minute concert, which mainly was made up from repertoire of her 2018 album 'Things You Leave Behind'. Outstanding her compositions and the way this band treated them – her vocal delivery on songs like 'True North', 'Closer' and on her cover of 'Hotel St. Pauli' was outstanding and full of emotions and brought a few tears to the eyes of the audience. Other highlights from earlier albums included her compositions 'Mina's Dream', a wonderful 'Powder Room Collapse' and the covers 'Little Drop Of Poison' from her Tom Waits album with the same title, plus 'Ghost In This House', which was absolutely beautiful and touching.

2019, Rebekka Bakken and band, Madrid

Her take of the Norwegian church song 'Korset Vil Jeg Aldri Svike' went from a captivating acapella song into a piece of psychedelic and spaced-out music, before returning to the simplicity of the beginnings. Bakken was at the top of her game, told stories that matter in her songs and performed them with a band that fully understood who she is as a musician and singer. Yolanda and I had lunch with the guys the day after and really had a lot of fun and some beautiful time with them and Rebekka.

In the last few months the music world lost many great and important artists, some of them I had the pleasure to see perform or work with: Ginger Baker, the outstanding rock and jazz drummer of his generation I saw at the Cream reunion concerts in London in 2005 and once before many years back with his Airforce band; Joseph Jarman, member of the Art Ensemble Of Chicago, which I had seen many times in Austria; Jacques Loussier, whose 'Play Bach' recordings were some of my fathers most played jazz albums at home; Joao Gilberto, whom I saw in Umbria joining Caetano Veloso on stage and the two then just created some musical magic; Pianist Milcho Leviev I heard first through his two duo recordings with Dave Holland, but as well liked his solo or group recordings. He was one of Europe's most underrated, but best, pianists. Producer Gerry Teekens I met a few times at North Sea Jazz and liked his enthusiasm for jazz, which he brought to his wonderful label Criss Cross and all its productions. Jan Erik Kongshaug was not only one of the best sound engineers of all time, but as well a warm and gentle human being. I had the pleasure meeting him and working with him on a few occasions and always enjoyed his company and professionalism.

We saw in the movies the amazing 'Parasite' by Bong Joon-ho, 'Once Upon A Time In Hollywood' by Quentin Tarantino, which was interesting and well done and greatly acted and '1917' by Sam Mendes, which was a typical English war film and nothing spectacular or new. I read the second part of Ketil's biography, this time about his life in the 70's and settling in the jazz world to a degree, but still as well having a foot in the classical scene. Musical and spiritual influences are laid bare, as well as internal struggles of which way to go artistically. A truly honest and thought-provoking book.

My favourite albums of the year, beside my two OKeh releases, were:
Betty Carter – The Music Never Stops

Haftor Medboe / Jacob Karlson   EP
Kevin Hays / Lionel Loueke – Hope
Dave Holland / Zakir Hussain / Chris Potter – Good Hope
James Brandon Lewis – An Unruly Manifesto
Joanna Wallfisch – Far Away From Any Place Called Home
Ketil Bjørnstad – The World I Used To Know
Michael Leonhart Orchestra – Suite Extracts, Vol. 1
Rymden – Reflections & Odysseys
Zela Margossian – Transition

In December news broke that a novel coronavirus was identified in Wuhan, China. The Chinese authorities spoke about a highly infectious virus that was transferred via airborne droplets and ordered a lockdown in Wuhan and other cities, but failed to contain the outbreak and it quickly spread to other parts of mainland China and around the world.

Mid December my nephew Patrick and his wife Avi, plus the kids Sorlannguaq and Pipaluk, came to visit us in Madrid. We had some great food at home and at Paco's, they visited a fun fair and we showed them around town a bit. And, as true Real Madrid fans, they went on a tour of the stadium. Patrick's teenage son really liked the city and asked to come back the following year. It is always great to see family, especially the one that lives far away, as these guys, who are based in Greenland.

2019, with Pipaluk, Patrick, Avi and Sorlannguaq

We decided to travel again for Christmas with Maria and picked Cadiz, as Maria hadn't been there for a while. We just had, but going to this place again was no problem at all. We booked a restaurant for the dinner on Christmas Eve and generally had a good time there in the warmer south of Spain. And of course, we visited our favourite restaurants there again. The day before New Year's Eve we had a lunch with Cecilie and Yngve and their friends, who had come to Madrid, as well as Alex and Estefania and by accident, Javier and Luci were actually eating in the same place. Great to have such fun company. We let the year end with a nice meal at home, celebrating the new year with Maria and our Mexican friend Claudia, who came to visit us for a few days.

2020

January started differently in 2020, as I didn't go to New York for the Jazz Connect Conference nor Winter Jazz. In the last few years Sony would have covered the costs for that trip and I didn't see a major reason to spend around $ 2000, as I didn't have any important meetings concerning my future lined up. Discussions were ongoing with several people, but nothing had been concreted yet. Burkhard had got back to me to tell me to wait a bit as they were finalising the books for year-end and then we would talk again. Sten had some ideas for Jazzland, but on a more project by project basis and the same was true for Dave at Edition Records. While the WHO declared the spread of the Covid 19 virus a Public Health Emergency Of International Concern, we brought Maria to the hospital with pneumonia or so we were told. Thankfully, after two weeks we could take her home again, weak, but ok.

In my blog I wrote the following: *"The start of 2020 is a good reason to have a look back into the roaring 1920's ... a period known, beside other names, as the Jazz Age. Post WW I the global economy was showing constant growth and modernity, the word for this time, brought the radio, movies and cars. Cities like Berlin, London, Paris, Sydney, Los Angeles, New York and Chicago had the cultural edge. The period became known for Prohibition, Art Deco, the Harlem Renaissance, women liberation and getting voting rights in many countries, Freud and his theories, to name just a few major developments. The name Jazz Age is definitely correct as in these times some of the most important jazz recordings of all time were made – above all the eternal Louis Armstrong Hot Five and Hot Seven recordings on OKeh, but as well the music by Bix Beiderbecke, Duke Ellington, Sydney Bechet, King Oliver, Jelly Roll Morton, and and and ... Blues recordings became hits in the US and the first country songs were recorded as well ... labels like OKeh, Black Swan, Broome, ARTo, Vocalion, Ajax and many others, as well as the big ones: Victor and Columbia were driving this new musical output. But the 1920's ended with a bang: Black Tuesday on Wall Street in New York on October 29th, 1929, the result of the London Stock Exchange crash from September 20, which send uncertainty into global stock markets and the years of speculation came to a tragic end that led into the Great Depression of the following years, culminating in WW II. So how does that compare with the start of our 2020's? Different set of problems ... mostly environmental, which, if done right, could as well lead to an upswing in a currently slow growth economy. On the other hand, modernity could be a good word for our times as well ... all going into one gadget that can do everything: phone, TV set, camera, satellite navigation system, medical equipment, ... Politically the move to the right looks like it will continue globally – a scenario in which jazz, for obvious reasons, usually thrives. Only time will tell if these years will yield everlasting new recordings as well. And let's see if mankind learned enough to avoid another Black Tuesday ... but the bubble of companies like Spotify, Uber, etc. which hardly ever made a profit (if at all) and are valued at billions of dollars might need to be addressed in some form at some time. For me it looks like the 2020's are neither going to be roaring nor boring!!"*

Sadly 2020 started with the loss of a few very important jazz musicians ... Jimmy Heath – 'Little Bird' was still playing aged 93; he had been a true jazz giant who mentored generations of musicians and was a wonderful human being.
Claudio Roditi – Brazilian jazz trumpet player with a distinguished career in the US and beyond and European jazz legend, pianist and keyboarder Wolfgang Dauner, whom I had the pleasure to meet a few times. I first heard of him as a player with saxophonist Hans Koller, then through his own recordings for MPS and later the Mood label, which he co-founded in 1977 with Albert Mangelsdorff, Volker Kriegel and others. Beautiful his solo piano albums and of course his work in the powerful United Jazz+Rock Ensemble, whose first album 'Live Im Schützenhaus' is still one of the

top selling jazz recordings of all time in Germany. When I was executive producer for the 1988 Konstantin Wecker album 'Wieder Dahaom – Live in Wien und Graz', Dauner was in the band that recorded these concerts and we had some fun doing the gigs ... and spend that New Year's Eve together with Wecker in Berlin. Dauner was a leading improviser and played Avantgarde, modern jazz as well as fusion, always seeking for new sounds and ways to express himself.

A month later Covid 19 was declared the official name for the new virus and the resulting illness, which was spreading around the globe with frightening speed. While the US reached a conditional peace agreement with the Taliban and started withdrawing its troops from Afghanistan, we had invited twelve friends to our flat for a Goulash lunch, which was a lot of fun and really nice. We often had been invited over the last year by some of these guys and therefore decided to have them all over and cook a Hungarian Goulash with potato dumplings or rice. We cooked it the day before and warmed it up before the guests arrived, as then it will taste best, and they all loved it. Little did we know at the time that this would be our last meal with friends before one of the most severe Covid lockdowns in Europe.

2020, lunch with Justina, Merche, María, Antonio, Cristina, Inma, Cesar, Luis, Rosario, Jorge, Susana & Julio

On Tuesday February 24th a new trio formed by pianist Daniel Garcia Diego, bassist Pablo Martin Caminero and drummer Shayan Fathi had their first ever concert at Madrid's Café Central. The trio, billed by the venue as Trio Flamenco, sees itself as a jazz group that has its base in Flamenco and performs a complex mix of the two styles. The repertoire included compositions by Daniel as well as Pablo and Paco de Lucia, Chick Corea and others. The way the group mixed the complex rhythms of Flamenco with jazz improvisation left the audience in awe of their musicianship. The trio mainly worked as a unit, supporting as well when one of them played a solo and therefore constantly changing colours and creating an intense atmosphere. Paco de Lucia's 'Zyryab' was a firework of rhythms and explosive interactions, but the compositions by Daniel and Pablo also caught the ear of the listener for their beauty and power and when the group got into Lyle Mays 'Travels' as an encore and tribute to the late musician, respect and emotions were flowing through the performance and captivated the attentive audience. As debuts go, this was a top one.

Five Days later we had the pleasure to hear one of the longest performing small groups in European jazz: the Marcin Wasilewski Trio, which was working and recording together for 26 years then. Their communication and understanding were incredible and gave them space to constantly exchange ideas when improvising.

2020, Marcin Wasilewski Trio, Madrid

The sold-out concert in the Sala Camara of Madrid's Auditorio Nacional featured mainly Wasilewski's compositions, some known from previous recordings, as the wonderful 'Night Train with You' and 'Austin', as well as three new ones, 'Glimmer Of Hope', 'Amour Fou' and 'Passing Sorrow', which confirmed once again what a great composer Wasilewski is. These three songs would be on a forthcoming, already recorded, album and were the base of another great record by the trio. Slawomir Kurkiewicz on bass and drummer Michal Miskiewicz were outstanding and made the piano trio really sound like a group, not just three musicians playing together. They can swing, lay back in ballads and groove, as they did in the last song of the concert, Herbie Hancock's 'Actual Proof', before coming back for a touching rendition of Krzysztof Komeda's 'Lullaby' from the soundtrack to 'Rosemary's Baby' … this was wonderful melodic jazz performed on the highest level!

While not working in A&R I still thought about what it means in our times and blogged a short observation on A&R in Jazz then: *"A&R (Artists and Repertoire) used to be the core of any jazz label – being the direct work with the artists to discuss projects, song selection, side men, recording studios and special guests, producers and engineers – but that has changed a lot over the last few years. Today any artist can easily produce the record he or she wants to do and then, after the recording is done, look for a label or service provider that puts the record out physically and/or digitally. The label function therefore is less A&R oriented and more focused on distribution, marketing and promotion. At new labels like Edition Records or Ropeadope, to name just two of many, artists make license deals for their recordings and work together with the label on marketing and PR by using all social networks and traditional marketing means. These labels act more like collectors, putting together a selection of releases based on what they want on their labels … some more narrow in their musical selection process, others more open. In this climate the process of A&R in jazz seems to fall more to the team around the artist, like managers, agents and producers (in case the artist isn't self-producing), as they are in more direct contact with the musician than most labels are today. This doesn't mean that jazz labels today don't need A&R people, they do, as the discussion on future projects once an artist is licensing his/her music to a label is obviously happening, but A&R people need to be and need to know more than in the past – they have to have a knowledge on modern communication and marketing concepts, to make sure the music they get on the label gets heard. Personally, I have always tried to make the best record I could with the artist in question at any given time. Which means for me not to pressure the artist to make the record I think is the right one, but to listen to what the artist wants to do and guide and give direction to these wishes and ideas and make them happen in the best possible way. There is now obviously as well the possibility of a form of 'indie A&R', as many artists, who recorded their music do not know to which label to go with it, or how to approach a label when not having the right contacts. Such a person would not only need to know the musicians, but as well most major and indie label personnel and have contacts there to provide them with new recordings that are needing a home. If one understands the philosophy and musical direction of any label and is able to place recordings that fit within these parameters, it is a win-win situation for the label and the artist and as well for the independent music broker, as I think that describes this activity the best. I am sure we will see more indie A&R, for the lack of a better description, in the future".*

And to a degree that was already what I was doing occasionally, by getting my OKeh artists and their recordings a new home or by sequencing new recordings for the artists, as they occasionally needed someone from the outside to listen and let them know what the best sequence would be. Harpist Julie Campiche came to me with such a request and released her stunning album 'Onkalo' in early 2020 with my suggested sequence and Kurt Elling released his outstanding new album 'Secrets Are The Best Stories', featuring Danilo Perez, on Edition Records, after I introduced his manager Bryan and Dave Stapleton via email. Beside that I had found a home for the new and very impressive album by Ellen Andrea Wang, 'Closeness', at Ropeadope Records. Louis Marks there seemed to trust my taste and was always listening to what I sent him and later signed as well the new Badi Assad record 'Around The World', and Clifton Anderson's straight ahead jazz album 'Been Down This Road Before', which I helped him to sequence as well. All these records were released in the fall of 2020 and did well for the respective labels.

I had cancelled in February my subscription to the gym across the road, as I didn't make the trip often enough to justify the expenses, but wanted to continue exercise, only at home. Therefore, Yolanda and myself bought a stationary bike and a vibrating platform to be able to work out at home together. Meanwhile Italy implemented a nationwide quarantine to fight Covid 19, now officially declared a pandemic by WHO. As every year, on March 8th there were many big demonstrations planned for Women's Day, but we decided that under the circumstances we wouldn't go this year. Maria wanted to go with some neighbours, but Yolanda could convince her that with the virus going around it would be better not to go and that all the demonstrations should be cancelled anyway. A neighbour and good friend of ours, who went to the demo, was ill with Covid 19 within 10 days and a week later she had passed away. When something like that hits so close to home it was time to react. We went into voluntary confinement to protect Maria, who has some underlying health issues, which made her extremely vulnerable and ourselves on March 10th and the Spanish government declared a nationwide quarantine and confinement from March 14th, which was to last three months. Too late. By that time, due to the massive March 8th demonstrations, which for political reasons weren't cancelled, and some Champions League games of Spanish teams in England and Italy, which weren't cancelled either, the virus had spread fast in Spain.
When health becomes a political issue instead of a medical one, which was the case there and would continue to be, people will suffer or die, which is exactly what happened in Spain and in many other countries. The EU closed its external borders, but didn't have any regulated travel policy for within their borders, so the spread of the virus continued for much longer.

We had the previous year arranged for a family meeting at my brother Thomas' house, but he wrote to all of us that someone within the family of his wife Heidi had been diagnosed with cancer and they didn't think to have a party was the right thing to do. He finally told us that this person was him and that he was fighting the cancer for two years already and had been in and out of the hospital for the last few months. The doctors had decided to let him go home, as there was nothing, they could do for him anymore. He got his medicine and Heidi in addition gave him some natural remedies for his overall health, but according to the doctors he had weeks, with some luck, months, to live. After the initial shock we decided two things as a family: as money was tight for them, we would cover the costs for the additional natural medicine Heidi got for him and started a Müller Fund for that, where all brothers and sisters paid in what they could afford and our mother contributed as well and secondly, we started to skype every Friday afternoon and who ever had time would be part of it. Mom, the six kids of her and Hannah, Patrick and Alexander were part of this group and Thomas joined on days he was feeling strong enough to do so.

While being at home, we opened our windows every day at 8 pm and went out on our terrace to applaud the people working in the health service in Spain and around the world to fight the disease. All neighbours joined and it was always a special and emotional moment of saying 'Thanks', but as well, being part of a community that suffered the same fate. Gladly Yolanda and myself were used to be home together, as we had worked jointly from home for many years by then and we had an appartement big enough to go out of each other's way, when someone needed space. And we had a big enough terrace to run around there a bit and taking in some sun and fresh air. During the first most strict three months of home confinement in the EU, all our shopping was delivered to our door from the nearby supermarket or our favourite fruit shop around the corner. I left the flat only to bring the rubbish down, as you weren't even allowed to go for a walk. When going shopping later I did that always with masks and a plastic shield to protect me and the people around me. We found our rhythm, did exercise, read, listened to music, watched TV – like everyone else.

The one amazing thing about being locked in was, that people got in touch, some you hadn't heard from in ages, just checking in how you are and we did the same. Strange times indeed, but times to focus on oneself and the ones close to us and to make sure we all get through this together.

2020, the typical outfit for outside …

And of course, music was helping a lot by giving emotions and distraction, taking us to other worlds. At one point during the initial confinement, exactly on March 18th 2020, Yolanda had the idea to send out a song to our friends in Madrid to cheer them up a bit while being at home. Sting's version of 'My Funny Valentine' with Herbie Hancock was the choice and the reactions were throughout positive. Based on that, we decided to give them a song every day until the lockdown would be over. And we did, ending up with a playlist that had 61 songs, from artists from all over the world. I too compiled a corresponding playlist on Spotify, which I opened up for our friends, so they had all songs there in the correct order as well. Only five songs I didn't find on Spotify, but I found other versions by the same or another artist and used these. The final two songs were Mercedes Sosa's wonderful and fitting 'Gracias A La Vida', as well as Silje Nergaard's Norwegian version of this song 'Jeg Vill Takke Livet'. We had fun selecting a new song every day and our friends were happy to have a bit of a daily distraction as well. We called the playlist 'Canciones Del Querer' and in total it runs for over 4 hours and 30 minutes.

I had seen many artists doing concerts in that time from their homes and streaming them online, which in general was a good idea and a nice gesture to help through these difficult times, but (and this is a big BUT) these shouldn't be always for free! There are ways to have people pay for access to these streams and performances and in times when concert income was more or less zero, this was more than needed – so my advice was: Do Not Give Away Your Music For Free!!!! Especially having in mind that a 'normal' concert schedule and with that its income, most likely might not be available until the following year.

The pandemic had put a stop to all live concerts, 'jazzahead' was cancelled and there was a big question mark hanging over all the summer jazz festivals, which meant the main income source for all jazz musicians, clubs, booking agents, concert halls, festival promoters was gone. And that was only one industry hit hard by this, others like hotels, travel agencies, airlines etc. etc. were in the same mess. The economic impact of the pandemic was massive. Personally, it put a stop to my efforts of finding a new job in the jazz world, as records were delayed as artists couldn't tour nor promote them properly and that had a financial impact on all labels. It was time to consider retirement as I would turn 65 in October 2020 anyway. I was sure that I could give more to the jazz business, but realistically it would take some time until that was even a remote possibility.

While Donald Trump, in the middle of all this, which he didn't seem to take too seriously, despite the US being one of the most affected countries, decided to stop funding for the World Health Organization, the official number globally for Covid 19 cases reached one million and the registered death climbed over 100.000 worldwide.

In my family the various and different by country restrictions for Covid 19 were experienced in many ways: my mother didn't feel that much on her island of Bornholm and when she had to stay at home, as in her age she was more vulnerable than others, she had my sister Barbara close by to do some shopping for her. Barbara had to do her teaching for a while via Zoom and worked from home, but restrictions in Bornholm or Denmark in general were much less than in Spain, which was hit considerably harder. My sister Christine came back from her short retirement and worked again as a nurse, as manpower was needed as well in her part of Denmark. Jürgen spent most of the confinement at his house in the countryside, walking the dogs and in general not feeling much of the situation. Hannah in the UK had to work from home and her workload increased over time as some people were let go and she had to take on a few more tasks. She had gotten a sewing machine and started to use the available time to work with that a bit. Her boyfriend Oliver also worked from home, but at least they still could go out for a walk once a day. Which we couldn't for three months. I had started to put order in my digital music files, which over the past few years I had stored on various hard drives and then had the time to work with them. Some didn't have the right sequence, as the software I had downloaded them with didn't give the tracks numbers, so it was a detailed job, which I could do thanks to Discogs and other online info sites. Yolanda needed occasionally to go with her mother to do tests in the hospital and she told me how empty the streets in Madrid were, as only few people were allowed to leave home for work - basically all essential workers, but no one else.

My friend John Cumming passed away on May 17th. I was aware how seriously ill John was, as in his last weeks we had exchanged some emails, but it still was a shock. I first met John in the early 1990's after having moved to London to work as International Jazz Marketing Director for PolyGram. Both moving in the jazz circle, we of course met and started chatting about the state of jazz, the business, new acts and were hanging out at gigs at Ronnie Scott's and other venues. We started to discuss the artists I was working with and with which and how to work together, built them for the UK market, an often-frustrating undertaking in a pop-oriented marketplace, but always continuing. What struck me immediately when meeting John was his incredible passion for music and his understanding that without the creative forces, without the artists, there would be nothing. This got him the respect of his peers as well as the artists he worked with. Later on, we not only met in London, but as well in New York at APAP or Jazz Congress or at gigs during Winter Jazz, then at 'jazzahead' and at North Sea Jazz occasionally. John and my friend Wolfgang Puschnig knew each other too from way back – in 1991 Puschnig made a record called 'Alpine Aspects' which combined a 16-piece traditional Austrian brass band and a jazz group and John brought the whole gang over to London for a gig. That album was one of the early ones in my career as executive producer. When Serious started the Take Five educational program for young jazz musicians John invited me to come and talk about the music business from the perspective of a major label and since then I have done most of them: the English ones, the Scottish, the Swiss and the two European ones. In the end, I talked about the music business and labels in general, not being connected to Universal anymore and we did the session as a kind of interview, where John would ask me the questions and tried to get answers that gave the young audience something to take away with them. So, the lecture became more like a chat between friends and still had lots of info about the music business included. These events also gave us time to talk and have a drink together. They are unforgettable memories for me. John played different roles for different people: husband, father, colleague, friend, agent, manager, mentor, educator, etc., but first of all he was a wonderful, warm, passionate human being, open for new adventures and always having an hear for upcoming new talent. I truly loved working with him, talking and thereby learning, listening to gigs together with a drink in our hands. The night of his passing I had a glass of a wonderful single malt whisky, a 1990 Bladnoch with the name 'Jam Session' – a gift from my friend Wolfgang Puschnig and I silently toasted to the life of John Cumming, who will be sorely missed, but he will always be in my memory.

with John Cumming, 1948 - 2020

Yolanda and I had booked tickets to fly to London to visit Hannah for a few days in May, but due to the high infection rates in Spain these flights were cancelled and so were the flights to Bornholm I had booked to see my mother in July. No travel for us that year it seemed, as there were no summer jazz festivals either, no touring at all to be precise.

In May the German Bundesliga started again with matches played in empty stadiums and the UK and other countries followed swiftly. Too early for my taste, but it seemed that business is business. End of May and slowly the restrictions imposed were eased here in Madrid, but there was still a long way to go … we still could only leave the house when really needed. We had set times when we could go out for walks, but then everyone in our age group was going out at that time and most people couldn´t wear masks, as they were not available for the general population, which kind of made us uncomfortable. By summer, some images of overcrowded plazas or beaches were simply shocking … not only in Spain, but the US, Italy, the UK and so on …. for me hard to understand, as I prefer in this case a 'better safe than sorry' lifestyle. But then you have people like Trump and Bolsonaro, who played down the danger of the virus, despite the fact that their countries were suffering horribly. And people saw it all as a lie and a conspiracy and just simply refused to wear a mask. And that after it was announced in June that meanwhile officially 10 million people worldwide had the illness and over 500.000 had died from it. Unofficially that number was surely much higher, as in a lots of countries the higher-than-average mortality rates given by the funeral homes were much higher than the official ones. Finally in June we could start having walks in our neighbourhood again, without having to do it at a certain time and infection numbers started to fall slowly.

The death in the US of George Floyd by the hands of a police officer brought the Black Lives Matter movement back on the streets. An estimated 20 million people demonstrated against police brutality in the US alone, with further demonstrations happening around the world. But this is a problem that isn't reduced to black lives. For me it is All Lives Matter, as no-one should suffer from racism, religious oppression or any other injustice, no matter where it occurs. In the historical context of what has happened and still is happening in the USA, I can see why the focus on black lives makes sense there, even so I can imagine that some people with Latin roots would have to say something as well on their treatment in that country. All Lives Matter, period!

While Yolanda, Maria and myself had our first beer on an outside terrace again in July, the Spanish government decided that from this point in the pandemic all restrictions and decisions on these would have to be taken by the local governments of the various regions in the country. The initial confinement was decreed by the national government and they would have to take responsibility to help some industries from the fall-out of these three months of inactivity in many ways. But from then on this would not be decided by the national government anymore – the responsibility was regional. With that in Spain happened what had happened in Europe before: there was no real and binding regulation of what would have to happen when a region or country would have a certain level of infections. In Austria for example the regions had a clear mandate to act when certain levels would have reached and the restrictions were clear laid out by the government. Not so in Europe, not so in Spain.

2020, enjoying a beer on a terrace

As the infection rate dropped further, we had our first meal in a restaurant for four months, with the restaurant only allowed to run at 50% of capacity. Both Yolanda and I missed going out with our friends, having a drink in a bar or a dinner together with them and this was, as we hoped, a first step back into the right direction. In August we even went to have a Barbecue with Javier Pouso and his wife Luci at their house just outside of Madrid, with Alex and Estefania being there as well. Both Javier and Luci had been in the hospital with Covid 19 in April, he even in the ICU for a few days, but had recovered well physically. Mentally it was still difficult for Javier to talk about the horror he had witnessed in the first wave of the pandemic in the Madrid hospital, where they were completely overwhelmed with the amount of people they had to treat. The afternoon with friends was balm for our souls and we really enjoyed being out. We both had lost some weight, due to the fact that we were actually eating healthier and did every day a one-hour exercise in our little gym at home.

During the same week, Maria told us that she would have a lunch with a friend of Jorge, who had checked in on her earlier. Yolanda told her that this wasn't a great idea, as the guy was working and travelling and seeing a lot of people and surely that was in times like this a huge risk. She went to have the lunch anyway and a few days later started to cough and we took her to our doctor who said they should take an X-Ray of her lungs, which showed she got Covid 19. The friend she had met with called to let her know that he tested positive and therefore we brought her immediately to the hospital to be taken care of. And, as we had been in touch with a person who had the illness, we had to take a test to see if we were infected as well. A week after we took the PCRs but the results only came back ten days later due to the huge backlog at that point: Yolanda was negative, I was positive. I had no symptoms at all, but right after we had to quarantine for two weeks to make sure we were fine and had to have masks on at home as well, sleep in different rooms and keep apart as much as we could. Thankfully I didn't develop any symptoms and neither did in the end Yolanda and after the quarantine we were fine to go out again.
Meanwhile the first Covid 19 vaccine was approved in Russia, while some European and American groups were working on more vaccines as well, but were still in a trial phase. Maria came home from hospital, but still needed additional oxygen for a while to slowly recover her strength overall and in her lungs.

A massive explosion of ammonium nitrate, stored at the Beirut harbour, killed over 200 people and injured thousands, leaving over 300.000 people without a home. And Bayern Munich won the Champions League final, played without audience, against Paris Saint Germain. Hannah and Oliver had gotten a cat, with permission of her landlord and now, as they needed to renew their rental agreement the landlord told them that she would love to do so, but changed her mind and wouldn't allow the cat in the new agreement. Luckily for them a friend just had moved out of a nice little flat in East London, an area where the two had a lot of friends, and so they arranged with their friend's old landlord to move into this flat. And there, cats were allowed! Now it was just Oliver and her and they really liked the new place, which again had enough space for both of them to work from home.
My brother Thomas was fighting hard and hanging in. It was great so see him sometimes on the family skype and have a chat and that he still did have his sense of humour. He dealt with his situation with dignity and power, putting up a fight, the doctors told him he should have lost already. The part of the family living in Denmark visited him, when possible, but Jürgen and I couldn't, as international travel was still restricted to Denmark from certain countries. Unfortunately, Austria and Spain, where infection rates went up again, were on that list.
By September 1st the world mourned over 1 million deaths from Covid 19 and comparisons with the Spanish Flu pandemic from 1918 were made. That pandemic had four waves over two years and cost an estimated 50 million lives worldwide. Thankfully the medical care over the years since then had improved and hospital care was much better, but there were a few similarities which are interesting to point out: some people didn't believe in its danger or when asked to wear masks in public, a lot of people objected, even demonstrated against it and for their freedom. History repeats itself, by different means maybe but it does and always it looks like mankind either doesn't remember or doesn't want to or simply hasn't learned anything from the past at all. At the end of

September Madrid was in the stronghold of a second wave of the Covid 19 pandemic – certain neighbourhoods were closed off (including where we live) and new restrictions were in place. Too little, too late, if you ask me, but better than nothing. And the same was happening in the UK and many other countries. Whoever had thought that we were over the worst might had to re-think.

On October 24th of 2020 I turned 65 and with that started my retirement. I had no farewell party and I didn't give myself a golden watch or anything, just had a nice meal at home with Yolanda and began time as a pensioner, like my brother had done the year before me. We both would have liked to enjoy the time a little bit better, as the pandemic put a lot of restriction of what one could do. But we have time, so no stress about that and we were healthy and loved.

As we couldn't go to the movies, we saw a lot of TV series and some great films on Netflix or Amazon Prime, which we both have subscribed to. 'Borat Subsequent Moviefilm' by Sacha Baron Cohen was not only funny, but had political undertones as well, that seemed to have been targeted mostly on the US audience before the elections there. Concerning TV series, which we watched a bit more than usual, as we didn't go out at night, we really liked 'Unorthodox', 'Lost Girls', 'Caliphate', 'Babylon Berlin', 'Little Fires Everywhere'' 'Selfmade', 'The Queen Gambit' and the Harry Bosch series, based on the books by Michael Connolly.

I was reading more in these weeks and months as well, including Ben Sidran's 'The Ballad of Tommy LiPuma'. Pianist, keyboarder, writer, and producer Ben Sidran here tells the story of Tommy Lipuma, one of the most successful music producers of the last 50 years. From Tommy's childhood to the Grammy awards he received; this book is a lovingly told story of a man who made it in music. Sidran gives all the facts but tells them from the perspective of a friend and therefore gives them emotions and a human touch. As someone who had the pleasure to work with Tommy LiPuma when he was running Verve Records and beyond, I can say that the portrait of the man I knew turned out exactly as I would have wished and recounted. Not wanting to give anything away, this is a book of stories with artists and managers etc. and it has a great human being at its centre.

Al Schmitt with Maureen Droney: 'Al Schmitt on the Record: The Magic Behind the Music' is the story of sound engineer and producer Schmitt, who interestingly worked a lot with Tommy LiPuma and had been on his side when many of LiPuma's greatest successes were recorded. Schmitt's book tells some of these stories and others about his work in the studio with known and unknown acts, but first of all it is a study of how he worked, how he set up the studio for a recording. A more technical approach in terms of how to set up the right microphones, get the best sound out of a studio … but nevertheless interesting and captivating.

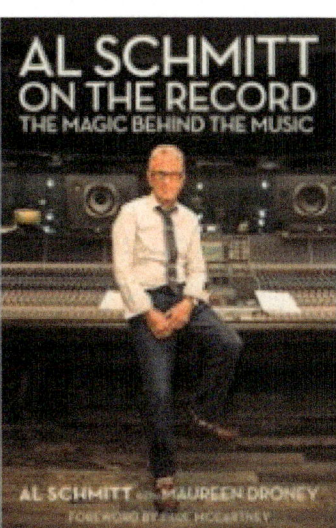

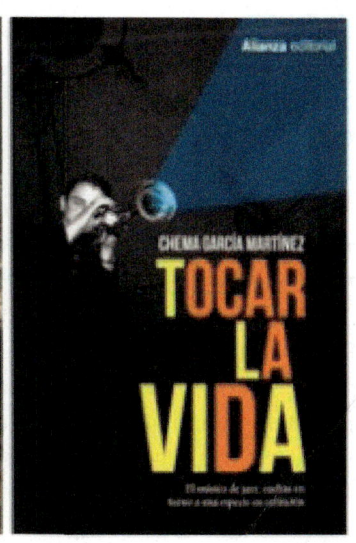

Chema García Martínez's 'Tocar La Vida' is a Spanish language book, which is a collection of articles and other writings by journalist García Martínez, giving evidence what it means to 'Play The Life'. Chema is a jazzman who writes with passion, insight, understanding and honesty. A wonderful and educating read by a real nice guy, whom I have met a few times in Vitoria and Madrid. Other books I read that year include the fifth adventure of the vinyl Detective by Andrew Cartmel and the first two books of the 'City Blues Quartet' by Ray Celestin, featuring a young Louis Armstrong. Crime stories with a connection to music is for me a wonderful combination. Unfortunately, there wasn't the third instalment of Ketil's biography in German yet, Covid 19 had delayed that release.

Christian Kellersmann had gotten a new job at BMG as head of Classics & Jazz worldwide, releasing his signings on the new Modern Recordings label. He is a true specialist when it comes to modern composers, but he is also well connected in the jazz world. One of his first jazz releases was the Mino Cinelu / Nils Petter Molvaer album 'SulaMadiana'. These two artists I knew individually for about 20 years and had over that time worked on various projects with them. When Nils Petter told me that they would record an album together I was truly excited, as I could clearly imagine what they could do together and they exceeded these expectations by far!! Percussionist, guitar player and singer Mino Cinelu and trumpeter Nils Petter Molvaer created (with the help of some electronics) a wonderful and captivating musical landscape. 'New York Stroll', a groovy instrumental with Molvaer laying New York impressions over the beat, is a great example of how the difference backgrounds of these musicians can create a wonderful blend of sounds and expressions. 'SulaMadiana' incorporates Cinelu's grooves, guitar and vocals to construct a captivating and touching song, dedicated by the musicians to Many Dibango. Sula is the Norwegian island where Molvaer grew up and Madiana is a synonym for Martinique, where Cinelu's father came from. "SulaMadiana" combines therefore both artists history and present, culturally, and musically, but with an eye on the tomorrow. 'Kanno Mwen' is another beauty of musical expression, crossing genre borders with ease. 'Rose Of Jericho' is a powerful and dynamic piece and next to the title track one of my favourites on the album.

Ropeadope Records finally released the new Ellen Andrea Wang album 'Closeness'. For her third album, Wang recruited young British guitar player Rob Luft and Swedish drummer Jon Fält to form a trio extraordinaire! She too wrote all the music on the album, except for the Traditionals 'Nobody Knows' and 'Wayfaring Stranger', as well as 'Lonely Woman' by Ornette Coleman and 'This Is Not America' by Metheny, Bowie and Mays. The opener 'Erasmus' is the perfect showcase for Wang's writing skills and the musicality of each member of the trio. The closeness between the three musicians is evident right from the start: Fält setting the pace, Wang adding the beat and steadiness and Luft flying over their infectious groove and delivering an outstanding solo. Their reading of the Spiritual 'Nobody Knows' is delicate, laid back and in perfect support of Wang's vocals. They play with immense respect for each other and the material they are performing, and the communication between them is immaculate and therefore they sound like a group that has played together for a long while. 'Strange Flower' and all other Wang compositions give the musicians the chance to shine and they do – individually and as a unit. 'Lonely Woman' opens with a beautiful bass intro, before Wang's voice enters, and bass and vocals continue together until guitar and drums carefully enter to enhance the touching atmosphere and take the song further out. A stunning version!!! And so is 'This Is Not America' with Fält setting the groove, Wang's voice comes in and Luft lets fly into a wonderful guitar solo again. The album closes with two quiet numbers: Wang's 'Silence' and 'Wayfaring Stranger', both with incredible vocals by Wang. Her bass sound is deep and full, and she grooves, swings, and sets the heartbeat for all songs with ease. From the song selection and even through her own songs one can hear that this record is as well a wonderful tribute to bass master Charlie Haden.

In September we lost in the jazz world Gary Peacock, bass player extraordinaire with the Keith Jarrett Trio, whom I had the pleasure to hear and see many times over the years, either performing standards or improvising freely. I totally love Gary's recording with Ralph Towner, 'Oracle' and 'Muthspiel, Peacock, Muthspiel, Motian', a 1993 release by the brothers Wolfgang and Christian Muthspiel, for which I was executive producer.

Toni Belenguer (1978 – 2020) was a trombone player, who had a massive impact in the Spanish jazz scene and I saw him perform a few times with the Pablo Martin Caminero group and witnessed his outstanding talent. Beside this group and his own formation, he performed among others with the Michael Brecker Quindectet, Perico Sambeat and Albert Sanz. Lyle Mays, keyboard player in the Pat Metheny group, and Jon Christensen, whom I had seen many times and met in Oslo once, also passed away that year, as did the unique pianist McCoy Tyner and the pianist and father of Wynton and Branford, Ellis Marsalis.

Toni Belenguer, 1978 – 2020, here with Ariel Bringuez (left) and Pablo Martin Caminero (right)

Sonny Rollins had his 90th birthday that September and I gave him a call, as I still do every second or third week. We chatted a bit about getting older and not celebrating birthdays anymore, but he sounded healthy and content with his life, trying every day to be a better person than the day before.
I had helped my wonderful friend, guitarist and singer Badi Assad to get a deal with Ropeadope and for me a new solo album by her is always something to look forward to. And 'Around The World' is no exception: performing her own material and some wonderful arranged covers, Badi is at her best – creating intimate atmospheres and touching moments of simple musical beauty. The opener 'Zoar' is a song she already recorded on her 2006 album 'Wonderland', but this new version sets the tone of the record: sublime vocal skills and wonderful guitar performances. 'Around The World' is connected to Badi's first book, released in 2018 and titled 'Around The World In 80 Artists', as the covers on the record come from artist from all corners of this world – New Zealand's Lorde, UK indie rockers alt-J, Irish singer Hozier and Islandic icon Bjork, whose 'Bachelorette' is getting the Badi Assad-treatment with stunning results. A through and through enjoyable album finishes with one of Badi's best compositions 'Ondas', recorded as well as 'Waves' on her 1998 release 'Chameleon', and here re-created in a wonderful, simple and captivating way. This album confirms once more, that Badi Assad is one of the most original artists of our time.

In November Joe Biden was elected the 46th president of the US, despite Trump ranting about a stolen election. America after the election looks like it has been given a chance – to bring back respect and direct communication in politics, to bridge the internal divisions and differences, to fight racism and to finally get rid of an old and complicated voting system. A chance to lead the fight for climate change, to mend relations internationally, and to improve an image that has taken a nose dive in the previous four years. What the world needed was a willingness for compromise over confrontation, for discussion instead of defamation and for unity instead of selfishness. There is only one world, which we all need to protect together.

Hundred years back then, in November 1920, singer Mamie Smith released her second recording, a song titled 'Crazy Blues'. OKeh Records had taken the chance to record the first Afro-American female blues singer and landed a million-selling single with 'Crazy Blues', opening doors for other Afro-American artists. It was a true pity that Sony Music, current owners of the OKeh catalogue, was not celebrating this historic event – as they didn't celebrate in any form the 100th Anniversary of the label in 2018. A chance missed to learn from history.

Mamie Smith, 1920 OKeh pr shot

The American JazzTimes magazine, celebrating its 50th Anniversary, asked their audience to vote for the ten best records of each of these five decades and the result doesn't really wield any surprises, except that there are only two albums that are not led by an American artist, which are the 1981 album 'Friday Night In San Francisco' by Paco De Lucia, John McLaughlin & Al Di Meola and the Dave Holland Quintet release from the year 2000 'Prime Directive'. The other 48 are all North American artists and are deservedly in a list which is compiled from a mainly US based audience, even so a great number of these recordings originated in Europe on labels like ECM, Emarcy or Verve France. A trend that continued as well in their lists with the votes from the jazz critics – one for each decade from the 1970's to the 2010's and only in the first decade three European artists made into the critics best list – John McLaughlin with the Mahavishnu Orchestra, Joe Zawinul with Weather Report and Dave Holland in 2010 with 'Aziza', his group with Chris Potter, Lionel Loueke and Eric Harland. It seems that there still is a long way to go until essential albums by artists like, Albert Mangelsdorff, John Surman, Nils Petter Molvaer, Till Brönner, Dhafer Youssef, E.S.T., Harry Pepl and many others, will get the same recognition in the US they have over here. In the critics list I found as well a few recordings I worked for on the global marketing campaigns and three in which I was involved more directly in some form: Michael Brecker's last statement 'Pilgrimage', the Roy Hargrove master piece

'Earfood', both released on Emarcy and the previous year's outstanding 'The Secret Between The Shadow and The Soul' by the Branford Marsalis Quartet on OKeh Records.

Our neighbour, living in the flat below us, came to tell us that she had water damage on her ceiling, which must have come from our flat. It turned out that some part of our small terrace was leaking and needed to be closed up, which took months to be done correctly. Not what you need at a time when you don't really want to have strangers coming to your house, but in the end it all worked out fine. As due to the colder weather we couldn't really run outside on the big terrace anymore, we had bought a treadmill, which was delivered early December and completed our little gym.

In December, when the world had 80 million confirmed Covid 19 cases with 1.5 million deaths, Russia started the first vaccination program with their Sputnik V vaccine. The vaccines from Pfizer and AstraZeneca were approved for use as well. It was an incredibly amazing achievement to have a vaccine ready for a new virus within a year. Normally this process of development and testing would take years, but mankind didn't have that amount of time and in such pressing circumstances seems to be able to come up with working solutions. The doctors called my brother Thomas a miracle, as he was thankfully still with us, enjoying to be close to his family and overall doing much better than anyone had expected.

I was invited to write a guest article at the Marlbank blog in the UK and, as it was the end of the year, included some records from the following extended list of my favourite albums of the year:

Thana Alexa / ONA – All songs were composed by Alexa, except her wonderful vocal arrangement for Massive Attacks 'Teardrops' and Tears For Fears 'Everybody Wants To Rule The World', which she totally makes her own. Powerful in their messages they confirm that Alexa is a jazz singer for our times – a masterful performer and writer, relevant in her messages and statements.
Lakecia Benjamin / Pursuance: The Coltranes – alto saxophonist extraordinaire Benjamin pays with her third album homage to Alice and John Coltrane. Co-produced with bass player Reggie Workman, who played with both Coltranes, this album is a strong statement of individuality and musical power.
Ketil Bjornstad & Guro Kleven Hagen / The Personal Gallery – Bjornstad composed especially for this cooperation with young classical violinist Guro Kleven Hagen and the music is melodic, touching and beautiful. These compositions have a classical background and a jazzy feel and gorgeous little melodies that make the listener smile. The performances by both musicians are outstanding, telling the stories of the pictures in this gallery with emotion and passion.
Carla Bley, Andy Sheppard, Steve Swallow / Life Goes On – This trio is working together on and off since 1994 and now has developed into one of the most exciting small jazz groups around – and the intelligent and witty compositions by Carla get the best out of the three players. 'Life Goes On' is a three-suite album that showcases the trios chamber music qualities, with a bit of blues thrown in.
Julie Campiche / ONKALO – On her first record, Swiss harpist Julie Campiche is creating wonderful soundscapes and spaces for improvisation for her band. Her sound on the harp is very individual and captivating, her music from groovy to contemplative, from ambient to modern jazz, with deep musical content, at the same time accessible and challenging and rewarding when listening closely.
Silvia Perez Cruz, Marco Mezquida / MA Live in Tokyo – The musical communication between the two is stunning, the way pianist Mezquida supports her is sensitive and touching and Perez Cruz' voice floats over the spare notes and emotionally captivates the audience.
Kurt Elling featuring Danilo Perez / Secrets Are The Best Stories – Elling is at his usual best, it seems there is nothing this man can't do with his voice ... and pianist Danilo Perez is giving colour and power to the proceedings. One album that shouldn't be missed – lyrically and musically essential for our times.

Bill Frisell / Valentine – This first outing of a new Frisell Trio featuring Thomas Morgan on bass and Rudy Royston on drums is a lesson in musical communication, creative freedom, and sublime individual performances.

Nubia Garcia / Source – Soulful compositions, energetic performances and a modern approach rooted in the tradition, make this a wonderful jazz record, multicultural and rooted in its time, without losing its focus.

James Brandon Lewis & Chad Taylor / Live At Wilisau – This music is full of dynamics, roughness, and beauty, covers it all and is in a category of its own – free as well as structured, melodic, and full of groove. The raw energy of the performance is even on the recording amazing and captivating.

Rob Luft / Life Is The Dancer – Luft's compositions are strong and engaging, his guitar playing that of a future star on his instruments and his group an ensemble that is completely at home with the leaders writing and way to tell stories.

Jesse Markowitz & various artists / Palladium 2020 – this 22-track tribute to the music of Wayne Shorter is stunning, as each of the performances just enhances the awe one had already for Wayne Shorter as a composer and musical visionary. A tribute album that sits comfortably next to some of Hal Wilner's productions.

Brad Mehldau / Suite April 2020 – This simply outstanding solo piano recording features 15 tracks, 12 are featured in the 'Suite April 2020' and the last three are covers of Neil Young's 'Don't Let It Bring You Down', Billy Joel's 'New York State Of Mind' and Jerome Kern's 'Look for a Silver Lining'

Wolfgang Muthspiel / Angular Blues – This outstanding trio moves beautifully between subtle swing and groovy little numbers as well as pensive ballads. Muthspiel switching between electric and acoustic guitars makes this album more colourful, his clear and beautiful sound is a pleasure to listen to and the musicianship and communication and understanding between the musicians makes the music deeper and touching.

Kasia Pietrzko / Ephemeral Pleasures – Pianist Kasia Pietrzko is for me one of the most interesting young artists to emerge in Europe. She writes with her Polish and European classical background in mind but gives within songs composition and improvisation equal importance.

Rymden / Space Sailors – Their eclectic mix of electronic and acoustic jazz with prog and psychodelia and shots of rock got tighter, more intense, and powerful. A true European power trio!

Christian Scott Atunde Adjuah / Axiom – Chief Adjuah is in blistering form and his horn wails, calls, and whispers when necessary. You can hear the past as well the present and future of improvised music, performed by musicians who are listening to each other, reacting, and creating on the spot beauty in sound.

December was quiet, with us living through the third wave in Spain. Depending on the region, restrictions were tougher or hardly existing, like in Madrid, were the regional government kept bars and restaurants open, despite having one of the worst infections rates in Europe. We stayed mostly at home, went out for walks occasionally, but still had our shopping delivered to us. My sister Marlis had her 70th birthday on December 16th, but without any celebrations, as no-one was allowed to travel. She decided to have a party in June or July of the following year, in the hope that by then we would be able to attend. Christmas and New Year's Eve we spent with Maria in our place, preparing some wonderful food and enjoying a good bottle of wine with it.

2021

So, 2021 had arrived …. And the first weeks weren't too promising!!! Covid19 was still a massive problem around the world with over 2 million victims and vaccinating was not up to speed by then, so we had a few more months with restrictions and being careful and responsible. Political horror in the US was making the news and shocked the world when Trump's followers stormed the Capitol, even so it was not that much surprising that he had something up his sleeve and maybe there might be even more to come, but for the time being, there was hope with the new president sworn in and active. Global warming let Spain drown in snow and shiver from arctic frost while Scandinavia had relative mild temperatures.

2021, snow in Madrid!

I never had seen that much snow in Madrid than what we had on January 8th during the Filomena storm and for a whole week the temperature plummeted to minus 9 degrees or less. All over the city branches were broken off trees by the heavy snow and roofs and terraces collapsed. We too had to clean out our three terraces, which were covered in tons of snow.

I still hoped that 2021 would be better than the previous year and we would be able to go out the way we did before the pandemic, see concerts and festivals or travel to meet friends and family. "Patience" and "Responsibility" were the words of these times. Yolanda and I were extremely careful and cautious as we needed to protect her mother and ourselves and everyone around us. We might seem for others extreme in our precaution, but this is about our lives and I do not want to be living with the fact that I gave someone I love the virus with horrendous results. We took it easy and we will continue to do so until we feel secure in going out, seeing people and spent time in public places indoors.

The beginning of the year unfortunately saw the passing of many great jazz musicians, some of them I had the pleasure to hear live or even meet, or their music was part of my life at some point:
Howard Johnson, the adventurous tuba player and baritone saxophonist, who gave the tuba a renewed place in jazz and whom I met when he recorded and toured with his band Gravity for Verve in 1996/1997, the German office of it to be precise, led at the time by Christian Kellersmann, who as well acted as Executive Producer on the two albums. Outstanding records both of them, with the second album featuring Taj Mahal. The third and last of the Gravity recordings was released in 2017 and in January that year I met Howard again at the Jazz Conference in New York, where he gave me the album.

2016 with Howard Johnson, 1941 - 2021

Pianist Bobby Few was probably more known in Europe than in the US, having lived in Paris since 1969 and toured the region frequently with his own projects, Archie Shepp or Steve Lacy, with whom I had the pleasure hearing Few perform in the early 1980's. As an exemplary improviser and attentive sideman, he was the perfect companion for adventurous jazz musicians like Shepp or Lacy.

I heard of the late cellist David Darling first through the amazing 1984 ECM album 'EOS', recorded with guitarist Terje Rypdal, followed by Darling's wonderful 1992 solo album 'Cello' and then the outstanding duo and quartet recordings he did with my friend, pianist and composer, Ketil Bjornstad between 1995 and 2000. The duo albums 'The River' and 'Epigraphs' are extremely touching and The Sea Quartet recordings powerful and captivating. His final recording, 'Homage To Kindness' from 2019, is a neo classical album featuring some wonderful compositions.

Armando Anthony 'Chick' Corea, who passed away, much too early, on February 9th, aged 79, will always be remembered for being an outstanding pianist and keyboarder, winner of 23 Grammy awards, as well as the man who wrote the song 'Spain'. For me Chick means so much more than this: his music was a big part of the soundtrack of my life ever since my friend Ewald Volk introduced me to 'Return To Forever' in 1973. I had heard about him being part of Miles Davis's group in the late 1960's, but until that point, I had not acquainted myself with his own music. The ease with which he switched from straight ahead jazz to fusion and Latin was not heard of before, his compositions outstanding and played by many other musicians throughout his career. For me it was beside RTF the album 'My Spanish Heart' and the duo recordings with Herbie Hancock that really touched me. The music with Gary Burton is also incredible and so are the albums he did with classical musicians like Friedrich Gulda and Nicolas Economou. 'The Children Songs' then became one of my favourite Corea albums of all time and not to forget 'Play', one of the albums he recorded with Bobby McFerrin. In 1992 Chick started Stretch Records for his releases, having them distributed by Concord shortly after that. That's when I met him for the first time and started to work on his releases via Concord, which had a distribution deal with Universal Music, for whom I did global jazz marketing at the time. We talked a lot about how to utilise his vast catalogue better, as Universal was now holding most of his music and we worked on the marketing of the new recordings, of which the solo piano albums are still my favourites. Chick invited me to the opening of the Blue Note in Milano in 2003 and we discussed the release of a project he had done with Philips Electronics – the surround sound recording of a series of shows at the Blue Note in New York, featuring a lot of special guests. I signed this project on to license from his label for global release and this album, 'Rendezvous In New York' feels a bit like a snapshot of Chick's career, featuring the crème de la crème of improvised music: Bobby McFerrin, Roy Haines, Miroslav Vitous, Christian McBride, Joshua Redman, Terence Blanchard, Gary Burton, John Patitucci, Dave Weckl, Steve Wilson, Avishai Cohen, Jeff Ballard, Tim Garland, Steve Davis, Gonzalo Rubalcaba, Eddie Gomez, Steve Gadd and Michael Brecker. What a wonderful recording!!! Whenever possible I saw Chick and his manager Bill Rooney on tour, we had dinners or lunches together or just chatted a bit. Once he sent me a new iPod, the so-called 'Chickpod' with a little video message on it … and when I got married in July 2007, he sent a little song, 'Wulf's Wedding Song', from wherever he was at the time on tour … something my wife and I value a lot. That year he released, only in Japan, a box set with 4 different piano trios – simply outstanding! And he followed that up with a trio featuring Christian McBride and Brian Blade – both double albums of this band Trilogy are among the best of his tremendous output. And so is the final album he released, 2019's 'The Spanish Heart Band – Antidote', a powerful reminder of his love for Flamenco, which he had shown many times before while collaborating with guitarist Paco De Lucia. I saw the Spanish Heart Band at the 2019 North Sea Jazz Festival and it was one of the best shows of that weekend – and it was the last time I saw Chick as well … he will be missed by many, but never forgotten.

Chick Corea, 1941 - 2021

In February my brother Jürgen called and asked if I would want to go with him to Denmark to visit our brother Thomas. Who was still doing fine under the circumstances, but Jürgen thought that if he wasn't going then, it might be too late. I was all up for the trip, but with a ten-times higher infection rate in Spain than in Austria, it was to be impossible. Jürgen got a PCR test and result within a week, which for me would have taken at least double the time, therefore he decided to make the trip on his own. I skyped with Thomas and explained to him why I still couldn't travel and he said, that he hadn't expected that Jürgen could make it happen that fast, but was happy about it.

Biden meanwhile fulfilled his election promise to re-join the Paris Climate Agreement and in general tried to build bridges. In Minneapolis began on March 8th the murder trial against four police officers in the George Floyd killing and the global vaccination program gathered pace.

Thomas's situation got worse and he lost a lot of energy trying to fight and, in the end, he decided to let go. He had his kids and wife with him when he drifted away. As our father, he took control and willed himself to make the final step. And as our father he left his wife Heidi with clear instructions about what he wanted in terms of a celebration of his life. I can't even start to understand what his passing meant for my mother, who had been strong through all his illness, but one could see a deep sadness written in her face in the days after his death. Of all of us six, he was the most artistic one, very good with anything he could do with his hands – drawing, painting, wood carving and carpentry. He loved his music: blues and Irish folk music most of all, best consumed with a triple distilled Jameson whiskey. I remember him as the little brother with whom we played around with our dogs in Berlin, who later would invite me to his summer house on a small Danish Island and we would sit and talk and have a drink together. We would talk about music, exchanged recommendations for albums or artists to check out. He came to Madrid for my 50th birthday, which I really appreciated, as he didn't like to travel, especially flying. But he had a great time in Madrid and enjoyed the lifestyle and the prices for drinks here, in comparison to Denmark. I remember as well very clearly the baptism of Alexander, which was held at home, as was custom in our family, in Ikast, Denmark. Riegers had come for that and we kids were there as well and my mother played the flute, which until then we didn't even know she could. It was so hilarious, that we all struggled not to burst out laughing aloud. Thomas's shirt was a bit tight and, in his struggle, it simply broke and had a big hole at the back, which was the last straw for us and we screamed with laughter. Thomas's incredible sense of humour and kindness made an impact on everyone who met him. There are no words to describe the emotional connection which was always there when we met, even it was a few years apart.

Remembering my brother Thomas, 1959 - 2021

His daughter Monika wrote the words that describe him best, as this is the man, we all loved and liked to be around:

"Yesterday morning passed our dearest father away, he was the strongest man. He wasn't only strong because he fought his cancer so fierce, which shocked the doctors again, and again. He was so strong of mind and love, he taught me that all people are equal and matter, that ignorance is a choice and to never judge a person before I at least have taken the time to learn some of their story. He taught me how to properly hold a pen, and paintbrush. I learned so much from him, that if I were to write it all down, I would never finish.

He was always there and understood my struggles and how I felt, even when I was unable to put them into words. He never made me feel weird about myself, or making me think that something was wrong with me. Instead, he understood without saying anything but instead he showed it in his actions. I have learned so much from him and what's important in this life.

He died peaceful in his sleep on the day he decided it was time, when he had seen and said his goodbyes to all his brats. In the meantime, until we see him again, will we continue to make trouble and spread love so we have something to tell him and make him laugh".

As there were still too many restrictions for most of us for international travel, we had to postpone the memorial service for him and the celebrations of his life until the end of August, when we hoped to be able to travel.

Singer Sachal Vasandani had called me and told me that he had recorded a new album, just with Romain Collin on piano and that he was looking for a home for this record. I remembered that Dave Stapleton at Edition told me once that he had seen Sachal in concert and really had enjoyed the show, so I gave him a call. He told me that someone already had spoken to him about this and that he would love to hear the music. I asked Sachal to send it to him and finally, the record 'Midnight Shelter' was released. I love Sachal's voice and his control and the way he makes everything he touches his own. And not to forget his writing as well. 'Midnight Shelter' is another proof of his unbelievable talent and the intimate setting with the wonderful and perceptive pianist Collin fits Sachal very well and puts the focus clearly on his vocal delivery. The album starts with one of three originals, the touching 'Summer No School', leading into interpretations of songs by Bob Dylan, Nick Drake, Abbey Lincoln and others. Recorded in 2020 this album reflects the anxiety of that challenging year, but leaves the listener with hope for the future. An album that soothes and caresses the soul. Sachal sings with emotion and love and transports these feelings within every word. This is art as seldom heard, powerful, true and touching. Just listen to his version of Wayne Shorter's 'Dance Cadaverous' to which he wrote lyrics or Abbey Lincoln's classic 'Throw It Away'… A true and timeless expression of humanity.

Meanwhile Maria had gotten her first vaccination and I was called as well in early May to get my first. Yolanda was last to receive hers, but second to have the vaccination completed, after her mother, as my AstraZeneca vaccine needed more time in-between the two jabs than the other ones.

On May 29th Chelsea won the Champions League final in Porto against Manchester City by 1:0, with the only goal scored by Kai Havertz. An audience of 14.000 people were allowed to see the game, but no travelling fans were included. Originally the game was supposed to be played in Istanbul, but the high Covid 19 numbers there made a switch necessary. Shortly after the final, the Euro 2020 finally kicked off, having been postponed for year. As a family we had a few countries to support – Germany, Denmark, England, Spain and Austria and from Yolanda's side Italy came into play as well. Over the next four weeks there was plenty of drama and good games until Italy won the final against England.
I do like football not only because I played myself when I was young, but because it has so much in common with jazz: it is a group effort, but with individual contributions, which in jazz and football are called a solo. Painting is something close to jazz as well, as it has structure and improvisation and I knew a lot of jazz musicians that painted, like Linda Sharrock, Ornette Coleman, Ute Lemper, Hans Koller, Silje and many others. And cooking belongs into this category too, as you have the structure of the recipe, but the improvisation of adding the spices the way you like.

We had, after a year's break, a beer on a terrace and it tasted wonderful!! And we went to a restaurant as well for the first time in a year and enjoyed eating out some incredible food. Restrictions were slowly winded down, but one still needed to be careful, as new variants of the virus constantly popped up, some of them very infectious. While deaths through Covid 19 globally reached the 4 million mark, I got my second vaccine on July 9th and therefore was in a better position to travel to Denmark in August.

July saw as well the release of the new Julian Lage album 'Squint', his first for Blue Note. The new trio with 'old' band mate Jorge Roeder and drummer David King is extremely tight and intense, but always playful and melodic and Julian's writing is as strong as ever. A real step forward for this amazing guitar player.

We had watched some really good TV series that year so far, including 'Interrogation', the sixth and final series of 'Line Of Duty' and the best of them all. 'Lupin' was as enjoyable as predictable it was and 'Silent Witness' was recommended to us by Blanca, our friend from Vitoria, and we did enjoy season 22 to start with. Films we watched included 'The Mauritanian' with Jodie Foster and 'Ma Rainey's Black Bottom' with Viola Davis and Chadwick Boseman and a soundtrack by Branford Marsalis. I loved reading the collection of short stories 'First Person Singular' by Haruki Murakami, especially the one titled 'Charlie Parker Plays Bossa Nova'. Murakami at his best! I read as well Richard Osman's charming 'Thursday Murder Club' and the wonderful and positive 'The Midnight Library' by Matt Haig, as well as Alex Michaelides's 'The Silent Patient' a psychological thriller with many interesting and surprising twists.

I had arranged to meet my brother Jürgen on August 19th in Copenhagen, spend the night there and pick up our mother and sister Barbara the next day at the Copenhagen airport, rent a car and head off to Højer for the memorial service for Thomas, to be held at the house he used to live in. We met at the hotel and I was kind of shocked to see that no-one in Denmark was wearing a mask. Not one person. Not inside nor outside! Coming from Madrid, this was kind of unusual. But the infection rate in Denmark was very low, compared to Spain. We went to have a beer outside the town hall and then walked to Nyhavn for a delicious seafood dinner. As Jürgen had to drive the next day, we took it easy and went back to the hotel to get some rest. It was great to see our mother again and Barbara and we had a lot of fun, under the circumstances, during the 4-hour ride with a short break for lunch. Friday afternoon and evening we spent at Heidi and Thomas's house, setting up the tent in the garden for next day's celebrations of his life, chatting and drinking beer and Jameson whiskey. Christine was there already, as were Heidi's son, and Kristian and Alexander.

2021, our mother at 93

The rest, that is Marlis, Thomas's kids Monika and Stephanie, Katia and Mikael, who was really emotional to meet our mother again, would come the next day. Mikael is Thomas's son from his second marriage and used to go to see my parents a lot as a child. When his parents separated things got a bit out of control and Thomas and him hadn't seen each other or spoken for many years, until Kristian called him when Thomas was near his end and Mikael came by. The two of them spoke for hours and Mikael was brought back into the fold of the family. Friends and neighbours of Thomas joined us Saturday afternoon and for a dinner. Thomas's letter to all of us was read by Heidi and Barbara and was full of love and very emotional. We all cried a little bit, then laughed telling stories and had a few Jameson's on our brother, father, uncle, friend and neighbour Thomas. It was a sending off he would have approved of for sure. And it was great to say 'Farewell' together, let the grief behind us and celebrate his time on earth. Amazing how strong and composed our mother with her 93 years looked, but I am sure inside she was suffering. We left on the Sunday, Jürgen driving us again to the airport in Copenhagen from where I took my flight to Madrid, Barbara and mother theirs to Bornholm and Jürgen to Vienna. The weekend after, Marlis finally celebrated her 70th birthday with Christine and Barbara and parts of their families being there and of course Marlis' family and friends. Mikael brough his wife and kid as well and again enjoyed being back with his father's family. Jürgen and myself didn't attend, as we didn't want to hang around In Denmark for a week, as that didn't make much sense.

Rolling Stones drummer Charlie Watts passed away at the end of August and when I had my usual call with Sonny Rollins, I asked him how it was to record with them in 1981. Sonny told me that it was Charlie Watts, who had asked for him to play the sax on three songs, but Sonny initially refused, he didn't think their music was that 'great'. But his wife thought that it would be good for Sonny to do the session, and she convinced him to do the uncredited recording and so he appeared on the album 'Tattoo You', including the single 'Waiting On A Friend'. According to Sonny, Charlie Watts was a fan of his and this was his chance to play with him and it worked.

Paul Dankmeyer, former booker of the North Sea Jazz Festival and in the last years the artistic director of the Java Jazz Festival in Jakarta, passed away in August 2021. I had met Paul when I was working with the jazz festivals in the 90's and we had become friends, as I liked his incredible knowledge of music and interest in new acts to present at his festivals. We always stayed in touch and he kept going to present jazz to many people in Indonesia, but almost every year returned to North Sea to meet friends, including myself. A really great guy who was respected equally by the artists he worked with and his peers.

The unusual hot and dry weather in Greece and Spain resulted in wild fires of unheard intensity and size. Global warming and some people setting consciously fire to areas they wanted to use for something different, are to blame for these catastrophes. The withdrawal of the US troops in Afghanistan brought the Taliban back to power and thousands of citizens were trying to flee the country in fear of their regime. European countries at least tried to get people out who had worked with their embassies there, but it wasn't enough. Covid 19 meanwhile had officially infected more than 200 million people worldwide and almost 5 million people had died from the virus. And we continued to live a cautious life ... as I wrote once before: better safe, than sorry!

On the first of September Hannah had her first day in her new job as a teacher. She had trained over the summer and was now starting with her first reception class and she really enjoyed this new challenge. She is a bit like my father, as she seems to need a new challenge when her current job becomes routine. I guess this one, as she is now directly dealing with people, will not that easy become routine for her, especially as this is something she spoke about to do already many years back. I am sure she will be a great teacher to these children and by giving them something for their lives, she will as well gain something for herself.

It was mid-September 2021 when I was writing these closing words, so finishing the musical chronicle of my life until then. Something I really enjoyed doing – looking back, reflecting, remembering and smiling throughout the process. I had been lucky all my life and continue to be so and now are looking forward to enjoy my retirement with my family, my records and books and new music to discover.

PS
While correcting, editing and generally improving this text with Yolanda, 2021 came to an end – the first year in over 50 when I didn't see one live concert!!!! It felt kind of weird writing this, but it is true. Even so there were a few gigs in Madrid in the second part of the year, I didn't go, as I wasn't prepared to venture into a closed space with people not wearing masks.

2021, a drink outside before the 6th wave of the pandemic hit Spain ... photo by Patricia Borda

In November another wave of the pandemic hit Europe hard. In December it took a grip of Spain, but for economic reasons, the government didn't do anything except making, too late, masks mandatory again outdoors. Decisions not based on the actual situation of the health of the people, but on political and economic terms. A pity.

The twelve records I liked most in 2021 came from a variety of countries around the world and really stood out of the music I heard that year. Here they are in no particular order:
Florian Arbenz – his exploratory series of collaborations 'Conversations' 1 to 4!!!
Sachal Vasandani feat. Romain Collin – 'Midnight Shelter'.
Tania Giannouli – 'In Fading Light'
Marc Johnson – 'Overpass'. (Solo bass)
James Brandon Lewis – 'Jesup Wagon'
Dave Holland / Kevin Eubanks / Obed Calvaire – 'Another Land'

Hakon Kornstad – 'For You Alone'
Julian Lage – 'Squint'
Gretchen Parlato – 'Flor'
Kurt Elling – 'SuperBlue'
Nils Petter Molvaer – 'Stitches'
Ketil Bjornstad – 'Flagstad, The Opera'

I was thinking for a while how to close this chronicle and didn't find a good final sentence, until I remembered the cartoons I watched as a kid, which always ended with:

That's all, Folks!

Wulf Müller, December 2021

2022

Last addition

While doing with my wife Yolanda the ultimate corrections for this book, I reacted to the events in our world by writing a blog on March 3rd, 2022, which I want, slightly updated, to add to my story. Here it is:

ABSOLUTELY NOTHING!

For a few days I didn't find any words within me to express the shock and anger of the Russian invasion of the Ukraine. A war in Europe in 2022? Hadn't we really not learned our history lessons?? How easy history can repeat itself – it just needs one man to bring the world close to a devastating third world war. The dream of rebuilding a powerful Soviet Union, of not only having access to the natural resources of Russia, but as well to control distribution to Europe completely, could destroy our world.
The two countries have a problematic history, just look at the Crimea and let's not forget what happened in the Russian speaking parts of the Ukraine over the years and that Ukraine didn't comply with the Minsk Agreement they signed. But this is no justification for war and what has happened in Mariupol and other places - war is never the answer, nor the solution.

The reaction of the West had been hesitating for a few days, but then we had a more or less united Europe, ready to sanction the aggressor, even if these sanctions will be felt at home as well. While the people of Ukraine were fighting for their survival, Europe, the UK, US and others were fighting an economical war with Russia, hoping to hit the economy hard enough for Putin to re-think his actions. Will Putin, as threatened, use nuclear bombs to retaliate to this economic 'aggression' of the West? Who knows how far both sides will go in the end, if the rest of the world isn't standing united against any invasions from any military power? India, who has good political relations with Russia and the West, is trying a balance act, that will fail in the end, as in a situation like this, one has to take a side. China is holding back, not condemning the invasion. Maybe they just watch to see what the world would do in case they move for Taiwan ….

"WAR: what is it good for? ABSOLUTELY NOTHING!" *These words are from the song 'War', penned in 1969 by Norman Whitfield and Barrett Strong, which was released as a single with singer Edwin Starr in 1970 and it became the most famous and successful protest song ever. Time to play it again and again and again ....*

I have immense respect for the people of Russia who go out to demonstrate against the war their leader started, even so if it could mean to be arrested for expressing their anger. School kids and elderly people are among the around 6000 imprisoned already for demonstrating for peace. And I have a lot of respect for the people around the world who take in the ones fleeing the war in their country – above all the people of Poland who opened their borders and hearts to help in an unprecedented way.
Let's all do what we can: donate, demonstrate, talk to each other and help in any way possible. Let's forget the 'Me' for a while and think 'Us', as in human beings.

Love, Peace and Happiness to all of us.

And I want to add as well, what my father wrote to Hannah in his 1996 letter to her, referring to the state of the world then, with conflicts in Yugoslavia, Africa, Palestine, Sri Lanka and the Far East:

"How can there be peace, if nobody wants to stop hating?
Franz Grillparzer wrote in 1848 during the Austrian and German Revolution:
'The war of modern man
is going from Humanity
via Nationality
to Bestiality.'
How true and correct, still after 150 years."

2022, Self-Portrait

Wulf Müller – a kind of discography

The below listed albums are only from artists which I personally did sign to the label in question and was involved in the making of the record in one or the other form – as executive producer, associate producer, album co-ordinator .... etc., but never as album producer, as this is not what I do.

I see myself as an A&R executive, someone who signs artists, makes things happen, brings musicians together and gives them a platform to express their creativity.

The year given is the year of the original release of the record.

Label: amadeo   **PolyGram Austria**

Karlheinz Miklin	Echoes of Illyria	1986	
	Carlitos	1986	
	Fegefeuer/Purgatory	1989	
Woody Schabata	May-Rimba	1986	
Duo Due	Focus It	1987	
	Tre	1989	
Airmail	Light Blues	1987	
Roedelius / Czjzek	Weites Land	1987	
Karl 'Bumi' Fian	Fian	1988	
Wolfgang Puschnig	Pieces of the Dream	1988	
	Alpine Aspects	1991	
	Mixed Metaphors	1995	
	Spaces (with Mark Feldman)	1998	
	Roots & Fruits	1998	
Konstantin Wecker& Die Band	Live in Austria	1988	Polydor
Red Sun & SamuNori	Red Sun – SamulNori	1989	
	Nanjang – A new horizon	1996	
R. Dahinden / C. Muthspiel	Trombone Performance	1989	
Wolfgang Muthspiel	Timezones	1989	
	The Promise	1990	

	Black & Blue	1992
	In&Out	1993
	Loaded, Like New	1995
Harry Pepl	Schoenberg Improvisations	1990
Werner Pirchner	A-NAA-NAS BA-NAA-NAS	1990
Linda Sharrock	On Holiday	1990
	Like a River	1994
	Live in Vitoria-Gasteiz	1997
Chr. & W. Muthspiel	Muthspiel-Peacock-Muthspiel-Motian	1993
Christian Muthspiel Octet Ost	Octet Ost	1992
	Octet Ost II	1994
Vienna Art Orchestra	Blues For Brahms	1989
	The Innocence of Clichés	1990
	Chapter II	1991
	Live in Vienna – Highlights '77-'90	1992
	Fe&Males	1992
	Standing ... what?	1993

From 1992 onwards I was more involved in the international marketing of releases by Verve, JMT, Emarcy and amadeo, than working in A&R, which I still did a bit for the amadeo acts I had signed before moving to London.

There I oversaw the global marketing for the releases by top artists like Joe Henderson, Herbie Hancock, Diana Krall, Wayne Shorter, John Scofield, Dee Dee Bridgewater, Betty Carter, Abbey Lincoln, Shirley Horn, Charlie Haden, Roy Hargrove, Michael Brecker, Melody Gardot and many others.

I helped the local Universal markets with their jazz signings and with the A&R for these and so got involved with artists from all over the world, like Maria Joao, Till Brönner, Eleftheria Arvanitaki, Anna Maria Jopek, Bugge Wesseltoft and his Jazzland Recordings, Monday Michiru, Jef Neve, Ketil Bjørnstad, Karen Mok and Sergio Mendes among many more from various countries.

Label: Emarcy   **Universal Music**

Joe Zawinul	The story of the Danube	1996	Philips/Decca
Chick Corea	Rendezvous in New York	2003	Grammy winner
Peter Wolf	The Other Side	2003	
	Nussknacker und Mäusekönig OST	2004	
Pepl/Pirchner/Polanski	Live At Miles Smiles	2003	
Tuck & Patti	Chocolate Moment	2002	
	A Gift Of Love	2004	
	Live in Holland (CD plus DVD)	2005	
	I remember You	2008	
Andreas Vollenweider	Vox	2004	
Matt Bianco	Matt's Mood	2004	
Terry Callier	Lookin' Out	2004	
	Live in Berlin (DVD)	2005	
Randy Crawford & Joe Sample	Feeling Good	2006	
	No Regrets	2008	Grammy Nominee
Madeleine Peyroux	Careless Love	2004	
	Half the perfect world	2006	
	Bare Bones	2008	
	Standing on the rooftop	2011	
Dee Dee Bridgewater	J'ai deux amours	2005	Grammy Nominee
	Red Earth	2007	Grammy Nominee
	Eleonora Fagan – To Billie with Love	2010	Grammy Winner
Ketil Bjørnstad	Grace	2001	
(signed to UNI Norway,	Before The Light	2001	
my A&R)	Old	2002	
	The Nest	2003	
	Seafarer's Song	2004	

	Floating	2005	
	Rainbow Sessions	2006	
	Devotions	2007	
	The Rainbow	2009	Compilation
Sonny Rollins	Sonny, Please	2006	Grammy Nominee
	Road Shows, Vol. 1	2008	
	In Vienne (DVD)	2009	
	Road Shows, Vol. 2	2011	Grammy Nominee
Michel Camilo & Tomatito	Spain Again	2006	
Michel Camilo	Piano Concerto #1/Caribe	2001	Decca Classics
	Mano A Mano	2011	
John Scofield	This meets That	2007	
	Piety Street	2009	
	54 (Metropol Orkest/V. Mendoza)	2010	Grammy Nominee
	A Moment's Peace	2011	
Medeski Scofield Martin & Wood	Out Louder	2007	
Michael Brecker	Pilgrimage	2007	Grammy Winner x 2
The Bad Plus	Prog	2007	
	For All I Care (with Wendy Lewis)	2008	
	Never Stop	2010	
	Made Possible	2012	
Roberta Gambarini	You are there	2007	
	So in love	2009	Grammy Nominee
James Carter	Present Tense	2008	
	Caribbean Rhapsody	2011	
	at the crossroads	2011	
Clifton Anderson	Decade	2008	
Roy Hargrove	Earfood	2008	
	Live at The New Morning (DVD)	2008	
	Emergence (Big Band)	2009	Grammy Nominee
Bill Frisell	All Hat (soundtrack)	2008	

Nicola Conte	Rituals	2008	
Medeski Martin & Wood	Radiolarians Box Set	2009	
Julian Lage	Sounding Point	2009	Grammy Nominee
	Gladwell	2011	
Gerald Clayton	two-shade	2009	Grammy Nominee
	Bond	2010	Grammy Nominee
Charlie Haden	Rambling Boy	2008	
	Sophisticated Ladies	2010	
	Come Sunday (with Hank Jones)	2011	
Bobby McFerrin	Vocabularies	2010	
Jane Monheit	Home	2010	
Nailah Porter	ConJazzNess	2011	
Sergio Mendes	Celebration: A Musical Journey	2011	Compilation
	Rendezvous	2013	Japan only
China Moses	Crazy Blues	2012	
Karen Mok	somewhere I belong	2013	

I signed as well a deal with Branford Marsalis for his Marsalis Music label and arranged all marketing and PR for these releases internationally and worked the Montreal Jazz DVD series internationally.

Label: OKeh **Sony Music**

Artist	Title	Year	Notes
John Medeski	A Different Time	2013	
MSMW	Juice	2014	
Bob James & David Sanborn	Quartette Humaine	2013	
Bill Frisell	Big Sur	2013	
	Guitar in the space age	2014	Grammy Nominee
	When you wish upon a star	2016	Grammy Nominee, ECHO Nominee, Dutch Edison Winner
	Music IS	2018	Billboard Jazz # 1
Michel Camilo	What's Up?	2013	Latin Grammy
Dave Holland	PRISM	2013	ECHO Winner
Craig Handy	2nd Line Smith	2013	
Dhafer Youssef	Birds Requiem	2013	Edison Nominee
	Diwan Of Beauty And Odd	2016	2x ECHO Nominee, Dutch Edison
Jeff Ballard	with Lionel Loueke & Miguel Zenon	2014	ECHO Winner
Nir Felder	Golden Age	2014	
James Brandon Lewis	Divine Travels	2014	
	Days Of FreeMan	2015	
Magos & Limon	Dawn	2014	
Theo Croker	AfroPhysicist	2014	
	DVRK FUNK EP	2015	digital only
	Escape Velocity	2016	ECHO Nominee
	Star People Nation	2019	Masterworks, Grammy Nominee, Nom Academy du Jazz
Sonny Rollins	Road Shows, Vol. 3	2014	

Somi	The Lagos Music Salon	2014	
	Petite Afrique	2017	NAACP Jazzalbum
			ECHO Nominé
Sergio Mendes	Magic	2014	Grammy Nominee
Branford Marsalis	In My Solitude	2014	ECHO Winner
	A love Supreme Live in Amsterdam	2015	CD/DVD re-issue
feat. Kurt Elling	Upward Spiral	2016	Grammy Nominee
			ECHO Winner
			Edison Nominee
	The Secret between the Shadow and the Soul	2019	Billboard # 3
			Grammy Nominee
			#1 Album Jazzwise UK
			JJA Jazz Album
			Nom Germ Jazzpreis
Sachal	Slow Motion Miracles	2015	
Dee Dee Bridgewater, Irvin Mayfield Jr. & NOJO	Dee Dee's Feathers	2015	
David Sanborn	Time and the River	2015	
Soundtrack	Playing Lecuona	2015	
Kurt Elling	The Beautiful Day (sings Christmas)	2016	Jazz FM Nominee
	The Questions	2018	Grammy Nominee
Till Brönner & Dieter Ilg	The Good Life	2016	
	Nightfall	2018	
Dee Dee Bridgewater	Memphis ... Yes, I'm Ready	2017	ECHO Nominee
Thomas Quasthoff	NICE 'N' EASY	2018	

Beside that I was involved in or oversaw local releases within the OKeh family by Kat Edmonson, The Bad Plus, Regina Carter, Jo-Yu Chen, Nils Petter Molvaer (Spellemans and 2 x ECHO Nominee 2017 for Bouyancy), Robin McKelle, Silje Nergaard, Camille Bertault, Baptiste Trotignon (Echo Winner 2018), Mario Biondi, Stacey Kent (Japan Jazz Award 2018), Hugh Coltman, Bria Skonberg (Juno Winner 2017, Juno Nominee 2018), triosence (ECHO

Nominee 2018), Markus Stockhausen (ECHO Winner 2018), BamesreiterSchwartzOrchester (2 x ECHO Nominee + 1 x Winner 2018), the Polish trio RGG, Rebekka Bakken, Lisa Ekdahl, Magos Herrera (Grammy Nominee 2019) and Sly & Robbie meet Nils Petter Molvaer.

2019 / 2020
I helped the following artists to get record deals:

Jeff Ballard to Edition Records with album 'Fairgrounds'
The Bad Plus to Edition Records with album 'Activate Infinity'
Kurt Elling to Edition Records with album 'Secrets are the best stories' feat. Danilo Perez
Ellen Andrea Wang to Ropeadope Records with album 'Closeness'
Badi Assad to Ropeadope Records with the album 'Around The World'
Clifton Anderson to Ropeadope Records with the album 'Been down that road before'

2019/2020
Sequenced the album 'ONKALO' by Julie Campiche for a 2020 release
Sequenced the album 'Been down that road before' by Clifton Anderson

2022
Café Drechsler to O-Tone Music with new album 'Let It Touch You'
Zela Margossian to Ropeadpe Records for new album 'The Road'
Claudia Acuna to Ropeadope Records for new album ….